D0202820

The Theory and History of Ocean Boundary-Making

The Theory and History of Ocean Boundary-Making

DOUGLAS M. JOHNSTON

McGill-Queen's University Press
Kingston and Montreal

ISBN 0-7735-0624-1

Legal deposit fourth quarter 1988
Bibliothèque nationale du Québec

Printed in Canada on acid-free paper

This book has been published with the help of a grant from the Social Science Federation of Canada, using funds provided by the Social Sciences and Humanities Research Council of Canada.

Canadian Cataloguing in Publication Data

Johnston, Douglas M., 1931–
The theory and history of ocean boundary-making
Includes index.
Bibliography: p.
ISBN 0-7735-0624-1
1. Territorial waters. 2. Maritime law.
I. Title.
JC323.J64 1988 341.4'48 C88-090120-9

Contents

PART THREE THE FUNCTIONALIST APPROACH TO OCEAN BOUNDARY-MAKING

Figures

Preface

The literature on boundary-making is one hundred years old. The oldest writings, on the history of frontier relations between neighbouring states, have long since been supplemented by detailed case studies of specific boundary disputes. In recent years psychologists, anthropologists, and sociologists have concentrated on the behavioural aspects of boundary-making. Geographers, political scientists, and international lawyers have described and compared the texts of boundary treaty settlements. A voluminous legal literature has subjected specific boundary adjudications to intensive textual analysis. Surveyors, hydrographers, and other specialists in the measuring sciences and technologies have produced studies on the techniques of boundary-making. In some degree, this present work draws upon most of these sectors with a view to presenting a composite picture of the various aspects of boundary-making as a human activity. However, its major purpose is to develop a new approach to boundary-making based on distinctively oceanic realities and requirements. I have made a special effort to avoid undue disciplinary bias, even though it has been necessary to give considerable weight to the new ("post-classical") law of the sea.

The "functionalist" rationale presented here is the product of several years' involvement in the Boundary Project of the Dalhousie Ocean Studies Programme. More than a dozen of my colleagues have contributed in important ways to this work, yet all remain immune from blame or guilt by way of association. Above all, I am deeply indebted to Aldo Chircop and Phillip M. Saunders for their numerous insightful comments and thoughtful assistance. Peter Mushkat was diligent in tracking down sources off the beaten path, and Marilee Matheson and Ena Morris were unfailingly helpful and efficient in converting my manuscript to a readable text.

The final stage in the production of the manuscript was completed after my appointment to the University of Victoria. I am grateful to Sheila

Talbot of the Faculty of Law for undertaking the last of the typing, especially on the bibliography. Finally, I wish to thank Kathy Johnson for her expert guidance and extraordinary diligence in editing the text and notes. Like most scholarly books, this is the product of a team effort. I am most appreciative of the contributions of the other players.

Introduction

The purpose of this monograph is twofold: first, to trace the history of all modes of boundary-making in the ocean, and, second, to provide a conceptual framework for the analysis and evaluation of all ocean boundary claims, practices, arrangements, and settlements. Because most thinking about the subject has been derived from experience on land, it will be useful to provide a preliminary review of the conceptual framework for boundary-making in general. It is hoped that in this way potential analogies between land and ocean can be identified and the influences of land-based ideas on ocean boundary-making appraised.

The problems of boundary-making in the ocean have not been a major preoccupation of governments until very recently.[1] Until the 1950s ocean technology in most regions of the world was confined largely to vessels of one kind or another, and most human activities in the ocean were dependent on an international legal system that was designed essentially to facilitate the movement of ships.[2] The post-war period has witnessed the advent of extensive zones of coastal state jurisdiction around the world,[3] especially since the early 1970s.[4] These trends in state practice have been confirmed through detailed and elaborate provisions negotiated at the Third United Nations Conference on the Law of the Sea.[5] The new law of the sea has been characterized, above all, by dramatic intrusions of national (and subnational) authority over an expanding range of activities in distant offshore areas. With the extension of coastal state jurisdiction far out into the ocean, these activities will now be brought increasingly under zoning and other regulatory policies and practices applied within the appropriate sector of a national system of public administration.[6] This extensive administrative presence in offshore areas of the ocean creates a totally unprecedented array of boundary-making requirements.[7]

The theory of land boundaries arrived rather late, in the final quarter of the nineteenth century.[8] In that period most writers on the subject blurred the now-familiar distinction between a boundary and a frontier.[9] Many of the early land-oriented theorists were motivated, more or less consciously, by considerations of national or imperial interest and often used theory to justify conquest for territorial aggrandizement.[10] Some were practitioners who drew upon their personal experience in surveying or boundary negotiations.[11] Systematic and objective treatment of land boundary-making might indeed be said to belong to the neo-colonial period.[12]

The theory of ocean boundary-making has arrived suddenly, as a matter of necessity, at the beginning of a period when the foundations of equitable and efficient ocean development and management must be laid. Bizarre or grossly self-serving approaches to maritime boundary-making are unlikely to be encouraged, or even tolerated, in an age of globally orchestrated efforts to create a fair and rational order for the oceans.[13] Virtually all problems and processes associated with ocean boundaries have an international aspect,[14] even in the case of boundaries designed to delimit zones within an area of national jurisdiction.[15] In short, the theory of ocean boundary-making will be developed on the basis of much more sophisticated considerations than existed at the same stage of theory-building for land boundaries.

Those considerations will be drawn not only from the earlier, land-dominated theory of boundary-making in general, but also from three recent sources of ideas about boundary-making in the ocean: the global negotiations at the First and Third United Nations Conferences on the Law of the Sea (UNCLOS I and UNCLOS III), which resulted in five major "law-making" conventions;[16] a proliferation of bilateral negotiations, which by the end of 1987 had produced over 130 international maritime boundary agreements between neighbouring states;[17] and a thin but apparently growing stock of adjudicative settlements and guidelines.[18]

It is unlikely that any one of these three sources will acquire saliency over the others in the development of "principles" governing ocean boundary-making. Each has limited contributions to make. The first four of the law-making conventions are the product of UNCLOS I, held at Geneva in 1958. These agreements belong to the "neo-classical" period of the law of the sea, and essentially for that reason have not been adopted by half or more of the nations that constitute the contemporary system of nation-states. It is difficult to maintain that their provisions on boundary-related matters reflect contemporary customary international law, except to the extent that some elements of 1958 Geneva law have been preserved and confirmed in the more recent law-making process of UNCLOS III.[19] The 1982 Convention on the Law of the Sea will have indeterminate status under the law of treaties until the early 1990s, and there may be continuing debate on its precise significance in the contemporary customary international law of the sea.[20] In any event, it seems that the most important contribution of UNCLOS III to boundary-making is not any particular provision on delimitation per se, but its general recognition that boundary-making may be conducted in two distinct but not unrelated processes: *negotiation* and *dispute management*.[21] Understandably and sensibly, the UNCLOS III Convention gives primacy to negotiation, as a matter of principle, in the case of a boundary issue between two neighbouring states.[22] But the Convention goes beyond the purpose of supplying general guidelines and creates a system of "settlement" for those boundary disputes that cannot be resolved through normal bilateral diplomacy.[23] In addition to these two modes of boundary-making, through negotiation and dispute management, the 1982 Convention also recognizes the need for unilateral boundary-making in certain situations through the national process of bureaucratic *administration*.[24]

Of the 130-odd bilateral agreements on maritime boundary delimitation negotiated in modern times, all but a few have been concluded in the UNCLOS III period.[25] In most of these agreements, the contemporary trends in global negotiations at UNCLOS III are reflected in the language of the bilateral text, and as a direct result of this convergence factor at the global level the bilateral agreements have contributed to the concordance of state practice.[26] It seems likely that, as bilateral treaty-making continues, significant boundary delimitation patterns will emerge, providing additional empirical data that may be crucial to the future theory of boundary-making in general.[27] Some of the more innovative of these bilateral instruments might even prove useful in non-oceanic contexts of boundary-making and natural resource management, such as Antarctica, airspace, and outer space, and some major international lakes, rivers, and internal seas.[28]

Last, but not necessarily least, the theory of boundary-making will be influenced by the way in which tribunals settle ocean boundary delimitation disputes. At present there are few such adjudicative settlements, but it seems reasonable to anticipate a growing number of submissions to third-party adjudication, especially after the 1982 Convention comes into force.[29] The theoretical influence of judicial settlements will be limited by the degree of geographical specificity adopted by tribunals.[30] If each adjudicated maritime boundary dispute is treated as unique, or nearly unique, it may not be easy or even desirable to extract general principles for the purposes of theory-building. Although it may be hoped that tribunals will make an important contribution to boundary-making theory through doctrinal development, perhaps even more should be expected from the development of *guidelines* through non-adjudicative modes of dispute management, such as conciliation and mediation.[31]

PART ONE

The General Framework of Boundary-Making

CHAPTER ONE

Terminology and Basic Concepts

BOUNDARY AND RELATED CONCEPTS

It seems surprising today, but the early theorists of boundary-making did not always make a sharp distinction between a boundary and a frontier. Until the end of the First World War, the two words, at least in the English language, were often used interchangeably.[1] Only in the 1920s did it become common to distinguish between the linear nature of a boundary and the zonal character of a frontier. Today, in normal English usage, the term "boundary" almost invariably refers to a line, and the term "frontier" to a type of boundary zone.[2]

In the context of ocean boundary-making, it may seem too early at the present stage of theory-building to predict that the frontier concept will prove useful.[3] Already certain trends in bilateral maritime boundary delimitation arrangements suggest that a variety of maritime boundary zones will be developed in state practice, but it may be questioned whether the term "frontier" should be applied to such zones. Given the prospect of a proliferation of national and subnational zones in the sea, it is likely that the land concept of a frontier will have to be rejected and replaced by a family of terms that reflect more accurately the precise functional characteristics of zones in boundary or transboundary areas of the ocean (see chapters 7 and 15).

TYPES OF BOUNDARIES

Boundary theorists today are inclined to question the usefulness of efforts to classify boundaries. The modern tendency is to emphasize the special, if not unique, characteristics of each boundary and of the problems associated with it.[4] Yet, in looking at the present (early) period of maritime boundary-making, we may find it useful to review some of the types of boundaries suggested by theorists.

International and Intranational Boundaries

Most of the literature of land boundary-making focuses on international boundaries. Boundaries between nations are generally more productive of controversy and even conflict, and access to archives on international boundary-making is usually easy for the scholarly researcher. Many citizens may be less familiar with the history and problems of intranational (that is, internal) boundaries (for example, federal, municipal, or communal), although their daily lives are likely to be more directly affected by them than by international boundaries.[5]

International ocean boundaries are much more publicized than internal ocean boundaries,[6] but federal maritime boundary disputes are becoming more common because of the extension of coastal state jurisdiction over the continental shelf and exclusive fishing zones.[7] Although the public administration of the ocean is less developed than that of the land, owing to the virtual absence of human settlements beyond the shoreline, the zoning of ocean areas for a growing number of specific administrative purposes underlines the importance of internal boundaries in ocean boundary theory.

Natural and Artificial Boundaries

One of the first distinctions to be drawn was that between natural and artificial boundaries.[8] The early theorists tended to stress the strategic value of a "strong" border,[9] and some of them argued that "natural" boundaries, based on physical features such as lakes, rivers, and mountain ridges, were more easily defended than artificial boundaries.[10] It has been argued that natural boundaries on land serve the administrative purposes of simplicity and visibility, but in practice this kind of boundary-making has been common mostly in conditions of maximum convenience, as in vast and lightly settled territories such as those of North America and Australia.[11] Today, most land boundary theorists tend to be sceptical of any a priori advantages in a "natural" boundary, however defined.[12] Given their scepticism, it will be interesting to examine, later in this monograph, the role that nature (geography, ecology, and geomorphology) has played so far in the delimitation of ocean boundaries. At this stage it may be sufficient to note that the more one takes "human geography" into account and gives weight to the socio-economic dependency of coastal communities on ocean resources, the more one is required to question the normal assumption that a "fixed and final" boundary must be immutable.[13] In short, if it seems normatively appropriate to emphasize the relevance of human geography in maritime boundary delimitation, the theory of ocean boundary-making may have to incorporate the concept of a flexible or mobile boundary.[14]

On the other side of the same coin, one encounters various kinds of artificial (or "geometrical") boundaries. In the first half of the twentieth century it was common to distinguish three kinds of artificiality: astronomical, mathematical, and referential.[15] Most political geographers today doubt that this kind of classification is any more useful a priori than its "natural" counterpart. But trends in ocean boundary-making, especially baseline delineation, show that a boundary today is often perceived in terms of the balance to be struck between natural and artificial factors and techniques (see chapter 10).

Formal and Informal Boundaries

Some of the difficulties involved in determining the appropriate range of criteria of boundary delimitation can be reduced by admitting the distinction between formal and informal boundaries. Since the idea of formality is usually associated with official (governmental) participation in the act of boundary-making, and with the production of a legal instrument such as a boundary treaty, the distinction between "formal" and "informal" is similar to the lawyer's distinction between de jure and de facto.[16] Such a distinction can be justified on the grounds that it reflects the variety of boundary arrangements that exist in practice and serves to remind officials that it is sometimes wise to leave certain kinds of boundary delimitation arrangements on an informal or de facto basis. Conversely, the distinction serves to highlight the fact that existing informal arrangements may be inadequate and should receive official attention.

In ocean boundary-making theory, it may be even more important than in land boundary theory to promote and develop the concept of an informal boundary. First, many coastal states, especially developing coastal states, may find it difficult and expensive to make formal boundary settlements or arrangements with their neighbours through negotiation or adjudication or a combination of both. Indeed, it may not be in their interest to do so in advance of appropriate regional or bilateral arrangements for the development and management of shared or shareable resources in offshore and adjacent areas.[17] Second, legal theorists are bound to recognize that many ocean boundary issues today seem to require an examination of modern claims to "historic rights" that were never formalized in indisputably binding and legally unchallengeable instruments. Legal entitlements sometimes evolve from sources that date back to earlier times, when "neighbourhood" arrangements were often handled in an informal manner.[18]

Political, Cultural, and Administrative Boundaries

Land boundary theorists have applied a number of adjectives to boundaries in an effort to clarify the primary purposes the boundary-makers were attempting to serve by the act of delimitation. For example, the term "political boundary" has been used to describe a boundary that is more or less explicitly designed to settle a political issue.[19] Usually such a boundary will have a formal (that is, official) status, and will therefore be expressed in legal form. But occasionally, in circumstances where political expediency suggests the need for informal arrangements, the term "political boundary" is used to distinguish an informal but politically significant arrangement from a formal, jurisdictionally significant, and legally binding boundary line.[20] In the interest of terminological precision, it may be best to avoid the use of the term "political boundary" in ocean boundary theory.

The term cultural boundary usually has been applied to divisions of a territory that are based on ethnic or religious groupings of a population.[21] A cultural boundary may have considerable political and administrative significance, internally if not externally,[22] but it is unlikely to serve basic jurisdictional purposes.[23] Ocean boundary theory should perhaps take cognizance of the cultural boundary concept, since a few recent maritime boundary agreements are based explicitly on the recognition of a need for special arrangements for certain traditional subcultures within a larger statist framework.[24] To the extent that subcultural variables are officially taken into account in ocean management, it may be necessary to recognize the utility of the cultural boundary concept for the purposes of ocean boundary-making and for subsequent administrative purposes.[25]

The concept of an "administrative boundary" has also been common in land boundary-making from the earliest times, and was used especially by the great empires.[26] As public administration became more complicated and more sophisticated, particularly within the bureaucratic structure of the British empire, administrative boundaries helped to avoid unnecessary conflicts with neighbouring peoples that might have been generated by a more visible and provocative use of formal legal or political boundaries. The term "administrative boundary" is certain to be useful in ocean boundary theory and practice as more and more variants of zoning in the ocean are introduced for regulatory and other administrative purposes. Some boundary-making experience in international lakes and rivers may provide useful analogies.[27]

Unilateral and Bilateral Boundaries

In early China and Rome frontier-making was an imprecise and, of course, a unilateral administrative act. In more modern times the first recorded land boundary delimitation, by Charlemagne in 806, was also a unilateral act, albeit one designed to serve familial (or dynastic) rather than administrative purposes.[28] Now that imperial and dynastic boundary-making belong to the past, it seems that unilateral boundaries almost invariably are drawn to perform some fairly specific administrative function, either formally or informally. The first recorded ocean boundary was imposed unilaterally by Pope Alexander VI, in response to competing claims to the New World by Spain and Portugal.[29] Today, the tasks of public administration of the ocean are likely to multiply under the conditions of modern technology. The need for more precise differentiation of agency mandates and for equitable allocation of coastal community rights creates the need for a proliferation of internal unilateral (as well as bilateral) ocean boundaries.

Bilateral international boundaries are a fairly modern invention. In 1222 six English and six Scottish nobles were commissioned to delimit the boundary between the two kingdoms, but the project miscarried.[30] In 1718 a boundary between France and the Austrian Netherlands was fixed with a degree of precision, but even by the end of the eighteenth century only a few land boundaries had been delimited bilaterally – as distinguished from frontiers that had been consented to by neighbouring states.[31] At sea, only a handful of boundary agreements existed between opposite or adjacent states prior to the Second World War.[32] Today, however, most land boundary theorists, and all governments, tend to approach international boundary-making as a transactional undertaking: "[T]wo countries should agree on a line and stick to it, as individuals agree on property lines."[33] But in the ocean we can expect a combination of bilateral and unilateral boundary-making, for both internal and international purposes, varying with the location, nature, and purpose of the boundary.

Territorial and Functional Boundaries

As ocean management and regulation continue to develop, more and more ocean boundaries will take on an explicitly administrative significance, whether of the international or intranational sort. It will be argued later that the theory of ocean boundary-making should be developed in the light of the theory of ocean management; that the primary, if not exclusive, purpose of ocean boundaries should be to delimit administrative zones of one kind or another; and that this approach to the theory of boundary-making should be designated the "functional" approach.

In the 1980s, however, some confusion has arisen from the terminology of UNCLOS III. In their determination to reach a compromise agreement on an intermediate zone of (primary) coastal state jurisdiction between the high seas and the territorial sea, the delegations accepted the term "exclusive economic zone" (EEZ).[34] What was adopted was not only a zone, but also a regime. For clarity, these two terms should be used quite distinctly: "zone" should refer simply to an officially designated area, and "regime" should refer to an authoritatively established system of legal principles, concepts, institutions, rules, practices, and procedures, which may or may not be spatially coextensive with an officially designated ocean area.

The theory of ocean boundary-making was further complicated by the fact that UNCLOS III in effect recognized and promoted the modern concept of functional jurisdiction, as distinguished from the traditional concept of territorial jurisdiction.[35] The EEZ regime, for example, is conceived and articulated in terms of a designated range of multifunctional competences of the coastal state, subject to various limitations, exclusions, and qualifications, within the two-hundred-mile exclusive economic zone.[36] The continental shelf regime is conceived and articulated as a composite of a few unifunctional zones of coastal state authority, subject to certain constraints, within the defined limits of the continental shelf zone.[37] Moreover, the traditional territorial sea regime might be regarded as virtually omnifunctional in conception and articulation.[38]

Despite these confusions and complications, it may be useful to distinguish two kinds of ocean boundaries now emerging in legal theory: territorial and functional. However, it seems premature to suggest that this distinction has been adopted by boundary theorists as part of their accepted terminology.

PHASES OF BOUNDARY-MAKING

Most of the early theorists focused chiefly on the history of international frontiers; they were interested in tracing the "evolution" of a boundary.[39] In many cases political boundaries could be seen to have passed the stages of preparation, decision, and execution. Today, most political geographers distinguish four stages: (1) *allocation* of political territory by virtue of agreed-upon general principles; (2) *delimitation* of a specific boundary site by the application of precise criteria and techniques; (3) *demarcation* of a boundary line on the ground by markers; and (4) *administration* of various official acts and services associated with the maintenance of a border.[40]

This classification is difficult to apply to maritime boundaries. UNCLOS III was clearly the all-important stage of allocation (or reallocation); but the stages of delimitation and administration vary with the type of maritime boundary,[41] and demarcation will not normally exist as a stage of boundary-making in the ocean.[42] The term "delimitation" in ocean boundary-making should be used with particular care. The coastal state's unilateral promulgation of baselines and closing lines across the mouths of bays and other coastal indentations should be described as an act of "delineation," and the unilateral-multilateral boundary-making process for the seaward limits of the continental shelf beyond the two-hundred-mile limits of the EEZ should be termed "determination." The term "delimitation," it is suggested, should be used only for the drawing of bilateral boundaries between two neighbouring states with opposite or adjacent coastlines.[43]

PROCESSES OF BOUNDARY-MAKING

Contrary to the popular impression that most boundaries are negotiated, the largest number of boundaries on land, those of the intranational sort, emerged from bureaucratic processes. Since the style of bureaucracy varies considerably from culture to culture and from government to government, it is impossible to generalize accurately about the characteristics of the bureaucratic "forum" of boundary-making. In most countries, many bureaucratically determined boundaries, especially those of the non-federal (internal) sort, are not submitted to the legislature for final approval and may not be easily discerned from published maps or other public sources.[44] Even federal intranational boundaries of a fundamental jurisdictional character may have resulted from bureaucratic decisions of an earlier colonial administration, like many of the international boundaries dividing nations that have emerged from colonial status.[45]

Today, of course, most international boundaries on land, as well as the bilateral boundaries of the ocean, are the product of negotiation.[46] All political boundaries, both intranational and international, are now deemed to be "transactional" or "contractual" in character.[47] International boundary negotiations are intended to result in a formal treaty. Normally, a boundary treaty is conceived of as being more permanent than most other kinds of treaties, and is therefore sometimes classified as "dispositive" or "resolutive."[48] Since negotiating style, like bureaucratic style, varies from culture to culture and from government to government, it is difficult to obtain a clear picture of how political boundaries are negotiated.

Lawyers in particular have always been intrigued by the adjudication of international boundary disputes. Most states are reluctant to submit to an international process of adjudication, whether in the form of litigation or arbitration. But national pride is often at stake in a boundary dispute, and the human obsession with territoriality (a topic discussed in chapter 2) seems to account for the relatively high incidence of boundary-related issues among disputes that are submitted to international adjudication.[49]

In the context of ocean boundary-making, it will be useful to compare the behavioural characteristics of negotiating teams and tribunals in order to provide a basis for predicting boundary-making outcomes from the processes of negotiation and adjudication. Special attention will be given to the emergence of non-adjudicative intermediary procedures for the treatment or "management" of ocean boundary problems.[50] It may be expected that parties to an ocean boundary dispute will often prefer conciliation or mediation, or will seek the intervention of an appropriate international organization.

BOUNDARY ISSUES AND RESPONSES

It is sometimes useful to draw a distinction between boundary issues and transboundary problems. The term "boundary issue" should be used to refer to an issue that is related directly to a claimed or accepted boundary line, such as an issue concerning the basis of allocation or the specific criteria to be applied to the act of delimitation. By contrast, the term "transboundary problem" should be applied to a cluster of issues concerning a set of activities in an area adjacent to a claimed or accepted boundary line: that is, issues that straddle the line and raise questions about the actual or potential relationship between the regimes, orders of jurisdiction, or administrative systems divided by the line. Taken together, both kinds of issues are "boundary-related."

It is fairly common to refer to the "evolution" of an issue. Frequently, an issue begins as an unthreatening *difference* of (official) opinion or policy. Once such a difference is officially recognized as an actual or potential problem (and one that must be articulated carefully), it can be characterized as an *issue*. At this stage some kind of official treatment is perceived to be necessary. If events reveal a deterioration of the relationship between the parties, the issue will be elevated to the status of a *dispute*, usually formulated with sufficient precision to make it justiciable or otherwise capable of treatment by means of legal ideas and institutions. A further and truly serious aggravation of a dispute may change the perception of the parties and introduce the terminology of *conflict*, with its connotation of coercive sanction or even potential violence.[51]

The range of official modes of treatment of a boundary or transboundary issue, dispute, or conflict is discussed at length in chapters 17 and 18. At this stage, it is sufficient to distinguish "arrangements" and "settlements" on the ground that the latter, unlike the former, represent a dispositive or resolutive response to a dispute or conflict.[52] Moreover, whereas boundary "arrangements" may be so diverse as to defy classification, boundary "settlements" are easily assigned to one of the three categories – agreements, awards, or other (intermediary) modes of settlement, involving conciliation, mediation, or some other non-mandatory form of third-party participation.

CHAPTER TWO

Factors

VALUES

The objectives of boundary-making can be described in terms of values. The range of human values at stake in the boundary-making process may be expected to vary from one context to another. Six "base values" are likely to have some weight in most contexts of boundary-related issues and to be reflected in the mode of treatment: these are security, self-respect, well-being, wealth, knowledge, and efficiency.

Security has generally been associated with the phenomenon of human territoriality, and therefore with issues of territorial boundary-making. The security argument for territorial boundaries has been made in two distinguishable forms. The first was based on the need for protection against a foreign enemy and was thus cast in strategic or military terms.[1] Originally, this approach assumed the primacy of the national or imperial need for strong, defensible boundaries. More recently, this line of argument has been buttressed by reference to the evidence that aggression is inherent in human behaviour,[2] and that political boundaries are a psychological necessity even in the absence of a direct military threat. The second form of the security argument is based on the need for protection from tribal, cultural, or other non-military intrusions into a group's living space. Many theories have been advanced to support the contention that boundaries are essential to human autonomy because they serve to institutionalize our separateness from others, even our closest neighbours.[3] The last two or three decades have produced a voluminous literature on aggression and territoriality in animal behaviour,[4] which has generated considerable controversy among behavioural and social scientists.[5] Military defence considerations played a prominent role in early ocean boundary-making, as reflected in the idea that the breadth of the territorial sea should be directly proportionate to the existing range of gunfire.[6] Today, with advances in military technology, such considerations have much less weight in the process of ocean boundary-making. A functional approach to ocean boundary-making might, however, provide for military security zones, and thus for special military security boundaries, in appropriate circumstances.[7] Moreover, in the modern period of UNCLOS III some of the motivation for the seaward extension of national jurisdiction has been attributed to the need for environmental security.[8]

A related but distinguishable value motivation behind certain kinds of boundary claims is the demand for *self-respect*. The movement towards extended coastal state jurisdiction in Latin America, for example, has been explained by reference to a national or cultural concept of patrimony – a sense of natural entitlement.[9] Frequently, especially in the case of an international boundary, problems related to boundary allocation, delimitation, demarcation, or administration are aggravated by the emergence of an issue with a symbolic significance that transcends the substantive interests at stake. At worst, this kind of situation can make the issue impossible to resolve through normal trade-off diplomacy.[10]

The *well-being* of the population at large, or of the communities most directly affected, is often put forward as a significant value at stake in a boundary-related issue. An effort may be made to focus on the food and other resources that represent the actual or potential sources of survival for the inhabitants of the disputed boundary area. Special emphasis may be given by a boundary claimant to the value of the area for grazing, hunting, or other modes of food production. The well-being argument for a boundary may also be made by reference to non-physical welfare requirements – that is, to social and psychological rather than ecological considerations.[11] Some theorists have held that the state is dependent for its survival on the preservation of a balance between centrifugal and centripetal forces,[12] and that interstate boundary-making is a balancing process that may necessitate occasional adjustments of boundary function, if not of definition or location.[13] Others, focusing on territoriality, have emphasized the need for stimulation and identity, as well as security, in human behaviour.[14] Still others have approached territoriality and boundary-making by underlining the significance of the "periphery," as distinguished from the "core," in human affairs.[15] Generally speaking, these non-physical welfare theories of boundary-making seem less applicable to the ocean than to the land. In fact, human territoriality applies to the ocean only by virtue of a more or less convenient legal fiction. Yet in certain atypical ocean areas some of these social and psychological theories might serve to qualify the argument for an excessively linear or developmental approach to ocean boundary-making.[16]

Frequently, of course, the prospect of significant *wealth* may be the strongest incentive for making a boundary claim at a particular time or place, or for making it in a particular manner. Characteristically, a wealth-based demand, focused on specific resources, envisages, for the nation as a whole or for a special interest, enrichment beyond the level of preservation or basic human need (which tends to be associated with a well-being demand). At UNCLOS III wealth was the primary value at stake in negotiations on issues related to the determination of seaward limits[17] and the delimitation of lateral boundaries between opposite or adjacent states,[18] and to a lesser extent the delineation of baselines and closing lines.[19] Many national claims to expanded offshore zones have been justified, more or less overtly, by reference to new economic development opportunities through access to previously unutilized fishery species or unharvested stocks or to newly available mineral resources in the offshore.[20]

To a lesser extent, some boundary claims are motivated in part by the desire for greater *knowledge* and *efficiency*. In the case of ocean boundary-making, the trend to a two-hundred-mile seaward limit for the exclusive economic zone owed much to the developing coastal states' resentment that the traditional regime of a narrow territorial sea deprived them of secured access to scientific data derived from the waters adjacent to their coastal zone.[21] Moreover, many new boundary claims of this sort can be attributed to a more or less generalized desire to enhance national capabilities through the development of technical and organizational skills applied to resources in the area claimed.[22]

INTERESTS

Any theory of interests applied to boundary-making is bound to begin with the distinction between common and special interests.[23] Common interests are clearly represented in globally negotiated and accepted principles and criteria for boundary delimitation and related matters, such as those formulated or reaffirmed at UNCLOS III.[24] Similarly, globally approved principles and criteria for boundary-making in airspace and outer space can easily be identified, but international boundary-making on land has depended very largely on a negotiated or adjudicated accommodation of special interests.[25] In the case of bureaucratic and diplomatic boundary-making, special interest groups may be effective in influencing the outcome through lobbying.[26] Resort to an intermediary represents an escape from special interest pressures.

In the typical case of a bilateral boundary delimitation issue, each claimant establishes an initial negotiating position or legal argument which, if it prevailed, would result in a zero-sum outcome as between the parties. More often than not, the actual outcome represents a compromise. Accordingly, both parties to a boundary issue have a mutual secondary (fall-back) interest in reaching some kind of compromise in order to avoid unnecessary conflict.[27] Normally, there is no element of reciprocity in a boundary delimitation arrangement or settlement, unless it is accompanied by some kind of transboundary arrangement such as an agreement for reciprocal rights of access.[28] Occasionally, a transboundary arrangement, such as a joint development agreement, is based on joint interest.[29]

ATTITUDES

Those who participate in the boundary-making process are influenced by a number of predispositional factors – environmental, professional, and personal.

Environmental conditioning has national, cultural, and ideological aspects. National background seems to have some effect on generalized attitudes, which are reflected in bureaucratic, diplomatic, and judicial boundary-making. Most countries can be said to exhibit national styles of bureaucracy.[30] Since international diplomacy is either bilateral or multilateral, no one style will prevail, but distinct national approaches to negotiation can be identified.[31] Moreover, all lawyers have to be trained within one national legal system or tradition, and it may be possible to distinguish various national approaches to international law.[32] Cultural influences are discernible in all three of these forums,[33] and it may also be possible to identify the impact of ideological attitudes within all three of these sectors of official behaviour.[34]

Professional attitudes also seem to play an important role in the boundary-making process, cutting through national, cultural, and ideological influences. The professional negotiator is likely to approach a boundary issue more or less like other issues: namely, as a challenge to his bargaining skills. The expected outcome of negotiation is a mutually beneficial compromise agreement. The professional bureaucrat is more likely to seek a boundary that serves administrative convenience (or managerial efficiency) and appears free of political controversy at home.[35] Sometimes, however, an administrator's boundary may be subject to internal diplomacy, especially in a large and complex federal state.[36] The professional adjudicator will see boundary-making in terms of doctrinal development (rule clarification) or the quest for justice in a choice between two adversarial claims. (On the considerations to be addressed in the adversarial system of judicial boundary-making, see chapter 19.) Generally, it might be expected that of these three professional approaches to boundary-making, the diplomatic approach is likely to be the broadest, at least potentially, and the judicial the narrowest.

Personal attitudes must also be supposed to have some influence on the process of boundary-making, though admittedly they are difficult to document. The bureaucratic approach probably tends to be the most impersonal of the three professional forums, but the significance of the personality factor in diplomatic and judicial boundary-making must vary considerably with the number and hierarchical arrangement of those participating.[37]

RELATIONSHIPS

In the context of international bilateral boundary issues, the relationship between the parties often has a decisive effect on the mode of treatment and on the outcome itself. Cultural or ideological affinity, or some other form of uncontrived congeniality, is presumed to be conducive to the negotiation of boundary or transboundary arrangements, but the history books are filled with examples of spectacular failures on the part of apparently "natural" partners. Conversely, some of the most stable borders are maintained by neighbours with little in common with each other. In the case of new boundaries at sea, the crucial relationship may be that of the two neighbouring economic or administrative systems, rather than that of the political or ideological system they represent.[38] Less conspicuously, internal political and administrative boundaries on land – and perhaps their emerging counterparts in the ocean – may be influenced by federal and inter-agency relationships.[39]

MILIEU

All forms of boundaries – unilateral, bilateral, and multilateral – can be seen as the product of the milieu within which they evolved or were established. The term "milieu," as used by political scientists,[40] is broadly defined to include a wide range of historical, geographical, cultural, ideological, political, economic, administrative, and institutional factors. These variables represent the total environment of actual and potential interactions and influences on official outcomes. There is almost no limit to the number of ways one might characterize the milieu of boundary-making at any particular place or time – for example, as a boundary of imperial conquest, non-imperial conquest, colonial administrative convenience, domestic administrative convenience, tribal government, technological contingency, linguistic division, religious segregation, military security, conflict avoidance, joint development, joint management, and so on. In each case the boundary is characterized by reference to a particular purpose or motivation, which in turn is inferred from one's own perception of what was salient in the milieu at the time the boundary was established. From this milieu perspective, many of the new international ocean boundaries are likely to be characterized as resource development and management boundaries because of the urgency of resource needs in the present milieu of government affairs.[41]

PHYSICAL SETTING

Boundary-makers have often found it convenient to attach special importance to the physical setting and to use the salient geographical features of the border region as the primary criteria for delimitation. In many cases, this use of "neutral" or "objective" factors has been found to be the best way of depoliticizing, or otherwise desensitizing, the boundary and related issues. Today, the concept of a natural boundary is widely criticized by theorists, but the relevance of the physical setting in ocean boundary-making has received increased emphasis in recent years. In delimitation adjudications, for example, weight has been given to the general "macro-geographical" characteristics of the region affected by the dispute as well as the special "microgeographical" characteristics of the boundary area and adjacent waters (see the section entitled "Modern Dispute Management" in chapter 11). In the context of baseline delineation and seaward limit determination (beyond two-hundred-mile limits), the formulae that have been devised reflect an awareness of the central significance of the physical setting. (This point is discussed in more detail in chapters 9 and 10.)

TECHNOLOGY

Military armaments were probably the first form of technology to be consciously applied to the theory and practice of boundary-making. In the eighteenth century the range of gunfire was the determinant of the seaward limits of the territorial sea. In modern times, military and non-military aviation technology has played a major role in the determination of boundaries in airspace and outer space.[42] In the 1950s an effort was made to determine the seaward limits of the continental shelf by a formula that included an explicit reference to "exploitability" – that is, to the present limits of drilling technology in the oil industry.[43] Whether or not this is the only modern example of the potentially short-lived character of technologically dependent boundaries, it serves to remind the theorist that ocean boundary-makers may be particularly vulnerable to the temptation to seek sophisticated boundaries within some kind of technological framework.[44] Although it may be unwise in most situations to use technology as the basis of international boundaries, the trend to technologically differentiated zones in public administration seems likely to result in an increased use of technological factors in the making and maintenance of internal administrative boundaries, both on land and at sea.

TIME

It it evident that the mode of treatment of boundary issues as well as specific outcomes may be affected significantly, and even chiefly, by the time of the undertaking. From any historical perspective, it is easy to distinguish important differences between ancient, modern, and contemporary practices in the allocation, delimitation, demarcation, and administration of boundaries. In the contemporary period, imperial conquest and the colonial style have given way to the principle of consent in the delimitation of international boundaries between neighbours. At sea, and to some extent in outer space, the concept of territoriality has yielded to the much greater specificity inherent in a functional approach to boundary-making. The advent of zoning as an administrative technique on land, in the air, on water, and underneath land and water surfaces underlines the regulatory significance of boundary-making much more than ever before. It seems likely that future approaches to ocean boundary-making will place less emphasis on permanent and inflexible settlements, and more emphasis on imaginative and sophisticated arrangements for the allocation and administration of ocean space. With further scientific and technological advances in ocean management, it may be expected that the concept of boundary maintenance inherited from the land will yield to an increasing diversity of post-settlement ocean-boundary-related arrangements.

CHAPTER THREE

Conceptual Approaches

THE NEED FOR OPERATIONAL STANDARDS

Even today, boundary-making tends to be as complicated in practice as it is in theory. Complexity arises from the diversity of values and other factors involved in the process. Even in the context of unilateral boundary-making, it is usually necessary to address a wide variety of factual and normative considerations and to reconcile different kinds of bias or saliency reflected over a broad range of expertise. In bilateral boundary-making, the need for compromise often results in a strenuous effort to co-ordinate various kinds of concepts and data to reduce the issues to a more easily negotiable form.

Not least, it is important to reduce the values at stake to a set of relatively specific objectives which can be easily accepted by the participants as the appropriate operational framework. Suitably articulated, these objectives may serve as operational standards for those involved in the bureaucratic, diplomatic, and adjudicative (or other intermediary) processes of boundary-making.

THE MODERN FOCUS ON EQUITY AND EFFICIENCY

In modern international law and diplomacy, there has been a general tendency, in many different contexts, to give primacy to the objectives of equity and efficiency. This conceptual framework seems to have become especially useful in global contexts of north-south issues, such as that of ocean development and management issues negotiated at UNCLOS III. The duality in the framework seems to many to be a suitably simple way of expressing the need for balance between, on the one hand, fairness in the distribution or redistribution of resources and, on the other hand, a degree of rationality in the management of those resources and in the organization and deployment of the requisite capital and labour.

An equity-efficiency approach to boundary-making seems especially appropriate in the oceanic context during the present early stage of the new law of the sea, when dramatic extensions of coastal state jurisdiction around the world have created unprecedented issues in the allocation of ocean space between neighbouring states at the same time that new uses of the ocean have introduced the need for much higher levels of organizational efficiency. As a result of the rising demand for justice in the international legal system,[1] equity was given more weight than efficiency at UNCLOS III, not least in the formulation of the principles of boundary allocation.[2] Yet it seems likely that a more nearly equal balance between equity and efficiency will be sought in ocean boundary and transboundary arrangements in the years ahead.

It is less easy to apply the modern equity-and-efficiency framework of criteria to the history of land boundary-making, but there is a general sense in which all boundaries, both internal and international, must be evaluated by this dual standard of seeming to be fair and proving to be workable in some organizational or sociological sense.

THE CONCEPTUAL FRAMEWORKS

The complexity of boundary-making always permits and usually requires the involvement of different kinds of specialists. Each area of specialized knowledge or experience relevant to boundary-making reflects a highly developed and clearly identifiable body of concepts, terms, techniques, and methodologies – a conceptual framework, in short. Most of these specialized frameworks reflect an intellectual perspective associated with a particular discipline or a cluster of related disciplines. Each of these perspectives represents a "source of knowledge," a distinct mode of theorizing about boundaries, and a particular focus on what is perceived to be relevant information.[3]

To the extent that each of these conceptual frameworks represents a distinguishable approach to the theory of boundary-making, and therefore a different kind of potential input into the process, it seems important to identify the principal examples. Six types of framework deserve special mention: physical, political, socio-cultural, economic, juridical, and managerial.

The Physical Framework

Since boundary-making is, in large part, a matter of drawing lines, the process has always depended on those who specialize in the techniques of delineation based on a knowledge of plane geometry. An equidistance line is only one of many examples of the linear or *geometric* approach to boundary-making.[4] In the nineteenth century, the physical framework incorporated spatial (frontier or zonal) approaches to the theory and practice of boundary-making; more recently, especially in the case of ocean boundaries, the task has sometimes been perceived in three-dimensional terms.[5]

Another branch of physical theory puts emphasis on the *geographic* rather than the geometric aspect of the problem. In early times this approach rested on the premise that special importance should be attached to the natural features of the terrain: mountain ridges, watersheds, valleys, rivers, lakes, streams, and specific morphological or vegetational characteristics. Nowadays, the geographic approach is usually broad enough to include human as well as physical factors: for example, the edge of a desert area is likely to be perceived not only as a convenient linear criterion, but also as an ethnically or sociologically significant dividing line between two cultures or lifestyles.[6] In the case of ocean boundaries, judicial resolution of a boundary dispute may be influenced above all by the way the adjudicators choose to characterize the configuration of the coastline or the boundary region as a whole.

In ocean boundary-making, the doctrine of the continental shelf created the need to inject *geological* (and geomorphological) characteristics of the seabed and subsoil into the stock of criteria relevant to certain kinds of boundary-making. (On the role of geographical characterization and the use of geological data, see chapter 19.)

The advantage of using a framework of physical concepts is that it places emphasis on objective and (normally) unchanging factors that are capable of empirical verification and are beyond the scope of political manipulation.[7] The disadvantage of the physical approach is that it tends to be perceived as unduly arbitrary from the perspective of equity: it puts a premium on technicality rather than reason. It is also somewhat deceptive in that it tends to conceal the fact that the use of nature is still essentially a matter of political choice, and therefore more subjective than it purports to be.[8]

The Political Framework

A totally different approach begins with the premise that boundary-making is, and must be perceived as, a political act. This line of theorizing stresses the governmental character of almost all boundary-makers. The actors involved in the boundary-making process are to be understood as representatives of national, subnational, or sectional interests. Even when a boundary dispute is submitted to third-party adjudication, the quasi-governmental character of the process is reflected in the fact that governmental agents normally retain control over the terms of the reference, and therefore over the scope of the issues submitted;[9] frequently, they also possess a virtual veto over the choice of individual adjudicators or the tribunal.[10]

The political character of boundary-making is especially evident at the first stage, that of allocation.[11] The next stage (delimitation) is likely to involve a more balanced mix of political and technical considerations.[12] The third stage (demarcation) is almost entirely technical, but the final stage (administration) is, of course, political in the broad sense that public administration, however routine or technical in purpose, is likely to reflect major influences in the political system as a whole.[13]

The chief effect of the political approach to boundary-making is to underline the fact that most boundaries, especially those of the bilateral sort, are the product of a political process. The political theorist is trained to furnish data and ideas that may have explanatory, predictive, and prescriptive value. Special insights can be derived, for example, from a study of the dynamics of negotiations at global, regional, national, and subnational levels. Through the application of bargaining theory and other approaches to conflict avoidance, the social scientist can help the parties limit the frequency or seriousness of mistakes and misunderstanding.[14]

On the other hand, a political approach can be criticized for introducing too much uncertainty into the theory and practice of boundary-making by seeming to elevate the virtue of flexibility, even at the price of principle, tradition, geography, and other agents of stabilization, permanency, and predictability. The negotiation theorist might also be criticized for leaning too heavily on the merits of finessing difficult issues in an ad hoc manner that overlooks some long-range implications.[15]

The Socio-Cultural Framework

Anthropologists and sociologists join "human geographers" in stressing the socio-cultural implications of boundary-making. They are likely to emphasize the need for contact as well as separation in a transboundary area,[16] and thus to warn against the creation of formal divisions which may be expected to generate resentments within the affected community. Such theorists also play a useful role in clarifying intracommunity and intercommunity patterns of trade, communications, and other significant flows that are unlikely to be accurately reflected in official statistics. In the case of ocean boundaries, the movements between fishing communities in a boundary area may underline the arbitrariness of a proposed line. Moreover, the socio-cultural perspective on boundary-making is often a local one, and thus serves as a corrective of the statist or macroregional perspectives that are likely to be adopted, consciously or unconsciously, by the boundary-makers.[17]

By the same token, the socio-cultural framework can be regarded as too narrow if the boundary is perceived as serving larger interests than those of the local, boundary-contingent communities. Those who profess to adopt a dispassionate or technical approach to boundary-making may even perceive the socio-cultural approach as representing an unduly romantic view of a problem of statecraft or international relations.[18]

The Economic Framework

The economist is likely to give special weight to the resource implications of a boundary-making issue. Like the socio-cultural theorist, he can be expected to draw attention to the potential relationship between boundary settlements and transboundary arrangements;[19] and like the political theorist, he will wish to look at any bilateral boundary delimitation issue with a view to the overall economic and political relationship between the two parties.[20] His training tends to foster a preference for a dispassionate mode of analysis that permits an even-handed appraisal of the costs and benefits associated with a proposal. Accustomed to analysis both at the micro and macro levels of economic planning, the economist is likely to be relatively comfortable with the intellectual framework of the military strategist, who will look at a boundary issue as only part of a much larger consideration of national or international security.[21] On the other hand, the economist is vulnerable to the charge of accentuating considerations of efficiency at the expense of equity, and perhaps even to that of dehumanizing the issues.[22]

The Juridical Framework

The lawyer's contribution to boundary-making is particularly evident in the late twentieth century. His practical utility lies in his versatility in such diverse professional skills as negotiation, drafting, counselling, advocacy, and judicial decision-making, which are applied in the arts of bureaucracy, diplomacy, and intermediation. Since lawyers are used so frequently today in all three of these processes, the juridical framework is also of importance in the theory of boundary-making. It may be assumed, for example, that the jurist tends to control the nature and direction of argument in any adversarial situation, and dominates the planning of strategy in the diplomatic and adjudicative processes. Since lawyers almost invariably draft the final product – whether a decree, statute, regulation, treaty, or award – it can also be said that their influence in the language of boundary-making is paramount.

Apart from his role as orchestrator of strategy in diplomatic and adjudicative settings, the lawyer exerts a disciplinary influence of his own. Typically, the legal framework consists primarily of principles, practices, and lines of argument that are assumed to have precedential value. The lawyer's mind is programmed in favour of predictability; he is trained to pursue the logic of linear reasoning from premises that are both "reasonable" and "established."[23] The conceptual framework of a lawyer is skewed towards equity rather than efficiency. But a training in the common law tradition may be likely to direct a search for carefully articulated "equitable principles" than for equity itself, based on the sense of justice or injustice.[24]

In sum, it might be suggested that the chief merit of the juridical framework is that of verbal precision. On the debit side of the account, the jurist often tends to be rigid in circumstances where a degree of intellectual flexibility or imaginativeness would be more productive. The sharpening of focus produced by legal analysis, under an appropriate head of legal doctrine, usually represents a kind of reductionism that results in a narrowing of the issues and an exclusion of certain kinds of information that may be irrelevant to the legal issues but central to the extra-legal purposes at stake.[25]

The Managerial Framework

At least in the most complex boundary-making situations, each of the five conceptual frameworks outlined above can be seen to be unduly limited. The need for a more comprehensive, less reductionist approach to boundary theory can be met more readily by combining them within an all-encompassing framework that might be characterized as managerial. Most official boundaries today are intended primarily to serve a regulatory, or at least an administrative, purpose. Accordingly, boundaries should be required, both in theory and practice, to pass some kind of functional test that is appropriate to the type of zone delimited by the boundary in question. (See chapter 15 on the test of functionality.)

The case for the managerial framework seems strongest in the ocean, where the task of boundary-making is most closely associated with the concept of management or, more properly, ocean development and management. This proposition, which will be developed throughout this monograph, is derived from the observation that coastal states are rapidly developing the administrative process of zoning areas of the ocean, especially coastal areas, and from the prediction that ocean boundaries will be required increasingly to serve administrative purposes by reference to the overriding rationale of ocean development and management. It is in the ocean that boundary-making problems of unprecedented complexity will be encountered and that the managerial perspective will be most useful.

The chief merit of the managerial framework is its inclusiveness, a mark of special sophistication in the most complex boundary-making situations. The suitability of a boundary will be evaluated by reference to the management functions to be served by the boundary: data acquisition, allocation of research effort, distribution of harvesting rights, monitoring authority, enforcement of regulations, and so forth. In situations where a boundary is directly related to several different sectors of management – such as offshore mineral development, fishery development and management, conservation of species, pollution control, the regulation of scientific research, and vessel traffic management in the exclusive economic zone – the managerial framework will have to be broadly ecological or environmental in scope.[26] In short, in the most complex situations the manager's view of boundaries will be systemic.

The most obvious weakness of the managerial framework of reference is that it lacks the conceptual tightness or rigour of a disciplinary framework. Its credibility depends to some extent on that of a general theory (or pre-theory) of ocean management. Although it is potentially innovative, the managerial approach is subject to the criticism that it is eclectic at best and internally self-contradictory at worst – an amalgam of inconsistent notions of development, management, conservation, regulation, and administration that will be forced to yield in practice to expedient political compromises.

CHAPTER FOUR

Processes and Outcomes

ACTORS

Bureaucracy

The chief actors in the bureaucratic process of boundary-making are, of course, government officials, although occasional use is made of professional consultants and academic experts.[1] Government officials are of crucial importance at all four stages of boundary-making (allocation, delimitation, demarcation, and administration), but the range of agencies represented, and the mix of expertise, is likely to vary from stage to stage. In the case of international boundaries, the foreign ministry is likely to be the lead agency during the allocation and delimitation stages, but other agencies possessing surveying, hydrographic, scientific, and administrative expertise are likely to assume primary responsibility in the later stages, unless an unexpected diplomatic incident occurs.

International boundaries are normally the preserve of national government, although a national government may find it necessary or useful to consult with a subnational state or province whose interests might be affected by the boundary or transboundary arrangement under consideration.[2] Internal boundaries usually involve county, township, or city governments, and may also involve private consultants.[3] Intergovernmental organizations operating at the global or regional level rarely have occasion to participate in boundary-making, but binational commissions have contributed both to boundary maintenance and transboundary management.[4] The role of regional organizations may be expected to become more important as the regional implications of ocean boundary-making, especially in semi-enclosed seas, become more evident.[5]

Diplomacy

Although international boundary-making negotiations are almost invariably directed by a nation's foreign ministry, it is necessary to involve officials from a number of other national agencies in order to provide the appropriate range of expertise.[6] It is not unusual for a national team negotiating an international boundary to include a number of officials from the subnational level of government, or even industry representatives, when transboundary arrangements are involved in the negotiations.[7]

Whether international or internal, bilateral boundary negotiations tend to be heavily laden with emotional freight. Even when kept secret or private they are likely to become disputatious.[8] Because of their symbolic significance they usually attract the attention of politicians and the public at large more than most other kinds of diplomacy.[9] Not infrequently, therefore, the negotiators of a boundary dispute find they are not the only actors, and that they are required to negotiate with relatively little flexibility in accordance with high-level political directives, which in turn may be perceived as a direct expression of public opinion (or at least coloured by an awareness of public sentiment).[10]

Adjudication

Three principal kinds of actors are involved in the adjudicative process of boundary-making: researchers, advocates, and judges.[11] The number and diversity of researchers involved will be tailored according to the requirements of legal argument and counter-argument. Once the terms of the *compromis* (the agreement to submit to adjudication) have been negotiated by the parties to the dispute, those responsible for preparing the case on each side are free to determine the range of relevant or useful research. For any one kind of boundary dispute there may be a very considerable difference between a narrow, legalistic interpretation of the research required and a broad "Brandeis brief" approach. If the latter course is adopted, many of the researchers may be non-lawyers.[12] Either way, the direction, scope, and rigour of the research are controlled by those responsible for the advocacy. The judges in a boundary dispute are usually legally trained, although they may call upon "assessors" or experts for advice on certain non-legal matters.[13]

Of the three processes, the adjudicative is the least dominated by government officials. In boundary disputes it is common for governments to engage scholars and professional consultants to assist in preparation of the case and to evaluate the other party's arguments.[14] It is also common for governments litigating an international boundary dispute to engage both foreign and native jurists in an advocacy role.[15] The judges, of course, serve in their individual capacity, although each of the parties may be permitted to nominate a national to the tribunal.[16] Similarly, in the case of an internal boundary dispute, scholars, professional consultants, foreign experts, and independent judges may all contribute to the adjudicative process, thereby considerably reducing the influence of the governments involved on the final outcome.

In addition, reference should be made to the principal forms of intermediation other than adjudication: conciliation, mediation (or good offices), and reference to an international organization. In each case the third party is asked to provide "mediational" services. To the extent that intermediation is an exercise in persuasion, its purpose may be best described as quasi-diplomatic, but it can also be characterized as partly adjudicative. Even so, members of a conciliation commission need not be lawyers, and even when they are they may serve the quasi-diplomatic purpose at hand more effectively by refraining from taking an unduly legalistic approach. A single mediator may be an expert, a professional diplomat, or some other person of considerable prestige or moral authority. A named sovereign, the pope, the secretary-general of the United Nations (or their personal representatives) have acted as mediators. Often what is needed, above all, is someone who can be depended upon to display patience, good will, and understanding, as well as strict impartiality, as in the normal process of adjudication.

ROLES

Bureaucracy

Most of the actors involved in bureaucratic boundary-making play out their roles on a darkened stage. Particularly in the case of unilateral boundaries, a well-lit set is not conducive to the solution of technical problems. Internal boundary-making at the local level is usually kept out of the glare of publicity, unless it is of the sort that has an immediate political significance, such as the revision of the existing boundaries of an electoral district.[17] Today, internal administrative boundary-making is carried out under zoning rather than boundary-making authority, and the public interest is likely to be attracted to non-boundary aspects of the zoning issue.

It follows from all of this that the actors in bureaucratic boundary-making are likely to fill technical rather than political roles. Most of these actors probably see their roles as substantive rather than representative, although, when agency interests or mandates conflict, some of them may find that their roles are also quasi-representative within the bureaucratic system and therefore quasi-political.

Diplomacy

In a negotiating situation, all the key participants serve in a representative capacity, even many of those who provide substantive or technical support. Today, however, the concept of a "diplomatic representative" is more blurred than it was in the nineteenth century, when foreign ministries and professional diplomats were closer to self-sufficiency. The widespread use of agencies other than foreign ministries in foreign affairs has extended the concept of diplomatic representation beyond the class of foreign service officers. For ocean boundary negotiations, government-employed geographers, geologists, geodesists, hydrographers, cartographers, and other experts usually have to be supplied by several different departments. Within federal states, moreover, the need for internal diplomacy between different levels of government for a growing variety of purposes, including boundary-making, has forced subnational states and provinces to create a new class of specialists in intergovernmental negotiation.

Adjudication

On the face of things, the roles of the actors in the adjudicative process of boundary-making are more fixed than in the bureaucratic and diplomatic processes. Certainly there are professional traditions and binding rules of procedure that define the roles of advocate and judge and prescribe the acceptable mode of conduct for both. But the senior advocate enjoys considerable latitude in the preparation of the case, and the tribunal normally has a very high degree of discretion in its disposition of issues.[18]

The senior advocate usually will have sufficient discretionary authority over the setting and planning of strategy – within the limits of the negotiated terms of the *compromis* in the case of an international boundary dispute – that he might be likened to a general preparing for battle. Before appearing in court, his role is organizational in the largest sense, rather than technical or representative, and his approach in organizing the data and the arguments is essentially personal, reflecting his own legal philosophy.

The tribunal normally is assigned a resolutive role, subject to the terms of reference agreed to by the parties to the suit. But the characteristics of judicial boundary-making will be determined ultimately by the way in which the adjudicators choose to interpret their mandate. They may give more weight to the *declaratory* or *facilitative* aspects of their role than the terms of reference request. Because of the larger "problem" behind the "issue" presented, the adjudicators may choose to define their role in facilitative as well as resolutive terms, even when the terms of reference seem purely resolutive. An international and multicultural tribunal in a boundary dispute may have difficulty in finding an approach to the merits of the case that is philosophically acceptable to all members. The need to produce a majority viewpoint may result in an arduous process of intellectual debate, which is likely to acquire at least some of the characteristics of compromise diplomacy. To that extent the adjudicative role can be said to be quasi-diplomatic, at least in the more difficult cases.

Non-adjudicative intermediary processes such as conciliation and mediation involve the assignment of explicitly facilitative roles contemplating the need for future negotiation between the parties.

RELATIONSHIP BETWEEN STAGE AND PROCESS

Bureaucracy

In the case of most internal boundaries, bureaucratic inputs are dominant, and often unchallenged at all four stages of boundary-making: allocation, delimitation, demarcation, and administration. Political influences outside the bureaucratic process do, of course, often intrude at the allocation or delimitation stage, but almost never during demarcation and only occasionally in subsequent administration. In the case of international boundaries, the bureaucratic input tends to yield to the diplomatic during allocation and delimitation, but even at those stages it is reflected to some extent in the preparations for negotiations. The demarcation and administration of an international boundary are, essentially, bureaucratic processes, although the former invariably and the latter frequently are undertaken as joint (usually bilateral) arrangements.

Diplomacy

The diplomatic process has been applied mostly to international boundaries, but in recent years zoning and related arrangements have created the need to negotiate new kinds of internal boundaries for administrative reasons, especially within federal states. External or internal diplomacy may be required at any of the four stages of boundary-making. In the case of international boundaries, the diplomatic input is invariably the primary input during allocation and delimitation, but it may also be present as a secondary input during demarcation and administration.

Adjudication

The adjudicative process is likely to be applied only at the stage of delimitation, usually only after the failure of diplomacy. Very rarely there may be occasion to have an issue resolved in a judicial or quasi-judicial manner during allocation, demarcation, or administration. Conciliation and mediation are often used at an earlier stage, when the parties are still deadlocked over basic questions of allocation. Often the secret of successful mediation or conciliation is the ability to reformulate the boundary issue as a distributive problem of resource development and management, which lends itself to a number of alternative solutions in the form of arrangements as well as settlements.

RELATIONSHIP BETWEEN INPUT AND PROCESS

Bureaucracy

Bureaucratic boundary-making may be influenced by any combination of the six intellectual inputs (conceptual frameworks) reviewed above: physical, political, socio-cultural, economic, juridical, and managerial. The physical input may receive no more and no less weighting in bureaucratic boundary-making than it does in diplomatic or adjudicative, but significant variations may occur in the weight assigned to the five other inputs. Above all, it seems likely that the managerial input would be weighted more heavily in the bureaucratic process than in the diplomatic or adjudicative, and the four remaining inputs seem likely to receive moderate weighting.

Diplomacy

In boundary negotiations the physical input will be weighted according to the political perception of the parties; that is, it will vary with their perception of the fairness or unfairness of using the objective facts of geography or geology, or the neutral techniques of geometry. As to the other kinds of inputs, the diplomatic process will tend to give primacy to political, socio-cultural, and economic perspectives and considerations, and intermediate ranking to juridical and managerial.

Adjudication

Judicial boundary-makers may be tempted to use geography or geology and the techniques of geometry for reasons of familiarity or impartiality; their degree of reliance on physical criteria may finally depend on whether they believe it will have an equitable effect. Adherence to a traditional juridical framework usually means that little if any weighting will be given to political, socio-cultural, economic, and managerial considerations. Typically, mediators and conciliators try to present a broader view of the problem than adjudicators in a court of law or an arbitral tribunal, even to the point of envisaging a range of alternative diplomatic and bureaucratic solutions.

RELATIONSHIP BETWEEN STAGE AND INPUT

The allocation stage of boundary-making deals primarily with political problems, and it should be assumed that the political perspective will have primacy over other inputs, whether the allocation issues are global, binational, or unilateral. At the delimitation stage the juridical, economic, and socio-cultural inputs will receive more weighting than at the other three stages. Whether they also will receive more weighting than the other inputs will depend on the circumstances. The physical input may have considerable influence on the delimitation of a boundary, although it may receive even more weight at other stages, especially that of demarcation. Physical factors and criteria will be paramount at the demarcation stage, almost to the exclusion of all other inputs. Finally, the managerial perspective is more likely to be prevalent at the administration stage than at any of the earlier stages. In the case of ocean boundaries, boundary maintenance will take the form of complex boundary-related arrangements that require the application, more or less constantly, or a wide range of inputs.

OUTCOMES

The interaction and inputs reviewed above are intended to result finally in one or more of four types of boundary settlements or transboundary arrangements: textual, organizational, special, and routine. A "boundary settlement" is an outcome of a boundary-making process that deals only with the allocation, delimitation, or demarcation of a boundary line. A "transboundary arrangement" is an outcome of a boundary-making process that deals with any matter that arises or is likely to arise in a transboundary (or frontier) area as such. The term "boundary-making process" is used widely to include efforts to maintain (or administer) a boundary after the line has been finally and precisely drawn.

Formal Texts

Most boundary arrangements include a formal text of one kind or another. The text is likely to take one of five forms: international treaty, constitutional provision, executive decree, statute, or subordinate legislation.

In the case of international boundaries, a formal treaty is almost invariably the final form of settlement. It is unlikely that an international boundary issue will be regarded as resolved until a legally binding international agreement has been concluded. A formal bilateral boundary treaty, addressed to the task of delimitation in the traditional sense, is indeed the classic example of a resolutive agreement, and thus distinguishable from other functional categories of treaties. (On the functional classification of treaties, see chapter 17.) The special nature of boundary treaties and other kinds of resolutive agreements has long been recognized by writers on international law, and is sometimes described as "dispositive" in effect.[19]

It is fairly common for a national constitution to include a provision on the official political boundaries of the state.[20] Counterpart provisions in subnational constitutions are also familiar.[21] Great variations exist, however, in the specificity of the language employed. In earlier times constitutionally defined boundaries were almost always land boundaries only, but since 1945 it has become less unusual to promulgate ocean boundaries in constitutional form.[22] The inclusion of airspace boundaries in national constitutions is still rare.[23]

In many countries both international and internal boundaries are promulgated by an executive decree of one kind or another.[24] The practice is most closely associated with countries having a presidential system of government, presumably because most countries with a parliamentary system adhere, by and large, to the British tradition of parliamentary sovereignty, and boundary-making is regarded as too important to leave entirely to the executive branch.[25]

Under both presidential and parliamentary systems it is common to promulgate a wide array of internal boundaries in normal statutory form. This trend is likely to become more pronounced as zoning becomes a more widely accepted technique of regulation in public administration. The trend to statutory boundaries will inevitably lead to an increased use of subordinate legislation for the delineation of local administrative zones on land, in airspace, and at sea.[26]

Permanent Organizations

The idea of creating permanent commissions to administer international transboundary arrangements, after agreement is reached on allocation, delimitation, and demarcation, seems to have originated in Europe in the nineteenth century.[27] The most famous examples are the commissions established to administer transboundary arrangements in international rivers and lakes.[28] Somewhat analogous is the organization created to administer the Suez Canal.[29] In North America, the International Joint Commissions between the United States and Canada and between the

United States and Mexico have developed further organizational functions in transboundary areas on land, in water, and in the superadjacent airspace.[30]

In some situations it has been preferred to entrust transboundary arrangements to an existing permanent organization rather than create a new body specifically for that purpose, either by adding a new component to the organization's committee structure or simply by introducing new administrative practices or procedures.[31] Occasionally, permanent organizations are entrusted with responsibility for administering internal transboundary arrangements.[32]

Special Arrangements

During the processes of allocation, delimitation, and demarcation, special temporary arrangements are made to facilitate those phases of boundary-making. Examples of such special arrangements abound in the history of international boundary-making. Special boundary arrangements may also take the form of projects, studies, or public inquiries.[33]

Routine Arrangements

It should not be overlooked that boundary-making often results in unpublicized acts or services of a routine governmental sort, either on a regular or irregular basis, such as the exchange of reports[34] or the practice of giving notice of an event of transboundary significance to the neighbour on the other side of the boundary.[35]

SOURCES

For evidence of these outcomes, one may refer not only to the five forms of formal texts, but also to a number of less formal sources: to unilateral declarations by governments or individual officials; to official press releases; to ministerial statements; to resolutions of international organizations; to official maps; to archival materials; to reports of lands and surveys departments; and to monographs, memoirs, and unofficial maps.[35] In the case of ocean boundaries, charts as well as maps may have an important evidentiary role.[36]

CHAPTER FIVE

Techniques

Most of the literature on boundary-making has focused chiefly on international boundaries, and the discussion has been dominated by political geographers, diplomatic historians, and international lawyers. Because of the structure of their respective disciplines, the geographers have generally given emphasis to the criteria and methods used, the historians to the factors at work, and the lawyers to the principles that were or should have been applied. Geographers often confine their analysis to the text of negotiated boundary settlements, lawyers to the text of adjudicated boundary settlements. For these reasons, neither of these two disciplines has been able to deal fully and even-handedly with the variety of techniques that can be applied to boundary-making.

The difficulty of attempting this task is compounded by the fact that the text of an international boundary agreement conceals more than it reveals of the principles, criteria, and methods that were actually applied by the negotiators. The traditional confidentiality of government documents has prevented disclosure of this kind of information for decades after the completion of negotiations, thereby leaving the investigation to diplomatic historians, who are not necessarily interested in the technicalities of boundary-making. Lawyers, on the other hand, focusing as they do on the published outcome of the latest adjudication, rarely resort to careful comparative analysis, and in any event their training in international rules and principles tends to produce a predisposition in favour of norms that are presumed to govern the outcome. The lawyer's normative bias is reinforced by the flow of the adjudicator's reasoning, which normally devotes more attention to the applicable rules and principles than to the criteria and methods used.

In the case of ocean boundaries, another discipline that attempts to deal specifically with the techniques of boundary-making is hydrography, which has been defined as the science of measuring and depicting those parameters that are necessary to describe the precise nature and configuration of the seabed, its geographical relationship to the land-mass, and the characteristics and dynamics of the sea.[1] The parameters encompass bathymetry, geology, and geophysics, and therefore tides, currents, waves, and certain other physical properties of sea water.[2]

Until modern times, the outer limits of ocean boundaries were relatively close to shore, and the sufficiency of the hydrographer's input into ocean boundary-making was determined by reference to the cartographic order of precision. In other words, the hydrographer's input consisted in large part of data collected essentially for the purpose of compiling nautical charts designed specifically to meet the requirements of marine navigation. Nautical charts are generally compiled on the Mercator projection and carry a gradation of latitude and longitude. (For the history of the nautical chart, see chapter 8.)

Today, ocean boundaries usually are shown on nautical charts.[3] Under the 1982 UN Convention on the Law of the Sea, the "normal" baseline for measuring the breadth of the territorial sea is to be marked on large-scale charts recognized officially by the coastal state.[4] No provision is made, however, for the scale of charts showing baselines that may deviate from the normal.[5] In the case of delimitation of "lateral" boundaries between opposite or adjacent states, the reference is to "charts of a scale or scales adequate for ascertaining [the] position" of such limits.[6] The same provision applies to archipelagic baselines.[7]

The scale of any chart is governed by two factors – navigational considerations and the scale at which the original survey was conducted. It is fairly common in charting practice to conduct surveys at about twice the scale of the intended navigational chart, but the International Hydrographic Office recommends various scales for various types of surveys.[8]

In recent years, however, the seaward extension of ocean boundaries hundreds of miles from the nearest shore has raised the prospect, and arguably the need, for greater precision. Today geodesists use highly sophisticated instruments of measurement to define the figure of the earth, and every variation on it, with unprecedented precision. Since very large areas of sea are now enclosed by ocean boundaries, distortions and inaccuracies in modern ocean boundary-making may be very considerable, but the techniques of marine geodesy are available to attain a higher standard of precision than has ever been available to boundary-makers on land.[9] The need for the highest degree of precision varies with the type of zone and regime involved, and perhaps with the interests and values at stake. The need for precision in the granting of petroleum concessions, for example, may be greater than in the enforcement of fishery conservation jurisdiction. Increasingly, the need for a higher order of precision in ocean boundary-making casts doubt on the adequacy of the Mercator chart for

EEZ and continental shelf areas extending far beyond the twelve-mile limits of the territorial seas.[10]

The technical difficulties involved in choosing the best method of delineation are most acute when a straight line is to be used, as in the case of a straight baseline or an equidistance line for delimitation between opposite or adjacent states. A straight line may be a rhumb line (or loxodrome), as depicted on a Mercator chart; or a small circle arc, such as all parallels of latitude, except the equator; or a great circle, such as the equator and all meridians; or a geodesic, which is the shortest distance between two points on the earth's surface.[11] In the case of very long ocean boundaries, especially in high latitudes, the difference between a rhumb line and a geodesic can be significant.[12] In these circumstances the geodesic is certainly the most accurate straight line. In ocean boundary-making practice, it is becoming more common, especially on the part of developed coastal states, to use geodesics as an accurate means of delimiting offshore zones.

To this further complications can be added. The geodesist has to choose from eight or more principal "spheroids" (geodetic reference systems), and "horizontal datums." Choices must also be made among many "vertical datums," especially tidal elevations, for baseline delineation purposes.[13] The need for charts underlines the need for choice not only in chart scales,[14] but also in projections. Moreover, geodesists and geometricians have different ways of measuring rounded surfaces.[15]

The result of this complexity, which arises from the capacity for precision in boundary-making, is confusion in the minds of the bureaucrats, diplomats, and adjudicators who are assigned the primary tasks of ocean boundary-making. From the perspective of hydrographers, geodesists, geometricians, and cartographers, precision-related choices remain to be made after their less technically minded colleagues have agreed on the choice of general principles, criteria, and methods – and perhaps also corrective tests, such as equidistance, median line, straight line, perpendicular line, "general direction of the coast," low-water, "half-effect," and proportionality. Moreover, lawyers have been unable to agree among themselves on the articulation and precise connotation of the legal principles applicable to ocean boundary-making. Indeed, the recent history of boundary adjudication suggests that the elucidation and distinction of judicially recognized principles, criteria, and methods is still at an early stage of evolution.

PART TWO

The History of Ocean Boundary-Making

CHAPTER SIX

The Evolution of Ocean Uses and Regimes

The ocean, like airspace and outer space, is much more limited than the land in the variety of human uses it supports. In recent times, however, we have witnessed a dramatic growth and diversification in the uses of the ocean. The introduction of these new uses, like the development of older ones, can be attributed directly to the emergence of new modes of technology.[1] Indeed, technology has not only played the crucial role in the development of ocean resources, but has also created the need for management of the marine environment. Yet, although technology is the key to ocean development and management, the hand that turns the key can only be described in terms of human values, interests, attitudes and relationships, and other factors discernible in the milieu of human initiatives. Together with emerging technology, these factors constitute the effective demand, and this creates the need for appropriate responses in legal and institutional form.

It is a commonly accepted fact of modern society that only government is expected to respond to demands of this sort. Within the nation-state system, obligations to respond to major social demands fall, above all, on the national government. Yet because so much of the ocean has traditionally been treated as extending beyond the limits of national jurisdiction – that is, beyond the limits of territorial jurisdiction – the obligation to respond to new ocean use demands has often been accepted at the international rather than the national level, within an appropriate intergovernmental forum, either regional or global. In recent years, however, the proliferation of ocean uses has necessitated multiple responses at all existing levels of government, including the local level. Indeed, the need for effective regulation and management of ocean uses can be met only within a split-level system of authorities.[2]

Over the centuries government has responded in various ways to new or altered demands for ocean use: by the assertion of general *spatial claims* to entitlement in the name of national or imperial authority (for example, *dominium maris*); by the assertion of *non-spatial claims* to authority protective of a particular kind of activity (for example, flag state jurisdiction over navigation and related activities); by the development of jurisdictional *regimes* of principles, rules, procedures, and institutions designed for the resolution of "first-order" legal issues (for example, the regime of the continental shelf); and, not least, by the delineation of more or less precisely defined *zones* for designated purposes of allocation or regulation, or both (for example, a contiguous zone).

Boundary-making is, of course, the delimitative aspect of the spatial allocation of authority. At sea, as on land and in the air, authority has been spatially allocated, within designated boundaries, in order to serve a variety of legal and administrative purposes: to assert rights, to acknowledge responsibilities, and to clarify the scope of designated kinds of official action. Two institutional devices – regimes and zones – have been developed over the centuries to facilitate these legal and administrative purposes in the ocean. Both have proliferated in modern times, to the point that a great deal of conceptual confusion has arisen in attempting to describe the contemporary system of public order in the ocean.

In the interest of clarity in dealing with the theory and history of ocean boundary-making, it seems important to draw a careful distinction between a regime and a zone. The term "regime" should be used *only* to refer to a system of principles, rules, procedures, and institutions. It is essentially a *legal* concept, designed primarily to serve the interests of public law. The term "zone" should be used to describe an area that has been spatially defined for separate or special treatment within a functionally defined context of official action. It is essentially an *administrative* (or quasi-administrative) concept, designed to serve certain designated purposes of public administration, including a wide range of ocean development, management, and regulation concerns. In the modern era it is necessary, for legal reasons, to rationalize the exercise of authority within an ocean zone by reference to the appropriate regime; and increasingly it has been found useful, if not essential, to develop zones, both international and intranational, in order to implement the rights and responsibilities under an ocean regime with an appropriately high degree of administrative efficiency.

The confusion between regimes and zones seems to be due to a number of causes. First, a regime, though essentially legal in purpose, has administrative implications. With the emergence of functional jurisdiction in the modern law of the sea we witness the seaward extension of public administration under new functional regimes, such as the regimes of the continental shelf and the exclusive economic zone.[3] Second, the creation of a zone, although essentially administrative in purpose, provides the opportunity for clarifying and developing the legal implications of the regime under which the zone is to be administered. The existence of precise spatial boundaries around a zone permits precise treatment of legal questions regarding the allocation of authority. Third, most regimes and most zones are alike in having both spatial and functional characteristics. Both, therefore, tend to have spatial boundaries that can or should be drawn in accordance with a functional theory of boundary-making. Fourth, further confusion arises from terminology: the most famous modern regime, the EEZ, is described as a zone in the 1982 Convention on the Law of the Sea.

Because of this confusion, it may be useful to mention several obvious differences between a regime and a zone, other than the basic distinction between public law and public administration purposes served. First, the *system* of ocean regimes, taken as a whole, is the outcome of the world constitutive process, and to that extent reflects the balance struck in the common interest between inclusive and exclusive uses of the ocean.[4] Ocean zones, on the other hand, are very largely coastal or offshore in orientation, reflecting chiefly the exclusive or special interests of the coastal or nearest adjacent state.[5] Second, the law developed specifically for a zone is likely to be composed largely of national elements, whereas a regime is an expression of international law. The law of a zone must be consonant with the regime with which it is associated, and to that extent the law of the zone is subordinate to the regime.[6] Third, the primary purpose of an ocean regime is allocative rather than regulatory, whereas the priorities tend to be reversed in the case of an ocean zone. This distinction can be expressed another way: in a regime, equity (an allocative value) tends to be primary, whereas, in a zone, efficiency (an operational value) predominates. Fourth, regimes tend to be broadly cast in spatial and functional terms; zones tend to be more restrictive geographically, and more specifically conceived, even precisely developed, on a functional plane.

Those trained in international law emphasize the relevance and saliency of the characteristics of the appropriate regime in dealing with regulatory questions that arise in the context of ocean development and management. Others may find it useful to focus more sharply on the features of the appropriate zone, especially if the questions arising fall within the context of public administration policy. But when the questions are directly related to boundary-making, the characteristics of the appropriate regime, and the features of the appropriate zone, and the relationship between the two must be taken into account. Accordingly, in describing the history of ocean boundary-making, it is necessary not only to review the evolution of ocean regimes, but also to trace the emergence of ocean zones. Since the former topic is a familiar history, and is described at length in many textbooks, it can be briefly summarized here.

Although it is easy to make the modern distinction between ocean regimes and ocean zones, it is difficult to view the histories of those concepts as separate trends in the development of the law of the sea. Each of the concepts represents a mode of thinking about the assertion of land-based authority over areas of the ocean and activities at sea. "Zonal thinking" focuses relatively clearly on a specific type of activity to be regulated and a specific geographical area for administering that authority. "Regime thinking," in contrast, reflects an effort to elaborate a kind of legal system within which the claimant authority is free to exercise a range of competences, albeit subject in some cases to certain constraints designed into the system. Zonal thinking is the hallmark of the administrative mind, and regime thinking is the hallmark of the legal mind. Both kinds of thinking have always been present throughout the history of the public law and administration of the oceans, inextricably linked and difficult to disentangle.

Of these two modes of thinking about the assertion of authority in the ocean, legal thinking has tended to dominate the literature of the legal and political history of the ocean. Accordingly, modern perceptions of regulatory issues in the ocean have been chiefly influenced by the observer's familiarity with the evolution of such legal regimes as the high seas, the territorial sea, and the continental shelf. Even non-lawyers have tended to assume that the nature and characteristics of the appropriate regime are the most normal and useful point of departure for the investigation of a regulatory issue in the ocean. Although the modern dominance of regime thinking now seems to be diminishing owing to the resurgence of ocean zoning, it is necessary to review the major trends and events that gave rise to the prevalence of legal thinking in the modern era.

It may be sufficient to begin that review in the period of Roman antiquity, although the history of claims to control over the ocean reaches back much earlier, both in the East and in the West.[7] The Romans were, of course, chiefly interested in the sea for the purposes of conquest and trade. Unlike the Greeks, the Roman conquerors were eventually able to impose their will by force on virtually the entire Mediterranean basin, which then became the centre of a wealthy and powerful empire.[8] Under the *pax romana*, the merchants of the Mediterranean became dependent on the Roman system of public administration and on the legal guarantees that existed in conditions of stability.[9] In the absence of serious rival claims to political authority over the region, Roman jurists were able to rationalize the undivided nature of Roman authority in terms of *imperium* and cognate concepts of legal doctrine.[10] This early effort by jurists to provide a rationale for the assertion of coastal state authority in generic rather than functional terms marks the beginning in the Western world of regime thinking about maritime jurisdiction and control.

Despite the universal language of Roman legal doctrine, the concepts of *imperium* and its variants were based on regional (Mediterranean) experience.[11] With the dawning of the Renaissance, man's horizons began to expand dramatically, and the Age of Discovery revealed the truly global dimensions of the world community.[12] By the end of the fourteenth century, ambitious princes were turning aggressively to the ocean for the commercial advancement of their city-states.[13] Their desire to attain sweeping political authority over extensive coastal areas required the services of legal scholars, who were able to rationalize their clients' claims in the tradition of the Roman *imperium*.[14] In succeeding centuries the same relationship between client prince and legal scholar became a familiar feature of the early development of the modern nation-state, giving the scholastic mind a prominent role in the rationalization of political ambitions in the sea.[15] By the sixteenth century serious rivalries in commerce and diplomacy, especially in western Europe, were increasing the political and economic stakes in the struggle for dominance over ocean space and certain ocean resources. Legal scholars serving the interests of a particular prince were now required to display a high degree of political astuteness in designing a system of legal regimes that would accommodate diverse and legitimate claims to authority over ocean space and resources. The early seventeenth century marked the first systematic effort to provide such a system, an effort dramatized by the great debate between Hugo Grotius, the advocate of *mare liberum*, and John Selden, the supporter of *mare clausum*.[16] Over the next two hundred years legal scholars were concerned with the development and refinement of such a system, and sought the balance between the requirements of coastal state control under the regime of the emerging territorial sea and the requirements of freedom of navigation and trade under the regime of the high seas.[17] By the beginning of the nineteenth century it was accepted virtually everywhere that the nation-state system, which by then had evolved, was best served by a universal public order system based on the principles of uniformity and reciprocity.[18] Above all, the interests of international trade and colonization required a legal system of great simplicity and clarity.

From the mid-nineteenth century, however, it gradually became apparent that the requirements of the modern state were less a matter of sovereign prerogative than of administrative responsibility. With the growing burden of state bureaucracy, which reflected the acceptance of governmental responsibility for a widening range of ocean-related concerns, government officials began to recognize the inadequacy of the simple dualistic system of regimes. By the second half of the nineteenth century, several states began to accept the need for a compromise on functional grounds and intermediate modes of coastal state authority between the classical poles of territorial sovereignty and navigational freedom. Although these administrative claims to a contiguous zone beyond the territorial sea were generally conceded to be necessary, they were not legitimized within a fully developed regime until the second half of the twentieth century.[19] By that time a much more radical change in the perception of the ocean had taken place, leading jurists to think systematically about the status of the sea bed.[20] This debate resulted in the emergence of the modern regime of the continental shelf and the contemporary doctrine of the common heritage of mankind applied to the deep ocean floor beyond the limits of national jurisdiction.[21]

Since the end of the Second World War, regime thinking about the ocean has been characterized by the political need to codify and develop the international law of the sea through global conference diplomacy. Within the span of twenty-five years, three major efforts have been made to consolidate and reformulate the legal architecture of ocean regimes.[22] This exciting experiment in legal development has been motivated largely by the desire of coastal states to acquire exclusive authority over newly available resources within an extensive coastal zone and increased entitlements to jurisdiction and control over a wider range of activities within those offshore areas.[23] In this contemporary period the advent of the two-hundred-mile exclusive economic zone is universally accepted as a dominant motif in the new system of spatial regimes.

CHAPTER SEVEN

Trends in Ocean Zoning

INTRODUCTION

Regime thinking has been the dominant mode of thought about claims to authority in the ocean in the modern era. The outline in the preceding chapter of the emergence of the various ocean regimes is likely to be familiar to most readers. Yet it is crucial to a proper understanding of the public law and administration of the oceans to appreciate the long history and continuous development of zonal thinking. Because this side of the story is less well known, it is important to trace these trends in greater detail.

The preceding chapter reviewed the emergence of ocean regimes by reference to the role of the legal scholar, especially in his capacity as a rationalizer of his client's political or commercial interests. Particularly in the service of a client prince, the jurist often tended to develop legal doctrine in a broad transempirical manner, more broadly sometimes than was necessary to justify the specific assertions of coastal authority advanced by the client under the conditions of the day.[1] But not all jurists surrendered to this temptation to broaden the claims by virtue of the doctrine of sovereignty, or some variant of all-encompassing political authority such as territorial jurisdiction. Indeed, many of the medieval and early Renaissance jurists tried to limit the discourse of maritime claims so as to deal specifically with the fishery protection, commercial regulation, or military security concerns of the day.[2] Even in those early days of doctrinal development there was a tension between those jurists who were tempted to extrapolate beyond the specific requirements of the coastal authorities and those who were careful to restrict doctrinal development to specific categories of interest.

Most of the history of ocean zoning lies outside the history of legal doctrine. It can be shown that inshore, coastal, and offshore zones have been established under many categories of interest for many hundreds of years. Some zoning practices antedate the advent of the territorial sea in the late eighteenth century, and therefore can be properly designated as traditional. Even after the acceptance of the territorial sea regime around the world, which seemed to reflect a victory for regime thinking in the public law and administration of the ocean, it was found necessary to resort to a variety of administrative control zones that extended beyond the three-mile limit of the territorial sea. In the modern era we have witnessed the proliferation of coastal and offshore zones designed chiefly for the purposes of resource development and management, especially in the period since the end of the Second World War.

TRADITIONAL ZONING PRACTICES

Mariculture

Aquaculture has been conducted for thousands of years in many parts of the world: in freshwater ponds, in brackish inlets and estuaries, and in containable inshore areas of the sea.[3] The origin of pond culture may be almost as ancient as that of agriculture, around 10,000 BC. References to the tilapia pond culture of the Middle East date from 2000 BC, and carp culture was being practised in China by that time, although the first Chinese treatise on fish culture, ascribed to Fan Li, did not appear until 475 BC. In India fish were almost certainly being reared in ponds earlier than 600 BC.[4] Marine aquaculture, usually referred to as mariculture,[5] can also be traced back to 2000 BC and the early efforts of the Japanese to raise oysters in sea water. By 1000 AD the Javanese had begun to build the first of their great estuarine fish pond systems, and when the Polynesians settled in Hawaii around that time they brought a well-established maricultural tradition with them.[6]

The need for zoning in mariculture depends upon the method used. Methods vary from extensive open systems, which involve a minimal departure from natural conditions (for example, certain modes of oyster cultivation) to intensive closed systems, which involve almost complete control over the organism and its environment (for example, Japanese prawn culture, and most trout and salmon culture).[7] For sea farmers the most important groups of organisms are molluscs (clams, oysters, mussels, cockles, and abalone), crustaceans (shrimps, crayfish, crabs, and lobsters), finfish (flounder, turbot, bass, mullet, salmon, catfish, and yellowtail tuna), and seaweeds and algae.[8]

Although the principles of aquaculture in general are similar to those of agriculture, there are unique characteristics associated with the aquatic medium, and the marine environment in particular presents special problems of control and management. These problems in turn cause difficulties in the legal regulation of aquacultural development. Unlike capture fishing, which is legally analogous to hunting, mariculture depends on a legal system that can secure the entrepreneur's rights to a site and protect his investment in the stock with something akin to a private property entitlement.[9] Moreover, the aquacultural entrepreneur may have to acquire special legislative protection from other conflicting uses in the designated area.[10] In modern conditions successful maricultural development is likely to depend on some kind of horizontal or vertical zoning of coastal waters, and on the observances of leasing or licensing requirements.[11]

Mariculture may now be on the brink of spectacular world-wide development, even in regions like North America where aquaculture has not traditionally been a profitable form of fish production.[12] Advocates of such development point to the virtually unlimited growth potentiality of fish culture, in contrast with that of fish capture. Moreover, mariculture can be conducted with fewer uncertainties about conservation.[13] Developing coastal states in particular may find it economically attractive to apply their capital and skills to the production rather than the extraction of food in the sea.[14] In combination with either agriculture or coastal fishing,[15] sea farming seems likely to become a major use of coastal waters and an important reason for further resort to ocean zoning.

Mineral Extraction

In recent decades the sea has attracted legal controversy mainly because of its growing importance as a source of mineral resources, but mineral extraction in coastal waters is one of the oldest uses of the ocean.[16] It is likely that salt was the first mineral to be derived from sea water. The human craving for salt is believed to have actuated the neolithic trend to the sea, and since then sea water in estuaries, inlets, and other coastal areas has been one of the principal sources of this universally sought-after commodity. Salt played an important part in shaping the development of trade in ancient times, and in many cultures it came to be used directly as a medium of exchange. Because of its considerable commercial and even strategic value, salt-mining has traditionally required a degree of regulation, and the designated and restricted use of coastal water areas for salt production must be considered one of the earliest examples of ocean zoning.[17]

In modern times it has been discovered that important coal mines extend beyond the shore, sometimes stretching several miles under the sea. The Chinese seem to have been the first to appreciate the versatility of coal, and were certainly much more aware of its uses than the Greeks and Romans. Specific references to sea-coal (*carbo maris*) can be traced back to early thirteenth-century Scotland, when coal was available on the shore of the Firth of Forth.[18] Today the mining of coal seams under the sea, essentially an extension of land-bound technology, also represents an extension of land-based regulations, and is an example of the special use of designated areas of the coastal zone.[19]

Among the other mineral uses of the sea, none has acquired greater saliency in the modern world than the production of oil. Offshore oil production began in the Gulf of Mexico at the end of the nineteenth century, but technical difficulties delayed attempts at large-scale production until the discovery of the Creole field in the late 1930s.[20] In 1947 the arrival of the new age of offshore technology was dramatized by the construction off the coast of Louisiana of the first platform beyond the sight of land, and in 1948 by the completion of the first offshore pipeline.[21] Since then, the world has witnessed a spectacular proliferation of new technologies for the production and transportation of offshore oil and gas around the world.[22]

Technological development has enabled man to reach much farther out into and under the sea in the search for minerals, but the now-familiar pattern of allocative and regulatory zoning of the ocean for petroleum and other mineral resources on and beyond the continental margin can be seen as a projection of much earlier inshore zoning practices.

Ports

Seaports, spatially defined by one of a number of alternative methods,[23] have for centuries been subject to particular types of zonal control. Long before any serious claims were advanced to sovereignty over territorial seas, coastal states exercised varying degrees of criminal, civil, and commercial jurisdiction over zones designated as port areas.[24] Both Carthage and Rome fulfilled such functions within their ports.[25] Since ancient times similar powers were claimed by the emperor of China,[26] and the legal writer Hales noted that in England supervision of port areas was "from the earliest times" considered a royal prerogative.[27] Although some early claims to control over ports were advanced on grounds of national sovereignty, it is apparent that jurisdiction was normally limited to the particular interests – such as commercial advantage, national security, and public order – which the port state was seeking to protect in a given instance.[28] The universal acceptance of ports as internal waters in the territorial sea era did not fundamentally alter this position, for in practice the jurisdiction of the coastal state over foreign vessels within its ports has always been restricted to something less than that exercised in internal waters generally, although more than that found in the territorial sea. The strongest elements of coastal state jurisdiction have been identified as those most directly affecting the interests of the port state, such as vessel safety, public health, security, and pollution control.[29]

The extension of jurisdiction over port areas, whether or not supported by a claim to state sovereignty, has always tended to be spatially coextensive with a range of specific administrative purposes. The emergence of ports as internal waters has not lessened the relevance of zonal thinking to the effective administration of ports. Rather, the focus of zoning has become intranational as various levels and agencies of government participate in a spatial sharing of authority over the complex functions of a modern port.[30] Ports exist as distinct zones both internationally and intranationally, subject to a unique set of legal and administrative arrangements designed to serve the needs of the port state on the one hand and ocean transportation on the other.

Fishing

The protection of fishing rights (as opposed to the protection of fish) has probably been a concern for coastal communities since the origin of ocean fisheries. The explicit designation of zones within which such authority may be exercised is perhaps a more recent phenomenon, but it certainly has antecedents prior to the advent of modern fishery zones. In the twelfth century, kings of Scotland asserted the right to exclusive fishing in limited areas of the coast, areas that came to be defined as all bays and firths, and coastal waters within a distance from the coast of fourteen to twenty-eight miles. Similar restrictions in England were less successful, but by the early nineteenth century Great Britain claimed control over sedentary fisheries such as the Ceylon pearl banks which lay beyond territorial waters – fisheries which by their static nature defined a zone.[31] This claim was rationalized by assertions of property rights in oyster and chank stocks dating back to the sixth century BC.[32]

It is interesting to note that by the nineteenth century British claims to the assertion of authority beyond the territorial sea were being justified in terms of "use and occupation" and "historic title"[33] – legal concepts introduced to rationalize early administrative activities as part of a sovereign right. In their early manifestations, however, the spatial claims to authority over certain fisheries were more often based on coastal community needs and interests than on extension of sovereign territorial control in the ocean.

Military Security

Many early claims to offshore jurisdiction, even before the territorial sea, were founded at least partly on the need to maintain the security of the coastal state and protect its seaborne commerce.[34] There are, however, examples of security zones of a purely military origin dating back at least to the Romans, when Pompey established "districts" in the Mediterranean during his campaign against the powerful pirate fleets that threatened the security of Rome.[35] By 1521 it was accepted in England, and provided in a treaty with France, that in specified coastal areas belligerent acts by the ships of one foreign state towards those of another were forbidden[36] – an early example of the "neutrality zone" concept that has reappeared throughout the history of the law of the sea.

The evolution of military technology ensured the continued development of zonal thinking about military activities at sea. It is possible to identify at least four distinct types of military or security zones that may exist as a part of, or independent of, any spatial legal regimes. *Coastal security* zones exist to prevent the use of a defined coastal zone for purposes detrimental to the security of the coastal state. Such zones may be coextensive with the territorial sea or may extend beyond it for limited purposes.[37] *Neutrality* zones are national or international areas within which belligerent acts by any state against any other are prohibited.[38] A refinement of this concept is found in the Indian Ocean "zone of peace," which seeks to remove the possibility of belligerency by disallowing entry of certain weapons.[39] *Blockade* zones, as opposed to high-seas interdiction of vessels, establish areas within which ships are subject to the blockade regulations. This variant of security zone is normally, but not exclusively, imposed in times of war.[40] The final category of military zone might be termed the *peacetime exclusion* zone, which either excludes all non-sanctioned vessels owing to the nature of some planned military activity within the zone,[41] or excludes one or more dangerous classes of intruders by reason of their expected actions once inside the zone.[42]

MODERN ADMINISTRATIVE CONTROL ZONES

Fiscal and Customs Control

The movement of contraband by sea has been a perennial problem for coastal states.[43] By the mid-eighteenth century the emergence of national bureaucracy had led to intense conflict between governments on the one hand and smugglers and tax evaders on the other.[44] As a result of the difficulties involved in the apprehension of violators on shore or in territorial waters, states came to recognize the need for preventive enforcement of national customs and excise laws within specified distances from the coast, independent of any claims to a territorial sea. In 1736 Great Britain introduced the first of its "hovering acts," which imposed national customs and excise jurisdiction upon vessels within five miles of the coast. Similar legislation in 1784, 1802, 1833, and 1853 varied the distance and the nature of jurisdiction, but the general intent remained the same, and the legislation was duplicated by other states.[45] Although the British modified their laws in 1876 so as to restrict jurisdiction to British vessels, many states continued with the broader approach until the development of the contiguous zone. Occasional refinements, such as the American regulations during Prohibition, either extended or limited coastal state controls in particular detail.[46]

The extension of fiscal regulation – a fundamental element of domestic law and administration – into the ocean represents zonal thinking at its most explicit. The tax-collecting interest of the coastal state was furthered by the creation and maintenance of a zone of limited jurisdiction in the absence of any claim to territorial sovereignty. The twentieth-century acceptance of the contiguous zone has not ended the assertion of state claims to limited jurisdiction for fiscal purposes in offshore zones, as is evidenced by Canada's recent declaration of a two-hundred-mile "customs zone" for the purpose of control over rigs and ships involved in oil and gas production.[47]

Public Health

The impact of shipborne disease upon the welfare of coastal states can be traced to the beginnings of maritime commerce,[48] and the interest of the coastal state in enforcing some measure of sanitary or public health control over vessels approaching the shore seems clear. By the mid-eighteenth century such public health concerns were finding expression in the declaration of "quarantine" restrictions, under which ships approaching the coast were subjected to requirements of notification and isolation if certain diseases were actually or potentially present.[49] A British act of 1753, for example, declared that all ships coming from areas of bubonic plague infestation must, when they neared the coast, signal all other vessels in the area. In this act, as in virtually all similar legislation, the coastal state jurisdiction to enforce quarantine measures was stated in terms of a zone – for the United Kingdom, a zone extending four leagues from the coast.[50]

By the nineteenth century the enforcement of public health regulations beyond territorial waters on the part of the coastal state was generally accepted, although the basis for this jurisdiction was held to be the assent of flag states rather than any legal "right" on the part of the coastal state.[51] This perception altered over the next century, so that by the mid-twentieth century jurisdictional powers of this type were acknowledged to be within the lawful competence of the coastal state.

Immigration

Immigration control is a relatively modern administrative practice.[52] Coastal states do not seem to have resorted to extraterritorial zoning for immigration control purposes prior to the twentieth century. In the period up to the Second World War, several states began to extend their immigration control authority beyond their territorial sea limits,[53] but no uniformity in state practice existed before the 1950s. When the International Law Commission began its debate on the purposes of the contiguous zone, it did not seem that there was sufficient state practice to justify the inclusion of immigration control in the package of administrative responsibilities that would be discharged out to the twelve-mile limit of the contiguous zone.[54] But when the delegates assembled for the United Nations Conference on the Law of the Sea at Geneva in 1958, they decided to include immigration control, and the concept of the contiguous zone acquired a fourfold administrative significance; the coastal state was empowered to enforce its "customs, fiscal, immigration, [and] sanitary regulations."[55] In the years since 1958, the inclusion of immigration control in the contiguous zone has been accepted throughout the world in state practice, and at UNCLOS III the same fourfold classification including immigration control was preserved when the contiguous zone was extended from twelve to twenty-four miles.[56]

Environmental Protection

The problem of marine pollution in offshore areas appears to be a legitimate interest of the coastal state with respect to areas beyond its territorial waters, but until the latter part of the twentieth century there was little or no activity directed towards zoning of the sea specifically for anti-pollution purposes. Even in the modern period of growing environmental awareness, this issue has been dealt with largely in the international arena through the adoption of a series of bilateral and multilateral agreements on marine environmental pollution.[57] Some elements of zonal thinking have been incorporated in such agreements, in that a number of bilateral and regional conventions on environmental protection specify the spatial extent of their application.[58] In this way, a form of international zoning takes place, for the areas defined by such conventions are identifiable both in terms of the function to be performed by all participating states – that is, the regulation of a certain category of ocean-based activity – and by the area within which it may be performed.

The controversial Canadian Arctic Waters Pollution Prevention Act of 1970 serves as the major example of a national zone created solely for promotion of environmental protection; provisions of that act represent an extension of jurisdiction for limited purposes in a specified area, a clear expression of zonal thinking.[59] It is likely that the expansion of coastal state jurisdiction over marine pollution under the regime of the EEZ will obviate the necessity for further national, unifunctional initiatives along the lines of the Canadian Arctic legislation.[60] This new regime may, however, give greater saliency to the intranational zoning difficulties associated with the division of national, local, and agency-by-agency authority for environmental protection.

Vessel Traffic Control

The first proposals for co-ordinated systems of vessel traffic control originated in the mid-nineteenth century, but no progress resulted until the institution of relatively informal passenger ship routing in the North Atlantic in 1898. These early efforts were voluntary and were not examples of zonal control in a strict sense. The first traffic separation scheme to rely on the creation and administration of inshore and offshore zones was the system implemented in the Dover Strait in 1967, involving Britain, France, and Germany and planned with the assistance of the Intergovernmental Maritime Consultative Organization (now the International Maritime Organization). The functions of traffic separation and management in the modern era include passive monitoring of vessel movements, establishment of routes or sea-lanes, and active shore-based control of vessels.[61] Zoning has proved relevant to these activities not only in defining acceptable routes of passage for the ships entering the area of the scheme, but also in separating the areas of administrative responsibility of different coastal states or internal agencies and regions. Thus, zonal provisions for the purposes of vessel traffic control may identify the state exercising control, or simply the various internal divisions of authority necessary to the effective management of the system.

Improvements in the available technology, coupled with an increased concern for the safety of life and vessels at sea, have led in the past fifteen years to a wider acceptance of national and, to a lesser extent, international vessel traffic control schemes beyond the confines of ports, most involving some degree of zoning activity. This trend can be expected to continue, with the major remaining question being the extent to which the resulting zones will be international, as opposed to national, in their planning, establishment, and administration.[62]

RESOURCE DEVELOPMENT AND MANAGEMENT ZONES

Fishery Development, Management, and Conservation

As noted above, there is a long history of efforts by coastal authorities to enclose inshore waters so as to reserve fishing rights to the nationals of the coastal state. These early fishing-zone practices were particularly conspicuous in regions such as the North Sea, which experienced the impact of efficient and vigorous distant fishing fleets.[63] In modern times, beginning in the later nineteenth century in the North Sea, fishery scientists began to realize the impact of overfishing.[64] As their investigations proved the need for some kind of conservation or management program, there began to emerge an awareness of the need for inshore or offshore zones for the protection of threatened stocks. Some of the protection zones were established under national or local authority, but in the period when the territorial sea was still restricted to a breadth of three miles, most fishery management and conservation zones were placed under international auspices in accordance with an international agreement negotiated by the countries with a common interest in the conservation of a high-seas fishery.[65]

When these international arrangements proved inadequate, there ensued a difficult period of unilateral claims by coastal states to extend their fishery jurisdiction far beyond the limits of the territorial sea in order to strengthen management and conservation controls and to assert exclusive or special fishing rights for nationals.[66] In the last two decades this trend to extensive fishery zones has been accelerated by the need of developing coastal states to secure to themselves an uncontested authority over all living resources adjacent to their shores, so that those resources can be integrated into their economic planning. All these factors have culminated in the legitimization of a two-hundred-mile exclusive economic zone designed partly to secure those ends.[67]

Offshore Mineral Production

Minerals have been extracted from inshore areas for two thousand years, but the zoning practices associated with those interests were of minor legal (if not economic) significance compared with the modern ocean zoning that has resulted from the discovery of massive hydrocarbon deposits in offshore areas. In a period of no more than forty years the offshore technology of the petroleum industry has advanced to such a point that exploration and production can be conducted at a depth of over 1000 metres and distances of several hundred miles offshore.[68] It appears that it soon will be technically and economically feasible to produce oil and natural gas from any major hydrocarbon deposit under the ocean floor. Accordingly, it might seem that coastal zoning will not be a sufficiently comprehensive administrative device to facilitate the regulation of hydrocarbon production throughout the world; but in the light of these expanding opportunities the world community has recently revised the definition of the continental shelf so as to permit exclusive coastal state jurisdiction over mineral resources of the seabed and subsoil beyond 200-mile limits, where circumstances permit, even to a distance of 450 miles from shore in a few exceptional cases.[69]

Zoning for offshore mineral production is not exclusively the concern of the nation-state, however. Because this kind of activity is industrial, zoning practices associated with it must be perceived in corporate as well as governmental terms. Accordingly, in addition to a division of the continental shelf along statist lines, bringing the non-living resources of the national zones of the shelf under the "sovereign rights" of the adjacent coastal state, there has been established a vast world-wide network of smaller areas leased to oil companies.[70] Most of the companies involved in offshore activities are foreign-controlled or foreign-owned, but are increasingly subject to coastal state jurisdiction.[71] It is important to note that these special commercial zones have often been established by agreement between the coastal state and a multinational corporation in circumstances of uncertainty about the seaward extent of the coastal state's jurisdiction over the continental shelf, and in circumstances where bilateral boundary disputes with neighbouring states remain unsettled.[72] This kind of special commercial zoning can exist virtually independently of a formal system of legal regimes under international law.

Coastal Zone Management and Sea Use Planning

Less universally publicized but equally significant in the history of ocean zoning are the trends to sea-use planning and coastal zone management.[73] These two terms are cognate to the extent that they both describe administrative efforts to organize, integrate, and co-ordinate the planning and management activities of various agencies with ocean-related responsibilities. But the concept of coastal zone management, which originated in the United States, refers specifically to a narrowly defined area at the interface between the land and the ocean,[74] whereas that of sea-use planning refers to both offshore and inshore areas and is not always linked to related land-based activities on the shoreline.[75] In these slightly dissimilar ways these two concepts envisage a highly sophisticated cross-sectoral approach to zoning: a system of interlocking zones, each designed to serve a specific unisectoral purpose but also designed within a larger framework of cross-sectoral planning and management. Whether or not these twin trends will prove to be the most successful method of advancing administrative efficiency in ocean development and management in the late twentieth century is difficult to predict. It is also too early to judge whether sea-use planning and coastal zone management can be developed at the international level in co-operation with two or more neighbouring states, or whether they are bound to be limited to the national level of public administration.[76]

THE RELEVANCE OF ZONES IN THE POST-UNCLOS III ERA

The foregoing discussion reveals that the history of the public law and administration of the ocean has been one of more or less continuous confusion between two rival modes of thought about the distribution and administration of authority in the ocean. Regime thinking has been supported by the theoretical need for overarching legal systems; zonal thinking has been propelled by the practical need for administrative schemes. In this sense, the tension between regime and zone can be said to reflect the need for accommodation between general theory and specific practical requirements. What seems to be important in the contemporary period is to find innovative ways of reconciling the general with the specific, and the theoretical with the practical. The likeliest method of resolving the tension seems to be the adoption of a functionalist approach both to the concept of maritime jurisdiction and to the theory of ocean boundary-making. (On the functionalist approach, see chapters 12 through 20.)

As matters now stand, at the end of the UNCLOS III period, we are confronted with a proliferation of legal regimes in the international law of the sea. Fundamental confusion arises not merely from the multiplicity of regimes, but from their diversity. In greatly differing degrees, each of these regimes, both ancient and modern, now bears the imprint of functionalist thinking dictated by the administrative purposes that lie at the heart of each.

In the case of the territorial sea, UNCLOS III has retained the basic formulation derived from UNCLOS I and from the consolidation of customary international law of an earlier era, but has modified some features of the territorial sea regime along functional lines. The major changes to this regime at UNCLOS III were made in articles 19, 21, 24, and 25 of the 1982

Convention, on the right of innocent passage with a view to spelling out clearly, in precise functionalist manner, the categories of coastal state concerns within which the coastal state is entitled to take measures that might impinge on the right of innocent passage through the territorial sea.

Similarly, in the case of the regime of the high seas, although the general structure and rationale have been preserved from UNCLOS I and earlier eras, the freedoms of the high seas have been developed and clarified along functionalist lines in article 87.

The regime of the continental shelf, as developed and refined at UNCLOS III, is not fundamentally different from the regime codified at UNCLOS I, but the protracted debate over the definition of the continental shelf was dominated by the delegates' awareness of the economic opportunities for offshore mineral production at the present stage of technological development. The formula finally agreed to (in article 76) was certainly the product of functionalist, not doctrinal, logic.

Above all, of course, UNCLOS III is of historic importance for its espousal and vindication of the new regime of the exclusive economic zone. Unlike any other regime in the law of the sea today, the EEZ regime set out in articles 55–75 has been thought out de novo along explicitly multifunctional lines, designed as it is to govern matters concerning living and nonliving resources, environmental management, scientific research, energy production, and the construction and maintenance of installations in the 188-mile zone between the limits of the 12-mile territorial sea and the 200-mile EEZ. This regime could serve as a composite of several theoretically separate, functional zones, all brought together, somewhat incongruously, within uniform and universally applicable 200-mile limits. Because of its hybrid character, purportedly a spatial regime but actually a composite of functional zones, the EEZ signals the end of the neo-classical period marked by a simple bifurcation of the ocean between unshared national areas and the universally shared expanse beyond.

The 1982 Convention maintains or introduces several other minor regimes or quasi-regimes. Each of these lesser regimes can be shown to have a considerable degree of functionalist design built into it: the traditional variety of administrative purposes still provides the rationale for the concept of the contiguous zone (article 33); specific protective purposes are served by the provisions on ice-covered waters (article 234) and other special areas of the EEZ (article 211(6); and navigational and security interests are balanced in the regimes of international straits (articles 34–45) and archipelagic waters (or states) (articles 46–54).

The result of the trends reflected in the text of the UNCLOS III Convention will certainly be a proliferation of national, binational, and possibly multinational zones designed to institutionalize and operationalize the various rights and responsibilities assigned to the coastal state under the new law of the sea. Inevitably, these prospective zoning practices around the world will have a profound impact on the theory and practice of boundary-making.

CHAPTER EIGHT

Trends in Ocean Science and Technology

INTRODUCTION

Boundary-making can be viewed in various ways: as a tribal, local, or even personal necessity; as a political act; as an administrative process; or as an application of juridical principles. The history of boundary-making, therefore, has social, political, legal and other dimensions. In the case of ocean boundary-making, however, the uninhabitability of the marine environment has minimized, if not entirely precluded, the significance of social history; and the political and legal history of maritime boundary-making beyond the familiar limits of coastal and inshore waters has been dependent in large part on the development of ocean technology. Basically, therefore, the history of ocean boundary-making has been the story of the emergence of ocean technology; or, more precisely, of the evolution of the science and technology of location and measurement at sea. Before examining the modern legal, political, and diplomatic history of maritime boundary-making, it seems necessary to review the history of physical geography, geodesy, cartography, and hydrography, and of cognate disciplines and techniques of location, measurement, and related forms of investigation.

THE ORIGINS OF PHYSICAL GEOGRAPHY

Physical geography is the science that describes the earth's surface – its form, physical features, and natural divisions.[1] This field of investigation has an extremely long and well-documented history. Indeed, it seems likely that geographical knowledge must have begun to evolve as early as the neolithic age.[2] The Sumerians probably were the first civilization to attempt to map the world as they knew it, somewhere between 5000 and

4000 BC.[3] The Babylonians, in the period between 2000 and 500 BC, are generally credited with pioneering in mathematics (not least as the inventors of the concept of zero) and then astronomy. It was the Babylonians who first predicted accurately the solar and lunar eclipses, and invented the gnomon, a simple but ingenious device to indicate time as well as the sun's meridian altitude. They may also have been the first to discover the sphericity of the earth.[4]

The Phoenicians and Minoans contributed to practical geographical knowledge. Although no record has been preserved, these great seafaring peoples are known to have collected useful information on winds, currents, tides, weather variations, and on the features of unfamiliar distant shores. When the balance of power in the Aegean shifted from Minoan Crete to Mycenaean Greece, around 1600 BC, a more warlike era arrived, one that seems to have been hostile or indifferent to the collection and storage of geographical information. Soon, as the Bronze Age gave way to the Iron Age, an Aegean Dark Age descended. From this period only Homer survives as a documentary treasure of early geographical knowledge.[5] It seems likely that the Orient was making the most important contributions to geography during the Aegean Dark Age.[6]

The Greeks, in the classical period from 650 to 150 BC, made the most important contributions to early geography, though colonials living on the mainland of Ionia (southwest Turkey today) and in other Greek settlements (in southern Italy) achieved the greatest success in this field of scholarship.[7] The first of these was Thales of Miletus (640–546 BC), who virtually introduced geometry to the Greeks, and established a reputation by correctly predicting the solar eclipse of 28 May 585 BC. His special interest in the ocean seems to have derived from his insistence that water was the fundamental element, the basis for all life. But it was Thales's disciple, Anaximander (611–547 BC), also of Miletus, who was regarded by the Greeks as the father of geography. Although he seems to have discovered the gnomon from Babylonian records, he was credited with its invention and with the construction of one of the first world maps, albeit more than two thousand years after the first Sumerian world map.[8]

There is also a case to be made for crediting Herodotus (484–425 BC) with the parentage of geography as well as history. Certainly his famous history of the Greco-Persian wars contained vast amounts of geographical information, and he created the best world map produced up to that time.[9]

At the theoretical level, a much more influential scholar emerged in the person of Pythagoras (active c. 530 BC), the first Greek scientist to advance the concept of a spherical earth, the basic principle of physical geography.[10] Though the concept apparently was propounded much earlier by the Sumerians, the espousal of sphericity by Pythagoras and his followers was radical at a time when the great Ionian geographers, like their Chinese counterparts, still considered the earth to be flat. It would be over two thousand years before sphericity became widely accepted as a scientific fact.

Another ancient geographical issue on the same order of significance concerned the place of the earth in the universe. The geocentric view of things, which placed the earth at the centre, seems to have been first advanced by Parmenides (active c.539 BC), who founded the Eleatic school of philosophy at Velia (Elea) in the fifth century BC. This view, supported by scholars as diverse as Aristotle and the medieval churchmen, continued to be influential for two millenia until it was finally overthrown by the discoveries of Nicolaus Copernicus in 1543 AD.[11] But the heliocentric theory of the universe, which finally prevailed, was almost equally ancient in origin, dating from the age of Aristarchus of Samos (fl. c. 270 BC).[12]

While these great controversies were being debated by the Greek philosophers, mathematicians and other scientists of the same era were making major, if more prosaic, contributions to the development of physical geography. The earliest of the great geographers of antiquity was Eratosthenes (276–195 BC), the director of the famous museum library established at Alexandria.[13] Accepting the Pythagorean tenet of a spherical earth, which he recognized as crucial to the development of mathematical geography and to the efforts to draw an accurate world map, Eratosthenes produced the first geometry of our planet, based on estimates of the size of the equator, the distance of the tropic and polar circles, the extent of the polar zone, the size and distance of the sun and moon, the occurrence of total and partial eclipses, both solar and lunar, and changes in the length of day according to different latitudes and seasons. Although many of his estimates were inaccurate, Eratosthenes is acknowledged to have provided the basis of geodesy.[14] In his own day he was best known for his efforts to measure the circumference of the earth from the angular height of the sun and the linear distance between Alexandria and Syene.[15] Although his methods were sharply criticized by his contemporaries and successors, such as Hipparchus of Nicaea (fl. 146–127 BC)[16] and Strabo of Amaseia (64 BC–20 AD), posterity has united in hailing his amazingly accurate calculation[17] as one of the great achievements of Greek science.[18] He also displayed impressive accuracy in his measurement of the length of the Mediterranean; he was the first to maintain that the earth was predominantly covered by water, not land; and he was the first to suggest that the earth was not a perfect sphere.[19]

The Romans in general were less interested than the Greeks in theoretical or mathematical geography, but Polybius (c. 204–117 BC), chiefly a historian, produced a systematic geographical work in which he made full use of the practical knowledge acquired from Roman campaigns in various parts of the widening world around the Mediterranean.[20] In the first century BC Poseidonius of Apameia (c. 135–c. 50 BC) wrote a treatise, *On the Ocean*, repeating the Eratosthenian idea that there was but one ocean. He was one of the first to ascribe the rhythmic movement of the tides to the combined actions of the sun and the moon, calling attention to the phenomenon of extreme variation between spring and neap tides. Less successfully, he tried to improve on Eratosthenes' estimate of the size of the earth. His computation that a vessel sailing west over the Atlantic for 70,000 *stadia* would reach India was trusted for over fifteen hundred years, and had much to do with Columbian optimism and the accidental discovery of America![21]

Strabo of Amaseia compiled the first encyclopaedia of geographical knowledge, an astonishing work that seems beyond the capabilities of a single scholar.[22] Apart from transmitting the famous Poseidonian error, it represents an impressive effort to comprehend the entire field of human as well as physical geography.[23] The Roman scholar, Pliny the Elder (23–79 AD) attempted to go beyond Strabo; he compiled an encyclopaedia of natural history that encompassed areas of geographical thought, but much of what he included was error.[24] Finally, mention must be made of Claudius Ptolemaeus of Alexandria (75–15 AD) – usually referred to as Ptolemy, but not to be confused with Ptolemy I, the first governor of Alexandria and the founder of the famous library – whose great work represents the culmination of ancient geography.[25] Unlike Strabo, who was chiefly concerned with the habitable world, Ptolemy was interested in the entire planet and its relationship to the sun and moon. Above all, he was concerned with providing "a scientific basis for an accurate portrayal of the spherical earth in a conventional and readable form."[26] His main accomplishment was in extracting from his Greek and Roman predecessors the elements of scientific cartography and the fundamental tenets of modern geodesy.[27]

After the lifting of darkness fifteen hundred years later, it was to Ptolemy that the geographers of the Renaissance returned.[28] But now, in addition to better thinking and better science, better practical knowledge prepared the way for the discipline of physical geography. The idea of a round earth, for example, although it never died out, had been overtaken by theological dogma in the Christian world, and this medieval mould of thought might have remained intact but for the shattering revelations of the Polos and other great European travellers and explorers in the period between 1400 and 1650.[29] By the end of that period, the new thinking of Galileo, Descartes, and Newton had inspired geographers such as Bernard Varenius (1622–50) to attempt to systematize the accumulated body of geographical knowledge,[30] but he and his successors still lacked sufficient factual knowledge to succeed in this task. By the end of the eighteenth century, after the great exploratory voyages of Cook, Vancouver, Bougainville, and La Pérouse, most of the world had been visited and described with some degree of accuracy, and it became possible for Alexander von Humboldt (1769–1859) to write the first systematic treatise on modern physical geography.[31]

THE SEARCH FOR LATITUDE AND LONGITUDE

Of all the approaches to the problems of geographical location and measurement, none was more basic to navigation than the search for latitude and longitude. Curious as it may seem to the non-scientist today, these undertakings were quite distinct. Latitude proved to be measurable, and was measured with considerable accuracy, in the period of antiquity; longitude was difficult to measure with accuracy, especially at sea, until the second half of the eighteenth century.[32] Latitude, the measurement of location north or south of the equator,[33] is described by reference to a system of parallels – that is, lines drawn parallel to the equator. Within this system of measurement the area of the earth's surface is divided into degrees (°), minutes (′), and seconds (″): 1 degree equals 60 minutes, and 1 minute equals 60 seconds. From the equator to either pole is 90°, one-quarter of the surface of the (nearly) spherical earth. Thus, the greatest possible latitudes are 90° north and 90° south. The length of a degree of arc of latitude is approximately 69 (statute) miles, varying, because of the non-uniform curvature of the earth's surface, from 68.704 miles at the equator to 69.407 miles at the poles. Longitude, the measurement of location east or west of a standard point of reference,[34] is described by reference to a system of meridians. The universally accepted standard point of reference, the prime meridian, is the line that passes through Greenwich, England. Under this system the earth's surface is divided into degrees, minutes, and seconds, so that longitude can be measured up to 180° east and 180° west of the prime meridian, the two together making the full 360° of the earth's circumference. The meridians are plotted and drawn directly from pole to pole. At the equator, where the meridians are the farthest apart, the number of miles per degree of longitude is about 69.17 (statute) miles. At the poles, where all the meridians converge, the distance apart is, of course, zero. Location is measured by the combination of parallels and meridians, which establishes a framework or grid of intersecting lines by means of which exact positions can be determined by reference to the equator and the prime meridian.

The ancient quest for latitude owes much to Hipparchus of Nicaea (fl. 146–127 BC), perhaps the greatest astronomer of antiquity, a skilled mathematician, and an observer of extraordinary precision. Hipparchus apparently was attracted by the challenge of applying rigorous mathematical principles to the determination of places on the earth's surface. In the eyes of posterity, Hipparchus seems unduly critical of the work of Eratosthenes,[35] and he certainly created errors of his own,[36] but he was the first of the ancients to specify the mode of geographical location by latitude and longitude, and the first to insist on the need for astronomical accuracy and mathematical precision. In his own work he tried to measure latitude by utilizing the ratio of the longest day to the shortest day at a particular place, instead of following the customary (Babylonian) method of measuring the difference in length of day as one travels northward. Hipparchus also divided the then-known inhabited world into climatic zones (*klimata*),[37] and suggested that longitude could be determined by observing, from any place, the exact time when a solar eclipse began and ended. But this ingenious method, though theoretically acceptable for a small portion of the earth's surface, could not be implemented in the technological conditions of the era.

Many others after Hipparchus tried to find universally workable methods for determining latitude and longitude. Although the former undertaking had been accomplished at a high level of precision by the end of the period of ancient Greece, the search for longitude continued to be frustrated by the lack of reliable scientific data. The technological problem of measuring longitude remained unsolved until Galileo's proposal to use a pendulum clock proved workable in the hands of Christian Huygens (1629–95) in 1657. Even this breakthrough, using chronometry for the precise determination of location, did not permit the precise measurement of longitude at sea on board a rocking vessel.

In the modern era, the French were the first to take up this last challenge in the quest for longitude. In 1666, when the Académie Royale des Sciences was founded by Louis XIV at the urging of his brilliant minister, Jean-Baptiste Colbert, the discovery of an accurate method of determining longitude was given top priority for its distinguished members. After years of effort, the Académie finally proved the utility of a method based on the eclipses of Jupiter's satellites, but it was conceded that the sea was too boisterous for the necessary astronomical apparatus to be used on board a vessel.[38]

In 1675, in the reign of Charles II, the Royal Observatory was established at Greenwich, and by the early eighteenth century the "race for the longitude" was dominated by British scientists motivated by the admiralty's desire to facilitate the development of British maritime power and commerce around the world. In 1714 Parliament offered a handsome sum as a reward for the invention of a reliable method of determining longitude at sea, and a permanent commission, the Board of Longitude, was created to administer the open competition. After many years of intense effort, disfigured by professional rancour and lightened by popular satire, the chronometric inventions of John Harrison (1693–1776) were finally recognized as the solution to the ancient problem, and the last instalment of the promised reward was paid in 1773.[39] With Harrison's invention of an accurate marine chronometer, the ancient problem of determining longitude at sea with scientific precision was solved.

SEA CHARTS AND THE FOUNDATIONS OF MODERN CARTOGRAPHY

Mapping may be the oldest of the graphic arts. Its origins are lost to history. The earliest evidence available suggests that the need for a sketch, a map, a diagram, arose independently in many different cultures in separate regions of the world. It is likely that all cultures valued maps as a simple precaution against getting lost and falling into harm. For this reason, charts have always been of special importance to mariners, who must brave the perils of the deep. Sophisticated charts have been found, dating back to preliterate stages of cultural development of many seafaring peoples.[40] Unfortunately for the historian of cartography, early navigators were notoriously reluctant to keep records. Only a few fragments survive from early times to show the accuracy of the mariner's observations and of the charts he constructed from his practical knowledge of marine geography.[41] These early charts (*portolanos*) were entirely practical in the sense that they were intended solely to serve the purposes of navigation and "haven-finding" and they tended to focus on coastlines and coastal waters, where navigational dangers threatened the mariner seeking haven.[42]

The perils of navigation meant that sea charts attached even more importance to direction than to distances. Indeed, it is said that chart makers gave direction to cartography.[43] The early cartographic response to the mariner's need for directional guidance was the ancient "wind-rose." The wind-rose gave approximate wind directions that met the mariner's daily navigational needs. The simple Greek rose of four winds evolved into the later Latin rose of twelve winds (*rosa ventorum*), which was accepted by mariners throughout the Roman empire from Egypt to Spain, and remained in common use throughout the Middle Ages. Eventually it was replaced by a rose of thirty-two winds as the variability of winds became better understood.[44]

Eventually, however, the need for greater precision forced chart-makers to take advantage of theoretical cartography. As we have seen, many of the early Greek geographers applied astronomy and mathematics to the art of mapping. Later, in the second century AD, Marinus of Tyre developed these earlier ideas to construct a network of meridians and parallels, and this method was amended and improved by Ptolemy. It appears that

Marinus first suggested the idea of projections on maps: that is, the reduction to a plane surface of the whole or part of the earth's spherical surface.[45] But it is Ptolemy who deserves the name of father of scientific cartography. Following Marinus, he systematized astronomy and improved upon the trigonometry invented by Hipparchus, making it easier to deal with the mathematics of the circle, an important step in cartography and geodesy. In showing how to form a table of chords (the straight lines connecting the extremities of an arc of a circle), he introduced a new system of subdividing a degree into minutes and seconds. In developing the method of a grid of latitudinal and longitudinal points of reference, and in other ways, Ptolemy can be said to have formulated the first principles of scientific cartography. Within a projected framework of coordinates, Ptolemy laid out the world as it was known to him through the writings of his predecessors.[46]

When the science of cartography was rediscovered in the Age of Enlightenment, major improvements became possible for a variety of unrelated reasons. First, the invention of the magnetic compass around 1300 introduced a higher level of accuracy in directional location at sea.[47] Second, the development of tabular compilations of unprecedented accuracy such as ephemerides permitted a higher level of precision in celestial navigation.[48] Third, triangulation made it possible to validate the Newtonian theory that the earth was an oblate spheroid,[49] and thus to introduce the new precision of the ellipsoidal epoch of geodesy.[50] Fourth, mapping was simplified by the invention of the plane table,[51] and by a succession of measuring instruments, which were invaluable for more accurate surveying.[52] Fifth, the popular interest in unfamiliar and distant places, and therefore in geography and cartography, was stimulated by the invention of the printing press[53] and the reintroduction of terrestrial globes.[54] Sixth, daring navigators ventured out into uncharted seas under the patronage of empire promoters and wealth seekers such as Yung Lo of China, Henry the Navigator and John II of Portugal, Ferdinand and Isabella of Spain, Henry VII of England, and Francis I of France.[55] Seventh, geographical precision acquired political significance for the first time with the discovery of the New World.[56] Last, but not least, the great Renaissance cartographer, Gerardus Mercator (1512–94) found a way of "squaring the circle" by a breakthrough in map projection – that is, of translating the sphericity of the earth with relative accuracy into the flatness of a map.[57]

Mercator was the first modern cartographer. The importance of his contribution to mapping and charting lies partly in the age he was born into, when a flood of new geographical information was becoming available, enabling the unblinkered to discard virtually all the classical and medieval misconceptions that had retarded cartography for fifteen hundred years. Unlike Ptolemy, his last great predecessor, Mercator had the opportunity to view the world in truly global terms and to portray most of it at a relatively high level of scientific accuracy.[58] More than anyone else, Mercator is conceded to have raised the status of map-making to an exact science. Above all, his place in history is due to the great skill with which he developed the technically difficult science of projection.

Throughout the Middle Ages, and even into the sixteenth century, Western mariners had navigated on the basis of portolan charts.[59] These charts probably originated as graphic extensions of simple but accurate descriptions of ports, coasts, and customary routes contained in pilot books (ruttiers). But even with the advent of the magnetic compass, which enabled cartographers to base charts on direct observations by means of a directional instrument, courses had to be plotted from the straight lines radiating from wind-roses. Although navigation based on portolan principles was sufficient for short voyages in a narrow range of latitudes, it was not suitable for the more extensive ocean voyages that were becoming much more common and more important in the sixteenth century. What was needed in the new age was a type of chart, suitable for long voyages, that would enable the navigator to draw a straight line between two points and immediately determine the constant course he must steer. Because the earth is round, such a line of constant compass bearing (the rhumb line) is a long curve (a loxodromic curve). This line curves a little more than a great circle route, which is the shortest distance between two points on the surface of a globe but requires constant changing of the compass course. Mercator's great success was in finding a cartographic method of converting the curving rhumb line to a more easily plotted straight line.[60]

Map projection is a highly specialized branch of applied mathematics. Many methods of projection have been developed, but none, however ingenious, can escape the problem of distortion, which is inherent in the process of reproducing features of a round surface on a plane surface. Of the many types of projections that have been experimented with, the two best known groups are the equal-area (equivalent or authalic) and conformal (orthomorphic) projections. On equal-area projections, the areal scale is constant from point to point; the linear scale at a point, however, in general varies with direction, and differences of direction are distorted. On a conformal projection, the linear scale at a point is constant in all directions and angles around a point are shown correctly; in general, however, the scale varies from point to point. It is obvious that no map projection can be both equal-area and conformal.[61] Mercator's solution was to develop the conformal type of projection in such a way that all lines of constant azimuth (rhumb lines or loxodromes) are shown as straight lines perpendicular to the equator, not as lines converging (as they actually do) on the poles. Thus, the meridians of longitude and the parallels of latitude intersect at right angles. The Mercator method of projection proved immediately to be the most useful method of cartography for the practical navigator, and it has remained the most popular ever since, despite the gross distortion of large-scale features of the globe that results from it – and despite the geographical confusion it creates in the minds of high school students around the world.[62]

THE DEVELOPMENT OF MARINE SURVEYING AND MODERN HYDROGRAPHY

The evolution of precision in location and measurement at sea has been characterized, at all stages of history, by a combination of science, technology, and navigational experience. Throughout the sixteenth and seventeenth centuries, commercial and political promoters continued to sponsor exploratory expeditions into unknown and uncharted seas, adding immeasurably to the stock of geographical information. But among all these explorer-navigators, one stands out clearly as the most important in the history of geography, cartography, and related disciplines. James Cook (1728–79) was almost certainly the greatest navigator of any age, but in addition he was a superbly accurate observer and recorder of everything he witnessed or discovered.[63] Accordingly, Cook's voyages were of much greater scientific value than any previously undertaken.[64] Indeed, we can see in retrospect that his voyages represent the culmination of the great explorations of the Age of Discovery and the beginning of major oceanographic expeditions that were to be an important feature of the Age of Science.

Cook made two important contributions to the geographical sciences. First, he accomplished almost single-handedly the extraordinary task of discovering and describing most of the vast, previously unknown areas of the South Seas and Antarctica, disposing in the process of virtually all remaining myths about the unfamiliar peoples and places on our planet.[65] In Mercator's *Atlas* of 1650, almost the entire southern hemisphere, including most of the Pacific, was shown as unexplored space. After Cook's three great voyages,[66] most of the major islands or island groups in that huge ocean region had been discovered or rediscovered, and became a permanent part of our understanding of world geography. Second, everywhere he went, he surveyed and charted so accurately that even today most charts of the Pacific Ocean are based on Cook's findings.[67] Unsatisfied with the traditional method of marine surveying by means of a "running traverse," which involved depth-sounding by plumb-line and guessing at the ship's track or position, Cook invented a much more thorough technique using the newly developed theodolite for measuring angles between lines of sight and a brass telescopic quadrant for determining latitudes from celestial altitudes.[68] Wholly without formal training, Cook combined the techniques of land surveying with the traditional practices of marine surveying, and raised the latter to an unprecedented level of precision.[69]

After Cook, others continued the work of marine surveying and charting in distant and unfamiliar waters. The most important were George Vancouver (1757–1857), who had sailed under Cook for many years,[70] and Francis Beaufort (1774–98), who was the first to develop a modern hydrographic office on a scientific basis.[71] By Beaufort's time, the age of modern oceanography, had begun – and new discoveries were being made under the ocean's surface.

Until the early decades of the nineteenth century, it had hardly seemed necessary to challenge the prevailing view of the subsurface layers of the ocean as a vast and lifeless (azoic) abyss. In the absence of knowledge about the deep ocean, physical and biological myths abounded. After the preliminary work of Edward Forbes (1815–54) in the 1840s, it gradually became clear that an extraordinary and vital world subsisted under the ocean's surface.[72] By the 1860s scientists were beginning to realize that the deep ocean held some of the answers to the questions raised by Darwin's theory of evolution.[73] Meanwhile, the pioneering work of Charles Lyell (1747–1875)[74] had raised novel issues concerning the origin of the earth, which in turn created the need for geological studies of the seabed and subsoil and subjacent strata of rock formations. By the time the *Challenger* put to sea in 1872, the sea floor lying off many of the European and North American coasts had been mapped, and within a few years the possibility of laying telegraph cables under the ocean had begun to provide the necessary stimulus for deep-sea research over extensive mid-ocean areas.[75] With the publication of Matthew Maury's topographical map of the North Atlantic in 1854,[76] the scene was set for the modern period of ocean-bottom mapping.[77] Even now, a century later and two decades after the tectonic revolution in marine geology,[78] it is evident that our knowledge of the resources of the deep ocean floor is still rudimentary.[79] In this last frontier of hydrography we are still pioneering.

CONTEMPORARY TRENDS IN SENSING AND MAPPING

Since the end of the Second World War, the science of location and measurement at sea has been advanced dramatically by the invention and development of amazingly precise techniques and technologies. The war itself was chiefly responsible for some of these improvements, such as radar,[80] sonar detection,[81] aerial photography,[82] and other modes of monitoring and location.[83] More recently still, ocean surveying and mapping have been elevated to undreamt-of levels of precision by the new generation of high technology. Two sectors of technology, in particular, deserve special mention: remote sensing and computer mapping.

Remote sensing of the earth and its oceans began to evolve earlier in the century with the advent of the airplane and the camera. But since the 1950s aircraft have given way to satellites, and cameras have been replaced by much more sophisticated sensors of various kinds. Since 1972 the physical features and natural resources of our planet have been the object of remote sensing from outer space under programs such as the Earth Resources Technology Satellite (LANDSAT) program, and its successor EOSAT.[84] As one writer has reported, using LANDSAT data in conjunction with computer analyses, such as digital image enhancement, pattern recognition and classification techniques, analysts have inventoried millions of acres of crops and forests, estimated timber and crop yields, located millions of gallons of surface water, determined watershed characteristics, developed base maps and land-use maps for the world, studied urban growth patterns and demographic characteristics, monitored water quality and air and water pollutants, located geological faults, and answered basic questions about the quality of our environment.[85] In the oceans, LANDSAT surveys have even located better fishing grounds. Today EOSAT satellites orbit the earth every 103 minutes at an altitude of 571 miles (920 kilometres) above the surface. As a result of the high altitude, they encompass a field of vision extending to 185 square kilometres. The high resolution of the sensing devices on board makes the satellites capable of discriminating between ground features only 80 metres apart. Satellite data can be used to support a range of studies in oceanography and hydrography focusing on currents and circulations, ocean surface topography, salinity and other chemical properties, the distribution and abundance of marine life, characteristics of the land-sea interface, water colour, and water depth (bathymetry). In areas of relatively low turbidity, these satellites can even make depth measurements to the 20-metre isobath, and thereby contribute to the more accurate location of reefs and shoals.[86]

Advances such as these are, of course, derived as much from the high-precision sensing devices used as from the satellites themselves. Conventional cameras are limited to sensing visible light and some portions of the infrared spectrum, which is only a part of the total electromagnetic spectrum. In recent years a variety of sensors have been developed with a view to expanding the range of objects that can be studied by remote sensing. In the past, photographic film was the primary medium for capturing reflected and emitted radiation; nowadays, multispectral scanners detect a wider range of radiation, including visible light, infrared and heat radiation, and sometimes ultraviolet, and generate electronic signals from which photograph-like images can be produced. Moreover, longer wave-length sensors, including those "active" systems using microwave and radar, are becoming available to expand the range of remote sensing even further.[87]

Even more exciting capabilities in location at sea are just around the corner. Satellite technology has already proved to be of enormous potential value for the precise location of mineral deposits under the seabed.[88] The SEASAT system being developed by NASA will soon be able to detect all vessels entering two-hundred-mile and other zones of national jurisdiction and control. Part of an emerging multipurpose system of microwave sensors at numerous frequencies, SEASAT will be available even in bad weather to warn ships of approaching storms and to detect stress in ice-floes.[89]

Conventional cartography has been described as a "mixture of art and science, with a heavy emphasis on art."[90] However, in the 1960s, when maps began to be viewed as dynamic models – not least for reproducing the ever-changing conditions and characteristics of the marine environment – it became necessary to redefine the objectives and methods of ocean mapping and charting.[91] With the development of new techniques of computer cartography, it is now feasible to accelerate mapmaking despite the immense volume of relevant information to be portrayed, and to do so without any loss of accuracy.[92] The development of computer science and technology has also permitted geodetic undertakings of unprecedented magnitude, such as the readjustment of the North American Datum by the U.S. National Geodetic Survey.[93]

With these and similar breakthroughs in technology,[94] it can truly be said that boundary-making at sea – or on land or in the air – has entered the Age of Precision.

CONCLUSION: ACCURACY AND PRECISION IN OCEAN BOUNDARY-MAKING

Two dominant and related motifs stand out in the preceding review of trends in the science and technology of location and measurement at sea: accuracy and precision. Seen in this perspective, the mostly Western classical period reviewed above was essentially taken up with establishing some rudimentary facts about the nature and size of the earth and the distances from point to point. Despite the speculative genius of so many classical scholars in relevant areas of science and mathematics, the ancients made relatively minor contributions to empirical undertakings such as location and measurement at sea. By any modern standards, their work was wildly inaccurate.

Classical ignorance was compounded by dogma and superstition throughout the Dark Ages and the Middle Ages. The opening up of the Renaissance mind and spirit had enormous significance for the fostering of the empirical sciences, the development of technology, and not least for the gathering of practical information and experience. By the late nineteenth century, most of the major tasks involved in establishing scientific accuracy in location had been completed. But as far as the ocean was concerned, the victory over geographical ignorance was limited mostly to the surface waters of the earth.

In the last few decades, studies in the physical geography of the ocean have been pursued in three distinct contexts. It seems inevitable that the new age of boundary-making in the ocean will be profoundly influenced by all three. First, the marvellously accurate techniques of location now available will clarify man's understanding of the distribution and abundance of ocean resources which tend to be the focus of boundary disputes – living resources close to the surface of the ocean, non-living resources on or under the seabed, and even minerals suspended in the water column.[95] Second, the new methods of highly precise measurement now make it possible to conduct ocean surveying, mapping, and boundary-making at an unprecedented level of technical sophistication, higher than has ever been attempted on land, and higher, perhaps, than is economically necessary or politically desirable within the present systems of government.[96] Third, the current effort to explore the submarine world, in the last Age of Discovery on our planet, promises to provide the missing knowledge that will equip man finally with a complete three-dimensional, ecological understanding of the marine environment. This new knowledge will eventually enable us to see the ocean as it really is: a mass of global energy composed of accurately locatable natural systems and interactions. In the more distant future, this dynamic model of the restless sea seems certain to alter fundamentally our perception of ocean management requirements, and of the roles of zones and boundaries.

CHAPTER NINE

Determination of Seaward Limits

INTRODUCTION

Our thinking about ocean development and management in the course of the last half-century has been transformed. The change in our pattern of thought is so complete that we have almost forgotten how imprecise ocean boundary-making was until a few decades ago. During the earliest stage in the development of ocean law and policy, there was virtually no need for precision in claims to authority over ocean areas, much less in the criteria and techniques of ocean boundary-making. Today it is technologically possible to bring a high degree of precision to ocean boundary-making. The setting of precise ocean boundaries is also now juridically appropriate, commensurate with the degree of functional sophistication that has recently been invested in the development of ocean regimes and zones.

Of the three principal kinds of ocean boundaries – seaward limits, baselines, and "lateral" boundaries – seaward limits are the most difficult to deal with outside the context of spatial allocation of coastal state authority over the ocean. In our modern era, the problem of determining seaward limits of coastal state jurisdiction applies to five clearly distinguishable regimes: (1) internal waters; (2) the territorial sea; (3) the contiguous zone; (4) the continental shelf; and (5) the exclusive economic zone (and associated exclusive fishing zones). But the problems of determining seaward limits for most of these regimes are non-contentious, unlike the larger allocation questions with which they are associated. The seaward limits of internal waters are identical with the baseline of the territorial sea, and should be treated as such.[1] The exclusive fishing zone has been deprived of regime status during the period of UNCLOS III,[2] and should be treated merely as a variant of the exclusive economic zone. Moreover, UNCLOS III defined the extent of the territorial sea, the contiguous zone, and the EEZ by a fixed standard in nautical miles, thereby reducing the problem of determining seaward limits to one of measurement from their common baseline.[3] Finally, only a dozen or so states have a continental shelf regime extending far beyond the two-hundred-mile limits of their EEZ,[4] and only in these few geographical situations can it be said that the determination of seaward limits may be both politically controversial and technically complex. But before these contemporary difficulties are examined, it may be useful to review the past.

Unfortunately, the pre-modern history of coastal state claims to maritime jurisdiction is one of great confusion. The determination of seaward limits is the "delimitative" aspect of the larger question of spatial allocation - or, more accurately, it is a later stage of ocean boundary-making which requires no technical precision until after the politically controversial issue of allocation has been resolved.[5] The history of jurisdictional confusion is the subject of a voluminous literature,[6] and this section will deal only briefly with some features of the "primitive" and "classical" periods and with the breakdown of the classical system, which pivoted on a narrow territorial sea.

THE PRIMITIVE PERIOD

The earliest period in the history of ocean boundary-making, viewed from a post-UNCLOS III perspective, was one that lacked any degree of precision or sophistication. The period was primitive in at least five important respects: politically, legally, morally, technologically, and administratively.

First, prior to the mid-seventeenth century there was little experience of states acting in concert.[7] The lack of anything resembling the modern state system, and the even more modern system of international organization, meant the lack of any solid political foundation of international law and policy in maritime jurisdiction and ocean boundary-making.

Second, despite the nominally universalist heritage of Roman law, the primitive period was witness to a succession of political "lordship" claims to exclusive or special authority over ocean areas without any solid juridical foundation. Regime thinking followed a painful and protracted course of development, for political claims often conflicted and sometimes resulted in warfare at sea.[8]

Third, the primitive period of claim-making was lacking in any moral sense. Claims were advanced as assertions of unqualified right or prerogative without any reference to countervailing duties or responsibilities. The claims were morally unbalanced as displays of authority. In general, power was considered a sufficient basis for the claim.[9]

Fourth, the opportunities for use of the sea were, more or less, limited to a narrow range of technological capabilities. Concepts of maritime jurisdiction were primitive because the stakes were modest. Before the Age of

Discovery few seafarers ventured far beyond sight of land, except in some familiar regional seas such as the Mediterranean and those of East Asia.[10] Until the late Middle Ages fishing was essentially a coastal activity.[11] The technology for precise positioning and detection at sea did not exist.[12] No one guessed at the mineral wealth besides salt and coal in and under the sea.[13]

Finally, the early examples of ocean zoning reviewed in chapter 8 preceded the emergence of national government as the engine of ocean management. The modest purposes of port administration, revenue collection, and smuggling control made minimal demands on administrative capabilities. The great empires, such as those of China and Rome, did develop some capabilities in port administration and coastal management within large bureaucracies of central government, but at other places and in other times administrative control over ocean activities was shared, often uncomfortably, between local and central authorities.[14]

Under these primitive conditions no precision or sophistication was possible in the determination of the seaward limits of regimes or zones of coastal authority. Political claims to authority at sea had only a quasi-jurisdictional significance at best. They extended to whole seas,[15] or vaguely allocated regions,[16] or to notional (but undrawn) median lines.[17] Even by the Renaissance, as the technology of measurement was beginning to be developed, the medieval concept of *mare adjacens* (adjacent sea) was approximate, and not the subject of the serious measurement debate that was to be such a conspicuous feature of the classical period.

THE CLASSICAL PERIOD

The rediscovery of Roman law and the re-emphasis on the need for universal principles in human affairs were two of the major accomplishments of the Renaissance. An extraordinary fermentation of ideas and aspirations, as much as an accumulation of information, cultivated new concepts of world community and new ideals of uniformity and reciprocity for the emerging nation-states in the sixteenth and seventeenth centuries. In the "new dawn" of international law the ocean was immediately perceived as the battleground for contending interests in the evolving interstate community. Law, or the idea of law, was looked to as the chief hope for civilizing the conflict between two, more or less legitimate, demands within the community: the demand for freedom and the demand for protection. By the early seventeenth century, with the establishment of the nation-state as the primary form of political organization, the assertion of state authority rested on the political concept of sovereignty and on the legal concept of territoriality. On the other hand, the Renaissance and the Age of Discovery had revealed the benefits of freedom and movement in human affairs.

An accommodation between the need for protection and the need for freedom had to be found within a legal framework that could be respected by all nations on the basis of common interest.

The search for accommodation was conducted within the scholarly community, but through the process of advocacy. In the famous confrontation between Hugo Grotius and John Selden[18] an encyclopaedic effort was made by both jurists to marshal all the facts and ideas available in support of freedom and protection respectively. The outcome remained inconclusive for over a hundred years, but by the late eighteenth century most of the Western world, and all of the dominant powers, had agreed to treat special or exclusive rights in coastal waters as a matter of national entitlement, derived from the concept of sovereignty and justified by the legal fiction of territoriality. Within a narrow band of "territorial waters" the coastal state was conceded to have authority, not far short of absolute sovereignty, for most purposes other than navigation control, based on the common agreement that such a grant of state authority was justified by the need for self-protection. Beyond that narrow zone the oceans at large – the "open seas" – were left unregulated as "no law" areas as an inducement to free navigation and trade.

On the face of things, Grotius had won the debate with Selden. Yet the matter was not so simple. In the classical period of international law, and even in recent times, many writers have felt drawn to one of two models of world community law: either "the Grotian tradition of moral order, whereby the rules of international law have been elucidated by reference to what the society of mankind requires for its regular development," or "the Vattelian tradition of acquiescence and consent, whereby the rules have been promulgated by reference to the practice of States."[19] Most classical writers on the law of the sea identified with the Grotian tradition, as if morally obligated to support arguments upholding the principle of freedom. In the Grotian perspective, the previous primitive period of the law of the sea had been characterized by "vague and unfounded claims."[20] Yet other classical jurists, who tended to adopt the Vattelian model of international law, felt compelled by the evidence of state practice to conclude that a balance was needed between the principle of freedom and the principle of protection. For the neo-Vattelians today, the "primitive" period of the law of the sea is simply to be viewed in retrospect as the period preceding the advent of the nation-state system.

As we have seen, the period since 1650 has witnessed dramatic innovations in the precise sciences associated with positioning and detection at sea. Equally impressive advances have occurred in other sectors of ocean science and technology since the establishment of oceanography.[21] By the end of the classical period of the law of the sea in the early twentieth century, political organization, legal theory, and bureaucracy had acquired a new level of global responsibility, offering the prospect of an equitable approach to ocean boundary-making. The classical framework of the law of the sea, consisting only of two diametrically opposed regimes, was now too simplistic to meet the needs of a more sophisticated world community.

Throughout the classical period the determination of seaward limits was a matter that could be applied only to the measurement of the territorial sea. In the later stages of the primitive period, from the Middle Ages to the mid-seventeenth century, the spatial allocation of coastal state authority in the adjacent sea was a matter of increasing importance and concern, but there was no consensus on the method of measuring the limits of these coastal areas. In parts of northern Europe it had become common to claim special fishing rights within the range of human vision. Especially in Scotland, it was maintained that the fishermen of the coastal state were entitled to exclude foreign fishermen from "reserved waters" in all firths and bays and in coastal waters within a "land-kenning" – that is, "not nearer than where they could discern the land from the top of their masts."[22] A land-kenning was estimated at fourteen nautical miles. Scottish claims to exclusive fishing rights within a land-kenning seem to have originated in the fourteenth century or even earlier, and in certain situations the claim was extended to a "double land-kenning" – that is, twenty-eight nautical miles.[23] After the Union of the Crowns of 1603, when James VI of Scotland also became James I of England, the Scottish custom was exported to the south,[24] but the most strenuous diplomatic pressure from London failed to induce the Dutch to acknowledge the validity of the range-of-vision rule in the law of nations.[25] After Danish complaints, the Scots were obliged to acknowledge that the rule applied against themselves off the coast of the Faeroe Islands, and it was also recognized by Spain.[26]

In these countries and elsewhere, the range of human vision had to compete with other methods of measurement for determining the standard limits of coastal state authority in the ocean. In the North Sea, for example, arbitrary 60-mile and 100-mile claims were advanced in the late Middle Ages and into the sixteenth century,[27] and the mid-channel (or thalweg) also had its supporters as a line of division in narrow ocean areas such as the English Channel.[28] But before the establishment of a mileage formula for the territorial limit, the criterion that commanded widest support was the range-of-gunfire. The celebrated "cannon-shot rule" was apparently first proposed in 1610, when the Dutch ambassadors representing the States of Holland and the States General argued for the freedom of fishing. The spatial extent of coastal state authority was limited, they asserted, by considerations of power; no prince could "challenge farther into the sea than he [could] command with a cannon, except gulfs within

[his] land from one point to another."[29] Thereafter, the range of gunfire became an increasingly common criterion in state practice for the measurement of seaward limits of coastal state authority, until it was elevated to the level of a maxim by the Dutch jurist Cornelius van Bynkershoek (1673–1743):[30] *imperium terrae finiri ubi finitur armorum potestas* (the state's authority extends as far as the range of gunfire).[31]

Questions regarding the validity and scope of the "gunshot rule" fascinated jurists for three hundred years.[32] Even in the nineteenth century, when a mileage criterion seemed to have prevailed in most countries, usually in the form of a three-mile rule, jurists continued to take pleasure in debating the merits of using military technology as a measure of the extent of coastal state authority. By that period most viewed the cannon-shot rule and the three-mile rule as the major alternatives in defining the breadth of the territorial sea.[33] Placed in opposition to each other, each seemed to promise something valuable: flexibility in one case and certainty in the other. Most of the classical commentators assumed that uniformity and reciprocity were desirable, but that both would be assured with either rule.

Even when victory appeared certain for the mileage proponents, the relevance of technology in ocean boundary-making continued to assert itself, most recently in determining the seaward limits of the continental shelf (on the "exploitability" criterion, see the section of this chapter entitled "The New Law of the Sea.") But the reintroduction of technology as a factor in the determination of seaward limits would prove impossible within the classical frame of reference. The logic of technology would be given little weight until the world community was ready to adopt a measure of modern sophistication, rather than classical simplicity, in the development of regime thinking in ocean law and policy.

THE BREAKDOWN OF THE CLASSICAL SYSTEM

The classical system of the law of the sea began to break down early in the twentieth century. No doubt the principal causes are to be found in the "outside" milieu, such as the advances in ocean science and technology and the resulting changes in national perceptions of ocean needs and opportunities. Within the discipline of international law, old philosophical debates were resumed, enlightened by a new awareness of the political tensions between the competing principles of freedom and protection at sea.

Some jurists of the period espoused the Grotian philosophy, adopting the (normativist) model of international law as a moral order and invoking the supportive tradition of natural law. Others espoused the Vattelian philosophy, adopting the (scientific) view of international law as a reflection of states' consent or acquiescence and invoking the supportive tradition of positive law. On the specific issue of the extent of coastal state jurisdiction, many late classical jurists felt bound to inject political judgment into the debate. Some of these advocated support for the Grotian policy favouring freedom at the expense of protection. Others advocated support for the Seldenian policy favouring protection at the expense of freedom.

Between 1910 and 1945 most of the major writers on coastal state jurisdiction tended to move away, in some degree, from the Grotian policy position. Through historical research, both ancient and modern, they uncovered a story of doctrinal confusion and conflict and a contemporary pattern of divergent, rather than convergent, trends in state practice.[34] More or less consciously espousing the Vattelian philosophy of international law, most of them presented this evidence of divergence with a view to questioning the validity or adequacy of the simple classical system based solely on the universalist notion of a uniform three-mile territorial sea. Some, but not all, of these writers also tended to lean toward Seldenian policy.[35] For all of these late classical specialists in maritime jurisdiction, regardless of personal inclination, the determination of the seaward limits of coastal state jurisdiction was now seen to be much more complicated than the simple scheme envisaged by the earlier classicists.

Specifically, this particular type of ocean boundary-making was affected by three important features of contemporary state practice: first, the lack of unanimity on uniform limits for a general territorial zone (the territorial sea); second, the gradual acceptance of uniform limits for a general administrative zone for limited purposes (the contiguous zone); and, third, a mounting number of unilateral claims to widely varying limits for certain special functional zones.

First, by the end of the classical period, it had to be acknowledged that state practice revealed a significant disparity in territorial sea limits, varying from the neo-Grotian favourite of three nautical miles to the traditional Scandinavian limit of four nautical miles to more modern limits of twelve miles and other distances. Strenuous efforts to resolve the differences were made under the auspices of the League of Nations, but they were unavailing.[36]

Second, by the time the League of Nations was formed, the concept of a uniform contiguous zone had been proposed for the exercise of certain administrative powers by the coastal state beyond three-mile territorial limits. The "minimalist" states, which wished to maintain the narrowest possible territorial sea at the three-mile mark, rallied around the proposal for twelve-mile limits to a contiguous zone, which would lie adjacent to the seaward limits of the territorial sea. In this way it was hoped to restrict "extraterritorial" jurisdiction to a few unexceptionable areas of administrative responsibility associated with customs, taxation, health, and immigration. But no formal adoption of the suggested functional regime was possible before the Second World War.[37]

Finally, the end of the classical period was reached amid mounting evidence of the need to recognize special entitlements for certain coastal states on the basis of historic usage, historic waters or bays, vital interests, or new technology.[38] This feature of contemporary state practice seemed even further removed from any short-term prospect of consensus, but in the 1930s no one foresaw that precisely this kind of diversity of special jurisdictional claims would provide an important building-block in the construction of a radically different legal order half a century later.

THE NEW LAW OF THE SEA

The Territorial Sea

The question of the breadth of the territorial sea has been for centuries the most famous and best documented of all issues in the law of the sea. In a monograph on boundary-making it hardly seems necessary to recount the familiar history of events leading to a general acceptance of a twelve-mile territorial sea. It should be sufficient to note that the final decision on twelve-mile limits at UNCLOS III[39] followed failures at both UNCLOS I and UNCLOS II, and that the eventual diplomatic consensus on these limits at UNCLOS III was inextricably linked with consensus on two-hundred-mile limits for the exclusive economic zone regime and on other jurisdictional matters negotiated in the Second Committee of that conference.[40] Under the conditions of modern technology, no coastal state is likely to encounter technical difficulties in bringing precision to the actual determination of seaward limits for a twelve-mile territorial sea now that the politically controversial issue of allocation has been resolved. All the problems associated with this kind of boundary-making arise in the delineation of the baseline, not in the drawing of a parallel line twelve miles out.

The Contiguous Zone

The same comments apply to the determination of seaward limits of the contiguous zone, which were extended from the twelve-mile mark adopted at UNCLOS I[41] to the twenty-four-mile mark agreed to at UNCLOS III.[42] Again, the actual drawing of these limits is done simply by the seaward projection of the baseline of the territorial sea. Given the strictly administrative reasons for this regime, it may be of minimal functional relevance that this extension keeps these acts of the coastal state within the range of guns, albeit beyond the range of human vision.[43]

The Exclusive Economic Zone

The advent of the two-hundred-mile EEZ regime at UNCLOS III is generally regarded as the most important single change in the new law of the sea. To many international lawyers, this event above all reflects the breakdown of the classical system based on the Grotian principle of the freedom of the high seas. From a post-classical perspective, it represents in particular a new beginning in the development of the international law of fisheries.[44]

After a quarter-century of gradual evolution bridging the neo-classical and post-classical periods of international law, patrimonial sea and exclusive fishing claims acquired more rapid momentum after the convening of the UN Seabed Committee in 1968. By the summer of 1974, at the first substantive session of UNCLOS III proper, an overwhelming majority of the delegations declared their willingness to accept the principle of such a radical resource regime, although reluctantly in many cases and on the condition that concessions were made on critical issues related to transit rights. Since the final period of gestation of the EEZ regime coincided with the early years of UNCLOS III, the process for establishing the formula for the determination of these seaward limits was essentially political.

Although the crucial events in this period were taking place in the arena of conference diplomacy, uncertainties regarding the outcome also created difficulties in the process of adjudication. In April 1972 the United Kingdom instituted proceedings before the International Court of Justice against the Republic of Iceland in respect of an Icelandic claim to a fifty-mile zone of exclusive fishery jurisdiction, extending far beyond its twelve-mile territorial sea limits. Six weeks later, in May 1972, the Federal Republic of Germany instituted similar proceedings against Iceland before the same tribunal. In response, Iceland declined to confer jurisdiction on the ICJ and refused to appoint an agent, but the Court agreed none the less to entertain proceedings by both litigants. These two parallel *Fisheries Jurisdiction* cases were fully argued thereafter, despite Iceland's non-appearance and non-participation. In August 1972 the Court granted certain interim measures of protection for both the United Kingdom and the Federal Republic of Germany.[45] In judgments dated 2 February 1973, the Court found it had jurisdiction to entertain the applications filed by the two parties and to deal with the merits of the two cases.[46]

The United Kingdom asked the Court to find that "there is no foundation in international law for the claim by Iceland to be entitled to extend its fisheries jurisdiction by establishing a zone of exclusive fisheries jurisdiction extending to 50 nautical miles from the baselines hereinbefore referred to and that its claim is therefore invalid."[47] The Federal Republic of Germany asked the Court to declare that "the unilateral extension by Iceland of its zone of exclusive fisheries jurisdiction to 50 nautical miles from the present baselines ... would have no basis in international law and could therefore not be opposed to the Federal Republic of Germany and to its fishing vessels."[48] By a vote of ten to four the Court held that the Icelandic fishery regulations in question were "not opposable" to either of the applicant states,[49] but it did not deal directly with the basic question whether Iceland's jurisdictional claim was valid or invalid under customary international law.

The problem for the Court was how to deal judicially with the fact that many other states had made similar, or much more extensive, fishery claims, and that the trend to acceptance of the two-hundred-mile EEZ regime at UNCLOS III was already in evidence. As to that trend, the Court simply commented that it "cannot render judgment *sub specie legis ferendae*, or anticipate the law before the legislator has laid it down."[50] Although it declined to predict the outcome of UNCLOS III on the determination of seaward limits, the Court did allow itself to offer some observations on the nature and extent of the duty to conserve fishery stocks and on the nature and extent of preferential fishing rights; those observations were based on the evidence of current trends in treaty practice and diplomatic negotiation rather than on "established" principles of customary international law. Significantly, perhaps, these observations were offered with a view to facilitating future negotiations between the parties to the dispute. It might therefore be said that the Court was cautious in its declaratory or resolutive role, since that role brought it into collision with the law-making process at UNCLOS III, but less cautious in its facilitative role.[51]

As anticipated, but not acknowledged, by most of those participating in the *Fisheries Jurisdiction* cases, UNCLOS III did result in the constitution of a regime of extended fishery jurisdiction. Within the limits of a two-hundred mile exclusive economic zone, the coastal state would be agreed to possess

(a) sovereign rights for the purpose of exploring and exploiting, conserving and managing the natural resources, whether living or non-living, of the waters superjacent to the sea-bed and of the sea-bed and its subsoil, and with regard to other activities for the economic exploitation and exploration of the zone, such as the production of energy from the water, currents and winds;
(b) jurisdiction as provided for in the relevant provisions of this Convention with regard to:
 (i) the establishment and use of artificial islands, installations and structures;

(ii) marine scientific research;
(iii) the protection and preservation of the marine environment;
(c) other rights and duties provided for in this Convention.[52]

For these various purposes, the zone would not extend beyond "200 nautical miles from the baselines from which the breadth of the territorial sea is measured."[53]

As a matter of cartography, the drawing of these two-hundred-mile seaward limits seems only slightly more complicated than the drawing of twelve-mile limits for the territorial sea or twenty-four-mile limits for the contiguous zone.[54] But because the distance is so much greater, care will have to be taken to allow for geodetic considerations.[55] Indeed, a case can be made for greater precision in this kind of boundary-making by arguing the need for more effective resource management and enforcement.[56]

The Continental Shelf

In determining the seaward limits of the continental shelf beyond the two-hundred-mile EEZ regime, it is difficult to make a clear distinction between allocation and delimitation in the sequential sense given to these terms in the general theory of boundary-making (see chapter 1). Because of the nature of this particular type of ocean boundary, the sequence of boundary-making is best described by reference to the transition from the global process of conference diplomacy to the national process of bureaucracy. The global process is concerned with the negotiation of the principles, criteria, and procedures for this kind of boundary-making, and this undertaking goes beyond the general issues of allocation to the more precise tasks of delimitation. The national process is necessary first to complete the tasks of delimitation, and then to resort, if necessary, to physical demarcation of the shelf and to the devising of functional arrangements for the administration of the shelf in the seaward boundary areas.[57]

This type of ocean boundary-making, more than any other, places heavy demands on interdisciplinary understanding. In particular, the boundary-maker in this context depends on critical information from several sectors of ocean science, and needs to have an appreciation of developments and prospects in relevant sectors of ocean technology. Lawyers, because of their prominence in the determination of the seaward limits of the continental shelf, particularly at the global stage of the process, have a special need for an understanding of related considerations in ocean science and technology. In this kind of boundary-making, "international lawyers should employ concepts only when, and in so far as, they do not contradict the physical realities with which the concepts deal."[58] In practice, the lawyers involved in the determination of the seaward limits of the shelf, both at UNCLOS I and UNCLOS III, have found it necessary, at the very least, to understand geological terminology and concepts, such as "continental margin,"[59] "continental shelf,"[60] "continental slope,"[61] and "continental rise,"[62] the morphological features of the deep ocean floor,[63] the process of sedimentation,[64] and the composition of manganese modules and other mineral compounds.[65] Similarly, lawyers engaged in this process have also had to acquire some understanding of the technology of ocean drilling and of the economic and technical problems associated with offshore petroleum production.[66]

This kind of boundary-making has been further complicated by the resource significance of the shelf to claimant states. By the end of the classical period in the late 1930s, it was becoming known that enormous submarine petroleum reserves would be available for exploitation as soon as platform and drilling technology could be deployed in offshore areas. By the late 1940s offshore oil and gas had become the major source of revenue for several "geographically advantaged" coastal states in the Arabian-Persian Gulf. In the period since then dozens of coastal states in other regions have given priority to the acceleration of offshore exploration, and many have reached the stage of offshore production. Especially since the escalation of world oil prices that began in 1973, the prospect of an extensive continental shelf for the exercise of sovereign rights over the resources thereon has given a high degree of political saliency to the issues associated with the determination of the shelf's seaward limits.

But geography has created natural inequities. For every coastal state blessed with a fairly wide shelf and the prospect of significant offshore mineral resources, there are two or more other coastal states with narrow shelves and as many again that are land-locked or shelf-locked.[67] Taken together, these "geographically disadvantaged" and "narrow shelf" states form a large majority of states. In particular, most of the developing states included in these categories have looked to some form of arrangement that would help to compensate them for this inequity of nature. Compensation has been sought, for example, in the form of beneficial participation in a global scheme for deep-ocean mining of hard minerals in the international area of the ocean floor beyond the limits of national jurisdiction over the continental shelf.[68] Accordingly, the naturally favoured minority of states has had the strongest interest in an extension of seaward limits of the continental shelf, whereas the majority of naturally unfavoured states has had an interest in restricting encroachments on the international area of the deep ocean floor.

With the lines so drawn, this particular type of ocean boundary-making has been heavily influenced by political considerations of equity as well as scientific considerations of precision,technological considerations of flexibility, industrial considerations of stability, and juridical considerations of certainty and uniformity. Given the need to satisfy so many diverse value demands, an extraordinarily high degree of sophistication has had to be brought to the determination of the seaward limits of the continental shelf.

The effort to achieve functional sophistication in this complicated context must be traced over two stages of conference diplomacy, spanning a period of over thirty years. The first stage began in 1951, when the International Law Commission (ILC) commenced its deliberations on a definition of the continental shelf as part of its seven-year preparation for UNCLOS I, which was held at Geneva in 1958. This stage culminated in the adoption of the 1958 Convention of the Continental Shelf.[69] The second stage began with the convening of the UN Seabed Committee in 1968 and ended fourteen years later with the adoption of the UN Convention on the Law of the Sea at (UNCLOS III) in December 1982.[70]

The story of the first stage can be summarized. In its first attempt to define the shelf, the ILC was reluctant to emphasize any depth criterion,[71] and in 1951, at the end of the third session, the Commission decided not to specify a depth limit.[72] But in 1952 the International Committee on the Nomenclature of Ocean Bottom Features noted that the edge of the geological shelf was conventionally taken to be the 100-fathom or 200-metre isobath, though variations occurred in many parts of the world.[73] In the following year the ILC adopted the 200-metre criterion, hoping this would discourage the adoption of different limits by different states. No doubt this kind of scientific precision appealed to the legal mind. Although it was already apparent that it was only a matter of time before drilling could be conducted in deeper waters beyond the 200-metre isobath, it seemed wiser to give precedence to precision over long-term stability. Thereafter, various governments began to press the argument for long-term flexibility through the adoption of the functional criterion of exploitability, and in 1956 a formal resolution to this effect was adopted at a conference of Pan American states.[74] Sensitive to these political pressures, the ILC incorporated both the depth and exploitability criteria in its final draft articles,[75] and that wording was adopted at UNCLOS I. Under article 1 of the 1958 Convention on the Continental Shelf, the term "continental shelf" was given the following legal definition:

> For the purposes of these articles, the term "continental shelf" is used as referring (a) to the seabed and subsoil of the submarine areas adjacent to the coast but outside the area of the territorial sea, to a depth of 200 metres or, beyond that limit, to where the depth of the superjacent waters admits of the exploitation of the natural resources of the said areas; (b) to the seabed and subsoil of similar submarine areas adjacent to the coasts of islands.

This formula presented the two most popular, but contradictory, criteria:

a fixed depth criterion and the expandable criterion of exploitability. Faced with the obvious difficulty of interpreting when, under this article, a state's sovereign rights should be deemed to extend beyond the 200-metre isobath, lawyers reacted in various ways. Some, in the textualist tradition of treaty interpretation,[76] adopted the "ordinary meaning" rule of construction, and argued that exploitability must prevail over the depth criterion as soon as the conditions of technology created a conflict between the two.[77] Others, looking at the context of conference diplomacy and the emerging pattern of state practice, sought relevant factors that could serve as a test of reasonableness to limit the elasticity of the exploitability criterion. Still others, attempting a simple functional interpretation, argued that the major purpose of the definition was to provide short-term security in the first generation of ("near-shore") offshore development under the Convention and that the elasticity of the exploitability criterion should be severely limited.[78] Eventually, most commentators aligned themselves with either the "broad shelf" or the "narrow shelf" interpretation, essentially on the basis of policy preference with respect to the overall purpose of the Convention to confirm and extend the coastal state's sovereign rights to the resources of the shelf.[79]

Much of the textualist analysis pivoted on the term "adjacent" in the phrase "submarine areas adjacent to the coast" preceding the depth and exploitability criteria in article 1. Arguments whether the term "adjacent" should be considered a third criterion, and to what extent it should be deemed a limitation on the elasticity of the exploitability criterion, revolved around the semantic question of the relationship between "adjacency" and "proximity" or "propinquity," and their counterparts in other languages.[80] Further confusion ensued when the International Court of Justice introduced the concept of "natural prolongation of land-mass" into continental shelf doctrine in its decision in the *North Sea Continental Shelf* cases of 1969.[81] But the Court was dealing with shelf boundary delimitations between adjacent states,[82] not with the determination of seaward limits; and, more important, the "natural prolongation" concept was an attempt to elucidate the juridical nature of the regime and of the coastal state's rights thereunder, rather than a principle or criterion for boundary-making.[83]

The truth is, of course, that the debate was sterile. Technology had, quite predictably, bypassed the 1958 definition of the shelf. A new formula for the determination of its seaward limits had to be found in the *Sturm und Drang* of conference diplomacy at UNCLOS III. A final all-out effort would have to be made to accommodate the requirements of the seven most relevant value demands: equity, precision, feasibility, stability, flexibility, certainty, and uniformity.

After several preliminary efforts in the UN Seabed Committee, the delegations at UNCLOS III proper decided that for the majority of nations, which were not particularly well favoured by nature, the best solution to the problem of redefinition of the shelf was simply to apply the seaward limits of the newly approved regime of the exclusive economic zone – namely, the two-hundred-mile limit. For most nations this arbitrary mileage criterion offered sufficient precision, stability, certainty, and uniformity to be politically acceptable. But for the dozen "broad margin" states – the "margineers" whose geological shelf or continental margin extended far beyond the two-hundred-mile limit, that simple mileage criterion was quite unacceptable. Indeed, for some it would have meant rolling back existing claims and cancelling exploration permits already granted for areas beyond those limits in their offshore waters.[84] For these naturally favoured coastal states, strenuous compromise diplomacy would be necessary to achieve a more complex formula that would also satisfy the requirements of equity, feasibility, and flexibility.

In the interest of feasibility and flexibility, and arguably in the interest of equity for the coastal state, most of the margineer states looked to science to provide them with a formula that would satisfy their desire for an extensive area of exclusive rights to the resources of the shelf, far beyond the two-hundred-mile limit applied to less fortunate coastal states. Most of the margineer delegations had the benefit of scientific advisers who could agree on the desirability of precision in defining the limits of the continental shelf regime and on the attractiveness of the idea of using a natural boundary for this purpose. Most advisers were inclined to underline the relevance of the "continental margin" as that term was understood in the science community. The closest thing to a natural boundary at the "edge" of the margin was the bottom or base of the continental slope,[85] but since this point could not be located with complete precision the margineer delegations cheerfully accepted the prospect of a more arbitrary boundary farther seaward on the continental rise.[86]

Faced with this task, the margineers acknowledged the inevitability of a highly eclectic type of formulation with a mixture of many different kinds of components. The first scientific approach, which focused on the bottom of the slope, was supplemented by a second scientific approach, which focused on the sediments on the continental rise extending beyond the foot of the slope. Particularly on Atlantic-type margins, there is a broad wedge of sediments tapering off toward the abyssal plain; but how precisely to determine the legal boundary of the margin on this sediment wedge? As long as the sediment could be shown to have originated on the continental land mass or its seaward extension, such a limit was scientifically consistent with the "natural prolongation" doctrine of the International Court of Justice – a marriage of science and jurisprudence to satisfy all but the greediest of the "broad shelf" claimant states.

A solution to the cut-off problem was offered in a breakthrough proposal by the Republic of Ireland's delegation in April 1976.[87] This proposal envisaged a boundary determined by a ratio between the thickness of the sediment wedge and the distance seaward from the foot of the slope. A sediment depth of 1 per cent of the distance from the base of the slope was chosen, despite considerable controversy over the technical difficulties involved.[88]

However, in the eyes of many "narrow shelf" and other states, the Irish formula seemed unduly permissive of encroachments on the "international area" of the seabed. Accordingly, the political balance swung back to the idea of a fixed mileage cut-off,[89] and this element was introduced into the group of margineers in the form of a three-hundred-mile cut-off proposed by the Soviet Union.[90] After further negotiation[91] the Irish and Soviet formulae were merged into one (the "biscuit formula")[92] and adopted finally by the Conference as a whole. This formula is reproduced in article 76 of the 1982 Convention:

1 The continental shelf of a coastal State comprises the sea-bed and subsoil of the submarine areas that extend beyond its territorial sea throughout the natural prolongation of its land territory to the outer edge of the continental margin, or to a distance of 200 nautical miles from the baselines from which the breadth of the territorial sea is measured where the outer edge of the continental margin does not extend up to that distance.

2 The continental shelf of a coastal State shall not extend beyond the limits provided for in paragraphs 4 to 6.

3 The continental margin comprises the submerged prolongation of the land mass of the coastal State and consists of the sea-bed and subsoil of the shelf, the slope and the rise. It does not include the deep ocean floor with its oceanic ridges or the subsoil thereof.

4 (a) For the purposes of this Convention, the coastal State shall establish the outer edge of the continental margin wherever the margin extends beyond 200 nautical miles from the baselines from which the breadth of the territorial sea is measured, by either:

(i) a line delineated in accordance with paragraph 7 by reference to the outermost fixed points at each, of which the thickness of sedimentary rocks is at least 1 per cent of the shortest distance from such point to the foot of the continental slope; or

(ii) a line delineated in accordance with paragraph 7 by reference to fixed points not more than 60 nautical miles from the foot of the continental slope.

(b) In the absence of evidence to the contrary, the foot of the continental slope shall be determined as the point of maximum change in the gradient at its base.

5 The fixed points comprising the line of the outer limits of the continental shelf on the sea-bed, drawn in accordance with paragraph 4(a)(i) and (ii), either shall not exceed 350 nautical miles from the baselines from which the breadth of the territorial sea is measured or shall not exceed 100 nautical miles from the 2,500 metre isobath, which is a line connecting the depth of 2,500 metres.
6 Notwithstanding the provisions of paragraph 5, on submarine ridges, the outer limit of the continental shelf shall not exceed 350 nautical miles from the baselines from which the breadth of the territorial sea is measured. This paragraph does not apply to submarine elevations that are natural components of the continental margin, such as its plateaux, rises, caps, banks and spurs.

This formula is surely the most complicated, and perhaps also the most sophisticated, ever applied to a boundary-making problem at sea, on land, or in the air. Several features of the formula should be noted. First, it reflects the combined influences of geography, geology, geomorphology, and jurisprudence – a tour de force of interdisciplinary co-operation.[93] Second, the problems of interpretation bedevilling article 1 of the 1958 Convention were eliminated by excluding all three contradictory criteria under the earlier definition: the two-hundred-metre isobath, exploitability, and adjacency. Third, the "ridge" issue was resolved by including all submarine ridges (plateaux, rises, caps, banks, and spurs), and excluding all oceanic ridges. Fourth, the outcome was extremely favourable to the margineer states, and, from the viewpoint of equity, represents a highly generous disposition of the allocation issue by the international community.[94]

In addition to this technically sophisticated but complex formula for determination of the seaward limits of the continental regime beyond two hundred miles, UNCLOS III also had to negotiate a procedure for its interpretation and application. If the formula had been simple and precise, interpretation of those globally approved criteria would have raised few difficulties, and application could have been entrusted entirely to the adjacent coastal state. As it stands, the matter is not straightforward. In a sense, the formula is the product of negotiation between a few highly favoured coastal states and the rest of the international community; the latter is entitled to some kind of participation (or representation) in the processes of interpretation and application. Since the data that must be interpreted are scientific in character, it was agreed at an early stage of negotiations at UNCLOS III[95] that article 76 should also make provision for an international technical commission to review each national interpretation.[96] More controversially, it was argued by some delegations that an international review of this kind should be regarded as a required procedure of approval. The more this proposed arrangement resembled a veto system, the more unacceptable it became to some of the margineer states.[97]

They argued that the formula in article 76 represented in some degree a rolling-back of their sovereign rights over the continental margin, to the extent that it imposed a limitation on the scope of the exploitability criterion in article 1 of the 1958 Convention on the Continental Shelf.[98] If they agreed to accept article 76, they argued, it should be subject to their retaining the prerogative, as a matter of sovereign entitlement, to determine their own limits, albeit within the parameters of the globally negotiated "biscuit" formula. On this politically sensitive issue the Conference was forced to resort to intentionally ambiguous wording, and four procedural paragraphs were adopted as part of the boundary-making system under article 76:

7 The coastal State shall delineate the outer limits of its continental shelf, where that shelf extends beyond 200 nautical miles from the baselines from which the breadth of the territorial sea is measured, by straight lines not exceeding 60 nautical miles in length, connecting fixed points, defined by coordinates of latitude and longitude.

8 Information on the limits of the continental shelf beyond 200 nautical miles from the baselines from which the breadth of the territorial sea is measured shall be submitted by the coastal State to the Commission on the Limits of the Continental Shelf set up under Annex II on the basis of equitable geographical representation. The Commission shall make recommendations to coastal States on matters related to the establishment of the outer limits of their continental shelf. The limits of the shelf established by a coastal State on the basis of these recommendations shall be final and binding.

9 The coastal State shall deposit with the Secretary-General of the United Nations charts and relevant information, including geodetic data, permanently describing the outer limits of its continental shelf. The Secretary-General shall give due publicity thereto.

10 The provisions of this article are without prejudice to the question of delimitation of the continental shelf between States with opposite or adjacent coasts.

In article 2(1) of Annex II it is provided that the Commission will consist of twenty-one "experts in the field of geology, geophysics or hydrography, elected by States Parties to this Convention from among their nationals, having due regard to the need to ensure equitable geographical representation, who shall serve in their personal capacities." Normally, however, it is expected that the Commission will function "by way of subcommissions composed of seven members, appointed in a balanced manner taking into account the specific elements of each submission by a coastal State" (article 5 of Annex II). The subcommission will submit its recommendations to the Commission (article 6(1) of Annex II). The functions of the Commission will be:

(a) to consider the data and other material submitted by coastal States concerning the outer limits of the continental shelf in areas where those limits extend beyond 200 nautical miles, and to make recommendations in accordance with article 76 and the Statement of Understanding adopted on 29 August 1980 by the Third United Nations Conference on the Law of the Sea;

(b) to provide scientific and technical advice, if requested by the coastal State concerned during the preparation of the data, referred to in subparagraph (a)[article 3(1) of Annex II].

The coastal state concerned is required to submit "particulars of such limits to the Commission along with supporting scientific and technical data as soon as possible but in any case within 10 years of the entry into force of the this Convention for that State" (article 4 of Annex II). The coastal state, not the Commission, is authorized to "establish the outer limits of the continental shelf in conformity with the provisions of article 76, paragraph 8, and in accordance with the appropriate national procedures" (article 7 of Annex II); but where the coastal state concerned disagrees with the recommendations of the Commission, the state "shall, within a reasonable time, make a revised or new submission to the Commission" (article 8 of Annex II).

A brief comment on these precedural provisions may be appropriate. The Commission and subcommissions are confined to scientific and technical work. Clearly the review process is not political, much less judicial, in character. The Commission cannot be said to "represent" the international community in a politically operational sense, much less to be authorized to adjudicate or overrule the boundary-making act of the coastal state concerned. On the other hand, the subcommissions might be regarded as representative in a symbolic sense, with a view to the "balanced manner" of their appointment and the need for accommodation of national and international interests in the seabed. Moreover, the Commission seems to have been given powers tantamount to a right of approval or disapproval, albeit on strictly technical grounds within a system of recommendatory, not decisional, authority. A balance is designed into the system between the prerogative of the coastal state concerned, whose sovereign rights are affected, and an implied right of approval vested in an international technical body.[99]

Finally, it should be noted that features of both the formula and the procedure under article 76 have been subjected to criticism since the end of negotiations at UNCLOS III. The most severe criticisms have come from the scientific community. As to the formula, many scientists still regret that the geological concept of the "continental shelf" ever became a legal term,[100] but most of them acknowledged the inevitability of that process at the beginning of UNCLOS III.[101] In any event, although the regime rests on a legal concept of the continental shelf, the boundary-making problem of determining the seaward limits of the regime beyond two hundred miles pivots on the geological concept of the "continental margin."[102] At least one prominent scientist has adopted the functionalist position that boundaries in the sea should vary with the use to which they are put, and on that ground has criticized the two-hundred-mile shelf limit that applies to the majority of coastal states.[103] This same critic and others have pointed to several examples of imprecision, such as the inadequate definition of "the foot of the slope," which is one of the central elements in paragraph 4,[104] and the confusing terminology of "submarine rights" and "submarine elevations" in paragraph 6.[105] Several scientists question the technical feasibility of applying the sediment-thickness test,[106] and others emphasize the expensiveness of applying this "geological method" of determination.[107] The introduction of new depth criteria as far as the 2,500-metre isobath imposes strains on existing technology, for depth is more difficult to measure accurately than distance.[108] Others have pointed to related problems in geodesy,[109] cartography,[110] position-fixing,[111] and data-sampling.[112] A few commentators have been particularly critical of the neglect of the special boundary-making problems associated with islands.[113]

As to the procedure, most commentators have noted that the Commission cannot be brought into this particular boundary-making process in certain areas until the end of the century.[114] Moreover, the Commission seems to have been given a high degree of discretionary authority in interpreting its own terms of reference.[115] Particularly in view of this final uncertainty, it is difficult to assess the probable effectiveness of the boundary-making system under article 76.

It must be concluded that the determination of the maximum seaward limits of the continental shelf in the late twentieth century has become an extraordinary challenge to the theory and practice of ocean boundary-making. Never before have the formulae and procedures of boundary-making involved so many diverse elements in the form of concepts, definitions, principles, criteria, methods, and mechanisms. It may be many years before one can predict the outcome of continuing efforts to reconcile the technical need for precision and certainty with the political need for flexibility.[116]

CHAPTER TEN

Delineation of Baselines and Closing Lines

INTRODUCTION

Today, in our Age of Precision, it is accepted as elementary that a clear distinction must be drawn between the regime of the territorial sea and that of waters lying immediately adjacent to the shoreline. In legislative and judicial practice there is still some confusion about the relationship between overlapping jurisdictional concepts of the international and "municipal" (that is, national) legal systems.[1] Yet within the context of international law it is now established, as a general proposition, that a "baseline" is a boundary that separates the territorial sea from either the internal or archipelagic waters on the landward side. According to our contemporary regime thinking, a baseline is typically the exterior limit of internal and archipelagic waters as well as the interior limit of the territorial sea. The baseline of the territorial sea is also used for measuring the seaward limits of the contiguous zone, the exclusive economic zone, the continental shelf, and (for some coastal states) the exclusive fishing zone.[2] So the drawing of the baseline is, in theory, of pivotal significance in the allocation of coastal state jurisdiction.

In practice, however, the areal implications of baseline delineation vary enormously from country to country. The drawing of baselines, unlike the determination of seaward limits, is governed largely by the facts of geography. Because of the diversity of coastal geography from region to region, and the extreme variability of many coastlines, this particular form of ocean boundary-making cannot be brought within the ambit of a few simple rules. Complexity is inherent in baseline delineation. Admittedly, some coastal areas do lack any distinctive or special configuration, but although such areas may be thought of as "normal" and treated by the application of "standard" boundary-making criteria, paradoxically they represent the exception rather than the rule.[3] Most coastlines possess a variety of irregular natural features, such as bays, inlets, estuaries, islands, islets, and rocks, as well as numerous low-tide elevations. Moreover, the contour of many coastlines is further complicated by the introduction of artificial features in the form of harbour works (port installations), roadsteads, buoys, artificial islands, and other types of offshore installations. In these more common situations it has been necessary, in the interest of flexibility, to devise a variety of special rules that permit a weighting of specific geographical features as factors in boundary-making.

Although physical geography seems to have played the major role in the history of baseline delineation, it would be unwise to ignore the interplay of human interests and attitudes in the process. Sometimes the relevant predisposition is based on the central government's conception of national interest, sometimes on a subnational government's conception of regional interest. But in either case governmental interest may be expected to reflect the attitude of the coastal community in the affected area. Generally, the attitude of coastal communities has tended to exclusivity, favouring claims to baseline delineation criteria and methods that will have the effect of excluding inshore areas from foreign activities.[4] In the past, therefore, coastal states, on behalf of the coastal communities, have tended to take the maximum advantage of geographical features that present themselves in order to "close off" coastal waters. This effort has focused especially on estuaries, bays, inlets, and other semi-enclosed inshore waters, usually those that bear the closest physical, economic, or strategic connection with the shore. Accordingly, many modern versions of the baseline have their origin in "closing lines" of one kind or another, applied to historic or otherwise designated coastal waters deemed to be entitled to special protection under the sovereignty of the coastal state.[5] So it has become one of the purposes of the modern international law of the sea to devise rules to check the abuse of discretion by the coastal state in the delineation of such boundaries.[6]

Given the prevalence of "exclusivist" purposes in the traditional approaches to baseline delineation, it might be questioned, in the aftermath of UNCLOS III, whether the same degree of importance should now be attached to this type of ocean boundary-making, given the vast extension of coastal state jurisdiction that characterizes the new law of the sea. This question cannot be answered simply. The relative importance of seaward limits and baselines depends entirely on the facts of geography confronting each coastal state. Some states are geographically advantaged in one way but not another; others are favoured by nature in both ways; and a few unfortunate coastal states are precluded by geography both from the benefits of a two-hundred-mile EEZ and from the advantages of securing extensive inshore areas by reason of special coastal characteristics.

Before examining the contemporary system of rules governing baseline delineation, it may be useful to review briefly the relevant antecedents in the pre-modern period.

THE PRIMITIVE PERIOD

The early period in the development of international law, up to the early or mid-seventeenth century, was primitive, not least in the sense that the classical concept of the territorial sea had not yet been formulated. Indeed, the concept of the territorial sea regime did not jell in the minds of international lawyers until fairly late in the nineteenth century, and the distinction between territorial and internal waters did not emerge with clarity until the early twentieth century. Accordingly, the concept of the "baseline", which is now defined essentially as the division between those two regimes,[7] dates only from the end of the classical period.

In this monograph it would serve no purpose to examine the history of the confusion over the antecedents to those modern regimes. Early regime thinking was extremely fuzzy by modern standards, and casts little light on the contemporary problems of baseline delineation. Yet a few of the early exclusivist trends in state practice are relevant to the general theory of boundary-making.

First, it should be recalled that most of the early claims to exclude coastal waters from foreign use blurred the now-familiar distinction between interior and exterior limits of coastal state jurisdiction. It was deemed sufficient by coastal authorities in the primitive period of international law to mark off "their" waters from the open sea. The conditions for any greater precision simply did not exist.

Yet, despite this imprecision, coastal authorities were usually quite clear about their reasons for wishing to exclude. Sometimes the reasons derived directly from national security concerns, as in the case of the King's Chambers.[8] Sometimes they were based on an ancient local prerogative, as in the case of reserved fishing areas. (See the section entitled "The Classical Period" in chapter 9.) At other times the reasons lay in the need for a resolution of an intranational jurisdictional issue, such as the old English quarrel between the common law courts and the courts of admiralty, when a division had to be made in the area *intra fauces terrae* (between the jaws of land).[9] To resolve this issue of judicial jurisdiction, a statute was passed as early as 1391, in the thirteenth year of the reign of Richard II.[10] But the cognate issue of the "limits of the realm" persisted up to and beyond the famous *Franconia* case of 1867 (*R.* v. *Keyn*).[11] Moreover, many of the early experiments in zoning involved claims to interior as well as exterior limits of administrative jurisdiction, as in the case of the Cinque Ports.[12]

Third, early boundary delineation claims were often advanced in the process of private litigation, and were thus injected into an area of legal doctrine, such as that of property law or regalia,[13] which had little if any connection with the principles of public international law that emerged subsequently. Even today, in both legislative and judicial approaches to baseline delineation, the issues are as likely to be cast in the terminology of private law as in that of public international law.[14] Also, when constitutional issues arise within a federal state, the doctrine of international law may be given little weighting in this area of judicial boundary-making.[15] In this way baseline delineation may still be governed by the doctrine of municipal law, dating from the primitive period of international law, to a degree inconceivable in the more modern contexts of delimitation between opposite or adjacent states and the determination of seaward limits.

Today, the relevance of the distant past to ocean boundary-making is most likely to be urged in claims to "historic bays" or "historic waters."[16] In these special circumstances it may be necessary to trace the earliest evidence of a local or regional custom. In the *Anglo-Norwegian Fisheries* case both sides engaged in historical research extending back to the late medieval period. (See the section entitled "The Breakdown of the Classical System" later in this chapter.) It remains to be seen whether the codification of the rules of baseline delineation at UNCLOS I and III will have the effect of reducing the relevance of ancient usage.

THE CLASSICAL PERIOD

The classical period of international law lasted three hundred years, from the time of Grotius, or the Peace of Westphalia (1648), to the League of Nations. In matters of ocean boundary-making, the classical period witnessed a steady development of legal claims designed to exclude foreigners from inshore waters. Characteristically, these classical arguments focused primarily on the question of the status of the waters rather than on the more specific question of boundary limits; but eventually, toward the end of the classical period, measurement was seen to be inherent in the process of baseline delineation. Perhaps the best example of this trend toward mathematical precision is in the treatment of bays.

Bays

More than any other kind of coastal indentation, the bay has been the object of special or exclusive jurisdictional claims by coastal states for hundreds of years. For most of that time it has seemed reasonable, in the case of bays enclosed by a single state, to allow an exception to any general rule that might be agreed upon for measurement of the territorial sea, on the ground of the coastal state's special interest in its semi-enclosed inshore waters. Besides, if baselines in bays were not treated on a special basis, anomalous situations would arise, such as the creation of high-seas enclaves within large bays whose mouth does not exceed twice the width of the territorial sea.[17]

Throughout the classical period of international law, strenuous efforts were made to find a rational criterion for the delineation of baselines within bays enclosed by the territory of a single state. The oldest method was the headland-to-headland closing line, which evolved from the pre-classical era and was applied by England in the seventeenth century through the doctrine of the "King's Chambers." This doctrine was restricted to security considerations,[18] but the headland theory was invoked for fishery reasons in Scotland, where certain bays or firths were held to be "national" waters and beyond the reach of foreign fishermen.[19] In the treatment of bays, the United Kingdom practice was variable: while accepting a mathematical (ten-mile) rule in various European treaties, the British government continued to claim the validity of the headland rule in North America.[20] In 1910 it pleaded this rule in the *North Atlantic Coast Fisheries* arbitration with the United States,[21] but the Permanent Court of Arbitration "recognized [the rule's] defects in practice and recommended to the two litigant governments a compromise doctrine."[22]

Another ancient criterion for closing off bays was that of defensibility. This was eventually seen to be inadequate, "since through changing circumstances the size of water areas which can be controlled will vary as a result of technical progress."[23] But the gunshot rule proved durable for a period of two hundred years when the range of artillery remained fairly constant.

The range of vision rule was also applied to baseline delineation in bays, as well as to the seaward limits of the territorial sea, throughout the seventeenth century. This criterion was eventually judged impracticable in the special case, as in the general, though the criterion of visibility continued to play a role in the determination of a mathematical measurement.[24]

Some governments and commentators in the late classical period continued to assert that each coastal state should be free to determine its own criteria for baseline delineation within its own bays, on the ground that such criteria should reflect the particular local needs and concerns rather than a general or external set of considerations.[25] Since there was no consensus on a fixed legal rule until the end of the classical period, this approach had the appeal of simplicity, at least until the classical goals of certainty and uniformity could be attained. In any event, it had to be recognized that many coastal states had such a strong emotional investment in certain bays, which they designated "historic," that sometimes nothing less than a headland closing line would be politically acceptable.

Yet finally, in the normal situation of non-historic bays, it was the mathematical approach that prevailed. In the mid-nineteenth century a number of bilateral agreements between European states adopted a fixed limit within which the coastal state was entitled to exercise sovereignty, or exclusive fishing rights, in certain designated bays. Later, the 1882 North Sea Fisheries Convention, which stipulated a ten-mile bay baseline, became the first multilateral agreement to apply a fixed mathematical limit to bays.[26] Several years later, the Chamberlain-Bayard Treaty between Great Britain and the United States also stipulated a ten-mile rule for baselines in bays. Because this agreement was never ratified, the issue between the parties was submitted to the Permanent Court of Arbitration in the famous *North Atlantic Coast Fisheries* arbitration of 1910.[27] After extensive argument on both sides, the Court recommended the general application of the ten-mile rule: "In every bay not hereinafter specifically provided for, the limits of exclusion shall be drawn three miles seaward from a straight line across the bay in the part nearest the entrance at the first point where the width does not exceed ten miles."[28]

The trend to a mathematical measurement was evident in state practice by the time of the Codification Conference held at The Hague in 1930 under the auspices of the League of Nations. The preparatory committee discovered through a questionnaire that a considerable majority of those responding either already accepted a ten-mile baseline for bays or were willing to consider it. It was reported to the Conference that most delegations agreed to a width of ten miles, "provided a system were simultaneously adopted under which slight indentations would not be treated as bays."[29] But the Conference was unable to agree on a formula for the characterization of bays eligible for the ten-mile baseline delineation rule, and therefore that rule could not be formally approved.

"Normal" Coastlines

Throughout most of the classical period, states were content to measure the extent of their national waters from the coastline itself. In the case of coastlines lacking any special or distinctive configuration, the baseline was deemed to follow the "sinuosities" of the coast. In the late classical period the need for a degree of precision raised a more technical issue of delineation: whether to use the high-water or low-water mark.

By the mid-nineteenth century many treaties and statutes had incorporated references to the "coast," and courts had been obliged to place their own interpretation on this term.[30] On most navigational charts it is the high-tide, not the low-tide, elevation that is marked, in the portolan tradition. To the extent that baseline delineation has navigational implications, it might have been appropriate to use the high-water mark.[31] Indeed, this line of reasoning was adopted by a highly qualified boundary expert attending the Codification Conference at The Hague in 1930.[32] However, by this time the exclusivist tendency of coastal states to extend their jurisdictional limits seaward had produced a trend toward general acceptance of the low-water mark.

The first treaty reference to low water as a legal boundary was the Fishery Convention of 1839 between Great Britain and France.[33] Despite the merits of alternative criteria, such as high water, navigability, seasonal tidal variations, the placement of coastal batteries, and coastal state discretion, the low-water mark was adopted as the standard in the implementation of the North Sea Fishery Convention of 1882.[34] In 1930 the Hague Codification Conference confirmed the general acceptance of the low-water criterion as the "normal" baseline of the territorial sea.[35] By this time hydrographers were beginning to differentiate several low-tide elevations,[36] underlining the need for greater precision in this area of boundary-making, but the classical period closed without any legal resolution of these technical issues.[37]

Offshore Features

We have seen that the complexities inherent in baseline delineation were being grasped in the last fifty years of the classical period, even in the general case of "normal" coastlines and particularly in the special case of bays. On the other hand, virtually no attention was given before the 1930s to the baseline delineation issues associated with minor indentations such as inlets or fjords; and solutions were not yet available for similar problems related to offshore features such as islands, dry rocks, and reefs, and low-tide elevations of various sorts. But the problems created by offshore features were at least perceived.

The major issues were five: (1) what kind of natural offshore features to admit as basepoints; (2) what distinction, if any, to draw between natural and artificial offshore features; (3) whether to confine the list of admissible basepoints to permanently dry features, or to extend it, in certain circumstances, to drying rocks and other kinds of low-tide elevations; (4) whether to treat groups of islands as a unit (an archipelago) for baseline delineation purposes, or to treat each island separately; and (5) what mileage or other limitation to place on any system of straight baselines connecting admissible basepoints.[38]

None of these five issues had been seriously debated among international lawyers before the final decade of the nineteenth century. State practice was spotty, and there was little prospect of finding uniformity merely by waiting for events to happen. Solutions had to be found through active resort to legal development. In its final half-century, from the 1880s to the 1930s, the classical period witnessed a continuous effort to develop international law through codification, and much of that effort focused on the regime of the territorial sea. Institutes of international law accepted the problems of geographical complexity in baseline delineation as a challenge to the task of codification, and their reports and proposals increased in volume when the League of Nations called for a codification conference to be held at The Hague in 1930.[39] But the world community was not yet ready to provide an appropriate forum for law-making diplomacy, and the scholarly proposals presented at The Hague in 1930 merely signalled the end of the first phase of a much more protracted process.

THE BREAKDOWN OF THE CLASSICAL SYSTEM

As we have seen, the simple dualistic system of regimes was beginning to break down early in the twentieth century, introducing the possibility of a radical reallocation of coastal state authority in the seas and the prospect of new problems in the determination of seaward limits. Just as the need for these major substantive changes in the law of the sea was beginning to be felt, an equally profound change was being introduced into the procedural system of legal development.

Under the Covenant of the League of Nations a judicial system was introduced in the form of the Permanent Court of International Justice (PCIJ), which would be authorized to contribute, at least indirectly, to the development of international legal doctrine through the settlement of disputes and the provision of advisory opinions on disputes and questions submitted to it by the Council or the Assembly.[40] Despite the absence of any specific mandate in the Covenant, the League also undertook the task of codification, and thus contributed in a more direct and systematic fashion to the development of international law.[41] Problems in the law of the sea figured prominently in the League's efforts at codification, but, as we have seen, these labours failed to bear fruit.

Under the Charter of the United Nations the judicial system was retained and strengthened with the creation of the International Court of Justice (ICJ), the successor of the (PCIJ).[42] But the Charter went further in the direction of legal development by empowering the General Assembly to "initiate studies and make recommendations" for the purpose of "... encouraging the progressive development of international law and its codification."[43] The classical technique of codification was thus officially supplemented by the neo-classical technique of progressive development.[44] In November 1947 the General Assembly established a new mechanism for carrying out both of these purposes: the International Law Commission (ILC).[45] Especially in the case of progressive development, the ILC was obligated to maintain close contact with the member states, either directly or through the office of the secretary general.[46] In this way the system combined the technical inputs of the jurists appointed to the ILC with the political inputs of the governments,[47] and it was envisaged that draft articles would, in appropriate circumstances, become available as a basis for negotiation in the arena of conference diplomacy.[48]

In practice, most of the work of the ILC since 1947 has been characterized as codification, and yet has tended to come under political influence at all stages of the process, especially in more recent years. Indeed, it must be said that in several contexts the balance between technical and political inputs has shifted in favour of the latter, introducing a decline in the classical tradition of legal development as epitomized in codification. Nowhere is this trend more conspicuous than in the law of the sea. The process of legal development in this field as a whole has moved from one end of the spectrum to the opposite end: from the classical codification approach attempted at The Hague in 1930, through the neo-classical progressive development approach by the ILC prior to UNCLOS I, to what might be termed the "romantic" law-making diplomacy approach of UNCLOS III, which dispensed entirely with the ILC and placed its faith in conference diplomacy.[49]

In the subfield of ocean boundary-making, the effect of these changes in law-making procedure has been variable. The general question of allocation of state authority has, of course, been treated as intensely political in significance and simply not amenable to technical debate in the classical or neo-classical tradition. To some extent the more specific problems of determining seaward limits have also been coloured with political interests, not least in the special context of the limits of the continental shelf beyond two hundred miles. (See the section entitled "The New Law of the Sea" in chapter 9.) In the case of baselines, the problem of delineation has been treated, by and large, as a chiefly technical area of debate, albeit one with appreciable political significance for many coastal states. The largest potential gains or losses in real terms have been associated with the delineation issues posed by groups of islands (archipelagoes). Significantly, that politically controversial issue could not be resolved in the neo-classical process of the ILC in preparing for UNCLOS I. But most of the other, less controversial, issues of baseline delineation were dealt with in a largely technical manner by the ILC in the 1950s, and only minor changes had to be effected later in the intensely political atmosphere of UNCLOS III.

One further modern feature of international legal development should be noted. The availability of the ICJ and of arbitral tribunals to deal with ocean boundary disputes has produced an interesting, and potentially creative, tension between the judicial and the diplomatic approaches to legal development. The ruling of the ICJ in the *Anglo-Norwegian Fisheries* case of 1951[50] was the first dramatic example of this relationship (as discussed immediately below in the context of baseline delineation trends in the new law of the sea), but the mutuality of influences is best evidenced in the context of delimitation between opposite or adjacent states after the Court's ruling in the *North Sea Continental Shelf* cases of 1969.[51]

THE NEW LAW OF THE SEA

By and large, the contemporary rules on baseline delineation are the product of the neo-classical, rather than the current "romantic," phase of legal development. The rules contained in the 1982 UN Convention on the Law of the Sea are not much different from those proposed by the ILC in the 1950s and formally adopted at UNCLOS I. Yet at least four features of the modern approach to baseline delineation are clearly post-classical in origin.

First, most of these boundary-making issues have been resolved to the advantage of the coastal state. Either the rules have been developed in such a way as to permit the coastal state to exclude larger areas of inshore waters, in accordance with the general expansion of coastal state jurisdiction, or the interpretation of these rules has been left to the discretion of the coastal authorities. The treatment of archipelagic states is the most spectacular example of generosity accorded to the geographically favoured,[52] but in a more modest degree most other coastal states have gained spatially from the modern international law of baseline delineation.

Second, the new law of the sea has given further recognition to the complexities of coastal geography, thereby sacrificing the classical goals of simplicity and uniformity. The modern regime of baseline delineation rejoices in the diversity of nature. By the same token, these rules invite coastal states to plead uniqueness by virtue of unusual coastal configurations. This emphasis on the special nature of the individual situation is certainly a reflection of the contemporary "romantic" approach to legal development.

Third, these delineation rules emanating from conference diplomacy reflect an awareness of the actual and prospective impact of new technology in the coastal zone. The provisions for artificial installations seem likely to encourage functionalist thinking in this particular sector of ocean boundary-making.

Finally, some of the seemingly traditional rules, such as that of the low-water mark, have been retained, but with a new awareness of the need for a higher order or precision in their application, through a clarification of the technical choices available in tidal datum.

Bays and Other Indentations

When the International Law Commission met in 1952 to resume the neo-classical debate over the treatment of bays, it was confronted with a bewildering variety of proposals. It was clear at least that there was no consensus in state practice. There was no rule waiting to be codified. Some jurists had perceived a trend toward the ten-mile closing line, reflected in treaties and textbooks, but in the previous year the International Court of Justice had stated firmly that the ten-mile rule has not acquired the authority of a general rule of international law.[53] This uncertainty left the Commission with no choice but to adopt a legislative, or frankly prescriptive, approach to its task of progressive development in this context.

As a matter of policy, positions on the treatment of bays can be divided into three categories: maximalist, minimalist, and moderate. The maximalist position favoured the enclosure of bays in general, or of specified bays deserving of enclosure for protective purposes. This position tended to make the fullest use of geographical and historical considerations. The minimalist position favoured the treatment of bays, with few if any exceptions, in the same way as any other part of the coastline. The minimalists invoked the classical concept of a narrow (three-mile) territorial sea and argued for a six-mile closing line, no broader than twice the breadth of the normal territorial limits. The moderate position, focusing on the need for a compromise formula, looked to mathematics for the measurement of a reasonable, albeit arbitrary, closing line.[54]

What emerged from the ILC debate was a complex formula designed, in the spirit of compromise, to provide moderate criteria for the delineation of bay closing lines. The formula consists mostly of mathematical elements composed in such a way as to permit the application of precise measurement techniques, in highly diverse geographical situations, to indentations that could be described as bay-like in configuration. With a view to the need for a means of qualifying or disqualifying indentations, reliance was placed on the "semi-circle test"[55] as articulated and finally adopted at UNCLOS I in article 7(2) and (3) of the 1958 Convention on the Territorial Sea and the Contiguous Zone:

2 For the purposes of these articles, a bay is a well-marked indentation whose penetration is in such proportion to the width of its mouth as to contain landlocked waters and constitute more than a mere curvature of the coast. An indentation shall not, however, be regarded as a bay unless its area is as large as, or larger than, that of the semi-circle whose diameter is a line drawn across the mouth of that indentation.

3 For the purpose of measurement, the area of an indentation is that lying between the low-water mark around the shore of the indentation and a line joining the low-water marks of its natural entrance points. Where, because of the presence of islands, an indentation has more than one mouth, the semi-circle shall be drawn on a line as long as the sum total of the lengths of the lines

across the different mouths. Islands within an indentation shall be included as if they were part of the water area of the indentation.[56]

The primary purpose of article 7(2) is, of course, to exclude "mere curvatures" from the legal concept of bays, and in this it generally succeeds. But the language of that paragraph has been subjected to severe criticism. For example, the coexistence of the two sentences raises the question which of the two rules should be construed as the primary criterion.[57] The reference to "landlocked waters" in the first sentence adds to the difficulty of interpretation.[58] Moreover, the semi-circle test in article 7(2) would, by a literal interpretation, include inland seas as well as bays, although this apparently was not the intention of the drafters.[59] Article 7(3) has been criticized on the ground that a bay, in the geographical sense, is "rarely a simple feature susceptible of easy comparison of its area with the area of the semi-circle drawn from its natural entrance points."[60] Not every bay has only two promontories that obviously qualify as "natural entrance points"; in the case of bays at the mouth of a river, the reference to the low-water mark is difficult to reconcile with the provision for straight lines across river mouths in article 13 of the same convention; and it is difficult to apply the semi-circle test to "compound bays" with both primary and secondary indentations.[61]

For greater precision in the establishment of a closing line, it was agreed to establish a uniform mileage criterion. In 1954 the ILC reintroduced the 10-mile limit, despite the ICJ's unfavourable dictum in the *Anglo-Norwegian Fisheries* case in 1951, but after criticism by many governments this was replaced, first, by a 25-mile proposal, and later by a proposal for a 15-mile limit. A 24-mile limit finally was adopted in Geneva at UNCLOS I. The reason for choosing that mileage was never officially explained, but in the minds of the delegations pressing for a 12-mile territorial sea the 24-mile limit for bays no doubt seemed an appropriate minimalist position. The following language was incorporated in article 7 of the 1958 Convention on the Territorial Sea and Contiguous Zone:

4 If the distance between the low-water marks of the natural entrance points of a bay does not exceed twenty-four miles, a closing line may be drawn between these two low-water marks, and the waters enclosed thereby shall be considered as internal waters.

5 Where the distance between the low-water marks of the natural entrance points of a bay exceeds twenty-four miles a straight baseline of twenty-four miles shall be drawn within the bay in such a manner as to enclose the maximum area of water that is possible with a line of that length.

This language seems less open to criticism on the ground of construction, even admitting that in practice a choice may sometimes have to be made between alternative sites as candidates for the "natural entrance points."[62] For policy reasons some commentators have opposed the introduction of a 24-mile closing line on the ground that it permits the enclosure of extensive bay-like waters without any functional rationale.[63] Certainly the desire for certainty, uniformity, and precision played a major role in the mileage decision reached at UNCLOS I.

Finally, it should be noted that article 7 of the 1958 Convention does not attempt to cover every bay-like indentation. The UNCLOS I formula is explicitly limited to "bays the coasts of which belong to a single state,"[64] and it is made clear that the formula does not apply to "historic" bays or to situations eligible for the application of the straight baseline system of delineation provided in article 4 of the same Convention.[65] Moreover, there is no provision for the fairly common situation in which the bay contains the mouth of a river.

In light of these omissions and the criticisms summarized above, it might have seemed that some revision would be attempted in the fifteen years of negotiation devoted to UNCLOS III. On the contrary, however, the subject of bays and other indentations received no discussion at all, and the language of article 7 adopted at UNCLOS I was incorporated without change into article 10 of the 1982 Convention on the Law of the Sea. Arguably, the Convention's silence on these matters leaves a bay state with undue discretion in the delineation of closing lines.[66]

"Complex" Coastlines

Bays and other indentations are only one example of the diversity of coastal geography. The "normalcy" of a coastline may be disrupted not only by bays, inlets, fjords, inland seas, river mouths, and other non-bay indentations, but also by natural offshore features such as islands, islets, rocks, sandbanks, and other kinds of low-tide elevations. A coastline that is deeply indented or fringed with groups of islands and other offshore features may be characterized as "complex."[67] A coastline that has both kinds of irregularities may be termed "highly complex."

Few countries have a more highly complex coastline than Norway. The northern half of Norway's Atlantic coast, facing the North Sea, presents acute baseline delineation problems.

> Very broken along its whole length, it constantly opens out into indentations, often penetrating far greater distances inland: the Porsangerfjord, for instance, penetrates 75 sea miles inland. To the west, the land configuration stretches out into the sea: the large and small islands, mountainous in character, the islets, rocks and reefs, some always above water, others emerging only at low tide, are in truth but

an extension of the Norwegian mainland. The number of insular formations, large and small, which make up the "skjaergaard" is estimated by the Norwegian government to be one hundred and twenty thousand. [In the northern sector] the "skjaergaard" lies along the whole of the coast of the mainland; east of the North Cape, the "skjaergaard" ends, but the coastline continues to be broken by large and deeply indented fjords.

Within the "skjaergaard" almost every island has its large and small bays; countless arms of the sea, straits, channels and mere waterways serve as a means of communication for the local population which inhabits the islands as it does the mainland. The coast of the mainland does not constitute, as it does in practically all other countries, a clear dividing line between land and sea. What matters, what really constitutes the Norwegian coastline, is the outer limit of the "skjaergaard."[68]

FIGURE 1: Anglo-Norwegian Fisheries Case

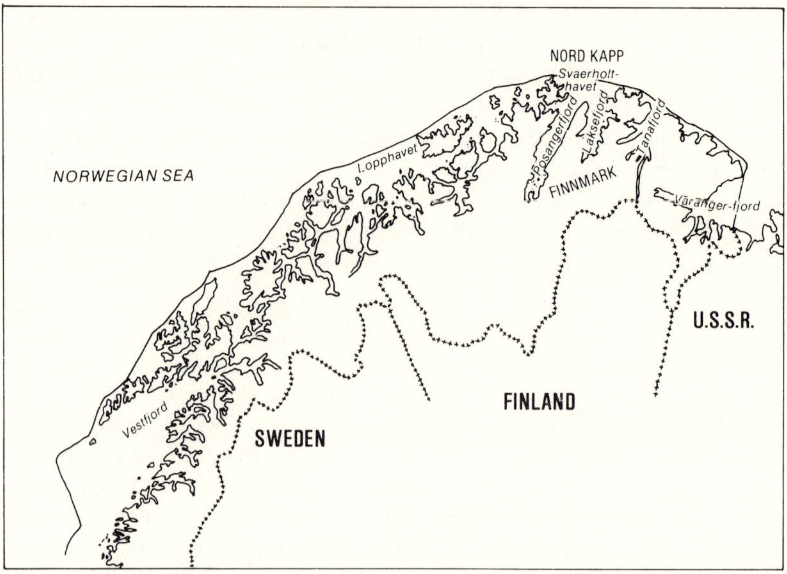

——— Norwegian straight baseline (upheld by the International Court of Justice, 1951).

Faced with a coastline of such exceptional complexity (see figure 1), the International Court of Justice was asked in 1951 to undertake the task of finding appropriate principles, rules, or criteria for the purposes of baseline delineation. The famous *Anglo-Norwegian Fisheries* case had been precipitated in 1933, when Norway delineated its territorial waters by a series of straight baselines connecting outlying points on the *skjaergaard* and various coastal promontories further north, in eastern Finnmark. In July of that year the United Kingdom protested against the use of what it alleged were unjustifiable baselines, but two years later, on 12 July 1935, Norway established a fisheries zone with the same baselines. Within this zone fishing was to be reserved to Norwegian nationals. Amendments to the enactment were made by a decree of 10 December 1937, adhering to the straight baseline method of delineation. This dispute led to negotiations and to the suggestion that the matter be referred to the Permanent Court of International Justice; but the war intervened, and it was not until September 1949 that proceedings were instituted before its successor, the International Court of Justice.

In challenging the validity of Norway's method of baseline delineation, the United Kingdom asked the Court to "declare the principles of international law to be applied in defining the baselines, by reference to which the Norwegian Government is entitled to delimit a fisheries zone, extending to seaward 4 sea miles from those lines and exclusively reserved for its own nationals, and to define the said baselines insofar as it appears necessary ... in order to avoid further legal differences between [the parties]."[69] In submitting the dispute to judicial process, the United Kingdom waived its right of challenge to Norway's once-contentious claim to a four-mile territorial sea. The U.K. challenge was limited to the manner of delineation used in the fisheries zone decrees, but since these baselines were identical to those introduced earlier for the territorial sea, the Court was left free to decide whether to distinguish between territorial and functional rationales.

The British case rested essentially on seven basic arguments:

3 That ... the base-line must be the low-water mark on permanently dry land (which is part of Norwegian territory) or the proper closing line ... of Norwegian internal waters.

4 That, where there is a low-tide elevation situated within 4 sea miles of permanently dry land, or of the proper closing line of Norwegian internal waters, the outer limit of territorial waters may be 4 sea miles from the outer edge (at low tide) of this low-tide elevation. In no other case may a low-tide elevation be taken into account.

5 That Norway is entitled to claim as Norwegian internal waters, on historic grounds, all fjords and sounds which fall within the conception of a bay as defined in international law, whether the proper entrance to the indentation is more or less than 10 sea miles wide.

6 That the definition of a bay in international law is a well-marked indentation, whose penetration inland is in such proportion to the width of its mouth as to constitute the indentation more than a mere curvature of the coast.

7 That, where an area of water is a bay, the principle which determines where the closing line should be drawn is that the closing line should be drawn between the natural geographical entrance points where the indentation ceases to have the configuration of a bay.

9 That Norway is entitled to claim as Norwegian territorial waters, on historic grounds, all the waters of the fjords and sounds which have the character of a legal strait ...

11 That Norway, by reason of her historic title to fjords and sounds, is entitled to claim either as territorial or as internal waters, the area of water lying between the island fringe and the mainland of Norway ...[70]

Norway contended that no rule existed to govern the method of delineating baselines. It was acknowledged that the baseline should bear some relationship to the configuration of the coast, but denied that it should invariably follow the sinuosities of the coastline. Norway was entitled to draw straight lines, and was not bound to employ the method of "trace parallele" or "arcs of circles" ("courbe tangente") in view of the unique characteristics of the Norwegian coastline. There was no principle of international law precluding the use of small islands or islets as base-points. In any event, the physical solidarity between the mainland and the *skjaergaard* was not the only element to be taken into account. Social reality, tradition, and effective usage were equally important considerations.[71]

The Court's initial response was to decline to pronounce upon the "abstract definitions, principles or rules" advanced by the United Kingdom.[72] Yet subsequently, as it dealt with the merits of the British arguments, it did pronounce indirectly on several of these propositions. For example, the Court explicitly agreed with the first of the British arguments set out above (point 3), which espoused the low-water mark as the normal baseline.[73] Equally clearly, it did not agree with point 4, which espoused the headland theory for bays, or with the British argument that Norway could draw straight baselines only across bays. "If the belt of territorial waters must follow the outer line of the 'skjaergaard,' and if the method of straight baselines must be admitted in certain cases, there is no valid reason to draw them only across bays, as in Eastern Finnmark, and not also to draw them between islands, islets and rocks, across the sea areas separating them, even when such areas do not fall within the conception of a bay. It is sufficient that they should be situated between the island formations of the 'skjaergaard,' *intra fauces terrarum*."[74] The Court rejected the alternative British argument in favour of a ten-mile rule by analogy to the rule for bays.[75] As to point 4 regarding low-tide elevations, the Court found it unnecessary to decide whether, as contended by the United Kingdom and denied by Norway, "drying rocks" were eligible as basepoints only if situated within four nautical miles of permanently dry land, since the Norwegian government had proved by charts that "none of the drying rocks used by [Norway] is more than 4 miles from permanently dry land."[76]

In oral argument the United Kingdom abandoned the contention that

Norway was bound to employ the trace parallele method of delineation. The Court held that this method, which "consists of drawing the outer limit of the belt of territorial waters by following the coast in all its sinuosities ... may be applied without difficulty to an ordinary coast, which is not too broken," but "where a coast is deeply indented and cut into, as is that of Eastern Finnmark, or where it is bordered by an archipelago such as the 'skjaergaard' ... the baseline becomes independent of the low-water mark, and can only be determined by means of geometrical construction. In such circumstances the line of the low-water mark can no longer be put forward as a rule requiring the coastline to be followed in all its sinuosities ... Such a coast, viewed as a whole, calls for the application of a different method: that is, the method of baselines which, within reasonable limits, may depart from the physical line of the coast."[77]

The Court further held that, as admitted by the United Kingdom, there is no obligation to use the arcs of circles (courbe tangente) method of delineation, whose purpose is "to secure application of the principle that the belt of territorial waters must follow the line of the coast." Several states had "deemed it necessary to follow the straight base-line method" and had "not encountered objections of principle by other States." This had been done "not only in the case of well-defined bays, but also in cases of minor curvatures of the coast line where it was solely a question of giving a simpler form to the belt of territorial waters."[78]

As to limitations on the length of the straight baselines drawn around the *skjaergaard*, the Court, having denied the existence of a ten-mile rule for the closing of bays, rejected the suggested applicability of a ten-mile limit to the much more complex formation of the *skjaergaard*. On this issue, "the practice of States does not justify the formulation of any general rule of law. The attempts that have been made to subject groups of islands or coastal archipelagoes to conditions analogous to the limitations concerning bays (distance between the islands not exceeding twice the breadth of the territorial waters, or ten or twelve sea miles), have not got beyond the stage of proposals."[79] The flexibility of the Court's position on the question of a mathematical measurement was made quite clear: "Furthermore, apart from any question of limiting the lines to ten miles, it may be that several lines can be envisaged. In such cases the coastal state would seem to be in the best position to appraise the local conditions dictating the selection."[80]

However, on the crucial issue of the extent of the coastal state's discretion in baseline delineation, the Court finally drew back from the extreme position towards which it seemed to be heading. "The delimitation of sea areas has always an international aspect; it cannot be dependent merely upon the will of the coastal State as expressed in its municipal law. Although it is true that the act of delimitation is necessarily a unilateral act, because only the coastal State is competent to undertake it, the validity of the delimitation with regard to other States depends upon international law."[81]

Overlooking that it was a fisheries zone whose boundaries had been challenged, the Court looked for guidance in "certain basic considerations inherent in the nature of the territorial sea" that "bring to light certain criteria which, though not entirely precise, can provide courts with an adequate basis for their decisions ..."[82] This line of reasoning brought the Court finally to what most commentators have regarded as the rationale of its decision upholding the validity of the straight baseline method of delineation:

Among these considerations, some reference must be made to the close dependence of the territorial sea upon the land domain. It is the land which confers upon the coastal State a right to the waters off its coasts. It follows that while such a State must be allowed the latitude necessary in order to be able to adapt its delimitation to practical needs and local requirements, *the drawing of base-lines must not depart to any appreciable extent from the general direction of the coast.*

Another fundamental consideration, of particular importance in this case, is the more or less close relationship existing between certain sea areas and the land formations which divide or surround them. *The real question raised in the choice of base-lines is in effect whether certain sea area lying within these lines are sufficiently closely linked to the land to be subject to the regime of internal waters.* This idea, which is at the basis of the determination of the rules relating to bays, should be liberally applied in the case of a coast, the geographical configuration of which is as unusual as that of Norway.

Finally, there is one consideration not to be overlooked, the scope of which extends beyond purely geographical factors: that of *certain economic interests peculiar to a region, the reality and importance of which are clearly evidenced by a long usage*[emphasis added].[83]

On the historical evidence, which was clear as far back as 1810, it was found that the Norwegian authorities had applied their system of baseline delineation "consistently and uninterruptedly" from 1869 until the time of the dispute in the 1930s. The Norwegian practice had been tolerated generally by foreign states and acquiesced in by the United Kingdom itself for a period of sixty years.[84]

Accordingly, the Court, by a majority of ten to two, held that the delineation method employed in the Decree of 1935 was not contrary to international law; and, by a majority of eight to four, that the baselines fixed in application of that method were not contrary to international law.[85]

The decision received a mixed reception from commentators.[86] It also proved to be controversial, but eventually greatly influential, in the debate of the International Law Commission on the treatment of "complex," as well as "highly complex," coastlines. Essentially, the ILC decided, after much controversy,[87] that the straight baseline of delineation should be available generally to any state whose coastline was "deeply indented and cut into" *or* to any state with "a fringe of islands along the coast in its immediate vicinity": that is, to many coastal states whose coastline was not nearly so complex as Norway's. Ironically, this generalized formulation, adopted at UNCLOS I, was rationalized in the same way as a judicial decision that pivoted on the uniqueness of Norway's coastal geography. At UNCLOS I the ILC's baseline delineation formula for complex coastlines was adopted after further controversy,[88] and prescribed in article 4 of the 1958 Convention on the Territorial Sea and the Contiguous Zone:

1 In localities where the coastline is deeply indented and cut into or if there is a fringe of islands along the coast in its immediate vicinity, the method of straight baselines joining appropriate points may be employed in drawing the baseline from which the breadth of the territorial sea is measured.
2 The drawing of such baselines must not depart to any appreciable extent from the general direction of the coast, and the sea areas lying within the line must be sufficiently closely linked to the land domain to be subject to the regime of internal waters.
3 Baselines shall not be drawn to and from low-tide elevations, unless lighthouses or similar installations which are permanently above sea level have been built on them.
4 Where the method of straight baselines is applicable under the provisions of paragraph 1 account may be taken, in determining particular baselines, of economic interests peculiar to the region concerned, the reality and importance of which are clearly evidenced by a long usage.
5 The system of straight baselines may not be applied by a State in such a manner as to cut off from the high seas the territorial sea of another State.
6 The coastal State must clearly indicate straight baselines on charts, to which due publicity must be given.

One commentator has noted that this formula is based on the principle that "both indentations and offshore features play a role in establishing the extent of the territorial sea, which varies according to whether they themselves lie within the primary territorial sea, whether they are permanently dry, and whether their interrelationship and their relationship with the mainland warrant the use of straight baselines."[89] It is true, of course, that the Convention does not provide precise guidelines as to when straight baselines may or may not be used, and to that extent concedes much to the discretion of the coastal state. The lack of a mathematical measure for limiting the length of straight baselines in article 4 is admittedly inconsistent with the mathematical approach to the limitation of bay closing lines in article 7 of the same Convention. In truth, state practice since the 1950s has, as widely predicted, "altogether failed to reflect either [the ILC's] limited view of the occasions when the method is available, or the notion that the length of straight baselines is inherently restricted by the concept of the 'general direction of the coast.'"[90]

Today, in the wake of UNCLOS III, these concerns must be surely viewed in light of the international community's support for "the rise of the coastal state." In the present "romantic" age of radically extended coastal state jurisdiction, many governments seem to consider it futile to continue the "classical" skirmishes of yesteryear. In the new law of the sea the reallocation of coastal state authority under the regime of the EEZ and the revamped regime of the continental shelf has had the effect of scaling down the ethical significance of expansionist trends in the application of the straight baseline method of delineation. This, at least, was the view of the majority of delegations at UNCLOS III.

At UNCLOS III only three relatively minor modifications were made to the 1958 formula for baseline delineation along complex coastlines. Article 7 of the 1982 Convention on the Law of the Sea preserves paragraphs 1, 2, and 4 of article 4 of the 1958 Convention in virtually identical language. Paragraph 3 was retained (as paragraph 4), but a clause was added that permits the drawing of straight baselines to and from low-tide elevations in situations where such practice "has received general international recognition." Paragraph 5 is retained (as paragraph 6), but the reference to the high seas is supplemented by a reference to the exclusive economic zone. The requirement that straight lines be indicated clearly on publicly available charts, contained in paragraph 6 of article 4 of the 1958 Convention, is found in a composite requirement of greater clarity in article 16 of the 1982 Convention.[91] Finally, a new provision is added(as paragraph 2) in response to the need to provide specifically for the special case of deltas.[92]

Despite some strengthening of the Geneva language at UNCLOS III, further precision is required to guard the straight baseline formula from abuse. State practice in the post-conference years has not encouraged hopes that all coastal states will delineate straight baselines in strict compliance with article 7.[93]

Non-coastal Archipelagoes

One of the most spectacular features of the new law of the sea negotiated at UNCLOS III is the concept of a special regime for archipelagic states – that is, for states that are "constituted wholly by one or more archipelagoes and may include other islands."[94] It is believed that over a dozen states qualify under this definition,[95] and are thereby entitled to draw archipelagic baselines in accordance with a formula designed especially for their benefit.

The legal history of this new entitlement is only part of the larger story of international efforts to deal equitably with the problem of determining territorial or jurisdictional limits for islands and island groups. As we have seen, the straight baseline system of delineation developed by the ICJ and the ILC in the 1950s offered a solution in the case of coastal archipelagoes, modelled on the *skjaergaard* lying off the northern coast of Norway. Within twenty years after UNCLOS I at least sixty-five countries had taken advantage of this method for measurement of their coastal jurisdictional zones.[96] The Hague Codification Conference of 1930 had failed to produce any article on archipelagoes.[97] During the period of preparation for UNCLOS I, a few mid-ocean archipelagic states began to formulate a national strategy based on the idea that all their islands *and the waters between them* should be accepted in international law as forming a single territorial unit. This claim, advanced especially by Indonesia and the Philippines,[98] was justified by reference to the security and economic needs and interests of these states, and not least to their status as developing countries entitled to this special perogative to assist them at a crucial stage of nation-building.

In 1958 both Indonesia and the Philippines had begun to adopt national legislation in support of their claims to special jurisdictional entitlements as archipelagic states, and some support for their position was beginning to emerge elsewhere.[99] At UNCLOS I the Philippines introduced two alternative versions of a proposal for incorporation into the proposed convention: either that the straight baseline method, which had been approved by the ICJ, should be extended to archipelagoes lying off the coast "whose component parts are sufficiently close to one another to form a compact whole, and have been historically considered collectively as a single unit"; or that island groups with those characteristics "may be taken in their totality and the method of straight baselines may be applied to determine their territorial sea." In both versions of the Philippine proposal it was made clear that the baselines "shall be drawn along the coast of the outermost islands, following the general configuration of the archipelago."[100] Both versions were rejected, and indeed almost ignored. At a law-making conference still dominated by maritime (as distinguished from coastal) interests, and classical (as distinguished from "romantic") concepts of legal development, the world community was not ready to resort to such a dramatic extension of coastal state jurisdiction.

At UNCLOS III, in a radically different climate of opinion, the outcome was bound to be different. Accustomed to other bold proposals for extension of coastal state jurisdiction, many delegations were no longer shocked by the notion of vast spatial gains at the expense of the classical regime of the high seas, provided that acceptable guarantees for transit could be agreed upon. Moreover, Indonesia and the Philippines had been joined by a dozen other states that could claim the status of mid-ocean archipelagic states, and their combined special interest was not significantly different from a host of other special interest claims advanced for consideration in the trade-off process of diplomacy at UNCLOS III.

The 1982 Convention on the Law of the Sea produced not so much a special baseline delineation *rule* for archipelagic states as a separate *regime* that included, with other provisions, a special formula for baseline delineation. The rationale for separate treatment of mid-ocean archipelagic states is reflected in the definition of "archipelago" in article 46: " 'Archipelago' means a group of islands, including parts of islands, interconnecting waters and other natural features which are so closely interrelated that such islands, waters and other natural features form an intrinsic geographical, economic and political entity, or which historically have been regarded as such." Once again, as with the concepts of "bay" and "continental shelf," ocean boundary-making requirements have induced diplomats to convert a relatively simple geographical concept into a much more complex legal concept.

Article 48 of the 1982 Convention provides that, under the regime of archipelagic states, the breadth of all four regimes or zones of coastal state jurisdiction – the territorial sea, the contiguous zone, the exclusive economic zone, and the continental shelf – "shall be measured from archipelagic baselines drawn in accordance with article 47":

1 An archipelagic State may draw straight archipelagic baselines joining the outermost points of the outermost islands and drying reefs of the archipelago provided that within such baselines are included the main islands and an area in which the ratio of the area of the water to the area of the land, including atolls, is between 1 to 1 and 9 to 1.
2 The length of such baselines shall not exceed 100 nautical miles except that up to 3 percent of the total number of baselines enclosing any archipelago may exceed that length, up to a maximum length of 125 nautical miles.
3 The drawing of such baselines shall not depart to any appreciable extent from the general configuration of the archipelago.
4 Such baselines shall not be drawn to and from low-tide elevations, unless lighthouses or similar installations which are permanently above sea level have been built on them or where a low-tide elevation is situated wholly or partly at a distance not exceeding the breadth of the territorial sea from the nearest island.
5 The system of such baselines shall not be applied by an archipelagic State in

such a manner as to cut off from the high seas or the exclusive economic zone the territorial sea of another State.

6 If a part of the archipelagic waters of an archipelagic State lies between two parts of an immediately adjacent neighbouring State, existing rights and all other legitimate interests which the latter State has traditionally exercised in such waters and all rights stipulated by agreement between those States shall continue and be respected.

7 For the purpose of computing the ratio of water to land under paragraph 1, land areas may include waters lying within the fringing reefs of islands and atolls, including that part of a steep-sided oceanic plateau which is enclosed or nearly enclosed by a chain of limestone islands and drying reefs lying in the perimeter of the plateau.

8 The baselines drawn in accordance with this article shall be shown on charts of a scale or scales adequate for ascertaining their position. Alternatively, lists of geographical co-ordinates of points, specifying the geodetic datum, may be substituted.

9 The archipelagic State shall give due publicity to such charts or lists of geographical coordinates and shall leave a copy of each such chart or list with the Secretary-General of the United Nations.

Given its complexity, this article is perhaps one of the most impressively drafted in the entire Convention. Although inevitably difficult to interpret and apply in inherently complex geographical situations, it is certainly the product of precise and sophisticated thought about ocean boundary-making. Yet, like a bride's ensemble, it includes something borrowed and something new. The obligation in paragraph 3 to conform with the general configuration of the archipelago is, of course, derived from the ICJ requirement to follow the general direction of the coast applied to straight baselines, and stipulated in article 4(2) of the 1958 Convention on the Territorial Sea and the Contiguous Zone and in article 7(3) of the 1982 Convention. The prohibition against cutting off a neighbour's access to the high seas or its EEZ, contained in paragraph 5, is the same as that in article 7(6) of the 1982 Convention, but third-party interests are further protected in a "traditional or vested rights" clause in paragraph 6, which is original, though comparable in purpose to the clause in article 69(2)(b) designed to protect the interest of neighbouring landlocked states. Paragraph 4 on low-tide elevations has two components, the first being identical to the first component of article 7(4) on straight baselines, the second being an original mathematical (twelve-mile) limitation of the sort suggested but not accepted for straight baselines. The provisions for charts in paragraphs 8 and 9 are, of course, identical to those in article 16 for the regime of the territorial sea. Originality is evidenced in the system of precise mathematical measurement developed in paragraphs 1 and 2 and in the geological refinement of paragraph 7. Taken as a complete system of baseline delineation, these nine paragraphs can be compared with the six paragraphs of article 10 on bays, or with the ten paragraphs of article 76 devoted to the determination of the seaward limits of the continental shelf.

The feasibility of this formula for the delineation of archipelagic baselines remains to be seen. Unlike the boundary-making system prescribed in article 76, the system in article 47 has no procedure for verification. Much is left to the discretion of the archipelagic state, but in some cases (such as that of low-tide elevations) more effort has been made to provide a precise limitation. Difficulty may be experienced in envisaging what constitutes an "appreciable" departure from the "general configuration of the archipelago," perhaps more so than in the comparable task of assessing departures from the "general direction of the coast." But the uncertainties generated by article 47 seem political rather than technical in origin. The future of this ingenious formula for baseline delineation is governed by the future of the archipelagic states regime as a whole. Part IV of the Convention, an original contribution of UNCLOS III and not yet unequivocably established in customary international law, may have an uncertain future if it is seen to be dependent on treaty ratifications and the vagaries of the law of treaties.[101]

Other Islands

As matters now stand, after the conclusion of UNCLOS III, the new law of the sea has fairly elaborate provisions for two kinds of island-related situations: that of coastal archipelagoes, where there is a fringe of islands along the coast in its immediate vicinity, is eligible for straight baselines under article 7 of the 1982 Convention, and that of mid-ocean archipelagoes is eligible under article 47 for archipelagic baselines. Yet there is no clear provision for islands in general, nor is there any comparable formula for other specific types of island-related situations.

As to islands in general, neither UNCLOS I nor UNCLOS III was willing to embrace the complexities of "legislating" systematically for the world's islands. At UNCLOS I the sole article dealing with islands per se was included in the 1958 Convention on the Territorial Sea and the Contiguous Zone. The decision was taken to limit the legal concept of an island to permanently dry natural formations,[102] and to acknowledge, though only implicitly, that an island may possess its own territorial sea, measurable in the same manner as mainland.[103] At UNCLOS III the 1958 definition was retained despite the emergence of improved technology for the construction of artificial and semi-artificial islands. Again, it was clearly implied that an island may possess its own territorial sea, but the 1982 Convention acknowledged its entitlement to a contiguous zone, an exclusive economic zone, and a continental shelf, all measurable in the same way as land territory.[104] The reluctance to declare an island's "entitlement" is understandable because of the breathtaking variability of island-related situations on the planet. At UNCLOS III one step was taken toward rational discrimination by the provision that rocks "which cannot sustain human habitation or economic life of their own shall have no exclusive economic zone or continental shelf," but no effort was made to distinguish rocks from islets, isles, or islands,[105] or to explain why "rocks" in general should possess a territorial sea or contiguous zone.

One specific type of island-related situation that remains to be dealt with juridically is that of a non-adjacent island, archipelago, or group of islands that fails to qualify as a mid-ocean archipelago under the new regime of archipelagic states. Reference may be made to the Galapagos Islands lying a considerable distance from the mainland of Ecuador; to Hawaii, which lies at an even greater distance from the mainland of the United States; and perhaps even to Rockall, far off the northwest coast of Scotland.[106] To deal with the baseline delineation problems in such circumstances, the state in question will be forced to resort to some form of analogical reasoning in the absence of any clearly applicable rule of international law.

"Normal" Coastlines

Since the establishment of the United Nations, baseline delineation issues have been almost solely concerned with geographically complex situations. As far as "normal" coastlines were concerned – that is, coastlines lacking any special or distinctive configuration – it was sufficient at UNCLOS I to codify the consensus reached at The Hague in 1930 that the low-water mark should serve as the normal baseline. With very little discussion by the ILC, agreement was reached on the language of article 3 of the 1958 Convention on the Territorial Sea and the Contiguous Zone: "Except where otherwise provided in these articles, the normal baseline for measuring the breadth of the territorial sea is the low-water line along the coast as marked on large-scale charts officially recognized by the coastal State." This codification seems to have secured the low-water rule in general, if not universal, conformity with national practices. At UNCLOS III virtually identical language was preserved in article 5 of the 1982 Convention.[107] This has given rise to inconsistencies in surveying, but it seems unlikely that this causes serious inconvenience to navigators.[108] To those familiar with hydrography and geodesy, the chief concern is that the choice of tidal datum is left open.[109] Most lawyers are likely to argue that when the experts in these disciplines can agree on standardization at the global level,[110] article 5 should be revised accordingly with a view to greater precision.

Low-Tide Elevations

After the ILC debate on "dry" and "drying" rocks and shoals,[111] it was agreed to treat low-tide elevations as eligible as basepoints for measurement of the territorial sea,[112] provided that they were located at a distance not exceeding the breadth of the territorial sea from the mainland or an island, and to apply the low-water line on the eligible elevation. This formulation was introduced and adopted at UNCLOS I as article 11 of the 1958 Convention on the Territorial Sea and the Contiguous Zone:

1 A low-tide elevation is a naturally formed area of land which is surrounded by and above water at low tide but submerged at high tide. Where a low-tide elevation is situated wholly or partly at a distance not exceeding the breadth of the territorial sea from the mainland or an island, the low-water line on that elevation may be used as the baseline for measuring the breadth of the territorial sea.

2 Where a low-tide elevation is wholly situated at a distance exceeding the breadth of the territorial sea from the mainland or an island, it has no territorial sea of its own.

This provision was preserved, in identical language, in article 13 of the 1982 Convention.[113]

Reefs

At UNCLOS III it was noted that the 1958 Convention had made no explicit provision for reefs. It was agreed to apply the low-water rule,[114] and accordingly article 6 was drafted and adopted: "In the case of islands situated on atolls or of islands having fringing reefs, the baseline for measuring the breadth of the territorial sea is the seaward low-water line of the reef, as shown by the appropriate symbol on charts officially recognized by the coastal State."

River Mouths

It was agreed at UNCLOS III that provision should be made for "normal" river mouths – that is, for the mouths of rivers that flow directly into the sea, and not through bays, deltas, or other natural features that may bring special delineation rules into play.[115] It was agreed to apply the "normal" low-water rule as expressed in article 13 of the 1958 Convention: "If a river flows directly into the sea, the baseline shall be a straight line across the mouth of the river between points on the low-water line of its banks." This is, of course, a special application of the headland rule, which was revived because of the controversiality of the most logical alternative, the concept of the "general direction of the coast." The use of the headland rule has the effect of assimilating river mouths to bays of less than double the width of the territorial sea.[116] Despite the uncertainty of applying the headland rule to certain estuaries with numerous shoals and sandbanks, the same language was incorporated into article 9 of the 1982 Convention adopted at UNCLOS III.

Artificial Features

Given the 1930 consensus that the territorial sea should be measured from the coast and not the mainland, it has become a matter of growing importance to decide whether artificial features should be eligible basepoints for delineation in situations where these man-made installations project any appreciable distance beyond the "normal" or otherwise applicable baseline. The most obvious examples are port installations (permanent harbour works that form an integral part of the harbour system) and roadsteads (anchorage grounds outside the nearest harbour that are used for the loading or unloading of ships).

Both kinds of artificial features invite functional treatment, since they are exclusively used, and indeed specifically designed, for one particular purpose. The question whether they should be eligible as delineation basepoints cannot be divorced from the question whether the proposed rule would facilitate that purpose. It has never been doubted that all harbour systems, including the outermost permanent harbour works, should be regarded as forming part of the coast. Accordingly, there was no opposition to the language of article 8 of the 1958 Convention on the Territorial Sea and the Contiguous Zone: "For the purpose of delimiting the territorial sea, the outermost permanent harbour works which form an integral part of the harbour system shall be regarded as forming part of the coast."

Between UNCLOS I and UNCLOS III new technologies for the construction of offshore installations and artificial islands emerged to force the issue of definition. It was decided, without much controversy, to exclude these new artificial features from the definition of permanent harbour works, and a provision to that effect was added to the 1958 rule in article 11 of the 1982 Convention.[117]

The treatment of roadsteads has been more controversial. Sometimes roadsteads are several hundred yards offshore, and yet it makes functional sense to assimilate them to ports. Normally a roadstead is the seaward extension of the port, and should therefore be governed under the same regime as the port it serves. At UNCLOS I several proposals were debated,[118] and the following version was finally adopted in article 9 of the 1958 Convention on the Territorial Sea and the Contiguous Zone: "Roadsteads which are normally used for the loading, unloading and anchoring of ships and which would otherwise be situated wholly or partly outside the outer limit of the territorial sea, are included in the territorial sea. The coastal State must clearly demarcate such roadsteads and indicate them on charts together with these boundaries, to which due publicity must be given."

At UNCLOS III it was decided to retain the first of these sentences in article 12 of the 1982 Convention. The second sentence was removed and replaced by a composite provision on charts and lists of geographical co-ordinates in article 16. The baseline delineation rules for artificial features have been formulated, contrary to functionalist logic, in such a way that ports fall within the regime of internal waters, whereas roadsteads, though extensions of ports, are brought within the regime of the territorial sea.[119]

General

It was found necessary at UNCLOS III to recognize that the coexistence of so many rules on baseline delineation, normal and special, might create the opportunity for a choice to be made between two or more methods that might be applicable in a particular geographical situation. It was agreed that the coastal state should have discretion in the matter, and that in complex circumstances it could choose a combination of suitable methods. Accordingly, a new provision permitting electicism was adopted in article 14: "The coastal State may determine baselines in turn by any of the methods provided for in the foregoing articles to suit different conditions."

CHAPTER ELEVEN

Delimitation of "Lateral" Boundaries

INTRODUCTION

It is important to avoid the general tendency to treat the delimitation of boundaries between neighbouring states as if it were typical of ocean boundary-making. Each of the three kinds of ocean boundary-making – determination, delineation, and delimitation – must be seen to have its own history and to possess its own distinctive characteristics. The delimitation of "lateral" ocean boundaries[1] is distinguishable from the two other kinds of ocean boundary-making by the nature and function of the boundary type, by the processes involved, and by the effects produced.

In the first place, the lateral boundary, unlike the baseline or the seaward limit, is bilateral in nature. It cannot be established unilaterally, and globally approved principles or criteria, though potentially useful, cannot remove the need for some form of bilateral action by the two neighbouring states. Moreover, lateral boundaries have not only an allocative significance, like all ocean boundaries, but also a specific distributive purpose. This kind of boundary-making takes place in a zero-sum situation: what one claimant gains, the other loses.

Second, the lateral ocean boundary, like its counterpart on land, calls for one or both of two kinds of processes: negotiation and adjudication (or an alternative intermediary procedure). Both processes involve confrontation over an "issue" or a "dispute." Negotiation contemplates resolution in the form of a treaty settlement or arrangement. Intermediation provides resolution or facilitation in the form of a judicial or arbitral award, a conciliation report, or some type of mediation proposal.

Third, "lateral" boundary-making, at sea as on land, holds a special fascination for lawyers. Because of their saliency as potential disputes, delimitation issues require legal treatment more immediately and more urgently than most issues related to the determination of seaward limits or the delineation of baselines. Determination and delineation issues are sometimes placed on the law-making agenda of the diplomatic community, or otherwise required to suffer the vicissitudes of state practice. Festering delimitation disputes may give rise to political as well as legal problems that place serious strains on the relationship between neighbouring states. Seen in more positive terms, delimitation is an opportunity for the orderly development of "considerations" relevant to ocean boundary-making.

The history of "lateral" ocean boundaries is extremely short. Admittedly, some of the considerations applied to this mode of ocean boundary-making can be traced to an early period in the legal history of rivers, lakes, and coastal areas, and lawyers tend to import analogies from other contexts to create a degree of continuity of legal reasoning. So a general review of these pre-modern analogies may be useful. But the history of awards and treaty settlements or arrangements concerned specifically with "lateral" ocean boundaries belongs essentially to the twentieth century.[2] Because of the relative unimportance of the pre-modern era in ocean boundary delimitation, separate sections on the primitive and classical periods can be dispensed with in favour of a combined account of early practices in legal and diplomatic history.

PRE-MODERN PRACTICES

Early Analogies with Rivers and Lakes

At an early stage in the evolution of the territorial sea regime, it was recognized that in certain geographical circumstances two neighbouring states with opposite or adjacent coastlines should reduce unnecessary conflict over the extent of their territorial jurisdiction by the establishment of a "lateral" boundary. The idea of formulating a rule of international law to govern ocean boundary delimitation seems to have been introduced by Samuel Pufendorf, who proposed a formula composed partly of the general principle of equality (or equal division) and partly of the more specific principle of proportionality.[3] Both of these principles were derived analogically from the treatment of boundary delimitation issues in lakes and rivers.[4] The strength of this reasoning seemed to depend on the existence of a physical resemblance between the coastal area in question and an enclosed or semi-enclosed area of fresh running water such as a river or lake. As soon as neighbouring states began to negotiate territorial sea boundaries, the analogy was found useful in the case of two opposite states facing each other across a narrow strait,[5] and in that of a gulf, bay, or estuary shared by two adjacent states.[6]

The resort to analogy with rivers and lakes had several effects on the theory and practice of ocean boundary-making. First, it brought equality considerations into competition with those of proportionality, or some other version of equity – an issue that continues to be central to many ocean boundary delimitation disputes today. Second, for opposite states it created the need to choose between the so-called rules of the median line and the thalweg. First applied to boundary-making on land, the thalweg is the line following the lowest part of a valley – the area to which all running water tends to drain. Applied to a river, the thalweg is the deepest channel in the riverbed, the most easily navigable part of the river. Particularly in the case of narrow straits, the analogy with navigable rivers or lakes suggested, by a kind of functionalist logic, that since navigation rights were primarily what was at stake, the boundary should be drawn in such a way as to secure to each state an equal (or at least a sufficient) area for safe navigation.[7] But the introduction of the navigability criterion to ocean boundary-making introduced a variety of interpretations of the thalweg, each representing a different degree of deviation from the median line,[8] and each reflecting a different view of equity.[9] Third, for adjacent states the analogy with lakes and rivers brought the median line method into conflict with other considerations. The navigability criterion could also be applied to the boundary-making problem in shared bays and estuaries, but the thalweg "rule" continued to make sense only to the extent that the thalweg itself continued to be discernible beyond the mouth of the river. In most coastal situations of this sort, the median line "rule" was also found to be inadequate unless qualified by the introduction of a method of delimitation that owed nothing to the analogy with rivers and lakes: for example, a line perpendicular to the general direction of the coast, or a line following a meridian of longitude or parallel of latitude, or a line of projection extending seaward the existing land boundary between the two adjacent states.

Late Classical Efforts to Consolidate Delimitation Norms

It is one of the characteristics of the late classical period that international lawyers generally attempted to reduce the complexity or intractability of international problems by bringing them under the governance of a few simple rules or principles. The late classical period of international law was of developmental significance in two ways: through the introduction of a more systematic approach to international adjudication[10] and through the involvement of leading jurists in the task of codification.[11] In both of these ways serious efforts were made to consolidate the rules and principles that seemed most relevant to the problem of ocean boundary delimitation between opposite or adjacent states.

FIGURE 2: Grisbadarna Arbitration

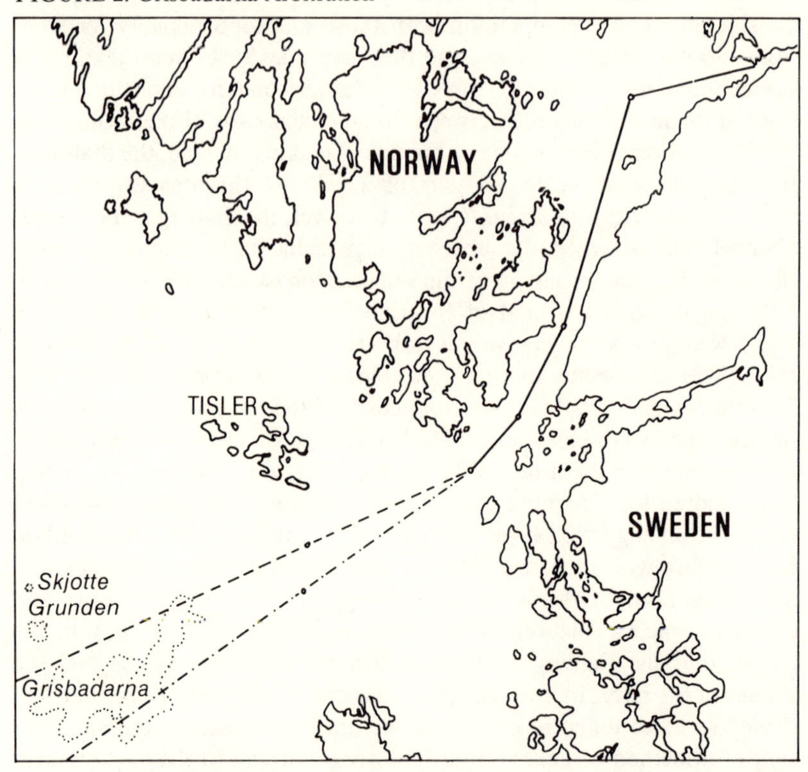

________ Line established by the project of Norwegian-Swedish commissioners on 18 August 1897.
------ Swedish claim (basis of arbitral award, 1909).
__ . __ . __ Norwegian claim.

The first adjudicative opportunity to attempt such a consolidation arose under the auspices of the Permanent Court of Arbitration in 1909, when Norway and Sweden agreed to arbitrate an ocean boundary delimitation dispute centred on the waters in the vicinity of the Grisbadarna bank between the Norwegian island of Tisler and the Swedish island of Koster off the northeastern coastline of the Skagerrak.[12] (See figure 2.) The tribunal was called upon to decide "how far the boundary line shall be considered to be, either wholly or in part, determined by the [fjord] boundary treaty of 1661, together with the chart appertaining to the same, and how such boundary line is to be traced, and also, insofar as the boundary line can not be considered as established by the treaty and chart in question, shall have power to determine the same, taking into account the circumstances of fact and the principles of international law."[13] Accordingly, the boundary delimitation issue in the *Grisbadarna* arbitration was characterized in the *compromis* primarily as a question of treaty interpretation; and the treaty in question preceded by over a century the crystallization of the territorial sea concept. Moreover, the tribunal chose to interpret the language of the *compromis* in a highly restrictive manner, holding that the outer boundary beyond the islands of Tisler and Koster, which fell outside the scope of the 1661 treaty, also had to be fixed according to the principles in force at that time, as if the entire matter had to be decided by reference to the presumed intention of the parties in 1661! So all the evidence presented on the relevant "principles of international law" that had evolved between 1661 and 1909 was discarded, and the opportunity to consolidate the norms was rejected. By limiting the relevant normative considerations in this way, the tribunal was obliged to hold that

(i) the rule of drawing a *median line* midway between the inhabited lands does not find sufficient support in the law of nations in force in the seventeenth century.
(ii) it is the same way with the rule of the *thalweg* or the most important channel ...;
(iii) we shall be acting much more in accord with the ideas of the seventeenth century and with the notions of laws prevailing at that time if we admit that the automatic division of the territory in question must have taken place according to the *general direction* of the land territory of which the maritime territory constituted an appurtenance, and if we consequently apply this same rule at the present time in order to arrive at a just and lawful determination of the boundary; and therefore,
(iv) ... the delimitation should be made today by tracing *a line perpendicularly to the general direction of the coast*, while taking into account the necessity of indicating the boundary in a clear and unmistakable manner, thus facilitating its observation by the interested parties as far as possible [emphasis added].[14]

Since the general direction of the Norwegian-Swedish coast swerves about 20 degrees westward from due north, it was held that the perpendicular line should "run towards the west to about 20 degrees to the south."

On the face of things, then, the delimitation issue was resolved by the application of the perpendicular line *method*, rather than by a "principle" or "rule" of international law. But it should be noted that the tribunal proceeded to consider some of the "factors," as if to test the reasonableness of its decision to apply the perpendicular line method. Noting that the line fell between the Grisbadarna and Skjottegrunde banks, and therefore had the effect of allocating the whole of the rich Grisbadarna lobster grounds to Sweden, the tribunal emphasized the reasonableness of this outcome by referring to two "circumstances of fact" of special relevance:

(a) The circumstance that lobster fishing in the shoals of Grisbadarna has been carried on for a much longer time, to a much larger extent, and by a much larger number of fishermen by the subjects of Sweden than by the subjects of Norway.

(b) The circumstance that Sweden has performed various acts in the Grisbadarna region, especially of late, owing to her conviction that these regions were Swedish as, for instance, the placing of beacons, the measurement of the sea, and the installation of a lifeboat, being acts which involved considerable expense and in doing which she not only thought that she was exercising her right but even more that she was performing her duty; whereas Norway, according to her own admission, showed much less solicitude in this region in these various regards ...[15]

Thus, the tribunal introduced what was purported to be a secondary consideration: the situational factor of specific historical usage. Moreover, in pressing this line of consideration, the arbitrators observed that "fishing is, generally speaking, of more importance to the inhabitants of Koster than to those of Hvaler, the latter being, at least until comparatively recent times, engaged rather in navigation than fishing; and from these various circumstances it appears so probable as to be almost certain that the Swedes utilized the banks in question much earlier *and much more effectively* than the Norwegians ... [emphasis added]."[16] These observations might lead a modern analyst to the conclusion that the tribunal was also influenced by two other considerations: the situational factor of socio-economic dependency, and the predisposition to achieve a result that would satisfy both the fairness and the effectiveness tests.

By modern logic, therefore, the outcome in the *Grisbadarna* arbitration seems to be most accurately explained by reversing the reasons given by the tribunal: first, there was a predisposition to draw a line (outside the ambit of the 1661 treaty) that would be fair and effective in light of the factual circumstances; second, the consideration of specific historical usage favoured Sweden; and third, to swing the decision in Sweden's favour it was convenient, given the geographical configuration of the coastline, to use the perpendicular line method of delimitation. The tribunal spared itself the pain of choosing between the competing rules or principles of international law that had evolved since 1661, and took the narrowest view of the terms of the *compromis* by purporting to be limited to the construction of the parties' intentions in its treaty of that date. By this analysis, the *Grisbadarna* decision was not so much a victory of the perpendicular line method over the median line "rule" as an early attempt to identify the range of considerations that should be weighed against one another by arbitrators asked to draw a lateral ocean boundary between adjacent states.

No other comparable opportunity presented itself for an adjudicative consolidation of the "rules" and "principles" of ocean boundary delimitation between opposite or adjacent states in the late classical period.[17] After the *Grisbadarna* arbitration, the median line "rule" was still seen to be in competition with the perpendicular line method in the case of adjacent states, just as the thalweg and median line "rules" were perceived as contenders in the case of opposite states. Given the lawyer's preference for uniformity and symmetry, it may not be surprising that the median line "rule" – or the "principle" of equidistance – continued to be the favourite of many lawyers in the late classical period.

When the League of Nations included the territorial sea among the areas designated for the progressive development of international law, jurists in various countries renewed their efforts to find an acceptable rule to govern ocean boundary delimitation between opposite and adjacent states. In the opposite-coast situation, most jurists agreed to give primacy to the median line. In his report for the League of Nations Committee of Experts for the Progressive Codification of International Law, the rapporteur Walter Schücking recommended that straits "not exceeding 12 miles in width whose shores belong to different States shall form part of the territorial sea as far as the middle line."[18] In the same year the Finnish jurist Björksten recommended the median line as a "presumptive sea boundary" between opposite states, with the possibility of agreement on the thalweg in certain circumstances.[19] In the United States, the Harvard Research team recommended in 1929 that "[i]n the absence of special agreement to the contrary, where two or more states border upon a strait, the territorial waters of each state extend to the middle of the strait in those parts where the width does not exceed six miles."[20] It seemed, then, that a convergence of views was taking place at least in the delimitation of straits between opposite straits, but the Schücking recommendation proved to be more controversial than expected and had to be withdrawn by the Second Committee of the Hague Codification Conference in 1930.[21]

The question of the applicable rule for the situation of adjacent states was more complicated. Björksten, for example, was prepared to accept one or more of a wide range of alternatives: not only a choice among the projection of the land boundary, the meridian, or latitude, but also the admission of supplementary exceptions, such as a median line between islands and the thalweg where the criterion of navigability applied.[22] The Harvard Research of 1929 acknowledged the use of the perpendicular line method in the *Grisbadarna* arbitration, but noted that "historical, vested, and other rights and conditions may be considered."[23] Schücking, wavering between the extension of the land boundary and the perpendicular line, and acknowledging the crucial importance of historical considerations, concluded that it would be preferable to "arrange for the conclusion of a special agreement between the States concerned, or for the settlement of the matter by arbitration or an ordinary tribunal, than to lay down an immutable principle."[24] Differences between Schücking and his colleagues led to the withdrawal of his recommendations on delimitation between adjacent states,[25] and the Hague Codification Conference limited itself to the special case of bays shared by two or more adjacent states.

After the failures of codification at The Hague, the delimitation debate shifted direction. Despite the lack of agreement on the applicability of the median line "rule," specialists took up the much more technical question of how to "demarcate" the median line. It had long been recognized that the median line could be drawn in different ways. To the layman, it was simply a line that was equally distant from two opposite shorelines; but such a line was shown to be technically impossible to draw even from one shore, and the result from the opposite shore was bound to be quite dissimilar.[26] A second conception of the median line was based on the notion of following the general lines of the two opposite shorelines and dividing the intermediate water area into two equal parts. But many kinds of lines could be drawn to this end: no one method of delimitation was suggested or required to satisfy this version of the "rule." So this conception served only as a way of testing whether a particular line had the effect of producing an equal, and therefore equitable, division of water area. A third version of the median line "rule," applicable to navigable rivers and straits, had linked the idea of equal division with rights of navigation, and thus drawn the line in such a way as to secure equality of access to the two opposite riparian states. This approach suggested demarcation through the mid-channel, but the mid-channel in practice was often difficult to identify. In theory, moreover, this version of the median line leaned more heavily on equity than equality, and introduced subjectivities that complicated the task of delimitation.

The technical debate on median line delimitation resulted eventually in the development of what may be called the "equidistance technique." This concept, as articulated by the American geographer Whittemore Boggs, envisaged a line "every point of which is equidistant from the nearest point or points on opposite shores."[27] Since only one such line could be drawn, it was shown to be more precise than any alternative version of the median line. Yet despite this important gain in technical precision, the equidistance line method of delimitation shared the deficiency of all other median line methods in that it would not always produce an equitable result, especially in the case of complex coastlines having marked indentations and scattered islands. Moreover, the equidistance technique was not as applicable to the adjacent-coast situation as it was to the opposite-coast situation.[28]

Despite these continuing difficulties in reconciling precision with equity in a single "rule" or "method," progress toward consensus on a formula was maintained throughout the 1930s and 1940s. Some of the alternatives to the median line began to drop out of contention. The projection of the land boundary between two adjacent states fell from favour, since it was conceded that land boundaries have no relationship, in theory or practice, to ocean-related purposes,[29] and the projection method tends to be inequitable unless the land boundary is approximately perpendicular to the general direction of the coast shared by two adjacent states.[30] Moreover, the general direction of the coast is not always possible to determine.[31] The thalweg method is applicable only to navigable waters, and the sharing principle underlying it depended on sufficiency, rather than equality, of access.[32] The perpendicular line method still had its supporters, but was increasingly seen as a special application of the median line method and this was subject to the general criticism that, if elevated to the status of a rule, it would often have an inequitable effect,[33] unless buttressed by historical usage, as in the Grisbadarna situation.

The final instalment of the territorial sea delimitation debate extended into the early years of the post-classical period. Although the International Law Commission initially limited its delimitation discussions to the case of straits, it was suggested in 1956 that the questions of straits and opposite states should be amalgamated.[34] At the First UN Conference on the Law of the Sea (UNCLOS I) in 1958 this amalgamation was approved, and it was agreed to merge the combined draft article on the two questions with the similarly worded draft article dealing with territorial sea delimitation between adjacent states. Accordingly, the following formulation, based essentially on the median line[35] and made applicable to both opposite and adjacent situations, was adopted as article 12 of the 1958 Convention on the Territorial Sea and the Contiguous Zone:

1 Where the coasts of two States are opposite or adjacent to each other, neither of the two States is entitled, failing agreement between them to the contrary, to extend its territorial sea beyond the median line every point of which is equidistant from the nearest points on the baselines from which the breadth of the territorial seas of each of the two States is measured. The provisions of this paragraph shall not apply, however, where it is necessary by reason of historic title or other special circumstances to delimit the territorial seas of the two States in a way which is at variance with this provision.
2 The line of delimitation between the territorial seas of two States lying opposite to each other or adjacent to each other shall be marked on large-scale charts officially recognized by the coastal States.

Although a few relatively minor questions remained to be dealt with under rather flexible principles of customary international law,[36] the UNCLOS I formulation was retained unchanged at UNCLOS III.[37] Although it appears to sanction the median line, in a simplified version of the Boggs equidistance technique, this solution does not apply where a deviation is justified "by reason of historic title or other special circumstances." To most legal analysts, the appropriateness of the 1958 formula depends chiefly on the scope of meaning to be assigned to the phrase "special circumstances." The alternative exception of "historic title" is narrower than "general or local custom" or "specific historical usage." For what it is worth, half a century later, the UNCLOS I ground of "historic title" could hardly be said to justify a deviation from the median line in the *Grisbadarna* arbitration.[38] If the phrase "special circumstances" is considered restrictively, merely as "any physical or geographical feature which can result in an inequitable division,"[39] as suggested in the context of the continental shelf, then the application of the median line under article 12 cannot be deflected by situational considerations of a non-physical sort, such as socio-economic dependency, development opportunity, or historic title. But it remains to be seen whether the concept of "special circumstances" will be interpreted narrowly or broadly by states negotiating a boundary under article 15 of the 1982 Convention.[40] By the same token, since article 15 is the only provision in the Convention that refers explicitly to the median line, it remains to be seen what use will be made of the "principle" of equidistance in future delimitation diplomacy in any other context.[41]

MODERN DISPUTE MANAGEMENT: ADJUDICATION AND ALTERNATIVE PROCEDURES

Delimitation Issues and the Law-making Process (UNCLOS I)

In retrospect, it is obvious that the post-classical period of international law has been a period of radical change in the law of the sea. But in 1945 no one predicted the extent of the impending transformation through the rise of the coastal state. Certainly no one then foresaw the emergence of a globally approved regime for a two-hundred-mile zone of surface and subjacent waters. Yet by the end of the 1940s one highly significant trend was clearly in evidence: the trend toward acceptance of a special regime of coastal state jurisdiction over the continental shelf.[42] In this totally modern concept we find the seeds of the contemporary approach to ocean boundary delimitation through negotiation and adjudication.

The prospect that each coastal state would be solely entitled to the resources of the adjacent continental shelf placed the issues of ocean boundary delimitation in a wholly different perspective. Long before the oil crisis of 1973, continental shelf delimitation became a matter of national importance, generating excitement and even a sense of urgency. In the late classical period delimitation had been a matter for technical debate within the context of a traditionally narrow territorial sea. By the late 1940s delimitation had become, almost suddenly, an issue of intense political interest and concern, threatening disputes between the friendliest neighbouring coastal states, and conflict between the most hostile. Indeed, the emergence of the continental shelf regime around the world altered the coastal state's perception of its "neighbourhood" in the ocean, and forced it to review the prospects of diplomacy with its newly perceived "neighbours" in the offshore. The geography of opposite- and adjacent-state situations had been expanded dramatically.

This new perception of the significance of delimitation issues coincided with fundamental changes in the law-making process. Under the League of Nations only fifty or so independent states contributed directly to the process of law-making conference diplomacy, and of those a dozen or so of the older states could be said to have had a dominant, if not decisive, influence in the juridical treatment of international issues. By the end of the 1940s, under the United Nations, it was apparent that a much larger number of nations would be able to participate effectively in the UN Conference on the Law of the Sea, which was scheduled to be held in the 1950s. The international community was becoming organized in such a way that it would be able to reduce its dependency on the subtleties of customary international law if it should choose to do so. In the new order of things, patience and moderation might have to yield to other virtues in the process of legal development.

It was in this changed milieu of expectations that the International Law Commission began its work on the law of the sea in 1950. Of the many issues confronting it, the concept of the continental shelf regime was almost certainly the most salient, although the breadth of the territorial sea and related issues were more divisive.

In the new ("progressive development") context of continental shelf delimitation, the ILC was not, of course, bound to look for precedent in the pre-existing norms of international law, as it may have felt bound in the older ("codification") context of territorial sea delimitation. The case for identical treatment of these two kinds of delimitation issues was hardly compelling. In the older context of a three-mile territorial sea, much could be said in support of the argument for continuity with the past, and to the extent that the median line "rule" had an ancient lineage in state practice it could not be overlooked as a candidate for primary status. In the new context of the continental shelf, more was at stake in economic terms, and it was understood that the doctrinal issue of rule primacy had to yield in priority to the political issue of procedure. That is, the matter to be emphasized was not the rule to be applied in the first instance, but the procedure to be adopted in the first phase. Accordingly, it was agreed to give chief emphasis, in the continental shelf context, to the transcendent significance of a negotiated solution to this kind of delimitation problem. The intensity of national interest in the shelf delimitation issue put a premium on diplomatic process rather than on legal formula.[43]

On the other hand, it was agreed that the diplomacy of continental shelf delimitation need not dispense entirely with at least a sense of the appropriate norms. Moreover, even if one were to concede that a normative vacuum might sometimes be conducive to a negotiated settlement, the prospect of diplomatic failure had to be provided for. So, as between the "formula" and "process" approaches to the problem, it was decided to suggest a formula only in the event of diplomatic failure.[44] This agreement on the limited or indirect role of formula meant that the main debate in the ILC focused on the respective merits of two competing schools of thought. The proponents of certainty and uniformity, invoking tradition and consistency with the treatment of delimitation in the territorial sea, argued that primacy should be given to the median line or equidistance "rule." The proponents of flexibility and equity, invoking the variability of geography and the need to proceed de novo under a totally different kind of regime, argued that special or equal weight should be given to "special circumstances." In the outcome, the need for compromise forced the ILC, and UNCLOS I, to admit both elements in a balanced package. Accordingly, article 6 of the 1958 Convention on the Continental Shelf was adopted:

1 Where the same continental shelf is adjacent to the territories of two or more States whose coasts are opposite to each other, the boundary of the continental shelf appertaining to such States shall be determined by agreement between them. In the absence of agreement and unless another boundary line is justified by special circumstances, the boundary is the median line, every point of which is equidistant from the nearest points of the baselines from which the breadth of the territorial sea of each State is measured.
2 Where the same continental shelf is adjacent to the territories of two adjacent States, the boundary of the continental shelf shall be determined by agreement between them. In the absence of agreement, and unless another boundary line is justified by special circumstances, the boundary shall be determined by application of the principle of equidistance from the nearest points of the baselines from which the breadth of the territorial sea of each State is measured.
3 In delimiting the boundaries of the continental shelf, any lines which are drawn in accordance with the principles set out in paragraphs 1 and 2 of this article should be defined with reference to charts and geographical features as they

> exist at a particular date and reference should be made to fixed permanent identifiable points on the land.

It can be said, then, that the UNCLOS I provision on shelf delimitation contemplated two processes and provided two formulae. Primacy was given expressly to the process of negotiation, both for opposite and adjacent states. Article 6 also contemplated the prospect of diplomatic failure, and although the Convention did not create or recognize a duty to resort to adjudication in that contingency, much less prescribe dispute settlement procedures, the two formulae were clearly intended for adjudicative purposes "in the absence of agreement." The first of the two formulae, applied to the situation of opposite states, consists of the median line "rule" or method and the consideration of special circumstances. The second formula, applied to the situation of adjacent states, consists of the "principle" of equidistance and the consideration of special circumstances. It is important to note, however, that in the opposite-state situation dealt with in paragraph 1 the boundary is the median line "unless another boundary line is justified by special circumstances," whereas in the adjacent-state situation dealt with in paragraph 2 the boundary "shall be" determined by reference to the "principle" of equidistance, subject to the same overriding consideration of "special circumstances." It should also be noted that the language of article 6(2) seems to admit the possibility of several methods of applying the "principle" of equidistance. Technically, then, the second paragraph does not prescribe an equidistance line method.

The North Sea Continental Shelf Cases (1969)

The effect of the 1958 Convention on the Continental Shelf was to promote a considerable volume of continental shelf delimitation agreements between opposite and adjacent states around the world. Among these agreements was a series in the North Sea region, negotiated shortly after UNCLOS I at a time when the littoral states were excited by the prospect of offshore hydrocarbon development.[45] In 1964 and 1965 the Federal Republic of Germany (FRG) entered into bilateral delimitation agreements with its neighbours, the adjacent states of Denmark and the Netherlands.[46] In 1966 Denmark and the Netherlands concluded a delimitation agreement that fixed a median line boundary further seaward.[47] But the two agreements with the FRG fixed only partial boundary lines on the shelf close to shore. Negotiations broke down on the boundary lines to be drawn within a triangular area converging on the point where the Danish-Dutch median line boundary took effect, as well as their separate median line boundaries with the United Kingdom. Both Denmark and the Nether-

FIGURE 3: North Sea Continental Shelf Case

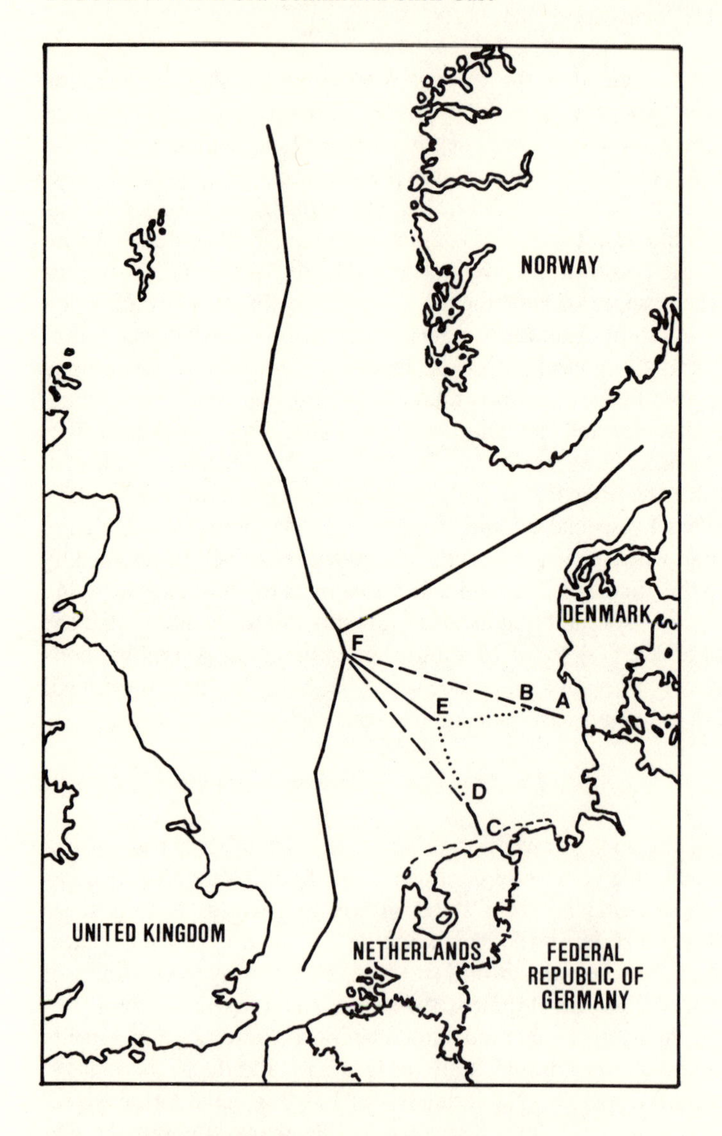

AB	Negotiated territorial sea boundary, 1965.
CD	Negotiated territorial sea boundary, 1964.
EF	Negotiated continental shelf boundary between Denmark and the Netherlands, 1966.
BE	Danish claim.
DE	Dutch claim.
DF BF	Presumptive German claim.

lands insisted on the use of the equidistance "principle" enunciated in article 6(2) of the Convention on the Continental Shelf, but in both negotiations the FRG which was not a party to that Convention, refused to accept equidistance as the basis of delimitation. Faced with this partial failure of agreement, the three countries agreed to submit their two disputes to the International Court of Justice. Because the issues were identical in both cases, the suits were conjoined.[48] (See figure 3).

The *North Sea Continental Shelf* decision is generally regarded as a landmark in international law, but less because of its disposition of the delimitation disputes than because of its coverage of a wide range of more basic issues. Much of the voluminous literature on this famous decision focuses on the Court's treatment of such problems as the formation of custom in contemporary international law,[49] the effect of a law-making treaty on third parties,[50] the juridical nature of the continental shelf,[51] and the weighting of criteria for determining seaward limits.[52] In this section we are concerned only with the Court's contribution to the problem of ocean boundary delimitation between adjacent states.

The Federal Republic of Germany contended that delimitation between the parties was governed by the "principle that each coastal State is entitled to a just and equitable share"; that the equidistance method was "not a rule of customary international law" and could not be employed "unless it is established by agreement, arbitration, or otherwise that it will achieve a just and equitable apportionment of the continental shelf among the States concerned"; and that the equidistance method was inapplicable "since it would not apportion a just and equitable share" to the Federal Republic of Germany. It was further argued that even if the equidistance-special circumstances "rule" of article 6(2) of the 1958 Convention was applicable, "special circumstances within the meaning of that rule would exclude the application of the equidistance method in the present case." The delimitation issue was a matter that had to be settled by agreement, and such agreement should "apportion a just and equitable share to each of the Parties *in the light of all factors relevant in this respect* [emphasis added]."[53]

Denmark and the Netherlands contended that the issue was governed by the "principles and rules of international law" contained in article 6(2) of the 1958 Convention, and that since "special circumstances" justifying another boundary line had not been established, the "principle of equidistance" should be applied. It was further argued that if these principles and rules were not applicable, the boundary should be determined "on the basis of the exclusive rights of each Party over the continental shelf adjacent to its coast and of the principle that the boundary is to leave to each Party every point of the continental shelf which lies nearer to its coast than to the coast of the other Party."[54]

It should be noted that the Court was not asked to draw the boundary lines, but merely to identify the applicable principles and rules of international law; it was assigned a declaratory role. But the two special agreements provided that with the Court's assistance the two sets of negotiations would be resumed with a view to completing the boundary-making task begun in the bilateral delimitation agreements of 1964 and 1965. The Court was asked to give chief emphasis to the minimally resolutive task of rule clarification, but in light of the need to facilitate future negotiations.[55]

The Court's majority judgment was supported by eleven votes to six.[56] The judgment is important not least because of its impact on the general theory and terminology of ocean boundary-making. In summarizing the arguments put forward by the litigants, the Court seemed to perceive an "equidistance line" as one based on the *principle* of equidistance. Somewhat confusingly, however, the Court proceeded to suggest that the equidistance line might consist either of a "median" line between "opposite" states, or of a "lateral" line between "adjacent" states. Later, it seemed to acknowledge the distinction between the equidistance line as a *method* and the equidistance line as a *rule*, but warned that the "factors" of "practical convenience and certainty of application ... do not suffice of themselves to convert what is a method into a rule of law, making the acceptance of the results of using that method obligatory in all cases in which the parties do not agree otherwise, or in which 'special circumstances' cannot be shown to exist. Juridically, if there is such a rule, it must draw its legal force from other factors than the existence of these advantages, important though they may be."[57] It concluded after further examination that, unlike the median line prescribed in article 6(1), the equidistance line method provided for in article 6(2) lacked the status of a rule in customary international law, and therefore it could not be binding on a non-party such as the Federal Republic of Germany. It may be inferred from the Court's language that the median line *rule* and the equidistance line *method* are both derived from the *principle* of equidistance, which is cognate with the principle of equality but not necessarily with that of equity; and that this was precisely the nub of the problem in the geographical situation it had to deal with.[58]

After holding that the FRG could not be shown, on the evidence presented, to have manifested its acceptance or recognition of the article 6 formula,[59] the Court proceeded none the less to comment on the wording of the provision. The wording of article 6(2) in particular seemed to the Court to pose the following dilemma: "in the absence of agreement on the matter, is there a presumption that the continental shelf between any two adjacent States consists automatically of an equidistance line – or must negotiations for an agreed boundary prove finally abortive before the acceptance of a boundary drawn on an equidistance basis becomes obligatory in terms of Article 6, if no special circumstances exist?"[60] The Court commented that the Danish-Dutch delimitation agreement of 1966 seemed to be based on the "tacit assumption" that the first of these questions should be answered in the affirmative, but that article 6 "provides only for delimitation between 'adjacent' States, which Denmark and the Netherlands clearly are not, or between 'opposite' States which, despite suggestions to the contrary, the Court thinks they equally are not ..."[61] In this dictum the Court gave the first indication of its intention, in appropriate factual circumstances, to accept the characterization of a delimitation issue as one that could not be dealt with solely under either the "opposite" or the "adjacent" rubric of article 6. A "mixed" geographical situation was accepted as a third possibility, although it had not been provided for in the 1958 Convention on the Continental Shelf.)

As to the rationale underlying the FRG's arguments, the Court took exception to the suggestion that it should engage in the task of "apportionment" with a view to securing to each of the adjacent states a "just and equitable share." On the contrary, the Court held, its tasks related "essentially to the delimitation and not the apportionment of the areas concerned, or their division into converging sectors. Delimitation is a process which involves establishing the boundaries of an area already, in principle, appertaining to the coastal State and not the determination *de novo* of such an area. Delimitation in an equitable manner is one thing, but not the same thing as awarding a just and equitable share of a previously undelimited area, even though in a number of cases the results may be comparable, or even identical."[62] This led the Court to enunciate its view of the nature of the continental shelf regime in customary international law – the famous "natural prolongation" doctrine[63] – which has much less logical relevance to an issue of delimitation between opposite or adjacent states than it has to the issue of determining the seaward limits of the shelf.[64] Taking the view that the concept of apportionment assumes there is something "undivided to share out," the Court concluded that this concept is inapplicable to delimitation, because any point of the shelf, as defined in customary international law, must "belong" to one of the adjacent states.

The truth is, however, that delimitation has an allocative-distributive aspect, which is of paramount interest to the parties, and in the orthodox theory of boundary delimitation, allocation, so-called, is the first stage of boundary-making. In practice, allocation merges, almost imperceptibly, into the second phase of delimitation, so-called. The facts of national interest and human psychology, as they operate both in negotiation and adjudication, challenge the Court's basic premise: that delimitation "cannot have as its object the awarding of an equitable share, or indeed of a share, as such, at all ..."[65] Instead, one might wish to suggest that a judicial boundary-maker, in weighing the relevant considerations, can hardly be expected to reach an equitable result if it decides predispositionally to overlook the distributive-allocative consequences of its delimitative decision. Yet any tribunal may properly be reluctant to undertake to balance all the equities in a quasi-allocative issue such as that of delimitation, especially in circumstances where the resource implications are largely unknown and what seems equitably apportioned today may not seem so tomorrow.[66]

Likewise, the Court was unconvinced by the central Danish-Dutch argument: the contention that continental shelf delimitation between adjacent states was governed by the "principle" of equidistance, or a cognate rule. By the Court's reasoning, this argument could prevail only if it was consistent with the nature of the continental shelf regime, as understood in customary international law; and this depended on the interpretation to be placed on the concept of adjacency. The concept of equidistance is consistent with adjacency only if the latter is understood to be equated with, or at least related to, the concept of proximity, because an equidistance line is a line of equally proximate points between two adjacent states. But the Court held that "there seems ... to be no necessary, and certainly no complete, identity between the notions of adjacency and proximity ... Hence it would see that the notion of adjacency, so constantly employed in continental shelf doctrine from the start, only implies proximity in a general sense, and does not imply any fundamental or inherent rule, the ultimate effect of which would be to prohibit any State (otherwise than by agreement) from exercising continental shelf rights in respect of areas closer to the coast of another State."[67] Nor could a "principle" of equidistance be spelled out of the doctrine of natural prolongation.[68] Accordingly, "the notion of equidistance as being logically necessary, in the sense of being an inescapable *a priori* accompaniment of basic continental shelf doctrine, is incorrect."[69]

Contrary to the Danish-Dutch contention, the Court held (1) that no one single method of delimitation was likely to prove satisfactory in all circumstances, and that delimitation should, therefore, be carried out by agreement (or by reference to arbitration); and (2) that it should be effected on equitable principles. This conclusion was based on current trends in state practice, originating with the 1945 Truman Proclamation on the Continental Shelf. After reviewing both the text and context of the 1958 Convention on the Continental Shelf, and especially article 6, the Court held also that the Convention "did not embody or crystallize any pre-existing or emergent rule of customary law, according to which the delimitation of continental shelf areas between adjacent states must, unless the Parties otherwise agree, be carried out on an equidistance-special circumstances base." The article 6 "rule" was "purely conventional." Finally, the

Court denied that the "rule" of article 6 had since 1958 "passed into the general corpus of international law," holding that if the 1958 Convention "was not in its origins or inception declaratory of a mandatory rule of customary international law enjoining the use of the equidistance principle for the delimitation of continental shelf areas between adjacent States, neither has its subsequent effect been constitutive of such a rule; and that State practice up-to-date has equally been insufficient for the purpose.[70]

These various determinations of law enabled the International Court of Justice to enunciate the applicable "principles and rules":

A the use of the equidistance method of delimitation not being obligatory as between the Parties; and

B there being no other single method of delimitation the use of which is in all circumstances obligatory;

C the principles and rules of international law applicable to the delimitation as between the Parties of the areas of the continental shelf in the North Sea which appertain to each of them beyond the partial boundary determined by the agreements of 1 December 1964 and 9 June 1965, respectively, are as follows:

1 delimitation is to be effected by agreement in accordance with equitable principles, and taking account of all relevant circumstances, in such a way as to leave as much as possible to each Party all those parts of the continental shelf that constitute a natural prolongation of its land territory into and under the sea, without encroachment on the natural prolongation of the land territory of the other;

2 if, in the application of the preceding sub-paragraph, the delimitation leaves to the Parties areas that overlap, these are to be divided between them in agreed proportions or, failing agreement, equally unless they decide on a regime of joint jurisdiction, user, or exploitation for the zones of overlap or any part of them;

D in the course of the negotiations, the factors to be taken into account are to include:

1 the general configuration of the coasts of the Parties, as well as the presence of any special or unusual features;

2 so far as known or readily ascertainable, the physical and geological structure, and natural resources, of the continental shelf areas involved;

3 the element of a reasonable degree of proportionality, which a delimitation carried out in accordance with equitable principles ought to bring about between the extent of the continental shelf area appertaining to the coastal State and the length of its coast measured in the general direction of its coastline, account being taken for this purpose of the effects, actual or prospective, of any other continental shelf delimitations between adjacent States in the same region.[71]

From a contemporary functionalist perspective, the *North Sea Continental Shelf* decision is a progressive effort to develop a rational foundation for this kind of boundary-making, rather than merely a judicial settlement of a delimitation dispute. First, the decision begins the effort to identify and distinguish types of considerations: for example, as far as norms are concerned, some effort is made to distinguiish specific "methods" from more general "principles and rules," and some of the relevant "factors" are identified without claim to a comprehensive listing. Second, the general tenor of the majority decision is conducive to flexibility rather than certainty, not least in the openness of the Court's approach to the choice of appropriate norms. Clearly, the majority wished to avoid an unduly doctrinaire approach to the analysis of "principles and rules," although this may have been due as much to the facts of the case as to the predisposition of the judges.

Third, the majority decision reflects an awareness of the need for a linkage between the type of boundary in dispute and the type of regime affected. It is clearly recognized that a solution that is appropriate for a territorial sea boundary delimitation problem between adjacent states may not be appropriate for a continental shelf boundary delimitation problem that is otherwise comparable in many respects. It might even be said that the Court, after reviewing various allegedly applicable principles and rules in a normal "legalistic" manner, with appropriate regard for the utility of doctrinal development, ended up with what essentially is a set of suggestions on how to deal with a delimination problem. The final adoption of this problem-solving approach is clearly due to the Court's awareness that it had been asked in effect to facilitate the negotiation of the boundaries, not merely to settle a dispute. In other words, the functionalist logic of the Court's recommendations is buttressed by the fact it had been asked virtually to perform good offices for the parties in the face of partial diplomatic failure.

Finally, of special interest from a functionalist perspective is the Court's acknowledgment that the parties to a delimitation dispute may be best served in a jurisdictional overlap situation by a negotiated "regime of joint jurisdiction, user, or exploitation." This early recognition of the need for joint development or management is further evidence of the Court's sensitivity to the functionalist implications of this kind of boundary-making problem.

Perhaps the most criticized element in the ICJ's majority decision has been the concept of "equitable principles," which because of its vagueness gives particular offence to those craving certainty in the aplication of norms. It should be remembered, however, that the Court in the *North Sea Continental Shelf* case was asked to clarify the applicable principles in light of the need to facilitate boundary-making by the parties, and that the concept of equitable principles was limited to the diplomatic frame of reference: "delimitation is to be affected *by agreement* in accordance with equitable principles ... [emphasis added]." Similarly the ICJ's concept of "natural prolongation of the land territory" is confined to the framework of diplomatic boundary-making. Both concepts are presented, more or less equally, along with "all relevant circumstances," as considerations to be weighted against one another in the negotiation process. The purpose of the formulation seems to be to deny primacy to any one norm, such as the "principle" of equidistance, or indeed to any one type of consideration, in the interest of flexibility.

The Mosaic: 1969-1977

By the time the *North Sea Continental Shelf* decision was handed down in 1969, it had become apparent that the theory of ocean boundary delimitation had become a mosaic of conceptual bits and pieces, each competing for the observer's attention. Shelf-related "bits" had firmly displaced territorial sea "pieces" from the centre of the picture. For the world community in general, the future of delimitation thinking seemed to lie with the median line, equidistance, and "special circumstances," as set out in article 6 of the 1958 Convention on the Continental Shelf, and especially with the principle of agreement or consent, which underlay that provision and article 12 of the Convention on the Territorial Sea and the Contiguous Zone.

The primacy of agreement, being incontestable, lent special importance to the emerging pattern of treaty practice around the world. For those who pictured delimitation theory in terms of unity rather than diversity, the danger was that the bilateral treaty-making process would be characterized by divergence rather than convergence. Fearful of undue diversity in the diplomatic process of ocean boundary-making, some jurists (the "unitarians") placed their faith in the unifying logic of doctrine rather than in the uncertainties of mutual interest. Boundary delimitation, it was felt by many, should be guided or even directed through doctrinal development by means of two concurrent processes: codification (or progressive development) and third-party adjudication of disputes.

By 1969 the UN Seabed Committee had begun to prepare the way for the Third UN Conference on the Law of the Sea, but it was much too early to predict the outcome for purposes of delimitation theory, or even to identify a majority trend of governmental opinion, much less give such a trend any juridical weight. In the years following the *North Sea Continental Shelf* decision, however, it became increasingly apparent in the UNCLOS III negotiations that the coastal states of the world were evenly divided between proponents of equidistance and those of equity (or "special circumstances").[72] Each state's alignment was based on its interpretation of its own national interest as it applied alternative formulae to its geographical situation. Normative considerations – in the form of principles, rules, criteria, and methods of delimitation – were accepted essentially as potential instruments of persuasion in diplomatic or adjudicative contexts. Norms were weapons for combat, along with situational and non-situational factors. Appeals to tradition, or continuity with the past, would be as suspect as any other form of argument.

By the mid-1970s, therefore, it semed to many UNCLOS III participants that the laying of a "common interest" foundation for the legal theory of ocean boundary delimitation could go no further than "procedural ethic": consensus would be limited to the primacy of agreement (the diplomatic mode) and the high value of a disinterested adjudicative procedure for balancing the equities in a given dispute. By sentiment, logic, and self-interest, a number of delegations were forced to the view that the convenience and relative certainty of equidistance (a form of equality) would have to yield, by any global formula of the "romantic" period,[73] to the consideration of equity. The chief test would have to be fairness, and if diplomacy failed in part or in whole, the adjudicator's responsibility would be to provide, above all, a fair result.

Yet the years following the *North Sea Continental Shelf* decision showed that the mosaic of delimitation theory would receive additional bits and pieces as the judicial process evolved in the quest for a fair result. Moreover, each subsequent adjudication, like the pioneer decision of 1969, would be scrutinized by commentators operating within two distinct frames of reference. The "unitarians" in the classical or neo-classical mode would continue to look for evidence of clarity and continuity in the development of norms, while the functionalists would be chiefly concerned with the adjudicator's facilitative role in ocean boundary-making. The theory of delimitation would be shaped, it seemed, in the heat of the debate between doctrinal and functionalist logic.

The Anglo-French Continental Shelf Arbitration (1977)

Like the *North Sea Continental Shelf* case of 1969, the *Anglo-French Continental Shelf* arbitration was the result of partial diplomatic failure. The British and French governments concluded four years of negotiation in 1974 by agreeing in principle on delimitation of a portion of the continental shelf in the English Channel eastward of 30 minutes west of the Greenwich meridian, and disagreeing over delimitation of all continental shelf areas to the west of that meridian (see figure 4). In some of these areas to the west the governments were able to agree in general terms on

FIGURE 4: Anglo-French Continental Shelf Arbitration

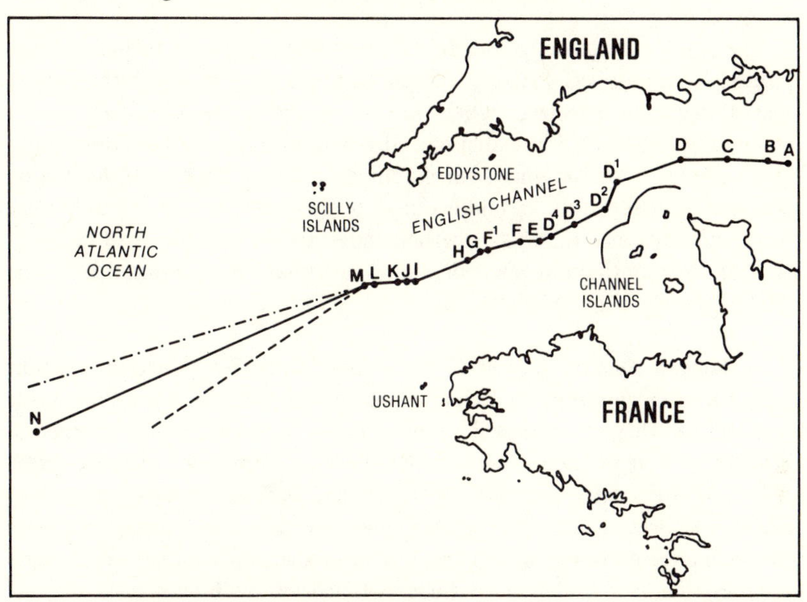

_ . __ . __ French claim in the Atlantic Region.
\- - - - - - UK claim in the Atlantic Region.
________ Boundary segments drawn by the Court of Arbitration, 1977.
12-nautical mile territorial sea enclaves for the Channel Islands established by the Court of Arbitration, 1977.

the applicability of the median line "rule," or the "principle" of equidistance, while they differed on the mode of application. In other areas of dispute, more fundamental differences arose. Accordingly, the governments agreed to refer all differences to arbitration, and for that purpose an arbitration agreement was signed in July 1975.

Under article 2(1) of the agreement the Court of Arbitration was mandated to determine "the course of the boundary (or boundaries) between the portions of the continental shelf appertaining to the United Kingdom and the Channel Islands and to the Republic of France" within the area westward of 30 minutes west of the Greenwich meridian as far as the 1,000-metre isobath. Under article 9(1) it was stipulated that the decision of the court would include "the drawing of the course of the boundary (or boundaries) on a chart," with the assistance of a technical expert or experts. Unlike the ICJ in the *North Sea Continental Shelf* case, the Court of Arbitration was asked to undertake the task of judicial boundary-making, and not merely to determine legal issues or provide guidelines for diplomatic boundary-making. Perhaps the nature of its role explains the extreme length of the court's decision[74] – five times that of the ICJ's majority decision in 1969 – as well as the need for a 112-page clarification of its decision.[75]

The court's treatment of the delimitation issues between France and the United Kingdom was strongly influenced by the way in which the area in dispute was characterized, which in turn was strongly influenced by the diplomatic history of the dispute. In their previous negotiations both governments had recognized the significance of the ICJ's 1969 distinction between opposite-state and adjacent-state situations in relation to the use of the equidistance method, whether under article 6 of the 1958 Convention on the Continental Shelf or under customary international law. The parties therefore agreed that

> throughout *the English Channel* where the coasts of the French Republic and the United Kingdom are opposite each other the boundary should, in principle, be the median line. They are in radical disagreement as to the appropriate method of delimitation in the *Channel Islands region*. Even in that region ... they are agreed that in the areas where the coasts of the Channel Islands and the coasts of Normandy and Brittany are opposite each other, the seabed and subsoil boundary should in principle be the median line. In short, leaving aside the special problems resulting from the position of the Channel Islands off the French coast, they are agreed that the geographical and legal frame of reference for the delimitation of the boundary is that of an "opposite States" situation; and that, in consequence, the appropriate method is in principle equidistance. In so agreeing, the French Republic bases itself on the rules of customary law, the United Kingdom on the provisions of Article 6 of the Convention; but the result is the same, which seems to confirm that under either head it is the geographical situation which indicates the applicable method of delimitation. In any event, this Court of Arbitration sees no reason to differ from the conclusion of the Parties that, in principle, the method applicable to the *English Channel* is to draw a median line equidistant from their respective coasts ...
>
> In the *Atlantic region* on the other hand, the Parties are in radical disagreement as to the correct characterization of the geographical situation for the purpose of delimiting the continental shelf. As a consequence, they are also in disagreement regarding the principle and method of delimitation to be applied in the region [emphasis added].[76]

The Court of Arbitration was more or less obliged to perceive the geographical situation as a whole in three distinct sectors: (1) the sector westward from 0° 30′ west longitude in the English Channel to the mid-channel point where the presence of the channel first begins to affect the application of the equidistance principle; (2) the sector so affected by the presence of the Channel Islands; and (3) the sector further westward as far as the 1,000-metre isobath, referred to as the "Atlantic region." Because of the emphasis placed by the parties on the principle of equidistance, the court also felt obliged to take a position on the significance of that principle both under article 6 and under customary law. Faced with the parties' choice of the equidistance "principle" on the one hand and the ICJ's emphasis on equitable principles in its 1969 decision on the other, the Court of Arbitration attempted a reconciliation, suggesting that

> the appropriateness of the equidistance method or any other method for the purpose of effecting an equitable delimitation is a function or reflection of the geographical and other relevant circumstances of each particular case. The choice of the method or methods of delimitation in any given case, whether under the 1958 Convention or customary law, has therefore to be determined in light of those circumstances and of the fundamental norm that the delimitation must be in accordance with equitable principles. Furthermore, in appreciating the appropriateness of the equidistance method as a means of achieving an equitable solution, regard must be had to the difference between a "lateral" boundary between "adjacent" States and a "median" boundary between "opposite" States.[77]

In agreeing with the governments' views on the utility of the median line method of delimitation in the opposite-state situation, the court held that there did not seem to be any legal ground for discarding the equidistance or any other method of delimitation in favour of a single physical feature such as the Hurd Deep-Hurd Deep Fault Zone, which was not considered a significant disruption of "the essential geological continuity" of the continental shelf in the arbitration area, either in the English Channel or Atlantic regions.[78] Compared with the deep Norwegian Trough in the North Sea, geological features such as these could only be regarded as "minor faults in the geological structure of the shelf." Yet the "essential geological continuity" of a continental shelf could not be said automatically to entail the continuous use of the same method of delimitation along the whole length of the shelf; otherwise the existence of "special circumstances" could have no relevance.[79] Consequently, the court accepted the task of determining the course of the median line in the English Channel both to the east and the west of the Channel Islands. With this in mind, it requested the governments, which had already agreed on the applicability of a "simplified" median line for the Channel,[80] to "identify precisely the respective terminal points of each of the agreed segments" of the boundary line in the Channel, to provide the relevant co-ordinates, and to trace these segments of the line on appropriate charts.[81]

In response, the British and French governments drew an agreed-upon simplified median line in the Channel east and west of the Channel Islands, with the exception of one portion of the line in the western segment. The negotiated line was in three segments: (1) from 0°30′ W longitude (point A) to 2°03′26″ W (point D); (2) from 3°42′44″ W (point E) to 3°55′47″ W (point F); and (3) from 4°21′46″ W (point G) to 5°18′00″ W (point J). The court then had to draw lines in the three remaining gaps: (1) in the English Channel between points D and E; (2) at the western end of the channel between points F and G; and (3) in the Atlantic region westward of point J to the 1,000-metre isobath (point N).

In addressing itself to the second gap, between points F and G, the court noted that the only difference between the parties concerned the status of Eddystone Rock and its relevance to the issue of boundary delimitation. On this point the court accepted the British argument for treating Eddystone as a relevant base-point for delimiting the continental shelf boundary in the Channel. Accordingly, the court drew a median line boundary between points F and G, equidistant between Eddystone Rock on the British side, and two base-points off the coast of Brittany on the French side.

As to the gap between points D and E, the court held that it must confine itself to delimiting the boundary in the areas to the north and west of the Channel Islands because of the French view that the court was not empowered under the arbitration agreement to delimit the seabed and subsoil boundary in the narrow waters situated between the Channel Islands and the coasts of Normandy and Brittany.[82] The exclusion of this particular area had the effect of tending, somewhat subtly, to downgrade the relevance of the Channel Islands to the court's perception of the area in dispute between points D and E. With the exclusion of the area to the south between the Channel Islands and the French coast, the Channel Islands was displaced from the centre to the periphery of the D–E area in dispute. With this perceptual shift to the north and west, it became correspondingly more difficult for the United Kingdom to convince the court that it should give "full effect" to the Channel Islands in the delimitation of the continental shelf in the western segment of the English Channel. So, once again, macrogeographical characterization had an important role in the process of judicial boundary-making.

The two governments had agreed that "the geographical and legal framework for determining the boundary is one of States the coasts of which are opposite each other; and that, in consequence, the boundary should, in principle, be the median line."[83] But they were sharply divided over the role of the coasts of the Channel Islands as coasts of the United Kingdom "opposite" those of France. France, treating the regime of article 6 of the 1958 Convention as inapplicable, invoked equitable principles under customary law, but contended in the alternative that, if article 6 were deemed applicable, the Channel Islands constituted a special circumstance justifying a departure from the median line. The United Kingdom, treating article 6 as applicable, invoked equidistance under the 1958 Convention, but likewise argued in the alternative that its position held good equally under the regime of customary law. The double basis of both submissions served to confirm the court's conlusion that "the different ways in which the requirements of 'equitable principles' or the effect of 'special circumstances' are put reflect differences of approach and terminology rather than of substance."[84]

In weighing the merits of the arguments advanced, the court found the "specificity" position of France the more persuasive of the two. By this view, the specific character of the problem arose from the location of the Channel Islands on "the wrong side" of the median line, "situated within a rectangular bay of the French coast and only a few nautical miles from it."[85] In consequence, the Channel Islands and the sea areas between them and the French coast should be perceived, France argued, as intrinsically linked with the continental land mass of France. The application of the eqidistance method proposed by the United Kingdom for the Channel Islands region would be inequitable in two respects: "First, it would involve a deep amputation of the French Republic's continental shelf in the Channel, which would result in a reduction of the area appertaining to the Republic and a corresponding gain to the United Kingdom wholly disproportionate to the size of the Channel Islands and the length of their coasts. Secondly, it would involve severing the continental shelf of France in the Channel into two separate zones."[86] Such a severance would jeopardize France's "vital interests" in military and economic matters. Accordingly, the automatic application of the equidistance method in the Channel Islands region would produce results of the "extraordinary, unnatural or unreasonable" sort that the ICJ in 1969 had characterized as the degree of inequity that justified a departure from the application of that method.[87] Instead, France proposed that a narrow (six-mile) enclave of British jurisdiction should be designated around the Channel Islands without affecting the delimitation of the shelf between France and the United Kingdom as opposite states at the western end of the Channel.

The court apparently was not particularly impressed by France's "vital interests" agument, and it explicitly rejected the suggested analogy between the doctrine of state equality and that of continental shelf entitlement; but it did give weight to the consideration of disproportionality and the "wrong side" depiction of the Channel Islands. While the court granted a certain weight to the equitable considerations invoked by the United Kingdom,[88] which "invalidated" the French proposal for restricting the Channel Islands to a six-mile enclave, those considerations did not appear to "justify the disproportion or remove the imbalance" which adoption of the United Kingdom's proposal would involve. It was concluded, therefore, that the specific features of the Channel Islands region called for "an intermediate solution that effects a more appropriate and a more equitable balance between the respective claims and interests of the Parties."[89] This intermediate solution was a twofold compromise, consisting of a combination of the median line and enclave proposals of the British and French governments respectively:

First, in order to maintain the appropriate balance between the two States in relation to the continental shelf as riparian States of the Channel with approximately equal coastlines, the Court decides that the *primary* boundary between them shall be a *median line*, linking Point D of the agreed eastern segment to Point E of the western agreed segment. In the light of the Court's previous decisions regarding the course of the boundary of the English Channel, this means that throughout the whole length of the Channel comprised within the arbitration area the *primary* boundary of the continental shelf will be a mid-Channel median line. In delimiting its course in the Channel Islands region, that is between Points D and E, *the Channel Islands themselves are to be disregarded, since their continental shelf must be the subject of a second and separate delimitation.*

The second part of the solution is to delimit a *second* boundary establishing, vis-a-vis the Channel Islands, the southern limit of the continental shelf held by the Court to be appurtenant to the French Republic in this region to the south of the mid-Channel median line. *This second boundary must not, in the opinion of the Court, be so drawn as to allow the continental shelf of the French Republic to encroach upon the established 12-mile fishery zone of the Channel Islands.* The Court therefore further decides that this boundary shall be drawn at a distance of 12 nautical miles from the established baselines of the territorial sea of the Channel Islands ... The result ... is to enclose them in an *enclave* formed, to their north and west, by the boundary of the 12-mile zone just described by the Court and, to their east, south and south-west, by the boundary between them and the coasts of Normandy and Brittany, the exact course of which it is outside the competence of the Court to specify [emphasis added].[90]

Finally, as to the Atlantic region to the west of point J, the court's approach to the delimitation was governed by its holding that the provisions of article 6 of the 1958 Convention were applicable and that the distinction between the opposite-state and adjacent-state situations was "not always uniform and clear-cut along the whole length of a boundary. In certain geographical configurations the relationship between the States may change from one situation to the other with the result that, as was observed in the Judgment in the *North Sea Continental Shelf* cases (paragraph 6), 'a given equidistance line may partake in varying degrees of the nature both of a median and of a lateral line.'"[91] After reviewing the British and French arguments for equidistance and special circumstances respectively, and identifying the distinguishing geographical characteristics of the Atlantic region,[92] the court held that "whether the Atlantic region is considered, legally, to be a case of 'opposite' States governed by paragraph 1 or a case of 'adjacent' States governed by paragraph 2 of Article 6, appreciation of the effects of any special geographical features on the equidistance line has to take account of those two geographical facts: the lateral relation of the two coasts and the great distance which the continental shelf extends seawards from those coasts."[93] Although the court was inclined to the opinion that the region falls within the terms of paragraph 1 (opposite-state situation) rather than paragraph 2 (adjacent-state situation), it felt little importance should be attached to the precise legal classification of the Atlantic region, since the "rules of delimitation" prescribed in those paragraphs are the same. "What is important is that, in appreciating the appropriateness of the equidistance method as a means of effecting a 'just' or 'equitable' delimitation in the Atlantic region, the court must have regard both to the lateral relation of the two coasts as they abut upon the continental shelf of the region and to the great distance seawards that this shelf extends from those coasts."[94]

The crucial question was what effect, if any, to give to the presence of the Scilly Isles west-southwest of Cornwall. To allow the islands as a base-point would "deflect the equidistance line on a considerably more south-westerly course than would be the case if it were to be delimited from the baseline of the English mainland." In the final analysis, the court held that "the additional projection of the Scilly Islands into the Atlantic does constitute an element of distortion which is material enough to justify the delimitation of a boundary other than the strict median line envisaged in Article 6, paragraph 1, of the Convention" and that the position of the Scilly Isles was a "special circumstance" as envisaged in that provision.[95] Yet the court could not accept the French contention for a median line delimited by reference to prolongation of the general directions of the Channel coasts of the two countries. The solution, it held, was to "take account of the Scilly Isles as part of the coastline of the United Kingdom, but to give them less than their full effect in applying the equidistance method."[96] The method of giving "half-effect" appeared to the court to be "an appropriate and practical method of abating the disproportion and inequity which otherwise results from giving full effect to the Scilly Isles as a base-point for determining the course of the boundary ... The function of equity ... is not to produce absolute equality of treatment, but an appropriate abatement of the inequitable effects of the distorting geographical feature."[97] Accordingly, the court drew a boundary line westward of point J by means of the equidistance method but giving only half-effect to the Scillies.

This unanimous decision by the Court of Arbitration was not the end of the story.[98] Less than four months after the court's decision was made known, the British government submitted an application seeking clarification of the meaning or scope of the decision with reference to two matters in dispute between the parties, namely, "(1) the techniques and methods employed for drawing on the boundary-line chart the 12-mile enclave boundary to the north and west of the Channel Islands; (2) the techniques and methods employed for drawing on the boundary-line chart the portion of the boundary west of point M out to the 1,000 metre isobath."[99] On the first of these matters, the burden of the United Kingdom's complaint was that the twelve-mile enclave boundary was improperly drawn, since the technical report attached to the court's decision showed that it used an incomplete listing of the relevant base-points from which the territorial sea of the Channel Islands had consistently been measured by the United Kingdom.[100] On the second matter, it was argued that the manner of drawing the segment M–N of the boundary line, as shown on the court's chart and as defined in its technical report, could not be reconciled with the "evident intention" of the court's half-effect solution applied in the *dispositif* of the decision.[101] These two technical difficulties had led to a dispute between the parties regarding the meaning and scope of the court's decision of 30 June 1977, or alternatively had revealed "internal contradictions" in the decision, either of which permitted the United Kingdom to seek a clarification under article 10(2) of the arbitration agreement of 10 July 1975.[102]

As a preliminary matter, the court agreed that a dispute had arisen between the parties regarding the meaning and scope of its decision, and held that the application should be regarded as a request for an interpretation of that decision. The court rejected France's contention that in providing a clarification it was limited, by virtue of the principle of *res judicata*, to the language of the *dispositif* and the boundary drawn in its chart. In determining whether there were "internal contradictions," the court was free to look at the reasons given as the basis of its decision.[103]

On the first part of the decision challenged by the United Kingdom, concerning the enclave boundary to the north and west of the Channel Islands, the court agreed that there was a discrepancy between its intention to draw a boundary twelve nautical miles seaward of "the *established* baselines of the territorial sea of the Channel Islands" [emphasis added][104] and the actual delimitation of the boundary in the *dispositif*. The discrepancy arose "purely and simply from technical causes," and it could properly be characterized as a material error analogous to "one resulting from a 'slip of the pen' or from the miscalculation or miscasting of arithmetical figures"; it therefore fell within the power of the court to rectify the error without violating the principle of *res judicata*.[105]

On the second part of the decision challenged by the United Kingdom, concerning the most westerly portion of the boundary in the Atlantic region, the court examined at length the arguments and counter-arguments concerning the technical aspects of delimitation,[106] and concluded that the method of calculating the course of the M–N line used by the expert and adopted by the court was not incompatible with its findings on the principles and method to govern the delimitation of that segment of the boundary. Since no incompatibility was established, the principle of *res judicata* applied, precluding the court from going "beyond the function of interpretation entrusted to the Court under Article 10 of the Arbitration Agreement as well as beyond its inherent power to rectify a material error."[107]

From any perspective, functionalist or otherwise, it must be said that the *Anglo-French Continental Shelf* arbitration was a complicated example of judicial boundary-making. Most of the difficulties of arbitration arose from or were associated with the treatment of the physical factors inherent in the "situation": that is, the general characterization of the "arbitration area" as a whole, or of the specific subareas in dispute, and the treatment of certain special features of designated subareas. With respect to the English Channel region east of the Channel Islands, the parties had had no difficulty in agreeing on the applicability of the median line "rule" in what was clearly an opposite-state situation, but it was left to the Court of Arbitration to decide how to apply the "principle" of equidistance elsewhere in the arbitration area with a view to reducing the inequities inherent in the macrogeography of the region and to correcting distortions caused by specific microgeographical features.

Counsel on both sides frequently referred to the "essential geological continuity" of the continental shelf throughout the arbitration area, but this kind of physical characterization served only to convince the court to apply the "principle" of equidistance without regard for minor faults in the geological structure, which was not in any event insisted upon by either side. The major "characterizational" issue was what weight, if any, to give to the location of the Channel Islands. A similar minor issue was the weight to be given to the location of the Scilly Isles. The "enclave" resolution of the major issue, granting no effect to the Channel Islands as far as the application of equidistance is concerned, was an important judicial initiative, albeit one of diplomatic, not juridical, origin.[108] The "half-effect" resolution of the minor issue, likewise of diplomatic origin, underlines the value of a two-way relationship between the judicial and diplomatic processes of ocean boundary-making.[109] In its decision dealing with the Atlantic region, moreover, the court performed a useful service in discouraging an unduly legalistic debate between "opposite-state" and "adjacent-state" characterizations of the situation, on the realistic ground that marine geography is much too variable to be categorized so neatly under paragraph 1 or paragraph 2 of article 6 of the 1958 Convention. The court's recognition that a situation may involve elements of both of adjacency and oppositeness seems a realistic approach to this particular kind of characterization.

On the normative side of the analysis the problem was simpler, but not so simple as it might appear. On the face of things, the general applicability of the principle of equidistance was not in dispute, even outside the English Channel region, but in reality the principle of equidistance came into conflict with the principle of equity under almost any method of application, given the distortiveness of certain geographical features. The conflict between these two general principles was resolved by adoption of the criterion of proportionality in the Channel Islands region, and by applying the "principle" of "special circumstances" to the Scillies in the Atlantic region. Although the solution to the normative issue in both situations pivoted on the process of characterization, the rationale of the court's reconciliation between equality and equity might be said to reside in its "abatement" theory of equity.[110]

The Aegean Sea Continental Shelf Case (1978)

For over three decades Greece and Turkey have been locked in conflict over a number of issues. Not the least of these is the question of entitlement to continental shelf areas in the Aegean Sea lying between the most easterly of the Greek islands and the Turkish coast.[111] This issue contributed to the embittered relations between the two governments in the period from late 1973 to late 1978, during which they disagreed sharply not only on the question of entitlement to the shelf but also on the appropriate method of dealing with the issue. Efforts at diplomacy and adjudication proved fruitless, but the history of the dispute offers important negative examples of both approaches to ocean boundary delimitation.

The dispute entered a critical stage in November 1973, when the Turkish government granted petroleum exploration permits for submarine areas of the Aegean close to the Greek islands of Samothráki, Límnos, Ay. Eustrátios, Lésvos, Khíos, Psará, and Antipsará. (See figure 5.) When Greece challenged the validity of these permits on the ground that they encroached upon the continental shelf appertaining to these islands, Turkey responded that the islands did not possess a continental shelf of their own since they were only "protuberances" on the natural prologation of Turkey's Anatolian coast.[112] In May 1974 the Greek government notified the Turkish government that it was "not opposed to a delimitation of the continental shelf between the two countries based on the provisions of present day positive international law, as codified by the 1958 Geneva Convention on the Continental Shelf," and several weeks later the Turkish government replied that it was ready to begin negotiations within the framework of the rules of international law, without any specific reference

FIGURE 5: Aegean Sea Continental Shelf Case

Area covered by Turkish exploratory permits, 1 November 1973
Area covered by Turkish exploratory permits, 18 July 1974

1	Samothráki	4	Lésvos
2	Límnos	5	Khíos
3	Eustrátios	6	Psará and Antipsará

to the 1958 Convention.[113] In July of the same year new exploration permits were granted by the Turkish government in areas further west of six of the seven Greek islands lying close to the Turkish coast, and in areas further south close to the islands of Ikarca and the Dodecanese, including Rhodes. Greece protested against this new aggravation of the dispute. In September Turkey rejected the Greek protest, but acknowledged that a mutually acceptable solution to the delimitation problem should be reached through negotiations.

Discussions between the two governments led to the Greek government's proposal in January 1975 that "the differences over the applicable law as well as over the substance of the matter" be referred to the International Court of Justice. The Turkish reply in February 1975 emphasized that "there seems to be no other alternative but to settle [the] disputes through negotiation ... with the aim of solving the differences on the Aegean continental shelf peacefully, in a just and equitable manner."[114] It added, however, that in principle it viewed favourably the Greek proposal to refer the dispute to the Court. To negotiate the terms of such a reference, Turkey proposed that the two governments initiate high-level talks. When the foreign ministers met in May 1975, the Greek delegation submitted a draft text of a *compromis* for negotiation, but the Turkish representatives argued that substantive negotiations should take place before adjudication. A subsequent meeting between the two prime ministers resulted in a joint communiqué, which referred to the need for negotiations and the prospect of resort to the Court, and called for acceleration of the process of diplomacy at the expert level. But throughout that summer the Turkish position hardened, to the point that by the end of September Turkey announced that it was "not in the interests of the two countries to submit the dispute to the International Court of Justice without first attempting meaningful negotiations" with a view to securing a "just and fair agreement based on equitable principles."[115]

By February 1976 it was clear that the two governments had committed themselves irreconcilably to two different national strategies on the delimitation issue; the situation was exacerbated by poor and deteriorating relations between them and by the deployment of hydrographic and naval vessels in the disputed area. After the commencement of seismic research in disputed waters by a Turkish vessel, the Greek government referred the matter in August 1976 simultaneously to the International Court of Justice and to the Security Council. Several days later the Security Council passed a resolution that emphasized the primacy of the diplomatic mode of settlement, called on the two governments to resume negotiations over their differences, and suggested that they "continue to take into account the contribution that appropriate judicial means, in particular the International Court of Justice, are qualified to make to the settlement of any remaining legal differences that they may identify in connection with their present dispute."[116] The two governments complied with the Security Council's request for further negotiations, but the diplomatic difficulties were aggravated by the continuance of judicial proceedings before the Court, which Turkey regarded as detrimental to the maintenance of good faith between the negotiating teams.

In September 1976 the ICJ denied Greece's request for "interim measures of protection" and decided that the written proceedings in the suit should first be addressed to the question of the Court's jurisdiction to entertain the dispute.[117] The memorial for Greece was duly filed, but the Turkish government sent a letter to the registry, stating that "it was evident that the Court had no jurisdiction to entertain the Greek Application in the circumstances in which it was seized thereof,"[118] and that consequently the Turkish government would neither appoint an agent nor file a counter-memorial.

In its original application, Greece asked the ICJ to declare that the Greek islands in question, "as part of the territory of Greece, are entitled to the portion of the continental shelf which appertains to them according to the applicable principles and rules of international law," and to determine "the course of the boundary (or boundaries) between the portions of the continental shelf appertaining to Greece and Turkey in the Aegean Sea in accordance with the principles and rules of international law which the Court shall determine to be applicable to the delimitation of the continental shelf in the aforesaid areas of the Aegean Sea ..."[119] At the close of the oral proceedings, Greece asked the Court to declare itself competent to entertain the dispute, and in conformity with article 53 of its statute the Court proceeded to address only the question of its jurisdiction.

At the outset the Court rejected the view of the Tukish government, as expressed in its *note verbale* of 29 September 1978, that there was no legal dispute for adjudication. Although "of a highly political nature," the situation was "clearly one in which 'the parties are in conflict as to their respective rights.' "[120] The Court then analysed at length the Greek argument that the Court's jurisdiction was founded on article 17 of the 1928 General Act for the Pacific Settlement of International Disputes. Despite the absence of Turkish arguments, the Court concluded that Greece's reservation to its ratification of the General Act was available to Turkey on the basis of reciprocity and had the effect of excluding the dispute from the application of article 17.[121] The key element in this decision was the holding that the dispute under consideration was a dispute "relating to the territorial status of Greece" within the meaning of Greece's reservation to the General Act. The judges had little difficulty in rejecting the Greek contention that delimitation was "entirely extraneous to the notion of territorial status":

> The basic question in dispute is whether or not certain islands under Greek sovereignty are entitled to a continental shelf of their own and entitled Greece to call for the boundary to be drawn between those islands and the Turkish coast. The very essence of the dispute, as formulated in the Application, is thus the entitlement of those Greek islands to a continental shelf, and the delimitation of the boundary is a secondary question to be decided after, and in light of, the decision upon the first basic question ... The question for decision is whether the present dispute is one relating to the territorial status of Greece, not whether the rights in dispute are legally to be considered as "territorial" rights; and a dispute regarding entitlement to and delimitation of areas of continental shelf tends by its very nature to be one relating to territorial status ... In short, continental shelf rights are legally both an

emanation from and an automatic adjunct of the territorial sovereignty of the coastal State. It follows that the territorial regime – the territorial status – of a coastal State comprises, *ipso jure*, the rights of exploration and exploitation over the continental shelf, to which it is entitled under international law. A dispute regarding those rights would, therefore, appear to be one which may be said to "relate" to the territorial status of the coastal State.[122]

The Greek effort to found the Court's jurisdiction on the joint communiqué issued by the two governments in May 1975 also failed.[123] Accordingly, by twelve votes to two, the International Court of Justice found that it was without jurisdiction to entertain the application filed by Greece.[124]

For the purposes of this monograph, two aspects of the *Aegean Sea Continental Shelf* decision are of special interest. The first is the reluctance of the Court to discontinue proceedings during negotiations, and indeed even to admit to the primacy of diplomacy as a mode of ocean boundary-making.

Negotiation and judicial settlement are enumerated together in Article 33 of the Charter of the United Nations as means for the peaceful settlement of disputes. The jurisprudence of the Court provides various examples of cases in which negotiations and recourse to judicial settlement have been pursued *pari passu*. Several cases ... show that judicial proceedings may be discontinued when such negotiations result in the settlement of the dispute. Consequently, the fact that negotiations are being actively pursued during the present proceedings is not, legally, any obstacle to the exercise by the Court of its judicial function.[125]

It does not seem to have occurred to the Court to ask itself whether the solution of the boundary-making problem would be facilitated more by the discontinuance than by the continuance of the proceedings. The boundary-making problem may, of course, have remained unsolved in any event, for overriding political reasons, but it is difficult to believe that continuance did not contribute in some degree to its intractability.[126] In retrospect, the Court's language can be criticized as incompatible with the spirit, if not the letter, of the 1982 Convention on the Law of the Sea. Article 83 of that treaty, which governs the delimitation of the continental shelf, clearly accords primacy to negotiations as a matter "procedural ethic."[127] Admittedly, in September 1976, when the Court agreed to accept written proceedings, the direction of UNCLOS III negotiations on this issue was still unclear.[128] To the extent that the 1982 provision reflects a new norm of the customary international law of the sea, it may now, after UNCLOS III, be considered more appropriate for the Court in similar circumstances to suspend proceedings until diplomatic failure is fully evidenced.

Many commentators have been unsympathetic to the Turkish government's position, not only because of its refusal to appear before the Court but also because of its denial that the Greek islands were entitled to a continental shelf of their own. This denial apparently was contrary to the language of article 1 of the 1958 Convention on the Continental Shelf,[129] and to the view that article 1 was declaratory of customary international law as far as the entitlement of islands was concerned.[130] At UNCLOS III many delegations emphasized their view that the 1958 Convention explicitly granted a continental shelf to *all* islands, and though some countries (including Turkey) proposed limiting amendments of one kind or another,[131] the final provision adopted in the 1982 Convention seems to have given further support to the Greek government's legal position on the issue of entitlement.[132] On the other hand, it must surely be conceded that to apply article 121(2) of the 1982 Convention and also a median line boundary to the continental shelf of the Eastern Aegean would be to produce an inequitable result. Because the easternmost Greek islands lie so close to the Turkish coast, it seems necessary for the parties to the dispute to find some kind of compromise, outside the framework of legal rules and principles, that would give appropriate weight to the unique geographical features, as well as the political sensitivities, of the region. A mediator or a conciliation commission, feeling the need to appease the Greek fear of "enclaves" around its easternmost islands and the Turkish fear of the overall "hellenization" of the shelf in the region,[133] would probably propose a package of negotiable settlements and arrangements as the means of achieving an "equitable solution" in conformity with article 83(1) of the 1982 Convention.[134]

The other matter of special interest from a functionalist perspective is the Court's dictum that delimitation in this case is secondary to the basic question of territorial status and entitlement. This pronouncement may be understandable in the context of the jurisdictional issue in question, but other reasons could have been given for rejecting the applicability of the 1928 General Act. Taken out of context, the pronouncement is potentially mischievous to the extent that it distorts the functional significance of ocean boundary-making. Moreover, the suggested relationship between delimitation and territorial status creates an unfortunate, and probably unintended, distinction between delimitation of the shelf and delimitation of the exclusive economic zone – one that is difficult to sustain within the framework of the 1982 Convention on the Law of the Sea.[135]

The Jan Mayen Continental Shelf Conciliation (1981)

In May 1980 the governments of Iceland and Norway concluded an agree-

FIGURE 6: Jan Mayen Continental Shelf Conciliation

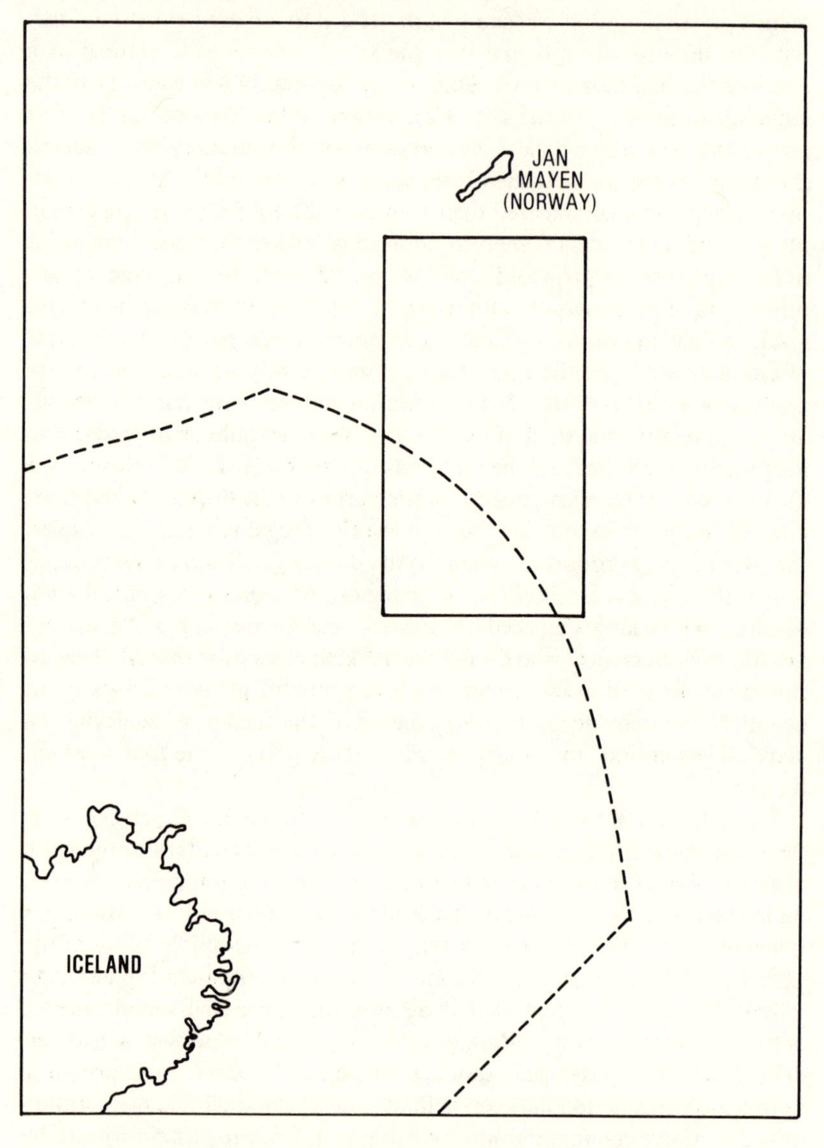

---- Icelandic claim to 200-nautical-mile exclusive economic zone.

☐ Joint development area suggested by Conciliation Commission, 1981.

ment concerning various fishery and continental shelf questions. Norway agreed to recognize Iceland's claim to a 200-mile exclusive economic zone, although Iceland and the Norwegian island of Jan Mayen are only about 290 nautical miles apart.[136] The Icelandic government also advanced a claim to a continental shelf extending beyond its 200-mile EEZ, motivated by the knowledge that the best offshore hydrocarbon prospects in the region existed under the northern part of the Jan Mayen Ridge, close to the island of Jan Mayen. (See figure 6.)

Since the parties could not agree on the delimitation of the shelf in the area, it was agreed to refer the matter to a conciliation commission established for that purpose.[137] The commission's mandate was to make recommendations on the delimitation issue, and it was asked to "take into account Iceland's strong economic interests in these sea areas, the existing geographical and geological factors and other special circumstances."[138] The recommendations of the commission were not to be binding on the governments, but during further negotiations they did agree to pay "reasonable regard" to them. Although less than a tribunal, the commission was established to operate in a quasi-adjudicative mode with a view to facilitating the diplomatic process of boundary-making in the region.[139] Since the two national members of the commission had participated in all previous negotiations, and since the governments had asked for recommendations within five months, it was decided to dispense with formal and time-consuming procedures.

As ambassadors deeply involved in UNCLOS III negotiations, the members of the commission began by invoking the relevant provisions of the current UNCLOS III text, the Draft Convention on the Law of the Sea (Informal Text) issued on 27 August 1980. The commission accepted article 121 on the regime of islands, quoted above, as a formulation that "reflects the present status of international law on this subject," and held that Jan Mayen was entitled to a continental shelf as well as a territorial sea and EEZ.[140] The commission also invoked the primacy of the principle of agreement, as confirmed in articles 74 and 83 on delimitation of the EEZ and the continental shelf respectively. After receiving a geological report, the commission concluded that the concept of natural prolongation "would not form a suitable basis for the solution of the outstanding issues."[141] Accordingly, it set itself the task of ascertaining "possible guidelines for the practicable and equitable solution of the questions concerned" in light of the interests, factors, and circumstances mentioned in the agreement between the governments.

In reviewing the variety of ocean delimitation solutions to be found in state practice,[142] the commission quoted the International Court of Justice's view of the "balancing of equities" process inherent in diplomatic ocean boundary delimitation: "In fact, there is no legal limit to the considerations which States may take account of for the purpose of making sure that they apply equitable procedures, and more often than not it is the balancing-up of all such considerations that will produce this result rather than one to the exclusion of all others. The problem of the relevant weight to be accorded to different considerations naturally varies with the circumstances of the case."[143] The commission concluded that the proper approach should take into account "both the fact that agreement by Iceland and Norway on Iceland's 200-mile economic zone has already given Iceland a considerable area beyond the median line and the fact that the uncertainties with respect to the resource potential of the area create a need for further research and exploration." Rather than propose a demarcation line for the continental shelf, the commission recommended the adoption of a joint development agreement covering "substantially all of the area offering any significant prospect of hydrocarbon production."[144] The commission suggested co-ordinates for a joint development area comprising 45,475 square kilometres, almost three-quarters of which would lie beyond the northeasterly seaward limits of Iceland's 200-mile EEZ.

Thus, instead of proposing a "settlement" in the form of a line, the commission suggested a system of co-operative "arrangements" for joint development in the designated area, covering the pre-drilling, drilling, and development stages. In discussing the final (development) stage, the commission described the four main types of joint co-operation arrangments in common use around the world,[145] and expressed its preference for a joint venture agreement as the most viable for the two governments in question. Financial and legislative implications were discussed, and recommendations were made on unitization, exploitation, and distribution procedures in the event that a petroleum deposit was found to extend on both sides of a demarcation line.[146]

Despite the fact that the commission went beyond its terms of reference in its facilitative role – that is, in its suggestions for co-operative seabed arrangements – its recommendations were accepted in toto by the two governments. The two national members of the commission were appointed to draft a second Norwegian-Icelandic agreement based on the commission's report, and that treaty was signed in October 1981. The parties agreed to participate in co-operative arrangements for the exploration and exploitation of the mineral resources within a designated rectangular area straddling the continental shelf boundary and to resort to conciliation in the event of a future dispute.[147] Such a flexible approach, accomplished through a combination of settlements and arrangements, can be recommended to other regions, although not many states will wish to be so generous as Norway was in its acceptance of the 1980 and 1981 Jan Mayen agreements.[148]

The Jan Mayen Conciliation Commission cannot be considered as representative of the adjudicative, much less the judicial, mode of ocean boundary-making. Yet its quasi-adjudicative task of weighting the relevant considerations ("balancing the equities") inherent in delimitation might be compared with that entrusted to tribunals. Since two of the three members of the commission were nationals of the states in dispute, this exercise in conciliation fell between the typical modes of diplomacy and adjudication. From a functionalist perspective, the resort to conciliation in this situation was an enlightened and imaginative approach to boundary-making. Informal and expeditious, it provided an opportunity to avoid voluminous and costly research and argument by eliminating extraneous data and issues and focusing attention on the most relevant facts and considerations. It is a model that deserves attention, especially by those who view adjudication as a facilitative rather than a resolutive process.[149] Especially useful is its identification of the six principal "solutions" and the four main types of co-operative "arrangements."[150]

Delimitation Issues and the Law-Making Process (UNCLOS III)

By the summer of 1974, when substantive negotiations began at UNCLOS III, it had become necessary, even for traditionally oriented lawyers, to concede that the Conference represented an unprecedented diplomatic effort to refashion the law of the sea. Specifically, the agenda seemed to commit the delegations to seek consensus on a new rule or formula for ocean boundary delimitation. In the years following 1974, it became increasingly perilous for adjudicators to ignore the changes in the making on the ground that it might be many years before the UNCLOS III Convention came into force under the law of treaties. The global process of negotiation at the Conference had to be accepted by jurists as a conspicuous part of the phenomenon of state practice reflecting the growth of the customary international law of the sea. At the Conference itself the delegates knew that the delimitation provisions to be negotiated would have to serve as both customary and conventional "rules" of international law. For that reason it was particularly important to secure the widest possible consensus.[151]

In the early years of UNCLOS III the delimitation proposals advanced by the delegations were heavily influenced by the adjudicative awards made since 1969. In that year the *North Sea Continental Shelf* award by the ICJ had given weight to the notion of equitable principles as the way to pursue a "basic norm" of delimitation. The United Kingdom-France Arbitration of 1977 had developed the earlier concept of a single equidistance-special circumstances "rule" derived from the 1958 Convention on the Continental Shelf, and had found some evidence of a trend to that form of compromise between the equidistance and equity factions negotiating at the 1976 sessions of UNCLOS III.[152] By 1977, however, the UNCLOS III negotiations on delimitation had become more active, and in the years thereafter the influence of trends at UNCLOS III on adjudicative awards became more conspicuous than the reverse influence. As we have seen, the conciliation commission in the Jan Mayen dispute relied on the delimitation provisions of the draft convention prepared at UNCLOS III in August 1980.

The UNCLOS III negotiations dealt with the issue of opposite or adjacent states under three separate regimes: the territorial sea (article 15), the exclusive economic zone (article 74), and the continental shelf (article 83). Throughout the negotiating process the delegations focused on three principal issues: (1) the criteria for delimitation; (2) interim arrangements pending agreement between the parties; and (3) the settlement of delimitation disputes. Some of the features of the final outcome became discernible as early as 1975, when it was proposed that the territorial sea provision should be based on article 12 of the 1958 Convention on the Territorial Sea and the Contiguous Zone, and that the provisions on the EEZ and the continental shelf should be indentical, without differentiation between opposite and adjacent states. But despite progress toward consensus on interim arrangements and dispute settlement, consensus on delimitation criteria for articles 74(1) and 83(1) continued to be elusive.[153] Failing any compromise between the equidistance and equity groups, a new approach was taken in the late summer of 1981, at the initiative of the president (Tommy Koh of Singapore) assisted by the Fijian delegate (Satya Nandan). After intensive consultations between the two interest groups, this new proposal was accepted with minor amendments.[154] In their final form the identical provisions read as follows: "The delimitation of the exclusive economic zone/continental shelf between States with opposite or adjacent coasts shall be effected by agreement on the basis of international law, as referred to in Article 38 of the Statute of the International Court of Justice, in order to achieve an equitable solution."

This final formulation is, admittedly, very different from what the delegates had been trying to negotiate for so many years. With this provision the equity group achieved the elimination of any express reference to equidistance, and substituted the vague reference to an "equitable solution" for the more familiar concept of "equitable principles." The provision has been severely criticized by the advocates of equidistance or some other reasonably precise guide.[155]

The open-endedness of the final outcome is even more marked in the second paragraph of articles 74 and 83, which requires that the parties to a delimitation issue that cannot be resolved by agreement "within a reasonable period of time" shall resort to a chosen form of dispute settlement, but fails to provide any guide, however imprecise, to the adjudicators:

"2. If no agreement can be reached within a reasonable period of time the States concerned shall resort to the procedures provided for in Part XV."

Less controversially, the remaining paragraphs of the articles provide for interim arrangements and special situations:

3. Pending agreement as provided for in paragraph 1, the States concerned, in a spirit of understanding and cooperation, shall make every effort to enter into provisional arangements of a practical nature and, during this provisional period, not to jeopardize or hamper the reaching of the final agreement. Such arrangements shall be without prejudice to the final delimitation.
4. Where this is an agreement in force between the States concerned, questions relating to the delimitation of the exclusive economic zone shall be determined in accordance with the provisions of that agreement.

From a "unitarian" perspective, the open-endedness of articles 74 and 83 can be criticized as a lost opportunity to develop or consolidate legal rules, principles, criteria, or methods for the delimitation of boundaries between opposite or adjacent states. In particular, it can be criticized for the omission of any linkage with the language of adjudication, such as equidistance, "special circumstances," or "equitable principles." The reference to an "equitable solution," limited to the purposes of negotiation, is regarded as too vague to be of any value as a guide to the making of boundary agreements.

From a functionalist perspective, however, the open-endedness of these law-making provisions is construed less as a problem of treaty interpretation than as an encouragement to negotiators and adjudicators to concentrate on the boundary-making problem in a particularistic manner, with minimal constraints by reason of extra-situational considerations. The need for innovation and ingenuity within this context of ocean boundary-making is seen to outweigh the need for certainty as to the applicable norms. At present, the first priority should be to help negotiators and adjudicators find equitable, but also effective, solutions to the problems of establishing appropriate "boundary and boundary-related settlements and arrangements," and articles 74 and 83 appear conducive to that end.

The Tunisian–Libyan Continental Shelf Case (1982)

The prospect of offshore petroleum production has generated boundary delimitation disputes around the world, but only in the Mediterranean have such disputes been referred to adjudicative proceedings on three separate occasions. The first occasion was the unsuccessful effort by Greece to effect judicial settlement of its Aegean Sea continental shelf boundary dispute with Turkey. The second concerned the continental shelf area adjacent to the coasts of Tunisia and Libya. The third Mediterranean resort to adjudication was by Libya and Malta only a few years after the dispute between Tunisia and Libya was submitted to the International Court of Justice.

Unable to settle their boundary dispute through diplomacy, the governments of Libya and Tunisia signed a special agreement in June 1977, setting out the terms of reference to the International Court of Justice.[156] In article 1 of the special agreement the parties asked the ICJ to determine the applicable "principles and rules of international law," and in rendering its decision to "take account of equitable principles and the relevant circumstances which characterize the area, as well as the recent trends admitted at the Third Conference on the Law of the Sea."[157] They also asked the Court to "specify precisely the practical way in which the aforesaid principles and rules apply in this particular situation, so as to enable the experts of the two countries to delimit those areas without any difficulties." In article 2 it was agreed that as soon as the Court's judgment was delivered, the two governments would meet to put these principles and rules into effect through a negotiated boundary delimitation treaty. If such a treaty could not be negotiated within three months, the two governments agreed (in article 3) that they would "together go back to the Court and request such explanations or clarifications as may facilitate the task of the two delegations, to arrive at the line separating the two areas of the continental shelf, and the two Parties shall comply with the Judgment of the Court and with its explanation and clarifications."[158]

In its majority judgment,[159] the Court noted the three "factors" of decision-making stipulated in the special agreement, and, though it was "bound to have regard" to all the legal sources specified in article 38(1) of the Statute of the Court, seemed to accept a prevalent obligation under the same article to apply the provisions of the special agreement. Accordingly, its judgment was framed around the three stipulated "factors": (1) equitable principles; (2) the relevant circumstances that characterized the area; and (3) the newly accepted trends at UNCLOS III. While the first two categories were acknowledged to be in "complete harmony" with the jurisprudence of the Court since the *North Sea Continental Shelf* case of 1969, the inclusion of the third required the Court to take a less tentative view of UNCLOS III trends than it had in the *Fisheries Jurisdiction* decision of 1974. (See the section entitled "The New Law of the Sea" in chapter 9.) In a significant sentence, the Court conceded that it "would have had *proprio motu* to take account of the progress made by the Conference, even if the Parties had not alluded to it in their Special Agreement, for it could not ignore any provision of the draft convention if it came to the conclusion that the content of such provision is binding upon all members of the international community, because it embodies or crystallizes a pre-existing or emergent rule of customary law."[160]

The mandate in article 1 requiring the Court to clarify a "practical method" for the application of the appropriate principles and rules was understood to impose a facilitative role on the Court. In oral proceedings, it was noted, both parties had agreed that the present case "would seem to lie between the *North Sea Continental Shelf* cases of 1969, in which the Court was asked only to indicate what principles and rules of international law were applicable to the delimitation, and the *Franco-British Arbitration on the Delimitation of the Continental Shelf* of 1977, in which the court of arbitration was requested to decide what was the course of the boundary between the portions of the continental shelf appertaining to each of the Parties in the relevant area." Faced with a difference between the parties in the interpretation of the original Arabic text, the Court found there was no substantial distinction between a "method of delimitation" and a "practical method for the application ... of principles and rules," only a "difference of emphasis as to the respective roles of the Court and of the experts of the two countries."[161] A difference of interpretation had also arisen over article 3 of the special agreement, but the Court held that it was premature to arrive at a determination of that issue.

In their written and oral arguments, both Libya and Tunisia leaned heavily on the meaning and applicability of the ICJ's own doctrine of "natural prolongation" as enunciated in the *North Sea Continental Shelf* decision of 1969.[162] But the Court rejected the major premise of both parties that the concept of natural prolongation had a central role in the legal theory of boundary delimitation, at least on the facts presented. Without going so far as to deny explicitly the ratio decidendi status of that doctrine in its 1969 decision, the Court emphasized that the concept of natural prolongation served as the basis of a coastal state's "legal title to continental shelf rights," but did not necessarily provide "criteria applicable to the delimitation of the areas appertaining to adjacent States."[163] The inclusion of the words "natural prolongation" in article 76 of the Draft Convention on the Law of the Sea did nothing to increase its utility as a delimitative principle. In the first place, that article dealt with the determination of seaward limits and was stated to be "without prejudice to the question of delimitation of the continental shelf between States with opposite or adjacent coasts."[164] In the second place, the redefinition of the continental shelf in article 76(1) had changed dramatically from the language of article 1 of the 1958 Convention on the Continental Shelf. Not only had the exploitability "test" been discarded, but a distance criterion – "mere distance from the coast" – had been introduced, in certain (indeed, normal) circumstances, as the basis of the coastal state's entitlement to a continental shelf. Accordingly, the UNCLOS III definition in article 76 afforded "no criterion for delimitation in the present case."[165] Instead, the Court continued, the most relevant trend at UNCLOS III was the change of focus in article 83(1), in its new formulation introduced by the president of the Conference in August 1981, with an emphasis on the need for an "equitable solution." In this new formulation, "any indication of a specific criterion which could give guidance to the interested States in their effort to achieve an equitable solution has been excluded. Emphasis is placed on the equitable solution which has to be achieved. The principles and rules applicable to the delimitation of continental shelf areas are those which are appropriate to bring about an equitable result ..."[166]

This turning away from the "natural prolongation" doctrine to a search for an "equitable solution" resulted in a considerable scaling down of the significance of the geological evidence presented by the parties. The Court firmly declined the invitation to choose between two competing interpretations of natural prolongation as a geological concept, noting that "for legal purposes it is not possible to define the areas of continental shelf appertaining to Tunisia and to Libya by reference solely or mainly to geological considerations. The function of the Court is to make use of geology only so far as required for the application of international law. It is of the view that what must be taken into account in the delimitation of shelf areas are the physical circumstances as they are today ... It is the outcome, not the evolution in the long-distant past, which is of importance."[167]

Counsel for both parties fared little better with the evidence presented from the fields of geomorphology and bathymetry. In holding that the physical structure of the seabed area in dispute "does not contain any element which interrupts the continuity of the continental shelf," the Court emphasized that "the physical factor constituting the natural prolongation" was only "one of several circumstances considered to be the elements of an equitable solution"; that is, configurational considerations of this kind, resting on geomorphological and bathymetric evidence, must be evaluated within the context of a larger examination of the "relevant circumstances which characterize the area."[168]

Obliged to decide the case on the basis of "equitable principles," as requested in the special agreement, the Court had the same difficulty as counsel in focusing on any specific set of norms. "This terminology, which is generally used, is not entirely satisfactory because it employs the term equitable to characterize both the result to be achieved and the means to be applied to reach this result. It is, however, the result which is predominant; the principles are subordinate to the goal. The equitableness of a principle must be assessed in light of its usefulness for the purpose of arriving at an equitable result ... The principles to be indicated by the Court have to be selected according to their appropriateness for reaching an equitable result."[169] Accordingly, the Court seems to have come close to saying that the phrase "equitable principles" is essentially an undesignated reference to the entire realm of "normative considerations," serving to emphasize the need to weigh those considerations, in the light of all relevant circumstances, with a view to the all-important purpose of providing an equitable solution.

Finally, the Court turned to an examination of the "relevant circumstances which characterize the area." Above all, this task required the judges to "determine with greater precision what is the area in dispute between the Parties and what is the area which is relevant to the delimitation." In defining the area that was to be the focus of the delimitation issue (the "focal area") the court rejected the argument that the whole of the coast of each of the neighbouring states must be taken into account. "It is clear from the map that there comes a point on the coast of each of the two Parties beyond which the coast in question no longer has a relationship with the coast of the other Party relevant for submarine delimitation. The sea-bed areas off the coast beyond that point cannot therefore constitute an area of overlap of the extensions of the territories of the two Parties, and are therefore not relevant to the delimitation."[170] The focal area was defined to lie between Ras Kaboudia on the Tunisian coast and Ras Tajoura on the Libyan coast (see figure 7).

Among the elements considered was "the general configuration of the coasts of the Parties, as well as the presence of any special or unusual features" as specified in the ICJ's *North Sea Continental Shelf* decision.[171] In this examination, however, the Court went beyond the facts of geography and geomorphology to a review of alleged maritime limits resulting from the conduct of the States concerned, the historic rights claimed by Tunisia, and a number of economic considerations urged as relevant by one or other of the governments.[172] Because of the Court's final dispositon of the delimitation issue, it was unnecessary to deal with the legal effect of Tunisia's historic rights. Economic considerations were held to be "virtually extraneous factors which could not be taken into account for purposes of delimitation, being variables which unpredictable national fortune or calamity, as the case may be, might at any time cause to tilt the scale one way or the other."[173]

In addressing itself to the task of choosing a practical method of delimitation, the Court made it clear once again that equidistance had no preferential legal status, at least in the situation of adjacent states. There was no presumption in favour of equidistance.[174] That the Court had found it necessary to define the focal area between Ras Kaboudia and Ras Tajoura did not imply that the area was considered to possess "such geographical homogeneity as to justify the application of a single method of delimitation throughout its extent."[175] On the contrary, the area close to the coasts of the neighbouring states had to be treated differently from the areas

FIGURE 7: Tunisian-Libyan Continental Shelf Case

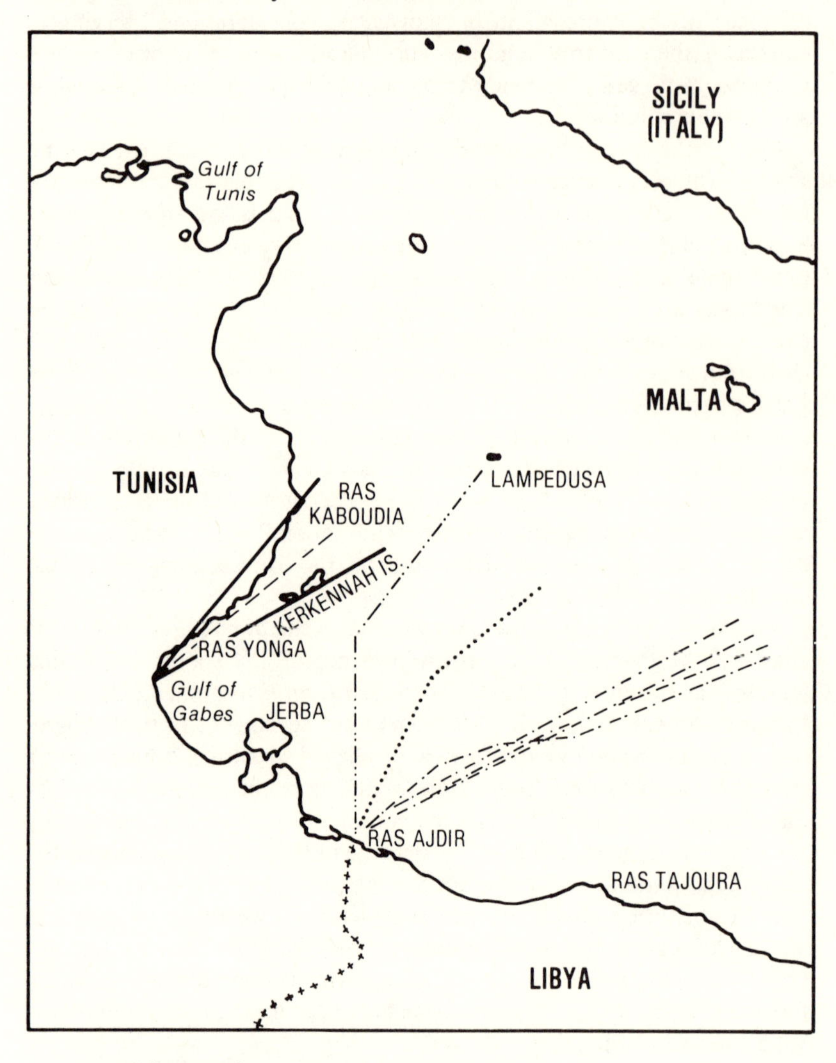

_ .. __ .. __ Libyan claim.
__ . __ . __ Tunisian claim (sheaf of lines).
— — — Line used by International Court of Justice to illustrate result of assigning half-effect to the Kerkennah Islands.
.... Line illustrating judgment of International Court of Justice, 1982.

further offshore. Accordingly, the Court divided the focal area into two sectors for differential treatment.

In the area closer to shore, the court was strongly influenced by the fact that both countries, in their separate petroleum concessions, had followed a de facto straight line that lay at an angle of 26° to the meridian. Adopting the logic of functionalism, the Court found this de facto line to have "great relevance." Its acceptability as a legal boundary was reinforced by reason of its earlier use by France and Italy, when they were colonial powers in the region, as a modus vivendi for the delimitation of fishing areas, drawn from the land frontier between the two territories at an angle of approximately 26° to the meridian, which was proposed on the basis of perpendicularity to the coast. The Court recalled that "in the context of delimitation of the territorial sea the methods of delimitation, other than equidistance, examined by the Committee of Experts for the International Law Commission in 1953 were the continuation in the seaward direction of the land frontier, the drawing of a line perpendicular to the coast at the point of its intersection with the land frontier, and the drawing of a line perpendicular to the line of general direction of the coast."[176] Accordingly, the 26° de facto line had the further merit of some precedential basis in legal and diplomatic history. This line was, therefore, extended seaward to the point of intersection with a parallel of latitude that was selected because of the abrupt change in the general direction of the Tunisian coast to the west of the Gulf of Gabes. In any event, the Court noted, "a line drawn perpendicular to the coast becomes, generally speaking, the less suitable as a line of delimitation the further it extends from the coast," even without such an abrupt change in its general direction. Moreover, the delimitation line should be drawn, further seaward, in such a way as to give some effect to the location of the Kerkennah Islands, "surrounded by islets and low-tide elevations, and constituting by their size and position a circumstance relevant for the delimitation."[177] By giving half-effect to the Kerkennahs, the Court introduced a deviation further seaward from the 26° line, veering northeast at an angle of 52° to the meridian.

In conclusion, the majority emphasized the specificity or particularity of the reasoning employed. "Clearly each continental shelf case in dispute should be considered and judged on its own merits, having regard to its peculiar circumstances; therefore, no attempt should be made here to overconceptualize the application of the principles and rules relating to the continental shelf."[178]

The majority decision was strongly challenged by three of the four dissenting judges, Judges Gros and Oda and Judge (ad hoc) Evensen. Judge Gros's dissenting opinion seems to acquiesce in the downgrading of the natural prolongation doctrine for the purposes of delimitation, but to object to the relegation of equidistance. Although the majority decision purported to deal even-handedly with all potentially applicable methods of delimitation, Judge Gros felt that no serious effort had been made to test the equitableness of the effect of applying the equidistance method;[179] nor, indeed, of any other method, including the actual use of a perpendicular line.[180] In drawing lines the majority not only eliminated geology but also effaced the Tunisian coastline. As to the 26° line drawn by the Court in the near-shore sector of the area in dispute, Judge Gros criticized the justifications offered by the majority, which were based on the concordance of three kinds of facts: the historical fact that the line had been fixed unilaterally by Italy, as a colonial power, as early as 1919; the functional fact that the same line had been used by both Libya and Tunisia for the administrative demarcation of petroleum concession areas; and what might be termed the diplomatic fact that use had been made, in some delimitations between adjacent states, of perpendicular lines, including the line perpendicular to the land frontier. From these "chance encounters" the majority judgment had deduced "something more than mere factual concordance: namely proof of the equitable character of the line delimiting the continental shelf as between the Parties."[181] The Court's reliance on "controversial and fragile arguments" raised fundamental questions about its approach to the determination of an equitable solution, which was characterized by Judge Gros as "subjective." But above all he dissented from the majority's acceptance of a facilitative role in the proceedings. The role of the ICJ was to "declare the law, not attempt a conciliation" between the parties.[182]

Judge Oda's dissenting opinion consists of a lengthy critical analysis of the issues and evidence presented,[183] and it differs from the majority decision on several essential matters. First, in Judge Oda's view, the Court failed to arrive at a proper appreciation of the "trends" at UNCLOS III. Second, the Court failed to develop the "positive principles and rules of international law" applicable to ocean boundary delimitation. Third, no attempt was made to prove how the application of the equidistance method would lead to an inequitable result. Fourth, the line suggested by the Court was "not grounded on any persuasive considerations," and, in particular, the way in which the Court justified the veering-off of the line further seaward at an angle of 52° to the meridian was "entirely obscure."[184]

On the first point, Judge Oda regretted that the Court had chosen to give weight to the current delimitation provisions of the Draft Convention on the Law of the Sea at a time when the negotiation process was not formally completed. The familiar treaty-law requirements of signature and ratification served to qualify the juridical significance of mere "trends" at a treaty-making conference, but these new delimitation provisions were too recent to be reflected in state practice in the form of bilateral delimitation agreements. Judge Oda likened UNCLOS III to a laboratory that had not yet provided a finished product, and critized the Court for not casting its net more widely.[185]

On the second and third points Judge Oda was even more explicitly "unitarian" than Judge Gros, emphasizing the importance of the ICJ's role in developing a coherent body of doctrine to govern ocean boundary delimitation. Faced with the apparent primacy of diplomatic boundary-making, Judge Oda was prepared to espouse the extreme view that the "equidistance/special circumstances" method of delimitation prescribed in article 6 of the 1958 Convention on the Continental Shelf should be supported by the Court as "a normal basis of agreement as well as of third-party determination," even though this interpretation was clearly not intended by the drafters of the Convention.[186] On the third point, Judge Oda expressed his regret that the Court had virtually neglected the merits of equidistance, which he blamed on the Court's earlier decision to reject equidistance in the *North Sea Continental Shelf* cases.[187] As if to save himself from the suspicion of underrating the juridical significance of UNCLOS III, Judge Oda criticized the majority for neglecting the linkage effected there between delimitation of the shelf and delimitation of the EEZ.[188] Although he adopted a conservative view of the status of the EEZ in international law,[189] Judge Oda suggested that the logic of the linkage required the Court to give some weight to distance criteria in delimitation cases, since distance is now intrinsic to "the latest concept of the continental shelf" as well as to that of the EEZ.

As to the practical method to be employed, Judge Oda admitted to confusion over the Court's justifications for the suggested two-segment line of delimitation: "In fact," he averred, "the Court fails to adduce any cogent ground for either segment of the line, or for the line as a whole, a line which does not exemplify any principle or rule of international law."[190] The Court had engaged in a highly discretionary process of boundary-making with minimal regard for the principles and rules of international law, as if the matter had been submitted for adjudication *ex aequo et bono* instead of by reference to equitable principles. He concluded by recommending a line of delimitation equidistant from the coasts of Libya and Tunisia that disregards all the low-tide elevations off both coasts and the existence of the Kerkennah Islands.

Judge Evensen agrees with Judge Oda that the Court should have given much more weight to the juridical significance of the UNCLOS III linkage between the shelf and the EEZ, since "it is hardly conceivable in the present case to draw a different line of delimitation" for the two regimes.[191] The majority judgment was too restrictive in maintaining that the applicable principles and rules of international law must be derived from the concept of the continental shelf itself. He agreed with Judge Oda that the Court should have been more scrupulous in maintaining the "very delicate" distinction between a decision based on equitable principles and a decision *ex aequo et bono*. To avoid a blurring of this distinction, "the equity considerations to be applied must be placed in some legal context," and one legal principle "which obviously may play a role in this case as a corollary to equity considerations" is the equidistance principle.[192] In its "almost total disregard or belittlement" of the equidistance method, the Court was clearly at variance with its own acknowledgment in 1969 that equidistance possessed the merit of convenience and could be used "in almost all circumstances." Likewise, the Court had disregarded "the fact that the equidistance/median line principle is the only concrete principle added to the broad reference to equity" at UNCLOS III for the purposes of shelf and EEZ delimitations between adjacent and opposite states.[193] The Court had also disregarded the use of equidistance in the *Anglo-French Continental Shelf* arbitration, and in "numerous delimitation agreements and enactments" for both the shelf and the EEZ.[194] Judge Evensen objected to the "relegation of the equidistance principle to the last rank of practical methods."[195] Giving only half-effect to the Kerkennah Archipelago and at the same time disregarding completely the low-tide elevations surrounding it was "not warranted in law and does not correspond to equity." Like Judge Oda, he was "deeply concerned" that the 26° line was "discretionary rather than equitable." The choice of a perpendicular line was criticized, as was the Court's "elevation" of the "proportionality test," applied as a "mathematical formula," to the "status of international law." Accordingly, "the equidistance principle would, in the present case – adjusted or tempered by considerations of equity – have given a more equitable and a more verifiable solution than the line given by the Court."[196]

At the end of his dissenting opinion, Judge Evensen added the functionalist suggestion that the parties negotiate an arrangement for "joint exploration, user or even joint jurisdiction over restricted overlapping areas" as "a corollary to other equity considerations," working together on the basis of a joint policy of exploration and exploitation, in the spirit of the "principle of co-operation."[197]

Neither the majority judgments nor any of the separate or dissenting opinions made reference to the application for permission to intervene in the *Tunisian-Libyan Continental Shelf* case filed by the government of Malta in January 1981. That application was based on the contention that Malta, as the opposite state only two hundred miles distant from the African coast, had "an interest of a legal nature which may be affected by the decision in the case," in the language of Article 2 of the Statute of the

International Court of Justice. Malta's legal interest in the outcome was said to be founded on the following considerations:

> In Malta's case there is a continental shelf boundary with both Libya and Tunisia, and the boundaries between all three States *converge at a single, as yet undetermined, point*. Given the proximity of Libya, Tunisia and Malta, "principles and rules of international law" applicable to the delimitation of the Libya/Tunisia boundary are bound to be relevant to the delimitation of the Malta/Libya and Malta/Tunisia boundaries. Furthermore, there is a substantial probability that many of the "relevant circumstances" – geographic, geologic, geomorphic, economic, and other – which affect the determination of the boundary between Libya and Tunisia would also be relevant to the determination of Malta's boundaries with those two States. The Court's treatment of such factors in the *Libya/Tunisia* case is thus bound to affect the treatment of the same factors in a subsequent case involving Malta's boundaries.[198]

However, in a judgment dated 14 April 1981, the Court found that Malta's request could not be granted. By seeking a "direct yet limited form of participation in the subject-matter of the proceedings," Malta was also seeking "an opportunity to submit arguments to the Court with possibly prejudicial effects on the interests of either Libya or of Tunisia in their mutual relations with one another. To allow such a form of 'intervention' would, in the particular circumstances of the present case, also leave the Parties quite uncertain as to whether or how far they should consider their own separate legal interests vis-à-vis Malta as in effect constituting part of the subject-matter of the present case."[199]

The rationale of this unanimous decision by the Court[200] is not quite clear. Either it is that the third-party intervention mechanism should not be used in any way that might be prejudicial to the interests of the parties initiating the litigation, since the aplicant has not "submitted" to the Court in the sense of agreeing to be bound by its eventual decision; or it is that intervention must not be permitted to obligate the Court to refrain from adopting or applying norms it might otherwise consider appropriate as between the litigants. By either form of reasoning it was left uncertain how such an application could succeed.

The matter was not resolved by the Court's judgment on the merits of the case between Libya and Tunisia dated 24 February 1982. In accordance with article 2 of the special agreement of 10 June 1977, the two governments met on several occasions to attempt to implement the Court's ruling in a negotiated boundary delimitation treaty, but they were unable to agree on the interpretation of the majority judgment. Accordingly, in July 1984, after two years of fruitless negotiations, Tunisia submitted an application for revision and interpretation of the 1982 judgment. Tunisia's difficulties concerned the determination of the straight line constituting the delimitation line in the first sector indicated by the Court, and the identification of the point determining the parallel which marks the change in the bearing of the delimitation line in the second sector.[201] Until these two points were clarified, it was argued, the two countries could not proceed to the application of the "practical method" favoured by the Court "in such a way as to draw a delimitation line as precisely as possible, using the most efficient marine geodetic techniques, which nowadays produce results accurate to within a few yards."[202]

Since this was the first time the ICJ had been asked to *revise* a boundary award, Tunisia set out the legal bases for its applicaton at some length. In accordance with article 61 of the Statute of the Court, Tunisia attempted to show the discovery of a new fact, a "decisive factor" that was not known to the Court at the time of its decision – namely, the discovery of the text of an official Libyan document which determines the true course of the north-western boundary of Libyan concession No. 137, a course which ... is very different from the one emerging from the descriptions Libya gave during the written and oral proceedings."[203]

In the event that the Court did not agree to revise its judgment in light of this "new fact," Tuisia requested an *interpretation* of the judgment by means of clarification of "the hierarchy to be established between the criteria adopted by the Court." This request for an interpretation did not concern the legal reasoning of the Court or the principles advanced in the decision, but only "those elements of the Judgment of which the Parties' experts can make direct use for the drawing of the line," such as the exact location of the starting-point of the delimitation line and, above all, the identification of the most westerly point of the Gulf of Gabes.[204]

In its judgment the Court concluded that Tunisia, with proper diligence, could have ascertained the co-ordinates of the oil concessions granted under the Libyan Petroleum Regulations of 1955, and therefore could not be said to have satisfied all the conditions of admissibility of a request for revision laid down in paragraph 1 of article 61 of the statute.[205] Moreover, although the Court found the Tunisian request for interpretation in the first sector to be admissible, it rejected Tunisia's submission as to the correct interpretation.[206]

In conclusion, four comments can be offered on the *Tunisian-Libyan Continental Shelf* case of 1982. Two are of special relevance to the functionalist theory of ocean boundary-making, and two are of a more general sort. First, the decision underlines the ICJ's attentiveness to its facilitative role in ocean boundary delimitation. To the dismay of "unitarian" dissenters and commentators, the majority revealed a disposition to focus on the need for an equitable solution to the boundary-making problem even at the expense of any juridical contribution to the consolidation of normative considerations. In virtually abolishing the doctrine of natural prolongation as a concept relevant to the task of delimitation, the Court threw out one of the props in the doctrinal edifice erected by counsel. In responding to the arguments for Tunisia, it re-emphasized that equidistance should not be accorded any particular normative status. Indeed, the Court went further in treating equidistance as simply one of several possible methods, one which, on the facts, did not seem the most appropriate for producing an equitable solution. There is no textual evidence that the majority relegated equidistance to the "last rank of practical methods" as suggested in the Evensen dissent, although it is unfortunate that the judges did not give reasons for rejecting that method, given its utility and widespread use in many parts of the world. The majority's justifications for choosing perpendicularity over equidistance drew upon non-situational rather than situational factors, to the further detriment of "unitarian" logic, which, in the absence of a firm doctrinal base, seeks to sharpen the focus on the circumstances of the situation, especially the physical features presented through geological, geomorphological, and bathymetrical evidence. In accepting the subjectivity inherent in any explicit quest for an equitable, as distinct from a strictly legal, solution, the Court exposed itself to the charge of adopting a discretionary approach which compounds the difficulty of case preparation for counsel in future litigation befor the ICJ. Unintentionally, the majority decision may have rendered futile the alleged *substantive* distinction between an "equitable solution" decision and a decision *ex aequo et bono*.[207]

Second, from the functionalist viewpoint, the majority's acceptance of the subjectivity inherent in the quest for equity would have been more appropriate if a more determined effort had been made to supplement the test of equity with that of effectiveness. If the majority had been prepared to admit to the conciliatory aspect of the facilitative function entrusted to the Court, it might have begun the judicial process of developing criteria for determining the functionality of the proposed line as a line conducive to the exploration and exploitation of the shelf. In acknowledging the "great relevance" of the concession line accepted de facto by both governments, the Court came close to admitting that weight should be given to the consideration of operational convenience, but it was left to Judge Evensen in dissent to point out the need for sensible joint development arrangements. In the spirit of discharging its facilitative task, the Court might have endorsed the concept of joint development or similar co-operative arrangements between two adjacent states.[208]

Third, the *Tunisian-Libyan Continental Shelf* decision raised questions about the kind and volume of data that should be presented as evidence in a boundary case. The subjective tendencies inherent in a quest for an equitable solution might seem to put a premium of the objectivity of hard data obtained from geology, geomorphology, and bathymetry, but the significance of such evidence was discounted considerably in this case. It is difficult to know whether this was due chiefly to the volume of factual information presented, or to its technical nature, or merely, as the majority judgment suggests, to judicial reluctance to choose between scientific schools of interpretation. At the same time, it should be noted, the Court tried to discourage resort by counsel to the soft (or less hard) data required to support arguments based on economic considerations. This decision seems to raise more questions than it answers about the choice of evidence to be presented and the risk of overburdening the Court.

Finally, the trend to assigning a facilitative function to an adjudicative body raises the difficult question, What is an appropriate degree of technical precision to expect of such a body in the actual drawing of a line on a rounded surface, or even in the furnishing of guidelines prior to that process?[209] Whatever the answer, by the end of 1987 the parties had not yet negotiated a boundary agreement based on the Court's facilitative award.

Canadian-U.S. Maritime Boundary Case: The Gulf of Maine (1984)

The Gulf of Maine dispute between Canada and the United States originated in the 1960s, at a time when these countries were beginning to explore for hydrocarbon resources off the continental shelf in the offshore waters of the northwest Atlantic. Both governments began to issue exploration permits in the Gulf of Maine in 1964, and in 1966 they initiated diplomatic talks that soon revealed the need for formal delimitation negotiations. By the end of 1969 the existence of an official "issue" involving the continental shelf boundary in the region was clearly established, and formal negotiations were begun in July 1970.

The Canadian position during negotiations was that no special circumstances existed in the area and that the continental shelf boundary should therefore follow the equidistance line as contemplated by article 6 of the 1958 Convention on the Continental Shelf, to which Canada had just become a party. In ratifying the Convention, Canada had appended a declaration that "the presence of an accidental feature such as a depression or channel in a submerged area should not be regarded as constituting an interruption in the natural prolongation."[210] This declaration, which drew a formal objection from the United States, was intended to protect Canada's position on the juridical significance of the Northeast (or Fundian) Channel between Brown's Bank and Georges Bank in the Gulf of Maine area (see figure 8). During negotiations the U.S. government asserted the inequitableness of the equidistance line in view of the existence of "special circumstances" and proposed that the continental shelf bound-

FIGURE 8: Gulf of Maine Case

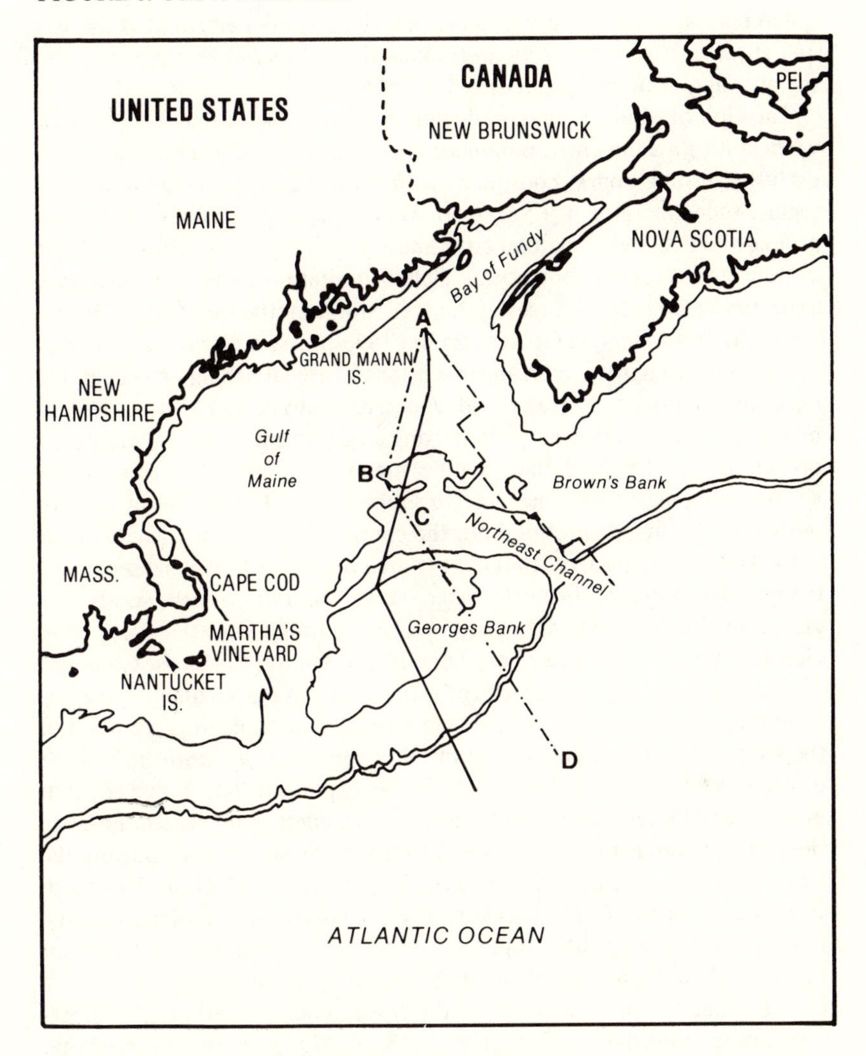

- - - - Revised US claim, 1982.
——— Revised Canadian claim, 1977.
-.-.-. Boundary line drawn by Chamber of International Court of Justice, 1984.

ary follow the Northeast Channel. The parties were unable to resolve their differences at the negotiating table, and the dispute deteriorated in 1975 and 1976 as the U.S. government took additional measures preparatory to the granting of oil and gas leases.

The Gulf of Maine boundary dispute acquired a new dimension in 1976, when both governments announced their intention to establish 200-mile exclusive fishing zones, consonant with the concept of the 200-mile EEZ regime then emerging at UNCLOS III. With these fishing zones established around the U.S. and Canadian coastlines early in 1977, the Gulf of Maine dispute grew from a continental shelf delimitation issue to a boundary issue concerning all resources in the area, not least the rich scallop fishery in the shallow waters on Georges Bank.[211] Despite some temporary success in negotiating an interim arrangement for reciprocal fishing privileges, the injection of fishery interests and concerns complicated the process of boundary-making diplomacy. Reflecting a new emphasis on fishery development in New England, the U.S. government formalized its preference for a "common maritime zone" in November 1976 by publishing the coordinates of a line delimiting both the continental shelf and fishery zones in the Gulf of Maine area. In the inner area of the Gulf, this line separated the fishing grounds of the northeastern sector from those of the southwestern sector. In the outer area the U.S. line separated Brown's Bank from Georges Bank, reaching the continental slope via the Northeast Channel.

One year later, in November 1977, the Canadian government gave notice of an adjustment of its equidistance line based on its interpretation of the Court of Arbitration's award in the *Anglo-French Continental Shelf* decision rendered on 30 June 1977. It was explained that in light of that award Canada believed it was entitled to a boundary to the southeast of the original equidistance line, which would be drawn by disregarding the Cape Cod peninsula and the islands of Nantucket and Martha's Vineyard. In rejecting the new Canadian claim, the U.S. government contended that a line drawn in accord with "equitable principles" would take into account the coastal configuration of the area, including the concavity of the U.S. coastline and the protrusiveness of the Nova Scotia peninsula. In a subsequent note, published in September 1978, the United States asserted that Georges Bank is a natural prolongation of U.S. territory; that in view of the special circumstances in the region, neither the original nor the revised version of the equidistance line was in accordance with equitable principles; and that there was no justification in international law for discounting the effect of Cape Cod or the neighbouring islands in determining the course of the maritime boundary.

These were the basic positions of the two governments when an agreement was reached in March 1979 to submit two negotiated treaties to the processes of ratification: the Agreement on East Coast Fisheries Resources and the Treaty to Submit to Binding Dispute Settlement the Delimitation of the Maritime Boundary in the Gulf of Maine Area. These two instruments were made interdependent, designed to come into force together, but when the Fisheries Agreement proved to be controversial within the New England fishing industry and was withdrawn from consideration by the U.S. Senate, Canada agreed, somewhat reluctantly, to proceed to adjudication of the boundary dispute under the treaty despite the severance of the link with the agreement. In November 1981 Canada and the United States concluded a special agreement for the reference of the case to a chamber (that is, a panel) of the International Court of Justice – the first reference of its sort in the history of the Court.[212]

The special agreement asked the chamber, "in accordance with the principles and rules of international law applicable in the matter," to determine the course of "the single maritime boundary that divides the continental shelf and fisheries zones" of the two countries within a designated triangular area in the Gulf of Maine.[213] But the chamber was asked to go further and actually draw the boundary "in terms of geodetic lines, connecting geographic coordinates of points," and to depict the course of the boundary on designated charts, with the assistance of a technical expert nominated jointly by the two governments.[214] Because the Court was requested for the first time in its history to draw the actual boundary line, and to do so with precision, the chamber and its technical expert were required to utilize a number of technical criteria set out in the special agreement.[215] The decision of the chamber would be accepted by the parties as final and binding upon them; each agreed not to "claim or exercise sovereign rights or jurisdiction for any purpose over the waters or seabed and subsoil" on the other side of the judicially delineated boundary.[216] As to the seaward extension of the booundary – beyond the designated triangular area to which the chamber's jurisdiction was confined – the special agreement added provisions for negotiation or, if necessary, third-party settlement, which included the possibility of returning to the chamber for a second adjudication.[217]

Early in its majority judgment, which was rendered in October 1984, the chamber drew a distinction between the maritime boundary (*frontière maritime*), which was sought by the parties, and "a real *frontière* (boundary) between two sovereign States," suggesting that because "sovereign rights" or "partial jurisdiction," and not "sovereignty," were at stake, the "rights of third states in the areas in question cannot be in any way affected by the delimitation which the Chamber is required to effect."[218] Shortly thereafter the chamber again expressed its discomfort with the concept of a single maritime boundary, noting uneasily counsel's reference to article III, paragraph 1, of the special agreement, which envisaged that the boundary to be drawn "should be applicable to all aspects of the jurisdiction of the coastal State, not only jurisdiction as defined by international law in its present state, but also as it will be defined in future" (paragraph 26). However, it had been asked to draw the line "in accordance with the principles and rules of international law applicable in the matter as between the Parties," and the chamber proceeded in effect to ignore the significance of article III in the special agreement. Observing that the governments had "simply taken it for granted that it would be possible, both legally and materially, to draw a single boundary for two different jurisdictions," but had "not put forward any arguments in support of this assumption," the chamber conceded, with apparent unhappiness, that "there is certainly no rule of international law to the contrary, and, in the present case, there is no material impossibility in drawing a boundary of this kind" (paragraph 27).

The chamber adopted a minimalist position on the scope of existing "principles and rules" of customary international law deemed to govern ocean boundary delimitation, and especially on the scope of the elusive "equitable principles" held out as having special relevance to judicial boundary-making. Employing Occam's razor, the majority held that "the association of the terms 'rules' and 'principles' is no more than the use of a dual expression to convey one and the same idea," and expressed preference for the term "principles" because of its "more general and more fundamental character" (paragraph 79). Second, the chamber deemed it essential to stress the distinction between "principles and rules of international law" (or simply "principles") and "the various *equitable criteria* and *practical methods* that may be used to ensure *in concreto* that a particular situation is dealt with in accordance with the principles and rules in question [emphasis added]" (paragraph 80). The chamber's minimalist and differential approach to normative considerations was explained in the following language (at paragraph 81):

In a matter of this kind, international law – and in this respect the Chamber has logically to refer primarily to customary international law – can of its nature only provide a few basic legal principles, which lay down guidelines to be followed with a view to an essential objective. It cannot also be expected to specify the equitable criteria to be applied or the practical, often technical, method to be used for attaining that objective – which remain simply criteria and methods even where they are also, in a different sense, called "principles." Although the practice is still rather sparse, owing to the relative newness of the question, it too is there to demonstrate that each specific case is in the final analysis different from all the others, that it is monotypic, and that, more often than not, the most appropriate criteria, and the method or combination of methods most likely to yield a result consonant with what the law indicates, can only be determined in relation to each particular case and its specific characteristics ...

In this emphasis on the need for specificity in the treatment of ocean boundary delimitation issues, the chamber followed the previous adjudicative trend and reissued a judicial warning against the temptation to overconceptualize judicial awards in this area of international law.

Applying this scheme of terminology to article 6 of the 1958 Convention on the Continental Shelf, the chamber held that only the primacy of boundary-making by agreement, in the first sentence of paragraphs 1 and 2, could be described as a "principle." The thrust of this principle of consent (or agreement) was "to establish by implication that any delimitation of the continental shelf effected unilaterally by one State, regardless of the views of the other State or States concerned, is in international law not opposable to those States." By corollary, this principle of consent was perceived to entail application of the related rules as to the *duty to negotiate* with a view to reaching agreement and to do so in *good faith*, with a genuine intention to achieve a positive result [emphasis added]" (paragraph 87). This principle of consent, and the corollary duty to negotiate, and the rule of good faith, which are present in article 6 of the 1958 convention, were described as "principles already clearly affirmed by customary international law, principles which, for that reason, are undoubtedly of general application, valid for all States and in relation to all kinds of maritime delimitation" (paragraph 90). On the other hand, the second sentence of paragraphs 1 and 2 of article 6, which referred to "equidistance" and "special circumstances," contemplated "the use of specified *criteria* and *methods* for effecting the delimitation in cases where it has proved impossible to reach agreement [emphasis added]" (paragraph 88). This use of terminology was held to be consistent with usage in earlier adjudication and with the current boundary-making thinking reflected at UNCLOS III, where the 1982 obligation to achieve an "equitable solution" was added to the 1958 principle of consent, through the identical language of articles 74 and 83, thereby serving to "open the door to continuation of the development effected in this field by international case law" (paragraph 95).

After this clarification of delimitation concepts, the chamber turned, at the parties' request, to the task of identifying any "fundamental norm" of international law that could be said to govern any delimitation of the kind envisaged for the Gulf of Maine. According to Canada, the fundamental norm should require that the boundary be determined "according to the applicable law, in conformity with equitable principles, having regard to all relevant circumstances, in order to achieve an equitable result" (paragraph 99). The U.S. definition was identical, except for the omission of the phrase "according to the applicable law," but in oral arguments the U.S. counsel waived any objection to the phrase.

The parties were divided, however, on the identification of any other "rules" or "corollaries" of mandatory application to ocean boundary delimitaton. The chamber denied the existence of any "rule" based on the concept of adjacency, proximity, or distance, as suggested by Canada. Such arguments were invalid, being nothing more than "another attempt to turn equidistance into a genuine *rule of law*, one to which general international law has supposedly given expression while yet tempering it to take account of special circumstances, and thus into something other than it is in reality: a *practical method* that can be applied for the purposes of delimitation [emphasis added]" (paragraph 106). The equidistance method had "rendered undeniable service in many concrete situations, and is a practical method whose use under certain conditions could be contemplated and made mandatory by a convention like that of 1958. Nevertheless, this concept, as manifested in decided cases, has not thereby become a rule of general international law, a norm logically flowing from a legally binding principle of customary international law, neither has it been adopted into customary law simply as a method to be given priority or preference" (paragraph 107).

Likewise, the chamber rejected the U.S. argument based on the distinction between coasts defined as "primary" simply because they followed the general direction of the mainland coastline as a whole or were parallel to it, and coasts defined as "secondary" simply because they deviated from that direction. The purpose of the suggested distinction was to establish the preferential nature of the relationship between the "primary" coasts of Maine and the Atlantic seaboard of Nova Scotia and the "maritime and submarine areas situated frontally before them," so as to accentuate the adjacent-state nature of the Gulf of Maine region and thereby diminish the appropriateness of the median line "rule" as proposed by Canada for what might otherwise be characterized as an opposite-state situation between Cape Cod in the south and the Nova Scotia peninsula in the north (paragraph 108). Like the Canadian adjacency argument, the U.S. "primary-secondary" argument was based on a false premise. "The error," it was held, "lies precisely in searching general international law for, as it were, a set of rules which are not there" (paragraph 110). In a similar fashion, the chamber repudiated other efforts to advance mere "considerations" as well-established rules of law, such as "the idea advocated by Canada that a single maritime boundary should ensure the preservation of existing fishing patterns which are vital to the coastal communities in the area concerned, or the idea advocated by the United States that such a boundary should make it impossible to ensure the optimum conservation and management of living resources and at the same time reduce the potential for future disputes between the Parties." These and other concepts, such as those of "non-encroachment" and "no cutting off," might in given circumstances constitute equitable criteria, provided no attempt was made to elevate them to the status of established rules endorsed by customary international law (paragraph 110).

This important section of the chamber's majority judgment concluded with a formulation of the requested "fundamental norm" (at paragraph 112):

1 No maritime delimitation between States with opposite or adjacent coasts may be effected unilaterally by one of those States. Such delimitation must be sought and effected by means of an agreement, following negotiations conducted in good faith and with the genuine intention of achieving a positive result. Where, however, such agreement cannot be achieved, delimitation should be effected by recourse to a third party possessing the necessary competence.
2 In either case, delimitation is to be effected by the application of equitable criteria and by the use of practical methods capable of ensuring, with regard to the geographical configuration of the area and other relevant circumstances, an equitable result.

The chamber concluded that special international law, not general customary international law, was "the proper place in which to seek rules specifically prescribing the application of any particular equitable criteria, or the use of any particular practical methods" as between the parties in the present case (paragraph 114). If the delimitation of the continental shelf alone had been in issue, there would have been no doubt as to the mandatory application of the "method" prescribed in article 6 of the 1958 Convention, to which both Canada and the United States were parties. But given the dual function of the proposed "single maritime boundary", it was unacceptable simply to apply the "method" of article 6, which was clearly limited to delimitation of the continental shelf. Employing similar functionalist logic, the chamber found nothing in the 1958 Convention on the Territorial Sea and Contiguous Zone "comparable with the reservation of the exclusive rights of exploitation of resources of a maritime area extending to 200 miles; there is therefore nothing which could justify the idea of an extension thereto of criteria and delimitation methods expressly contemplated for the narrow strip of sea defined for a quite different purpose" (paragraph 120). In short, the chamber rejected any attempt to turn the delimitation provisions of either of the two 1958 Conventions into a "general rule applicable as such to every maritime delimitation" (paragraph 124). Moreover, the chamber was not persuaded that the United States had acquiesced in Canada's use of a median line for delimitation of the shelf in the Georges Bank area, or that Canada could properly invoke the doctrine of estoppel on this issue (paragraphs 126–148).

Because the parties were not bound by any rule of treaty law, or any other rule, to apply any particular criteria or methods for delimitation of the single maritime boundary proposed, the chamber was free to select the most appropriate criteria and methods from the theoretical range of possibilities put forward by counsel.[219] As to the criteria, their equitableness could be assessed only in relation to the circumstances of each case, and "for one and the same criterion it is quite possible to arrive at different, or even opposite, conclusions in different cases" (paragraph 158). Unlike the equitable criteria by which delimitation must be guided, the "practical methods" available had been subjected to intensive analysis in previous adjudication, but "the greater or lesser appropriateness of one method or another could only be assessed by reference to the actual situation in which they are used. There was no method of which it could be said that it must receive priority." Accordingly, a judicial boundary-maker must be willing to adopt "a combination of different methods whenever that seems to be called for by differences in the circumstances that may be relevant in the different phases of the operation and with reference to different segments of the line" (paragraph 163).

The chamber proceeded to evaluate the appropriateness of the criteria and methods used in the four lines drawn by the parties. The original U.S. line, drawn in 1976, was found to be based on natural criteria, especially geomorphological and ecological, and the method used amounted virtually to the adoption of the line of the greatest depth. The main objective was to keep the various ecosystems in the area intact through single-state management, which would justify awarding the resources of Georges Bank in toto to one of the parties – namely, the United States. But the chamber had initial difficulties with the concept of a "natural boundary," especially in the ocean environment,[220] and observed that "a delimitation, whether of a maritime boundary or of a land boundary, is a legal-political operation, and ... it is not the case that where a natural boundary is discernible, the political delimitation necessarily had to follow the same line. But in any event the problem does not arise in the present instance, since ... there are no geological, geomorphological, ecological or other factors sufficiently important, evident, and conclusive to represent a single, incontrovertible natural boundary" (paragraph 56). In rejecting this "natural boundary" line of argument, the chamber seems to have been influenced by what it regarded as undue use of ecological data for a line that was to serve both fishery and non-fishery purposes. It left the impression that the ecological argument should in future be used more selectively – confined to particular segments of a single maritime boundary rather than made to serve as the rationale for an entire multifunctional boundary (paragraph 186).

The revised U.S. line of 1982 was based on a macrogeographical characterization of the Gulf of Maine region, which depended on the suggested distinction between primary and secondary coasts and on the idea that the "projection or frontal extension of the primary coastal front" should be identified with the natural prolongation of the land mass "in the geographical sense." In short, it was a natural prolongation argument in disguise, skewed so as to reduce the saliency of the opposite-state characteristics of the region, and buttressed by consideration of equitable criteria such as non-encroachment, no cut-off, and proportionality (paragraph 170). The method proposed was that of a line perpendicular to the general direction of the coast, comparable with that employed by the ICJ in the *Tunisian-Libyan* decision of 1982. But adjustments to such a line were necessary to take account of the configuration of the region, including the location of Grand Manan Island and the Nova Scotia peninsula, and to preserve the unity of distinct ecosystems. What resulted was essentially a compromise between "two fundamentally different methods": a geometrical method and an ecological (or ecogeographical) method (paragraph 173). But the chamber found that the fictitious distinction between primary and secondary, which was crucial to the U.S. argument, was too weak to "resolve the insurmountable difficulties that result from the forced application of a criterion and of a method which are not at all appropriate, having regard to the real geographical configuration of the area" (paragraph 177).

The two Canadian lines of 1976 and 1977 were considered together, since both were based on the same criterion (equal division) and employed the same method (equidistance). Just as the chamber felt the U.S. lines were less appropriate for the shelf than for the water column, so it found the Canadian lines less appropriate for the water column than for the shelf. But this aspect was de-emphasized in its treatment of the Canadian government's argument, as it focused on the rationale of Canada's 1977 revision in the light of "other special circumstances" that had been previously overlooked. The chamber held that although the relative length of the coastlines of the two states was neither a criterion nor a method of delimitation, it could be used as a test of the appropriateness of a provisional delimitation effected initially on a different basis. In the chamber's language, "a maritime delimitation can certainly not be established by a direct division of the area in dispute proportional to the respective lengths of the coasts belonging to the parties in the relevant area, but it is equally certain that a substantial disproportion to the lengths of those coasts that resulted from a delimitation effected on a different basis would constitute a circumstance calling for an appropriate correction" (paragraph 185). The chamber also questioned the use of what was essentially an equidistance line throughout a "mixed" situation, where the adjacent-state relationship predominated closer to shore and the opposite-state relationship predominated further seaward (paragraphs 186–9).

Having rejected all four lines drawn by the parties, the chamber proceeded to formulate its own solution independently of the proposals advanced by counsel. The first consideration was the need to preclude the application of "any criteria, however apparently equitable in themselves, which can now be seen as inappropriate to the delimitation of one or other of the two objects" that the special agreement requested the chamber to delimit. That the criteria applied in earlier adjudications were found equitable and appropriate for the delimitation of the continental shelf did not imply that "they must automatically possess the same properties in relation to the simultaneous delimitation of the continental shelf and the superjacent fishery zone" (paragraph 192). In a case like the present one, it was necessary "to rule out the application of any criterion found to be typically and exclusively bound up with the particular characteristics of one alone of the two natural realities that have to be delimited in conjunction" (paragraph 193). For example, in seeking to serve a dual purpose such as this, it was difficult, if not impossible, to adopt an ecological criterion, and a geological or geomorphological criterion would be equally inadequate. What was needed was a criterion or a combination of criteria that did not give "preferential treatment to one of these two objects to the detriment of the other, and at the same time is such as to be equally suitable to the division of either of them." Indeed, it could be foreseen "that with the gradual adoption by the majority of maritime States of an exclusive economic zone and, consequently, an increasingly general demand for single delimitation, so as to avoid as far as possible the disadvantages inherent in a plurality of separate delimitations, *preference will henceforth inevitably be given to criteria that, because of their more neutral character, are best suited for use in a multi-purpose delimitation* [emphasis added]"(paragraph 194).

With a view to the need for more "neutral" criteria, the chamber concluded that much must be made of geographical considerations: "The Chamber's basic choice should favour a criterion long held to be as equitable as it is simple, namely that in principle, while having regard to the special circumstances of the case, one should aim at an *equal division* of areas where the maritime projections of the coasts of the States between which delimitation is to be effected converge and overlap [emphasis added]" (paragraph 195). Yet in many situations, such as that of the Gulf of Maine region, geographical diversity requires that the criterion of equal division be "adjusted or flexibly applied to make it genuinely equitable, not in the abstract, but in relation to the varying requirements of a reality that takes many shapes and forms." In such a situation use must be made of "auxiliary criteria." In the Gulf of Maine region, "a fair measure of weight should be given to a by no means negligible difference within the delimitation area between *the lengths of the respective coastlines* of the countries concerned [emphasis added]." Weight should also be given, for corrective purposes, to the need not to apply the basic criterion of equal division in such a way that would result in cutting off one coastline, or part of it, from its appropriate projection; and to the need to grant some effect, however limited, to the presence of a geographical feature such as an island or group of small islands lying off a coast "when strict application of the basic criterion might entail giving them full effect or, alternatively, no effect" (paragraph 196).

Given the geographical nature of the basic and auxiliary criteria, geometrical methods of delimitation were appropriate; but they should not be used in such a way as to follow "a complicated or even a zigzag path, made up of a succession of segments on different bearings" (paragraph 202). Such a boundary might be acceptable for dividing the seabed alone, but not for delimiting fishing areas: "Exploitation of the sea's fishery resources calls for the existence of clear boundaries of a constant course, that do not compel those engaging in such activity to keep checking their position in relation to the complicated path of the line to be respected" (paragraph 202).[221]

In accordance with the chamber's characterization of the Gulf of Maine region, it was held that regardless of the practical method selected, the boundary in the inner sector of the delimitation area should be a "lateral" line between what were primarily adjacent states, whereas in the outer sector it should be essentially a "median" line between what were primarily opposite coastlines. Moreover, geography also dictated that the median line should be almost parallel to the two nearly parallel coasts of Massachusetts and Nova Scotia (paragraph 206).[222] Applying these methods in light of the basic and auxiliary criteria, the chamber drew the boundary by means of a two-stage process, the second part of which required an adjustment of the first-stage line by reference to the ratio between the coastal fronts of the two neighbouring states.[223]

In its closing comments the chamber defended its heavy reliance on geographical criteria and geometric methods by discounting the need for historical and socio-economical considerations in order to achieve an equitable solution to a boundary-making problem of this sort. As to the U.S. argument of historical predominance in the region, the chamber confirmed its decision not to accord any "decisive weight" to the "antiquity or continuity of fishing activities carried on in the past" beyond the Gulf proper, noting that "whatever preferential situation the United States may previously have enjoyed, this cannot constitute in itself a valid ground for its now claiming the incorporation into its own exclusive fishery zone of any area which, in law, has become part of Canada's" (paragraph 235). Nor could Canada claim entitlement to a single maritime boundary designed to "ensure the maintenance of the existing fishing patterns that are in its view vital to the coastal communities of the region" (paragraph 234). There was no reason to effect a delimitation with a view to the displacement or redistribution of fishing rights of the neighbouring states, or of third-party states, under the new law of the sea. The chamber did concede that the littoral states were entitled to a degree of concern "lest the overall effect ... should unexpectedly be revealed as radically inequitable, that is to say, as likely to entail catastrophic repercussions for the livelihood and economic well-being of the population of the countries concerned" (paragraph 237). But there seemed no reason to fear that any such effect might be caused by the chamber's boundary in the Gulf of Maine. Any problems arising should be amenable to solution through negotiation by two neighbouring states with a long history of success in cooperative arrangements (paragraphs 238–40).

In paragraph 3 of his dissenting opinion, Judge Gros protested that the majority had missed an opportunity to "strengthen rather than erode the law on the delimitation of maritime expanses." To this "unitarian" view of the chamber's adjudicative function he added an "anti-consensual" perspective on ocean boundary-making, challenging the parties' entitlement to ask the chamber to draw a single maritime boundary without being able to demonstrate the legal grounds for such a boundary. UNCLOS III had eroded the "equidistance-special circumstances rule of the 1958 Convention on the Continental Shelf without replacing it with any rule at all in Articles 74 and 83 of the 1982 Convention on the Law of the Sea. All the gains represented by the legal edifice of 1958, the 1969 Judgment and the 1977 Decision, have thus been destroyed by the effect of those two articles of the 1982 Convention, which take no account of that jurisprudence and efface it by the use of an empty formula" – that is, "equitable solution" (paragraph 8). The majority were therefore to be criticized for not applying the 1958 Convention, the only treaty binding both parties, even if the effect of doing so would be to give "preferential treatment" to shelf considerations to the "detriment" of fishery considerations in the water column.

Expressing a degree of hostility to UNCLOS III in particular, and to the trend to jurisdictional expansionism in the new law of the sea in general, Judge Gros deplored the emergence of a normative vacuum if the "equidistance–special circumstances rule" were to be pronounced dead, and regretted the chamber's subjective approach to the interpretation of "equity." "One must not narrow down the law of delimitation to two words, agreement plus equity, only to equate that equity with judicial discretion" (paragraph 29). In following the vague prescriptions of UNCLOS III, the ICJ in the *Tunisian-Libyan Continental Shelf* decision of 1982 had "given equity in maritime delimitation this doubtful content of indeterminate criteria, methods and corrections which are now wholly result-oriented. A decision not subject to any verification of its soundness on a basis of law may be expedient, but it is never a judicial act. Equity discovered by an exercise of discretion is not an application of law" (paragraph 37).

Indeed, it was doubtful whether "international justice can long survive an equity measured by the judge's eye" (paragraph 41). The majority's approach was better suited, he concluded, to an "amicable conciliator" than to a court of law (paragraph 48).

These strong words in Judge Gros's dissenting opinion certainly serve to underline the seriousness of the jurisprudential rift opened up by the ICJ's decisions of 1982 and 1984, a rift essentially between the "unitarian" and the "facilitative" (or functionalist) views of the adjudicative function in ocean boundary delimitation. It seems unlikely that the "unitarians" would have been satisfied with anything less than a reinstatement of the "rule" of equidistance and the doctrine of natural prolongation and an application of the 1958 Convention, albeit to a bifunctional boundary for which the Convention was not designed. This approach could be justified only by adopting the "unitarian" view that the primary purpose of adjudication is to develop a coherent body of rules rather than to help solve a problem or to administer justice (or equity) between the parties.

From a functionalist viewpoint, the most important features of the case were that the chamber was assigned a maximal facilitative function (to draw an official boundary that would be binding on both parties and to define the chosen line with technical precision) and that the boundary to be drawn was to serve two distinct purposes. The circumstances of the case were therefore totally inappropriate for the reinstatement of the old case law, even if the majority had been disposed to adopt the "unitarian" view of the juridical process. The chamber had no choice but to grant judicial primacy to the result-oriented equitable-solution approach finally prescribed in UNCLOS III. To the extent that the chamber had to deal with a "juridical vacuum" in the field of ocean boundary delimitation, it had to accept the inevitability of a somewhat discretionary approach to the treatment of equity, and attempt to reduce the subjectivity inherent in this approach by resort to relatively neutral facts. To complain that even geographical facts are not totally neutral merely registers a quibble over semantics. Arguably, no set of facts is totally free of disputes over interpretation, but geographical facts in general speak more clearly, at least to non-scientists on a tribunal, than do geological or ecological facts in general.

Finally, it might be suggested that from a functionalist viewpoint the most important feature of the *Canadian-U.S. Maritime Boundary* decision is the chamber's clarification of the delimitation considerations put forward by counsel. Even "unitarians" should benefit from a clarified distinction between principles (and "rules"), criteria, and methods. It is to be hoped that future tribunals will be encouraged by this decision to differentiate various categories of "factors" and perhaps "approaches" as well as "norms."[224]

The Beagle Channel Case (1967–1984)

Like the Aegean Sea dispute between Greece and Turkey, the Beagle Channel dispute between Argentina and Chile consisted of several different issues, reflecting a difficult and often hostile relationship between two neighbouring countries. Unlike its counterpart in the eastern Mediterranean, the ocean boundary delimitation issue between the two South American states seems finally to have been resolved, but only after many years of effort at direct bilateral diplomacy, facilitated by arbitration and mediation. If the final settlement of 1984 proves secure, the Beagle Channel case must be regarded as a successful, albeit arduous, example of ocean boundary-making through a complex diplomatic/intermediary process.

For several decades the dispute between Argentina and Chile focused attention on the eastern sector of the Beagle Channel, which runs in a general east-west direction at the latitude of parallel 55° south, at the tip of the South American continent. (See figure 9.) Efforts by the two governments to deal with the problems of that area (known as the "Southern Region") can be traced back as far as 1904. The boundary delimitation issue in the Beagle Channel has always been closely associated with a territorial dispute over three fairly large islands – Picton, Nueva, and Lennox – and a large number of smaller uninhabited islands in more or less adjacent waters (the PNL group). Both the territorial and boundary issues have involved questions of interpretation arising out of a (chiefly land) boundary treaty concluded in 1881.[225]

In December 1967 the dispute erupted again when Chile initiated steps to have both issues submitted to arbitration under the General Treaty of Arbitration signed by Argentina and Chile in 1902,[226] under which the parties agreed to submit any dispute to the British government as permanent arbiter. Chile asked the British government to intervene in that capacity to settle the dispute, but Argentina denied the applicability of the 1902 Treaty of Arbitration and invited Chile to resume negotiations.[227] Further diplomacy resulted in two agreements. First, in July 1971 the three countries signed an arbitration agreement (*compromiso*) whereby the Beagle Channel dispute was submitted to ad hoc arbitration instead of to the permanent system established in 1902.[228] Second, in January 1972 Argentina and Chile signed a treaty providing for the judicial settlement of disputes, which was designed to establish the jurisdiction of the International Court of Justice in place of the arbitral role of the British government under the 1902 treaty.[229] This new treaty of 1972 was denounced by Argentina, but Chile reserved its right to resort to the ICJ for settlement of the Beagle Channel dispute. After further disagreement over dispute settlement procedure, the two countries agreed to proceed with ad hoc arbitration of the Beagle Channel dispute in accordance with the 1972 agreement.

FIGURE 9: Beagle Channel Arbitration/Mediation

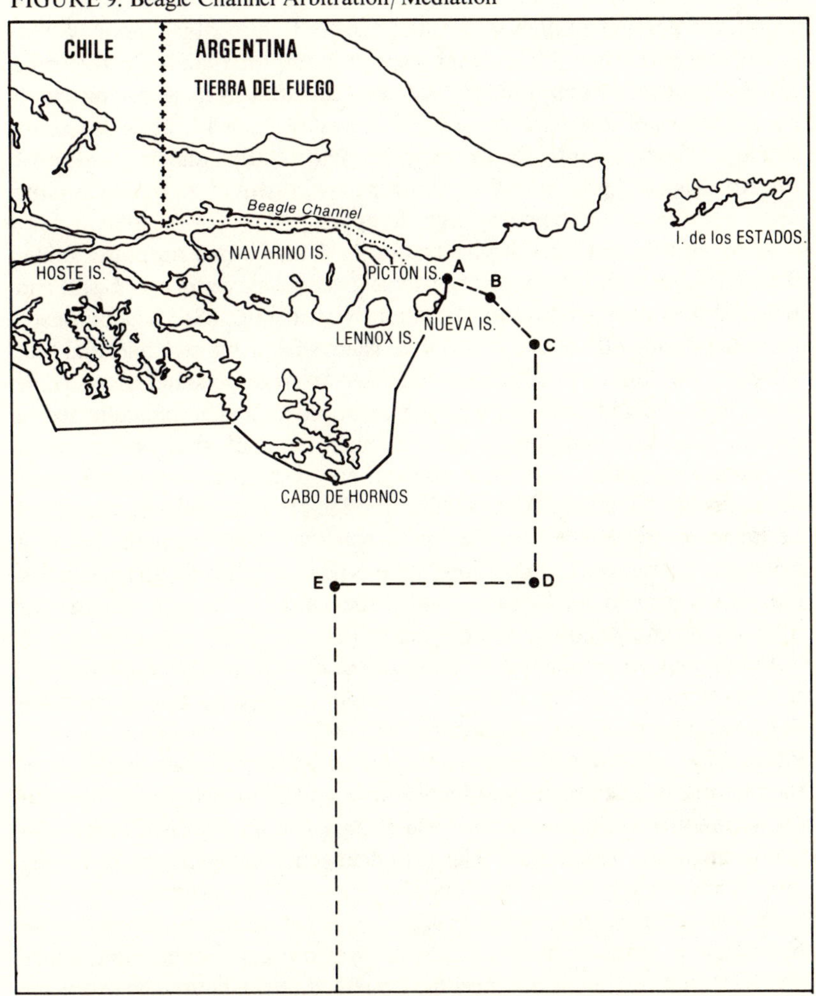

++++++ International land boundary (1881 Treaty).
——— Chilean straight baselines.
·········· Beagle Channel boundary drawn by Court of Arbitration, 1977.
- - - - Maritime boundary (1984 Treaty).

Under the *compromiso* it was provided that the dispute would be settled by an ad hoc arbitration tribunal consisting of five members of the ICJ chosen by the government of the United Kingdom,[230] and that the decision of that court would become effective only upon ratification by the United Kingdom in accordance with the 1902 treaty. The Court of Arbitration was asked, in article 1, to determine the boundary line between the maritime jurisdictions of Argentina and Chile from meridian 68°36′38.5″ W within the designated area in dispute, and to declare which country possessed territorial jurisdiction over the PNL group of islands. In the same article the court was required to "reach its conclusions in accordance with the principles of international law."[231] It was also provided that the court would be "competent to decide upon the interpretation and application of the Arbitration Agreement," and that the award would be legally binding upon both parties without any right to appeal.[232]

In its award the Court of Arbitration held that it had no power under the *compromiso* or otherwise to reach a conclusion *ex aequo et bono*, and relied almost exclusively on the boundary treaty of 1881. Unanimously, the court decided that the PNL group of islands belonged to Chile, and that the waters to the north of the line belonged to Argentina and those to the south to Chile. The line drawn was in principle a median line, adjusted in certain relatively unimportant respects for reasons of local configuration or better navigability. The court added that "in so far as any special steps are necessary to be taken for execution of the present Decision, they shall be taken by the Parties."[233] In April 1977 the UK government issued a statement ratifying the "decision" of the ad hoc tribunal and declaring that it constituted an "award" under the 1902 treaty. The award was officially promulgated two weeks later in May 1977.

Public and governmental reaction to the award in Argentina was extremely negative. As the nine-month period assigned for implementation of the arbitral award approached its end, without any prospect of reconciliation, diplomacy was elevated to the presidential level. But shortly after the first meeting between Presidents Videla and Pinochet, Argentina officially announced its rejection of the Beagle Channel award, despite its commitment to accept it.[234] The presidents met again in the following month and issued the Declaration of Puerto Montt, dated 10 February 1978, outlining a three-stage process of negotiation to deal with the boundary problems in the Southern Region and other contentious issues.[235] By this time it had become evident that the boundary problems were of more than merely symbolic significance. Seismic studies indicating the possible presence of oil in the Southern Region led to the authorization of offshore drilling by the government of Argentina, and in April 1978 drilling was begun near Tierra del Fuego. These and other provocations on both sides led to an even more serious deterioration in relations, and military forces were deployed in the frontier area. By December 1978 the two countries found themselves on the brink of war.

The imminence of open military conflict finally forced the governments, in January 1979, to sign the Agreement of Montevideo, by which they accepted the mediation of the Holy See in the person of Cardinal Antonio Samore, special representative of Pope John Paul II. The governments welcomed the offer of intermediary assistance in the solution of the Southern Region problem and promised "to consider any ideas which may be expressed by the Holy See." At Cardinal Samore's request, the governments also agreed not to resort to force and to "abstain from taking measures that might affect harmony in any sector."[236] Officially, efforts at mediation began in May 1979, and signs of progress appeared in December 1980, when the Holy See issued a papal proposal for the resolution of the Beagle Channel dispute.[237] In that document a boundary line was proposed for division of the Argentinian and Chilean exclusive economic zones in the "Southern Sea" extending seaward from the Beagle Channel, and drawn so as to keep the PNL group under the territorial jurisdiction of Chile. The premise to this proposal was the mediator's request that the validity of the 1881 boundary treaty should be recognized by both parties in conformity with the principle of *pacta sunt servanda*.

This proposal became the basis of intense diplomatic activity over the next four years. Throughout this crucial period Cardinal Samore constantly emphasized the "mission of peace" aspect of the mediation and reiterated the need for co-operation between the neighbouring states and for a general system of settlement for all future disputes between them. In September 1982 he managed to persuade the governments to extend the 1972 General Treaty on the Judicial Settlement of Disputes until such time as a final treaty providing for a "complete and definitive solution" could be concluded.[238] The mediator's facilitative efforts were rewarded with the signing of a joint declaration in January 1984, and finally with the conclusion in November 1984 of a formal Treaty of Peace and Friendship.[239]

The 1984 treaty is based squarely on the papal proposal of 1980 as far as the Beagle Channel boundary issue is concerned. It incorporates a line that extends to the seaward limits of the parties' exclusive economic zones in the "Sea of the Southern Region" and preserves the territorial integrity of the PNL group of islands on the Chilean side of the line in conformity with the 1881 boundary treaty, essentially as interpreted by the ad hoc Court of Arbitration in 1977. But with a view to securing peace and friendship, the parties went further and promised that in the event of future diplomatic failure to agree on another means of peaceful settlement of disputes between them, they would resort to a permanent Argentine-Chilean Conciliation Commission to be established under chapter 1 of Annex 1 to the treaty. In the event of failure of this conciliation procedure, either of the parties would be permitted to submit the dispute to arbitration by means of the procedure provided for in chapter 2 of Annex 1.[240] The treaty also provided, in article 12, for the creation of a permanent binational commission to work co-operatively in such sectors as land communications, mutual concession of ports and free zones, land transport, aviation, telecommunications, natural resource exports, tourism, and protection of the environment. The final outcome of this complex diplomatic/intermediary process was a complicated package of treaty settlements and arrangements serving a wide variety of demonstrative, administrative, and distributive, as well as resolutive, purposes. It is to be hoped that the ratification of this treaty by both states has finally resolved the difficult and potentially dangerous Beagle Channel dispute.[241]

Guinea-Guinea Bissau Maritime Boundary Arbitration: Gulf of Guinea (1985)

In February 1983 a maritime boundary dispute off the northwest coast of Africa was submitted to a three-member ad hoc arbitration tribunal by the French-speaking country of Guinea and by Guinea Bissau, its tiny Portuguese-speaking neighbour to the north. All three members of the tribunal were non-nationals of the two states in question; each government nominated one arbitrator, and those two nominees chose the third, who served as president of the tribunal.[242]

Under article 2 of the 1983 arbitration agreement, three questions were put to the tribunal: (1) Did the Franco-Portuguese Treaty of 12 May 1886 determine the general maritime boundary between Guinea and Guinea-Bissau? (2) What was the juridical value of the protocols and documents annexed to the 1886 treaty for the purposes of interpretation of that instrument? (3) In light of the answers to these two questions, what was the course of the line delimiting the "maritime territories" of Guinea and Guinea-Bissau? In article 9(2) of the arbitration agreement, the tribunal was asked to depict the boundary on a chart with the assistance of a technical expert chosen by the tribunal.

Because of the nature of the first two questions, almost two-thirds of the award dealt with the problems of interpreting the 1886 treaty and related instruments concluded by two of the former colonial powers in the region, France and Portugal. By applying the Vienna Convention on the Law of Treaties,[243] the tribunal concluded that the annexed protocols and document did have an important role in the interpretation of the 1886 treaty, and that the treaty could not be interpreted as determining the maritime boundary between French and Portuguese possessions in West Africa at that time.

On the third question, Guinea-Bissau argued in favour of an equidistance line drawn from the low-water mark along the coasts of the two neighbouring countries; Guinea argued for a southwesterly line extending from the thalweg in the Cajet river connecting with the line of latitude 10°40′ N, and then for a second segment following that parallel of latitude to the seaward limits of the parties' coastal state jurisdiction. (See figure 10.) Having answered the first question in the negative, the tribunal was

FIGURE 10: Gulf of Guinea Arbitration

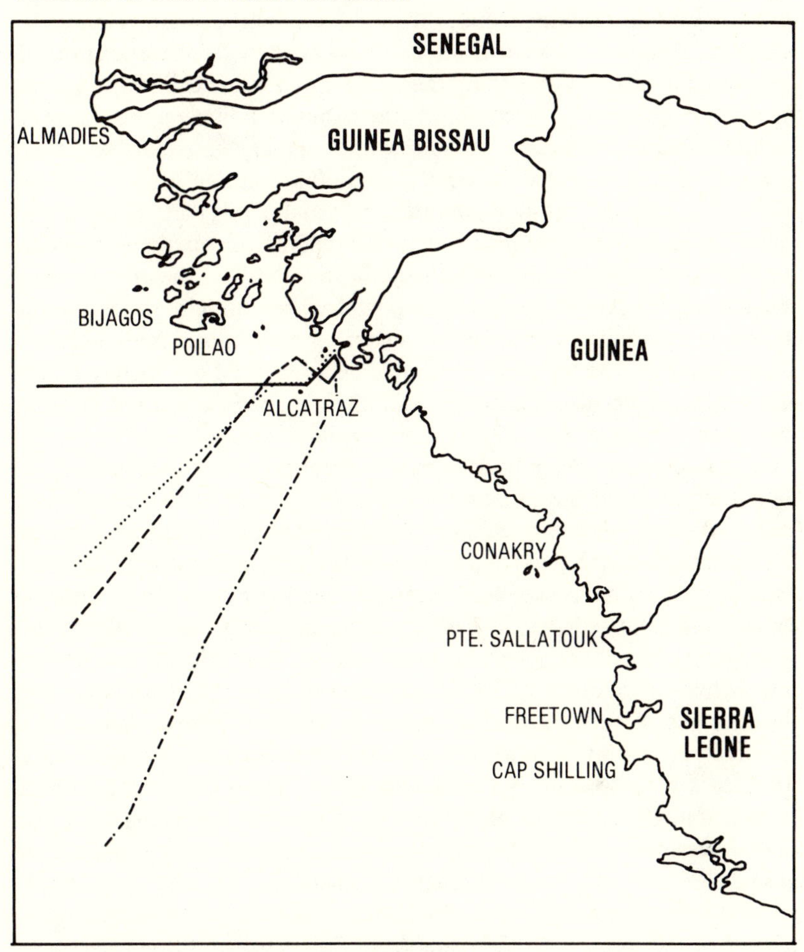

________ Guinean claim based on 1886 treaty.
– – – – – Guinean adjusted equidistance claim.
–.–.–.–. Guinea-Bissau equidistance claim.
.... Boundary line drawn by the arbitration tribunal, 1985.

free to respond to the suggested lines and the accompanying arguments by reference to all three regimes of maritime jurisdiction under the new law of the sea (territorial sea, continental shelf, and the EEZ) without involving itself in historical or ethical issues arising from the application of "inter-temporal law."[244]

Both parties agreed on the appropriateness of invocations to three sources of law: custom; judicial and arbitral decisions; and "especially conventions concluded under auspices of the United Nations." As to the 1982 Convention resulting from UNCLOS III, both parties were prepared to recognize many of its provisions as "consistent with the evolution of international custom concerning the contemporary trends" in the law of the sea (paragraph 43). Accordingly, the tribunal, following the chamber of the ICJ in the *Canadian-U.S. Maritime Boundary* case of 1984, began by applying the "essential purpose" ("equitable solution") provisions on ocean boundary delimitation contained in articles 74(1) and 83(1) of the 1982 Convention, which purport to govern delimitation on the EEZ and on the shelf respectively. Like other adjudicative bodies, the tribunal felt obliged to deny that this undertaking involved the exercise of discretionary power or implied a mandate to render an *ex aequo et bono* decision (paragraph 88). The tribunal's equitable decision must not merely reflect the arbitrators' personal conviction and their sense of justice, but must be "based on considerations of law" (paragraphs 88 and 90).

On the matter of geographical characterization of the area in dispute, Guinea argued that the situation was wholly that of two adjacent states; Guinea-Bissau, which was seeking an equidistance line, described the area as a mixed situation having opposite-state as well as adjacent-state characteristics. The tribunal declined to resolve this matter on the terms presented, but indicated that it was not inappropriate to take note of the macrogeographical configuration of the region to which the area in dispute belonged in order to rest the delimitation on "an equitable and objective base." Accordingly, it might be necessary to take account of the coastal configuration of at least two of the other states in the region to the north of Guinea-Bissau (Senegal) and to the south of Guinea (Sierra Leone). It might be impossible to determine an equitable boundary of the kind requested without regard to other delimitations of a similar kind effected, or requiring to be effected, elsewhere in the region (paragraph 92).

Most of the complications arising from the presence of three classes of offshore islands were put aside by the tribunal on the ground that they involved baseline delineation, not delimitation, and did not directly concern the tribunal in its task at hand (paragraphs 95–6). The location of the islands was of relevance chiefly for measuring the lengths of the two adjacent coastlines following their general direction: if the Bijagos islands were included, each coastline was approximately 154 miles long; but if they were excluded, Guinea-Bissau's coastline was only 128 miles long (paragraph 97). If the coastlines of the two countries were considered separately, Guinea's was concave and Guinea-Bissau's convex (if the Bijagos islands were included as part of Guinea-Bissau's coastal configuration). But if the two were taken together, the coastline of the area in dispute was concave, and the concavity was accentuated if account was taken of the presence of Sierra Leone to the south of Guinea. The manner in which one drew an equidistance line and the question of what would constitute an equitable boundary were therefore affected by the way one chose to characterize the coastal configuration of the region in the broader sense, or of the area in dispute in the narrower sense (paragraph 103).

The parties agreed that the question was not one of "refashioning geography," and that the effects of "amputation" and "enclavement" should be avoided as much as possible. But they differed on the choice of method. Guinea-Bissau, citing the *Anglo-French Continental Shelf* arbitration, argued that the tribunal should first consider the appropriateness of an equidistance line before proceeding to the question of possible modifications by other methods because of special circumstances. Guinea, citing the *Tunisian-Libyan Continental Shelf* decision, argued that no priority should be given to any one method of delimitation. The tribunal chose to follow the second course (paragraph 102).

Having decided to give no special priority to equidistance, and thereby avoiding some of the problems of distortion arising from its chosen characterization of the area or region, the tribunal viewed the total bearing of the coast of West Africa as relevant to the delimitation before it, even though this approach involved a perceptual simplification of the larger regional situation. By taking a broad view of the region, not just the area in dispute, the tribunal admitted that its approach had implications for at least two third-party states that were not parties to the suit, namely, Senegal and Sierra Leone (paragraphs 109–10). Accordingly, the tribunal boldly drew a straight line connecting Almadies Point on the Senegal coast and Cap Shilling on the Sierra Leone coast for the purpose of determining the general direction of the coast from which a perpendicular line could be drawn as the second segment of the delimitation line between Guinea and Guinea-Bissau.

As to the continental shelf aspect of the delimitation issue, the tribunal noted the anomalous coexistence of two concepts of shelf entitlement in the law of the sea: "natural prolongation" as developed doctrinally by the ICJ in 1969, and mere distance (two hundred miles) as prescribed in article 76 of the 1982 Convention. As between these two incompatible "rules," the tribunal refused to recognize any "priority" or "hierarchy" (paragraph 116). What was important was the "unity" of the shelf shared by the two neighbouring states as admitted by their counsel. Geomorphological variations were not significant enough to constitute valid considerations for the purposes of delimitation (paragraph 117).

Like other adjudicative bodies, the tribunal chose to treat proportionality as a corrective criterion for evaluating the equitableness of a proposed line rather than as a criterion in the first analysis (paragraph 118). Again, in the established line of adjudicative reasoning, the tribunal held that socio-economic considerations were too changeable to constitute a reliable basis for the purpose of permanent ocean boundary delimitation (paragraphs 121–5).

In conclusion, the tribunal drew a three-segment line, the first segment of which proceeded from the thalweg in the Cajet River, and the third (and by far the longest) segment of which followed a line perpendicular to the straight line drawn between two points to the north of the coast of Guinea-Bissau and to the south of the coast of Guinea. The decision was unanimous.

This arbitral decision can be interpreted in different ways. For many "unitarian" commentators it represents further evidence of an adjudicative body's methodological bias against equidistance. The easy dismissal of equidistance in favour of perpendicularity for the third and longest segment of the line can be criticized in much the same way as the decision in the *Tunisian-Libyan Continental Shelf* case of 1982 was criticized by the dissenting judges."Unitarian" objections might also be raised against the decision to use a straight line between points outside the territories of the litigant states, to the extent that this admits "non-adversarial" elements into the adjudicative process. This bold decision by the arbitration tribunal might be defended more comfortably by functionalist commentators on the ground that the broad characterization of the region, justified by reference to potential third-party interests, introduced a regional perspective conducive to the purposes of ocean development and management in West Africa as a whole.[245]

Libya-Malta Continental Shelf Case (1985)

The Libyan-Maltese dispute over continental shelf areas in the central Mediterranean originated in Malta's claim to a median line as early as 1965. The Republic of Malta, consisting of four inhabited islands (Malta, Gozo, Comino, and Cominotto) and the uninhabited rock of Filfla, lies 183 nautical miles north of the nearest point of the Libyan coastline. (See figure 11.) When the two governments submitted the dispute to the International Court of Justice under a special agreement dated 23 May 1976, it became the first adjudication of a delimitation dispute exclusively between opposite states.

By an application dated 23 October 1983 Italy requested permission to intervene in the case, arguing by reference to article 62 of the Statute of the Court that it had "an interest of a legal nature which may be affected by the decision in the case." It was contended that Libya's and Malta's claims "extend[ed] to areas which would be found to appertain to Italy if a delimitation were to be effected between Italy and Libya, and between Italy and Malta, on the basis of international law." The whole bed of the

FIGURE 11: Libya-Malta Continental Shelf Case

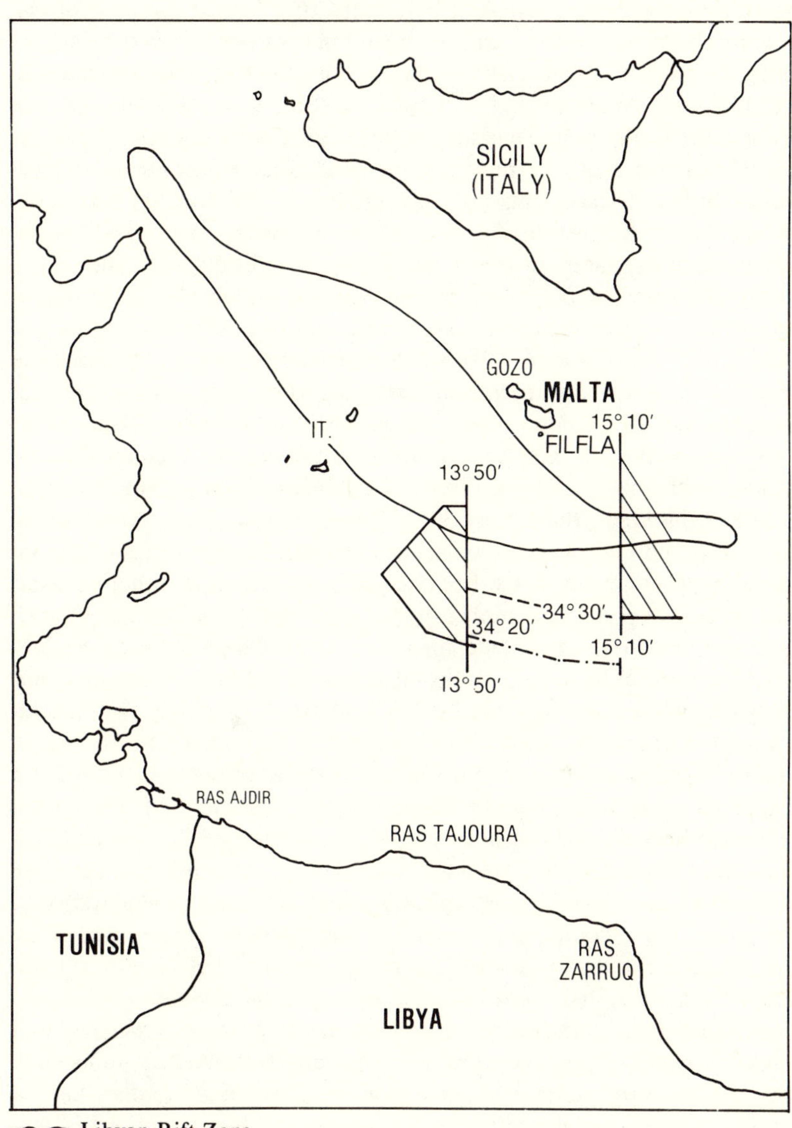

Libyan Rift Zone.

Limits of Italian claim.

Provisional hypothetical equidistance line drawn by the International Court of Justice.

Final adjusted line proposed by the International Court of Justice, 1985.

sea area in dispute was said to be "part of the continental shelf, within the meaning of the definition in Article 76 of the 1982 United Nations Convention on the Law of the Sea, and the greater part of such sea-bed consists of areas of overlap" of the rights of the littoral states of central Mediterranean.[246] Italy emphasized that it was not seeking to intervene solely to inform the Court of its own claims, but so that the Court could give the parties "all the requisite guidance to ensure non-encroachment on areas over which Italy has rights" (paragraph 16). Both Libya and Malta opposed Italy's request for permission to intervene, principally on the ground that the nature of Italy's interest was insufficiently specific.

Despite Italy's disclaimer of any intention to ask the Court for a determination of its own continental shelf delimitation disputes with Libya and Malta, the Court held that his would nonetheless be the effect, in some degree, of a decision to permit intervention. The Court could not sustain the suggested distinction between a request that it "safeguard" Italy's legal interests as reflected in its continental shelf claims, and a request that the Court "recognize" or "define" Italy's legal interests (paragraph 17). "If in a case of this kind a third state were permitted to intervene so as to prevent its claims and indicate the grounds advanced as justifying them, then the subsequent judgment of the Court could not be limited to noting them, but would, expressly or implicitly, recognize their validity and extent." Italian intervention would tend "inevitably to produce a situation in which the Court would be seised of a dispute between Italy on the one hand and Libya and Malta on the other, or each of them separately, without the consent of the latter States; Italy would thus become a party to one of several disputes which are not before the Court at present. In this way the character of the case would be transformed" (paragraph 32). Yet, though it denied Italy the right of intervention, the Court could not "wholly put aside the question of the legal interest of Italy as well as other States of the Mediteranean region" (paragraph 41). These third-party interests would be taken into account as they were in the *Tunisian-Libyan Continental Shelf* case of 1982–by acknowledging the existence of claims and and disputes in areas adjacent to the area under present dispute.

The case between Malta and Libya was heard between November 1984 and February 1985 by a court of seventeen judges, the largest number ever to adjudicate an ocean boundary dispute. Four of the judges had no previous experience in judicial boundary-making (paragraph 41).[247] The judgment, handed down in June 1985, was supported by a majority of fourteen to three.[248]

In article 1 of the special agreement the parties asked the Court to determine "[w]hat principles and rules of international law are applicable to the delimitation of the area of the continental shelf which appertains to the Republic of Malta and the area of continental shelf which appertains to the Libyan Arab Republic, and how in practice such principles and rules can be applied by the two Parties in this particular case in order that they may without difficulty delimit such areas by an agreement as provided in Article III." It became apparent at the outset that the wording of the second part of the question had given rise to difficulties between parties while the text of the special agreement was being negotiated. What resulted was a compromise formula. Malta wanted the Court to be asked to draw the delimitation line (thereby assigning the Court a role close to the maximal facilitative function), while Libya wanted it only to pronounce on the applicable norms of international law (a declaratory task close to the minimal facilitative function). "Libya would not accept that the line itself should be drawn by the Court, since, in its view, it was preferable that this should be done by agreement between the Parties. Malta did not agree that the matter [should] be left to the Parties since it [was] of the view that the reference of the dispute to the Court would then fail to achieve its main purpose."[249]

The Court noted that the special agreement contained no reference to a choice of methods of delimitation, but concluded that since it was required to decide how the principles and rules of international law could be applied in order to enable the parties to negotiate a delimitation "without difficulty," it was responsible for naming the method or methods it considered appropriate in the light of the applicable rules and principles. Whether the Court should indicate an actual delimitation line would depend, in some degree, on the method or methods found appropriate. In no event was the special agreement to be interpreted as debarring the Court from indicating "at least an approximate line which could be illustrated on a map" (paragraph 19).

Also arising out of the special agreement was a question of interpretation regarding the spatial scope of the Court's decision. Both Malta and Libya took the position that it should extend to all areas of the central Mediterranean which "appertained" to one or other of the parties, and should not be limited to the shelf area in which those were the sole competing claims. But the Court, citing its disposition of Italy's request for permission to intervene in the case, affirmed that it was bound to take note of third-party interests, such as those of Italy and Tunisia. The actual decision, however, must be limited in geographical scope so as to leave Italy's claims unaffected: that is, it must be confined to the area in which Italy had said it had no claims to continental shelf rights. Accordingly, the Court's decision would be limited to the area between the meridians 13°50′ E and 15°10′ E (paragraphs 20–3).

Since Libya was not a party to the 1958 Convention on the Continental Shelf, the delimitation provision of article 6 was not applicable. The 1982 UN Convention on the Law of the Sea, which both had signed, was not yet operative under the law of treaties. The special agreement was open-ended and made no stipulations on the substantive law deemed to be applicable. Nor were there any bilateral or multilateral agreements of any relevance to be considered. The parties were agreed that the matter was to be governed by customary international law. It was agreed that some of the relevant provisions of the 1982 Convention reflected customary international law, but the parties could not agree on the identification of those provisions (paragraphs 26–9).

Faced with a minimal stock of applicable principles and rules, the Court felt obliged to follow its *Tunisian-Libyan Continental Shelf* decision of 1982 in holding that, despite the absence of any reference to "equitable principles" in the 1982 Convention, it was bound to decide the present case on that basis and to produce an equitable result. This was consonant with the view of the parties that these two requirements, "equitable principles" and "equitable solution," formed part of the customary international law to be applied, but not with the chamber in the *Gulf of Maine* case, which preferred to focus on "equitable criteria" rather than "equitable principles."

The parties were also divided over the legal basis of title to continental shelf rights, which the Court accepted as pertinent to the issue of delimitation (paragraph 27). For Libya, only the reference to "natural prolongation" corresponded to customary international law; for Malta, the reference to a distance criterion (two hundred miles) represented a "consecration" of the "distance principle" (paragraph 34). The Court was unable to accept Libya's contention that distance from the coast was not a "relevant element" in a continental shelf delimitation under customary international law, and stated (at paragraph 34):

> Although the institutions of the continental shelf and the exclusive economic zone are different and distinct, the rights which the exclusive economic zone entails over the sea-bed of the zone are defined by reference to the regime laid down for the continental shelf. Although there can be a continental shelf where there is no exclusive economic zone, there cannot be an exclusive economic zone without a corresponding continental shelf. It follows that, for juridical and practical reasons, the distance criterion must now apply to the continental shelf as well as to the exclusive economic zone; and this quite apart from the provision as to distance in paragraph 1 of Article 76. This is not to suggest that the idea of natural prolongation is now superseded by that of distance. What it does mean is that where the continental margin does not extend as far as 200 miles from the shore, *natural prolongation*, which in spite of its physical origins has throughout its history become more and more a complex and juridical concept, *is in part defined by distance from the shore, irrespective of the physical nature of the intervening sea-bed and subsoil. The concepts of natural prolongation and distance are therefore*

not opposed but complementary; and both remain essential elements in the juridical concept of the continental shelf [emphasis added].

Libya argued that the intervening seabed consisted of two distinct shelves separated by what it termed a "rift zone" located much closer to the Maltese islands than to the Libyan coastline. Accordingly, Libya maintained that natural prolongation, in the physical sense, was still the "primary" basis of title to continental shelf. Malta denied that juridical significance could be attached to any "rift" in an area of fundamental geological continuity; that distance was now the "prime element" and that equidistance was virtually a required method, at least between opposite coasts, if only at the first stage of delimitation. The Court, emphasizing the primacy of the distance criterion, said there was no reason to ascribe any role to geological or geophysical factors within two hundred miles from the coast, "either in verifying the legal title of the States concerned or in proceeding to a delimitation as between their claims" (paragraph 39). Nor was there any reason why a factor "which has no part to play in the establishment of title should be taken into account as a relevant circumstance for the purposes of delimitation" (paragraph 40). Accordingly, in seabed areas that fell within EEZ limits, it was no longer relevant to point to marked disruptions or discontinuances of the seabed as a factor in delimitation. Accordingly, Libya's "rift zone" argument, based on geomorphological data, was rejected.

The Court also dismissed Malta's argument that the new criterion of distance conferred primacy on the equidistance method of delimitation, even as "a starting point of the delimitation process" (paragraph 42). The Court could not accept that "even as a preliminary and provisional step toward the drawing of a delimitation line, the equidistance method is one which *must* be used, or that the Court is 'required, as a first step, to examine the effects of a delimitation by application of the equidistance method' " (paragraph 43). The application of equitable principles in particular circumstances might still require the adoption of another method or combination of methods.

Given agreement between the parties that shelf delimitation under customary international law must be effected by the application of equitable principles in order to achieve an equitable result, the Court proceeded to offer a list of five "well-established" equitable principles.[250] This undertaking seems to reverse the trend toward a more open-ended appraisal of appropriate criteria and methods exhibited by the chamber's decision in the *Gulf of Maine* award of 1984 and by the arbitration tribunal's decision in the *Guinea-Guinea Bissau Maritime Boundary* arbitration of 1985, but it is difficult to say what weight was given by the Court to any of these equitable principles. Without fully explaining the applicability of the principles to the case at hand, the Court went on to deal with a mixture of related and unrelated matters. It rejected Libya's claim that the land mass behind the coast as well as the coastline itself should be accepted as a relevant consideration (paragraph 49). It dismissed Malta's argument that relevant equitable considerations, facilitating the assessment of the equitableness of a delimitation otherwise arrived at, should include economic factors such as the absence of energy resources on the island of Malta, its requirements as a developing island state, and the range of its established fishing activity (paragraph 50). It denied the relevance of Malta's security and defence interests (paragraph 51). It conceded that it was not irrelevant to boundary delimitation that the islands of Malta constituted an independent state, but spurned the notion that the doctrine of the equality of states could be invoked in support of the equidistance method of delimitation (paragraphs 52–4).

The Court then proceeded to consider the role to be assigned to proportionality, quoting from earlier adjudications to show consistency in using proportionality as a "factor" in correcting distortions ("disproportions"), not as a "rule" or "principle" of delimitation in the first instance, as implied by Libya. It rejected the Libyan argument suggesting that the difference in length of the respective coastlines was "of itself determinative of the seaward reach and area of continental shelf proper to each party," since this would "go far beyond the use of proportionality as a test of equity" (paragraph 58).

After reviewing these considerations, the Court was ready to draw a "provisional line" – a line of first instance – by using "a criterion and a method both of which are clearly destined to play an important role in producing the final result" before proceeding to the second stage of examining the "provisional solution in the light of the requirements derived from other criteria, which may call for a correction of this initial result" (paragraph 60). The Court had no doubt that the appropriate criterion of first instance, directly related to the basis of the state's legal title to the continental shelf, was that of distance (or the "principle of adjacency as measured by distance"). As to the method, the Court considered the median line to be the most judicious first step toward an equitable result. The equidistance method, the Court stressed, was not the only method applicable to the dispute, and it did not even have the benefit of a presumption in its favour: it must be shown to lead to an equitable result. In the circumstances, it was found equitable not to take account of the uninhabited island of Filfla in the construction of the provisional median line, so as to avoid the disproportionate effect a median line would have had in the first instance (paragraphs 61–4).

The provisional line was then subjected to adjustment by reason of certain relevant circumstances. Among the considerations dismissed as irrelevant, for the purposes of adjustment, was the comparative land-mass size of Malta and Libya. The marked disparity between the lengths of the two coasts, on the other hand, was held to be a relevant circumstance that warranted significant adjustment of the provisional median line. It was felt necessary to consider the general (regional) context in which the delimitation had to be effected. In regional perspective, although the delimitation related only to the continental shelf appertaining to two states, it was also "a delimitation between a portion of the southern littoral and a portion of the northern littoral of the Central Mediterranean." From this macrogeographical viewpoint, the "southward location" of the coasts of the Maltese islands was a geographical feature that constituted a relevant circumstance. Malta was seen as a relatively small feature in a semi-enclosed sea. Taking these two circumstances into account – disparity in the length of coastlines and Malta's "southward location" in a semi-enclosed region – it was necessary to adjust the delimitation line so that it would lie closer to the coasts of Malta. The need for this northward adjustment was reinforced by the fact that the unadjusted provisional median line was controlled on both sides by a few salient points on a short stretch of coast: two points eleven miles apart for Malta, and several points concentrated east of Ras Tajoura for Libya (paragraphs 66–71).

The Court then established the extreme limit of a northward "transposition" of the provisional median line by reference to a hypothetical model based on Malta's relative proximity to the Italian land mass (paragraph 72). By this reasoning an equitable boundary between Libya and Malta must be to the south of a notional median line between Libya and Sicily. The Court concluded that a shift of about two-thirds of the distance between the Malta-Libya median line and the line located 24′ further north gave an equitable result, and that the line was to be produced by "transposing" the median line northwards through 18′ of latitude. It was left to the parties and their experts to determine the exact point of intersection (paragraph 73).

In conclusion, the Court held that it was unnecessary in the circumstances to apply the test of proportionality based on the ratio between the lengths of the respective coasts and the areas of shelf attributed. It was possible to make a broad assessment of the equitableness of the result without resorting to precise measurement, which in any event presented practical difficulties because of the existence of basepoints on third-party territories.

Judges Mosler, Oda, and Schwebel dissented, and no fewer than seven of the majority of fourteen appended separate opinions expressing various degrees of discomfort with the reasoning in the majority judgment. Of the seven concurring, Judge (ad hoc) Valticos (nominated by Malta) came closest to dissenting, observing that in the present case, "which is a classic and straightforward situation of opposite coasts without complications of any kind, a solution based on the median line pure and simple would have had a more general relevance," and deploring the introduction of the "coast-length factor" and other "relevant circumstances" for the purposes of adjustment of the median line.[251] Judge Sette-Camara, also concurring, took exception to the majority judgment on several important points: for example, he criticized the continuing "relegation" of equidistance; he asserted that the "distance" criteria in article 76 of the 1982 Convention were not yet established as "rules" of customary international law, and that "natural prolongation" was still the only such "rule" governing delimitation of the shelf; he denied the relevance of EEZ criteria in the customary international law governing a delimitation issue restricted to the shelf; and he opposed the introduction of a regional, macrogeographical perspective on the central Mediterranean beyond the area in dispute between the litigant states.[252] Three other members of the majority, Judges Ruda, Bedjaoui, and Jiménez de Aréchaga, objected to the majority's silence with respect to Malta's "excessive and unjustified" *trapezium* ("a radical projection of its coasts in all directions").[253] Judge Mbaye objected to the majority's suggestion that the considerable distance between the two coastlines was a relevant consideration requiring adjustment of the preliminary median line, and attempted to reinforce the majority's contention that the natural prolongation and distance criteria are complementary rather than contradictory concepts.[254] Judge El-Khani merely observed that "a reasonable degree of proportionality, taking into account the lengths of the coasts of the two Parties," should have produced a line lying further north than the line drawn by the court.[255]

The dissenting judges departed even further from the majority decision. Judge Mosler, taking a strict "unitarian" view of the judicial task by emphasizing its declaratory purpose,[256] denied the existence of any special geographical circumstances that would justify departing from the median line, which he regarded as the "equitable solution" in the circumstances of the case. He deplored the majority's decision to exclude the northeastern sector of the area in dispute between Malta and Libya by reason of third-party claims to that sector.[257] Judge Schwebel was similarly opposed to the "undue truncation" of the Court's delimitation line in deference to Italy's claims in the northeastern sector, and was sharply critical of the majority's unnecessarily vague references to "relevant circumstances" in support of its transposition of the median line.[258] The longest dissenting opinion was rendered by Judge Oda. In a forty-six-page critique, he began by identifying five "misconceptions" in the majority judgment. First, he challenged the majority's contention that the natural prolongation and distance criteria were complementary concepts, suggesting that such a statement was nothing more than an attempt to keep natural prolongation alive "by artificial respiration." Second, he questioned the Court's decision to restrict its task of delimitation to a narrow area "merely in order not to risk interfering with a third State's claim," and regretted the Court's earlier decision to reject Italy's application for permission to intervene. Third, he criticized the majority's "misapplication" of the proportionality test, and, fourth, its "maladjustment" of the equidistance line. Finally, he departed from the majority treatment of the opposite-state situation for the purpose of applying the preliminary median line. He noted the failure of UNCLOS III to indicate "positive rules" for the delimitation of the continental shelf, and proceeded to reappraise at length the equidistance-special circumstances rule of 1958 and to comment on the "misunderstanding" of proportionality and half-effect in the ICJ's judgments of 1982 and 1984. He then suggested his own line of delimitation.[259]

In view of these criticisms, it must be questioned whether the official 14–3 decision truly reflects the extent of the split among the judges participating in the case. In five of the separate opinions, the divergence from the majority's reasoning is sufficiently marked to constitute de facto dissents. All five, in a less charitable mood, might have chosen to join the three dissenters, but were apparently persuaded by the majority not to do so in order to preserve the appearance of some degree of judicial unity. In reality, however, it seems accurate to say that the split in the Court was closer to 9–8 than 14–3. From a "unitarian" viewpoint, at least, this judgment seems to show the International Court of Justice in serious disarray.

"Unitarian" disappointment with the majority judgment may be attributable chiefly to the Court's treatment of its own provisional median line. It is not irrelevant to note that the Court's "adjustment" of the provisional line northwards was so massive that it was obliged to describe it as a "transposition." Even functionalists might wonder why, in a straightforward opposite-state situation, it was found appropriate to deviate so far from the traditional median line, especially at a time when the need for equality of treatment between opposite states may seem to have been reinforced rather than reduced by the merger of EEZ and continental shelf delimitation criteria at UNCLOS III.

On the other hand, functionalists are likely to welcome the Court's treatment of the third-party-interest problem as an ingenious effort to provide a truly effective facilitative service to the parties. A facilitative judgment, it may be argued, is wholly prospective and problem-oriented in character, and should not be constrained unduly by the bilateral, or bifurcatory, frame of reference traditionally associated with adversarial proceedings. To have said that the problem was solely one between the litigant states would have been to introduce a procedurally convenient fiction in the face of facts already brought to the Court's attention. To have denied these facts might have contributed, in some degree, to the satisfaction of the "unitarian" sense of judicial propriety, but would have introduced an element of artificiality into a problem-solving process. For functionalists it seems a step forward, not backward, for a tribunal to give weight to the regional (or subregional) characteristics of the physical situation with which it must deal and to acknowledge the relevance of third-party interests in that region without prejudgment of other disputes that should be settled, preferably through negotiation.[260]

Despite criticism of the Court's decision, and despite Maltese disappointment with the outcome, the award became the basis of a continental shelf delimitation agreement concluded by Libya and Malta in 1986.

Conclusions

A number of major trends can be discerned in the emerging pattern of adjudication in the field of ocean boundary delimitation.

1 Since the first of the relevant modern adjudications (by the ICJ in 1969), there has been a clear trend toward an explicit acceptance of the facilitative role of the tribunal, although the scope of the facilitative function assigned to the tribunal varies from case to case, as does the tribunal's interpretation of it.

2 Chiefly because of the facilitative nature of their role, tribunals have been obliged to adopt a particularistic approach to the settlement of delimitation disputes. In warning against the danger of over-conceptualization, they have underlined the need to give maximum attention to the "circumstances" of each situation, especially the geographical features of the area in dispute.

3 The situation-specific approach, involving an emphasis on the relatively "neutral" facts of geography, has resulted in a corresponding de-emphasis on the traditional discussion of applicable rules and principles of international law at an abstract level. The "factors" rather than the "norms" represent the engine of adjudication.

4 Doctrinal difficulties in the application of norms have been compounded by contextual difficulties in the weighting of factors. In some cases, confusion over "applicable rules and principles" has given way to confusion over "relevant circumstances."

5 Questions concerning the juridical (and possibly political) significance of UNCLOS III as a law-making process have contributed to a split among the judges of the International Court of Justice in the context of ocean boundary delimitation. This split seems to be widening. It has been aggravated by jurisprudential questions concerning the appropriate judicial exercise of an explicitly facilitative function, which clearly

goes beyond the "unitarian" task of merely declaring the law and tends toward a more discretionary form of judgment.

6 The declaratory function has now been discharged through the provision of a "basic norm" of delimitation by a chamber of the ICJ, but the full court has not yet validated this formulation. This formulation serves a useful "unitarian" purpose, but its importance may be less than it now appears to be if the trend to facilitative awards continues.

7 Tribunals seem to be agreed on the need to produce an "equitable solution" to a delimitation problem, but they are divided over the utility of the quest for "equitable principles." Those who support the search for such principles justify their effort on the ground that the pursuit of equity must be based on law. Those who prefer to describe the process as a choice of "equitable criteria" come closer to acknowledging the result-oriented nature of the task, but they are reluctant to concede the subjectivities inherent in the process, and they deny especially that it is indistinguishable from a decision *ex aequo et bono* by treating the latter solely as a procedural concept.

8 The general downgrading of legal rules and principles as the chief foundation of judicial boundary-making is reflected in a consistent relegation of equidistance from the level of "rule" or "principle" to that of "method". Tribunals have consistently denied the primacy of equidistance, even as a method, and have sometimes appeared to be biased against the use of equidistance (or median line), even in a straightforward opposite-state situation.

9 To the extent that tribunals have reflected a bias against equidistance even as a method of delimitation, they have created a divergence from treaty-making practice, in which equidistance is still a common and important element in ocean boundary delimitation.

10 The earlier doctrine of natural prolongation has been reduced by tribunals to a very low level of relevance in the delimitation of the continental shelf (as distinguished from the determination of seaward limits). "Unitarian" efforts to extract delimitation criteria per se from the natural prolongation doctrine have been unsuccessful, partly because of the logical weakness of the suggested analogy, and partly because of the prevalence of distance criteria at UNCLOS III in the determination of the normal seaward limits of the shelf and the EEZ. Yet many judges are still reluctant to kill off the doctrine of natural prolongation, and hope to keep it alive by "artificial respiration," in Judge Oda's words, through the fiction that it and distance are complementary concepts essential to the juridical concept of the continental shelf.

11 The relegation of natural prolongation for the purposes of continental

shelf delimitation has resulted in the virtual demise of geological and geomorphological arguments, except possibly in conspicuous cases of geological discontinuity which might still be assigned weight as a special circumstance beyond the two-hundred-mile limit of the EEZ.

12 Despite references to the new distance criteria of UNCLOS III for the determination of seaward limits, the tribunals have not yet decided whether these criteria have the force of a rule of customary international law, much less what relevance they have to the task of delimitation. For these and related reasons, the relevance of adjacency considerations is still obscure.

13 Because of the de-emphasis on geomorphology and geology, the tribunals are more reluctant than ever to recognize the concept of a natural boundary on the continental shelf. Similarly, in the case of fishery zone or EEZ boundary delimitation disputes, they have tended to reject arguments based on ecology.

14 In recent adjudications little weight has been given to historical considerations. In the *Tunisia-Libya* case colonial history received some weight in support of a perpendicular line, but only in conjunction with other functional considerations of effectiveness.

15 There is a clear trend to the rejection of socio-economic considerations, despite their relevance to questions of equity (at least in the sense of distributive justice). This rejection usually is justified on the ground that socio-economic status is changeable in the short term, and that delimitation must be effected on the basis of permanent circumstances such as those of geography.

16 There is a recent tendency to adopt a macrogeographical perception of the physical situation, and thus to place the delimitation dispute in a larger regional (or subregional) perspective if geography permits. This perceptual disposition of tribunals seems to be explained by the logic inherent in the adoption of an explicitly facilitative approach to the task of adjudication.

17 It is not yet clear what trend is emerging by way of third-party intervention in the adjudication of ocean boundary delimitation disputes. Italy's and Malta's efforts to intervene failed in a technical (procedural) sense, yet both succeeded, in varying degrees, in bringing the relevance of third-party interests to the Court's attention, and thereby in reinforcing the argument in favour of adopting a regional (or subregional) perspective on the dispute being adjudicated.

18 There is some evidence of a growing realization by governments in-

volved in litigation or arbitration of the need to have a judicial delimitation effected with a high degree of technical precision. Especially when the tribunal is assigned a close-to-maximal facilitative role, as in the *Anglo-French* and *Gulf of Maine* adjudications, some care is taken to specify the desired level of geodetic and cartographic precision, and to provide the tribunal with technical assistance.

19 Despite the important changes that have taken place in the law of the sea since 1969, and despite the demise of the natural prolongation doctrine in the context of ocean boundary delimitation, the ICJ and other adjudicative bodies are reluctant to deny the juridical significance of many of the dicta offered in the *North Sea Continental Shelf* case. Most lawyers still look upon that decision as a landmark.

MODERN DELIMITATION TREATIES AND THE PATTERN OF STATE PRACTICE

Delimitation Agreements and State Practice

The post-classical period of international law has been a period of phenomenal growth in the treaty system of the world community. Since the end of the Second World War tens of thousands of agreements of every possible form and nomenclature have been concluded on virtually every subject matter of public concern, cutting across cultural, ideological, political, and economic lines. Consent, as expressed through treaty-making, has become the dominant value in bilateral diplomacy, binding states together in an ever-widening global network of negotiated settlements and arrangements.[261] In the post-classical period the nation-state system has become, in effect, a system of official transactions assisted in various ways by consensus-based outcomes of global and regional organizations.

Before the beginning of continental shelf doctrine, ocean boundary delimitation was limited to narrow areas of territorial sea between neighbouring states. Prior to the Second World War relatively few delimitation agreements were concluded: most sources refer to only two territorial sea boundary agreements – between Denmark and Sweden (Limits in the Sea 26) and between Italy and Turkey, both concluded in 1932.[262] Significantly, the first "early modern" ocean boundary treaty, concluded ten years later by Venezuela and the United Kingdom (for Trinidad and Tobago), concerned the delimitation of the continental shelf (LITS 11). In the following twenty-two years only six more ocean boundary agreements were negotiated. But beginning in 1965, when no fewer than seven were concluded in the same year, the resort to treaty for ocean boundary-making purposes accelerated. Fourteen treaties were concluded in 1971, and eleven in 1974; and by the end of 1980 at least 80 had been negotiated in the preceding sixteen years. By the end of 1987 it appeared that over 130 ocean boundary agreements were in existence, including the early listed ones dating from 1932.

In the history of ocean boundary delimitation nothing is more dramatic than this proliferation of (mostly) bilateral agreements. Almost 300 bilateral ocean boundary issues remain to be dealt with solely or partly through agreement with neighbouring states. Even allowing for the intractability of many of these issues, it is conceivable that well over 200 delimitation agreements may be in existence by the year 2000. Whatever the figure, it is likely that the final third of the twentieth century will be regarded by posterity as the golden age of boundary-making.

Even now, the mounting volume of delimitation agreements signifies that treaties provide the principal evidence of state practice in the delimitation of "lateral" boundaries, just as national promulgations provide the principal evidence of state practice in baseline delineation and the determination of seaward limits. As noted above, some recent trends in the adjudication of delimitation disputes have raised concern precisely because they constitute a divergence from the pattern of state practice as reflected in contemporary treaty-making. Unfortunately, it is not possible, at least in a monograph of this sort, to trace the diplomatic history of all delimitation agreements in existence, and the texts themselves reveal only part of the story.[263] Indeed, most of the texts are so sparsely written that the reader is left to guess which considerations carried the most weight during the process of negotiation. Until a more revealing history can be put together from many case studies focused on different countries and regions, only a few general trends in this form of treaty-making and patterns of state practice can be discerned.

Types and Variations

Of seventy-six delimitation treaties examined, all except four are bilateral.[264] The near-monopoly of the bilateral approach to ocean boundary delimitation may not be surprising, but, particularly in view of the trend in the adjudicative process toward taking judicial notice of third-party interests, excessive bilaterialism in boundary-making can aggravate the problem of promoting regional or subregional arrangements in ocean development and management.[265]

Most of the early modern delimitation agreements, from the period beginning in 1942, were concerned exclusively with delimitation of the continental shelf. Of the 76 instruments examined, 36 were exclusively or mainly concerned with the shelf. Of those 36 agreements, 3 also dealt with non-shelf matters. In addition, 10 others dealt mainly with the delimitation of the shelf, although their scope was more broadly defined in their titles. Thirty of the 76 instruments were concerned, both in title and in fact, with a maritime boundary that includes the water column and normally extends to those areas that come under the regime of the exclusive economic zone.

No more than seven of the delimitation agreements are limited in title and in fact to the territorial sea. But the vast majority of delimitation agreements deal wholly or chiefly with areas of the ocean beyond territorial limits, the areas of functional jurisdiction, such as the continental shelf, the EEZ, or exclusive fishing zones consonant with the EEZ regime. The continental shelf or fishing zone delimitation agreements may be characterized as unifunctional in purpose and the others as multifunctional. Since 1973 the most important trend in ocean boundary treaty-making has been the trend to multifunctional boundary treaties, most of which are explicitly or implicitly modelled on the UNCLOS III multifunctional concept of the exclusive economic zone extending to the seabed and subsoil as well as the superjacent waters.

Another distinction can be drawn between ocean boundary settlements and ocean boundary arrangements. Of the 76 instruments examined, at least 58 can be characterized as settlements in the sense that they are confined entirely to the final and permanent resolution of the linear issue of boundary location, with no provision for revision or adjustment procedures, much less any cross-boundary or other arrangements related to the maintenance of the boundary or the administration of the boundary area. Only 18 at most can be characterized as arrangements in any operational sense. Though still a minority, these treaty arrangements may increase proportionately as the interdependencies of hydrocarbon development, fishery development and management, pollution control, and other activities governed by the EEZ regime are more clearly perceived and translated into co-operative arrangements in state practice. As the administration of the EEZ (and the adjoining shelf) becomes more complex and more sophisticated, a trend to a wider variety of bilateral boundary-related arrangements between neighbouring states can be expected.

Finally, an examination of the geographical areas covered by the 130 existing instruments may make it possible to divide them into opposite-state and adjacent-state agreements. A superficial reference to the map suggests that two-thirds of these instruments fall into the opposite-state category, some 32 into the adjacent-state category, and the remaining 15 or so into a mixed category. But it is certain that a closer look at the areas negotiated would show that a black-and-white distinction between the first two categories cannot be easily maintained, and that many more than a dozen have elements both of oppositeness and adjacency in the situations dealt with.

Principles, Criteria, and Methods of Delimitation

It is often difficult when looking only at the texts of agreements to infer the principles, criteria, or methods of delimitation that were used by the parties, and it is virtually impossible to obtain a clear picture of all the other considerations injected into the negotiating process. Yet a few carefully qualified impressions can be derived from a comparison of the texts.

In almost all of the opposite-state agreements it is made explicit that the notion of equidistance has played an important role in the delimitation effect, sometimes as the "basis," sometimes as a "guiding principle."

In the adjacent-state and mixed agreements, equidistance is sometimes mentioned as an element, but as a rule delimitation between adjacent states seems to have been effected by a combination of methods, with no single "principle" or "criterion" given any saliency. In the adjacent-state agreements one finds frequent use of perpendicular lines, sometimes drawn against a parallel of latitude or meridian of longitude, sometimes against what appears to be the general direction of the coast, but more often against a straight line connecting basepoints selected from conspicuous coastal features. In other adjacent-state agreements the delimitation is essentially, or initially, a seaward projection of the land boundary drawn from the land terminus. It seems impossible to find any general pattern in the selection of basepoints in different coastal situations.

As to islands, rocks, and other offshore features, it is impossible to establish any general pattern in the way parties to opposite-state or adjacent-state delimitation agreements have agreed to grant or withhold "effect." Indeed, it seems unlikely that any pattern of state practice will ever be discernible in the choice of turning-points or basepoints in ocean boundary delimitation. When parties to a delimitation agreement negotiate adjustments to a preliminary or provisional line suggested at an earlier stage of negotiation, it may be presumed that both accept that such adjustments must be based on equitable considerations. But it seems improbable that adjudicators will ever have the benefit of empirically verifiable state practice in the weighing of such considerations for the purpose of boundary adjustment.

Continental Shelf Agreements

Of the agreements that are exclusively or mainly concerned with delimitation of the continental shelf, regardless of title, no fewer than thirty-four had been negotiated by the end of 1971 – that is, before the concept of a multifunctional regime had been advanced. These pre-UNCLOS III agreements on continental shelf delimitation were developed mostly by the littoral states of Europe (both western and eastern) and the Gulf. Of the thirty-four, only five were concluded outside those regions. Whether owing to regional or other factors, the similarity of the agreements is striking. Moreover, the similarities persist in the wording of continental shelf delimitation agreements concluded after 1971, to the extent that one suspects a widespread practice of imitation of preceding agreements.

Most of the basic elements of the standard type of continental shelf delimitation agreement had come together by the end of 1965 through the treaty-making practices of the Gulf and European states, which were heavily influenced by the corporate policies and practices of the petroleum industry, and presumably by the similarity of technologies deployed on their shelves. By the end of 1971, two years after the ICJ's ruling in the *North Sea Continental Shelf* cases, the mould had been set. The years thereafter were a period of global imitation with only a few relatively unimportant variations.

In its standard form, the continental shelf delimitation agreement consists typically of five to ten dispositive articles, limited to the purpose of resolving the linear issue of boundary location. The agreement begins, typically, with a preamble or article outlining the purpose for which the agreement was negotiated (for example, the exploration and exploitation of the natural resources of the shelf), and then refers to the general principle or criterion governing the delimitation (usually equidistance, especially in the case of opposite-state agreements). The principal method of delimitation (for example, median line) is often identified before the specific points (co-ordinates of longitude or latitude) through which the line is to be drawn are set out. Frequently, the chosen geometric technique for delineation is also named: for example, by straight lines, by geodetic lines, or by arcs of the great circle. A subsequent article sometimes designates a joint body, or two separate national agencies, to complete the process of delimitation with technical precision.

Generally, there is a provision dealing with the possibility of a natural resource deposit that straddles the boundary. A "single geological structure" or "straddling" clause usually provides that the sharing of such a deposit or of the revenues derived from its development will be settled through "negotiation" or "consultation" between the parties in a fair and equitable manner. This consensual method is usually the only one mentioned for the settlement of any dispute arising from the agreement. Frequently there is also a clause emphasizing that the agreement is limited to the purpose of delimitation described in the preamble or opening article, and is not to be used for any cognate purpose such as the allocation of jurisdiction over superadjacent waters or airspace. The final clauses of the treaty usually deal with the method of ratification and the manner in which the treaty will come into force.

Despite the similarities among most of these continental shelf delimitation settlements, there are, of course, some deviations from the norm. In some instruments the delimitation is effected with sufficient precision that reference to a technical body is deemed unnecessary. In a few – not more than six – a third-party dispute settlement method, or at least a policy, is agreed to. Usually arbitration is the chosen method, but in three agreements the parties agree to submit a dispute to the International Court of Justice.[266] In more recent years some delimitation settlements have been extended beyond the seabed and subsoil to the superjacent waters, consonant with the purposes of the EEZ regime, and in a few cases an effort has been made to incorporate some form of co-operative arrangement.

The most significant deviation in the form of arrangement is an agreement to resort to joint development, which avoids the difficulties of precise delineation of a delimitation line by defining a joint development zone within the boundary area in dispute. Provision is made for a joint commission to facilitate development within the designated zone. Detailed arrangements can be added for the establishment of a regime to govern co-operative arrangements for the exploration and exploitation of the natural resources of the shelf in that area. The two most conspicuous examples of a joint development treaty arrangement are those concluded by Japan and the Republic of Korea in 1974 (Francalanci et al.) and by Malaysia and Thailand in 1979. An interstate joint development arrangement based on treaty is to be distinguished from an intercorporate unitization or alternative arrangement, which may arise from the discovery of a "single geological structure" straddling a previously delimited boundary, and which may or may not be reflected in a subsequent treaty arrangement between the states.

Of special interest is the emergence of a few post-adjudicative agreements designed to effect, complete, or revise the delimitation of a continental shelf area after the parties have obtained an award, as requested, from an adjudicative body of their choosing. For example, after the ICJ decision in the 1969 *North Sea Continental Shelf* cases, the Federal Republic of Germany negotiated delimitation agreements with Denmark and the Netherlands in 1971.[267] In the same year, the United Kingdom's delimitation agreements with the Netherlands and Denmark, negotiated in 1965 and 1966 respectively, were revised in light of the ICJ's 1969 decision.[268] The 1981 Jan Mayen agreement on continental shelf delimitation was negotiated in light of the Conciliation Commission's report and recommendations to the governments of Iceland and Norway published in the same year, and in 1987 Malta and Libya concluded an agreement based on the ICJ's award in the 1985 continental shelf case.

Other Agreements

Of the remaining (non-shelf) ocean boundary agreements, only seven are concerned solely with delimitation of the territorial sea, but the vast majority are ocean boundary settlements and/or arrangements for water and seabed areas beyond the outer limits of the territorial sea. Normally, the reference is to a "maritime boundary," and the settlement or arrangement usually can be construed as the negotiated division of the EEZs of the two neighbouring states that are parties to the agreement. Despite their greater potentiality for variance, these EEZ-type boundary agreements are mostly as short and simple as their earlier continental shelf counterparts. In most cases only one all-purpose delimitation line is drawn, and the elements that constitute the body of the agreement are essentially the same as those that constitute the shelf agreements. By and large, their outstanding features are simplicity and, given the inherent complexity of EEZ administration, a lack of sophistication. It may still be too early to perceive any clear pattern in state practice in the replacement of simple delimitation settlements for the shelf with more complex and sophisticated settlements and arrangements for the EEZ.

A conspicuous and impressive exception is the famous Torres Strait treaty concluded by Australia and Papua New Guinea in 1978.[269] Of all the agreements in existence, this instrument stands alone as a functionally sophisticated approach to ocean boundary-making under the conditions of the new law of the sea in the late twentieth century.[270] Parts II through V of this long and complex treaty are worthy of special notice.

Part II consists of articles 2, 3, and 4. In article 2 each party recognizes the other's sovereignty over designated islands whose territorial status had not previously been clear or settled. "Sovereignty over an island" includes sovereignty over its territorial sea, the airspace above the island and its territorial sea, the seabed and subsoil beneath its territorial sea, and any island, rock, or low-tide elevation that lies within its territorial sea. Article 3 delineates territorial sea boundaries and the outer limits of the territorial seas for various designated islands in the treaty area. Article 4 develops the concept of maritime jurisdiction and, consonant with the UNCLOS III concept of functional jurisdiction, distinguishes three subsets for the purposes of the treaty: seabed jurisdiction, fisheries jurisdiction, and residual jurisdiction (which relate to such matters as the preservation of the marine environment, marine research, and the production of energy from the water, currents, and winds).

Part III, which consists of articles 5 through 9, deals with sovereignty and jurisdiction over various "related matters." Article 5 makes provision for existing petroleum exploration permits. Article 6 is an improved version of the standard "single geological structure" clause of continental shelf delimitation agreements. Article 7 contains detailed provisions designed to protect the freedoms of navigation and overflight in designated areas. Articles 8 and 9 deal with the provision and maintenance of navigational aids and the entitlement to wrecks.

Part IV creates a protected zone in the Torres Strait consisting of "all the land, sea, airspace, seabed and subsoil" within a designated sub-area of the larger area covered by the treaty. The principal purpose of the parties in establishing the zone, as explained in article 10, is "to acknowledge and protect the traditional way of life and livelihood of the traditional inhabitants, including their traditional fishing and free movement." To this end Part IV elaborates special arrangements for "free movement and traditional customary rights" (article 12); for protection of the marine environment (article 13); for protection of fauna and flora (article 14); for prohibition of mining and drilling of the seabed (article 15); for immigration, customs, quarantine, and health (article 16); for "implementation and coordination" (article 17); for "liaison arrangements" (article 18); and for the establishment and maintenance of an advisory and consultative body for the Torres Strait (article 19).

Finally, Part V establishes a special regime, or subregime, for commercial fisheries to be permitted in the protected zone of Torres Strait. Article 20 grants priority to traditional fishing. Subsequent provisions relate to "conservation, management, and optimum utilisation" (article 21); "conservation and management of individual fisheries" (article 22); sharing of the catch of the commercial fisheries in the protected zone (article 23); "transitional entitlement" (article 24); "preferential entitlement" (article 25); licensing arrangements (article 26); third-state fishing in commercial fisheries of the protected zone (article 27); and inspection and enforcement procedures (article 28).

The sophistication of this treaty owes much to the special characteristics of the region in question, and is not easily duplicated elsewhere. Yet it sets a new and ambitious standard for ocean boundary-making in the age of extended maritime jurisdiction and multiple regimes of functional jurisdiction. Other efforts at ocean boundary-making should be judged against this standard.

Some "post-adjudicative" agreements of the EEZ type may be expected in the years to come – for example, between Canada and the United States, in view of the award of the chamber of the ICJ in the *Gulf of Maine* case of 1984, or between Guinea and Guinea-Bissau, in light of the 1985 award by the ad hoc arbitration tribunal established by those two states. Such agreements will provide a useful barometer for gauging the feasibility of entrusting an adjudicative body with a facilitative function in a context having a potentially high degree of functional sophistication.

Regional Trends

A regional breakdown of 100 delimitation agreements shows a wide variance in the frequency of resort to this kind of treaty-making. Northern Europe easily leads with 30 instruments, followed by Asia (14), Central America and the Caribbean (13), and the Middle East (10). More revealingly, of the 30 northern European agreements no fewer than 24 deal exclusively or mainly with delimitation of the continental shelf, and almost all of those 24 are in conformity with the standard form of a continental shelf settlement. The trend to multifunctional boundary-making and more complex and more innovative arrangements lies outside Northern Europe, and indeed outside Europe as a whole. These data from Europe seem to project the image of a conservative continent reluctant to follow the main directions of UNCLOS III, at least in ocean boundary-making practices.

Some other regional patterns are worthy of comment. Despite a close association with the early modern movement to extended jurisdiction, South America has shown little interest in ocean boundary-making initiatives or innovations. Africa, with a much larger number of littoral and coastal states (36), has a long way to go in ocean boundary-making. Most of the innovation seems to have come from the South Pacific and East Asia. The Gulf states have been content for many years with their early initiatives in continental shelf delimitation settlements. Innovative regional (or subregional) boundary-related arrangements have not yet been attempted in those regions that seem most likely to benefit from such initiatives: for example, West Africa, Southeast Asia, and the Caribbean and Central America.

In other respects it is more difficult to draw regional distinctions. The Northern European continental shelf delimitation agreements seem to lean heavily on equidistance-related considerations, but apparently not much more so than agreements of the same kind negotiated in other regions. Most of the 100 treaty instruments are too sparsely written to permit interregional variations to be discerned by content analysis. Work of this kind will have to be left to in-depth case studies.

Conclusions

The first generation of ocean boundary treaty-making in the post-classical era, in the thirty-year period beginning 1942, had four primary characteristics. First, it was largely preoccupied with the prospect of offshore petroleum development on the continental shelf. Second, a large proportion of these shelf delimitation agreements, emanating mostly from the Gulf and Northern Europe, achieved a high degree of conformity with an early model of short, simple, and entirely dispositive settlements, complicated only by the hint of possible future arrangements in the standard "single geological structure" clause. Third, most of these continental shelf settlements were clearly influenced by the parties' agreement that significant weighting should be given to equidistance-related considerations, and presumably, though less clearly, that the effect to be given to special geographical circumstances should be negotiated with a view to reaching an equitable outcome. Fourth, it seems clear that the negotiation of these continental shelf delimitation settlements at the intergovernmental level was closely linked with previous or concurrent negotiations or consultations on future arrangements at the intercorporate level. The apparent rigidity and simplicity of these treaty instruments is therefore somewhat deceptive. The approach to this kind of ocean boundary-making in the first generation was almost certainly much more sophisticated than the texts of these governmental documents imply.

The second generation of bilateral treaty-making, beginning with the advent of UNCLOS III in the early 1970s opened up a very different prospect of ocean boundary-making for the final years of the twentieth century. The emergence of the EEZ regime of multifunctional jurisdiction has begun to generate a more diversified approach to the negotiation of ocean boundary delimitation settlements and arrangements. It is too early to discern any general pattern in this new mode of treaty-making, and it may be shown in succeeding years that this area of state practice resists the tendency to patterned behaviour that is normally found in treaty-making. There is some evidence, persuasive rather than compelling, that the new trend will be to longer, more complex, functionally sophisticated, boundary treaty arrangements designed to be flexible and conducive to co-operative ocean development and management. But it may take a decade or more for the functionalist approach to ocean boundary-making to be clearly reflected in treaty behaviour around the world.

PART THREE

The Functionalist Approach to Ocean Boundary-Making

CHAPTER TWELVE

The Theory

THE FUNCTIONS OF AN OCEAN BOUNDARY

Boundary-making is a primordial activity. We have always felt the need to make and maintain boundaries around ourselves, our personal spaces, and the possessions we cherish.[1] At least throughout the history of the modern nation-state, we have institutionalized our instinct for territory by elevating the "official" boundary to the level of a social imperative. Indeed, at the present stage of human development, boundaries in national form have sometimes been allowed to assume a symbolic significance that transcends mere reason or common sense. We purport to be bound to define the limits of national society even as we acknowledge the nonsense of partitioning the human environment.[2] We behave as if the core of our existence can be protected only by establishing its periphery.[3]

In the age of nationalism, our collective aspirations have focused on the institutions of government within the limits of state territory. The assertion of sovereignty within these national spaces has been seen as the best hope that welfare will be promoted, order maintained, and loyalties rewarded. Over and above the mystique of national consciousness, the national boundary represents the limits of government agency powers and responsibilities. Yet, despite the importance of its administrative function in the modern era, the land boundary defies rational analysis.

The prospect of rationality in boundary-making seems to rest with the ocean boundary. With the extension of high technology and public administration far beyond the shoreline, new questions must be asked about the purposes of boundary-making in the modern world. How much land boundary-making theory can be adapted usefully to the sea? How much should the future course of boundary-making at sea be influenced by the history of boundary-making on land? How much stock do we wish to place in land-to-sea analogies? How much emotional capital can we afford to invest in ocean boundaries, and in the processes that set them apart from boundaries on land?

The functionalist approach to these questions begins with the distinctiveness of ocean boundaries. The modern era of ocean boundary-making has begun at a time when new boundaries need not carry a heavy freight of symbolism. At least until the advent of artificial island communities in the sea, ocean boundaries cannot impinge directly on human settlements. Some local boundaries in the sea may be emotionally significant for the neighbouring coastal communities, and certainly some modern offshore boundary issues are divisive because of their economic or industrial consequences. But most maritime boundaries that must be drawn under the conditions of the new law of the sea are designed essentially to serve *specific administrative purposes* that can be easily identified and clearly distinguished. According to their degree of suitability for these specific purposes, ocean boundaries should be drawn and maintained by reference to their "functionality." For the first time we have to examine the case for rational boundary-making.

Within a rational frame of reference, we should be prepared to question the certitudes of the past. Should all ocean boundaries be fixed and permanent settlements, regardless of future events? Should they have some relationship, wherever possible, to the constancies of nature? Should ocean boundaries be drawn with the greatest possible precision by means of the best available technology? Is an ocean boundary just a line?

In the general theory of land boundary-making, the linear concept of a "boundary" is sensibly distinguished from the areal concept of a "frontier." The earlier and rather vague concept of a frontier has given way to the more precise institution of the "border," which may or may not give rise to the need for a designated "border zone," if necessary to serve a specific administrative purpose. In the ocean we are likely to have a greater need to preserve the concept of a "boundary zone" for the purposes of joint development or co-operative management. Given the certainty of a wide variety of future arrangements for ocean development and management purposes, across accepted or preconceived boundaries of one sort or another, a strictly linear conception of the ocean boundary seems unlikely to endure. In practice, the history of ocean zoning goes back much further than was generally understood, and the current need to engage in "sea-use planning" with some degree of sophistication has generated a need for managerial thinking about the making as well as the maintenance of ocean boundaries. (On managerial thinking about boundaries, see chapter 3.) Especially at the subnational level, ocean management may be hindered rather than helped by an unduly simple and strictly linear conception of an ocean boundary.

The nature of an ocean boundary is bound to be affected by two concurrent trends in ocean development and management. The first of these is the trend toward a proliferation of *extensive zones of national administrative authority under "regimes" of functional jurisdiction vested in the coastal state*.[4] The sophistication and effectiveness of zonal practices at sea will vary widely with the coastal state's capabilities in public administration. In many situations it must be expected that "patrimonial" sentiment associated with national spaces, which may be characterized as "quasi-sovereign," will continue to curtail the prospects of a fully rational approach to ocean boundary-making. On the other hand, there is also in evidence a newer trend toward the building of *regional or subregional "regimes" of negotiated arrangements designed to facilitate co-operation in ocean development and management*.[5] This second trend, supported by the "co-operative ethic" of UNCLOS III,[6] is likely to be conducive to a flexible approach to ocean boundaries, which will require a balancing of the areal and linear implications of the boundary-making process. It reflects region-building as much as nation-building.[7]

According to the functionalist approach to ocean boundary-making, the making of the boundary should be strongly influenced by the administrative reasons for the boundary in question and by the anticipated administrative problems associated with its maintenance. On the one hand, the delineation of baselines and the determination of seaward limits should be influenced by the kind of administrative responsibilities to be discharged by the coastal state's agencies within the zone of adjacent waters, subject to the provisions of the relevant regime of coastal state jurisdiction. On the other hand, the delimitation of "lateral" boundaries between neighbouring (opposite or adjacent) states should be influenced by the need for co-operative development and management by these states in transboundary and adjacent ocean areas, subject to the provisions of the relevant regime.

Baselines and seaward limits should be regarded as "dysfunctional" when they seem to obstruct rather than facilitate the globally approved purposes which the relevant zone and regime are designed to serve. These two kinds of ocean boundaries should, therefore, be regarded as capable of at least minor adjustment as to location and nature, but since the relevant provisions governing baselines and seaward limits under the UNCLOS III Convention are presented in the form of rules and formulae, any deviation from the provisions should be justified by the coastal state by reference to legitimate and demonstrated administrative need. The classical view, reflecting the "unitarian" perspective on legal development, is that these provisions – especially those delineation provisions carried over from UNCLOS I and customary international law – are strictly binding *rules* and that no significant deviation should be countenanced. It might be feared that some coastal states will be tempted to adopt a post-classical view that the provisions are merely *guidelines* and that it lies within their discretion to disregard them or to modify them at will. A functionalist compromise would be to accept the UNCLOS III provisions on the delineation of baselines (and closing lines) and the determination of seaward limits as globally approved and legally obligatory *criteria*, and to acknowledge that the weight of the coastal state's burden to justify a deviation increases with the significance of the deviation (see chapter 14).

"Lateral" boundaries between opposite or adjacent states are, on the other hand, the outcome of bilateral diplomacy. At UNCLOS III it was stipulated only that they should be "equitable." This kind of boundary is intended to be consonant with the neighbouring states' needs in ocean development and management, and especially with their need for co-operation in transboundary and adjacent waters, but the outcome is above all a negotiated agreement. The "lateral" boundary is either a relatively simple linear *settlement* designed essentially to resolve the issue of precise location and measurement, or it is part of a more complicated *arrangement* designed to promote and regulate co-operative transboundary management.

To the extent that the treatment of a delimitation problem should be influenced by the need for legal certainty, technical precision, and political stability, or even permanence, it should be governed by the logic of settlement. To the extent that the treatment should be influenced by the need for social and economic flexibility and administrative efficiency, it should be governed by the logic of arrangement. The weighting assigned to these competing value considerations will vary with the way in which one characterizes the delimitation problem, the approach to be adopted, and the area of relevance. (See chapter 8.) A broad characterization is likely to draw attention to the need for flexible and efficient institutional arrangements, whereas a narrow characterization focusing on issues will tend to attract the logic of settlement. In functionalist theory, therefore, ocean boundary delimitation can be said to serve the two functions of settlement and arrangement.

According to this view, ocean boundary-making should be treated not as a discrete act, but as a process or even as a mode of behaviour.[8] The process is characterized as consisting not only of one or more acts, but also of an indefinite succession of administrative actions. Consequently, the functions of an ocean boundary refer to the entire range of values, interests, and other factors associated with foreseeable outcomes of the boundary-making and boundary-maintenance processes.

THE INHERITANCE OF FUNCTIONALIST THEORY

Any approach to boundary-making theory that places emphasis on the functions of boundaries may properly be considered a "functionalist" approach. The term "functionalism," however, has been used in most of the biological, social, and behavioural sciences, as well as in philosophy and the humanities, in widely varying ways for widely varying purposes.[9] This monograph is not derived from any of those functionalist approaches or theories, but it should be acknowledged that some of the elements of the functionalist approach to ocean boundary-making have been borrowed from functionalist theory in international law and political science.

Above all, the approach developed here is an adaptation of the "policy science" approach to the study of world order developed systematically by Harold D. Lasswell and Myres S. McDougal. Especially in its problem orientation and contextuality, it is believed to owe most to the policy science school of international law.[10] In this manner it departs from traditional, rule-oriented models of law, and offers in their place a more dynamic paradigm of legal development which requires resort to an interdisciplinary frame of reference. Some of the specifically functionalist elements – for example, the emphasis on international organization and regional co-operation – have been associated with international lawyers such as Wilfred Jenks, Wolfgang Friedmann, Oscar Schachter, and Richard Falk.[11]

The functionalist approach to ocean boundary-making may also owe something to earlier functionalist and neo-functionalist theorists in the fields of international organization[12] and regional integration,[13] but contemporary political theory seems to have most to offer in the theory of regime-building developed by scholars such as Oran Young.[14]

In common with most of these writers, I believe that the development of a safe, equitable, and effective world order is most likely to be achieved through a disciplined interaction of states. Such an interaction would be characterized by various modes of collaboration in functionally designated areas of shared interest in circumstances that require the assistance or active participation of international agencies.[15] It might even be questioned whether all forms of international collaboration must depend on the constant political will and frequent political initiative of national governments.[16] More trust is to be placed in the collaborative behaviour of *los tecnicos* than in the competitive behaviour of *los politicos*.[17] Regional interest in co-operation may sometimes be better served by a regime of arrangements designed specifically for ocean development and management rather than by reliance on an existing structure.[18] Form follows function. Accordingly, in conformity with functionalist theory in political science, it seems that safe, equitable, and effective boundary-making in the ocean is attainable, under conditions of near-rationality, only if the concept of an ocean boundary is desymbolized and the boundary-making task is assigned as far as possible to the appropriate experts and technocrats.

CHAPTER THIRTEEN

The Processes

THE BUREAUCRATIC PROCESS

Inputs

Between 1968 and 1982 – a period of intense global diplomacy – most of the controversy over boundary-making focused on the diplomatic process required for delimitation between neighbouring states[1] and the "monitoring" process required for the determination of the seaward limits of the continental shelf beyond two hundred miles (see the section entitled "The New Law of the Sea" in chapter 9). Yet implicit in the phenomenon of extended jurisdiction is the inevitability of a trend to zoning by national agencies within greatly extended limits of coastal state jurisdiction (see chapter 7), at least in those countries with an ambitious style and tradition of public administration, and matching capabilities.

Because of the great variances in the styles and traditions of public administration at the national level, and the even greater disparity in capabilities, we may expect to see leadership initiatives by some governments provoking imitation by others. A great deal of money already has been spent on international research and training programs in ocean-use planning, zoning techniques, and boundary-related arrangements.[2] If this kind of imitation happens fairly quickly on a widespread scale, national bureaucratic participants in the ocean boundary-making process may discover that an international mode or standard exists to guide them. But even under the impact of external influences, bureaucratic ocean boundary-makers at the national level will find themselves required to engage in some degree of internal diplomacy between representatives of two or more agencies of national government, especially in the case of federal states with subnational levels of government. At least in the matter of baseline delineation, the provisions of the 1982 Convention will be available to help relax the tensions that build up in the course of internal negotiations.

Because of the nature of the bureaucratic process, which is devoted to the purposes of public administration, bureaucratic boundary-making should emerge as the most rational approach to the task. Compared with the diplomatic and intermediary processes, it should suffer from fewer temptations to expand the scope of reference, as in diplomacy, or to restrict it, as in adjudication. It also seems to offer the best prospect of an appropriate interdisciplinary mix of data and viewpoints, and to be conducive to the adoption of a managerial approach to ocean boundary-making.

In theory, the bureaucratic process seems also to be the most likely of the three to remain within the control of the appropriate experts. *Los tecnicos* are the persons most aware of the managerial and operational implications of ocean boundary-making, and thus are the best equipped to approach those tasks with a view to their effectiveness, tested by practical experience in inter-agency and intergovernmental co-operation and in the day-to-day implementation of measures for administration and enforcement. In practice, of course, interference from the political managers of government and industry (*los politicos*) may introduce distortions or biases that threaten to impair the functional rationality of the bureaucratic undertaking. Whether this happens will depend on whether an ambitious politician, industrialist, or interest group perceives an advantage to be gained by creating an issue out of the boundary-making exercise, and on the reaction to the issue within the responsive sector of the political system.[3]

Stages

In the determination of seaward limits and the delineation of baselines and closing lines, the bureaucratic boundary-making process can involve as many as six stages.

The first stage must be a process of *consultation*. Even within a country where boundary-making is assigned exclusively to one agency at one level of government, without a political or legal requirement to consult the public, some consultation will be necessary among colleagues with different inputs within the agency. Lawyers must collaborate with hydrographers, cartographers, and scientists of various kinds. With a view to the allocative implications of the undertaking, consultation normally will extend to two or more agencies, often to two or more levels of government, and sometimes to the constituencies affected. Since both kinds of unilateral ocean boundaries always have an international aspect, it may occasionally be necessary to engage in private consultations with neighbouring or other states with a potential interest in challenging the validity of the proposed boundary.

In certain circumstances, consultations may have to be followed by a more formal process of *negotiation* with other agencies and levels of government. Especially in a large and complex federal state, some degree of internal diplomacy may be necessary to advance the boundary-making process. It is less likely that the government will wish to acknowledge the need for formal negotiations with another state, however important the need for consultation with it.

The third stage is the drawing of the baseline, closing line, or seaward limits with some degree of technical precision – the *delineation* stage. This stage concludes with a cartographic representation of the boundary and the statutory determination of the co-ordinates of longitude and latitude.

Delineation is sometimes followed by a *validation* stage, during which the line is challenged and tested by reference to constitutional or treaty criteria. In circumstances where the constitutionality of the boundary is questioned, the validation is an entirely domestic matter. If the baseline or closing line is alleged to be drawn in violation of the applicable provisions of a law-making treaty, such as the 1958 Convention on the Territorial Sea and Contiguous Zone or the 1982 UN Convention on the Law of the Sea, validation may be entrusted to an international tribunal. After the entry into force of the 1982 Convention, the validation process for seaward limits of the continental shelf beyond the two-hundred-mile EEZ regime, drawn by the coastal state in accordance with the formula prescribed in article 76, will involve the Commission on the Limits of the Continental Shelf.

If the line is deemed or demonstrated to have passed all legal challenges, it becomes established in the continuing and routine process of *administration*. This stage might also be described as "boundary maintenance," except that this phrase gives an inappropriately permanent or static appearance to what in reality may be a dynamic interaction of bureaucratic procedures and arrangements related to the boundary.

Indeed, the realities of boundary administration might be such as to require eventually a final stage of *revision*, designed to ensure that the boundary facilitates and does not obstruct the administrative purposes it is intended to serve. The likelihood that the appropriate agencies might be induced to revise an ocean boundary for reasons associated with ocean zoning requirements is probably greater than in land boundary-making.

THE SIMPLE DIPLOMATIC PROCESS

Inputs

A "lateral" ocean boundary between neighbouring states usually is drawn at the end of a bilateral negotiation process. If the process remains direct throughout, and no resort to any kind of intermediary is necessary, it can be characterized as "simple," though not necessarily easy.

UNCLOS III has given primacy to the diplomatic process for the purposes of delimitation between opposite or adjacent states. By the end of 1986, over 120 ocean boundary delimitation agreements had been negotiated since the 1950s,[4] and the rate of treaty-making seems likely to be maintained, if not accelerated, for a decade or more. We may expect well over 200 ocean boundary delimitation agreements to be in existence by the end of the twentieth century. Both external and internal diplomacy will play a central role in the shaping of the second generation of ocean boundaries in the post-UNCLOS III era.

International negotiators belong, more or less consciously, to a worldwide community of specialists who pride themselves on a combination of characteristics – toughness, reasonableness, flexibility, and sensitivity, with only minor modifications by reason of culture, ideology, or political stature. Much more so than the bureaucratic approach, the diplomatic mode of ocean boundary-making seems to be vulnerable to the influence of personality and group dynamics.[5] Yet that appearance is deceptive, for in practice boundary negotiators are hedged in by a thicket of preconceptions, positions, and considerations of bureaucratic origin. Also, because of the saliency of international boundary issues, diplomatic negotiators may be constrained by specific instructions from the cabinet level of government. Unsuccessful boundary negotiations are often doomed before the negotiators sit down, and sometimes even the most painstaking diplomacy may be thwarted by domestic political interests after the conclusion of successful negotiations.

Despite these constraints, diplomacy seems to introduce the best prospect for ingenuity in ocean boundary-making. The interplay of values, interests, and attitudes at the negotiating table provides an opportunity for an imaginative balancing of linear and areal thinking about boundary-making applied to the uses of the ocean through a blend of distributive and integrative diplomacy.[6] As the theory of ocean boundary-making becomes more sophisticated in the functionalist mode, diplomatic boundary-makers are likely to have the best chance to experiment creatively in the mixing of linear settlements and areal arrangements. Indeed, in semi-enclosed regions (such as the Mediterranean, the Caribbean, the South China Sea, and the Gulf)[7] and "compacted" regions (such as West Africa)[8] the littoral states have a special inducement to look at their ocean boundary-making problems in both regional and national perspective to ensure that binational boundaries serve the larger regional interest in the various functions of ocean development and management. As the regional interest in ocean boundary-making becomes more widely accepted, the normal bilateral process of negotiation may have to be expanded, in certain regions, to admit third-party neighbouring states and even global or regional organizations. As the management frame of reference becomes more critical for success in this area of diplomacy, political interests and concerns may have to compete with increasingly compelling considerations of efficiency and feasibility.

Stages

The simple diplomatic process of ocean boundary-making may consist of as many as eight stages. The first stage in the making of a lateral ocean boundary is normally the promulgation of a *claim* to jurisdictional authority of some sort, normally by reference to the appropriate regime: territorial sea, continental shelf, or EEZ. The initial claim may be described in general spatial language or in precise linear terms, or with an intermediate degree of specificity. Whatever the form of the claim, it is almost certain to provoke a *response* from the neighbour, which may be only a protest or may constitute what amounts to a counterclaim. By the end of the response stage, the positions of the two neighbouring states on the boundary-making problem have been made known to each other. Almost invariably there is at least a "difference" between claim and response, and normally that difference will be characterized as an "issue," unless both countries take special care to avoid giving the matter any saliency. If the issue is aggravated by later events, it may acquire the status of a "dispute," which assumes the need for a negotiated settlement. At worst, the matter may escalate into a "conflict."

At some point after the mutual perception of a difference between claim and response, the neighbouring countries enter into the stage of *consultation*. Usually this private and relatively informal process of communication between governments is devoted to a clarification of the questions both parties are willing to submit to the next stage.

The next stage is, of course, the formal and official process of *negotiation*. By this stage, if not earlier, the governments have pooled all their available talents and resources for effective ocean boundary-making. The inputs are in place. If successful, the negotiation produces agreement at least on the general question of "allocation." Sometimes it may be taken further and produce agreement on a linear settlement described with a degree of technical precision, and occasionally even on some kind of boundary-related arrangement, at least of a preliminary or provisional sort.

The final stage of *drafting* the settlement/arrangement outcome of successful negotiations is sometimes detached from the negotiations themselves, and may be treated as a separate stage in the overall boundary-making process.

Usually, the product of negotiation, in treaty form, is subject to *validation* by whatever method of ratification is prescribed by the constitutional systems of the parties. Both in one-party systems and in parliamentary systems, validation usually is automatic after some form of internal debate. In some more complex systems, however, validation may be entrusted to a legislative body that is more or less detached from the executive branch of government and may refuse to consent to ratification as required under the national constitution.

After validation, the parties are ready to initiate the indefinite and routine process of *administration*, subject to any arrangements for consultation or co-operative management that were agreed upon.

Traditionally, most land boundary treaties are not made subject to review and revision, although there is nothing to prevent the parties from choosing to re-negotiate. In the case of "lateral" ocean boundaries, it may become more common for the neighbours to resort to *revision* of treaties when changes occur in their shared perception of related ocean development and management requirements.

THE COMPLEX DIPLOMATIC-INTERMEDIARY PROCESS

Inputs

Not infrequently, the process of direct bilateral diplomacy cannot cope unaided with the problems of ocean boundary-making, and it becomes necessary, if the problems are serious, to consider recourse to some form of intermediary procedure. In this situation the boundary-making process is complex in the sense that it is complicated by third-party involvement after some kind of diplomatic or political failure. Normally this requires the parties to adjust to an adjudicative or quasi-adjudicative frame of reference. Almost invariably the boundary-making and related problems are not finally and fully resolved through intermediation, and the parties must return to direct bilateral negotiation and thus readjust themselves to the diplomatic frame of reference.

By the late classical period of international law, many governments considered it best in such circumstances to resort to third-party adjudication, preferably by an international court that could be depended upon to interpret and apply the appropriate rules and principles of public international law. Such a resort was not uncommon even in the sensitive context of land boundary-making.

In the western world, centuries of legal tradition have conditioned non-lawyers as well as lawyers to place their trust in the judicial process for the settlement of virtually every kind of dispute. Indeed, in the most litigious cultures the judiciary is such a revered institution that legal disputes are sometimes welcomed, despite the costs involved, because they are perceived as stepping-stones to firmer safeguards of justice. The tradition of trust in judicial impartiality has been secured by the legal profession's commitment to the rule of law, which requires all judges, however elevated, to follow the established lines of doctrinal development so as to maintain the maximum degree of consistency in the application of legal rules and principles. Within this tradition it is usual for lawyers to accept a measure of inflexibility as the affordable price for achieving certainty and predictability in the legal system. In these (mostly western) cultures, the rule of law, the judicial process, and the logic of doctrinal development are honoured and cherished as society's most durable protection against the abuse of authority.

Moreover, the western experience in third-party adjudication has accentuated the virtues of adversarial proceedings. For centuries, direct confrontation through litigation in public courts of law has been the preferred mode of settlement. Even now, when western countries have discovered arbitration, mediation, conciliation, and other forms of alternative justice, judicial process through the adversarial system, despite its deficiencies, is by far the most common mode of dispute settlement.

Accordingly, it comes naturally to most western-trained or western-influenced international lawyers to view the judicial organs of the international community not only as a valuable method for the peaceful settlement of international disputes but, more idealistically, as the best check against the abuse of authority.[9] Reflecting this classical bias in favour of the rule of law through judicial process and doctrinal development, many western jurists abhor the emergence of more frankly political modes of legal development during the present "romantic" period.[10] Law-making by self-serving majorities through the modern political process of conference diplomacy, such as that of UNCLOS III, is judged by classicists to be a distasteful and inadequate approach to legal development compared with the involvement of disinterested judges in the technical process of litigation. Given the relative infrequency of recourse to the International Court of Justice, classical lawyers tend to seize every opportunity to emphasize the Court's responsibility for doctrinal development. Faced with an ocean boundary dispute, they expect adjudicators to give primacy to the "unitarian" task of contributing to the clarification, reconciliation, and consolidation of legal rules and principles.

Outside the western world, many countries have developed significantly different models of legal development, influenced by different cultural traditions and different attitudes to governmental authority. In most of these non-western countries, a less adversarial approach to dispute settlement is espoused, and the judiciary is less exalted as the protector of justice and fair dealing. For many countries, recourse to the ICJ seems an alien as well as a costly method of dispute settlement.[11]

The reluctance of non-western governments to submit justiciable disputes to the ICJ, or even to an arbitration tribunal, is no doubt partly due to their view that international adjudication tends to be dominated by western habits of thought, organization, and procedure.[12] If so, that reluctance is likely to be reinforced by the prevalence of the "unitarian" approach to the adjudication of ocean boundary disputes. To the extent that western-style classicists continue to emphasize the importance of the logic of doctrinal development in the abstract, rather than the fairness of the result in the given situation, the doubters and sceptics may continue to withhold their trust in the adjudicative process of ocean boundary-making.

The reluctance of so many states, especially non-western states, to accept third-party adjudicative procedures that entail binding decisions, either in the form of judicial decisions or arbitral awards, may be expected to result in a trend to conciliation, mediation, and other non-adjudicative intermediary procedures after a diplomatic or political failure in ocean boundary-making. The use of such procedures may be expected to produce facilitative rather than resolutive outcomes, in the form of recommendations instead of decisions or awards. Facilitative recommendations are likely to address broader boundary-related problems as well as the specific issue of delimitation, and thus to focus on a combination of possible arrangements and settlements.

Yet a significant number of states have been willing to submit ocean boundary disputes to third-party adjudication in recent decades. Through the terms of reference, presented in the *compromis* or treaty of arbitration, the parties to adjudication attempt to control the outcome. Normally, the terms of reference in adjudicative proceedings are framed around the traditional assumption that the tribunal's role is resolutive rather than facilitative.[13] Emphasis invariably is placed on specific legal issues rather than on related problems. At one end of the spectrum of possibilities, the parties may try to limit the tribunal to a merely declaratory role, whereby the adjudicators confine themselves to a declaration or clarification of the applicable rules or principles. At the opposite end, the parties may go so far as to assign the tribunal a dispositive role, whereby the adjudicators are requested to draw the boundary line with the highest possible degree of technical precision.

In practice, however, it may be difficult for the parties to prevent the adjudicators from going beyond the resolutive language of the terms of reference and from making facilitative observations or recommendations. In recent years most of the tribunals engaged in ocean boundary delimitation disputes have tended to interpret the terms of reference liberally rather than restrictively, and to assume both a facilitative and a resolutive role (see the section entitled "Modern Dispute Management" in chapter 11). On the other hand, there is almost always a minority, and occasionally a majority, of tribunal members who prefer to adhere closely to the resolutive language of the terms of reference, or even to confine themselves to the declaratory role if the parties are so inclined.[14] They are usually, though not always, lawyers trained in the classical western tradition of international law, dominated by the civil and common law heritage of judicial theory and practice.

Stages

The complex diplomatic/intermediary process of ocean boundary-making may have as many as twelve stages. The first four are the same as in the simple diplomatic process: *claim*, *response*, *consultation*, and *negotiation*. When a diplomatic or political impasse occurs and agreement is reached on the need for resort to some kind of intermediary procedure, the parties proceed to the fifth stage, *advocacy*. Regardless of the form of intermediation, each of the parties is required to attempt to persuade the third party of the reasonableness and propriety of its position. Frequently the change of circumstances requires some shift in the scope, nature, or emphasis of the arguments offered, or even in the data presented.

The *drafting* of the settlement or arrangement awarded or suggested by the intermediary must be organized within a selected framework of considerations and determined in accordance with selected weightings assigned, either at the discretion of the intermediary (as in the case of adjudication) or in consultation with the parties (as in the case of non-adjudicative modes of intermediation).

Thereafter, the parties are almost invariably required to return to the process of direct diplomacy. Normally this will involve a second resort to *consultation* and *negotiation*, and the *formulation of a negotiated settlement or arrangement* based at least in part on the settlement or arrangement awarded or suggested by the intermediary. Thereafter, of course, it is necessary to proceed through *validation* to *administration*, as described above, and perhaps eventually to *revision*.

CHAPTER FOURTEEN

The Factors

DETERMINATION OF SEAWARD LIMITS

Values

Through recent developments in state practice, including UNCLOS III and related law-making diplomacy, international law has gone far towards the goal of universally prescribed seaward limits for all regimes of coastal state jurisdiction, and thus for all zones subsumed under these regimes and spatially coextensive with them. These limits are generally considered to be "established" in customary international law: that is, their validity is not dependent on the bringing into force of the 1982 Convention on the Law of the Sea under the law of treaties. The allocative issue regarding the location of these limits has been resolved in favour of coastal states seeking satisfaction of their value-based demands for more extensive national areas in the ocean. Accordingly, it might be said that the primary value at stake in this form of ocean boundary-making is conformity with these newly prescribed limits, as set out in the 1982 Convention.

For three of these regimes (territorial sea, contiguous zone, and EEZ), the limits are prescribed by the application of a single mileage criterion (12 nautical miles, 24 nautical miles, and 200 nautical miles, respectively), all measured from the baseline of the territorial sea.[1] These three products of distributive diplomacy may be said to reflect a widespread desire for uniformity and certainty. This "distance" approach to boundary-making has the virtue of simplicity and it is widely, if not universally, expected to result in stability. The only "value" question is whether to countenance exceptions to these new rules, based as they are on legal values and reflective of a classical response to the quest for justice in the law of the sea.[2] From a functionalist perspective, ocean boundaries generally should be approached with a view to the administrative purposes they serve, and therefore should be governed by administrative rather than legal considerations. But of all three forms of ocean boundaries, seaward limits should be the least influenced by administrative values such as flexibility and convenience. Although these limits are arbitrary, from any managerial viewpoint, the arbitrariness should be reduced, if at all, through special treaty arrangements for appropriate ocean management purposes, not through unilateral extensions of the boundaries.[3] For the international community at large, it seems that more would be lost than gained by permitting much flexibility in the location of seaward limits. The advantages gained in having globally settled limits should not be sacrificed for the sake of management requirements, which can be met through special negotiable arrangements.

On the other hand, is it fair or realistic to expect all coastal states, regardless of technological capability, to conform to the highest possible standard of precision in the determination of seaward limits that are far distant from the shoreline? Most developing coastal states have not been able to apply geodetic precision to ocean boundary-making, but the new high technology will soon be widely available through appropriate technical assistance programs.

More difficult questions arise from the new provision on the seaward limits of the continental shelf beyond the two-hundred-mile EEZ under article 76 of the 1982 convention (see the section entitled "The New Law of the Sea" in chapter 9). The formula offered for this kind of boundary-making is complex, and the difficulties of interpretation may prove politically sensitive, as well as technically divisive. Indeed, it remains to be seen whether the formula and procedure are workable in the way intended by the delegates at UNCLOS III.

Other Factors

Under article 76, the expansionist *interests* of the "broad margin" claimant state are balanced by the anti-expansionist interests of the international community through the introduction of a complementary, but somewhat ambiguous, *relationship* between the claimant state and an international body, the Commission on the Limits of the Continental Shelf. Article 2(1) of Annex II to the Convention shows that this relationship is technical in orientation: "the Commission shall consist of 21 members expert in the field of geology, geophysics, or hydrography." The relationship cannot be tested until the Commission is established after the 1982 Convention comes into force, perhaps no earlier than 1991. No provisional arrangements are in force. It is hoped that in the meantime the "broad margin" claimant states will exercise self-restraint in the interpretation and application of the formula in article 76(4), (5), and (6).

When the intended "dialogue" begins, it will be a technical discourse between scientific specialists in designated fields. The prevailing *attitude* is therefore likely to be professional.[4] It remains to be seen whether the specialists' training in scientific objectivity will be offset by the quasi-adversarial nature of their relationship, and whether the members of the Commission will be consciously influenced by the *milieu* of the political debate on deep-ocean mining after the establishment of the International Seabed Authority. Obviously the *timing* of the dialogue will be of some relevance, to the extent that it is perceived by the "broad margin" claimant state as an important factor in attaining a higher degree of national self-sufficiency in oil and gas or other minerals. Not least, the coastal state's posture may be profoundly influenced by prevailing cost and price levels within the relevant industrial sectors at the time of the dialogue, and thus by the state of the relevant *technology* of capture.

As a matter of basic legal values, it seems important that the dialogue between the Commission and the coastal state should be conducted and viewed as an attempt to secure a balance between the special interest of the claimant and the common interest of all other nations. From a functionalist perspective, it also seems important to preserve the technicality of the proceedings, given the nature of the formula accepted by the world community as a whole. A politicization of this explicitly technical form of ocean boundary-making would almost certainly be dysfunctional, and would tend to promote precisely the kind of unilateralism that the international community should be most anxious to avoid.

DELINEATION OF BASELINES AND CLOSING LINES

Values

As in the case of determining seaward limits, modern international law has gone far in the prescription of fairly precise, if incomplete, rules to govern the delineation of baselines and closing lines as set out in the 1982 Convention.[5] Once again, considerable weight should be given to the legal values of conformity and certainty. But, in contrast with the determination of normal seaward limits, delineation tends to be complicated. Its complexity arises from the variability of coastal geography, which has forced boundary-makers to embrace diversity instead of uniformity. This kind of ocean boundary-making gives rise to three kinds of value issues: first, how far to tolerate deviations from the normal (or classical) legal goal of uniformity; second, whether to yield to the administrative argument for flexibility rather than stability in the light of coastal zoning requirements;

and, third, how hard to press for the highest possible standard of precision.

As to the second of these questions, the case of flexibility in delineation should, in a functionalist perspective, depend on the nature and importance of administrative zoning requirements in coastal and adjacent waters. (This topic is discussed in chapter 15.) As to the third question, the case for precision should depend on the economic availability of the best science and technology (as discussed in chapter 16). As to the first question, the prospect of diversity in state practice, it is necessary to examine the interplay of interests, attitudes, and physical setting, as well as values.

Other Factors

On the face of things, all international lawyers should be able to agree on the desirability of conformity with globally negotiated provisions on the delineation of baselines and closing lines. Although incomplete – by reason, for example, of the omission of provisions on the thorny question of historic bays and other waters, and the underdevelopment of the regime of islands – these delineation rules and formulae are ingenious compromises between the coastal and transit *interests*: between coastal interest in protection and the non-coastal interest in freedom of transit. Any significant deviation from the provisions might be construed unfavourably as a disturbance of that carefully contrived balance of interests.[6] A widespread disregard of delineation provisions, such as article 7 on the straight baseline method, might even be viewed as a threat to the credibility of the Convention in a larger sense.

However, despite these legitimate fears, and despite the admitted need to monitor state practice with a view to minimizing deviations from the Convention, each apparent departure from the rules and formulae on baselines and closing lines should be examined within its own context. First, it should be recalled that these provisions were conceived within a strictly statist frame of reference; and yet, of all the boundaries in the ocean, baselines and closing lines come closest to impinging directly on the coastal community.[7] Article 7 in particular is designed to reflect the legitimacy of the "economic interests peculiar to the region concerned, the reality and the importance of which are clearly evidenced by long usage." In view of the centrality of communal interests and attitudes in this provision, it seems reasonable to permit some limited degree of flexibility in appropriate circumstances, both in interpretation and application and conceivably in revision.

Second, it should be noted that the delineation provisions in the post-classical law of the sea are designed to reflect unique or special features of the physical setting. They must be understood as an attempt to construct an *extension* of the coastline. Built into these rules is a tension between the natural and the artificial elements of boundary-making. Especially in the case of highly complex coastlines, some flexibility should be tolerated in the balancing of geographical and geometrical considerations.

It may be concluded, then, that we should not rely too heavily on a single formula or rule as a solution to all possible issues of delineation for complex coastlines. But article 7 in particular is wracked with tension, and has already been subjected to widespread abuse.[8] Delineation problems may also arise from the formula designed for archipelagic states, especially as coastal archipelagic states attempt to validate baseline claims by analogy with provisions in the Convention.[9] Given the unilateral nature of the delineation process, it is desirable that challenges should be referrable to some form of intermediary procedure, whereby "deviationist" states would be answerable to the world community and required to justify their deviation in functionalist terms. As suggested in chapter 12, these delineation provisions should be regarded as globally approved and legally obligatory *criteria*, permitting only functionally justifiable deviations.

DELIMITATION OF "LATERAL" BOUNDARIES

Values

The delimitation of "lateral" boundaries between opposite or adjacent states, especially for the EEZ and the continental shelf, has not proved amenable to precise governance by legal rules. Despite protracted efforts to find an acceptable formula incorporating both of the favourite elements, equidistance and equity, UNCLOS III ended with compromise language that merely emphasized the need for agreement between parties and limited the normative reference to the negotiation process, requiring that the agreement be based on international law and directed to the achievement of an "equitable solution." Failing agreement, parties to a delimitation dispute are required to resort to third-party adjudication, but no guidance is offered to the adjudicators.[10] A very high degree of flexibility is given to the negotiators of a delimitation dispute, and even more discretion is vested in adjudicators: there is not even an explicit requirement that they provide an "equitable solution."[11]

This outcome has been a disappointment to many international lawyers. Some, pointing to the lack of certainty, may even characterize the final result in articles 74 and 83 as a failure of the law-making process at UNCLOS III. In the functionalist perspective, however, certainty is a questionable value in this context of ocean boundary-making. The bilateral process of negotiation should not be constrained by a priori or extrinsic considerations in the form of legal norms that appear reasonable in the abstract, especially if those norms have been haggled over at the global level of conference diplomacy. The paramountcy of the principle of agreement (or consent) seems to require that the initial process of negotiation should be left unregulated by substantive legal rules, however well-intentioned. The duty to produce an "equitable solution" through negotiation is hardly constraining, and the reference to equity, however vague, serves at least to give substance to the duty to negotiate in good faith.

The failure to provide any normative guidance to adjudicators is less easy to defend. Certainly, those adopting the "unitarian" view of adjudication have criticized the lack of any globally approved "basic norm," or set of general principles, conducive to the consolidation of legal rules. But the matter depends on how one characterizes the role of a tribunal in an ocean boundary delimitation dispute. The functionalist view is that the court, tribunal, or commission should be asked in effect to perform a *facilitative* role: that is, to facilitate the negotiation of the delimitation and other boundary-related issues between the parties, in light of the circumstances in which the diplomacy to date has stalled, and with special emphasis on the relevance of the "situation." Given the primacy of the principle of agreement, it seems essential that the intermediary process, whether adjudicative or not, should be viewed as ancillary to the process of diplomacy. From this contextualist premise, it follows that tribunals should be discouraged from giving undue weight to extra-contextual "norms," as against contextual "factors." (See chapter 19.)

Although the Convention does not require that intermediaries (as distinguished from negotiators) must base their decision or recommendations on international law with a view to achieving an "equitable solution," this seems to be a reasonable interpretation, but an implied requirement to apply international law cannot be imposed indiscriminately on all kinds of intermediaries. Given the range of dispute management procedures available under Part XV of the Convention,[12] different weights will and should be assigned by different kinds of intermediaries to the rules and principles of international law. On the other hand, there is no reason why the achievement of an "equitable solution" should not be equally imperative for all kinds of intermediaries. Accordingly, the language of articles 74 and 83 on the delimitation of "lateral" boundaries is viewed more kindly when placed in a functionalist, as distinguished from "unitarian," perspective.

The principal functionalist criticism of the delimitation provisions of the Convention is that the "fairness test" approach inherent in the requirement for an "equitable solution" should have been complemented by an "effectiveness test." The new law of the sea in general, as reflected in the Convention, seems best approached, in value terms, as an attempt to reconcile the value demands of equity and efficiency in ocean development and management in the conditions of the late twentieth century.[13] Since so much more emphasis was placed on equity rather than efficiency throughout the text of the Convention, it is scarcely surprising that UNCLOS III failed to prescribe an "effectiveness test" to balance the fairness test in articles 74 and 83. In the functionalist theory of boundary-making, equal consideration should be given to equity and efficiency (or effectiveness) by negotiators and adjudicators in their approach to the delimitation of "lateral" ocean boundaries between neighbouring states. They are equally significant components of functionality.

Other Factors

The open-endedness of the delimitation provisions of the Convention serves, of course, to invite controversy over the mix of value considerations and other factors that should affect the outcome of the diplomatic and intermediary processes applied to delimitation.

As to the interplay of *interests* between neighbouring coastal states, it may be worth recalling that the normative open-endedness of international law in this context arose from the futility of seeking a global reconciliation between two competing interests – those favouring the "principle" of equidistance and those favouring the "rule" of special circumstances. Delegations at UNCLOS III studied their own ocean or coastal geography – their *physical setting* – to discover where their national advantage lay. No one pretended that values could be divorced from interests.

The UNCLOS III debate originated, of course, in the equidistance-versus-special circumstances debate at UNCLOS I, which resulted in the balanced language of article 6 of the 1958 Convention on the Continental Shelf (see the section entitled "Modern Dispute Management" in chapter 11). Most delegations arrived at UNCLOS III hoping to tilt that balance to their national advantage, but the issue of delimitation had been greatly complicated by the emergence of the two-hundred-mile EEZ concept, overlapping and extending beyond the continental shelf of most coastal states. The prospect of a single maritime boundary delimiting the water column as well as the seabed and subsoil presented difficulties that could not be handled in the old terminology of UNCLOS I. The conversion of the "special circumstances" position in that earlier debate to the "equity" position at UNCLOS III reflected in part the influence of newcomers motivated by fishery rather than hydrocarbon interests.

After UNCLOS III, as continental shelf boundaries gradually give way to EEZ boundaries, governmental *attitudes* to ocean boundary delimitation may be influenced by the broader considerations of renewable resource development and management rather than by the narrower considerations of non-renewable resource production. In many cases, an attitudinal shift of this sort might be expected to create a demand for something less simple than a line, such as a package of boundary settlements and boundary-related arrangements. Such a shift may encourage the parties to view their *relationship* in a more potentially co-operative light.

The UNCLOS III conversion to the value of equity seems also to have granted primacy to context over general principle, as well as to flexibility over certainty. This change in value orientation will require adjudicators and other intermediaries to apply situational ethics, which will lead inevitably to charges of subjectivism. They may essentially be obliged to "fashion a result in a case unguided by articulated rules of law."[14]

With the primacy of the principle of agreement confirmed, government negotiators have been relieved of legal constraints on the negotiating process. In theory, this should have the effect of encouraging the negotiation of appropriate boundary-related settlements and arrangements. Since ocean boundary-making by treaty continues at a fairly brisk rate, it is difficult to say that UNCLOS III has failed in its purpose. The treaty-making rate may be accelerated by consideration of all the options available, as is suggested in chapter 17.

The open-endedness of the language of articles 74 and 83 may deter a few classically oriented governments from resorting to third-party adjudication if they demand certainty and consistency in the application of legal rules and principles before committing themselves to the rigours of case preparation. They may be forgiven for shrinking from an undertaking that seems to have some of the characteristics of a lottery. But it also seems conceivable that a larger number of otherwise reluctant litigant states may now be encouraged to submit to some form of adjudication precisely because of the even chance that disinterested adjudicators will be won over to their view of the equities of the situation, and committed, as most adjudicators now accept they should be, to the avoidance of an inequitable result. It is too early to guess whether the battle against reluctance will be won.

As to other effects on attitudes, it is already evident that the UNCLOS III contextualist ("equitable solution") approach to delimitation has created a jurisprudential split among counsel, judges, and commentators. Those attracted to the "unitarian" view of the adjudicative process, who emphasize the declaratory rather than the facilitative role, seem to be in the majority among western-trained counsel and commentators. Those attracted to the functionalist view, who emphasize the need for balance between facilitative and resolutive roles, seem to be in the majority among the adjudicators. The majority-minority split among the adjudicators may, of course, deter some governments from resorting to adjudication. If the personal attitudes or judicial philosophies of individual adjudicators cannot be easily discerned, the jurisprudential split will add to the uncertainties of litigation, especially before the full bench of the International Court of Justice. If the attitudes can be determined, the split will add to the difficulty of agreeing on the choice of panelists or arbitrators. This uncertainty could have the effect of encouraging states to resort to conciliation rather than litigation or arbitration. In the functionalist view of things, this would add an interesting, and probably constructive, dimension to this form of ocean boundary-making.

For many lawyers, crucial questions about the judicial function will arise out of these comments. Should the functionalist approach to adjudication of ocean boundary disputes, with its emphasis on the facilitative role of tribunals, be carried so far as to encourage tribunals to give what is *substantively* or morally equivalent to an *ex aequo et bono* decision, even though the parties, as a matter of procedure, have not requested proceedings on such a basis? Conservative lawyers can be expected to shrink from such a prospect, and others who might welcome judicial innovation in other forms may be fearful that the acknowledgment of such a judicial attitude will be damaging to the cause of international adjudication. But the time may have come, at least in the specific context of ocean boundary delimitation, to welcome the unacknowledged but apparent trend to what are virtually *ex aequo et bono* decisions, often reached in a quasi-conciliatory spirit for clearly facilitative purposes. Such a trend seems wholly compatible in principle with the functionalist policy assigning precedence to the achievement of fair and sensible boundary settlements or arrangements over certainty and consistency in the application of legal rules and principles. To acknowledge the trend would raise the level of frankness in legal debate, and might strengthen the case for resort to international adjudication in ocean boundary delimitation. Whether the trend should be encouraged in other contexts is arguable, depending on the nature of the "problem" involved in each situation.[15]

CHAPTER FIFTEEN

The Relevance of Ocean Zoning

THE ADMINISTRATIVE PURPOSES OF OCEAN BOUNDARY-MAKING

The history of ocean zoning goes back thousands of years to the earliest practices of regulating mariculture in coastal waters. Traditional zoning practices for other purposes, such as mineral extraction, port administration, fishing, and military security, have been succeeded by the creation of regulatory arrangements in administrative control zones (fiscal and customs control, public health, immigration, environmental protection, and vessel traffic control), and more recently by the establishment of increasingly sophisticated arrangements in resource development and management zones (fisheries, offshore minerals, and coastal zone management).

From a functionalist perspective, great significance is attributed to these ancient and modern practices in ocean zoning. For the purposes of development and management of ocean uses, the trend to further zoning seems assured, both within and beyond limits of national jurisdiction. For each designated zone in the sea a system of functionally designed administrative arrangements will surely evolve in association with the appropriate regime of regulatory authority. Eventually, each zone will "belong," in some functional sense, to a network of zones linking functionally related administrative arrangements and settlements effected at regional, subregional, national, subnational, and local levels of regulatory or managerial authority.

The emergence of functionalist logic in the new law of the sea is apparent not only in the advent of new regimes of functional jurisdiction (for example, continental shelf, the exclusive economic zone, the contiguous zone, straits used for international navigation, and the "international area"), but also in the elucidation of functionally defined exemptions and special privileges (for example, various rights of transit or passage, historic fishing rights, landlocked states' rights of access to fishery resources, and special environmental controls). The functionalist cast of the 1982 UN Convention on the Law of the Sea reflects only the beginning of modern functionalist logic applied to ocean law and policy around the world.[1] Despite the continuing force of nationalist sentiment and symbolism in the post-classical period of international law,[2] economic self-interest seems to ensure the continuance of ocean zoning in all regions, and thus the further application of functionalist logic in administrative practices in ocean areas.

Especially within the appropriate sectors of bureaucracies – at global, regional, subregional, national, subnational, and local levels – it will be clearly discerned that ocean zoning and ocean boundary-making are governed by essentially the same range of administrative values and considerations, and therefore linked by the same kind of functionalist logic. Inevitably, the questions why, whether, how, when, and where to draw lines in the ocean will be dealt with by reference to the relevant administrative purposes to be served and to what is perceived, in the appropriate bureaucratic sector, to be the affected ocean area.

THE ADMINISTRATIVE TEST OF FUNCTIONALITY

At the present stage of ocean development and management, it is difficult to predict the rate of conversion to functionalist logic in ocean boundary-making. But at least in the case of bureaucratically derived baselines and seaward limits, and especially in the case of internal boundaries for national, subnational, and local ocean zones, it seems only a matter of time before it is widely accepted, in conformity with the administrative rationale of zoning, that existing boundaries of these kinds should be subject to review and potential revision if they fail the test of administrative effectiveness. To the extent that bureaucratic rationality reflects the political requirement of satisfying social pressures on government, administrative logic is likely to represent a balance between the competing needs of efficiency and equity.[3] Ocean boundaries, placed in the context of ocean zoning requirements, will be regarded by administrators as changeable rather than permanent in nature. If the stakes are high enough, existing boundary settlements and arrangements will be revised, and the line itself altered, if they can be shown to have failed the administrative test of functionality.[4]

It is more difficult to make predictions in the case of internationally negotiated or adjudicated ocean boundaries, which may continue to attract nationalist sentiment or symbolism. In those situations functionalist logic may not always prevail. The contest between logic and sentiment may be complicated, moreover, by important and legitimate differences in the measurement of related costs and benefits.[5] An international boundary that cannot be renegotiated may simply have to remain unchanged, and the resulting irritants will have to be absorbed within the political relationship between the neighbouring states.

The administrative logic of zoning and the administrative test of functionality are of central significance for the future of ocean boundary-making, and unduly parochial and unilateral action may result unless ocean boundaries are also viewed from a regional perspective. Administrative logic must look outwards as well as inwards, and the efficiency-equity test of functionality must take stock of both external and domestic policy options. Within the overall framework of national ocean policy, constant attention should be given to the regional implications of existing ocean boundary delimitation settlements and transboundary arrangements and of unresolved boundary problems and issues. Above all, care should be taken that a contemplated change in the administrative status quo does not threaten to impair existing co-operative arrangements with neighbours and other littoral states in the region, or with transit and other interested states with treaty and other legal entitlements. All regional and other international responsibilities and opportunities should be included in a full accounting of costs and benefits by the appropriate sector of bureaucracy.[6]

CHAPTER SIXTEEN

The Relevance of Ocean Science and Technology

GENERAL

Science

The functionalist approach to ocean boundary-making begins with the expectation that boundaries at sea, unlike most on land, can be made and maintained in a relatively rational manner. This assumes that there will be a role for science in the treatment of ocean boundary problems, including the design and development of appropriate boundary delimitation settlements and boundary-related arrangements. Functionalist logic tends to assign priority to the "managerial framework" as an intellectual input into ocean boundary-making, and ocean management rests to a large extent on a scientific foundation.[1]

However, there is no assurance that science will invariably be given a central role in the treatment of ocean affairs generally, or in the shaping of ocean law and policy specifically. Whereas biology and ecology have virtually a controlling influence on the design of most regimes for the protection of the marine environment,[2] those same disciplines have lost ground in the remaking of the international law of fisheries.[3] Some observers even fear that the advent of a "consent regime" for the regulation of marine scientific research inside EEZ limits[4] may impair the growth and vitality of vessel-based oceanography in certain parts of the world, and thus detract from the rational basis of ocean settlements and arrangements.[5]

As an outgrowth of policy science, the functionalist approach to ocean boundary-making prescribes, but does not predict, a role for science. But science pulls in different directions. The life sciences, such as ecology and biology, and certain physical sciences, such as geology and geomorphology, might seem to favour the rationality of a natural boundary in the sea,[6] but most of the social sciences, such as economics, sociology, and human geography, are more likely to emphasize the rationality of an institutional settlement or arrangement that satisfies the criteria of efficiency and equity.[7] Law, when seen as a social science, might be expected to balance such values of certainty and flexibility, and thus to remain neutral between these diverging tendencies among other sciences. Any multidisciplinary approach to ocean boundary-making, functionalist or otherwise, seems bound to avoid any normative predisposition. The case for science in general, and for particular sciences, varies with the context; the boundary-maker's perception of the situation must be expected to guide the selection and weighting of the intrinsic, or most relevant, factors and the selection and evaluation of the most pertinent data. Not least, the role of science will vary with the type of boundary involved.[8]

Technology

Almost all uses of the sea are directly dependent on technology. As ocean technology develops, ocean zoning will become more usual, more sophisticated, and more diversified (see chapter 15). As this process evolves, it may become increasingly difficult to justify fixed and immutable ocean boundaries. In the functionalist perspective, it is the role of technology and bureaucracy together to test the functionality of ocean boundaries.

On a different plane, law and technology are sometimes viewed together as important instruments for use in nation-building, and to some extent in the economic development of regions. In the context of ocean development and management, technology is chiefly important as conducive to efficiency in the use of the ocean, whereas international law in the post-classical age is chiefly important as conducive to equity. Accordingly, legal settlements and arrangements for the treatment of ocean boundary problems must take cognizance of current developments in ocean technology, but the relevance of ocean technology, like that of ocean science, may vary with the type of boundary.

DETERMINATION OF SEAWARD LIMITS

Science

The EEZ regime was established primarily to secure coastal state control over the development and management of living resources. It has sometimes been asserted that the uniform two-hundred-mile limit prescribed for the EEZ regime has a scientific basis, since it is a verifiable fact that most species are concentrated within two hundred miles from the shore. But this line of reasoning rests on the commercial fact of stock availability rather than on the scientific fact of species distribution, and most coastal states do not need such an extensive zone to secure control over most of the non-migratory stocks adjacent to their coast. The larger truth is that there is little constancy in the marine environment, and that an immovable and uniform ocean boundary serves legal and political rather than scientific ends.

The facts of fishery science are relevant to the question whether a deviation from the two-hundred-mile rule should be countenanced in circumstances where major stocks, constituting a "unit of management," are found to straddle what is, from the managerial (and scientific) perspective, an arbitrary boundary. To yield to this argument for deviation in the name of science would be to confuse the function of settlement with that of arrangement. If a credible scientific argument can be mounted in support of a single transboundary management regime in such circumstances, the solution suggested by functionalist logic is a co-operative management arrangement involving users and managers on both sides of the line, rather than a further seaward extension of the line. Only in a scenario of extremely uncooperative behaviour, which seriously threatens the sustainability of the coastal state's renewable resource, does it seem conscionable on that scientific ground to claim a further extension of the EEZ limit as a last resort to preserve the major benefit intended to accrue to the coastal state under the EEZ regime.[9]

In the case of hydrocarbon and other non-living resources, the argument for a maximum and uniform two-hundred-mile limit was overcome at UNCLOS III. Coastal states possessing a broader continental margin and contemplating the prospect of hydrocarbon production further seaward, were to benefit from a provision permitting a more extensive and non-uniform boundary at the edge of their margin, determined in accordance with a complex and highly scientific formula.[10] In this context, scientific findings are of the highest relevance, more so than in the making and maintenance of any other kind of ocean boundary, or indeed any boundary on land. The relevant UNCLOS III provisions call for a technical dialogue between scientists after a boundary is determined by the "broad margin" coastal state. The international body that will participate in the dialogue has no adjudicative authority, and so it cannot be described as a science court. Yet the process envisaged is devoted to scientific validation which would be the primary purpose of a "science court,"[11] and the empirical scientific methods of observation and investigation are the only means of making and evaluating this kind of boundary.

A new science, marine geodesy, has acquired an increasingly important role in the determination of seaward limits. Highly precise geodetic techniques of measurement accentuate the distortive effects of traditional cartography based on the Mercator projection, especially when applied to very long ocean boundaries in high latitudes. For coastal states capable of meeting the highest technical standards, science in the form of marine geodesy brings a new order of precision to this kind of boundary-making. The history of ocean science is an impressive account of the quest for accuracy and precision (see chapter 8), and navigation and other ocean uses seem likely to benefit from further advances in the science of measurement and positioning.[12]

Technology

Artillery was the first form of technology to be applied to the determination of seaward limits, when the breadth of the territorial sea was measured by reference to the range of gunfire. This early resort to functionalist logic was based on the assumption that national security was the dominant value served by the grant of territorial jurisdiction at sea. Modern warfare, of course, has demonstrated the indadequacy of a technology-dependent ocean boundary for the territorial sea in an age of immense disparities in military technology. Similarly, in the 1950s the inclusion of "exploitability" (drilling capability) among the criteria specified in the 1958 Geneva definition of the continental shelf gave rise to confusion, and some consternation, in the face of a widening range of national capabilities in that sector of ocean engineering. (See the section entitled "The New Law of the Sea" in chapter 9.) There is general agreement on the need for uniformity in seaward limits in the form of globally negotiated mileage provisions, and technology has only a minor role in this context of ocean boundary-making, through the techniques of hydrography and the related sciences centrally involved in the drawing of seaward limits. This auxiliary role is likely to be of the greatest importance in the case of "broad margin" coastal states that are eligible to apply the complex scientific formula for determining the limits of their shelf beyond the EEZ under article 76 of the 1982 Convention.

DELINEATION OF BASELINES AND CLOSING LINES

Science

Given the nature of the globally accepted rules and formulae prescribed for delineation, it seems that hydrographers will draw chiefly upon geography and geometry in this sector of boundary-making. Each scientific team will have to find its own way of resolving the tension inherent in the formulae between the flexibility and certainty criteria represented by the natural and artificial elements of geography and geometry respectively. To the extent that each science tends to be geared for precision, the delineators may be inclined to interpret and apply the geometric criteria strictly, but political and social pressure can be expected in many circumstances to support the case for flexibility. In such a context it may fall to science to exercise a moderating influence and thus discourage unconscionable deviations from the language of the Convention.

Technology

The technologies ancillary to surveying and charting are the technologies most directly involved in ocean boundary-making, especially in the preparations required for delineation as envisaged in the 1982 Convention. A functionalist approach to ocean boundary-making tends to emphasize the value of precision in the drawing of baselines and closing lines, more so than in the case of seaward limits and "lateral" boundaries, where precision may receive less weight in competition with other values. With a view to raising the level of precision in delineation, it is hoped that the leading national hydrographic bureaus will be given the support necessary to provide training to developing coastal states in surveying and charting, and related technologies.[13]

DELIMITATION OF "LATERAL" BOUNDARIES

Science

It is difficult to specify the role of science in the delimitation of an ocean boundary between neighbouring states. In circumstances where both parties agree on the need for a simple linear settlement rather than a package of settlements and arrangements, fishery science, ecology, geology, geophysics, and other sciences may be seen by nervous politicians and their foreign policy advisers as being likely to introduce unacceptable complications, delays, and expenditures into the boundary-making process. Many "lateral" ocean boundary agreements in existence today seem to have been negotiated with minimal reliance on the findings of science. In the functionalist perspective, the makers of such boundaries should be prepared to consider the need for revision if future scientific findings prove the dysfunctionality of the original boundary settlement. In these circumstances, the role of science is to furnish enough accurate information on the border environment and its resources to permit an evaluation of the functionality of the boundary.

Where bilateral diplomacy fails to produce agreement and the parties resort to intermediation, the role of science may vary considerably with the type of intermediary procedure adopted. In such circumstances, resort to adjudication before the ICJ or an arbitral tribunal has often resulted in heavy reliance on the relevant sciences for the purposes of case preparation. Commitment to international adjudication has been interpreted as requiring the litigant states to prepare a highly systematic, sophisticated, and rational argument based on a massive volume of scientific information representing a wide range of disciplines. In extreme cases, such as the *Gulf of Maine* adjudication between Canada and the United States, the investment in science has been spectacular. However, in light of recent judicial and arbitral decisions, there may be a tendency in the coming years for litigant states to invest more modestly, or more selectively, in science for adjudication of a "lateral" boundary dispute. In the functionalist perspective, it seems wise to accept the unlikelihood that any tribunal consisting solely of lawyers will wish to base a decision squarely on a scientific foundation.

The non-adjudicative modes of intermediation seem even less well suited to heavy investment in science. One of the chief advantages of resort to conciliation, mediation, or a regional organization is that it is expeditious and inexpensive, since it is freed from the heavy burden of documentation that so often descends on adjudicators of an ocean boundary dispute. Given the explicitly facilitative nature of their undertaking, non-adjudicative intermediaries might be expected to look to science only for general guidance as to the approach that should be taken to the larger problem of designing appropriate boundary settlements and boundary-related arrangements.

In general, it might be conceded that it is less crucial to have a scientific basis for a linear settlement than for a boundary-related arrangement. Functionalist logic suggests that the case for science in the delimitation of a "lateral" boundary depends on whether the neighbouring states perceive a close link between the nature and location of such a boundary on the one hand and their ocean development and management needs and opportunities in adjacent waters on the other. The closer the link the more crucial the need for investment in science.[14]

It also seems necessary to emphasize the role of science for the purposes of boundary revision. Since no one can evaluate the functionality of an ocean boundary without reference to the relevant ocean science and technology, a rational approach to the maintenance of a "lateral" boundary requires a constant investment in scientific and technological research. By the same token, a rational approach requires an open mind on the possibility of revision of the location and nature (functions) of the boundary. Both parties must be prepared to regard the boundary as changeable if they are to respond rationally to new findings that suggest the need for adjustments in accordance with a shared perception of efficiency and equity.

Technology

Like science, technology is more likely to play an important role in the treatment of a delimitation problem when the parties contemplate the need for co-operative arrangements. For example, neighbouring coastal states that agree on the establishment of a joint development zone have in effect placed their faith in technology, or the prospect of technology transfer. Similarly, neighbours that agree on the creation of a joint (or subregional) management regime for fishery development or environmental purposes have committed themselves, in some degree, to the treatment of any problem of competing or incompatible technologies that may emerge. Even if the neighbouring states choose a simple linear settlement, technology is still important as the means by which the parties hope to attain an enhanced enforcement capability. But especially in the case of long "lateral" boundaries, it may be more cost effective for a coastal state with limited resources to invest more heavily in the industrial technology suggested by a boundary arrangement than in the enforcement technology suggested by a linear settlement. In short, a choice between autonomous and co-operative behaviour in ocean development and management may be essentially a choice to invest in a particular type of technology.

CHAPTER SEVENTEEN

The Range of Choices in Direct Bilateral Diplomacy

MODES OF BILATERAL DIPLOMACY AND NEGOTIATION

Most "lateral" ocean boundaries between neighbouring states are the outcome of bilateral negotiation. Because of the primacy of the principle of agreement in this context of ocean boundary-making, the functionalist approach must incorporate components both of the theory of negotiation and of the theory of treaty-making.

In theorizing about international negotiation, an initial distinction should be drawn between "symbolic" and "non-symbolic" (or "operational") diplomacy. The former is devoted to the treatment or modification of attitudes; the latter is concerned with the attainment of specific objectives. Symbolic diplomacy or negotiation draws upon the human faculty for good will, bolstered if possible by cultural affinity, ideological compatibility, or a shared heritage. Operational negotiation involves the art and science of bargaining. Sometimes the conditions for an operational approach to ocean boundary diplomacy may be lacking. Instead of undertaking a bargaining process, neighbouring states may find it more sensible and less risky to resort to symbolic diplomacy with a view to negotiating some kind of generally worded instrument whose soothing assurances of good will may improve the prospect of future boundary negotiations of a more operational sort. Even an agreement to disagree may be better than nothing.

Operational ocean boundary negotiation may be conducted according to two models of negotiation behaviour: "competitive" and "integrative." The competitive behaviour model emphasizes the purpose of winning advantages through the techniques of persuasion, threat, and "positional commitment."[1] This is essentially a static model of bargaining, whereby "a fixed set of rewards is divided in a single set of negotiations between two parties." It has been suggested that this approach to negotiation, associated especially with contract bargaining, may have grown out of western concepts of the adversary process, and out of "tendencies to view agreements as legal documents divorced from economic, social and political influences."[2] The integrative model, on the other hand, emphasizes collaboration with the other party in a joint search for a mutually acceptable solution.[3] Integrative bargaining depends on the possibility of "co-ordinative behaviour" between the negotiators, which in turn depends on their mutual trust and a genuine sharing of the goal of co-ordination.[4]

In the functionalist theory of ocean boundary-making, it is prescribed as desirable, in reasonably congenial circumstances, for the two negotiating teams to adopt integrative bargaining methods based on co-ordinative behaviour. Whether in the unifunctional context of the continental shelf or in the multifunctional context of the EEZ, negotiation of a delimitation issue should be conducted with a view to the requirements for co-operation in ocean resource use and management in adjacent waters.

FOUR CATEGORIES OF BILATERAL TREATIES

Most bilateral treaty instruments are devoted to one subject area, and can therefore be classified in discrete, and more or less mutually exclusive, categories. Moreover, within each general subject category one can usually discern a single overriding purpose. Accordingly, it is possible to classify bilateral treaty instruments according to primary function. In the functionalist theory of treaty-making, there are four major categories of such instruments: distributive, administrative, demonstrative, and resolutive.[5]

Distributive (bilateral) agreements are those designed primarily to serve the purpose of distributing or redistributing designated resources, goods, or services. Most trade agreements fall into this functional category, as do agreements for scientific or cultural exchange and international development assistance. Distributive agreements make up nine-tenths or more of all existing bilateral treaty instruments.

Administrative agreements are those designed primarily to serve the purpose of initiating, maintaining, or regulating designated interstate (or otherwise state-controlled) services. Most consular, banking, transportation, and communications agreements belong to this group.

Demonstrative agreements are those designed primarily to serve the purpose of demonstrating or dramatizing attitudes conducive to the consolidation or improvement of official friendship or good will between the parties. These products of symbolic diplomacy (and non-operational negotiation) are exemplified in treaties of friendship, peaceful coexistence, and general co-operation, as well as in joint communiqués that may or may not be legally binding as instruments of "treaty character."

Resolutive agreements are those designed primarily to resolve in a more or dispositive manner a policy difference, issue, or dispute between the parties. This category is exemplified in treaties of peace that terminate a state of war, most land boundary treaties that simply draw a line, and agreements negotiated to settle legal disputes over such matters of entitlement as nationality, copyright, and protection of aliens.

By traditional thinking, boundary treaties are examples of resolutive agreements. By modern functionalist criteria, however, boundary treaties belong to a family of boundary and boundary-related settlements and arrangements. Even in the case of land boundaries, the members of this family can be seen to consist of distributive, administrative, and demonstrative, as well as resolutive, siblings and cousins, all descended from a resolutive parentage and sharing resolutive traits in varying degrees. The family of ocean boundary and boundary-related settlements and arrangements is just beginning to grow up; the best functionalist guess is that this family will exhibit fewer of these resolutive traits as it matures, and more of the administrative and distributive. Moreover, demonstrative ocean boundary instruments seem to be the best outcome immediately available for non-congenial neighbouring states not yet ready to bargain specific settlements or arrangements.

ELEVEN DIPLOMATIC OPTIONS

The various modes of diplomacy and negotiations and the four categories of treaties open a wide range of diplomatic options to neighbouring coastal states confronted with an ocean boundary delimitation issue. In functionalist theory, each such state has at least eleven options for the diplomatic treatment of an international delimitation problem in its offshore.[6]

1 Do-Nothing Policy. A coastal state may be so inhibited by a hostile relationship with its neighbour that the safest and wisest course may be to do nothing. This wholly passive strategy of inaction may be justified if the relationship is so bad that any reference to the boundary issue is likely to be misunderstood or misrepresented by the neighbouring state and added to the list of existing irritants, thereby increasing the risk of serious conflict.[7]

2 Agreement to Disagree. Almost always, however, a hostile relationship between two neighbouring states is too serious to be left untreated. Except possibly in the most acute cases of political conflict or paranoia, the hostile neighbours can usually be persuaded to discover that it is to their mutual benefit to agree to disagree. This option assumes a willingness on the part of the two states to admit publicly, perhaps in some kind of joint communiqué that requires resort to at least some minimal form of symbolic diplomacy, that an ocean boundary delimitation issue or dispute exists between them, but that the matter cannot be resolved under present conditions. This use of publicity concedes by implication that the matter calls for tact and moderation on both sides. If such a statement is followed by a good-faith effort by the neighbours to adhere to a policy of non-provocation or self-restraint, then, after a reasonable period, conditions may improve to the point that a bolder attempt at accommodation becomes possible.[8]

3 Agreement to Designate. At the third point, still close to the "minimal" end of the spectrum of diplomatic possibilities, the neighbours can enter into an agreement designating the boundary area acknowledged by them to be at issue. Such a designation can be implemented at various levels of precision. If the parties can agree on the longitude and latitude of the area at issue, they and interested third parties are put on notice that reasonable boundary-related arrangements may be acceptable outside the defined area, but that similar arrangements within those limits are likely to be provocative to at least one of the claimant states. This kind of conflict-avoidance policy, if successfully conducted, creates more flexibility in national and regional ocean development and management than is possible under the second option, and prescribes an area as well as an issue for future negotiation.[9]

4 Agreement to Consult. Somewhat more positively, the neighbouring states may conclude an agreement on consultation or a limited degree of co-operation within the defined area at issue. For example, there may simply be an agreement that each has an obligation to notify the other when some national initiative is being considered within the designated area. Or there may be a relatively informal bilateral arrangement between the neighbours to exchange certain kinds of data, such as the results of scientific research or the reports of task forces on resource policy questions. At best, this policy of low-cost or routine co-operation may result in an agreement on involvement in scientific co-operation if the parties can agree that co-operative investigation need not be deferred or postponed simply because the governments cannot agree on how to delimit a formal boundary within the designated area in dispute.[10]

5 Agreement on Access. Closer to the middle of the diplomatic spectrum is the option to negotiate an agreement on access to the designated boundary area for specified purposes. This policy of provisional utilization envisages a range of possible user arrangements that may be negotiated pending an eventual settlement of the delimitation issue, such as a provisional agreement on reciprocal or special fishing rights, provisions for marketing the fishery products derived from the disputed area, common standards or guidelines for fishery conservation or other environmental purposes, or agreed-upon conditions for rights of transit by oil tankers or other designated classes of vessels.[11]

6 Preliminary Joint Enterprise Policy. At the sixth level, the two neighbouring states may be sufficiently motivated by the prospect of resource development in the disputed area to negotiate a preliminary joint undertaking that contemplates future production based on some unspecified form of co-operation. This policy of preliminary co-operation assumes that a relatively friendly relationship exists or has been cultivated, even though the parties are still unable or unwilling to agree on a boundary settlement. They may be close to agreeing, at least in principle, on a strategy of co-operative development, with or without a boundary settlement, in their coastal and offshore waters. Such an arrangement might take the form of a formal agreement on joint prospecting for mineral resources in the designated offshore area, with or without the participation of third-party states, an international organization, or a transnational corporation. This kind of arrangement focuses on preparations for resource development without stipulating the form that such development will take. It may be chiefly concerned with the scale of potential production on a cost-sharing basis, and may be negotiated for a temporary experimental period without risking longer-range commitments that might not be easily fulfilled. A final decision to proceed to joint or national production can be postponed until the resource potentiality has been determined and the relationship between the neighbours further tested.[12]

7 Operational Joint Development Policy. More boldly, the two neighbouring states may have reached the stage of policy commitment that permits the negotiation of a joint development agreement for designated (fishery or hydrocarbon) production purposes within the disputed area. This strategy assumes that the development prospects for both states are favourable, that a formula for sharing production costs and benefits can be negotiated, and that the two governments can agree on detailed conditions of operation for the entrepreneurial and managerial institutions that will be involved. Commitment to a joint development policy usually implies at least a medium-term postponement of the linear boundary delimitation settlement within the area subject to the joint development arrangement. But this option represents a limited co-operative strategy to the extent that it focuses on a particular sector of ocean use and is confined to a project based on a renewable or terminable arrangement.[13]

8 Agreement on Sharing of Services. Rather more ambitiously, the neighbouring states may be able to agree on the sharing of specified state services related to ocean uses in the boundary area. Such a policy of administrative co-ordination requires a formal and continuing commitment over an indefinite period, and may involve costs that exceed revenues in the early years. A cost-sharing arrangement may be easier to negotiate, initially, in an area of strong mutual concern (rather than interest), such as a joint contingency plan in the event of a major oil spill or some other kind of environmental emergency. Such an arrangement is designed primarily to increase administrative efficiency or reduce administrative cost, and if sufficiently technical in purpose can sometimes be concluded and successfully maintained without arousing political sensitivities or popular mistrust.[14]

9 *Agreement on Limited Joint Management Arrangements.* In certain circumstances, the neighbouring states may recognize that a linear boundary settlement is not necessarily a primary objective in their ocean-use planning, and that proceeding with a joint development policy is unlikely to be effective without some degree of joint management, at least for an experimental period. In these circumstances they may wish to negotiate an agreement for the establishment of joint management arrangements limited to the purposes of their existing or projected joint ocean development projects. These arrangements are likely to cover the entire boundary area at issue, and may extend for certain purposes to undisputed national waters adjacent to the boundary area still in dispute. Functionally, however, an arrangement of this sort is essentially based on a policy of sectoral management, and is incomplete if it does not stipulate how all ocean management functions are to be assigned among the agencies of the neighbouring states.[15]

10 *Agreement on Permanent Joint Management.* The most ambitious option is the negotiating of an agreement for the establishment of a full-scale joint management system. This type of treaty applies not only to the area in dispute but also to extensive adjacent waters defined in accordance with accepted management requirements. Based on a policy of multisectoral management, the arrangements for co-operation are systematically conceived, and include provisions for the assignment of all management functions among the appropriate agencies of the two governments and perhaps for the creation of a joint commission or council having some degree of executive authority. This system of joint management requires the drawing of internal administrative lines within the overall area of joint management, lines that are the product of external negotiation as well as administrative logic.[16]

11 *Final Boundary Treaty.* The end of the diplomatic continuum is a formal treaty containing a complete package of negotiated settlements and arrangements. This outcome constitutes a fully developed regime that reflects the need for both the certainty of a settlement and for the flexibility of co-operative arrangements. A final boundary treaty is ambitious, complex, and possibly prone to diverse interpretations, but where a congenial

relationship exists between neighbouring states it represents the ultimate in a rational and sophisticated approach to the treatment of ocean boundary problems.[17]

The difficult question, in functionalist theory, is at what point on the continuum of diplomatic options it is in the interest of two neighbouring coastal states to resort to resolution of the linear issue of delimitation per se. How early or how late should the states give priority to settlement? At sea, as on land, there are definite advantages in having a fixed and permanently installed "fence" between neighbours; a fence often serves as the final answer to quarrels about space and entitlement. Especially in a strategically sensitive region (such as the Arctic), or in a region where the hostility between two armed neighbours has reached dangerously threatening proportions (such as the Arabian-Persian Gulf), the paramountcy of the need for security may put a premium on reaching a boundary settlement as early as possible. But functionalist theory, when applied to more normal situations of neighbour relations, underlines the irrationality of resorting to a premature settlement.

Many coastal and island states today find themselves confronted with a national dilemma in ocean boundary-making policy. At their present stage of nation-building, it may be unwise to resort to the making of fixed and purportedly final ocean boundaries with their neighbours. Too little may be known about the resources at stake, and it may be too early to decide how much to invest in procuring or developing the expertise required for effective ocean development and management. Moreover, the tasks of nation-building coexist with those of region-building, and it is certainly too early to assess unerringly the link that should be forged between the national and regional levels of ocean development and management. The age of experimentation in the design of international regimes for the management of ocean uses and resources is just beginning. From either or both of these national and regional viewpoints, an intermediate course lying between the do-nothing option at one end and the final boundary treaty at the other may represent the wisest choice.

The question for many coastal states is not whether but how and when to settle their ocean boundary issues. An early linear settlement may confer a net advantage on both parties, when they come to later bilateral or regional negotiations, if the settlement is temporary or provisional or is agreed to be subject to review and possible adjustment at a specified time. Both the policy of postponement and that of subsequent adjustment would give each of the two neighbouring states time to make and correct mistakes in ocean use planning at the national level, and to take advantage of improvements in ocean management thinking on the part of competent international organizations. Especially in the case of developing coastal states, it may be in the interest of both neighbours to defer a final boundary delimitation until the region as a whole has assembled an equitable and effective strategy for ocean development and management, with careful thought given to the regional implications of bilateral boundary-making.[18]

CHAPTER EIGHTEEN

The Range of Choices in Resort to Intermediation

MODES OF ADJUDICATION

In the field of international law, two principal modes of adjudication can be distinguished: litigation and arbitration. In most contexts, international litigation involves resort to the International Court of Justice, which is the principal judicial organ of the United Nations. The Court, which now consists of fifteen members, is authorized to deal with disputes submitted to it by applying

a international conventions, whether general or particular, establishing rules expressly recognized by the contesting states;
b international custom, as evidence of a general practice accepted as law;
c the general principles of law recognized by civilized nations;
d subject to the provisions of Article 59, judicial decisions and the teachings of the most highly qualified publicists of the various nations, as subsidiary means for the determination of rules of law.[1]

If the parties to the dispute agree, the Court may instead decide a case *ex aequo et bono* – that is, on an equitable basis rather than in strict accordance with the rules of international law.[2]

The 1982 UN Convention on the Law of the Sea provides an alternative method for the litigation of disputes arising out of the Convention, including certain types of ocean boundary disputes, in the International Tribunal for the Law of the Sea.[3] The twenty-one members of the Tribunal will be elected by the parties to the Convention within six months of its coming into force, perhaps not before 1991.[4] The Tribunal will be authorized to decide all disputes and applications submitted to it by applying the 1982 Convention and "other rules of international law not incompatible" with the Convention.[5] Where the parties agree, the Tribunal may decides a case *ex aequo et bono*.[6] Following the model of the ICJ, the Tribunal is empowered to lay down its own rules of procedure.[7]

The Court and the Tribunal are alike in that "chambers" (panels made up of a smaller number of judges) may be used in place of the full bench, at the parties' request, in particular kinds of disputes, including ocean disputes. The chamber procedure of the ICJ was first used by Canada and the United States in the *Gulf of Maine* boundary case, which was decided by a chamber consisting of four members of the Court (selected by the parties) and one *ad hoc* judge. Future litigants in an ocean boundary dispute submitted to the Tribunal could request a chamber composed of three or more members "determined by the Tribunal with the approval of the parties."[8] The 1982 Convention also provides for the use of more expeditious summary procedures within the framework of the Tribunal.[9] Accordingly, parties that wish to refer their ocean boundary dispute to litigation have a choice of five procedures: two under the Court (full bench and chamber) and three under the Tribunal (full bench, chamber, and summary procedure).

In the alternative, parties willing to submit their ocean boundary dispute to third-party adjudication may opt for some form of arbitration. Resort to arbitration, like litigation, requires the parties to accept in advance the adjudicated outcome as legally binding upon them, subject only to their right to clarification or revision in certain carefully defined circumstances. The main difference between the two types of third-party adjudication is that arbitration allows the parties a higher degree of control over the adjudicative process, especially in the selection of the adjudicators, the procedural system to be employed, and the scope and nature of rules and other considerations to be applied.[10]

Essentially, arbitration in any form proceeds by virtue of a treaty or treaty provision negotiated by the parties, and in principle it can be restricted by whatever limitations the parties choose to impose upon it. In practice, however, the arbitral body created or appointed by the parties often has as much discretion in the interpretation of its role, and in its choice of approach, as a court of law. Sometimes arbitration has the effect of putting a special burden of responsibility on the chairman, who may be the only independent arbitrator appointed by both parties, in contrast to the large number of independent judges on the full bench of the Tribunal (twenty-one) or the Court (fifteen). Often, however, the differences between arbitration and litigation are more apparent than real, judged by the nature and quality of the final outcome. This is a matter of some importance to the states that become parties to the 1982 UN Convention on the Law of the Sea. Under the provisions governing "compulsory procedures entailing binding decisions," parties to a dispute concerning the interpretation or application of the Convention are required – at signature, ratification, or accession – to choose one or more of four designated modes of adjudication: the Tribunal, the Court, "an arbitral tribunal constituted in accordance with Annex VII," or "a special arbitral tribunal constituted in accordance with Annex VIII for one or more of the categories of disputes specified therein."[11] It seems that the third of these options could be used in the event of certain kinds of ocean boundary disputes if the parties are unable to reach a settlement by recourse to section I of Part XV of the Convention. Annex VII envisages that the secretary general of the United Nations will maintain a list of arbitrators consisting of four nominees designated by each state party to the Convention. The arbitral tribunal will be empowered to determine its own procedure, and under article 293 will be authorized to base its award on exactly the same legal or equitable grounds as the Tribunal. It may be worth noting that whereas the members of the Tribunal under Annex VI are expected to be persons "of recognized competence in the field of the law of the sea,"[12] members of the arbitral tribunal under Annex VII are expected to be persons "experienced in maritime affairs."[13] On the face of things, Annex VII is clearer than Annex VI in envisaging the use of non-lawyers as well as lawyers in the process of adjudication.

MODES OF NON-ADJUDICATIVE INTERMEDIATION

"Non-adjudicative intermediation" refers to the range of procedures for third-party "problem management" (rather than dispute settlement) that do not involve a binding adjudicative award. In the context of ocean boundary problem management, it is sufficient to distinguish three basic modes: conciliation, mediation (or good offices),[14] and consideration by an appropriate international organization.

As in the *Jan Mayen* dispute, parties to an ocean boundary dispute may refer the problem to *conciliation* and establish a special commission for this purpose. In the *Jan Mayen* dispute, Norway and Iceland limited the commission to three members, consisting of one nominee of each party and an agreed-upon chairman from a third country. All three were prominent experts in the law of the sea. But a conciliation commission may consist of any number of members chosen by the parties, and need not be composed of lawyers. A conciliation commission holds meetings and discussions among the members, with external assistance if necessary, with a view to reaching agreement on recommendations to be submitted to the parties to the dispute. The conciliators' report is not binding on the parties, and the mandate usually is explicitly facilitative, although there is nothing to prevent a commission from recommending a "settlement" instead of, or in addition to, some kind of "arrangement."

In practice, a conciliation commission is likely to try to clarify the choices in direct bilateral diplomacy available to the parties, but it may also use the opportunity to clarify the applicable principles of international law and other pertinent considerations. The conciliators might even go so far as to draw a suggested boundary line, but a commission normally is not sufficiently equipped with technical expertise to perform such a task with the highest degree of precision. To the extent that the parties' nominees (that is, nationals) participate in the work of a commission, this method of problem management might be described as quasi-diplomatic.

It is important to note that the 1982 UN Convention on the Law of the Sea provides for conciliation in the event of a dispute concerning the interpretation or application of the Convention, and therefore of certain types of ocean boundary disputes. This procedure depends on the consent of both parties, but once proceedings have been initiated, they can be terminated only in accordance with the prescribed procedure, unless the parties otherwise agree.[15]

Under the Convention, conciliation may be conducted either in accordance with the procedure under Annex V, section 1, or by "another conciliation procedure."[16] If the former is chosen, the parties may, if they wish, establish the procedure to be used by the conciliation commission, and they may, if they wish, specify that the proceedings are to be informal.[17] The commission is mandated to "facilitate an amicable settlement of the dispute,"[18] and there is no requirement that the rules of international law be followed, as in litigation and arbitration. Consistent with the open-ended nature of conciliation, members of the conciliation commission under Annex V are expected only to be persons "enjoying the highest reputation for fairness, competence and integrity."[19] Freed from technical constraints, they are obligated only to "hear the parties, examine their claims and objections, and make proposals to the parties with a view to reaching an amicable settlement."[20]

The second non-adjudicative mode may be described as *mediation*, although this term should be conceived broadly as subsuming the procedure of good offices. Broadly defined, mediation of an ocean boundary problem would normally involve a single person engaged by the parties to "commute" between them with a view to helping them explore possible solutions. If he is successful, the mediator will have facilitated future negotiations between the parties, and in that sense the mediation process can be characterized as indirect bilateral diplomacy supported by intermediary assistance. Sometimes the mediation is conducted, at the parties' request, by a highly prominent person, such as the UN secretary-general or the pope, or their personal envoy or representative, as in the final stage of the *Beagle Channel* dispute between Chile and Argentina (see the section entitled "Modern Dispute Management" in chapter 11).

In principle, mediation may be said to possess the greatest flexibility of any form of third-party dispute management. The outcome of the process is entirely and continuously within the control of the parties, who may choose to avoid publicity before, during, or after the period of engagement. Since mediation usually is conducted in circumstances of extreme political delicacy, it may be counter-productive to publish any document or otherwise disclose the nature of the mediator's input. But, as in the case of conciliation, the success of the mediation is measured in terms of persuasiveness, and successful mediation brings the parties to (or back to) the negotiating table, if not to an actual agreement on a boundary settlement or arrangement.

Finally, non-adjudicative third-party assistance may be sought through recourse to some form of conference diplomacy in the arena of an appropriate *international organization*, global or regional. If an ocean boundary dispute is perceived as a conflict constituting a threat to the peace, as in the case of the *Aegean Sea Continental Shelf* dispute between Greece and Turkey, one of the parties may refer the problem to the UN Security Council or General Assembly under chapter VI of the United Nations Charter. In the alternative, one or both of the parties may refer the problem to an appropriate regional organization, if such a body exists in the region where the dispute has arisen. Several existing regional organizations offer conciliation, mediation, or consultation services to member states engaged in bilateral disputes that have not been resolved through direct bilateral diplomacy. Given the regional or subregional implications of most bilateral ocean boundary disputes, reference to a regional system of dispute management may sometimes be the wisest course of action.[21]

THE PROBLEM OF PROCEDURAL STRATEGY

In the event of a diplomatic failure at the negotiating table, or an adverse political reaction after successful diplomacy, the parties to an ocean boundary dispute may be forced by mounting pressures to submit to some mutually acceptable form of intermediation. The choice of procedural strategy may be affected by a variety of values, interests, and attitudes.

The fundamental question is whether or not to use some form of adjudication. Many governments, especially in Western Europe, regard resort to the International Court of Justice as the most principled, and therefore the most honourable, method of third-party dispute settlement. A decision or an offer to rely on the ICJ to do so may be perceived as a value-based position to the extent that it is seen to reflect a national commitment to the rule of law. Such a position is essentially based on trust in the impartiality of the judicial process, but may be rationalized in various ways: for example, in the "unitarian" mode, by reference to an obligation to support the Court in its function of contributing to the consolidation of legal rules and principles, and by reference to the need for uniformity and consistency in dispute settlement.

States willing to refer an ocean boundary dispute to the ICJ may, however, differ on whether to use the full court or a chamber. The only apparent advantage in the chamber option is that it seems to give the parties a marginally higher degree of control over the outcome through control over the selection of judges. If the Court as a whole is perceived as becoming more divergent – culturally, ideologically, and juridically – it may be expected that the chamber procedure will be chosen occasionally, on grounds of mutual interest, by litigant states anxious to select only those judges who are regarded as sharing their own orientation to the application of international law in an ocean boundary context. (On the jurisprudential split in the ICJ, see chapter 14.)

After the entry into force of the 1982 Convention on the Law of the Sea, states willing to refer an ocean boundary dispute to international litigation may resort to the International Tribunal on the Law of the Sea. In that situation, as noted above, litigants will have three procedural options: full court, chamber, or summary proceedings. Conceivably, all three procedures could be available for ocean boundary-making purposes. The supposition is that the Tribunal will consist entirely of law-of-the-sea specialists, and may therefore be preferable to the Court for its collective expertise. But reference to the Tribunal requires that the boundary-making problem be presented so that it turns on a question concerning the interpretation or application of one or more of the boundary-related provisions of the Convention. A litigant otherwise willing to use the Tribunal may be reluctant to do so if it involves characterizing the issue in a way that seems to distort the real boundary-making problem.

States willing to refer an ocean boundary dispute to the Tribunal may differ on whether to use the full bench (with twenty-one members), a chamber (with, say, three to seven members), or summary proceedings (with five members). Because of the uncertainties involved, it seems unlikely that many states will wish to refer an ocean boundary dispute to a judicial body of twenty-one members representing all geographical regions, cultures, ideologies, and juridical traditions, except perhaps a test case. It is also difficult to envisage the use of summary proceedings in a matter as weighty as an ocean boundary dispute. It seems likely that parties to an ocean boundary dispute will not make frequent use of the Tribunal, and that when they do the chamber procedure will be the preferred mode.

It may be, however, that most states willing to contemplate adjudication of an ocean boundary dispute will choose arbitration. At least notionally, arbitration seems to offer the same prospect of impartiality as litigation, and a similarly binding and resolutive outcome, without the same degree of commitment to the reduction of the boundary-making problem to a set of relatively narrow legal issues. Where concern over undue "legalization" is a factor, resort to arbitration may seem more attractive if the parties believe that they can retain a slightly higher degree of control over the interpretation of their terms of reference, and that they can influence the tribunal's orientation through the selection of non-lawyers, or "non-legalistic" lawyers, as arbitrators. It may, of course, be questioned whether these beliefs are warranted.

For the settlement of an ocean boundary dispute, resort to modern arbitration can be almost as elaborate and expensive as resort to the ICJ, as in the case of the *Channel Islands* arbitration between France and the United Kingdom. Similarly, judged by the scale and cost of the *Gulf of Maine* dispute between Canada and the United States, it is doubtful whether reference to a chamber of the ICJ involves any saving of money and effort. In theory, arbitration appears to be potentially more economical than litigation, but in practice it seems that economies in international adjudication can be effected only if the parties have an equal interest in limiting the volume of research and documentation and the size of the teams involved.

Many governments today seem unwilling to use any form of adjudication for the settlement of anything as weighty as an ocean boundary dispute. In most of these situations, the reluctance seems attributable to attitude as much as to values or interests. For reasons of ideology (for example, in the case of Eastern Europe) or culture (for example, in the case of Asia and Asia Minor), there is a tendency on the part of many countries to avoid the kind of adversarial confrontation that is inherent in litigation and arbitration.[22] In some regions the anti-adjudicative sentiment is so strong that it is difficult to imagine what it would take to induce the parties to seek such a resolution of their dispute.

In addition to attitudinal barriers, one or both of the parties may feel that it is not in their mutual interest to deal with a multifaceted problem by the kind of legal reductionism inherent in the process of adjudication, and many governments are frankly unwilling to accept the risk of losing in a legal contest. Moreover, most of the "reluctant" states emphasize the primacy of the principle of voluntary negotiation as a matter of values, almost to the point of denying the need for any alternative method of dispute settlement.

But an ocean boundary dispute may have such important resource implications, especially for a developing coastal state, that an indefinite postponement of a settlement or arrangement is simply unacceptable. In this situation the parties to the dispute may be induced to think of it as a problem that could be managed more effectively with the assistance of some kind of non-adjudicative intermediary. In circumstances of this kind, the choice of mode might be made almost wholly on the grounds of national interest, with minimal constraint by reason of attitudes or values. The relative advantages of resort to a conciliation commission, a mediator, or an international organization can be assessed only within the context of a particular dispute, but it may be surmised that conciliation is the most likely to be attempted. When the 1982 Convention comes into force, in 1991 or thereabouts, conciliation under section 1 of Part XV is likely to become a preferred choice of non-binding intermediary procedure.

With a view to the future applicability of the Convention, it should be noted that article 298(1)(a)(i) permits a party to declare its non-acceptance of any one or more of the "compulsory procedures entailing binding decisions" contained in section 2 of Part XV for the settlement of "disputes concerning the interpretation or application of articles 15, 74, and 83 relating to sea boundary delimitations ..." States making such a declaration are obligated to resort to conciliation under section 2 of Annex V. If the parties are unable to negotiate an agreement based on the report of the conciliation commission, they "shall, *by mutual consent*, submit the question to one of the procedures provided for in section 2, *unless the parties otherwise agree* [emphasis added]."[23] The double qualification seems to have the effect of reducing this apparently obligatory provision to the status of "soft law," which may mean that in diplomatically difficult situations conciliation will be both the first and the last resort to third-party intermediary treatment of a boundary problem.

When all considerations are weighed in the balance – values, interests, and attitudes – it is likely that most coastal states confronted by a serious ocean boundary problem that cannot be solved through normal direct bilateral diplomacy will resort to conciliation. If conciliation fails, it may prove difficult to induce the parties to proceed to any form of adjudication. As to those states willing to submit an ocean boundary dispute to adjudication either in the first or second resort, arbitration seems likely to become the favourite mode of treatment. If such a pattern emerges, it may be expected that intermediaries of both sorts will deal facilitatively, rather than resolutively, with ocean boundary disputes.

THE PATTERN OF INTERMEDIARY PROCEEDINGS

The full range of choices available in the resort to intermediation would become apparent in a comprehensive functionalist analysis of the evolving pattern of intermediary proceedings. All such proceedings, except the abortive attempt to settle the *Aegean Sea* dispute between Greece and

THE INTERMEDIARY PROCESS

PROCEEDING	MODE		ORIENTATION OF PARTIES		ROLE ASSIGNED				MAJOR INFLUENCES ON INTERMEDIARY				APPROACH BY INTER-MEDIARY		ROLE DISCHARGED				OUTCOME	
	A	N/A	Issue	Prob.	Interp.	Declar.	Resol.	Facil.	P	R	T	M	Restr.	Lib.	Interp.	Declar.	Resol.	Facil.	Settl.	Arrang.
Grisbadarna (Norway v. Sweden)	X		X		X	X					X		X		X	X			X	
Anglo-Norwegian Fisheries	X		X			X					X		X			X			X	
North Sea Continental Shelf	X		X		X	X		X				X		X	X	X		X	X	
Fisheries Jurisdiction	X		X			X						X	X			X				
Channel Islands (Anglo-French)	X		X		X		X						X			X	X		X	
Beagle Channel I (Argentina v. Chile)	X		X		X		X						X		X		X			
Jan Mayen (Iceland v. Norway)		X		X				X	X	X	X	X		X				X		X
Tunisia-Libya Continental Shelf	X		X			X		X				X	X			X				
Gulf of Maine (Canada v. U.S.)	X		X				X			X		X	X			X	X		X	

Beagle Channel II (Argentina v. Chile)		X		X			X	X	X	X		X		X			X	X	X	X
Gulf of Guinea (Guinea v. Guinea-Bissau)	X		X		X		X		X			X		X	X		X	X	X	
Libya-Malta Continental Shelf	X		X			X		?	X				X				X		X	

A = adjudicative
N/A = non-adjudicative
P = perceptual (parties' perception of problem situation)
R = relational (relationship between parties

T = technological (parties' technological opportunities)
M = milieu-related (world community expectations)
Interp. = interpretive
Declar. = declaratory

Resol. = resolutive
Facil. = facilitative
Restr. = restrictive
Lib. = liberal
Settl. = settlement
Arrang. = arrangement

Turkey, are characterized in the accompanying table. In the absence of full-scale case studies of these disputes, the compilation of such a table involves some guesswork, especially in the identification of factors that might have influenced the intermediary.

As suggested in the table, the parties to the dispute have choices not only in the mode of proceedings (adjudicative or non-adjudicative) and in their orientation to the situation (issue-oriented or problem-oriented), but also in the roles assigned to the intermediary (interpretive, declaratory, resolutive, and facilitative). If it is relatively uninfluenced by various factors beyond the issues and arguments presented, the intermediary may restrict itself to the orientation of the parties and to the role(s) they have assigned it. On the other hand, the intermediary may regard these factors as relevant to the task of delimitation, adopt a more "liberal" approach, and discharge a broader range of roles than those assigned. In functionalist perspective, it is of special interest to observe whether there is a trend toward a more "liberal" approach by intermediaries in the management of an ocean boundary delimitation dispute, and toward the discharge of an unsolicited "facilitative" role in various kinds of intermediary proceedings.

CHAPTER NINETEEN

Considerations in the Treatment of Ocean Boundary Problems

Perhaps the most difficult task in developing the theory of ocean boundary-making is to account for the diversity of mental elements involved in the boundary-making process. In functionalist perspective, ocean boundary-making should be treated both as decision-making and problem-solving. Persons officially authorized to make and maintain ocean boundary settlements and arrangements have to marshal and weigh a wide range of "considerations" to those ends. However difficult it may be, it is important for the theoretician to try to organize the various considerations in a way that seems conducive to the development of a functionalist rationale for ocean boundary-makers.

This task is complicated by the impossibility of knowing the full range of considerations actually applied to all ocean boundary problems. In particular, the bureaucratic and diplomatic processes are virtually impenetrable by a scholarly observer, and even the lengthiest judicial or arbitral decision is unlikely to acknowledge all of the considerations addressed by the court or tribunal as a whole. However, to the extent that an adjudicative award sets out, albeit incompletely, the rationale of the decision, it represents the best available evidence of how one type of boundary-maker thinks through the process.

By default, therefore, the organization of relevant considerations is influenced to a large extent by the adjudicative model of boundary-making. But it should be remembered that adjudicators operate under constraints that usually have the effect, and almost invariably the purpose, of limiting the range of judicial or arbitral considerations. Above all, of course, the court or tribunal is constrained by the terms of reference in the *compromis* or arbitration agreement.[1] The range of considerations usually is limited by a number of self-imposed constraints accepted by the adjudicators as professionally appropriate, such as their reluctance to permit a third-party intervenor to participate in judicial proceedings, or their reluctance to acknowledge resort to *ex aequo et bono* reasoning without the parties' consent (see the section entitled "Delimitation of 'Lateral' Boundaries" in chapter 14).

To the extent that the functionalist approach is a problem-solving approach, it seems necessary to advocate a kind of lateral thinking that seeks to find a way around all sides of the problem.[2] It is inherent in the nature of any discipline that it offers only a particular perspective on a problem of any complexity, and therefore on the problem of problem-solving. Typically, an exclusively legal approach tends to limit the process of reasoning to legal issues, legal values, and legal norms in the form of rules and principles. In extreme cases, such an approach encourages an exercise in derivational logic, which is justified on the ground that the chief responsibility of the court or tribunal is to contribute to the consolidation and crystallization of mutually consistent rules and principles. Such an approach, characterized in this work as "unitarian," should be contrasted with the functionalist approach, which places emphasis less on extrinsic considerations such as legal rules than on intrinsic considerations found in the situation with which the adjudicator has to deal.

Since the intended outcome may take the form of a linear settlement, an institutional arrangement, or a combination of the two, the inquiry might vary from relatively narrow to extremely broad in scope. The maximal range of considerations is likely to be addressed in the context of what is perceived to be an important and difficult ocean boundary problem. The maximal range consists of three distinguishable types: perceptual, analytical, and instrumental. In practice it seems desirable to proceed sequentially in addressing these considerations, beginning with the perceptual and concluding with the instrumental.

The *perceptual* stage of the problem-solving process applied to ocean boundary problems involves the characterization of the "situation" that must be dealt with at the beginning. To determine the situation, the boundary-makers must characterize: (1) the problem of which the boundary-making issue or dispute forms a part; (2) the approach to be adopted in the treatment of the problem; and (3) the geographical area to be adopted as the most appropriate spatial frame of reference for the approach selected. After the problem, the approach, and the area have been characterized, it becomes easier to distinguish relevant intrinsic and extrinsic factors and to assess their degree of significance. The approach adopted may draw upon all or some of at least six distinguishable frames of reference: physical, political, socio-cultural, economic, juridical, and managerial (see chapter 3). A bureaucratic boundary-maker should be the least constrained in the characterization of problem, approach, and area; almost invariably an adjudicative boundary-maker is likely to be the most

The Process of Problem-Solving

Stage	*Goal*	*Elements*
Perceptual	Characterization of situation	• problem • approach • geographical area
Analytical	Evaluation of factors • identification (potential) • clarification • selection (actual) • weighting	• values • interests • attitudes • relationships • milieu • physical setting • technology • time
Instrumental	Application of techniques • identification • clarification • selection • final adjustment	• principles • criteria • methods

constrained. Functionalist reasoning prescribes that all ocean boundary-makers should be as free as possible from artificial or arbitrary limitations on this initial exercise in perceptual choices, and that problem, approach, and area normally should be characterized broadly rather than narrowly.

The *analytical* stage of the problem-solving process involves choices in the application of the various factors deemed to affect the boundary-making process – for example, values, interests, attitudes, relationships, milieu, physical setting, technology, and time (see chapter 14). In practice, factors as diverse and abstract as these are unlikely to be listed systematically in the bureaucratic or diplomatic environment, but the need for the rationalization of decisions may induce adjudicative or other intermediary boundary-makers to identify the relevant factors explicitly. A systematic ordering of such factors might be expected to proceed sequentially, from identification through clarification, if necessary, to selection and the final process of relative weighting.

The *instrumental* stage involves choices in the application of appropriate techniques: principles, criteria, and methods (see chapter 5). In practice as well as in theory, the instrumental stage should follow the analytical stage, and preferably in the same sequence, beginning with identification and proceeding through clarification and selection to final adjustment.

DETERMINATION OF SEAWARD LIMITS

The establishment of fixed uniform limits for the territorial sea, the contiguous zone, the continental shelf, and the EEZ has removed the need for any protracted problem-solving process in the determination of most seaward limits. In most circumstances, these limits have been predetermined at the global level of law-making and are established in provisions based on the criterion of distance. The only available method is that of parallel lines, straight or otherwise. Only the degree of geodetic precision to be applied is a matter for the unilateral consideration of the bureaucratic boundary-maker.

In a dozen or more coastal states, whose continental shelf extends farther than two hundred nautical miles seaward from the baseline of the territorial sea, the seaward limits must be determined in accordance with a complex formula rather than a simple mileage rule. In the technically difficult process of implementing the formula in article 76 of the 1982 Convention, the "broad margin" coastal state is expected to submit its continental shelf seaward boundary to validation by the technical experts who constitute the Commission on the Limits of the Continental Shelf. Anticipating a technical dialogue with the Commission, the boundary-maker will perhaps feel obliged to give careful thought to the factors involved as well as to the techniques that might be deployed. Apart from considerations of timing and technology, attention will focus on the physical setting and the relationship to be cultivated with the Commission. The Commission may respond initially by raising questions about the accuracy and reliability of the data presented as the basis of the proposed boundary. To that extent, the mode of validation is the scientific method of empirical investigation, based on the criterion of verifiability. But it is conceivable that in certain political circumstances the dialogue may eventually reveal a difference between the Commission and a coastal state on the selection and weighting of factors and the application of techniques (see the section entitled "The New Law of the Sea" in chapter 9).

DELINEATION OF BASELINES AND CLOSING LINES

Delineation is closely associated with the interests and attitudes of the adjacent coastal communities, and in some circumstances these factors might be regarded as prevailing over the value consideration of strict conformity with the delineation formulae prescribed in the 1982 Convention. Delineation is a non-negotiable sort of boundary-making, and consists essentially of a unilateral act or series of actions on the part of the national bureaucracy. It is to be hoped that the approach adopted will be tempered by the realization that this type of ocean boundary-making, like others, has an international legal aspect, and that the claimant coastal state is answerable to the international community for the way in which the boundary is made. Because other states will have legitimate navigational interests in adjacent waters, this kind of ocean boundary-making should be influenced by the evaluation of a wide range of factors as well as the application of alternative techniques.

In the case of normal baselines, the prescribed formula requires the use of the tidal (low water) method of delineation, based on the criterion of coastal curvature. The straight baseline approach to delineation involves the use of a formula that consists of a combination of geographical ("general direction of the coast"), socio-economic ("close linkage") and historical ("long usage") criteria. The selection of appropriate points for the purpose of applying the straight baseline formula or system prescribed in article 7 of the Convention is a discretionary act that should be tempered by a variety of international as well as national considerations, but the absence of any prescribed method (as distinguished from criteria) ensures that this kind of delineation will invite controversy. Less controversy should accompany the drawing of archipelagic baselines in accordance with article 47 and of bay closing lines in accordance with article 10 because of the relatively precise geometric methods injected into those two formulae. In both situations some controversy may occasionally erupt over the manner of delineation, despite the attempt to prescribe precise conformity, but such disputes probably will be limited to quarrels over techniques, such as the method of weighting islands (see the section entitled "The New Law of the Sea" in chapter 10).

It should be added that a wider range of factors will be addressed in claims and responses related to historic bays and other historic waters.[3] Because of the lack of clearly established criteria limiting such claims in international law, delineation practices by certain claimant states may be difficult to challenge effectively at the level of techniques.

DELIMITATION OF "LATERAL" BOUNDARIES

It is chiefly in the context of delimitation between neighbouring states that the wide variety of considerations constitutes a major intellectual problem. The problem is critical when the simple diplomatic process is unable to provide an acceptable settlement or arrangement and it becomes necessary to resort to a complex diplomatic/intermediary procedure, and when the parties resort to some form of third-party adjudication.

In the functionalist view, adjudicators called upon to deal with a delimitation dispute should proceed in a facilitative manner to the extent consistent with the terms of reference negotiated between the parties. Within the general parameters described in the *compromis*, the adjudicators should proceed immediately to a broad characterization of the problem behind the dispute, and with that problem in mind determine the role or approach to be adopted by the tribunal. Unless the *compromis* is clearly restrictive and assigns the adjudicators a strictly resolutive or merely declaratory role, the court or tribunal should characterize its approach as primarily facilitative in purpose. Such an approach should normally induce the adjudicators to characterize the geographical area of relevance broadly rather than narrowly, so as to ensure that important third-party interests and regional or subregional responsibilities are included among the appropriate considerations. Even if it is difficult, for procedural or other reasons, to admit an interested third party to the adjudicative proceedings, the tribunal should feel obliged, by functionalist reasoning, to give appropriate weighting to the need for regional or subregional settlements (such as "tri-junction" agreements) and related arrangements.[4] This approach is particularly desirable when the tribunal is confronted with a physical setting such as an enclosed or semi-enclosed sea, in which all littoral states are subject to a special obligation to co-operate in ocean development and management under the new law of the sea.[5] Again, in characterizing the situation with which it has been asked to deal, a primarily facilitative or problem-solving approach should influence the tribunal's determination of how to distinguish more important from less important considerations.

The facilitative approach to adjudication suggested by functionalist reasoning seems to require a tribunal to give primacy to situational over extra-situational factors. This approach would reduce the use of derivational logic, which tends to be inherent in legalism, and reduce or delay the weighting of historical considerations, since both types of factors are perceived as extra-situational.[6] Because of the overriding obligation in international law to produce an equitable solution, adjudicators should postpone recourse to law and history until they have examined the interplay of values and other factors in the situation.

The analysis of relevant values can, of course, be conducted at different levels. First, at a high level of abstraction, the prescribed requirement for equity should be supplemented by the need for efficiency; but at that level equal or subsidiary reference also can be made to other value categories, such as wealth, power, respect, knowledge, and well-being.[7] Second, there is a catalogue of values specifically related to the consequences of ocean boundary-making, such as certainty, uniformity, flexibility, precision, and stability. At this level of analysis one comes closer to discerning the criteria of functionality that should be applied to ocean boundaries. (On the value criteria for determining the functionality of an ocean boundary, see chapter 14.) Third, it is possible to approach the evaluation of an ocean boundary proposal or option in view of the kind of behaviour one wishes to facilitate in the larger context of regional ocean development and management – co-operative, competitive, or autonomous.[8] Fourth, it is useful to consider the values that take the form of first-order legal principles organized as a cluster and enunciated as a "basic norm."[9] Although extrinsic to the situation, all elements of the "basic norm" share the systemic characteristics of the equitable solution requirement, and can be accepted together as a normative predisposition of fundamental value to those responsible for the treatment of an ocean boundary delimitation problem. The term "solution" in the "basic norm" should be interpreted as acknowledging the existence of a "problem," one that is likely to be larger than the legal or technical issues associated with it.

The suggestion that only a "basic norm" in international law should have any preliminary weighting in the minds of adjudicators in a delimitation dispute means that other, secondary-level legal norms should be perceived as extrinsic considerations that should not be given undue saliency early in the problem-solving process. Ideally, secondary legal principles should be withheld from adjudicative consideration until the instrumental stage, when they should compete, in a sense, with criteria and methods for the tribunal's favour as potential techniques for achieving an "equitable solution." This suggested treatment of legal principles is less radical than it sounds, because of the artificiality of any distinction between legal and non-legal categories of techniques available at the instrumental stage of adjudication.[10]

The appropriate principles, criteria, and methods should be selected, in accordance with functionalist logic, in light of the following elements discernible in the situation confronted by the tribunal: (1) the general (macrogeographical) characteristics of the physical setting, within the appropriate area of relevance; (2) the special (microgeographical) characteristics of the physical setting within the area in dispute, and perhaps adjacent waters; (3) the opportunities and problems of ocean development and management in the disputed area and adjacent waters, with reference in appropriate circumstances to the prospect of relevant regional or subregional settlements and arrangements; and (4) the recent history of ocean uses and relevant relationships in the region.[11]

With these considerations in mind, a functionally oriented tribunal should proceed to the selection of the appropriate techniques with a view to achieving an outcome that is both efficient and equitable. Most of the available techniques can be characterized as criteria or methods: median line as a method based on the criterion of equidistance; proportionality as a "test" (that is, a method of testing equitableness) based on the criteria of distance, length, and area; the thalweg as a method based on the criterion of navigability or the principle of equal advantage; and so on.[12] The "principle" of natural prolongation has been virtually eliminated from the adjudication of delimitation disputes, and the precise role of the "principle" of special circumstances in delimitation seems more uncertain than ever since primacy was assigned to the need for an equitable solution in every situation (see the section entitled "Modern Dispute Management" in chapter 11). The discretion inherent in this requirement often will be exercised chiefly through the choice of methods for weighting islands.[13] A facilitative approach to adjudication, like conciliation, may result in non-binding guidelines or recommendations for the use of zoning techniques.[14]

The tribunals adjudicating delimitation disputes in recent years have consistently emphasized the particularistic orientation of their decisions, and have warned us not to try to extract general principles from them. Equally consistently, those warnings have been ignored by "unitarian" counsel and commentators, who seem to assume that the consolidation of legal norms is the primary function of any tribunal. The facilitative approach to adjudication recommended in this chapter comes closer to reflecting the current realities of judicial and arbitral behaviour in this context of ocean boundary-making, and is more likely to serve the larger purposes of ocean development and management around the world.

CHAPTER TWENTY

Conclusions

The functionalist theory developed in this book represents a contextualist, problem-oriented, and interdisciplinary approach to ocean boundary-making. It is a result of dissatisfaction with traditionalist approaches to boundary-making theory that seem too limited or too limiting because of their dependency on abstraction, their obsession with narrowly technical issues, or their bias toward one particular discipline.

The functionalist approach as set out here may seem to invite complexity in the name of sophistication. In practice, the drawing of an ocean boundary should often be approached initially as a relatively uncomplicated problem. But as coastal states strive for efficiency in the development and management of their ocean resources and in the regulation of ocean uses, it is unlikely that simple linear conceptions of ocean boundaries will survive the initial phase of national ocean policy formation. Despite the continuing advantages in the certainty of linear settlements, more and more coastal states are likely to proceed to a variety of internal and external arrangements as the public law and administration of the ocean evolve through the building of regimes and the proliferation of zones in the ocean. It is hard to believe that trends of this sort will not be accompanied by an increasingly sophisticated and complex approach to the making and maintenance of ocean boundaries. It might seem, therefore, that functionalism depends on a prediction of trends in ocean development and management around the world.

To what extent does a prediction of increasing complexity find support in current trends? Given the fishery development rationale of the EEZ, it is relevant to note the widespread evidence of diminishing regard for scientific evidence in the theory, and especially the practice, of fishery management. The highly eclectic fishery management provisions negotiated at UNCLOS III suggest that most coastal states prefer the political rather than the technical approach to this sector of resource management. It may be questioned whether this trend to eclectic and political management of fisheries is a trend to simplicity. It seems just as easy to draw the opposite conclusion.

The question of prevailing trends in ocean development and management is partly dependent on the prospect of a significant transfer of ocean science and technology from developed to developing coastal states in the next two decades, in what might be regarded as the preliminary period of national ocean development and management. Obviously, the general picture is one of considerable diversification among states. Most states can be expected to develop a policy that consists of both convergent and divergent features: that is, of norms, institutions, practices, and procedures that both converge with and diverge from those of neighbouring, transit, and other relevant states. Convergence might be expected in sectors of ocean development and management where co-operative behaviour is seen to be most beneficial, and divergence in sectors where competitive or autonomous behaviour is perceived as serving the national interest. Since each coastal state will develop its own pattern of co-operative, competitive, and autonomous policies, there may be considerable disparities in national approaches to ocean settlements and arrangements, and therefore to the treatment of boundary-related problems within limits of national jurisdiction. But there is little in this prospect that seems to challenge the prediction of increasing complexity or the assumption of a need for functional rationality.

Finally, even in the immediate aftermath of aggrandizement of ocean space, there is little evidence that coastal states regard their new boundaries in the ocean simply as territorial lines. Almost everywhere, the concept and logic of functional jurisdiction seem rooted in national ocean policy and practice. These boundaries are not the product of conquest or historic accident, but are the result of international planning and negotiation. The history of boundary-making on land has little to offer by way of example. The making and maintenance of boundaries in the sea should be viewed as a new beginning, offering a better hope for the world community.

Notes

INTRODUCTION

1 Because of the narrowness of the limits of the territorial sea permitted in general state practice before the Second World War – and the virtual non-existence of coastal state authority beyond the traditional twelve-mile limits of the contiguous zone – before 1945 states had little incentive to assign a high priority to ocean boundary-making. But since the seventeenth century jurists have addressed themselves to the principles that should govern ocean boundary delimitation. Samuel Pufendorf (1632–94) was apparently the first to do so in a systematic fashion. Rhee, "Sea Boundary Delimitation," 556–7.

2 See generally Gold, *Maritime Transport*.

3 The modern trend to extended coastal state jurisdiction around the world usually is said to originate in the two Truman Declarations of 1945, in which the United States laid claim unilaterally to exclusive jurisdiction over the continental shelf and to special conservation authority over certain fishery stocks in areas of the high seas adjacent to its territorial sea. McDougal and Burke, *Public Order of the Oceans*, 635–8, 966–8.

4 Johnston and Gold, "Extended Jurisdiction," 3–56.

5 The main provisions on coastal state jurisdiction negotiated (or renegotiated) at UNCLOS III are found in Part II ("Territorial Sea and Contiguous Zone"), Part IV ("Archipelagic States"), Part V ("Exclusive Economic Zone") and Part VI ("Continental Shelf") of the 1982 United Nations Convention on the Law of the Sea.

6 The so-called enclosure movement took two forms prior to UNCLOS III: extension-of-sovereignty claims and specific claims to functional jurisdiction. See Eckert, *Enclosure of Ocean Resources*, 21–32.

7 In 1979 it was estimated that extended jurisdiction has created the need for approximately 317 lateral ocean boundaries between opposite and adjacent

coastal states for fisheries and hydrocarbon purposes alone. Hodgson and Smith, "Boundary Issues," 426.

8 The first scholar to attempt a systematic study of land boundaries and frontiers was Friedrich Ratzel (1844–1904). For a summary of his ideas, see Prescott, *Boundaries and Frontiers* 14–16.

9 Most of these early practices took the form of spatial claims to designated areas of territory before the advent of linear claims to precisely defined zones of national jurisdiction or authority.

10 For a pre-modern treatment of conquest as a "proper legal title" to territory, see McMahon, *Conquest and Modern International Law*. See also de Martini, *Right of Nations* and Van Campen, *The Imperator*. On colonial boundary-making in Africa see McEwan, *International Boundaries of East Africa* and Prescott, *Evolution of Nigeria's Boundaries*.

11 For example, Col. T.H. Holdich based his work *Political Frontiers and Boundary Making* (1916) on his personal experience on boundary commissions.

12 From a modern viewpoint, none of the European pioneers in the boundary literature seems both systematic and objective, and several seem neither. Perhaps the first of the systematic and objective treatises are two American works: Boggs, *International Boundaries* (1940), and Jones, *Boundary-Making* (1945).

13 The viewpoint that the 1982 UN Convention on the Law of the Sea negotiated at UNCLOS III represents a "fair and rational order for the oceans" is not yet unanimous, mainly because of the controversial provisions on deep-ocean mining. But even in the few states dissenting, most law of the sea specialists support the non-seabed-mining provisions as possessing a uniquely significant legal status. In 1984 the members of a panel on the law of ocean uses in the United States described these provisions as "a workable regime that would promote order at sea and satisfy the complex of competing interests of different states." Letter reproduced in 79 *American Journal of International Law* 151 (1985). In urging the U.S. Administration to support the outcome of UNCLOS III, they invoked the "new opportunity for building a universal 'customary law' around the rules described by the Convention ..." Ibid., 153. For responses, see ibid., 154–8.

14 In the 1951 *Anglo-Norwegian Fisheries* case, the International Court of Justice observed: "The delimitation of sea areas has always an international aspect; it cannot be dependent merely upon the will of the coastal State as expressed in its municipal law. Although it is true that the act of delimitation [i.e., baseline delineation] is necessarily a unilateral act, because only the coastal State is competent to undertake it, the validity of the delimitation with regard to other States depends upon international law." ICJ Rep. 1951, 132.

15 Admittedly, the ICJ's famous dictum, applied to delineation of the baseline

of the territorial sea (or exclusive fishing zone), was enunciated during the neo-classical period in the history of the law of the sea, when the international regime of the high seas still impinged on waters close to shore and to the baseline around a coast. But the point of the dictum seems to have much less to do with geographical propinquity than with the origin and character of the rules or criteria governing the "delimitation of [all] sea areas." This reasoning seems not to be affected by the geographical extension of coastal state jurisdiction, since that phenomenon is solely the product of the international legal system. Even an internal administrative boundary drawn by a coastal state within its exclusive economic zone or on its continental shelf, designed to apply only to its own nationals, must still have a secondary, if not primary, "international aspect," since it may have an effect, intentionally or otherwise, on the rights and interests of other states and their nationals.

16 1958 Convention on the High Seas, 450 UNTS 82; 1958 Convention on the Territorial Sea and the Contiguous Zone, 516 UNTS 205; 1958 Convention on the Continental Shelf, 499 UNTS 311; 1958 Convention on Fishing and Conservation of the Living Resources of the High Seas, 559 UNTS 285; and 1982 Convention on the Law of the Sea, text reproduced at 21 *International Legal Materials* 1261ff (1982).

17 No complete listing exists. The best single source is the series of documents produced by the Office of the Geographer of the U.S. State Department entitled *Limits of the Seas*. For a 1983 listing of 84 bilateral ocean boundary delimitation agreements, see McDorman, Beauchamp, and Johnston, eds., *Maritime Boundary Delimitation*, 157–95. For an updated listing of 103 agreements, see Jagota, *Maritime Boundary* 331–44. For texts of, or references to, more recent agreements, see *Law of the Sea Bulletin* and *International Legal Materials*.

18 By late 1986 six major adjudications of ocean boundary-related disputes had been made by the International Court of Justice, namely, *Anglo-Norwegian Fisheries*, judgment, ICJ Reports 1951, 3; *North Sea Continental Shelf*, judgment, ICJ Reports 1969, 3; *Fisheries Jurisdiction*, judgments, ICJ Reports 1974, 3,175; *Continental Shelf (Tunisian/Libyan Arab Jamahiriya)*, judgment, ICJ Reports 1982, 18; *Delimitation of the Maritime Boundary in the Gulf of Maine Area*, judgment, ICJ Reports 1984, 246; and *Continental Shelf (Malta/Libyan Arab Jamahiriya)*, judgment, ICJ Reports 1985, 13; text also reproduced in 24 *International Legal Materials* 1189 (1985). In addition to the early (1909) *Grisbadarna* arbitration between Norway and Sweden, there have been three important modern arbitrations of ocean boundary disputes: *Arbitration concerning Territorial and Maritime Jurisdiction Issues in the Beagle Channel between Argentina and Chile*, decision of 2 May 1977, reprinted in 17 *International Legal Materials* 634 (1978); *Arbitration concerning the Delimitation of the Continental*

Shelf between the United Kingdom of Great Britain and Northern Ireland, and the French Republic, decision of 30 June 1977, 18 *Reports of International Arbitral Awards* 3, reprinted in 18 *International Legal Materials* 397 (1979); and *Arbitration concerning the Delimitation of the Continental Shelf between Guinea and Guinea-Bissau*, decision of 14 February 1985, reprinted in 25 *International Legal Materials* 251 (1986). The conciliation between Iceland and Norway in 1981 resulted in recommendations concerning the delimitation of the continental shelf area close to Jan Mayen Island. See "Report and Recommendations of Conciliation Commission," reprinted in 20 *International Legal Materials* 797 (1981). An important mediation procedure led to the settlement of the *Beagle Channel* dispute between Argentina and Chile: see Papal Proposal of 12 December 1980, reprinted in 24 *International Legal Materials* 7 (1985). Finally, it should be noted that in 1978 Greece initiated a suit against Turkey before the International Court of Justice concerning the delimitation of the continental shelf in areas of the Aegean Sea, but Turkey refused to appear or respond and the court refused to accept jurisdiction. All of these proceedings are reviewed in chapters 10 and 11.

19 Johnston, "Maritime Boundary Delimitation and UNCLOS III," 139–45.

20 See, for example, the discussion on the status of the non-seabed provisions as customary international law in Juda, ed. *The United States without the Law of the Sea Treaty*, 111–50.

21 Articles 15, 74, and 83, 1982 Convention on the Law of the Sea.

22 Both article 74 (on EEZ delimitation) and article 83 (on continental shelf delimitation) begin by emphasizing that delimitation "shall be effected by agreement on the basis of international law, as referred to in Article 38 of the Statute of the International Court of Justice, in order to achieve an equitable solution." On the other hand, article 15 (on territorial sea delimitation) imposes no clear duty to negotiate.

23 Article 15 provides that equidistance ("the median line") shall apply unless a deviation from that provision is justified by reason of *historic title* or *"other special circumstances"* Articles 74 and 83 merely provide that agreement shall be effected on the *"basis of international law"* so as to achieve an *"equitable solution."* Article 15 makes no reference to third-party adjudication, but articles 74 and 83 provide that "[i]f no agreement can be reached within a reasonable period of time, the States concerned shall resort to the procedures provided for in Part XV." This part of the Convention, consisting of articles 279–99, constitutes a highly diversified approach to dispute settlement on a wide range of issues arising out of the Convention.

24 Articles 5 through 14 and 47 through 50 deal with baseline delineation, and articles 3, 4, 33, 57, and 76 with the determination of seaward limits. All these acts are unilateral, but the act of determining seaward limits of the

continental shelf beyond two hundred miles, under article 76, is subject to the requirement that the coastal state submit information on such limits to an international body, the Commission on the Limits of the Continental Shelf, as set up under Annex II to the Convention.

25 Of the 84 agreements listed by McDorman et al., supra note 17, only 20 predate the UN General Assembly's decision in 1967 to convene the UN Seabed Committee.

26 On the impact of UNCLOS III on ocean boundary-making, see Jagota, supra note 17, 219–72.

27 For a region-by-region examination of many ocean boundary agreements, see Prescott, *Maritime Political Boundaries*, 155–354.

28 There is a general tendency to assume that international ocean boundary treaty-making is invariably a bilateral act, and therefore of limited relevance to boundary-making problems in Antarctica, outer space, lakes, and internal seas, which are generally assumed to be multilateral. But the "laterality" of the act may be less important than the range of considerations that should be regarded as relevant to the process of boundary-making. In short, ocean boundary-making should be seen in a regional as well as a national and a binational perspective. Johnston and Saunders, "Ocean Boundary Issues." Seen in a regional (and ultimately a global) perspective, state practice in the ocean boundary-making context is likely to be influential on boundary-making in these non-oceanic contexts.

29 In contemplating a decision on ratification, states have reacted to the 1982 Convention in two ways. The first group, a small minority, has proceeded on the ground of principle to make a decision one way or the other without a detailed examination of the costs and tasks of implementation involved. The remaining states have preferred to make such an examination before deciding whether or not to ratify. If the 1982 Convention comes into force with the sixty or more ratifications required under article 308, it will apparently be because a number of nations in the second group have decided after careful examination to undertake the costs and tasks of implementation, including those of boundary-making. It is assumed in this study that the Convention will come into force in the early 1990s.

30 Each major award to date has focused in considerable detail on the geographical features of the particular situation. Indeed, most of them might be interpreted as settlements of specific and geographically unique disputes rather than as a linear contribution to the process of jurisprudential or doctrinal development. On the "factors" that may be considered in the judicial process, see Charney, "Ocean Boundaries between Nations," and Charney, "Delimitation of Ocean Boundaries." In these articles Charney underlines the current uncertainty regarding the specific role that legal norms actually play in the judicial settlement of ocean boundary disputes.

But it has always been uncertain whether and how boundary-making on land should be governed by "principles." See, for example, Brigham, "Principles in Determination of Boundaries."

31 In the interest of doctrinal precision, the International Court of Justice already has begun the judicial task of clarifying and developing the UNCLOS III criteria of boundary delimitation. In the *Gulf of Maine* boundary case between Canada and the United States, a chamber (that is, a five-member panel) of the Court extended the guidelines contained in articles 74 and 83 of the 1982 Convention by postulating a "fundamental norm," that "delimitation is to be effected by the application of equitable criteria and by the use of practical methods capable of ensuring, with regard to the geographical configuration of the area and other relevant circumstances, an equitable result" (paragraph 112). It also held that, since it was dealing with a single maritime boundary, the equitable criteria established in earlier boundary decisions may be inappropriate, and that "preference will henceforth inevitably be given to criteria that, because of their more neutral character, are best suited for use in a multi-purpose delimitation" (paragraph 194).

CHAPTER ONE: TERMINOLOGY AND BASIC CONCEPTS

1 The confusion between the two concepts is due partly to the influence of Friedrich Ratzel (1844–1904). One of the first theorists of boundary-making, Ratzel is generally regarded as the father of the organic-state theory. He viewed the state as a living organizm that needed room for healthy growth (*Lebensraum*), and he wished to blur the division between two neighbouring states in the way that natural divisions, such as that between land and sea, are blurred or mobile. Ratzel denied the wisdom of drawing a sharp distinction between a linear boundary and a border zone or frontier. His concept of a "border fringe" between two countries consisted of three zones: the outer two were envisaged as peripheral frontier areas and the middle zone as the common core area where the characteristics and competences of the two states intermingled. Prescott, *Boundaries and Frontiers*, 14–16.

2 It has been suggested that a frontier is "outer-oriented," whereas a boundary is "inner-oriented." See Kristof, "The Nature of Frontiers," 271–4. Kristof portrays a frontier as a manifestation of "centrifugal" forces and an "integrating" factor, and a boundary as a manifestation of "centripetal" forces and a "separating" factor. The *Shorter Oxford English Dictionary* defines "boundary" as "[that] which serves to indicate the limits of anything; the *limit itself* (emphasis added). The word "frontier" is defined as "[t]he part of a country which fronts, faces, or borders on another country," and, in the American sense, as "[t]hat part of a country which forms

the border of its settled or inhabited regions." The first of these categories has been described as a "political frontier," the second as a "settlement frontier." Prescott, *Boundaries and Frontiers*, 33–53. In other languages the distinction is not so clear. In French, the word "frontière" usually means "the boundary line," but it can also mean "border zone." Today, French writers sometimes use the terms "frontière-zone" and "frontière-ligne" as equivalents to the English terms "frontier" and "boundary" respectively. See Blumann, "Frontières et Limites," 8. In German, the word "Grenze" also carries both linear and spatial meanings. See also Chao, "Legal Nature," 42–8.

In the past lines have sometimes been drawn for frontier rather than boundary reasons. On the role of the Great Wall of China in frontier delimitation, see Lattimore, *Frontier History* 97–118. In early China the "linear frontier" never existed except as a concept. Ibid., 115.

3 Although the term "frontier" offers flexibility, which may be useful in developing a functionalist theory of ocean boundary making, it seems rather too vague to suit modern boundary-making purposes. Especially, but not only, in its American sense of "wilderness frontier," the concept of a frontier has perhaps served too great a diversity of literary and other uses to be given any operational significance. "The harsh reality of the wilderness frontier encountered by the early American colonists ... has been subsequently a rich source of *metaphorical* and *mythological* inspiration [emphasis added]." Livingstone and Harrison, "The Frontier," 129. For the most famous work on the American frontier, see Turner, *Frontier in American History*. See also Wyman and Kroeber, *Frontier in Perspective*.

4 "By and large, the process of boundary-making is smoothed by considering each boundary a special case, with individuality more pronounced than resemblance to a theoretical type." Jones, *Boundary-Making* 11. Prescott, *Boundaries and Frontiers*, at 27–8, also finds it "regrettable that some geographers have persisted in their efforts to classify international boundaries instead of making detailed studies of particular cases."

5 For example, land boundaries of the intranational sort may have a direct bearing on the amount of tax (property tax, sales tax, and even income tax) that a citizen must pay, especially within a federal state; municipal boundaries determine the pattern of electoral representation; and neighborhood boundaries serve to distinguish zoning restrictions on the construction and renovation of buildings. As to the scope of nationality and citizenship, which appears to be determined by international boundaries, it is rare for delimitation issues concerning such a boundary to impinge directly on more than a tiny, border-dwelling minority of a polity, race, or culture. But this point, it should be noted, is obviously not valid if delimitation is confused with *allocation*. The concept of a transboundary zone has been developed by European theorists, and was derived from earlier works on frontier

theory by writers such as Lapradelle and Ancel. The modern concept of "voisinage" owes much to Andrassy, and it has been extended from the land to the ocean and air space. See, for example, Kiss, "La Frontière."

6 Jones, *Boundary-Making*, at 7 maintains that "[t]he most real distinction in boundaries is between internal and international. The presence or absence of an overriding sovereignty is the basis." The second statement, written in 1944, is, of course, of doubtful validity when applied to ocean boundaries. Under the conditions of the new law of the sea, the theory of functional (not territorial) jurisdiction governs the nature of authority to be exercised within the newer jurisdictional regimes determined by international ocean boundaries. On the relationship between internal and international ocean boundaries, see Warbrick, "Boundary between England and Scotland."

7 See, for example, Charney, "Delimitation of Lateral Seaward Boundaries."

8 The concept of a natural boundary may be of French origin, dating from the Age of Reason, when it was intellectually fashionable to derive human institutions from the law of nature. Pounds, "Origin of Natural Frontiers," and Pounds, "France and 'Les Limites Naturelles.'" See also Jones, "Boundary Concepts," 187, and Chao, "Legal Nature," 63–83.

9 Jones, *Boundary-Making*, 14–16. The case for a strong border, or more properly a strong frontier, was advanced early in the twentieth century by British, German, and French theorists, essentially from a geopolitical perspective. For an introduction to geopolitics, see Glassner and Blij, eds., *Systematic Political Geography*, 263–300. Influenced by the geostrategic line of reasoning set out by Alfred Thayer Mahan and Sir Halford J. Mackinder, British frontier experts such as Lord Curzon and Col. T.H. Holdich were concerned chiefly with the use of frontiers for defensive strategy to stabilize British territories abroad and to protect British military outposts in remote and vulnerable areas. The author of *Frontiers* (1907), one of the first studies of frontier-making principles, Curzon was particularly well-placed, as viceroy of India and later foreign secretary, to implement his own ideas. One of these, regarding the use of buffer zones of one kind or another, was put into practice in various parts of Asia and Africa. Curzon's influence is apparent in other British works of that period: for example, Fawcett, *Frontiers* (1918), and Holdich, *Political Frontiers and Boundary Making* (1916). A decade later, German adherents of *Geopolitik* approached the study of frontiers primarily with a view to the opportunities for the expansion of the German nation at home vis-à-vis France and other neighbouring countries. The most prominent representative of this aggressive approach to frontier-making was Karl Haushofer (1869–1946), whose chief work, *Grenzen in ihrer geographischen and politischen Bedeutung* (1927, rev. 1939), became extremely popular with the Nazi party and other Germans critical of the territorial provisions of the Treaty of Versailles. Some French writers, such as Ancel, *Géopolitique* (1936), accepted the

legitimacy of the geopolitical analysis applied to frontier problems but were sharply critical of Haushofer's use of these methods to justify German territorial expansionism at home and abroad. See Stausz-Hupé, *Geopolitics*, 196-217. From the geopolitical theory of boundary-making some writers have derived the concept of an "international frontier," in the sense of a "zone in which the Great Powers, expanding along their main lines of communication to the limits of their political and economic influence and defence needs, impinge upon each other in conflict or compromise." Hall, "International Frontier," 42. For a recent re-evaluation of the literature, see Zoppo and Zorgbibe, eds., *On Geopolitics*.

10 But some of the military-minded frontier experts, such as Colonel Holdich, warned that some natural features, such as a mountain ridge or a narrow mountain pass, might be more advantageous to the attacker than to the defender. There is a voluminous literature on the various factors involved in British imperial frontier-making. See, for example, Lamb, *McMahon Line*.

11 "Probably any government occupying or claiming vast, poorly mapped, lightly settled areas would be inclined to adopt simple boundaries. The common use of rivers as boundaries in such cases was not respect for 'The Law of Nature' but for the practical matters of exploration, transportation, and cartography. Rivers were conspicuous and seemingly precise on maps that showed mountains only vaguely." Jones, "Boundary Concepts," 190.

12 See, for example, East, *Geography Behind History*, 100-1.

13 In the *Gulf of Maine* case between Canada and the United States, a great volume of evidence was advanced on the relevance of human geography, but this evidence was almost ignored by the chamber of the International Court of Justice. See Sharma, "Relevance of Economic Factors."

14 The case for flexible or mobile ocean boundaries based on the human geography argument–that boundaries should be able to respond to the changing needs of the neighbouring coastal communities–might be compared, ironically, with the case for frontier zones put forward by some of the early strategic theorists of land boundary-making. For the orthodox view that all boundaries should be immutable, see Kaikobad, "Observations," which argues for a maximum degree of continuity and a minimum degree of change in boundaries, subject only to a few exceptional considerations.

15 All three of these categories might be subsumed under the general heading of geometrical boundaries. Jones, *Boundary-Making*, 151-62. Astronomical boundaries are those drawn along lines of longitude (meridians) or latitude (parallels). Mathematical boundaries are those drawn by means of arcs of great or small circles. Referential boundaries are those drawn parallel or perpendicular to some arbitrarily chosen reference line. On a famous anomaly created by excessive dependency on the 49th parallel, see Clark, *Point Roberts*. It seems better to regard these as alternative methods of boundary-making rather than as types of boundaries. In any event, the use

of long geometrical lines as boundaries requires some geodetic sophistication. Artificiality does not necessarily promote simplicity. Ibid., 190. For a sceptical view of the distinction between natural and artificial boundaries, see Brownlie, *African Boundaries*, 3–4.

16 Today it is most unusual for an official boundary-making exercise to be conducted outside the government system. Yet this is precisely what has happened recently in Canada, where a boundary to divide the Northwest Territories into two separate territories was negotiated by representatives of the indigenous peoples of the region. On one side, making up the Western Constitutional Forum, were the Dene Nation, the Metis Association of the Northwest Territories (NWT), and appointed members of the legislative assembly of the NWT residing in the western NWT. On the other side was the Nunavut Constitutional Forum, consisting of the Inuit Tapirisat of Canada, the Tungavik Federation of Nunavut, representatives of each of the regional councils, representatives of each of the regional Inuit associations, and appointed members of the legislative assembly of the NWT residing in the eastern NWT. For the text, see *Boundary and Constitutional Agreement for the Implementation of Division of the Northwest Territories*. With the "allocation" so agreed upon, the boundary was subject to popular approval through referendum in the spring of 1987. See the *Globe and Mail* (Toronto), 17 January 1987. This line, it might be added, is a land-and-ocean boundary. By the end of 1987 it appeared that this boundary issue had become too divisive to be politically acceptable.

Formal de jure boundaries must, of course, be publicized in published documents and maps. If they are bilateral, they are legally binding on the parties to the boundary-making transaction. The parties are therefore obligated to induce compliance through appropriate enforcement and other management measures. Normally the agreement is contained in a legal instrument of treaty character, so that a violation of the boundary may be construed as a violation of the treaty. Informal de facto boundaries are less easy to document, since their purpose is often to reduce the profile of the boundary issue. The absence of a permanent and binding commitment is assumed to facilitate relations between the parties in the case of a bilateral boundary by limiting the possibility of acrimonious recriminations over alleged violations.

17 Johnston and Saunders, "Ocean Boundary Issues."

18 The making of claims to special entitlements (for example, historic bays, archipelagic waters) often requires arguments to be advanced on the basis of relatively informal practices of the past. For an extensive treatment of customary practices in ocean boundary-making, see O'Connell, *International Law of the Sea*, passim. See also Westerman, *Juridical Bay*, passim.

19 Most political geographers today seem to treat all modern international land boundaries as political simply because their primary purpose is to

separate two adjoining territories, and territory is conceived to be the sine qua non of political authority within the nation-state system. See Gottmann, *Significance of Territory*, especially 134–43. The concept of a political boundary crystallized early in the history of boundary-making theory. See, for example, Holdich, "Political Boundaries," and Johnson, "Role of Political Boundaries." Most theorists would also classify internal boundaries of the federal sort as political. Victor Prescott terms all ocean boundaries "political," but it should be noted that he comes close to the extreme view that all terminological classifications, and indeed virtually all other kinds of generalization about boundaries, are best avoided. Prescott, *Maritime Political Boundaries*, xiv-xv, 1–10.

20 Of the hundreds of undelimited land boundaries in the world today, a large portion remain relatively stable because of the success of informal political arrangements. Sixty or more such boundaries are unstable precisely because of political difficulties between the neighbouring states or their governments. See Day, ed., *Border and Territorial Disputes.* For a similar listing of maritime boundary disputes, see Degenhardt, *Maritime Affairs*, 183–220.

21 The concept of a cultural boundary was of particular interest to German theorists. In the second half of the nineteenth century, during the period of the formation and consolidation of the modern German state, Germans were inclined to perceive boundaries in terms of national culture rather than natural features. In response to French invocations of the "law of nature," German scholars such as Johann Fichte (1762–1814) argued that common language and culture constituted a natural law higher than that of rivers and mountains. Jones, "Boundary Concepts," 187. Following the self-determination line of argument for national autonomy, later German theorists placed the prerogatives of *Kultur* at the centre of Nazi ideology. In the 1920s and 1930s Haushofer supported the view that German frontiers should be sufficiently expanded to encompass all German-speaking "Aryans."

22 The British seem often to have given minimal weight to ethnic homogeneity and nomadic movements in their boundary delimitation practices, especially in Africa. Whether British colonial administrators encouraged or discouraged migrational or other cross-boundary movements after the fact of delimitation may have been influenced in particular circumstances by considering whether the formally delimited boundary did or did not correspond with a pre-existing informal cultural boundary, but it may be assumed that the matter was evaluated chiefly by reference to British imperial interests, both commercial and military. See Brownlie, *African Boundaries*, 5–9.

23 The term "jurisdictional purposes" refers to administrative matters associated with the application of the formal legal system. In practice, British colonial administrators were often extremely flexible in permitting the con-

tinuance of traditional law in matters that did not threaten British imperial interests – as were the Romans much earlier. A dramatic exception to the general practice is the drawing of a 'basic jurisdiction' land- and- ocean boundary dividing the Northwest Territories of Canada by Inuit and Dene-Métis negotiators. If this line were implemented, the new territory to the west (Denendeh) would be inhabited predominantly by Denes and Métis, the area to the east (Nunavut) predominantly by Inuit. See supra note 16.

24 The best example is the Torres Strait boundary treaty between Australia and Papua New Guinea. (See the section entitled "Modern Treaties and the Pattern of State Practice" in chapter 11.) Sometimes a boundary-making issue impinges on an issue of access to a location of special ethnic or religious significance, as in the case of the ocean boundary negotiations between India and Sri Lanka in the early 1970s. For the solution to this problem, see Jagota, *Maritime Boundary*, 80.

25 In Canada, for example, sociological considerations compete with biological and economic concerns in the formulation of national fishery management policy. Internal fishing zones are, to a large extent, delimited with a view to the need to preserve an equitable balance among different fishing communities. Zonal boundaries of this sort are, therefore, "cultural" as well as "administrative" in nature. In the *Gulf of Maine* boundary dispute between Canada and the United States, both parties argued that the international boundary should be equitable in the cultural sense that it should preserve an appropriate balance between the fishing communities of the maritime provinces on the one hand and of New England on the other.

26 The boundary-making practices of imperial China and ancient Rome have many striking similarities, since both nations necessarily approached the problem as administrators of a vast and unwieldy empire. Jones, "Boundary Concepts," 184–7. Usually these administrative purposes were served by using imprecise boundaries.

27 Some international boundary commissions in these spheres have had to address specific administrative problems, such as navigation control and environmental management. See, for example, the 1985 *Activities Report* of the International Joint Commission.

28 East, *Geography behind History*, 98. In 806 Charlemagne planned a division of his empire between his two sons, and boundaries were drawn up for this purpose. The elder son died, however, and the entire estates passed to the younger, Louis of Aquitaine, in 813.

29 In 1493 Pope Alexander VI established a line of division from pole to pole 100 leagues west of the Cape Verde Islands. Spain was given exclusive rights to the region west of the line, and Portuguese expeditions were to keep to the east. Since the pope was himself Spanish and was acting at the request of the queen of Castile, the adjudicative process was suspect. In the following year, at Tordesillas, Spanish and Portuguese envoys met and negotiated

a treaty which, at the instance of the Portuguese, moved the line 270 leagues further west, running between 48° and 49° west longitude. This change was finally sanctioned by Pope Julius II in 1506.

30 Strausz-Hupé, *Geopolitics*, 201.

31 East, *Geography behind History*, 98.

32 Rhee, "Sea Boundary Delimitation."

33 Jones, "Boundary Concepts," 190.

34 1982 Convention on the Law of the Sea, Part VI.

35 In the strict sense, territorial jurisdiction applies only within the limits of the regime of the territorial sea, which at UNCLOS III were defined as extending "up to a limit not exceeding 12 nautical miles, measured from baselines determined in accordance with his Convention." Ibid., article 3.

36 Ibid., article 57.

37 Ibid., article 76.

38 Many of the rights and responsibilities of a coastal state within its territorial sea were spelled out in functional categories at UNCLOS III. Ibid., articles 19, 21, 24, and 25.

39 See, for example, Ratzel, *Politische Geographie*; Fawcett, *Frontiers*; and Lapradelle, *La frontière*.

40 Jones, *Boundary-Making*, 5–7. "Chronologically, these stages may overlap, may succeed each other promptly, or may be separated by gaps of many years. Allocating and delimitation may take place at a single conference. On the other hand, a general allocation of territory may be agreed upon long before boundaries are delimited. One part of a boundary may be demarcated before others are delimited. There are boundaries formally delimited years ago that have not yet been demarcated. Some boundaries have remained unadministered for many years, while others have been under *de facto* administration before they were delimited, or even before the final allocation of territory was decided." Ibid., 5. See also Chao, "Legal Nature," 49–67. Other specialists have preferred to distinguish the first three of these acts or phases from the fourth. Prescott, *Boundaries and Frontiers*, at 63–72, treats the first three as stages in the evolution of boundary definition, which is distinguished from boundary position (ibid., 72–5) and boundary function (ibid., 75–6). What Jones describes as boundary administration is deemed to fall into Prescott's category of boundary function. For a detailed study of boundary functions (or types of boundary administration), see Boggs, *International Boundaries.* For Boggs's summary of boundary functions, see ibid., 10. For a different view of boundary functions in the oceans context, see chapter 12 infra.

41 For example, in certain regions, two or more neighbouring coastal states have defined a "joint development" zone encompassing water and/or seabed areas that fall putatively under the jurisdiction of the states that are parties to the arrangement in spite (or, more probably, because) of the lack

of a delimitation line within the joint development area. In such a situation "administration" is designed to precede "delimitation."

42 Demarcation of a sort is, of course, now physically possible through the placement of fixed buoys at regular intervals. In certain areas, such as narrow, congested, coastal waters, the expense of installation and maintenance may be justified if visual detection is the key to compliance, and compliance is crucial to the avoidance of disputes.

43 The English version of the 1982 Convention on the Law of the Sea offers no more than partial support for this suggested choice of terminology. In the case of baselines and closing lines the term "delineate" does not appear at all, but the Convention permits a choice of "draw" (articles 7, 10, 47, and 50), "determine" (articles 3, 14, and 16), "establish" (articles 8 and 35), and "delimit" (article 12). At least the term "delineate" offers a degree of impartiality. In the case of seaward limits of the continental shelf, dealt with in article 76, the term "determine" (used only once) has to compete with "draw" (also used once) and with "establish" and "delineate" (both used three times). Only in the case of lateral boundaries between opposite and adjacent states do we find consistency of usage: only the word "delimit" is used as the functional verb and in these articles (15, 16, 74, and 83) the word is used as a synonym for "divide" and applied to the area, not the line. One prominent boundary specialist, finding no evidence that terms like "delimit" or "determine" had been used at UNCLOS III in "special and consistent ways," uses those terms synonymously with "delineate," "draw," "establish," and "construct." Prescott, *Maritime Political Boundaries*, xv. But he provides his own scheme of concepts for describing the "processes of international maritime boundary delimitation." Ibid., 80–8.

44 One writer distinguishes local government boundaries from field service boundaries. "Local government boundaries are usually precisely described and represented on published maps. If they are changed, the alterations must be published in government gazettes and often they will be justified in government statements ... Field service boundaries will sometimes be precisely described and represented on published maps; this is true, for example, of electoral boundaries and census district limits. However, many field service boundaries will be represented only by lines drawn with a coloured pencil on a map in some offices concerned with a single activity such as firefighters or the enforcement of regulations dealing with the production and sale of livestock ... Apart from electoral and census boundaries, field service boundaries are very easy to alter, and generally these alterations will not be announced." Prescott, *Boundaries and Frontiers*, 177.

45 Ibid., 167–72.

46 See generally Lall, *Modern International Negotiation*. A negotiated international boundary is deemed to be subject to the doctrine of state succes-

sion. On the effect of change of sovereignty on boundary treaties, see O'Connell, *State Succession*, vol. 2, 274–91.

47 Boggs, writing on international boundaries, assumed that such boundaries should be "contractual" in the modern era, and that if border friction had to be reduced, the proper course was to negotiate a "functional contract" whereby the function, not the location, of the boundary could be altered to the mutual benefit of the parties. Jones, "Boundary Concepts," 190.

48 "Resolutive" treaties are those designed primarily to resolve an issue or dispute between the parties (such as the definition, location, or function of a boundary). They are to be distinguished from the vast majority of international agreements, which are "distributive," and others that are "administrative" or "demonstrative." See Johnston, "Chinese Treaty Behaviour," 385–96. See also chapter 17 infra.

49 In the ancient Greek world the largest class of disputes submitted to arbitration arose out of conflicting territorial claims. Tod, *Arbitration amongst the Greeks*, 53–4. See also Ralston, *Arbitration from Athens to Locarno*. Between 1794 and 1970 some seventy-four international arbitrations of boundary disputes have been conducted. Stuyt, *International Arbitrations*. On the return to favour of arbitration as a method of settling boundary disputes, see Johnson, "International Arbitration." On the reasons arbitration might be preferred to judicial settlement, see ibid., 308–13. After surveying international arbitrations between 1945 and 1980, Johnson concludes that arbitration is especially suitable for disputes of a technical nature, such as boundary disputes, "where a certain flexibility of procedure is desired." Ibid., 327–8. For a lengthy and thoughtful evaluation of the adjudicative approach to boundary-making, see Munkman, "Adjudication and Adjustment."

50 For a review of UN intermediary procedures, see Raman, *Ways of the Peacemaker*. On the range of choices in intermediation in ocean boundary-making, see chapter 18 infra.

51 This suggested terminology may have an operational utility, like the official distinction between talks and negotiations. If a potential "issue" between two states is kept, by mutual agreement, at the level of a "difference," it signals the intention of both parties to leave the matter untreated because of more important considerations. Similarly, if one of the states begins to refer to an issue as a "dispute," it gives notice that the matter is being assigned a higher priority than previously and that the other state is expected to respond accordingly.

52 On the failure of UNCLOS III to link boundary settlements with transboundary arrangements, see the introduction to Johnston and Saunders, "Ocean Boundary Issues," 7–8.

CHAPTER TWO: FACTORS

1 In land boundary-making theory, the idea that a (territorial) boundary was essentially a requirement for military defence encouraged theorists to blur the distinction between the linear concept of a boundary and the zonal concept of a frontier. The existence of enemies was generally accepted as a "natural" condition of international relations, and at that time there was no experience of collective security in the form of international peace-keeping or otherwise.

2 Unfortunately, both social and political history provide an abundance of evidence in support of such a view of human nature. Modern research in human psychology also furnishes support for the view that aggression not only is a necessary human characteristic, but also can perform an important and useful function both for individuals and groups. See, for example, Starr, *Human Aggression*. This view is challenged by many feminist writers, who attribute aggression and domination in human affairs almost exclusively to males and portray those characteristics as entirely negative. See, for example, Sayers, *Biological Politics*, and Gilligan, *In a Different Voice*.

3 Some architects and designers have taken cognizance of the human individual's variable need for living ("personal") space. See Sommer, *Personal Space*, and Stea, "Space, Territoriality and Human Movements."

4 See, for example, Lorenz, *On Aggression*, and Ardrey, *Territorial Imperative.* Lorenz and other biologists have attempted to show that few animals could survive without aggressiveness; such is its selective value to the welfare of individuals, populations and species. Ardrey has distinguished the "biological nation" from the "noyau." The former is defined as "a social group containing at least two mature males which holds as an exclusive possession a continuous area of space, which isolates itself from others of its kind through *outward antagonism*, and which through joint defense of its social territory achieves leadership, cooperation, and a capacity for concerted action." Ibid., 191 (emphasis added). The "noyau" is a social group that adheres despite the apparent prevalence of *inward antagonism*. (Italy is held out as a noyau!) Unlike the noyau, the biological nation "spends its aggressive energies on enemies foreign, [and] wastes none on enemies domestic." Ibid., 214.

5 See, for example, Montagu, *Man and Aggression*, and Eibl-Eibenfeldt, *Biology of Peace and War*. Some scholars are sceptical that the findings of biology can be extended into the field of international relations. Burton, "Nature of Aggression." Others question that the desire for domination is deeply rooted in human emotion. Ruth Tringham, for example, denies that the notion of innate human aggression has any support in either archaeo-

logical or ethnographic evidence. "It is rather the simplistic ethnocentric concept of sophisticated, guilt-ridden Western investigators. By this concept they would justify the physical defence and demarcation of space by humans as normal behavioural phenomena. It is clear from archaeological and ethnographic evidence, however, that the defence and physical demarcation of territory is by no means universal and is dependent on a large number of interrelated factors." Tringham, "Territorial Demarcation," 463–4. Some theorists discern the demise of the "shelter function" of territory – and therefore of the concept of territorial sovereignty – and call for a new approach clarifying the modern functions and values of boundaries in delimiting territory. See, for example, Gottman, *Significance of Territory*, 127–43.

6 Walter, "Territorial Waters," and Kent, "Three-Mile Limit."

7 At least thirty-two coastal states have promulgated military security zones in offshore waters. Leiner, "Maritime Security Zones." In some, but certainly by no means all, of these cases an argument might be made that the state's vital interest in self-preservation (its right of self-defence) entitles it to special protection from foreign military movements immediately outside its territorial sea. An argument of this sort should rest, it seems, on factual evidence of a special vulnerability, not merely on a feeling of nervousness.

8 The demand for tighter control over marine pollution was a strong motivation behind the UNCLOS III movement for extended coastal state jurisdiction. Johnston, ed., *Environmental Law of the Sea*, passim. In the result, the 1982 Convention on the Law of the Sea conferred coastal state jurisdiction over "the protection and preservation of the marine environment" within the 200-mile limits of the exclusive economic regime (article 56(1)(b)). This provision should be read along with other provisions on coastal state jurisdiction over pollution, such as articles 208, 211, and 220.

9 The concept of the coastal state's "patrimonial right" to the resources in an extensive area of offshore waters was converted into that of the "patrimonial sea." By 1972, when ten Latin American states subscribed to the Declaration of Santo Domingo, the claim to a two-hundred-mile patrimonial sea covered only natural resources, not the area as a spatial whole, so that it would be differentiated from a claim to a two-hundred-mile territorial sea. O'Connell *International Law of the Sea*, vol. 1, 557–8.

10 Moreover, states that place a symbolic significance in claimed territory or a territorial boundary can be drawn into wars, such as the Falklands War of 1982, that cannot be justified by a vital national need for security or survival. Similarly, a symbolic boundary is more likely to be enshrined in a state's national constitution, making it exceedingly difficult to alter in response to changes in international law. Several Latin American states, for

example, have promulgated a two-hundred-mile territorial sea in constitutional form and now find that their constitution is no longer in conformity with the new international law of the sea, which does not now permit the extension of the territorial sea regime beyond twelve-mile limits.

11 The ecological theory of boundary-making stems from late nineteenth-century Darwinism, which placed man firmly among the animal species and offered an ecosystemic (environmental) perspective on his needs as the fundamental explanation of human group behaviour. Most social and psychological theories of boundary-making have a more complex heritage, owing something to the more recent findings of the behavioural sciences, something to the psychiatric theory of the subconscious, and something to the political theories of geopolitics and *Realpolitik*.

12 Hartshorne, "Functional Approach in Political Geography," 136–9. The basic centripetal force is "the idea of the state." Ibid., 139–41. See also Kristof, "Nature of Frontiers and Boundaries," at 169–70, where he uses Hartshorne's distinction to explain the difference between a frontier and a boundary. The frontier is described as an "integrating factor" and the boundary as a "separating factor."

13 Boggs, the chief proponent of this view, was a contemporary and fellow countryman of Hartshorne and gave a similarly positive emphasis to the potentiality of the border area as a contact zone, rather than a negative emphasis to the boundary as a barrier. The concept of a border area as a contact zone has generated many empirical studies. See, for example, Martinez, *Across Boundaries*.

14 A Scottish biologist, after studying territoriality in animal behaviour, identified the apparent need for stimulation (to combat boredom) as well as the need for security (to assuage anxiety). Darling, "Social Behaviour and Survival." Building on this, Ardrey, "Territorial Imperative," at 70, has added the need for identity (the avoidance of anonymity). Characteristically, Ardrey goes further than most scientists in insisting on the similarities between human and animal boundary-making behaviour. See also Evans, *Ourselves and Other Animals*, 155–7.

15 "Most attempts to create territorial models have involved a home-base area usually, and significantly, located centrally within the various layers of spatial territory." Porteous, "Home," 386. The security of the home involves a recognition of the Jungian concept of the sanctity of the threshhold. See Raglan, *Temple and House*; Newman, *Defensible Space*; Lyman and Scott, "Territoriality"; Ross, "Jurisdiction"; and Stea, "Space Territoriality." Ardrey has also applied "core" and "periphery" concepts to the theory of boundaries. "Building upon a metabiological theory of animal needs and the functions of territory, [Ardrey] suggests that while the frontier provides opportunities for conflict, adventure, social encounters, discharge of aggressiveness, and self-realization (stimulation and identity), the

centre provides security, rest, and the environment favourable to reproduction of the species (mating and rearing of the offspring). And, insofar as the security of the individual and the continuation of the species are the ultimate values in nature, the centre can acquire a sort of biological sacredness. On the other hand, groups build boundaries between them and the outside. Circle and centre are the sacred loci of identity and security of every human being; but human beings are social creatures and their individual spheres coalesce into an ordered cosmos. [In the *Weltanschauung* of many civilizations, there is] a fundamental distinction – a boundary – between cosmos, the ordered familiar world inhabited by fellow men, and chaos, the frightening outer world of evil forces and monsters." Strassoldo, "Periphery and System" 29. In most disciplines, as Strassoldo observes, one's attention is directed to the centre, the core of things, not to the margin. "Philosophers have recommended that we catch the essence of things and forget the marginal aspects; some logicians maintain that too precise definitions of terms and concepts, in order to discriminate marginal cases, are unnecessary and even stifling ... Sociologists have usually looked at societies as self-contained systems, whose boundary interactions with other societies and the environments are relatively uninteresting ... Modern societies tend to channel the attention of the masses to what happens at their centres" (44). Yet the contemporary shift, Strassoldo suggests, should be "from a consideration of boundaries as a line of separation between hostile political units to the consideration of *borders as regions of encounter and exchange between cooperating neighbor states* [emphasis added]."

16 In the ice-covered waters of the Arctic ocean, for example, the Inuit resident perceives the environment around his home base as the "core" in a much more significant sense than other, non-resident users of the waters. This kind of perception is one element in the sociological concept of "nordicity."

17 Negotiation of the seaward limits of the continental shelf regime (article 76) was closely linked, as a matter of wealth allocation, with negotiation of revenue-sharing arrangements related to the area of the shelf beyond two-hundred-mile limits (article 82).

18 In negotiating articles 74 and 83, delegations took a position favouring either "equidistance" or "equity" strictly in accordance with national economic advantage in light of resource distribution off their shores in boundary areas.

19 In some degree, which varies considerably from coastline to coastline, the method used for baseline or closing line delineation may affect the area of offshore resource wealth enclosed within limits of national jurisdiction: for example, by straight baselines, bay closing lines, and archipelagic baselines.

20 Many of the new international ocean boundaries that may now be drawn around the world are associated with the regime of the two-hundred-mile exclusive economic zone (EEZ), and most of the coastal states supporting the

EEZ did so for fishery reasons. For an evaluation of the probable economic consequences, see Anderson, ed., *Extended Fisheries Jurisdiction*.

21 For the outcome, in the form of a "consent regime" governing scientific research in the exclusive economic zone, see Part XIII of the 1982 Convention on the Law of the Sea.

22 For general comments on the distribution of efficiency and equity values at UNCLOS III, see Johnston, "Equity and Efficiency."

23 McDougal, Lasswell, and their associates have suggested that the crucial distinction is between inclusive interests and exclusive interests, and that a common interest consists of the reconciliation of these two as sanctioned by the organized world community. See, for example, McDougal, Lasswell, and Vlasic, *Law in Space*, 101–3. The truth is, perhaps, that any terminology of this order introduces theoretical difficulties in some, if not most, contexts.

24 The concept of common interest is of special importance in the context of international resources law. See Pardo and Christol, "Common Interest." Articles 74 and 83, on delimitation of the exclusive economic zone and the continental shelf, respectively, are products of compromise diplomacy resulting from the intransigent opposition of special interests – namely, those favouring "equidistance" and "equity." The common interest that prevailed lay in the agreement to leave the balance open between these two groups of special interest. Article 76, on determination of the seaward limits of the continental shelf, was, of course, an accommodation of the special interests of the broad margin states (with continental margins extending well beyond two hundred miles), but the common interest was to some extent reflected in the revenue-sharing arrangements agreed to in article 82 and in the counterbalancing provisions regarding the scope and powers of the International Seabed Authority in the deep ocean area beyond limits of national jurisdiction.

25 On the delimitation of cosmic spaces, see Kish, *Law of International Spaces*, 39–49. It might be questioned whether a common interest has yet emerged in the delimitation of Antarctica. Ibid., 28–38. The overall limits of the seabed, Antarctica, and outer space are now subject to the principle of the "common heritage of mankind," and within these areas the common heritage doctrine might be said to deny the possibility of international territorial boundaries. It does not, however, preclude the emergence of functional boundaries, which may prove to be necessary for administrative purposes. Many have urged in recent years that the uninhabited lands of Antarctica belong, or should belong, to the international community as a whole. To this end, the prime minister of Malaysia has proposed that the present claimant states should give up their territorial claims to Antarctica "so that either the United Nations administer these lands or the present occupants act as trustees for the nations of the world." Statement by Dato

Seri Dr Mahather bin Mohamad at the thirty-seventh session of the United Nations General Assembly, 29 September 1982, reproduced in Theutenberg, *Evolution of the Law of the Sea*, 259. A later speech by Dr Mahather bin Mohamad, at the seventh summit of non-aligned countries held at New Delhi in March 1983, explicitly linked this proposal with the concept of the common heritage of mankind which evolved at UNCLOS III: ibid. For supportive commentary, see Pinto, "Antarctica"; and Zam-Azrael, "Malaysian Perspective." For the alternative view that the international interest in Antarctica is better served by some version of the existing treaty regime, see Young, "Antarctic Resource Jurisdiction." The current campaign to introduce a global regime to Antarctica was revived in 1975 by Ambassador Shirley Amerasinghe when he served as the president of UNCLOS III. Quigg, *A Pole Apart*, 167–8. For a detailed analysis of the issue see Petersen, "Antarctic Implications." For a more recent comment, see Child, *Antarctica*.

26 For a recent examination of the lobbying process in general, see Pross, *Group Politics*.

27 At UNCLOS III a compromise of this kind was necessary to break the deadlock in the wording of the provisions on delimitation of the continental shelf and exclusive economic zone between opposite and adjacent states. See Jagota, *Maritime Boundary*, 239–45.

28 One of the strongest arguments for seeking a negotiated settlement of a boundary issue instead of resorting to third-party adjudication is, of course, that it permits the establishment of a treaty-based boundary that is contingent on reciprocal access arrangements, whereas a judicially determined boundary might be construed by the parties as a gain for one and a loss for the other. Access arrangements can be negotiated after the establishment of a judicially determined boundary, but the location of the latter might be regarded as inequitable by the losing party to the adjudication, so that the post-award negotiations would start in an atmosphere of resentment.

29 On the trend to offshore hydrocarbon joint development, see Valencia and Miyoshi, "Southeast Asian Seas," and Lagoni, "Oil and Gas Deposits."

30 Much has been written on the bureaucratic styles and traditions of Britain, the Soviet Union, France, China, India, and the United States. For example, on the French system, see Crozier, *Bureaucratic Phenomenon*, 213–314. On national variations, see Dalby and Wertham, eds., *Bureaucracy in Perspective*.

31 Much of the literature on this subject tends to be anecdotal and highly subjective, and is based on personal experience. See, for example, Lall, *How Communist China Negotiates*.

32 See Macdonald and Johnston, "International Legal Theory," 10–11.

33 It is convenient to treat as "cultural" the unchanging elements of national

bureaucratic style or tradition. Changes in bureaucratic behaviour or structure can be attributed to the variables in the national political system. On the cultural aspects of negotiation, see Anand, ed., *Cultural Factors*. On East Asian reluctance to resort to the judicial settlement of boundary disputes, see Rhee and MacAulay, "Ocean Boundary Issues."

34 It is, of course, notoriously difficult to separate ideological from cultural influences on bureaucracy. See, for example, Schurmann, *Ideology in China*. The evidence of continuity encourages cultural explanations, whereas the evidence of discontinuity is conducive to ideological (or economic or technological) explanations. The same difficulty arises in the analysis of legal (or judicial) development. To a lesser extent, perhaps, analysts of national diplomatic style may also find it difficult to distinguish cultural and ideological factors in negotiating style. See Gulliver, *Disputes and Negotiations*.

35 Since the pioneering work of Max Weber, most studies treat bureaucracy as an organization rather than a process, and as an organization with technical superiority over any other. In modern parlance, bureaucracy is a complex system. Any bureaucratic approach to a difficult, policy-related task is therefore generally assumed to be technical and complicated, and bureaucracies possess unmatched skills for such an approach to decision-making. Rourke, *Bureaucracy and Public Policy*, 39–61. The bureaucratic method of treatment demonstrates three kinds of deficiency: it falls short of optimum rationality; it exhibits a reluctance or inability to innovate; and it fails to deal compassionately with individual needs. Thompson, *Bureaucracy and the Modern World*. Yet none of these alleged deficiencies of bureaucratic behaviour seems likely to impair bureaucratic boundary-making.

36 Both federal ocean boundaries of a political sort and internal ocean boundaries of a more specifically functional character may have to be negotiated: between the national and subnational levels of government, between two subnational governments, or between two or more agencies at the same level of government.

37 Most of the literature on bureaucracy assumes that personality operates mostly through élite group behaviour rather than individual behaviour, because bureaucracy is perceived as a complex, hierarchically arranged organization. Compare Armstrong, *European Administrative Élite* (1973) with Blau, *Dynamics of Bureaucracy*. Treaty negotiations, on the other hand, though they emanate from bureaucracy, are delegated to small groups of specialists, and individual personalities, especially of the heads of delegations, may influence the outcome. Today, however, diplomatic boundary-making is likely to be conducted by larger teams than in the past, and respect for seniority may have diminished. Judicial boundary-making may be done by a small group of adjudicators, sometimes as few as three. The

force of intellect is presumed to be as influential as that of personality in judicial behaviour. See Eckoff, *Rationality in Decision-Making*.

38 Canada and the United States have a great deal in common politically, economically, and culturally, yet their ocean boundary issues have been found difficult to resolve. Perhaps the explanation lies in the close relationship between boundary (delimitation) issues and transboundary (management) problems at sea, for the systems of public administration are divergent and the attitudes of their coastal communities to the role of government are far apart and apparently widening. Johnston, *Canada and the Law of the Sea*, 125–30. It is sobering to recall that it took these neighbouring countries well over one hundred years to resolve all their land boundary delimitation issues.

39 In the Arctic Ocean, Canadian intranational boundary problems are complicated by the relationship between the federal government and the government of the Northwest Territories and by relationships among the Department of Indian and Northern Affairs, the Department of Energy, Mines, and Resources, and other federal agencies. On community involvement in Canadian intranational Arctic boundary-making, see chapter 1, notes 16 and 23. Talks between Canada and the United States over the Juan de Fuca Strait boundary have been held up for years because of the lack of agreement between the federal government of Canada and the government of British Columbia, and for other reasons.

40 See, for example, Sprout and Sprout, *Ecological Perspective* and *Ecological Paradigm*.

41 To some extent, the functional theory of ocean boundary-making rests on the possibility of agreement among the boundary-makers and those directly affected on how to characterize an ocean boundary in terms of the major purposes to be served by it. The theory of functionalism puts considerable weight on the relevance of milieu. See chapter 19.

42 It is often suggested that the maximum flight height of aircraft should determine the extent of (national) airspace, and that the minimum orbit height of spacecraft should constitute the lower limit of (international) outer space. Kish, *Law of International Spaces*, 43. However, many specialists believe that "until a serious problem can be identified that can only be solved through the delimitation of air space from outer space, there is no need for such a boundary now." Hosenball and Hofgard, "Delimitation of Air Space," 893. See Csabalfi, *State Jurisdiction*, passim.

43 1958 Convention on the Continental Shelf, article 1.

44 Technologically dependent boundaries need not become dysfunctional, provided it is understood that they represent a potentially flexible type of boundary. See chapter 16.

CHAPTER THREE: CONCEPTUAL APPROACHES

1 See Schachter, *World's Resources*, and Johnston, "Justice in International Law."

2 The emphasis on equity is best evidenced in articles 74 and 83 of the 1982 Convention on the Law of the Sea, which provide that a boundary between opposite or adjacent states should be drawn in such a way as "to achieve an equitable solution." However, it is questionable whether a sense of justice dictated the grant of generous entitlements to naturally favoured ("geographically advantaged") coastal states through the provisions for baseline and closing line delineation and the determination of seaward limits of the continental shelf beyond two-hundred-mile limits.

3 The neo-functionalist literature in political science assigns a central role to "sources of knowledge" in regime-building. This crucial input has been defined as "the sum of technical information and of theories about that information which commands sufficient consensus at a given time among interested actors to serve as a guide to public policy to achieve some social goal." Haas, "Why Collaborate?" 367–8.

4 Especially since the appearance of Shalowitz, *Shore and Sea Boundaries* (1962), technical specialists have been trying to develop geometric boundary-making techniques by drawing upon physical geography, geodesy, hydrography, surveying, and related disciplines. The time apparently has come for a systematic effort to co-ordinate these efforts in ocean boundary-making. See Alexander, "Technical Issues of Delimitation." For an example of similar writings, see also Beazley, "Maritime Boundaries"; Prescott, "Straight Baselines"; and Beazley, *Maritime Limits*. For some of the mathematical complexities that may be inherent in the geometry of boundary-making, see Mandelbrot, *Fractal Geometry*.

5 For example, in the *Gulf of Maine* case between Canada and the United States, a chamber of the International Court of Justice was asked to draw a "single maritime boundary" for both fishery (water column) and petroleum (seabed) purposes. See the section entitled "Modern Dispute Management" in chapter 11.

6 The environmental phenomenon of desertification – the encroachment of desert areas and the creation of dessicated desert-like lands in areas remote from the great sandy deserts – is a reminder that human beings should hesitate to put blind faith in the permanence of a natural boundary of this sort. On the general environmental problem, see Glantz, ed., *Desertification*, and Spooner and Mann, eds., *Desertification and Development*. On the legal aspects, see Johnston, "Systemic Environmental Damage."

7 Use of the physical setting tends to keep boundary-making in the hands of *los tecnicos*, rather than *los politicos*. See chapter 13.

8 For a challenge to the idea that physical factors are neutral, see Judge

Gros's dissent in the *Gulf of Maine* case, discussed in the section entitled "Modern Dispute Management" in chapter 11. An over-emphasis on geographical, geological, and geomorphological factors is subject to most of the criticisms of natural boundaries.

9 Even in the case of normal litigation before the International Court of Justice, the litigant states are responsible for drafting the *compromis*, which sets out the terms of reference and thereby purports to limit the scope of the Court's determination. In ad hoc arbitration the parties seem to have even greater control, since their treaty of arbitration may go further in stipulating the range or diversity of considerations, the procedures to be followed, and the type of outcome desired.

10 Even in resort to the International Court of Justice, the litigant states may choose to adopt the chamber method whereby five of the members of the Court are selected through negotiation between the litigants and consultation with the Court itself. This was the method adopted by Canada and the United States in the *Gulf of Maine* dispute, as discussed in chapter 11. In arbitration the parties are free to choose the adjudicators by whatever method they can agree upon, except that in resort to the Permanent Court of Arbitration they are required to choose from the (extremely lengthy) list of arbitrators on file with the secretary general of the United Nations.

11 The initial allocation stage of boundary-making is closest to the emotive political issue of territorial gain or loss, with its psycho-cultural and legal implications. In the case of international boundaries, which normally have to be negotiated bilaterally, the negotiators more or less consciously represent, not merely reflect, the political interests in the territory at stake. At UNCLOS III, where the principles to govern the allocating of ocean space were negotiated at the global level, the process was, of course, entirely political in character.

12 Delimitation involves the choice and application of boundary-making techniques (principles, criteria, and methods) within a general framework of politically determined guidelines of allocation.

13 Boundary administration (the maintenance and development of boundary functions) requires the application of relevant functional policies on both sides of the boundary, and in that sense is partly a political process. In the case of international ocean boundaries, boundary administration reflects the interaction of the national ocean development and management policies of the neighbouring states. In the case of internal ocean boundaries, the bureaucratic process of boundary administration may reflect federal and inter-agency tensions of a political character. See generally Rehfuss, *Public Administration*, and Sharkansky, *Routines of Politics*.

14 See, for example, Schelling, *Strategy of Conflict*; Stahl, *Bargaining Theory*; Deutsch, *Resolution of Conflicts*; Rubin and Brown, *Psychology of Bargaining*; Druckman, ed., *Negotiations*; and Bacharach and Lawler, *Bar-*

gaining. Most of this literature applies to labour negotiations.

15 Since it deals primarily with collective bargaining requirements in labour-management relations, much of the literature on negotiation theory envisages the need for short-term agreements of a contractual character serving chiefly a distributive purpose rather than the need for a long-term or permanent treaty that may have to serve resolutive and demonstrative, as well as distributive and administrative, purposes.

16 Some of the earlier land boundary theorists drew a distinction between frontiers of contact and frontiers of separation. For a modern treatment, see Prescott, *Boundaries and Frontiers*, 20.

17 At UNCLOS III, where the focus was confined to international ocean boundaries of one kind or another, little thought was given to the local or communal significance of such boundaries. Boundary-making issues were negotiated within a statist frame of reference. Yet the local impact of international ocean boundaries may be as great as that of intranational boundaries. On transboundary community problems on land, see Martinez, *Across Boundaries*.

18 For a comparison of industrial, communal, and scientific perspectives on national fishery policy and related issues, see Johnston, *Canada and the Law of the Sea*, 27–30.

19 The economist's interest in boundary-making begins with the initial issue of wealth allocation, but extends to all subsequent boundary-related questions of resource development and management. Therefore, in the economist's mind the problems of boundary settlements are inextricably linked with those related to transboundary arrangements.

20 It may make economic as well as political sense for negotiator X to make a boundary-related concession to negotiator Y in return for a concession by Y on a matter of interest to X that is unrelated to boundary issues or transboundary problems.

21 The military strategist's approach to boundary-making (and especially to boundary maintenance) is determined today less by the traditional concern with the defensibility of space than by a concern with the need to "manage" conflicts in sensitive areas through the limitations of risks. Risk limitation is a matter that calls for planning, rather like the economist's task of resource development and management.

22 A concern with resource benefits may, of course, be broad enough to include consideration of human resources, but sometimes the economist's emphasis on efficiency tends to screen out considerations of human or communal welfare that cannot be easily quantified in a cost-benefit analysis.

23 Most lawyers are trained to approach boundary-making, at least initially, as an exercise in doctrinal development: that is, as an opportunity, or even a responsibility, to clarify the appropriate rules and apply them consistently.

In the western world this professional or disciplinary attitude is associated particularly with so-called positivists, but probably most lawyers reflect this bias in some degree. To this extent, the legal ideal is one of uniformity of treatment. For strictures on the unduly legalistic ("unitarian") approach to judicial boundary-making, see chapter 19.

24 To most lawyers trained in the common law tradition, the concept of equity or justice is too vague to be of operational utility unless it can be formulated as a set of rules or principles that lend themselves to the sophisticated juridical process of doctrinal development, preferably by frequent recourse to professional adjudicators. Lawyers trained in the civil law tradition can usually operate more comfortably with high-order abstractions. On the use of the concept of equity in maritime boundary adjudications, see Jiménez de Aréchaga, "Conception of Equity."

25 This tendency is, of course, especially apparent when a boundary dispute is referred to adjudication, and legal arguments have to be organized within the framework of the relevant case law.

26 In the *Gulf of Maine* case the United States in particular leaned heavily on environmental factors in its natural-boundary argument for an EEZ boundary in that area, but the ICJ chamber had difficulty in relating this kind of argument and data to the continental shelf component of the situation. Colson, "Environmental Factors."

CHAPTER FOUR: PROCESSES AND OUTCOMES

1 Few if any government officials have the time or the resources to carry out the studies and analyses that must be applied to highly complex boundary problems of the modern age. Even intranational ocean boundary-making is complex, and present evidence suggests that many governments will choose to use academics and consultants as an extension of the bureaucratic process.

2 In preparing for the *Gulf of Maine* boundary adjudication before a chamber of the International Court of Justice, both the U.S. and Canadian federal governments secured the involvement of fellow officials from the states and provinces directly affected by the boundary dispute.

3 In the United States, at least, private consultants have also played an important role in the bureaucratic phase of intranational ocean boundary delimitation. Charney, "Delimitation of Boundaries."

4 The International Boundary Commission of Canada and the United States (IBC) is one of the most active boundary commissions. After a series of temporary commissions, the IBC was established in a permanent form in 1925 to supervise boundary maintenance on a continuing basis. Its tasks are "to inspect the boundary; to repair or replace damaged boundary markers; to maintain a clear boundary 'vista' or six-metre/20-foot swath through

brush and trees; to ensure the accuracy of the boundary through surveys; and to define any portion of the boundary that may be questioned by either government." IBC, *Annual Joint Report 1984*, 3. The commission also makes regulatory decisions on proposed projects that would cross or adjoin some part of the 5,526-mile-long boundary. Much more publicized is the work of the International Joint Commission of Canada and the United States (IJC), which was established under the Boundary Waters Treaty of 1909. The tasks of the IJC are better described as transboundary management than boundary maintenance. Whereas the IBC's work is almost exclusively technical, the IJC's is a mixture of technical and political. For a Canadian evaluation of the IJC's work, see Spencer, Kirton, and Nossal, eds., *Seventy Years On*. The 1984 Treaty of Peace and Friendship between Argentina and Chile, which resolved the Beagle Channel boundary dispute, established a permanent binational commission to "promote and develop initiatives" in transboundary as well as other contexts (article 12). For the text, see 24 *International Legal Materials* 11 (1985). It appears that this commission is intended to operate more in the manner of the IJC than in that of the IBC.

5 Johnston and Saunders, "Ocean Boundary Issues."

6 In preparing for the *Gulf of Maine* adjudication, the Canadian government drew upon the resources not only of its Department of External Affairs but also of several other agencies: the Department of Fisheries and Oceans; the Department of Justice; the Ministry of the Environment; the Ministry of Transport; the Department of Energy, Mines and Resources; the Department of Industry, Trade and Commerce; and others.

7 For example, Canada's preparations for the *Gulf of Maine* case involved provincial government officials representing Nova Scotia and New Brunswick, and required frequent consultations with representatives from the fishing and oil industries. A similar consultative approach seems to have been adopted by the Canadian government in its preliminary negotiations with France on matters related to ocean boundary-making in the waters between St Pierre and Miquelon and Newfoundland. But both of these communities felt they had not been sufficiently consulted by their respective national government and reacted angrily when the outcome of the preliminary negotiations was announced in late January 1987.

8 In the modern era there apparently has been a near-extinction of secret treaties, except for the occasional secret protocol to a public treaty. In modern treaty-making theory, a treaty is a public instrument that has little resemblance to a private, confidential contract. On the other hand, formal treaty negotiations are frequently preceded by private or informal "talks" which may be officially recorded without being publicly disclosed. Accordingly, the public-private distinction still applies to the negotiation process but rarely to the outcome of that process.

9 Perhaps the most acrimonious of ocean boundary disputes in recent years was the Beagle Channel dispute between Chile and Argentina. During the protracted period of controversy the two states came close to open conflict. Yet the symbolic significance of the negotiations between the two countries owed much to the fact that the dispute was territorial in character, arising from conflicting claims to several islands at the tip of Tierra del Fuego. See the section entitled "Modern Dispute Management" in chapter 11. The negotiations between Canada and France over the delimitation of the waters around the French islands of St Pierre and Miquelon, off the south-western coast of Newfoundland, were kept relatively confidential for many years. It appears that initially the French government attached a merely symbolic significance to this issue; the angry reaction to the outcome of preliminary negotiations early in 1987 proved that national sentiment was also strong in Canada both at the popular and political levels. On the substantive issues, see Symmons, "Canadian Fishery Limit." The dispute increased in visibility in France when it was elevated to the prime-ministerial level in mid-1987. In Canada the clearest examples of jurisdictional and boundary-making issues governed by national symbolic sentiment are those in the Arctic Ocean. In the Aegean Sea the limitations placed on diplomacy by Greek patrimonial sentiment are sadly apparent in the context of the continental shelf dispute with Turkey. See the section entitled "Modern Dispute Management" in chapter 11.

10 The efforts of Canada and the United States to negotiate a maritime boundary in the Gulf of Maine were watched with concern by the general public and especially the fishing communities in the affected region, New England and the Canadian maritime provinces. But in neither country could it be said that national passions were aroused in the degree or manner revealed in the Beagle Channel dispute between Chile and Argentina or in the Aegean Sea dispute between Greece and Turkey. Still, in all these situations diplomacy failed essentially for political-popular reasons.

11 For a recent description of the process, see Robinson, Colson, and Rashkow, "Perspectives on Adjudication."

12 A survey of the teams assembled to attend the hearings in recent ocean boundary adjudications shows that in general one-third to one-half of the team members have been non-lawyers. The researchers involved behind the scenes usually remain unidentified in public documents; most of these participants in the preparation of "Brandeis briefs" are also non-lawyers.

13 In cases where the tribunal is asked by the litigants to draw the line (and not merely to declare the applicable principles and rules of international law), it is usual for the tribunal to appoint a technical expert, usually someone skilled in hydrography or cartography, to render assistance.

14 Governments usually do not disclose the identity of consultants hired on a confidential basis. Personal communication suggests the existence of a

thriving industry of advisory and research services to litigant states involved in ocean boundary adjudication. It has been reported that "nearly a hundred professionals contributed to the U.S. case" in the *Gulf of Maine* dispute. Robinson, Colson, and Rashkow, "Perspectives on Adjudication," 588.

15 In the *Gulf of Maine* case the United States used only its own nationals for oral advocacy, unlike most other litigant states involved in ocean boundary adjudications, yet it had decided at the outset to engage a number of foreign legal consultants. "There were several considerations that went into U.S. thinking in this regard. We wanted to obtain the widest and most sophisticated insight into practice before the Court. We also wanted to ensure that the preparations were compatible with the different legal traditions reflected by the members of the Chamber. These foreign consultants were most helpful in discussing tactics and strategy and in making detailed comments upon the drafts of the written and oral pleadings that were initially prepared in-house." Ibid.

16 For example, in the *Gulf of Maine* adjudication, held before a chamber of the International Court of Justice, the United States chose to nominate the American member of the court (Judge Stephen Schwebel), which, of course, entitled Canada to nominate a Canadian (Professor Maxwell Cohen) as ad hoc judge.

17 Taylor and Gudgin, "Parliamentary Boundary Commissions"; Curtice and Steed, "Dreams into Reality."

18 In normal international adjudication there is often a tension between the prerogatives of the parties and those of the tribunal. The parties fix the terms of the submission as far as the issues are concerned, but the tribunal has the role of interpreting these terms, and in jurisdictional and procedural matters is master of its own house. This competition for control over the adjudicative process is evident when the adjudicators want to adopt a more facilitative role in the proceedings than was envisaged by the parties.

19 It should be noted, however, that the term "dispositive" is sometimes used in a narrow technical sense to describe treaties having the character of conveyances. McNair, *Law of Treaties*, 740–3.

20 It is not always easy to determine the scope of a constitution. Especially in a political culture lacking the tradition of a written document, the constitution may be found in various statutory texts deemed to be of constitutional character or significance. See, for example, Wiktor and Tanguay, eds., *Constitutions of Canada.* The boundaries of Canada's provinces evolved from a variety of international treaties, British and Canadian statutes, arbitrations, and court decisions. These provincial boundaries are now mostly in statutory form, but they can be altered by the Parliament of Canada only with the consent of the provincial legislature concerned. Ibid., vol. I, CIII. Boundary statutes may therefore be deemed to be of constitutional or

quasi-constitutional status. It might be argued that boundaries can acquire constitutional status only in association with a claim to virtually absolute territorial sovereignty. By this reasoning, ocean boundaries can acquire constitutional status only when they delimit internal waters, in the case of baselines and closing lines.

21 The states or provinces of federal states normally have their boundaries defined by constitution. See, for example, the Ontario Boundary Act, 1889, and the Ontario Boundaries Extension Act, reproduced ibid., C237 et seq.

22 The constitution of Hawaii (article XV, section 1) defines the state as consisting of "the islands, together with their appurtenant reefs and territorial and archipelagic waters included in the Territory of Hawaii on the date of enactment of the Admission Act."

23 In the 1940s and 1950s several states made claims to airspace boundaries in spatial terms, but in the present era national sovereignty over airspace is conceived in functional terms. On trends in space law, see Csabalfi, *State Jurisdiction in Space Law*. The view generally held is that the upper flight height of aircraft (some thirty miles) constitutes the functional limit of airspace, but there is little inclination to practise any boundary-delimiting of airspace from outer space. Kish, *Law of International Spaces*, and Hosenball and Holgard, "Delimitation of Air Space." Perhaps because the matter is not resolved in international law, states have been reluctant to claim an airspace boundary in constitutional form.

24 For example, the straight baselines of Italy's territorial sea were promulgated in 1977 by Decree of the President of the Republic no 816 (26 April 1977). In some respects the Italian system is a hybrid of presidential and parliamentary features, in which law-making is divided chiefly between central and regional levels of government. Amato et al., eds., *La Legislazione Italiana*, 2–7.

25 For example, the co-ordinates of the Republic of Vanuatu's archipelagic baselines are set out in its Maritime Zones Act of 1981. United Nations, *Law of the Sea Bulletin*, no 1, 64–73 (September 1983). The Soviet Union's ocean boundary arrangements are set out in detail in its national legislation, the Law on the State Frontier, of 24 November 1982. United Nations, *Law of the Sea Bulletin*, no 4, 24–30 (February 1985).

26 For example, the co-ordinates of two Italian conservation zones (*zone di tutela biologica*) were prescribed by a ministerial decree dated 10 August 1971 and 25 August 1972, both under the Law of Maritime Fishing of 14 July 1965. Amato et al., *La Legislazione Italiana*, 152–4.

27 The first Danube Commission was created by a treaty of 1856, chiefly to regulate navigation. Interestingly, the parties to the treaty (and the members of the commission) were not confined to riparian states. Great Britain and France were parties (and members), presumably because of their great power status. In addition to commissions entrusted exclusively with bound-

ary maintenance functions, permanent regional organizations are sometimes assigned boundary-related roles. Lyon, "Regional Organizations," 109–40.

28 International rivers administered by joint commissions include the Rhine, Danube, Scheldt, Oder, Elbe, Po, Pruth, St Lawrence, and Rio Grande. International lakes similarly co-managed include Lake Lucerne and the Great Lakes.

29 Baxter, *Law of International Waterways*; Obieta, *Suez Canal*.

30 The U.S.-Canada IJC was created by the Boundary Water Treaty 1909, TS no 548, and the U.S.-Mexico IJC by the Treaty on Utilization of Waters 1944, TS no 944. By the 1972 Canada-United States Great Lakes Water Quality Agreement, the IJC was given the additional function of monitoring and surveillance over the parties' pollution control programs on the lakes, and was empowered to publish its own reports and establish a regional office with a staff of scientific and professional experts. Munton, "Paradoxes and Prospects," 61. The scope of the U.S.-Mexican International Boundary and Water Commission is being re-examined. It has been proposed that the management of groundwater resources in the border areas be the subject of a new arrangement involving the creation of a new transboundary commission. Rodgers and Utton, "Ixtapa Draft Agreement."

31 For example, within the EEC many committees become involved in the regulation of environmental risks affecting international rivers and lakes and other transfrontier areas.

32 For example, the Northwest Atlantic Fisheries Organization works closely together with Canada and Greenland in the management of fishery resources that straddle the seaward limits of their EEZs in the Northwest Atlantic. This form of co-operation involves both NAFO and the neighbouring coastal states in an integration of zoning practices, which has internal as well as international boundary implications.

33 For example, a number of neighbouring coastal states (such as Canada and the United States) have negotiated contingency plans outlining co-operative procedures for clean-up operations in the event of a major oil spill in boundary waters.

34 Many river boundary commissions, such as the Joint Danube Fishery Commission, publish and exchange scientific and technical reports. Bekiashev and Serebriakov, *International Marine Organizations*. Less formally, France and Italy have agreed to create a joint boundary commission designed to facilitate the solution of neighbourhood problems (problèmes de voisinage) despite the absence of a defined maritime boundary. For text of Exchange of Notes, see *Gazzetta Ufficiale della Rèpubblica Italiana*, no 174 (26 June 1981), at 4092. This arrangement involves not only the central governments but also the governments of the provinces and départements.

35 Brownlie, *African Boundaries*, 5. Evidentiary problems of special difficulty may arise in the context of traditional boundaries. Murty, "Evidence on Traditional Boundaries." See also Hyde, "Maps as Evidence."

36 On the risks of cartography, see Troop, "Legal Liability of the Chart-maker."

CHAPTER FIVE: TECHNIQUES

1 Kapoor and Kerr, *Maritime Boundary Delimitation*, 9–10.

2 Ibid., 10. See also the UN *Report on Hydrographic Surveying and Nautical Charting*.

3 Many coastal states are dependent on the surveying and charting services provided by the hydrographic bureau of another state. They may also depend on old charts prepared by navigators of an earlier age, such as Cook and Vancouver. On the need for hydrographic assistance to developing coastal states, see Holden, "National Hydrographic Service," and Myres, "Survey Tasks."

4 UN Convention on the Law of the Sea, article 5. On the difficulties involved in the application of this provision in developing states, see Kapoor and Kerr, *Maritime Boundary Delimitation*, 20–1.

5 See, for example, the provision for reefs in article 6 of the UN Convention on the Law of the Sea.

6 See articles 16, 75, and 84 of the 1982 convention for delimitation of territorial sea, EEZ, and continental shelf boundaries respectively.

7 Article 47 of the 1982 convention.

8 For example, "an intricate area with irregular depths would merit a detailed examination on a large scale, whereas in a coastal area with fairly regular depths the scale might be reduced." Kapoor and Kerr, *Maritime Boundary Delimitation*, 19. See also Watson, "Ocean Charting."

9 Marine geodesy is a new science that might be said to have "come together" at the First Marine Geodesy Symposium held in 1966. Marine geodesy "unites the geosciences with the marine and space sciences and provides the basic geographical/geophysical framework to which all ocean studies, technologies and operations relate. It defines and establishes control points and related descriptive data with the ocean environment. Areas of interdisciplinary interest include topography and mapping (including satellite altimetry, bathymetry and remote sensing), positioning and precise navigation (including submersible navigation), boundary demarcation and determination, tsunamis, geoid determination, acoustic and space instrumentation, and ground truth and system calibration." Editorial, 1 *Marine Geodesy* 1 (1977). So broadly defined, marine geodesy may evolve as a new polydisci-

pline, separate from land-based geodesy. Compare Fischer, "Marine Geodesy," 165.

10 Mercator projection preserves the same angle of bearing with respect to intersected meridians as does the track of a vessel on a true course. But whereas any small area shown on a Mercator chart will generally maintain its true shape, large areas become distorted by changes in scale from point to point. Consequently, an equidistance line on the ground will not retain its dimensions when charted. Mercator charts are especially distortive in high latitudes, or when a boundary runs for some distance in a north-south direction. Kapoor and Kerr, *Maritime Boundary Delimitation*, 11. On the limitations of the nautical chart, see Drummond, "Nautical Chart." He suggests that errors in boundary-making on the ocean floor could cost as much as $1 million per metre (at 215). On legal liability for such errors, see Troop, "Legal Liability."

11 For definitions of these terms, see Kapoor and Kerr, *Maritime Boundary Delimitation*, 11–12.

12 Thamsborg, "Geodetic Hydrography," 157.

13 Kapoor and Kerr, *Maritime Boundary Delimitation*, 14–18.

14 Ibid., 19–21. On contemporary trends in nautical charting, see chapter 8.

15 See, for example, Dragomir et al., *Earth's Shape*, and Moritz, *Advanced Physical Geodesy*.

CHAPTER SIX: THE EVOLUTION OF OCEAN USES AND REGIMES

1 For example, some of the newly developed ocean uses are the direct result of advances in the technology of mining and mineral extraction. Borgese, *Mines of Neptune*.

2 Johnston, "International Law in the North Pacific," 82–3.

3 O'Connell, *International Law of the Sea*, vol. 1, 467–509, 552–81.

4 For a treatment of the common interest in the law-of-the-sea context, see McDougal and Burke, *Public Order of the Oceans*, 51–6. The "economic balance of exclusive and inclusive uses" cannot be looked for in each separate regime – although the new EEZ regime might be said to be designed to effect precisely such a balance – but only in the system of all regimes taken as a whole: that is, the traditional ("classical") regimes of the high seas, the territorial sea, internal waters, and international straits; the modern ("neoclassical") regimes of the contiguous zone and continental shelf; and the contemporary ("romantic") regimes of the "area," archipelago states, and the exclusive economic zone. One might add to this list the virtually inchoate regime of islands.

5 It is a misuse of language to describe the high seas or the "area" (that is,

"the seabed and ocean floor and subsoil thereof, beyond the limits of national jurisdiction") as a "zone." Presumably, more felicitous terms for the latter regime were tried and rejected in negotiations.

6 The appropriate regime language contained in the 1982 Convention on the Law of the Sea governs the extent to which national (and regional) measures may be taken within a zone in the exclusive or special interest of the coastal state and neighbouring states. To the extent that these regimes are, or are intended to become, mini-systems of law, we may see the emergence of legal principles operating to resolve intersystem conflicts as an oceanic counterpart of private international law or conflict of laws.

7 John Selden and other English advocates of *mare clausum* tried to prove that British dominion in the adjoining seas was anterior to the Roman occupation. Fulton, *Sovereignty of the Sea*, 25.

8 According to the orthodox view of things, Rome's triumph over Carthage for the mastery of the Mediterranean during the Punic Wars (264–146 BC) was due chiefly to Rome's superior sea-power. Mahan, *Influence of Sea Power*, 13–21. Yet Rome was never a great "maritime" power.

9 See generally Trakman, "Evolution of the Law Merchant."

10 The treatment of the sea in Roman law is difficult to summarize. Most of the later Roman jurists tried to distinguish between the (public law) concept of *imperium* (jurisdiction or right of control), which was vested in the sovereign, and the (private law) concepts of *dominium* (absolute ownership) and *proprietas* (right of property). The claim to *imperium* was never fully converted into any sort of property right in the sea itself: that is, the claim to *imperium* was not developed into a claim to *dominium*. There was never a Roman doctrine of *mare clausum*. Fenn, *Right of Fishery in Territorial Waters*, 3–32. "The occasional Roman claims to a *mare clausum*, like earlier Greek and Carthaginian claims, can only be regarded as military threats made to serve economic benefits in a hectic colonial age. They lacked substance in contemporary legal theory." Johnston, *International Law of Fisheries*, 158–9. On the relationship between *imperium* and *dominium* in the modern era, see O'Connell, *International Law of the Sea*, 14–18.

11 The Romans also acquired exclusive authority over the English Channel for a short period, but no formal legal claim to a *mare clausum* in that area seems to have been made in the Emperor's name. However, John Selden argued that the ancient Britons were "Lords of the North Sea" before they were subdued by the Romans, and that Rome succeeded to this lordship from the reign of Claudius for several centuries, even until the fall of Rome. Selden, *Mare Clausum* (reprinted as *Of the Dominion*), 201–4.

12 Boorstin, *The Discoverers*, 79–289.

13 Fenn, *Origin of the Right of Fisheries*, 224–31.

14 Feudal lawyers attributed to the king (or the client prince) certain exclusive

rights and privileges known as the *jura regalia*, whose origin lay in the Roman concept of *imperium*. Jurisdiction over coastal waters came to be included in the *regalia*. Three famous jurists developed the doctrine of *mare adjacens*: Bartolus of Sassofrato (1314–57), Baldus of Ubaldi (1327–1406), and Alberico Gentili (1552–1608). Their concept of *mare adjacens* later became the foundation of the classical doctrine of the territorial sea. Johnston, *International Law of Fisheries*, 160–3. Although none of these three men was engaged in royal service, the doctrine certainly served the interests of central government at the birth of the modern nation-state.

15 O'Connell, *International Law of the Sea*, vol. 1 1–18.

16 On the Grotius-Selden debate, see Fulton, *Sovereignty of the Sea*, 338–77.

17 Jessup, *Law of Territorial Waters*, passim.

18 The principle of uniformity may be said to rest on the value of efficiency (or convenience), whereas that of reciprocity clearly reflects an effort to achieve equality, which is a form of justice, or equity.

19 McDougal and Burke, *Public Order of the Oceans*, 75–81. See also O'Connell, *International Law of the Sea*, vol. 2, 1034–61.

20 Hurst, "Whose Is the Bed of the Sea?" Hurst argued for recognition of "special property rights in particular areas of the bed of the sea outside the marginal belt for the purpose of sedentary fisheries," which, he maintained, "does not conflict in any way with the common enjoyment by all mankind of the right of navigation of the waters lying over those beds or banks" (at 43).

21 1982 UN Convention on the Law of the Sea, articles 76–85, 133–191.

22 The First UN Conference on the Law of the Sea (1958) produced four conventions: the Convention on the High Seas; the Convention on the Territorial Sea and the Contiguous Zone; the Convention on the Continental Shelf; and the Convention on Fishing and the Conservation of the Living Resources of the High Seas. The Second UN Conference on the Law of the Sea (1960) failed to produce a two-thirds majority agreement on the issues presented. The Third UN Conference on the Law of the Sea (1973–82) produced the 1982 UN Convention on the Law of the Sea.

23 Johnston and Gold, "Impact of UNCLOS III."

CHAPTER SEVEN: TRENDS IN OCEAN ZONING

1 The transempirical tradition in this area of doctrinal development was sustained, of course, by political motivation in claiming, protecting, and extending rights of control over sea areas by reference to "sovereignty" and "territoriality." But in some countries the strength of the tradition of municipal prerogative, originating in royal grants to boroughs and guilds, has tended to offset general (sovereign) entitlements at the national level through a system of special (functional) entitlements at the local level.

2 As early as 1569, the English jurist Thomas Digges argued that the Crown had an exclusive right of property in the sea and in the fishing there. Fulton, *Sovereignty of the Sea*, 362. The Scottish lawyer Sir Thomas Craig (c. 1538–1608) adhered to the theory of *dominium maris*, declaring that the sovereign is the proprietor of the fisheries found in the coastal waters. O'Connell, *International Law of the Sea*, vol. 1, 4–5. But the first jurist to argue specifically that a coastal state should have exclusive fishing rights was the Scottish jurist William Welwood (1578–1622). Johnston, "Scottish Tradition in International Law," 26–7, 44. There is evidence that the Crown exercised authority over coastal fishing in late medieval England, but "it was only when the concept of sovereignty was adumbrated in the Renaissance period that a methodology was afforded whereby feudal jurisdiction rights in the sea could be rationalized by the lawyers as expressions of a claim to exclusive rule ... Since the Crown's government was inherently based on the Crown's feudal rights in the land, it was inevitable that the power of England to exclude foreign fishing from the Narrow Sea ... should theoretically be founded on the Crown's property in the sea." O'Connell, *International Law of the Sea*, 6.

3 "Aquaculture" as a generic term has been defined as "man's attempt, through inputs of labour and energy, to improve the yield of useful aquatic organisms by deliberate manipulations of their rates of growth, mortality and reproduction." Reay, *Aquaculture*, 1. In this broad sense, it is virtually synonymous with "aquafarming" and a little broader than "fish farming," "fish husbandry," "fish culture," and "fish cultivation."

4 Ibid. 4. See also Borgese, *Seafarm*, 16–17.

5 "Mariculture" is "a means to promote or improve growth, and hence production, of marine and brackish water plants and animals for commercial use by protection and nurture in areas leased or owned." Ivesen, *Farming the Sea*, 33. The term "sea farming" is a little narrower; it focuses on animal organisms and suggests an exclusive concern with food production.

6 Borgese, *Seafarm*, 18–19.

7 Reay, *Aquaculture*, 3–4. Reay classifies eight modes of aquaculture, from the most extensive or open-ended to the most intensive or closed.

8 For a comprehensive technical treatise on these aquaculturally valuable species, see Bardach, Ryther, and McLarney, *Aquaculture*.

9 Wildsmith, *Aquaculture*, 93–101, 103–14.

10 Marine aquaculture may conflict with agriculture, captive fisheries, industrial development, sand and gravel extraction, navigation, dredging, waste disposal, recreational activities, residential development, and other uses of coastal areas.

11 On Canadian legislative provisions and administrative practices, see Wildsmith, *Aquaculture*, 153–210. For a recent statute providing for zoning of this kind, see The Aquaculture Act, Stats. Nova Scotia 1983, c. 2.

12 Highly developed nations have found captive fisheries an efficient and profitable approach to food production through the use of industrial techniques that enable the entrepreneurs to enjoy the benefits of large-scale production. But it is doubtful whether these economies will continue to be available under the conditions of the new law of the sea, with its emphasis on coastal state jurisdiction over the major commercial fisheries of the world. For economic reasons the wealthier nations may be forced to import more fishery products from developing countries, and at the same time to develop at home non-industrial techniques of mariculture. For a nation-by-nation survey of current rends in mariculture, see Brown, *World Fish Farming*.

13 Pillay, *Aquaculture Development*.

14 Bell and Canterbery, *Aquaculture for Developing Countries*.

15 Many societies have found that aquaculture can be integrated most successfully with agriculture. Borgese, *Seafarm*, 21–41. But others, such as the Soviet Union, have emphasized the integration of aquaculture with fish capture rather than agriculture. Ibid., 185.

16 Tanzer, *Race for Reserves*; Leipziger and Mudge, *Seabed Mineral Resources*. For an early account of the making of salt from sea-water, see Georgius Agricola, *De Re Metallica* (1556), 546. See also Rickard, *Man and Metals*, vol. 1, 75.

17 Four-fifths of the total salt production of Ming China (1368–1644) came from the sea. Since one-third to one-half of all imperial revenues were derived from the salt tax, the regulation of offshore salt production was a matter of priority in that period of Chinese history. Chiang, "Salt Industry of Ming China." In Rome the salt industry was important enough to be reserved as a monopoly of the state. Mommson, *History of Rome*, 345. See also Multhauf, *Neptune's Gift*, 11–12, on the salt monopoly in Rome.

18 Rickard, *Man and Metals*, vol. 2, 788. It is believed that before the first working of a seam, coastal communities collected and used sea-coals washed in by the tide.

19 *Re Dominon Coal Co. Ltd. and County of Cape Breton* (1963), 40 DLR (2d) 593, 48 MPR 174. In this case, undersea coal workings of the corporation under territorial waters off the coast of Cape Breton were found to be assessable for the purpose of municipal taxation.

20 Owen, *Oil Finders*, 800–3.

21 Burns, "Offshore Platform Concepts."

22 For statistics on offshore activities around the world, see the *International Petroleum Encyclopedia*, which is published annually.

23 A seaport is distinguished from river, lake, and canal ports by its purpose of providing shelter from winds, waves, and swell. Morgan, *Ports and Harbours*, 13. Normally, a seaport consists of a harbour (or haven), which serves the purpose of shelter, and installations (or port works), at which "ships are dealt with and where especially the trans-shipment of mail,

passengers and cargo takes place." Ibid., 54. Installations include quays (wharves), piers, moles, docks, and other kinds of works.

24 Harper, *Port of London Act*, 1–3. This control extended to the setting of taxes and levies and the assigning of "legal" ports, and can be dated in England to the reign of King John.

25 Reddie, *Researches in Maritime International Law*, 27–35.

26 See, for example, the requirement of imperial authorization for the opening of the eight treaty ports to Western traders in 1862 and 1898. Greenfield, *China and the Law of the Sea*, 3, note 1.

27 This supervision extended to the very designation of the ports and the prohibition against landing goods elsewhere "under pain of confiscation" (4 Henry IV, c. 20). Harper, *Port of London Act*, 1.

28 Carthage prevented the landing of goods from vessels of states in commercial competition with Cathaginians. Reddie, *Researches in Maritime International Law*, 27–8. In the case of Rhodes, the extensive port-state law-making role adopted by the Rhodians did not prevent their going to war with Byzantium over restrictions placed on Rhodian vessels in Byzantine ports. Later, ports became customs posts and thereby acquired leverage on merchants with little choice between land and ocean trade routes. See, for example, Braudel, *Mediterranean World*, 293–5.

29 McDougal and Burke, *Public Order of the Oceans*, 99–116.

30 Oram and Baker, *Efficient Port*, 169–85.

31 Fulton, *The Sovereignty of the Sea*, 57–9, 82–4, 604, 697.

32 *Annakumaru Pillai* v. *Muthupayal* (1903), 23 Indian Law Reports, Madras Series 511, 553, as noted in Jessup, *Law of Territorial Waters*, 15: "Proceeding then to a consideration of the *situs* of the beds, the learned Chief Justice remarked 'that the rule as to the territorial waters of a country is founded on the principle that a proper margin is absolutely necessary for the safety and convenience of every country bordering on the sea' ... [I]t was noted that gulfs and bays stand upon an exceptional footing ... This gulf, with its rich products, had long been subject to the exclusive control of native princes and later of the British Crown. This claim had not been questioned by other powers, was supported by Vattel, and was believed to be unassailable."

33 Fulton, *Sovereignty of the Sea*, 12.

34 Ibid., 5: "In thus appropriating the seas adjacent to their territories ... the various nations were doubtless impelled by consideration of their own immediate interests. In most instances ... the principal object appears to have been to maintain a monopoly of trade and commerce as far as possible in their own hands, in accordance with the commercial spirit of the times." In a similar vein, Edgar Gold assesses the early (1300–1500) claims to large portions of the Mediterranean by city-states such as Venice: "Although always couched in imaginative legal terms, such claims were invariably

enforced by the use of military power and led to many a sanguinary war. However, the motivation was always the same – to preserve a commercial *status quo*." Gold, *Maritime Transport*, 30–1.

35 Greenhalgh, *Pompey*, 91. "[Pompey] had divided the Mediterranean area into thirteen districts, to each of which he assigned a legate with a powerful force of ships and troops ... [I]f hunted pirates managed to escape from one operational area into another, the pursuing squadron must retire and leave the enemy to take its chance with the neighbouring Roman commander or with the commander-in-chief ... Of the thirteen operational areas six were in Western waters and seven in the East."

36 Fulton, *Sovereignty of the Sea*, 119–20.

37 See, for example, the fifty-nautical-mile security zone established by North Korea. Park, "Military Boundary Zone"; Larkin, "East Asian Ocean Security Zones."

38 An early application of this concept is found in the South American Neutrality Zone created by the Declaration of Panama, 3 October 1939, which restricted belligerent operations within three hundred miles of the South American coast. For a discussion of this zone and its central role in the *Graf Spee* incident of December 1939, see O'Connell, *Influence of Law*, 27–39.

39 See Buzan, "Naval Power," and Ranjeva, "L'ocean indien et le nouveau droit de la mer."

40 Strange, "Cuba and After," 7.

41 Goldblat, *French Nuclear Tests*, 26–7.

42 Marston and Birnie, "Falkland Islands."

43 Fulton, *Sovereignty of the Sea*, 5 et seq.

44 Jessup, *Law of Territorial Waters*, 17.

45 Ibid., 10; Fulton, *Sovereignty of the Sea*, 77–8.

46 Jessup, *Law of Territorial Waters*, 279. "While maintaining the three-mile limit as the boundary of territorial waters, the United States asserted ... a right to effect seizures on the high seas." See also McDougal and Burke, *Public Order of the Oceans*, 594–6.

47 Customs and Excise Offshore Application Act, SC 1984, c. 17.

48 Cartwright, *Disease and History*, 29–53. Cartwright relates the history of the plague and (at 38) suggests that "[i]t is, however, possible that the infection was brought to Bristol by sea, or even that this may have been a new focus of infection, for Bristol was a port of considerable size and received many ships from Europe." He adds (at 41): "Inland waterways and coastal traffic (throughout Europe) would also favour the spread." Siegfried, *Germs and Ideas*, explains how cholera spread along the great sea-trading routes (at 41 et seq.).

49 Jessup, *Law of Territorial Waters*, 10.

50 Ibid.

51 McDougal and Burke, *Public Order of the Oceans*, 594.

52 Plender, *International Migration Law*, dates the beginning of modern immigration practices with the French Revolution (at 42 et seq.).

53 For a history of the development of immigration controls see ibid., 57–70.

54 On the Commission's narrow approach to the contiguous zone concept, see McDougal and Burke, *Public Order of the Oceans*, 604–5.

55 Article 24, 1958 Convention on the Territorial Sea and the Contiguous Zone.

56 Article 33, 1982 UN Convention on the Law of the Sea.

57 Johnston, ed., *Environmental Law of the Sea*, 20 *et seq*.

58 For example, the Oslo Dumping Convention (11 *International Legal Materials* 262) applies only to the Northeast Atlantic Ocean, a portion of the Arctic Ocean, and the North Sea; the Helsinki Convention (13 *International Legal Materials* 546) applies to the Baltic, the Gulf of Bothnia, the Gulf of Finland, and the entrance to the Baltic; the Barcelona Protocol (15 *International Legal Materials* 290) applies to the Mediterranean as a part of the Mediterranean Action Plan.

59 Rev. Stats. Can., c. 2 (1st Supp.), s. 3. Under this statute the national zone extends as far as one hundred miles seaward from the baseline of the territorial sea.

60 On Canadian legislative requirements for the purposes of environmental protection in the EEZ, see McDorman et al., *Caracas Convention*, 57–83. Canada's special concern in Arctic waters was met through the "ice-covered waters" provision in article 234 of the 1982 UN Convention on the Law of the Sea. See Johnston, *Canada and the Law of the Sea*, 18–20, 39–41.

61 Gold, "Vessel Traffic Regulation," 4–8.

62 For the argument that IMO and the coastal state should work together as "joint guardians" of the common interest in preserving the marine environment of a coastal state's EEZ waters, see Gold and Johnston, "Ship-Generated Pollution."

63 French and Flemish fishermen were prominent in the North Sea fisheries during the Middle Ages, and in the Baltic the cities of the Hanseatic League controlled the herring trade. But in the early fifteenth century the herring fishery along the British coast became the most important in Europe, and gradually the Dutch came to take the leading part in it. Fulton, *Sovereignty of the Sea*, 61–2.

64 Johnston, *International Law of Fisheries*, 3–81.

65 Koers, *International Regulation of Marine Fisheries*.

66 Johnston, *International Law of Fisheries*, 176–252.

67 Articles 56 and 57, 1982 UN Convention on the Law of the Sea.

68 See Burns, "Offshore Platform Concepts." In 1978 one platform was installed in 1,025 feet of water in the Gulf of Mexico. Steel jackets permitting instalment in even deeper waters have been introduced.

69 It seems that Argentina and Canada, for example, might be able to claim

sovereign rights to continental shelf areas exceeding four hundred miles in breadth under the formula provided in article 76 of the 1982 Convention.

70 See the annual editions of the *International Petroleum Encyclopedia*.

71 Indeed, it is sometimes required in certain countries that the foreign company enter into some kind of contractual arrangement with the national oil company of the coastal state.

72 In at least one area of the North Sea (Denmark-West Germany), and two areas of the Arabian Gulf, this kind of commercial "zoning" seems to have preceded formal boundary-making by the government concerned. In addition, joint development zones are sometimes negotiated by neighbouring states as a means of circumventing the need for a formally delimited boundary. Admittedly, these joint development zones are the product of formal treaty-making, but they are sometimes negotiated for industrial reasons, as in the case of Sudan-Saudi Arabia. Townsend Gault, "Offshore Boundary Delimitation."

73 Johnston, *Canada and the Law of the Sea*, 41–2.

74 Knecht, "Coastal Zone Management."

75 Couper and Smith, "North Sea."

76 For a Canadian perspective on national ocean management and related issues, see Johnston, *Canada and the Law of the Sea*, 39–63. Despite its national origin, coastal zone management was designated in the early 1980s as a priority for the United Nations Environment Programme, but it is not yet clear what can be initiated at global or regional levels.

CHAPTER EIGHT: TRENDS IN OCEAN SCIENCE AND TECHNOLOGY

1 Today the field of physical geography is generally perceived as a composite of all of those disciplines that contribute to our understanding of man's physical environment, such as descriptive geology, physical oceanography, hydrology, climatology, ecology, and the traditional study of land forms, soils, and vegetation. Many general textbooks also include chapters on certain aspects of astronomy, geophysics, geodesy, and cartography. See, for example, Strahler, *Physical Geography*, and Birot, *General Physical Geography*. Some approaches emphasize the distinctness of natural systems, such as the atmosphere, the hydrosphere, the geosphere, and the biosphere; see, for example, Hidore, *Physical Geography*, and Chorley and Kennedy, *Physical Geography*. Other works treat physical geography more explicitly as a human environment; for example, Rolars and Nystuen, *Physical Geography*. But it is normal today to maintain a distinction between physical geography and human, political, economic, and other aspects of the subject. For a modern physical description of marine geography, see Cotter, *Physical Geography of the Oceans*. Because of the fragmentation of

geographical knowledge into specialized compartments, it is difficult for physical geography, or geography in general, to retain its coherence as a discipline within the all-encompassing field of "earth sciences" on the one hand, and "environmental sciences" on the other.

2 Fuson, *Geography of Geography*, 3.

3 Ibid., 4–7. The earliest known map dates from the dynasty of Sargon of Akkad (about 2400–2200 BC). Brown, *Story of Maps*, 33; Wilford, *The Mapmakers*, 8.

4 Fuson, *Geography of Geography*, 8.

5 A vast amount of geographical description is contained in *The Iliad*, so much that many scholars regard Homer as the father of geography.

6 Fuson, *Geography of Geography*, 22–8; Wilford, *The Mapmakers*, 7–8; and Boorstin, *The Discoverers*, 111–13. The Sung dynasty (960–1279) witnessed the greatest flowering of indigenous Chinese science – astronomy, mathematics, meteorology, geology, geography, and cartography. But the Chinese developed an interest in geography much earlier. For example, in the early fourth century the Taoists started to produce a voluminous number of gazetteers on local topography, which are "probably unrivalled in any nation for extent and systematic comprehensiveness." Needham, *Science and Civilization in China*, vol. 1, 120. The study of geography on a larger scale began to flourish in China in the Yuan dynasty (1279–1368) as a result of contacts between East and West. The first great Chinese atlas was produced between 1311 and 1320. Ibid., 141.

7 But early geography also owes much to four Greeks from the heartland of Hellenic civilization: Plato, Aristotle, Alexander the Great, and Ptolemy I, (who was of Macedonian origin, although he later settled in Alexandria and founded there the greatest library in the world of antiquity). Fuson, *Geography of Geography*, 23–7.

8 Ibid., 15–16

9 Herodotus was one of the best-travelled scholars of his age, and he possessed a marvellous eye for detail. Like other great travellers (such as Marco Polo), he was insatiably curious and remarkably fair-minded, which makes his recorded observations especially reliable. Yet Herodotus seems to have had a low opinion of maps. Witness his ironic account of Aristagoras of Miletus, leader of the Ionian Revolt (499–494 BC), who tried unsuccessfully to recruit Cleomenes of Sparta to his cause by appealing to his territorial greed through the self-serving use of a map. Wilford, *The Mapmakers*, 10–11.

10 The concept of sphericity may have been put forward by Philolus of Tarentum (480–? BC), a disciple of Pythagoras, rather than by the master himself. Fuson, *Geography of Geography*, 22.

11 The heliocentric views of Copernicus, which revolutionized the field of planetary astronomy, were published in his one great work, *De revolutioni-*

bus orbium coelestium, which was completed only in the year of his death.

12 The heliocentric hypothesis does not appear in the one work of Aristarchus that is extant today (*On the Sizes and Distances of the Sun and Moon*). But a quotation from another of his works, which appears in the writings of Archimedes, has convinced posterity that Aristarchus was indeed the first to maintain that the earth revolves around the sun, and Copernicus himself acknowledged that Aristarchus had anticipated his great discovery.

13 The early Ptolemies, who governed the city, developed the original museum into the leading Greek university, attracting many of the greatest scholars of the classical age. From its establishment by Ptolemy I (c. 290 BC) to its destruction in the reign of Emperor Aurelian (c. 270 AD), this great library complex served as the nucleus of what was essentially the first international university. For an account of Eratosthenes' contributions at Alexandria, see Wilford, *The Mapmakers*, 15–24.

14 Geodesy is that branch of astronomy or applied mathematics which determines the figures and areas of large portions of the earth's surface, and the figure of the earth as a whole.

15 Brown, *Story of Maps*, 31; Boostin, *The Discoverers*, 95–7.

16 Hipparchus insisted that a world map should be constructed in such a way that every important place could be located according to its latitude and longitude, both to be determined by astronomical observation. Eratosthenes had divided the earth's sphere into 60 parts; Hipparchus developed a delineatory system consisting of 360 parts, which became the degrees accepted in modern global geography. These meridian lines are approximately seventy miles apart, as proposed by Hipparchus over two thousand years ago. Boorstin, *The Discoverers*, 97. It fell to the great geographer Ptolemy, in the second century AD, to build on the Hipparchean system by subdividing each degree into sixty minutes of the arc, and each minute into sixty seconds. Ibid., 98.

17 Sarton, *History of Science*, 104–6. Just how accurate Eratosthenes' measurement of the earth's circumference really was is still a matter of debate among scholars, since it is not entirely certain what his unit of measurement was. All geographers of Greek antiquity measured great distances by *stadia*: that is, the length of a stadium. But not every stadium of that period corresponded to one-eighth of a Roman mile. Some modern scholars believe that Eratosthenes came within fifty miles of the correct figure. See, for example, Lister, *Antique Maps*, 14; and Fuson, *Geography of Geography*, 28–9.

18 Thrower, *Maps and Man*, 18.

19 Ibid., 19; Fuson, *Geography of Geography*, 28.

20 Polybius travelled widely throughout the Mediterranean and beyond, and, like Herodotus, accurately recorded much of what he observed in his historical writings. Since he practised the non-sensationalist approach to his-

tory that he preached, the geographical information he provided was generally reliable.

21 Sarton, *History of Science*, 418. Following Poseidonius and Strabo of Amaseia, in the second century AD Ptolemy declared the earth to be 18,000 miles in circumference. "Together with this providential underestimate he made the mistake of stretching Asia out eastward to reach far beyond its real dimensions, for 180 degrees instead of its actual 130 degrees. On Ptolemy's maps this had the effect of grossly reducing the extent of the unknown parts of the world between the eastern tip of Asia and the western tip of Europe. How long might the European encounter with the New World have been postponed if Ptolemy had followed not Strabo but Eratosthenes? And then, if Columbus had known how large the world really was?" Boorstin, *The Discoverers*, 99.

22 Sarton, *History of Science*, 421.

23 Strabo's great work, *Geography*, is the only general treatise on the subject that has survived intact from the classical period. By the sixth century AD, it was established as a classic. Today it represents the most reliable source of information about the ideas and writings of the great geographers of antiquity, such as Eratosthenes, Hipparchus, Polybius, and Poseidonius. Strabo, like Hipparchus, stressed the geographer's need for scientific knowledge and mathematical precision, although he, like Polybius, leaned toward descriptive and historical geography.

24 Fuson, *Geography of Geography*, 40–2. Pliny's famous work, *Natural History*, has been described as a storehouse of ancient errors, but its influence on future generations was considerable. Books 3 to 6 of the work are devoted to geography and ethnography.

25 Fuson, *Geography of Geography*, 42–5. Ptolemy was a celebrated scholar in astronomy, mathematics, and geography. His reputation as a geographer rests on his monumental work, *Guide to Geography* (*Geographike Huphegesis*).

26 Brown, *Story of Maps*, 60–1.

27 Ptolemy's knowledge of astronomy and mathematics equipped him unusually well to become the leading classical authority on scientific geography and cartography. Yet his descriptive geography was less complete and less accurate than Strabo's, and he committed many errors, such as his espousal of Poseidonius' rather than Eratosthenes' calculation of the earth's circumference. See supra, note 21.

28 Fuson, *Geography of Geography*, 43–60; Crone, *Maps and Their Makers*, 65–72; Bagrow, *History of Cartography*, 75–86.

29 Crone, *Maps and Their Makers*, 73–94; Boorstin, *The Discoverers*, 107–38.

30 Crone, *Background to Geography*, 37–9. The effort by Varenius to produce a systematic treatment of geography culminated in the publication of *Geographia Generalis* (1650), a comprehensive work later issued in revised

editions with the assistance of Isaac Newton and others. Varenius was also one of the first to develop a treatise on "special" (regional) geography in his book, *Descriptio Regiae Japoniae*.

31 Crone, *Background to Geography*, 48–56. Humboldt was a naturalist, traveller, diplomat, and humanitarian of impressive productivity, insight, and versatility, and his influence on science and education has been long-lasting. His voluminous scholarly contributions to physical geography made careful use of his lifelong travels and observations in many parts of the world. He is best remembered today as the first student of the ocean currrent off the west coast of South America, which bears his name and which was to play an important role in the evolution of the two-hundred-mile exclusive economic zone of coastal state jurisdiction. Compare Hollick, "Origins of Offshore Zones."

32 Boorstin, *The Discoverers*, 46–53.

33 More precisely, latitude is the location of any place on the earth's surface by reference to the angular distance on its meridian north or south of the equator. Technically, there are different kinds of latitude – geographical, astronomical, and geocentric. But the differences between them are minor, and it is the geographical latitude, the kind used in mapping, that is most often applied to boundary-making.

34 More technically, longitude is the amount of arc created by drawing a line from the centre of the earth to the intersection of the equator and the prime meridian and another line from the centre of the earth to any point elsewhere on the equator.

35 Eratosthenes was one of the first to attempt to construct a network of parallels and meridians, but it was so lacking in scientific precision that even his contemporaries recognized its inadequacy. Hipparchus was particularly offended by the imprecision of the work. But Eratosthenes' contemporaries and immediate successors seem to have been moved by envy as much as by greater knowledge or superior judgment. See, for example, Sarton, *History of Science*, 101; Brown, *Story of Maps*, 49–50; Thrower, *Maps and Man*, 18–19; Fuson, *Geography of Geography*, 28–9; and Boorstin, *The Discoverers*, 96.

36 Hipparchus, like so many others before and after him, was a geocentrist. His work had a major influence on Ptolemy, whose geocentric theory was widely accepted in the Western world for fifteen hundred years, until it was overthrown in the age of the Renaissance.

37 Boorstin, *The Discoverers*, 94–5.

38 Much of this work was directed by Giovanni Dominico Cassini at the Paris Observatory, which was built between 1667 and 1671. Ibid., 215–23. For an account of the cartographic contributions of the Cassini family in Paris, see Wilford, *The Mapmakers*, 111-27, and Crone, *Background to Geography*, 73–81.

39 No less a sum than £20,000 was offered for a timekeeper that would enable longitude to be determined within an accuracy of half a degree at the end of a voyage to the West Indies: that is, within thirty nautical miles at the end of a six-weeks voyage. Such timekeeper would have to remain accurate within three seconds per day – a standard that had not been attained on land by the best pendulum clocks. Because of the difficulty of producing such an accurate device, Parliament also offered lesser sums for lesser accomplishments: £10,000 for any method capable of determining a ship's longitude within one degree, and £15,000 for a method within a 40′ margin of error. Harrison invented and constructed no fewer than four marine timekeepers. The fourth, which won the coveted prize, can be seen today, still in working order, at the Royal Observatory at Greenwich. See Wilford, *The Mapmakers*, 128–37; Boorstin, *The Discoverers*, 46–53.

40 The stick charts of the Marshall Islands, for example, were used long before Westerners first visited the South Pacific. Thrower, *Maps and Man*, 5–8.

41 "The history of sea charts and their makers is even more difficult to trace than maps and the men who compiled them, for next to professional lawbreakers no group of people in the history of mankind has been more reluctant to keep records than professional sailors ... They kept their knowledge to themselves." Brown, *Story of Maps*, 114. *The Periplus of the Erythraean Sea*, by an unknown author, is a rare example of early charting that has been preserved. This handbook for navigators contains very accurate sailing directions for the Red Sea, the Erythraean (Arabian) Sea, and the Persian Gulf. It also contains references to India, Ceylon, and other distant places, including Zanzibar in the "torrid zone," which many theoretical geographers of the time still regarded as impenetrable and uninhabitable. Fuson, *Geography of Geography*, 42. For illustrations of early charts, see Putnam, *Early Sea Charts*.

42 Since sea charts were aids to navigation, they allowed no room for theory or speculation. "They treated in a simple, direct way the problems which concerned navigators and ignored the rest. The safest place for a navigator and his ship is deep water – beyond soundings. It is when he heads for shore that he inevitably heads for trouble. Then he wants an accurate picture of the coastline he is approaching, with the location of prominent points from which he can check his position in relation to his chart. He must know the location of reefs and shoals and submerged rocks before he gets to them, not after." Brown, *Story of Maps*, 122–3. In the Mediterranean, even as late as the fifteenth century, mariners normally stayed close to the coastline, using familiar landmarks. But when Portuguese sailors started to explore southward down the western coast of Africa, they had no *portolanos* to guide them. "The Mediterranean was nowhere more than five hundred miles from its southern to its closest northern coast, which meant a difference of only some seven degrees of latitude. Mediterranean pilots therefore

seldom worried about their latitude, especially since the modes of defining latitude were still so wide. But the African continent stretched from 38 degrees north latitude to 38 degrees south latitude, one-fifth around the globe." Boorstin, *The Discoverers*, 148. Along unfamiliar coastlines and in uncharted waters, latitude was the best, and sometimes the only, way of defining a ship's position. By the early sixteenth century, after the early Portuguese explorations, marine charts began to show scales of latitude.

43 Brown, *Story of Maps*, 123.

44 Ibid., 123–5.

45 Crone, *Background to Geography*, 21; Lister, *Antique Maps*, 14–15.

46 Wilford, *The Mapmakers*, 25–33.

47 Ibid., 52–4.

48 An ephemeris is a table giving the position of one or more of the celestial bodies for stated points of time. It was developed in the fifteenth century by astronomers and mathematicians such as Johannes Müller (Regiomontanus) (1436–76) and Bernhard Walter (1430–1504).

49 Triangulation, a method crucial to modern mapmaking, makes it possible to measure the distance to remote objects by applying a simple principle of geometry: if one side and two angles of a triangle are known, the other properties of the triangle can be determined. On the story behind the validation, see Wilford, *The Mapmakers*, 99–110.

50 The first epoch of geodesy, the "spherical" epoch, was dominated by the belief that the earth was a sphere and characterized by mapping based on that belief. The second epoch, the "ellipsoid," benefited from more precise surveys, which led to the new conception of the earth as being less than perfectly round. The third, and contemporary, period, the "geoidal," is marked by highly sophisticated instruments of measurement that enable geodesists to define the figure of the earth and every variation on it with amazing precision. Ibid., 109–10.

51 A plane table consists of a smoothly finished drawing board mounted on a tripod and a metal sight rule (alidade) for taking accurate aim on the object to be plotted. It came into general use in the sixteenth century as the first mapping device for measuring and recording angles.

52 Some of these instruments were designed for the measurement of angles: for example, the theodolite and the altazimuth. Others, such as the odometer and the surveyor's chain, were used for measuring distances. Still other methods were adopted for measuring elevation: for example, spirit levelling, trigonometric levelling, and barometric levelling. Wilford, *The Mapmakers*, 96–8.

53 The invention of the Western printing-press is usually attributed to Johannes Gutenberg (c. 1398–1468) in 1440, though records are unreliable. By the 1470s printing presses had been established in many European cities, and books were being produced in great volume in response to a rapidly

growing reading public. Boorstin, *The Discoverers*, 510–32.

54 The utility of globes, small reproductions of the earth, seems to have been understood by the Greeks, but they did not become a familiar and popular mode of depiction until the lifetime of Martin Rehaim (1459–1507). Wilford, *The Mapmakers*, 59–61.

55 Yung Lo, who reigned early in the Ming dynasty, is best known in the West as the patron of Cheng Ho, the great Chinese navigator. Unlike the European promoters, Yung Lo and his successors were uninterested in the accumulation of further wealth. Their motivation in supporting expeditions seems to have been to display more widely the fame and glory of the Chinese empire, and to receive appropriate symbolic "tribute." Boorstin, *The Discoverers*, 186–201. Prince Henry (1394–1460) was the first modern promoter of exploratory expeditions. At Sagres, in the Algarve region of southern Portugal, he established an "academy of seamanship" composed of navigators, shipbuilders, astronomers, cartographers, and instrument-makers. There the first effort was made to organize the practical information of mariners and to collect the portolan charts they used on board. Henry's captains carried out much of the original exploration of the coastal waters of West Africa. Ibid., 156–68. The most famous of King John's navigators were Vasco da Gama and Bartholomew Dias. Ibid., 169–78. Ferdinand and Isabella were, of course, the sponsors of Christopher Columbus's first and most famous voyage of discovery to the New World in 1492–3. Ibid., 224–44. Under the patronage of Henry VII of England, John Cabot first explored the waters of Newfoundland, Cape Breton, and the St Lawrence in his voyages of 1497 and 1498. See Williamson, *The Cabot Voyages*. In 1534, Francis I sponsored the first of the three expeditions to North America undertaken by Jacques Cartier. See Jacques Cartier, *Voyages en Nouvelle-France*.

56 After the return of Columbus and Vespucci, Spain and Portugal quickly fell into conflict over claims to the New World. In response to a Spanish request, Pope Alexander VI promulgated a series of four bulls, announcing that all new territories discovered or yet to be discovered east of a designated line of demarcation (redrawn in 1494) would be assigned to Portugal, and all that lay west of the line would belong to Spain. This line of demarcation was a meridian of longitude drawn from pole to pole on a chart of the Western Ocean 100 leagues (300 nautical miles) from the Azores. This might have been a masterly example of Iberian diplomacy, except that no one knew where the line was. Curiously, the Portuguese navigator Ferdinand Magellan proposed to King Charles I of Spain (later Emperor Charles V) that he sail west to acquire practical proof of Spain's claim that the coveted Spice Islands lay within the Spanish, not the Portuguese, hemisphere. This seems to have been the first maritime boundary dispute of major political importance. It also represents the first example of a strong

political incentive to support the development of geography, cartography, and related disciplines. On the final outcome as negotiated in the Treaty of Tordesillas, see chapter 1, note 29, supra.

57 Wilford, *The Mapmakers*, 73–86; Bagrow, *History of Cartography*, 111–22; Boorstin, *The Discoverers*, 271–8.

58 Mercator's major maps were of Palestine (1537), the world (1538), Flanders (1540), Europe (1554 and 1572), and the British Isles (1564), besides his famous world chart of 1569, his edition of Ptolemy's maps, and his *Atlas*, which consumed most of his later years. Most of these works were characterized by a higher degree of accuracy than had been attained by any previous cartographer. His maps of Europe, for example, contained much more accurate measurements of the length of the Mediterranean than Ptolemy's excessive estimates.

59 Bagrow, *History of Cartography*, 59–66.

60 Apparently Mercator was neither the inventor nor the first user of the projection that bears his name, but he was certainly the cartographer mainly responsible for its general acceptance by seafarers.

61 *Encyclopaedia Britannica* (1966 ed.), vol. 14, 822–3.

62 Many cartographers since Mercator have, of course, introduced alternative methods and found ways of improving the Mercator projection. Wilford, *The Mapmakers*, 42, 77–86. For a review of recent advances in cartography, see McDonnell, *Map Projections*.

63 His extraordinary powers of observation set him on the road to fame. For someone self-taught in astronomy and mathematics, Cook made remarkably accurate observations of the solar eclipse of 1776 from the Burgeo Islands. His account of this phenomenon so impressed the Royal Society that two years later it appointed him as one of two observers in Tahiti of the transit of Venus, as part of an international scientific effort to determine the earth's distance from the sun. This voyage in the *Endeavour* was the first of his three great expeditions.

64 On board the *Endeavour* were two scientists, Joseph Banks and Daniel Solander, who would make important contributions to ethnology and biology and point the way to the great oceanographic expeditions of the nineteenth century, such as those of the *Challenger* and the *Beagle*. On the *Endeavour* voyage home, Cook lost one-third of his crew to scurvy. Aware this was the "normal" death rate from scurvy, Cook studied the existing knowledge of scurvy prevention and concluded that this scourge of the seafaring community could easily be eliminated if the proper precautions were taken. His paper on the subject so impressed the Royal Society that he was appointed a Fellow and received the prestigious Copley Medal.

65 Eighteenth-century man was full of bizarre and romantic misconceptions about exotic places and peoples. Belief in the existence of a great "southern continent" was the motivation behind the first two of Cook's expeditions.

Boorstin, *The Discoverers*, 278–89. Cook was able to dispel this myth, and, more important, he was the first explorer to make an intelligent and humane effort to establish significant contracts with the "savages" he encountered.

66 His *Endeavour* voyage lasted from 1768 to 1771; the second, in the *Resolution* and *Adventure*, from 1772 to 1775; and the third, in the *Resolution* and *Discovery*, from 1776 to 1779. See Barrow, ed., *Captain Cook's Voyages*. The classical, though uncritical, biography of Cook is Beaglehole's *Life of Cook*.

67 Most captains left chartmaking to others, as they do today. Chartmaking is a highly technical undertaking that requires long and rigorous training. Cook became "acquainted with the whole process" in a matter of days in the summer of 1758 after some conversation with Samuel Holland, a British Army surveyor. Soon afterwards he had an opportunity to practise his newly learned skills in a survey of Gaspé Bay off the coast of Quebec. After the end of the Seven Years' War, between 1763 and 1767, Cook perfected the technique of surveying and charting off the coast of Newfoundland. Wilford, *The Mapmakers*, 143–4.

68 Ibid., 144–5.

69 Cook's method was developed earlier off the coast of Newfoundland, around the islands of St Pierre and Miquelon. "Going ashore nearly every day, Cook measured a baseline by chain and marked the ends of the line by implanting flags. He fixed the latitude of the line by taking quadrant sightings on the sun. Then, using the theodolite, he determined angles between each end of the line and some distant point, a tree or rocky crag or implanted flag. This was the same technique of triangulation used with such impressive effect by the Cassinis of France. In time Cook obtained enough angles to plot a network of triangles, whereby it was possible to know the correct relation between many land features along the coast. A draftsman then sketched in the detail between the measured points. After running a series of triangles, Cook then took theodolite sightings on the mast of his ship, thereby linking his shore survey with any offshore soundings." Ibid., 145–6. In his later circumnavigations of the Pacific Cook was never to exceed these impeccable surveys of the Newfoundland coast. Off the coasts of New Zealand and the east coast of Australia, for example, Cook lacked the time for such thoroughness and was forced to settle for "running surveys." Despite the infrequency of triangulations on shore, without the benefit even of a chronometer, Cook achieved a degree of accuracy that is as astounding to us today as it was to his contemporaries and certainly stands as the most impressive feat in the history of practical hydrography. Later, in 1778, Cook conducted a remarkable reconnaisance survey of the west coast of North America, from Oregon to Alaska, which, though falling short of his own standards of exactitude, alone would have preserved his name in history. Ibid., 147–52.

70 Ibid., 153–6. For a full-scale biography of this great navigator-surveyor, see Anderson, *Surveyor of the Sea*.

71 Wilford, *The Mapmakers*, 157–60. By the time of his death, the British Hydrographic Office under Beaufort had produced no fewer than fifteen hundred new nautical charts. See Friendly, *Beaufort of the Admiralty*.

72 Schlee, *An Unfamiliar World*, 81–106.

73 Thomas H. Huxley, for example, turned to deep-sea research with a view to finding evidence in support of the Darwinian theory. Ibid., 95–8.

74 Lyell is widely regarded as the father of modern geology. His chief work, *The Principles of Geology* (3 vols., 1830–3), was the most comprehensive treatise produced on the subject. His other major works were *Elements of Geology* (1838), a standard treatise on stratographical and paleontological geology, and *The Antiquity of Man* (1863), in which he reviewed the arguments for man's early development. Like Thomas H. Huxley, Lyell was a close friend and supporter of Charles Darwin throughout their professional lives.

75 Schlee, *An Unfamiliar World*, 107–38.

76 Ibid., 55. Matthew Fontaine Maury (1806–73), one of the pioneers of oceanography in the United States, is known today chiefly for his seminal contributions to hydrography. His major work was *The Physical Geography of the Sea* (1855). Trained as a naval officer, he was primarily responsible for the first systematic collection of nautical charts and instruments in the United States, and for the later establishment of the US naval observatory and hydrographic office. Schlee, *An Unfamiliar World*, 26–63.

77 For recent descriptions of the ocean bottom, see Sarutton and Talwani, eds., *Ocean Floor*, and Nairn et al., *Ocean Basins and Margins*.

78 Ollier, *Tectonics and Landforms*; Toksoz et al., eds., *Oceanic Ridges and Arcs*.

79 The prospect of petroleum development in the offshore has resulted in dramatic advances in the techniques of offshore surveying. But most developing societies are seriously deficient in hydrographic surveying skills, and the International Hydrographic Organisation has recently called for the establishment of training programs and other remedial measures. See *International Hydrographic Bulletin*, March 1987, 76–8, and May 1987, 156–9.

80 Radar is an acronym for "radio detecting and ranging." This is the function of an electronic device that was developed independently in the United Kingdom, Germany, France, and the United States in the 1930s. The Scottish scientist Robert Watson-Watt may have been the first to establish its operational value with a successful experiment conducted in 1935. Radar detects and locates certain types of objects at distances and under conditions of limited light or darkness that make the unaided eye useless.

81 For recent contributions, see Bjφnφ, ed., *Underwater Acoustics*. On theory, see Urick, *Underwater Sound*.

82 Dickinson, *Maps and Air Photographs*. For another recent study of aerial surveying techniques, see Ritchie et al., *Mapping for Field Scientists*, 155–234.

83 For example, the locational science of underwater acoustics, which has been applied to such diverse undertakings as anti-submarine warfare navigation, fish detection, surveying, and communications and control. Haines, *Sound Underwater*. See also Spiess, "Acoustic Techniques for Marine Geodesy."

84 Teicholz, "Processing Satellite Data." In September 1985 LANDSAT was transferred by the US federal government to the private sector through a contract with the Earth Observation Satellite Company (EOSAT) a joint venture formed by Hughes Aircraft Company and RCA.

85 Teicholz, "Processing Satellite Data," 117.

86 Ibid., 118, 119–20. On the role of remote sensing as an aid to detection of hydrographic features not included on existing charts, see Watson, "Ocean Charting," 141–3. See also Weeks and Carsey, "Remote Sensing of the Arctic Seas."

87 Teicholz, "Processing Satellite Data," 125–6. It is believed that laser systems may have the greatest potentiality for remote sensing of water depths. Douglas and MacPhee, "Hydrography for the Year 2000."

88 Cronan, *Underwater Minerals*.

89 Teicholz, "Processing Satellite Data," 127–9.

90 Dutton and Nison, "Computer Cartography," 134.

91 On recent trends in ocean mapping, see Kerr, ed., *Dynamics of Oceanic Cartography*, and Perrotte, "Review of Coastal Zone Mapping."

92 Dutton and Nison, "Computer Cartography," passim; Carter, *Computer Mapping*; and Kerr, Eaton, and Anderson, "The Electronic Chart."

93 Kolata, "Geodesy." In geodetic terms, a datum is "a network of reference points, whose longitudes, latitudes, and in some cases altitudes must be known to an accuracy of within a few centimeters." Ibid., 421. Computer science and technology may also produce dramatic improvements in navigation control. Harris, "Navigation Control System."

94 For example, by the early 1990s a breakthrough will have occurred in radionavigation with the advent of the Global Positioning System (GPS). With the installation of twelve to eighteen GPS satellites, a much more accurate system of navigational location will become available relatively cheaply to shipowners around the world. It will be simple to operate and effective in all weather conditions. Stansell, "Global Positioning System." For the normal purposes of navigation, it has usually been sufficient to attain positional accuracy within a few hundred metres. Today, in seismic exploration, demands for accurate positioning of a moving vessel at sea are at the two-to-five-metre level. Before the end of the 1980s requirements are expected to approach the submetre level. Wong et al., "Integration of Inertial and GPS-Satellite Techniques."

95 It should be understood, however, that the present generation of sensing produces information limited to surface and near-surface waters.

96 Although ocean charts are still based on sparse and inadequate data, recent improvements are impressive. For example, at the time of writing, seventy-nine small-scale international charts are near completion; they will cover all ocean areas except the polar regions. Watson, "Ocean Charting," 128–41.

CHAPTER NINE: DETERMINATION OF SEAWARD LIMITS

1 Article 8 of the 1982 UN Convention on the Law of the Sea reaffirms that, except in the special case of archipelagic states, "waters on the landward side of the baseline of the territorial sea form part of the internal waters of the State."

2 For a discussion of the history and status of the exclusive fishing zone concept, see O'Connell, *International Law of the Sea*, vol. 1, 510–51.

3 The breadth of the territorial sea was fixed at 12 nautical miles (article 3), of the contiguous zone at 24 miles (article 33), and of the exclusive economic zone at 200 miles (article 57), all as measured from the baseline of the territorial sea.

4 The most conspicuous of these "broad shelf" coastal states are the Soviet Union, Canada, the United States, Australia, New Zealand, India, Brazil, the United Kingdom, Argentina, Indonesia, and Ireland.

5 "Delimitation" is used here in the sense of a stage of boundary-making, and not in the sense of the "lateral" type of boundary-making between two states with opposite or adjacent coastlines. See the section entitled "Phases of Boundary-making" in chapter 1.

6 Fulton, *Sovereignty of the Sea*, 537–692; Jessup, *Law of Territorial Waters*, 3–208; O'Connell, *International Law of the Sea*, 124–69. See also Riesenfeld, *Protection of Coastal Fisheries*, 125–263; and Colombos, *International Law of the Sea*, 87–177.

7 The first coming together of modern nation-states for common ("world community") purposes is usually said to have occurred at the peace conference that concluded the Thirty Years' War and adopted the Treaty of Westphalia. The great majority of European nations participated. On the conference's significance for the development of international law, see Gross, "The Peace of Westphalia." Like other scholars, Gross has divided the period after 1648 into four phases of development of international law: (1) the period following the Peace of Westphalia (1648–1815), when the development of legal theory pivoted on the concept of world order; (2) the period following the Congress of Vienna (1815–1919), when legal institutions based on the Concert of Europe began to evolve; (3) the period of the League of Nations (1919–45), when the first steps were taken toward the establishment

of a global network of international organizations; and (4) the period of the United Nations (1945 to the present), when most important legal developments occur within the all-encompassing UN system.

8 Perhaps the best-documented warfare arising from conflicting positions on maritime jurisdiction was the series of Anglo-Dutch wars in the seventeenth century. Fulton, *Sovereignty of the Sea*, 378–516.

9 Even today in the international legal system the concept of state responsibility is weakly developed, and the foundations of justice are unimpressive. See Johnston, "Justice in International Law."

10 On the importance of the shore in pre-modern coastal navigation, see Braudel, *Mediterranean World*, 103–8. On the conditions for discovery, see Parry, *Age of Reconnaissance*, 33–145.

11 It seems that the Dutch were the first to engage in ocean (non-coastal) fishing on an industrial scale, when they started to develop the North Sea herring fishery in the fourteenth century. On early fishing practices, see Johnston, *International Law of Fisheries*, 68–74.

12 See chapter 8. Even by the sixteenth century, the Mediterranean was not yet a sea "within the measure of man." Braudel, *Mediterranean World*, 355.

13 Borgese, *Mines of Neptune*, passim, and Baram, Rice, and Lee, *Marine Mining*.

14 For the great empires the balance between central and local control was determined chiefly by reference to fiscal and public order requirements. In the Ming and Ch'ing periods of imperial China, for example, the local magistrate was delegated a wide range of powers, but the raising of revenues and the maintenance of order were always paramount, and in these matters he was always answerable to the emperor. In the West local autonomy was a fact of life long before the consolidation of central authority, and accommodations had to be made between the two levels through guild arrangements that permitted merchants and artisans to retain local control in return for the tax revenues accruing to central governments. The balance was particularly critical in commercially important seaports, such as the Cinque Ports of England and the ports of the Hanseatic League.

15 From the age of antiquity numerous lords of the sea saw fit to puff up their pretensions to power and authority by claiming dominion over the whole sea washing their shores. Such was the practice of the Minoans, Lydians, Thracians, Rhodians, Phrygians, Cyprians, Phoenicians, Egyptians, Milesians, Carians, Lesbians, Phocaeans, Carinthians, Ionians, Naxians, Eretreans, Aeginians, Lacedemonians, Athenians, Tuscans, Carthaginians, Romans, and Britons, up to the Venetians. Jessup, *Law of Territorial Waters*, 53–4.

16 The earliest example of general allocation of ocean space was between Spain and Portugal through a series of papal bulls and then a treaty late in the twelfth century. See chapter 8, note 56, supra.

17 As early as the seventh century proposals had been made for the application of the thalweg (mid-channel) method of delimitation to rivers, and frequently during the Middle Ages the median line method was held out as applicable to regional seas such as the North Sea and to straits such as the English Channel. This form of claim was disavowed by Elizabeth I of England, and never clearly adopted, although extended jurisdictional powers had long been exercised in the English Channel under the auspices of the Cinque Ports. Fulton, *Sovereignty of the Sea*, 541–4. On thalweg and median line methods of delimitation, see chapter 11.

18 Hugo Grotius, *Mare Liberum* (1609, 1633); John Selden, *Mare Clausum* (1635).

19 Jessup, *Law of Territorial Waters*, ix.

20 Ibid., 4.

21 Schlee, *Edge of an Unfamiliar World*, 81–106.

22 Fulton, *Sovereignty of the Sea*, 84.

23 Ibid., 77, 78. A nautical mile equals 1853 metres, or 1.15 English statute miles. Therefore, a double land-kenning equals 51.884 kilometres, or 32.2 English statute miles. See O'Connell, *International Law of the Sea*, 643–5.

24 The Scottish right to reserved waters within a land-kenning was incorporated in the draft Treaty of Union between England and Scotland in 1604, and later declared to be valid by the Scottish Parliament and Privy Council, but the 1604 draft Treaty of Union was never ratified by the English Parliament. Fulton, *Sovereignty of the Sea*, 84, 192, and 223.

25 Throughout a long (twelve-year) period of bitter wrangling between Scottish and Dutch fishermen and their diplomatic representatives, the States General maintained the position that they had never heard of such a custom! Ultimately, in 1619, they adopted a conciliatory position without yielding on legal principle. "They objected, indeed, that fourteen miles was a greater distance than that at which a person could see the coast from the sea and this exceeded a 'land-kenning' or the range of vision, but they promised to issue orders to their fishermen to keep so far from the land as to be out of sight of people on the shore, and to strongly prohibit them from going nearer." Ibid., 193. This response was the closest the Dutch came to a formal acceptance of the range-of-human-vision rule. Ibid., 546.

26 In 1618 the King of Denmark complained to James I of England and Scotland of Scottish violations within a land-kenning of the Faeroes. Scottish guilt was clearly established, and the excuse that these violations were necessary because of Dutch violations off the Scottish coast was found wanting. A royal proclamation was issued, forbidding Scottish fishermen "to fish within sight of the land of the Isle of Faeroe, but to reserve the [fishings there] to the inhabitants of the said Isle," and to the subjects of the King of Denmark, directing them to "*conform to the law of nations*" under a penalty of confiscation of ships and goods of the persons offending

(emphasis added). Ibid., 176, 544–5.

27 Those supporting one-hundred-mile claims purported to derive legitimacy from the works of Bartolus of Saxo-Ferrato (1314–57), whose authority as a jurist in the Middle Ages was enormous. Supporters of sixty-mile claims claimed descent from Baldus of the Ubaldi (1327–1406), a pupil of Bartolus who had achieved almost equal stature. Ibid., 539–41.

28 The thalweg doctrine was applied to streams and rivers at an early stage of legal development, perhaps as early as the seventh century. But the mid-channel rule was never clearly adopted in the state practice of jurisdictional claims to the ocean. Ibid., 541–4. See chapter 11 infra.

29 Cited ibid., 156.

30 See ibid., passim; Jessup, *Law of Territorial Waters*, passim; O'Connell, *International Law of the Sea*, 124–9; and Colombos, *International Law of the Sea*, 92–4. Bynkershoek's work *De Dominio Maris* (1703) was widely influential throughout the eighteenth century in matters of maritime jurisdiction. More generally, his works on international law reflect the positivist tradition, which places emphasis on actual usage rather than theoretical precept. In this respect he was a philosophical predecessor of Vattel.

31 This famous maxim also appears in the literature as *terrae dominium finitur ubi finitur armorum vis*. By the time of Pufendorf, in the late seventeenth century, the doctrines of *dominium* (ownership) and *imperium* (jurisdiction) had coalesced in the form of the territorial sea doctrine, based on the concept of territorial sovereignty, so that the difference between the two versions of the gunshot rule was negligible, or non-existent.

32 Fulton, *Sovereignty of the Sea*, 680–92.

33 Faced with the choice between the three-mile rule and the cannon-shot rule, many early nineteenth-century writers were inclined to equate the two: that is, to adopt a legal fiction that three miles represented the range of gunfire. See, for example, Wheaton, *A Digest of the Law of Maritime Captures on Prizes* (1815), chapter 2, 55. As it became obvious later in the century that the firing range of guns at sea would exceed three miles, those who objected most strongly to restricting the breadth of the territorial sea to narrow three-mile limits rediscovered, as it were, the merits of the cannon-shot rule. Some insisted, quite logically, that the extent "must necessarily vary with the improvements in artillery." Fulton, *Sovereignty of the Sea*, 595. In espousing a critical view of the three-mile rule, which he regarded as inadequate for purposes of fishery protection, Thomas Wemyss Fulton was one of the early functionalists in the literature. He instinctively favoured expandable seaward limits of coastal state jurisdiction in accordance with expanding technology, and to that extent he was relatively sympathetic to the range-of-gunfire approach to the determination of seaward limits. It appears that Fulton's views, which were hostile to the conventional wisdom of his contemporaries in the field of international law, may have contrib-

uted to the neglect of his great treatise – in addition, perhaps, to resentment that a geographer presumed to write a major work on legal history! Johnston, "Scottish Tradition in International Law."

34 For a detailed account of these trends and counter-trends, see Riesenfeld, *Protection of Coastal Fisheries*.

35 The protectionist policy was described by Elihu Root during the proceedings of the *North Atlantic Fisheries* arbitration in 1910: "The sovereign of the land washed by the sea asserted a new right to protect his subjects and citizens against attack, against invasion, against interference and injury, to protect them against attack threatening their peace, to protect their revenues, to protect their health, to protect their industries. This is the basis and the sole basis on which is established the territorial zone that is established in the international law of to-day." Cited in Jessup, *Law of Territorial Waters*, at 5. In retrospect, it seems inevitable that a policy of protection directed at coastal industries would expand beyond the narrow three-mile limits of the traditional territorial sea.

36 McDougal and Burke, *Public Order of the Ocean*, 521–6.

37 Ibid., 623–7.

38 Many of these arguments were put forward in the form of claims to delimit the boundary between internal waters and the territorial sea. Ibid., 305–445.

39 1982 UN Convention on the Law of the Sea, article 3: "Every State has the right to establish the breadth of its territorial sea up to a limit not exceeding 12 nautical miles, measured from baselines determined in accordance with this Convention."

40 A twelve-mile limit was favoured from the beginning at the first substantive session held at Caracas in 1974. "Agreement on a 12-mile territorial sea is so widespread that there were virtually no references to any other limit in the public debate, although other alternatives are presented in the working paper. Major conditions for acceptance of 12 miles as a maximum limit were agreement on unimpeded transit of straits and acceptance of a 200-mile exclusive economic zone." Stevenson and Oxman, "The 1974 Caracas Session," 13–14.

41 1958 Convention on the Territorial Sea and the Contiguous Zone, article 24(2).

42 1982 UN Convention on the Law of the Sea, article 33(2): "The contiguous zone may not extend beyond 24 nautical miles from the baselines from which the breadth of the territorial sea is measured."

43 The range of human vision was once regarded as a sensible measure of the extent of coastal state jurisdiction. The new 24-mile limits for the contiguous zone take the outer area of that zone beyond the range of vision (even on a clear day, even from the top of a small hill near the shore). It has been argued that the range of human vision is a sensible criterion because of the

desirability of preventing the provocative sight from shore of unwanted or unfriendly foreign vessels, whether warships or fishing vessels. But warships continue to enjoy the right of innocent passage through the territorial sea. If such transit by any foreign vessel is deemed to be unacceptably provocative, the coastal state may, under article 25(3) of the 1982 Convention on the Law of the Sea, "without discrimination in form or in fact among foreign ships, suspend temporarily in specified areas of its territorial sea the innocent passage of foreign ships, if such suspension is essential for the protection of its security, including weapons exercises." As to provocative fishing activities by foreign vessels outside 12-mile territorial sea limits, but still within the range of human vision from the shore, the coastal state now has the authority to restrict and regulate foreign fishing within the 200-mile limits of the exclusive economic zone by virtue of the provisions of Part v of the 1982 Convention. The 24-mile limits apply only for the purposes of the special functional regime within the contiguous zone, as provided in article 33(1). "In a zone contiguous to its territorial sea, described as the contiguous zone, the coastal state may exercise the control necessary to: (a) prevent infringement of its customs, fiscal, immigration or sanitary laws and regulations within its territory or territorial sea; (b) punish infringement of the above laws and regulations committed within its territory or territorial sea." Within 24-mile limits, the coastal state has "an occasional, exclusive competence to control access by prohibition or regulation of entry for certain specified and limited purposes, usually also in relation to limited areas and for temporary periods." McDougal and Burke, *Public Order of the Oceans*, 575–6. It is difficult to envisage circumstances where the exercise of this entitlement would be materially affected by the mere invisibility (to the naked eye) of a foreign vessel entering the outer area of the 24-mile contiguous zone.

The range of gunfire used to be considered relevant to the question of the extent of coastal state jurisdiction. In the contemporary era, ship-to-shore or shore-to-ship gunfire is limited to warlike situations in which the limits of the contiguous zone have no possible relevance. Enforcement of the laws and regulations protected within the contiguous zone may, of course, lead to the use of force, but almost invariably from a vessel employed for that purpose by the coastal state. If the foreign vessel attempts to avoid enforcement measures, it is likely to become the object of hot pursuit under article III of the 1982 Convention. The right of hot pursuit is not, of course, confined within the limits of the contiguous zone, but extends as far as necessary throughout the EEZ and high seas to the territorial sea limits of another state.

On the future of the contiguous zone in the post-classical law of the sea, see Economides, "Contiguous Zone."

44 See Johnston, "International Law of Fisheries."

45 *Fisheries Jurisdiction (United Kingdom of Great Britain and Northern Ireland* v. *Iceland*), interim protection order of 17 August 1972, ICJ Reports 1972, 12; *Fisheries Jurisdiction (Federal Republic of Germany* v. *Iceland*), interim protection order of 17 August 1972, ICJ Reports 1972, 30.

46 ICJ Reports 1973, 3, 49.

47 *Fisheries Jurisdiction (United Kingdom* v. *Iceland*), judgment, ICJ Reports 1974, 3, at 6.

48 *Fisheries Jurisdiction (Federal Republic of Germany* v. *Iceland*), judgment, ICJ Reports 1974, 175.

49 ICJ reports 1974, 34, 205.

50 ICJ reports 1974, 23–4, 192.

51 Some of the judges felt that in offering these facilitative observations, the majority had exceeded the limits of its jurisdiction. See, for example, the dissenting opinion of Judge Petren, ibid., 151–63.

52 1982 UN Convention on the Law of the Sea, article 56(1).

53 Ibid., article 57.

54 The delimitation of a 200-nautical-mile boundary is not seen as a problem apart from defining the baseline from which it is measured." Kerr and Keen, "Hydrographic and Geological Concerns," 145. Yet the drawing of a two-hundred-mile boundary is not entirely without technical complications. "Two viable alternatives are available for [this kind of boundary-making]: either (1) intersecting arcs presently in vogue, or (2) geodetic lines connecting a discrete set of points." Orlin, "Offshore Boundaries," 90. On the problems associated with each, see ibid., 90–1. "Many states, it is believed, will attempt to delimit their 200 nautical mi exclusive economic zones on nautical charts by the arcs-of-circle principle. Owing to distortions caused by map projections and the great distances involved, most of the areas so drawn will not lie 200 nautical mi from the national baseline." Hodgson and Smith, "Single Negotiating Text," 253.

55 "Graphical measurement and plotting of the outer limit of the [EEZ] are liable to error due to the chart projection used. The plotting of this limit should be carried out from geodetically-computed points along the outer limits." Kapoor and Kerr, *Maritime Boundary Delimitation*, 60.

56 Ibid.

57 "Administration" in this context may take the form of regulatory arrangements for the management of conflict between exploration and exploitation of mineral resources on the shelf and fishing, navigation, and the laying of submarine cables and pipelines in superjacent waters or neighbouring areas. Under articles 60 and 80 of the 1982 Convention on the Law of the Sea, the coastal state is authorized for the purposes of conflict management to establish "reasonable safety zones" not exceeding five hundred metres in radius, around "artificial islands, installations and structures" within the exclusive economic zone or on the shelf beyond.

58 O'Connell, *International Law of the Sea*, 440–1.

59 "The continental margins are of particular significance in marine geomorphology because they cover the zone linking the continents with the deep ocean basins, two fundamentally different structural zones in the earth's crust ... Geomorphologically the continental margins can be subdivided into the coastal zone, the continental shelf, the continental slope, and the continental rise, extending from the land towards the deep sea basins." King, *Introduction to Marine Geology*, 68.

60 "The continental shelf links the continental slope to the land. It is a zone of shallow water, varying greatly in dimension from place to place ... It is defined scientifically as the shallow area extending out to the top of the continental slope, where there is a sudden increase of gradient. The depth at which this change of gradient occurs is variable, and so is the shelf width." Ibid., 99. The term "continental shelf" was apparently first used by oceanographers in 1891. Emery, "Geological Limits of the Continental Shelf."

61 The average gradient of the continental slope has been estimated as 4°17′ to a depth of 1,830 metres. The slope is rarely uniform, being diversified by valleys, basins, or canyons. On the whole, the slopes in the Pacific Ocean tend to be steeper (5°20′) than in the Atlantic (3°05′) or the Indian Ocean (2°55′). King, *Introduction to Marine Geology*, 119.

62 "The rise represents a thick apron of sediment, attaining 1.6 km thickness in places. The conformable layers of sediment involved in this great pile of material lap up onto the slope between 1200 and 2000 m. below sea level ... Most of the sediment on the rise has been derived from the land, probably since Cretaceous time." Ibid., 123.

63 In modern times scientists have made major discoveries concerning the relief of the deep ocean floor. Indeed, much of the evidence for the new global tectonics, which has virtually revolutionized the field of geology, is derived from the ocean basins. "The most important geomorphological discovery has been the location of the world-wide ocean ridge system. This system lies central in the Atlantic and Indian Oceans, but not in the Pacific or Arctic Oceans ... The significance of the ridge system is that it is the locus along which new ocean crust is forming. It is the line of sea floor spreading." Ibid., 29. But not all ridges in the ocean basins are similar in structural type and morphology. On the morphology of the open sea, see ibid., 147–90. These "oceanic" ridges on the deep ocean floor (including isolated guyots, sea mounts, and abyssal hills as well as the great mid-ocean mountain ridges) occur far from continental margins and are quite distinct, geologically and geomorphologically, from the "submarine" ridges on the margins.

64 On ocean sediments, see ibid., 191–252.

65 See Borgese, *Mines of Neptune*.

66 See Hall, *Drilling and Producing Offshore*, and the proceedings of the

annual offshore technology conferences held in Houston, Texas. See also Baram, Rice, and Lee, *Marine Mining*.

67 On the emergence of the geographically disadvantaged group at UNCLOS III, see Miles, "Global Ocean Politics," 152–3.

68 For the UNCLOS III provisions on the "common heritage" regime for deep ocean mining, see the 1982 Convention on the Law of the Sea, Part XI.

69 499 *UNTS* 311 (entered in force on 10 June 1964).

70 Text reproduced in 21 *International Legal Materials* 1245 (1982).

71 At its second session, in July 1950, the ILC began consideration of the continental shelf doctrine. "Within seconds, it was clear that the legal regime of coastal state rights over the seabed would not be limited to the geological concept of the continental shelf." Oxman, "Article 1 of the Convention on the Continental Shelf," 259. The prevailing scientific approach was to define the shelf by a depth criterion, such as the two-hundred-metre isobath, but the report of the special rapporteur (Professor François of the Netherlands) opposed such a limit on the ground that it would give different coastal states very unequal areas of the seabed. Instead, he proposed a fixed mileage criterion that would be the same for all states. Most members of the Commission were opposed to this approach but were divided on the merits of depth and exploitability criteria. Ibid., 254–68.

72 "The Commission considered the possibility of adopting a fixed limit for the continental shelf in terms of the depth of the superjacent waters. It seems likely that a limit fixed at a point where the sea covering the continental shelf reaches a depth of 200 metres would at present be sufficient for all practical needs. This depth also coincides with that at which the continental shelf in the geological sense generally comes to an end and the continental slope begins, falling steeply to a great depth. The Commission felt, however, that such a limit would have the disadvantage of instability. Technical developments in the near future might make it possible to exploit resources of the sea-bed at a depth of over 200 metres. Moreover, the continental shelf might well include submarine areas lying at a depth of over 200 metres, but capable of being exploited by means of installations erected in neighbouring areas where the depth does not exceed this limit. Hence the Commission decided not to specify a depth-limit of 200 metres in article 1." 2 *International Law Commission Yearbook* (1951) 141.

73 The committee defined the shelf as "[t]he zone around the continent, extending from the low-water line to the depth at which there is a marked increase of slope to greater depth." The continental slope was defined as "[t]he declivity from the outer edge of the shelf or continental borderlands into greater depths." "Scientific Considerations," reprinted in First United Nations Conference on the Law of the Sea, *Official Records*, vol. I (1958) 39, and cited in McDorman, "Definition of 'Canada Lands'" 196 note 2.

74 This was the 1956 Inter-American Specialized Conference on Conservation of Natural Resources: Continental Shelf and Oceanic Waters. Brown, *Legal Regime of Hydrospace*, 4.

75 On the final ILC debate on delimitation of the continental shelf, see Oxman, "Preparation," 454–72.

76 For a critique of the "textualist" or "plain and natural meaning" school of treaty interpretation, see McDougal, Lasswell, and Miller, *Interpretation of Agreements*, 3–13. This work sets out the case for a contextualist approach to treaty interpretation. Yet articles 31 and 32 of the 1961 Vienna Convention on the Law of Treaties stipulate an essentially textualist approach to treaty interpretation, offering an extremely narrow definition of context for this purpose.

77 For a summary of this approach, see Brown, *Legal Regime of Hydrospace*, 5–8.

78 Ibid., 8–30, 31.

79 In the late 1960s the debate between "narrow shelf" and "broad shelf" proponents took on something of a moral, if not a philosophical, tone. The former identified, more or less consciously, with a neo-Grotian policy favouring the international use of the seabed, and perhaps also with the Grotian normativist philosophy supporting the search for a better world order. The "broad shelf" proponents identified with a neo-Seldenian policy favouring the sovereign rights of the adjacent coastal state, and in the Vattelian empirical tradition pointed to supporting evidence for this position in the evolving pattern of state practice.

80 The prevailing view was that the term "adjacency," unlike "proximity," did not imply the need for a cut-off at some point of remoteness from shore. One writer pointed out that the term "should not be invoked independently of its context. Adjacency in the North Sea context will tell us little that is directly relevant to the South East Pacific." Goldie, "Lexicographical Controversy," 833.

81 ICJ Reports, 1969, 1. See the analysis in the section entitled "Modern Dispute Management" in chapter 11 infra.

82 In this litigation two separate suits were conjoined, since they presented identical issues for judicial resolution. Both were initiated by the Federal Republic of Germany, one against Denmark and the other against the Netherlands.

83 The Court's "most fundamental rule" of "natural prolongation" throws little light on the determination of the outer limits of the shelf, but the judges did contribute indirectly to that end by denying any necessary identity between "adjacency" and "proximity" under article 1 of the 1958 Convention on the Continental Shelf. The notion of adjacency implies proximity only in a general locational sense, but not so as to have a specific limitative effect. Brown, *Legal Regime of Hydrospace*, 31. Narrow shelf

advocates deplore the lack of a rationale for testing the reasonableness of coastal states' claims to extensive areas of the shelf. Some writers continued to debate whether "in view of the advances in technology, which indicate a prospective capability to exploit in any depth of water, it is, or will be, the test of adjacency as set forth in Article 1 of the [1958] Convention that determines the outer limit of coastal state national jurisdiction and control." Finlay, "Outer Limits of the Continental Shelf."

84 On the Canadian situation, for example, see Johnston, *Canada and the Law of the Sea*, 9-13.

85 It is generally acknowledged that the bottom of the slope is "the greatest topographical and structural discontinuity of the Earth." Emery, "Geological Limits of the Continental Shelf," 4. Some scientists suggested that the best seaward boundary of the margin for legal purposes would be the natural boundary between the ocean crust and the "pre-rift continental basement rocks." Ibid., 4-5. "The fact that the Earth's crust of the continents is thick and of a 'granitic' nature, while that beneath the oceans is thin and 'basaltic' in composition, suggested that their meeting point could be the boundary, and it would be in line with the concept of natural prolongation." Kerr and Keen, "Hydrographic and Geological Concerns," 141.

86 Because the bottom of the slope could not be precisely determined in all marginal areas of the legal shelf, a prominent geologist proposed that it should be used not as a line but as a *zone* within which the coastal state could firmly determine its limits by a series of straight lines. Hedberg, *National-International Boundary*, "Ocean Floor Boundaries." For a criticism of the Hedberg formula, see Hodgson and Smith, "Single Negotiating Text," 225-9. But others have supported the Hedberg zonal concept. "It was unfortunately found that there is not in fact a neat division between the two features, but ... rather a zone where it is quite difficult to say with certainty 'this' is oceanic and 'that' is continental." Kerr and Keen, "Hydrographic and Geological Concerns," 141.

87 Doc. NG 6/1. This proposal was based on ideas later published by Gardiner and Robinson in *Technology Ireland* (July 1977), and Gardiner, "Reasons and Methods," 145-70.

88 Kerr and Keen, "Hydrographic and Geological Concerns," 141.

89 Many delegations, including the Arab group, had taken the position that the shelf should not extend beyond two hundred nautical miles, but most were willing to accept a compromise formula in return for concessions on other issues, not least that of revenue-sharing from the exploitation of shelf mineral resources beyond two hundred miles. Oxman, "Seventh Session," 19.

90 Doc. C 2/Informal Meeting/14, 27 April 1978, noted ibid., 20, note 61. The main purpose of the Soviet proposal was to ensure that in no circumstances could the legal shelf extend beyond three hundred nautical miles from the baseline of the territorial sea, and to facilitate the determination of a sea-

ward limit for the "broad shelf" states between the two-hundred-mile and three-hundred-mile marks "on the basis of scientifically sound geological and geomorphological data," or in the absence of such data by reference to the second variant in the Irish formula, namely, a 60-mile cut-off measured from the foot of the slope. Brown, "Delimitation of Offshore Areas."

91 The three-hundred-mile cut-off suggested by the Soviet Union would have excluded "certain areas important to some broad-margin states. Accordingly, the idea emerged of alternative criteria for the cut-off, one expressed in terms of distance from the coast, and the other expressed in terms of distance from a readily identifiable seabed feature, in this case a specified isobath (depth contour) ... For determining the cut-off, the Chairman [Ambassador Aguilar] selected alternative criteria, of 350 nautical miles from the coast (baseline) or 100 nautical miles from the 2,500-meter isobath, whichever is further seaward ..." Oxman, "Eighth Session," 20.

92 "So stylized was the relationship between the opposing sides that for a considerable period, to symbolize its emergence from the center of the table rather than from any delegation, and perhaps to suggest a customary affection for tea among the original chefs, the proposal was called the 'biscuit.'" Ibid., 20 note 66.

93 Geography is represented by the inclusion of a depth criterion of 2,500 metres and of four mileage criteria (200, 60, 100, and 350 nautical miles). Geology is represented by the inclusion of the concept of the "continental margin," comprising "the submerged prolongation of the land mass of the coastal state" and consisting of "the sea-bed and subsoil of the shelf, the slope, and the rise"; and also by the reference to sedimentary rocks. Geomorphology is represented by references to the "foot of the slope," "oceanic ridges," and various "submarine elevations." Jurisprudence is represented chiefly by the inclusion of the phrase "the submarine areas that extend beyond [the] territorial sea throughout the natural prolongation of [the] land territory." This phrase is based on the natural prolongation doctrine enunciated by the International Court of Justice in its 1969 ruling in the *North Sea Continental Shelf* cases, and replaces the phrase "the submarine areas adjacent to the coast but outside the area of the territorial sea," which was incorporated in article 1 of the 1958 Convention on the Continental Shelf. Jurisprudence might also be said to be represented by the introduction of a system of straight lines (connecting fixed points), which is analogous to the straight baseline method for the delineation of baselines and closing lines in certain geographical circumstances.

94 It is somewhat surprising that the majority conceded as much as they did to the margineer minority. It can hardly be maintained that the trade-off on revenue-sharing beyond two hundred miles was especially generous. For a more generous view of a reasonable trade-off, see Hardy et al, *New Regime for the Oceans*, 48.

95 Serious discussion of the proposal to institute a technical commission began in the second substantive session of UNCLOS III, held at Geneva in the spring of 1975. Stevenson and Oxman, "The 1975 Geneva Session," 782. But the idea of a technical commission seems to have originated with Professor Hedberg as early as the late 1960s. See, for example, Hedberg, "National Jurisdiction over Natural Resources," at 164.

96 At least one perception of the original purpose of the suggested international commission was that it would "certify the result" of this kind of national boundary-making. Ibid.

97 Most "broad margin" states took the position that the system to be established should be one of consultation rather than approval; that the commission's function should be supervisory, not judicial or quasi-judicial. Johnston, *Canada and the Law of the Sea*, 90 note 82.

98 Canada, as one of the biggest potential gainers or losers on the margin issue, had taken a hard line in a November 1973 position paper, claiming "rights over the whole of the continental margin comprising not only the physical continental shelf but the continental slope and rise as well." Buzan and Middlemiss, "Canadian Foreign Policy," 25. Canada was, of course, well placed technologically to take advantage of the exploitability criterion throughout its extremely extensive margin in the Northwest Atlantic, and was therefore opposed to the 200-metre, 40-mile, and 200-mile limit proposals. On the other hand, the Canadian position on revenue-sharing and other related issues was more flexible. Ibid., 26–8.

99 "The last line of Article 76(8) is the key one: 'The limits of the shelf established by the coastal State *on the basis* of these recommendations (of the Commission) shall be final and binding.' (emphasis added). Previous wording had indicated that the coastal state would set the outer limit boundary 'taking into account' these recommendations. The crucial question is whether the coastal state can unilaterally set its outer limit boundary and only acknowledge the recommendations by the Commission. It was felt that the wording 'taking into account' would permit such unilateral undertakings. The wording 'on the basis' was an attempt to tie the broad-margin states to the recommendations of the Commission. Canada suggested that this wording 'appears to encroach upon the sovereign rights of the coastal State', and that the wording 'could be interpreted as giving the Commission the function and power to determine the outer-limits of the continental shelf of the coastal State.' Where the coastal state and the Commission agree on the location of the outer limit of the continental margin no problems will arise. It is expected that the broad margin state and the Commission will work together to reach an accommodation. It is in the situation of irreconcilable differences that uncertainty arises. The Commission is not a legally oriented body and is not equipped for dispute settlement. The coastal state is purportedly 'denied the extraordinary power to insist that all other parties to the Convention are bound to accept its views regarding the proper

application of Article 76.' While this may have been the general intention of the draftsmen, this is not clear from the language used and the lack of an expressly provided dispute settlement provision leaves the ultimate determination unclear." McDorman, "Definition of 'Canada Lands,'" 206–7.

100 Hedberg, for example, regrets that the 1982 Convention "persists in redefining the classic and very useful, geomorphic and geographic term 'continental shelf' to make it not a shelf at all but a legalistic or political term to indicate not only the true geomorphic continental shelf but also the continental slope and even the continental rise – and thus some of the deepest parts of the ocean. This is a completely needless and wanton procedure and will be an endless source of confusion. The term should be used in its original sense as a geomorphic unit of the continental margin." Hedberg, "Boundary Provisions," 339–40.

101 See, for example, McKelvey, "UNCLOS III Definition of the Continental Shelf," 465–6.

102 See the letter from Dr McKelvey published in 12 *Ocean Development and International Law* 343 (1983).

103 Hedberg, "National Jurisdiction over Natural Resources," deplores the "[c]onfusion of boundary needs for mineral resources with those for fishing," which is reflected in the multifunctional two-hundred-mile limit for the exclusive economic zone. "There is no reason why the boundaries for jurisdiction over *mineral resources* beneath the ocean should necessarily have to be the same as the boundaries for jurisdiction over *fish* in the waters of the ocean ... What we need is a simple base-of-slope-related boundary everywhere (continents and islands) for mineral resources ... and a simple distance-from-shore boundary (200 nautical miles from shore?) everywhere for fishing ..." (at 338). On this functionalist position, see Brown, "Continental Shelf and Exclusive Economic Zone," 383.

104 Hedberg, "Boundary Provisions," 329; McKelvey, "UNCLOS III Definition of the Continental Shelf," 470; Kerr and Keen, "Hydrographic and Geological Concerns," 145. In questioning the method of determining the foot of the slope by reference to "the point of maximum change in the gradient at its base," as provided in paragraph 4(b), Kerr and Keen note that "[i]n an examination of eleven detailed profile samples along the eastern Canadian continental margin, it was found that his method did not allow the base of the slope to be determined without ambiguity. The transition from the slope to the flat ocean floor was in most of the samples quite gradual ..." They challenge the claim that "it is now recognized that the base of the slope can be located for those margins that extend beyond 200 nautical miles." Ibid., 146.

105 McKelvey, "UNCLOS III Definition of the Continental Shelf," 468–9; and McMillan, "Extent of the Continental Shelf," 151. Paragraph 6 may be the most confusing part of article 76. The listing of "plateaux, rises, caps,

banks, and spurs" takes no account of the fact that these differences in geologic origin and composition are "only indirectly, if at all, reflected in the names that have been applied to their component geomorphic features. This is partly because many submarine features were named long before their geologic character was understood. Even more important, however, is the fact that one of the principles guiding the naming of undersea features is that the name describes only the topographic configuration of the feature and not its geologic origin or composition. Names such as ridges, rises and seamounts have thus been given to some undersea features that are a part of the deep-ocean floor and to others that are a part of the continental margin." McKelvey, "UNCLOS III Definition of the Continental Shelf," 468.

106 Ibid., 470–1; Kerr and Keen, "Hydrographic and Geological Concerns," 141; Hedberg, "Ocean Floor Boundaries." The sediment-thickness test requires sophistication in the use of seismic reflection techniques. McMillan, "Extent of the Continental Shelf," 152.

107 Kerr and Keen, "Hydrographic and Geological Concerns," 146; Crosby, "Definition of the Continental Shelf," 477.

108 "The measurement of distance and the location of position many miles offshore has reached a high state of refinement using modern satellite positioning systems. The location of the position of drilling platforms using satellite methods can now be obtained to better than 10 metres, and the position of moving vessels to 50 metres ... The measurement of depth of 2,500 metres is a much more difficult matter as acoustical science has moved more slowly. Hydrographers consider that, provided they have a reasonable knowledge of the density structure of the water column, they can measure depths to +/–1%. With considerable care in measuring the density during each echo sounding measurement, and by using narrow-beam echo sounding equipment, it is possible that the figure could be improved to perhaps half that amount, but such data is not generally available for the world's oceans. Although +/–1% of 2,500 metres is only [25] metres, it is to be realized that these depths normally occur in areas of the ocean where the slope of the sea floor is often less than one degree. This could result in a considerable horizontal offset in the position of the boundary in the order of several nautical miles." Kerr and Keen, "Hydrographic and Geological Concerns," 147.

109 Under paragraph 9 of article 76 the coastal state is required to deposit geodetic data with the UN secretary general. The commission established under the Convention will have to decide whether its task includes the scrutinizing of baselines from which the two-hundred-mile limit is measured, and thus will become involved in geodetic difficulties associated with the use of the vertical and horizontal datum. "In many parts of the world the configuration of the coastline is imprecisely known, particularly the position of off-lying islands and rocks. This situation may be aggravated

where there are large tidal ranges, pack ice, and even rough seas which obscure the precise position or elevation of the low-water line. The matter of vertical datum has been a matter for dispute in several cases, including the Anglo-French Arbitration with respect to the Eddystone Rock. The above matters are not unsolvable but may require the extensive use of precise geodetic control and photogrammetry and the establishment of a common vertical datum and definition of low water. In all cases where boundaries are to be defined in terms of geographical coordinates [as in paragraph 7 of article 76], they must be reserved to a horizontal datum, and ideally this should be a world-wide datum." Ibid., 145.

110 The drafting of foot-of-slope lines on a world map raises a variety of difficulties. "It must be cautioned that the bathymetric maps in some parts of the world have been interpreted from sparse data and that ideally the base of the slope should be determined from measured profiles, and that the bathymetric maps will normally provide only an approximate position for this keystone of the boundary delineation." Ibid., 146.

111 McMillan, "Extent of the Continental Shelf," 151–2.

112 Ibid., 150–3.

113 See, for example, Hedberg, "Boundary Provisions," 340–1.

114 See the letter from Professor Hedberg published in 12 *Ocean Development and International Law* 345, at 347–8 (1983).

115 "Certain technical and administrative matters must be examined in detail by the Commission, such as whether their task involves scrutinizing the baselines from which the territorial sea is measured, the use of horizontal and vertical datums, the precision of depth measurements, the interpretation of the base of the slope, the exact definition of an undersea feature in terms of its generic nomenclature, the methods and accuracy of determining the thickness of sediments, and the precision with which boundaries can be plotted on charts of different scales." Kerr and Keen, "Hydrographic and Geological Concerns," 147–8.

116 In September 1985 Chile claimed sovereignty over the continental shelves of Easter and Sala y Gomez Islands, extending to a distance of 350 nautical miles from its territorial sea baseline. One week later Ecuador claimed jurisdiction over the shelf between its mainland and the Galapagos. Both claims provoked protests from the United States as being in violation of article 76, but a case can be made that they are "cognizable" under that provision. Ramakrishna, Bowen, and Archer, "Outer Limits."

CHAPTER TEN: DELINEATION OF BASELINES AND CLOSING LINES

1 There are hundreds, and probably thousands, of national statutes around the world that are applicable to "national," "inland," "local," "patrimon-

ial," or otherwise designated areas of water described in terms that have no precise significance in international law. Often these national designations have no clear relationship to the coastal areas of "internal waters," "archipelagic waters," the "territorial sea," and the "contiguous zone," which are terms of art in public international law. A major task of reconciliation confronts jurists, drafters, and judges almost everywhere. To compound the problem, most judges on national tribunals, and most counsel arguing before them, have little knowledge of international law. With the extension of coastal state jurisdiction in the new law of the sea, the "interaction of international law and municipal law is today one of the main issues of legal action." O'Connell, *International Law of the Sea*, xii. This seems especially true of the problems of baseline delineation, but it also applies to issues involving vessels or rigs on the continental shelf, such as those arising from the conflict between flag state and coastal state jurisdiction. On some Canadian problems of "legal development" after UNCLOS III, see Johnston, *Canada and the Law of the Sea*, 52–5.

2 1982 UN Convention on the Law of the Sea, articles 8 (1), 49 (1), 33 (2), 57, and 76. The exclusive fishing zone, as such, was not dealt with at UNCLOS III, on the ground that it is subsumed under the new multifunctional regime of the exclusive economic zone. Given this subsumption, it must be supposed that in the customary international law of the sea its baseline should be drawn in the same way as that of the EEZ. O'Connell, *International Law of the Sea*, 510–51.

3 McDougal and Burke, *Public Order*, 307.

4 "The people in regions near the ocean, and sometimes of whole states, must on occasion rely for sustenance and general livelihood upon the produce of the ocean waters, and sometimes, in otherwise non-productive regions, these peoples come to be highly dependent upon ocean areas immediately adjacent to them. The result over a period of time may be the emergence of strong identifications with the proximate geographic areas and the formation of attitudes that outside groups must not intrude into such areas unless invited or forced to do so. Again, this attitude of exclusivity may ensue not from historical patterns of life, but from emerging and anticipated conceptions of new needs, caused by changes in technology and customs, whose satisfaction is expected to be partially derived from uses of maritime resources." Ibid., 308.

5 The concept of a closing line has been applied to several kinds of coastal waters, but especially to river mouths and estuaries, bays (including firths, gulfs, and channels), inlets (such as fjords), and other forms of historic waters.

6 "The most important policy issues relate to differential impact upon inclusive and exclusive interests ... In concrete terms, the policy issues involve delimitation of the areas over which comprehensive coastal competence

ought to be permitted from the areas in which all states should be permitted relative freedom of use. The problem is, in other words, that of achieving an appropriate balance between inclusive and exclusive competence and use by delimiting the areas within which the one or the other is to be given greater weight." McDougal and Burke, *Public Order*, 316–17. Since these words were published in 1962, the balance has shifted very perceptibly toward the "exclusive" (coastal state) end of the spectrum, as far as the allocation of authority over the ocean is concerned. By the same token, it is more important than ever to have clear criteria in international law to restrain geographically favoured coastal states from manipulating the rules of baseline delineation to their advantage, so as to acquire exclusive authority over excessively extensive areas of the ocean.

7 The distinction between these two coastal regimes has been described as "a contrivance of international law resulting from the development of the concept of innocent passage." O'Connell, *International Law of the Sea*, 107.

8 The King's Chambers were "the large as well as small indentations around the coasts of England and Wales within which hostile actions of belligerents were prohibited." Bouchez, *Regime of Bays*, 31. The doctrine of "King's Chambers" seems to have originated, and also expired, in the Stuart dynasty of England. "One of the first acts of James I was to cause to be laid down on charts the precise limits of the bays or 'chambers' along the English coast, within which all hostile actions of belligerents were prohibited. This sensible proceeding ... is not to be regarded as in any sense an assertion of maritime sovereignty or jurisdiction beyond what was customary; and it does not appear that any other prince or state contested the right of the king to treat these bays and arms of the sea as territorial in respect of neutrality." Fulton, *Sovereignty of the Sea*, 9. In 1605 the limits of the King's Chambers were delineated by the Jury of Trinity House. Ibid., appendix E, 753–4. Thereafter large semi-enclosed areas like Cardigan Bay, the Bristol Channel, the Wash, and the Thames estuary were claimed as neutral waters. See also O'Connell, *International Law of the Sea*, 339–41.

9 Early commentators on the *fauces terrae* doctrine differed over the rationale to be applied. Some applied merely the "range of vision" rule, others the "range of visual knowledge." By the former it is enough that the "other side" is visible from one side of an indentation; by the latter, an observer on one shore must be able to see "what is done" on the other. O'Connell, *International Law of the Sea*, 341–5. The difference between the two may be considerable.

10 13 Richard II, c. 5 ("in what places the admiral's jurisdiction doth run"), Statutes-at-large II, 340–1. This early statute prescribed that the Court of Admiralty should not meddle in any matter "within the realm, but only in things done on the sea." All "contracts, pleas and quarrels, and all other things rising within the bodies of counties, as well as by land as by water as

above, and also wreck of the sea, shall be tried, determined, discussed and remedied by the laws of the land, and not before nor by the admiral, nor his lieutenant in any wise." This statute was the source of the common law rule in England that the waters within the jaws of land where one could see from side to side were within the body of a county. Ibid., 343.

11 *Regina* v. *Keyn (The Franconia)* [1876] LR 2 Ex. Dir. 63. For an extended analysis and commentary, see O'Connell, *International Law of the Sea*, 93–106. The finding of the court was essentially that the territorial sea, in its modern sense, lay outside the counties adjoining. By at least one interpretation, this finding offered a distinction between the "realm," which was limited to the extent of all the counties of England, and the "territory," which extended to the seaboard limits of the territorial sea. O'Connell argues that the true ratio decidendi in *R.* v. *Keyn* was that common law judicial jurisdiction terminated at the low-water mark and that admiralty jurisdiction was confined to British ships, even though this interpretation means that the court thereby opened up a jurisdictional hiatus beyond that mark as far as non-British vessels are concerned.

12 For their administrative history, see Hull, ed., *Cinque Ports, 1432–1955*, and Jessup, *Cinque Ports*.

13 The doctrine of regalia, derived from Roman law, belongs to the municipal level of legal development. O'Connell, *International Law of the Sea*, 111–13.

14 See, for example, Herman, "Offshore Territorial Claims."

15 For a review of North American trends, see Charney, "Offshore Jurisdiction."

16 Blum, *Historic Titles*, 241–340. The origins of the theory of "historic bays" go back only to the nineteenth century, when it became necessary to fix the boundary between the high seas and "national" waters, but evidence of local usage, strategic significance, and other considerations may be found as early as pre-classical times. Historically, the concept of "historic waters" evolved from the more limited concept of "historic bays." The former concept denotes "all waters which, owing to an unusual geographical configuration, combined with overriding economic interests, strategic factors, etc. are subjected to the riparian State's authority, in derogation of the normally applicable rules of international law." Ibid., 261. See also O'Connell, *International Law of the Sea*, 417–38.

17 "The economic interests of the coastal state may manifest themselves in two ways. Firstly, the water area comprised by bays is often an important fishing area. Secondly, bays and especially estuaries of rivers give access to important industrial centres and, moreover, are the places which are by nature eminently fit for the construction of harbour works. The need to protect the vital centres, as well as the fact that bays in general can be easily defended, clearly prove the close relation existing between the bay or estu-

ary on the one hand and the enclosing territory on the other hand." Bouchez, *Regime of Bays*, 108.

18 This functional limitation created difficulties for Selden, who wished to use the precedent to support the much broader Stuart claims to sovereignty in the *mare clausum*. O'Connell, *International Law of the Sea*, 340.

19 In 1630, for example, the boroughs ("burghs") of Scotland petitioned to have foreign fishermen excluded from the Firth of Clyde, Moray Firth, Solway Firth, and the Firth of Lothian (now the Firth of Forth), by virtue of a system of straight closing lines. It was agreed by the boroughs that the reservation of these waters was essential for the subsistence of the people. The Scots wished to exclude the English as much as the Dutch, despite the Union of Crowns in 1603! A final solution was achieved in 1632, during the reign of Charles I, when designated areas within the Firths of Lothian and Clyde were reserved for Scottish fishermen. Fulton, *Sovereignty of the Sea*, 209–45. A similar concession for the Moray Firth was withheld, and this area of inshore waters was later to become the focus of diplomatic controversy and legal fame. Ibid., 718–40. For a brief account of the "great firths" of Scotland, see Bouchez, *Regime of Bays*, 33–41.

20 The British were reluctant to abandon the headland rule in North America, where they laid claim to sovereignty over large bays and gulfs of considerable military, as well as economic, significance. Ibid., 47. On the fishery interests at stake in the bay delimitation issue in the Northwest Atlantic, see Johnston, *International Law of Fisheries*, 190–205.

21 For the text of this award, see Scott, ed., *Hague Court Reports*, vol. 1, 1ff.

22 Jessup, *Territorial Waters and Maritime Jurisdiction*, 360.

23 Bouchez, *Regime of Bays*, 110.

24 Ibid., 111, 113.

25 Ibid., 114.

26 The conference agreed to apply the three-mile territorial sea limit to bays, the distance of three miles to be measured "from a straight line drawn across the bay, in the part nearest the entrance, at the first point where the width does not exceed ten miles," as provided in article 2 of the convention. Johnston, *International Law of Fisheries*, 178–9; Bouchez, *Regime of Bays*, 28.

27 The tribunal was asked, among other things, to construe the scope and meaning of article 1 of the 1818 Convention of Commerce. Britain contended that the United States had renounced the right to fish within all bays and within three miles thereof: that is, that the word 'bays' in the 1818 convention was used in both a geographical and territorial sense, thereby excluding American fishermen from all bodies of water on the non-treaty coast known as "bays" on the charts of the period. The United States maintained that the word "bays" was used in the territorial sense and

therefore limited to small bays; that only such bays whose entrance was less than double the Anglo-American marine league (that is, less than six miles) were renounced; and that in such cases the three nautical miles were to be measured from a line drawn across the bays where they were six miles or less in width. Johnston, *International Law of Fisheries*, 202–3.

28 It was held that the word "bays" must be construed in its geographical sense, and in the case of such bays "the three marine miles are to be measured from a *straight line drawn across the body of water at the place where it ceases to have the configuration and characteristic of a bay*. At all other places the three marine miles are to be measured following the *sinuosities of the coast* [emphasis added]." Scott, *Hague Court Reports*, 187–8. In view of the difficulties involved in the practical application of this rule, it was recommended that in the case of bays not specified in the 1818 treaty the limits of exclusion should be "three miles seaward from a straight line across the bay in the part nearest the entrance *at the first point where the width does not exceed ten miles* [emphasis added]." Ibid., 188. But for a few designated bays, "where the configuration of the coast and the local climatic conditions are such that foreign fishermen, when within the geographic headlands, might reasonably and bona fide believe themselves on the high seas," the tribunal recommended limits of exclusion between specified headlands. Accordingly, the Court introduced a diversified system of baselines for the bays of the North Atlantic coast of North America, and it is only partly correct to say that it adopted the 10-mile rule. Jessup, *Territorial Waters and Maritime Jurisdiction*, 363–82.

29 McDougal and Burke, *Public Order*, 354.

30 In the *Alaska Boundary Case* (UN Reports, vol. XV, 481 at 496, 498), Lord Alverstone said that the word "coast" has no recognized meaning in international law. Cited in O'Connell, *International Law of the Sea*, 170 note 1.

31 It can be argued that delineation of the baseline should be governed at least as much by land use as by sea use considerations; but to the extent that the adoption of a low-water mark introduces a conflict between law and cartography, it might be observed that navigation charts served well for centuries before the adoption of legal boundaries in the ocean.

32 The US expert S. Whittemore Boggs proposed that the baseline be located at points on "whatever line of sea level is adopted in the charts of the coastal State," which in practice meant the high-tide mark. McDougal and Burke, *Public Order*, 323.

33 In UN Legislative Series, *Laws and Regulations on the Regime of the Territorial Sea* (1957), 738–41.

34 Those who argued for the adoption of the navigability criterion maintained essentially that the flag state's right of innocent passage in the territorial sea should begin from the point where the sea first became navigable. Advocates of the tidal-variation criterion, focusing on the elevation of the tide at

the moment when the relevant event occurred, accepted a natural boundary that was mobile, not fixed. The view of those who supported the coastal batteries criterion was, of course, consistent with the range of gunfire criterion for the measurement of territorial waters. The discretionary argument rested on the notion of coastal state prerogative with a view to the "vital national interest" in security within the inshore area of coastal waters. O'Connell, *International Law of the Sea*, 172.

35 McDougal and Burke, *Public Order*, 322–4.

36 O'Connell identifies eight tidal levels: (1) lowest astronomical tide – highest astronomical tide; (2) mean low-water spring tide – mean high-water spring tide; (3) mean low-water neaps tide – mean high-water neaps tide; (4) mean sea level; (5) mean higher high-water; (6) mean lower high-water; (7) mean higher low-water; and (8) mean lower low-water (at 173–4). These terms continue to create technical difficulties. See, for example, Fischer, "Mean Sea Level," and Hamon and Godfrey, "Mean Sea Level."

37 At the Hague Conference, Germany proposed that a draft convention should refer to the "sea level adopted in the charts" of the coastal state that might be based on the geodesic principles applied by the state in question. O'Connell, *International Law of the Sea*, 172.

38 McDougal and Burke, *Public Order*, 373–98.

39 Four organizations or groups in particular made useful contributions to the codificatory process in the late 1920s and early 1930s: the Institut de Droit International, the American Institute of International Law, the International Law Association, and the Harvard Research.

40 Covenant of the League of Nations, articles 13 and 14.

41 The process of codification was first attempted through international conferences such as the First and Second Hague Peace Conferences of 1899 and 1907, and by jurists whose drafts were discussed at meetings sponsored by the League of Nations and other organizations such as the Pan-American Union. In 1924 the Council of the League of Nations appointed a committee of sixteen jurists to report on the need for codification of international law. The committee reported back to the Council in 1927 recommending seven subject areas as "ripe" for codification: (1) nationality; (2) territorial waters; (3) responsibility of states for damage done in their territory to the person or property of foreigners; (4) diplomatic privileges and immunities; (5) procedure of international conferences and procedure for the conclusion and drafting of treaties; (6) piracy; and (7) exploitation of the products of the sea. Three were related to the ocean. Oppenheim, *International Law*, vol. 1, 56–70.

42 Charter of the United Nations, articles 92–96.

43 Ibid., article 13(1)(a).

44 In article 15 of the Statute of the ILC the expression "codification of international law" is "used for convenience as meaning the more precise formu-

lation and systematization of rules of international law in fields where there already has been extensive state practice precedent and doctrine." In the same provision, the expression "progressive development of international law" is said to refer to "the preparation of draft conventions on subjects which have not yet been regulated by international law or in regard to which the law has not yet been sufficiently developed in the practice of States."

45 Resolution 174(II) of the General Assembly, 21 November 1947, GAOR, II, resolution (A/519), 105–10. For a description of the commission's work in the early years, see Briggs, *International Law Commission*.

46 Statute of ILC, articles 16–17.

47 The International Law Commission consists of fifteen members "who shall be persons of recognized competence in international law," in the language of article 2(1) of its statute, but the members are elected by a political process in the General Assembly.

48 The ILC is required to submit to the General Assembly a draft and explanatory report with recommendations, but article 15 of its statute assumes, in the case of progressive development, that the final draft will take the form of a convention suitable for negotiation in the diplomatic arena.

49 "Today ... we live in a romantic age. The structure of the nation-state system has put a premium on the notion of national sovereignty and the need for consent. The vast size of the system, still expanding, has created the need for immense and elaborate undertakings at the global level of international organization. The United Nations 'system' consists essentially of a succession of conferences, propelled by an assortment of governmental initiatives and maintained by an arsenal of secretariats ... The arena of conference diplomacy, an outlet for more or less reasoned expression of political sentiment, is a stage. Conference diplomacy is *drama*, both in structure and content. Viewed from this theatrical perspective, the requirements of 'good' legal development today are likely to be interpreted in accordance with an ideal composed of 'romantic' virtues. A universally acceptable legal instrument in the present age is not required to possess all the classical characteristics of the ideal code. Symmetry, clarity, consistency, and the other virtues associated with the classical ideal, are expected to compete with and often yield to a current of 'romantic' sentiments in favour of diversity rather than uniformity, justice rather than order, imagination rather than logic. Legal development is a matter for which passion may be appropriate. Participation and spontaneity are felt to be virtues in themselves, even to the point that the 'process' may be judged to be more important that the 'product.'" Johnston, "Political Thought in International Law," 198–9.

50 *Anglo-Norwegian Fisheries*, judgment of 18 December 1951, ICJ Reports 1951, 116.

51 *North Sea Continental Shelf*, judgment of 20 February 1969, ICJ Reports 1969, 3.

52 1982 UN Convention on the Law of the Sea, articles 46–54.

53 Supra note 50, at 131.

54 A mathematical solution to the problem of defining the relationship between the dimensions and configurations of bays was first attempted at the global level at the Hague Codification Conference in 1930. Mathematical proposals were offered by Britain, France, Germany, and the United States. During the conference the British and German proposals were withdrawn in favour of the American. For a description of the latter by its author, see Boggs, "Delimitation of the Territorial Sea." For a detailed analysis of the mathematical problems involved, see Münch, *Die Technischen Fragen des Küstenmeeres* (1934), 95 et seq., summarized in O'Connell, *International Law of the Sea*, 390–2. See also François, *Handboek van het Volkenrecht* vol. 1, 136–7.

55 The semi-circle test adopted by the ILC and UNCLOS I was a simplified version of the Boggs proposal presented in 1930. O'Connell, *International Law of the Sea*, 392–3.

56 516 *UNTS* 205.

57 "Do they contain independent standards, each of which must be satisfied? Or is the second sentence a specification of the standard in the first?" O'Connell, *International Law of the Sea*, 393. In the *Louisiana* case of 1969 (394 U.S. 11, at 54), the Supreme Court of the United States construed article 7(2) as treating the semi-circle test as a minimal requirement, which may not serve to establish what curvatures qualify as bays if other factors are absent. Ibid., 394.

58 "If it is taken literally, so as to mean that the waters of the bay are not directly open to the sea, then it restricts the category of bays susceptible of treatment under Article 7 to very few actual bays in the world. If it is to mean that the indentation has land on three sides, it adds nothing to the result achieved by applying the semi-circle test." Ibid., 393.

59 Bouchez, *Regime of Bays*, 20–1

60 O'Connell, *International Law of the Sea*, 398.

61 Ibid., 396–402

62 Kapoor and Kerr, *Maritime Boundary Delimitation*, 48–50. For a detailed analysis, see Beazley, *Maritime Limits and Baselines*, and Hodgson and Alexander, *Objective Analysis of Special Circumstances*, 3–22.

63 "The real or alleged economic (fishing) needs of coastal states unquestionably played a most important role in the events which led to the twenty-four mile baseline decision. The basic issue in the *North Atlantic Fisheries* case concerned access to fisheries, although in its decision the Tribunal emphasized other factors which might justify inclusion of bays within internal waters. The *Anglo-Norwegian Fisheries* case, too, involved conflicting

claims for access to coastal fisheries and the Court there placed explicit emphasis on the economic needs of the coastal populace, stressing also the unusually complicated geographic configuration of the Norwegian coast. Consideration of wealth and well-being, with most stress on the latter, were clearly influential here in leading the Court to reject the ten-mile baseline as part of the customary international law.

"The major defect of the twenty-four-mile baseline is that it bears no necessary relationship to the exclusive coastal needs which might warrant creation of internal waters. The result is that literally thousands of square miles of waters may now be removed from any type of inclusive use on the undemonstrated assumption that an allocation to exclusive use and competence is more productive of total values than alternatives permitting more inclusive use." McDougal and Burke, *Public Order*, 370.

64 1958 Convention on the Territorial Sea and Contiguous Zone, article 7(1). On the international law related to bays enclosed by the territory of more than one state, see Bouchez, *Regime of Bays*, 116–98, and Strohl, *International Law of Bays*, 369–98. In the case of bays with two or more bordering states, boundaries have to be negotiated and, as part of the diplomacy involved, agreement would be necessary on baselines delineated in accordance with provisions other than the bay closing line rule. Kapoor and Kerr, *Maritime Boundary Delimitation*, 43.

65 1958 Convention on the Territorial Sea and Contiguous Zone, article 7(6). On the international law related to historic bays, see Bouchez, *Regime of Bays*, 199–237; and Strohl, *International Law of Bays*, 231–368. On a recent controversy over a historic bay claim, see Spinnato, "Historic and Vital Bays." On the straight baseline method, see the section below on complex coastlines.

66 For a study of disputes arising out of the 1958/1982 treaty provision on the delineation of bay closing lines, see Westerman, *Juridical Bay*.

67 Coastlines with these characteristics have been described as "rugged and complex." McDougal and Burke, *Public Order*, 398.

68 ICJ Reports 1951, 127.

69 Ibid., 118–19.

70 Ibid., 120–1.

71 O'Connell, *International Law of the Sea*, 201–2.

72 "Points 3 to 11 appear to be a set of propositions which, in the form of definitions, principles or rules, purport to justify certain contentions and do not constitute a precise and direct statement of claim. The subject of the dispute being quite concrete, the Court cannot entertain the suggestion ... that the Court should deliver a Judgment which for the moment would confine itself to adjudicating on the definitions, principles of rules stated ... These are elements which might furnish reasons in support of the Judgment, but cannot constitute the decision. It further follows that, even under-

stood in this way, these elements may be taken into account only so far as they would appear to be relevant for deciding the sole question in dispute ..." ICJ Reports 1951, 126. These comments may be interpreted as a refusal by the Court to engage in judicial rule-making, especially as it was known that the International Law Commission was soon to begin a debate on many of these propositions in preparation for the law-making process of UNCLOS I. In short, it seems that the Court wished to focus merely on the question whether the Norwegian baselines were in violation of international law – that is, "not contrary to international law." Ibid., 124. It might be added, from a functionalist perspective, that the British advocacy in this case represents an extreme example of the "unitarian" approach to judicial boundary-making; and that the decision can be seen in retrospect as the first of the modern adjudications to strive instead for a contextualist approach.

73 "The Court has no difficulty in finding that, for the purpose of measuring the breadth of the territorial sea, it is the low-water mark as opposed to the high-water mark, or the mean between the two tides, which has generally been adopted in the practice of States. This criterion is the most favourable to the coastal State and clearly shows the character of territorial waters as appartenant to the land territory." Ibid., 128.

74 Ibid., 130.

75 "In these circumstances the Court deems it necessary to point out that although the ten-mile rule has been adopted by certain States both in their national law and in the treaties and conventions, and although certain arbitral decisions have applied it as between these States, other States have adopted a different limit. Consequently, the ten-mile rule has not acquired the authority of a general rule of international law." Ibid., 131.

76 Ibid., 128.

77 Ibid., 128–9

78 Ibid., 129, 130.

79 Ibid., 131.

80 Ibid.

81 Ibid., 132.

82 Ibid., 133.

83 Ibid., 133.

84 Ibid., 133–43.

85 Dissenting judgments were rendered by Sir Arnold McNair (at 158–85) and Judge J.E. Read (186–206). Judge Hsu Mo, in his separate opinion (154–7), agreed with the majority on the validity of the method, but dissented on the validity of certain baselines. Judge Alvarez, concurring, provided an individual opinion (145–53).

86 Conservative international lawyers, fearing encroachments on the freedom of the high seas, regretted the looseness of the Court's "general direction of the coast" constraint on the application of the straight baseline method of

delineation. Others, less concerned with retaining the narrowest area of territorial waters than with restricting the discretion of the coastal state, pointed out that some states would be likely to conclude from the Court's ruling that the use of baselines departing from the mainland coast is permissible for relatively non-complex coasts – for example, where only a relatively few islands are near the coast. McDougal and Burke, *Public Order*, 387. But many commentators hailed the decision as innovative, applauding the Court's willingness to recognize the coastal state's legitimate interests and especially the emphasis placed on its economic and social dependence on its inshore waters. O'Connell, *International Law of the Sea*, 205; and Johnston, *International Law of Fisheries*, 182. For a technical analysis of the straight baseline method applied to the Norwegian coastline, see Hodgson and Alexander, *Objective Analysis of Special Circumstances*, 23–44.

87 Most members of the Commission accepted the general thrust of the Court's decision. The main issue in the ILC debate concerned the degree of discretion to be allowed the coastal state in baseline delineation. This debate eventually focused on the question whether or not to have a mileage restriction on the length of straight baselines. On this question the ILC was evenly divided. At its sixth session the Commission considered a compromise proposal that, while ten miles should be the general rule, longer lines might be drawn, provided that no point on such a line is more than two miles from the coast. At the following session, by a one-vote margin, the Commission voted to delete this provision, ensuring a victory for the proponents of broad coastal discretion; but the extreme suggestion that the straight baseline system could be used even for coasts with only minor curvatures was defeated. On this debate, see McDougal and Burke, *Public Order*, 402–6.

88 Delegates at UNCLOS I, like the members of the ILC, were split on the question of a limitation on the length of straight baselines. While the majority agreed that such baselines should not exceed fifteen miles, except for historical reasons or in exceptional geographical circumstances, this provision did not obtain the necessary two-thirds majority in the plenary session. On the UNCLOS I debate, see ibid., 406–8.

89 O'Connell, *International Law of the Sea*, 208.

90 Ibid., 211.

91 "(1) The baselines for measuring the breadth of the territorial sea determined in accordance with articles 7, 9 and 10 or the limits derived therefrom, and the lines of delimitation drawn in accordance with articles 12 and 15 shall be shown on charts of a scale or scales adequate for ascertaining their position. Alternatively, a list of geographical co-ordinates of points, specifying the geodetic datum, may be substituted. (2) The coastal State shall give due publicity to such charts or lists of geographical co-ordinates

and shall deposit a copy of each such chart or list with the Secretary-General of the United Nations." This provision is at least a partial response to concerns that general criteria such as the "general direction of the coast" guideline would become meaningless unless relatively large-scale charts were used. O'Connell, *International Law of the Sea*, 205–6.

92 "(2) Where because of the presence of a delta and other natural conditions the coastline is highly unstable, the appropriate points may be selected along the furthest seaward extent of the low-water line, and notwithstanding subsequent regression of the low-water line, the straight baselines shall remain effective until changed by the coastal State in accordance with this Convention."

93 For a concise account of the various ways in which the article 7 provision has been ignored or circumvented, see Prescott, "Delimitation of Marine Boundaries." This prominent analyst of boundary-making practices concludes that article 7 is in danger of becoming a dead letter. Maritime powers are especially concerned that such abuses may close off considerable areas of navigable coastal waters under the regime of internal waters. The case for a stricter definition of terms is beginning to be made, especially in the United States. For a detailed analysis of many baseline delineation issues, see Scovazzi, *La Linea di Base del Mare Territoriale*. For illustrations of emerging national legislation on straight baselines, see Francalanci, Romanò, and Scovazzi, eds., *Atlas of Straight Baselines*, Part I.

94 1982 UN Convention on the Law of the Sea, article 46.

95 One expert analysis of article 46 limits the eligible states to eleven: Antigua, the Bahamas, Cape Verde, the Comoros, Grenada, Indonesia, Jamaica, the Maldives, the Philippines, São Tomé and Principe, and St Vincent and the Grenadines. This analysis questions the credentials of several states that have claimed entitlement to archipelagic baselines: for example, Fiji, Papua New Guinea, the Seychelles, the Solomons, and Tonga. Prescott, *Maritime Political Boundaries*, 70–2. Some of the "apparently eligible" have not yet claimed archipelagic baselines. Other territories that might be entitled under article 46 have acquired self-governing status only at or since the end of UNCLOS III: for example, Vanuatu, Tuvalu, Kuribati, the Marshalls, the North Marianas, and the Federated States of Micronesia. Eligibility often turns on whether the claimant purports to encompass the most remote of its islands or islets.

96 U.S. Dept. of State, Office of the Geographer, *Limits in the Sea: Series A*.

97 The delegations at The Hague could not agree whether every island should have its own territorial sea, whether an archipelago could be treated as a single unit, or what kind of baselines should be used. No effort was made to distinguish between coastal and mid-ocean archipelagoes. Tangsubkul, *Southeast Asian Archipelagic States*, 15.

98 Ibid., 27–50.

99 A sympathetic proposal along these lines was made by Jens Evensen of Norway. See "Delimitation of Territorial Waters of Archipelagos."

100 UN Doc. A/CONF. 13/C.1/L.98, 1 April 1958.

101 Significantly, the archipelagic states of Indonesia and the Philippines were, at the end of 1986, the only Southeast Asian states to have ratified the 1982 Convention. Other ratifying states with archipelagic claims or entitlements were the Bahamas, Fiji, and Jamaica.

102 1958 Convention on the Territorial Sea and the Contiguous Zone, article 10(1): "An island is a naturally formed area of land, surrounded by water, which is above water at high tide."

103 Ibid., article 10(2): "The territorial sea of an island is measured in accordance with the provisions of these articles."

104 1982 UN Convention on the Law of the Sea, article 121(2): "Except as provided for in paragraph 3, the territorial sea, the contiguous zone, the exclusive economic zone and the continental shelf of an island are determined in accordance with the provisions of this Convention applicable to other land territory."

105 Robert Hodgson, formerly The Geographer to the U.S. Department of State, suggested the following definitions: *rock*: less than .001 square mile in area; *islet*: between .001 and 1 square mile; *isle*: between 1 square mile and 1,000 square miles; *island*: more than 1,000 square miles. See Hodgson, "Islands," 150–1.

106 See, for example, O'Connell, *International Law of the Sea*, 194; Brown, "Limits of National Jurisdiction," 275; and Symmons, *Maritime Boundary Disputes*.

107 "Except where otherwise provided in this Convention, the normal baseline for measuring the breadth of the territorial sea is the low-water line along the coast, as marked on large-scale charts officially recognized by the coastal State."

108 Under the 1958 and 1982 conventions the coastal state has discretion in the choice of datum. "Herein lies the difficulty: nautical charts usually indicate the configuration of the coast, the nature of the sea-bottom, the depth of water calculated from the zero isobath, the location of reefs, shoals, wrecks, etc., and artificial aids to navigation, rise and fall of the tides, direction and strength of currents, and behaviour of the earth's magnetism. In the key marked on the chart, the relevant low-water plane will be indicated as the zero isobath, for sounding purposes, and depths will be indicated in figures accordingly. This will establish which low tide is the datum used. But ... it has not been the general practice to indicate on the chart a line other than the shoreline, and this has usually been the high-water line from which coastal elevations are measured, and the height indicated in figures. The reason for the selection of the low water plane for soundings and the high-water plane for elevation was that these gave the mariner the minimum

latitude of navigational risk or error. But the chart for this reason will not ordinarily indicate the low-water line from which he is to make his calculations respecting the exterior limit of the territorial sea, nor the actual point from which the baseline is to be drawn across bays for the purpose of that calculation. Strict definition of the low water datum has thus been more of a surveying question in boundary making than a navigational matter ..." O'Connell, *International Law of the Sea*, 178–9.

109 On the choice of tidal level, see ibid., 173–5, and Kapoor and Kerr, *Maritime Boundary Delimitation*, 16–18

110 On attempts at international standardization of the tidal datum, see O'Connell, *International Law of the Sea*, 176–8.

111 The key concept, developed by Schücking in 1930, was that the territorial sea should be measured from the "coast," not the mainland, and that "islands" might be included within the conception of the "coast" if they did not lie outside the limit of the territorial sea as measured from the mainland. For a comment, see O'Connell, *International Law of the Sea*, 132–3, and for a subsequent revision, see 142. This introduced the distinction between primary and secondary basepoints, and suggested a way of treating drying features such as rocks and islets – namely, as secondary basepoints. Ibid., 192–3.

112 The term "low-tide elevation" was substituted for "drying rocks and shoals," without objection, in response to a proposal by the United States. On the reasons for this change, see ibid., 193–4.

113 Kapoor and Kerr, *Maritime Boundary Delimitations*, 37–9.

114 Some commentators believed that the UNCLOS I dichotomy between primary and secondary basepoints and between high-tide and low-tide elevations did not deal adequately with reefs. Others pointed to historical usage in certain reef-infested regions. O'Connell, *International Law of the Sea*, 195–6. See also Kapoor and Kerr, *Maritime Boundary Delimitation*, 31–2.

115 Many river mouths are estuaries. "Looked at from the cartographic point of view, these are only bays, and do not require separate treatment, but looked at from the points of view of water physics, ecology, and the other scientific and sociological factors which today bear increasingly upon the law, estuaries are not in fact bays ... It follows that the determination of the baseline of the territorial sea in such cases can only be made after evaluation of all the relevant elements which distinguish a river from the sea ..." O'Connell, *International Law of the Sea*, 222.

116 Ibid., 224–5; Kapoor and Kerr, *Maritime Boundary Delimitation*, 41–2.

117 "For the purpose of delimiting the territorial sea, the outermost permanent harbour works which form an integral part of the harbour system are regarded as forming part of the coast. Off-shore installations and artificial islands will not be considered as permanent harbour works."

118 O'Connell, *International Law of the Sea*, 219–20.

119 However, it has been questioned whether under the twelve-mile rule for the territorial sea it will be necessary to invoke article 12 on roadsteads, even though very large wide carriers often anchor several miles offshore. Kapoor and Kerr, *Maritime Boundary Delimitation*, 52.

CHAPTER ELEVEN: DELIMITATION OF "LATERAL" BOUNDARIES

1 Normally the term "lateral" is applied only to boundaries between adjacent states. The adjective "median" has sometimes been used to describe all boundaries between opposite states, but this is unsatisfactory because the median line is a *method* of delimitation which has had to compete with the thalweg method and others which have been applied to the delimitation of an ocean, river or lake boundary between opposite states. See note 8 infra. Since delimitation problems between opposite and adjacent states are now treated together under the new law of the sea, it is more useful than ever to have a common adjective to apply to both situations, so as to distinguish such boundaries from baselines and seaward limits. It seems defensible to use the adjective "lateral" for both kinds of "neighbourhood" boundaries in the ocean.

2 The first documented adjudication of any ocean boundary delimitation was the 1909 *Grisbadarna* arbitration between Norway and Sweden. The first modern ocean boundary delimitation agreement may be said to have been the treaty between Italy and France, concluded in 1908, to delimit fishery zones between Corsica and Sardinia. But see notes 5 and 262 infra.

3 Samuel Pufendorf (1632–94) provided his formula for ocean boundary delimitation in coastal areas in his major work, *De Jure Naturae et Gentium* (1672). He proposed that sea boundaries should be established on the basis of the equal division principle in the absence of an agreement between them to exclude foreigners and share their waters. But this general principle was qualified by the phrase *pro latitudine terrarum*, which may be translated to mean "in proportion to the breadth of their respective shorelines." With only this textual evidence it is impossible to be sure whether Pufendorf intended to give primacy to the principle of equality or to that of proportionality. Rhee, "Sea Boundary Delimitation," 556–7.

4 For example, in 1526 a tribunal of the Holy Roman Empire settled a private family dispute over Lake Sant'Andrea by applying the principle of proportionality. The same principle was applied to the division of Lake Geneva among the five riparian states under the Treaty of Lausanne concluded in 1564. Ibid., 557. The median line rule was normally applied to rivers, and often to lakes. Bouchez, "International Boundary Rivers."

5 One of the earliest examples of an ocean boundary delimitation treaty

between two opposite states was that concluded between Norway and Sweden in 1661. This agreement fixed a boundary in a fjord in the Bay of Christiana by connecting certain median points between two opposite coastlines. Ibid., 558. Boundary treaties of this kind became more common in the first half of the nineteenth century, such as that between Finland and Sweden in 1809, when a median line boundary was applied to the Gulf of Bothnia and the Aaland Sea, and that between Great Britain and the United States in 1846 which drew a boundary through the middle of the Strait of Juan de Fuca, between territories that are now the province of British Columbia and the state of Washington. Ibid., 559–64.

6 The delimitation of lateral ocean boundaries between adjacent states was given little attention in the nineteenth century. During the period of a three-mile (or four-mile) territorial sea, such a boundary was generally of minimal concern to neighbouring states. For examples of early agreements between adjacent states, see ibid., 564–5.

7 "Measurement by reference to superficial area alone might deprive one coastal State of a necessary shipping channel, and such a situation is not infrequent where a strait is the continuation of a boundary river ... There is plausibility in the argument that in arms of the sea where analogous conditions occur, coastal States are just as entitled as riparian States to avail themselves of the means of communication which naturally exist." O'Connell, *International Law of the Sea*, vol. 1, 660.

8 "As a result of the invention of steamships and the increase in tonnage of vessels, mutual preservation of equal rights of navigation in the deep-water channel or thalweg was essential to co-riparian states. For this practical reason, the thalweg principle, which had emerged only in the early 19th century, soon challenged the traditional middle line principle. It prevailed to such an extent in navigable waters that numerous provisions for a median line in previous agreements were often misinterpreted as the middle of the stream, the 'middle of the channel,' the 'center of the main channel,' and so on." Ibid., 560–1.

9 "Equitable delimitation was thus sometimes achieved by the flexible application of the median line principle and sometimes by application of the rule of the main channel of navigation to preserve equal rights of navigation." Ibid., 562.

10 The development of regular adjudicative procedures for the international community was achieved in two ways: by the establishment of the Permanent Court of Arbitration (PCA) in 1899 and that of the Permanent Court of International Justice (PCIJ) in 1921.

11 See chapter 10, note 41 supra.

12 This three-member tribunal was not constituted under article 24 of the Hague Convention of 1899, which requires that tribunals be drawn up from members of the permanent panel of the PCA, but the parties availed them-

selves of the facilities of the PCA as permitted under article 26. Although not technically an award of the PCA, the decision is usually treated as such. See the editorial comment in 4 *American Journal of International Law* 186 (1910). Only one of the three arbitrators, the Swedish appointee (Mr Hammarskjold), was a member of the PCA.

13 Convention between Norway and Sweden for the reference to arbitration of the question of a certain portion of the sea limit between the two countries in connection with the Grisbadarna rocks (1909), article 3, reproduced in Scott, ed., *Hague Court Reports*, vol. 1, 133–5.

14 Ibid., 129.

15 Ibid., 130.

16 Ibid., 131.

17 Argentina and Chile signed a general treaty of arbitration in 1902, and the first of several protocols in 1915, with a view to the adjudication of the territorial and ocean boundary disputes between them in the Beagle Channel. In this dispute the boundary issue focused on channels or straits with the claimants on opposite coasts. Argentina based its position on the thalweg rule and Chile favored the median line rule. Rhee, "Sea Boundary Delimitation," 571–3. For more detailed treatment, see the section entitled "Modern Dispute Management" later in this chapter.

18 Report of Rapporteur Walter Schücking, LoN Doc. C44/M 21/1926, vol. 10, 33.

19 S.R. Björksten, *Das Wassergebiet Finnlands in Völkerrechtlicher Hinsicht* (1925), 93, cited in Rhee, "Sea Boundary Delimitation," 574.

20 Research in International Law (Harvard Law School) (hereinafter "Harvard Research").

21 Rhee, "Sea Boundary Delimitation," 574–7.

22 Björksten, supra note 19.

23 Harvard Research, 275.

24 Schücking, supra note 18, 16.

25 Rhee, "Sea Boundary Delimitation," 575–7.

26 Boggs, "Water Boundary Delimitation," 447–8.

27 Ibid., 448.

28 Rhee, "Sea Boundary Delimitation," 580–7.

29 Boggs, "Water Boundary Delimitation," 189.

30 In the *Grisbadarna* arbitration the tribunal had established the boundary by drawing a line perpendicular to the general direction of the coast. This method was followed by the Italian authorities in Libya in 1913, and tacitly accepted by the French authorities in neighbouring Tunisia. On the weight of this consideration in the *Libya-Tunisia* case before the ICJ in 1982, see the section entitled "Modern Dispute Management" later in this chapter.

31 Boggs, "Water Boundary Delimitation," 580–7.

32 O'Connell, *International Law of the Sea*, 662.

33 Gidel, *Le droit international public de la mer*, vol. 1, 710.

34 1956 *Yearbook of the International Law Commission*, vol. 1, 197–9, paras. 24–46.

35 In recommending a formula based on the median line, the ILC rejected three alternative methods of delimitation: a continuation of the land frontier; a perpendicular line on the coast at the intersection of the land frontier and the coastline; and a line drawn perpendicular to the general direction of the coast. Kapoor and Kerr, *Maritime Boundary Delimitation*, 73.

36 O'Connell, *International Law of the Sea*, 679–83. For example, article 12 of the 1958 convention does not deal with the situation of opposite states where the intermediate waters lie beyond, as well as within, territorial sea limits. But concerns related to "pockets of high seas" are subsumed under the 1982 Convention on the Law of the Sea, which recognizes the existence in the customary international law of the sea of the new regime of the EEZ, whose delimitation formula is provided in article 74 of the 1982 Convention.

37 In article 15 of the 1982 UN Convention on the Law of the Sea.

38 The *Grisbadarna* arbitration tribunal made no mention in its historical references to the existence of "title." It gave weight to Swedish historic usages for reasons of equity, without reference to ownership or analogous considerations.

39 This definition was offered by Robert Hodgson, Geographer of the U.S. State Department, during testimony presented in the *Texas* v. *Louisiana* boundary adjudication of 1974, cited in O'Connell, *International Law of the Sea*, 679.

40 On the geometric techniques available, see Kapoor and Kerr, *Maritime Boundary Delimitation*, 73–7. See also Hodgson and Cooper, "Delimitation of Equidistant Boundary."

41 See, for example, Langeraar, "Delimitation of Continental Shelf Areas."

42 On early trends, see Mouton, *Continental Shelf*.

43 The desirability of boundary-making by negotiation, and not by the application of norms through adjudication or otherwise, was emphasized by several members of the ILC at its first session in 1950. O'Connell, *International Law of the Sea*, 704.

44 The majority view was that, in light of the need for maximum flexibility in negotiation, the introduction of any "binding rule" would result in confusion between the diplomatic and judicial functions and work to the detriment of the entire boundary-making process.

45 Those North Sea agreements belonged both to the opposite-state and adjacent-state categories; the former generally preceded the latter. By 1969 the United Kingdom, on the western side of the North Sea, had entered into opposite-state delimitation agreements with Norway, Denmark, and the Netherlands, but not yet with the Federal Republic of Germany (FRG.

46 The delimitation agreement between the Federal Republic of Germany and

the Netherlands was concluded on 1 December 1964, and the delimitation agreement between the FRG and Denmark on 9 June 1965.

47 The delimitation agreement between Denmark and the Netherlands was concluded on 31 March 1966.

48 The procedure began with the simultaneous submission of separate special agreements between the FRG and each of the other two applicant states, and of a trilateral protocol that dealt with procedural questions affecting all three litigants. The Court found that the governments of Denmark and the Netherlands were "in the same interest" and joined the proceedings in the two cases. *North Sea Continental Shelf*, judgment, ICJ Reports 1969, 8. In its award the Court explained the effect of the joinder in these words: "Although the proceedings have thus been joined, the cases themselves remain separate, at least in the sense that they relate to different areas of the North Sea continental shelf, and that there is no *a priori* reason why the Court must reach identical conclusions in regard to them – if, for instance, geographical features present in one case were not present in the other. At the same time, the legal arguments presented on behalf of Denmark and the Netherlands, both before and since the joinder, have been substantially identical apart from certain matters of detail, and have been presented either in common or in close cooperation. To this extent, therefore, the two cases may be treated as one; and it must be noted that although two separate delimitations are in question, they involve – indeed actually give rise to – a single situation." Ibid., 19.

49 See, for example, D'Amato, "Manifest Intent." Many jurists have focused on the reasons given in support of the Court's decision that article 6(2) of the 1958 Convention on the Continental Shelf neither reflected nor generated a rule of customary international law binding upon all states, including non-parties such as the FRG.

50 A rule in a treaty may become binding on non-parties if it becomes part of general or customary international law. See the 1962 Vienna Convention on the Law of Treaties, article 38.

51 O'Connell, *International Law of the Sea*, 476–84.

52 Ibid., 488–95. Most of the commentary on this case is listed in McDorman, Beauchamp, and Johnston, *Maritime Boundary Delimitation*, passim. See also Jagota, *Maritime Boundary*, 127–39.

53 ICJ Reports 1969, 9.

54 Ibid., 11.

55 See article 1(2) of both special agreements. Ibid., 6, 7.

56 The dissenting judges were Vice-President Karetsky, Judges Tanaka, Morelli, Lachs, and Bengzon, and Judge (ad hoc) Sorensen.

57 Ibid., 23.

58 "It would however be ignoring realities if it were not noted at the same time that the use of [the equidistance line] method ... can under certain circum-

stances produce results that appear on the face of them to be extraordinary, unnatural or unreasonable. It is basically this fact which underlies the present proceedings." Ibid., 23–4.

59 It seems that, in so deciding, the Court might have been prepared, if necessary, to look at the FRG's "state practice" in a broad sense, including its actions and policy statements during the ILC debate preceding UNCLOS I and at the conference itself, as well as its conduct, public statements, and proclamations more generally. Ibid., 25–7.

60 Ibid., 27.

61 Ibid., 28.

62 ICJ Reports 1969, 23.

63 The Court held that "the rights of the coastal State in respect of the area of continental shelf that constitutes a natural prolongation of its land territory into and under the sea exist, *ipso facto* and *ab initio*, by virtue of its sovereignty over the land, and as an extension of it in an exercise of sovereign rights for the purpose of exploring the seabed, and exploiting its natural resources. In short, there is here an inherent right ..." Ibid.

64 In the determination of seaward limits, the contest is between national sovereignty, or "sovereign rights," with all the connotations of exclusive entitlement, and inclusive entitlement for the international community in general. Delimitation rests on questions of relative entitlement, which are not relieved in any way by reference to the "inherent" right of one or other of the claimant states.

65 ICJ Reports 1969, 22.

66 It should be recalled that at the time of these two disputes, none of the three countries involved had any clear idea of the location, much less the value, of the hydrocarbon resources presumed to be at stake. It is now known, many years later, that the area in dispute is of little commercial significance as far as oil and natural gas are concerned – an ironic final commentary on the dispute!

67 ICJ Reports, 1969, 30–1, 31–2.

68 Ibid., 32. In reducing the juridical significance of proximity, and therefore equidistance, in the delimitation of the shelf between adjacent states, the Court referred to the debate in the International Law Commission between 1950 and 1956 on the rationale of entitlements to the shelf. In the ILC's records, the Court noted, "there is no indication at all that any of its members supposed that it was incumbent on the Commission to adopt a rule of equidistance because this gave expression to, and translated into linear terms, a principle of proximity inherent in the basic concept of the continental shelf, causing every part of the shelf to appertain to the nearest coastal State and to no other, and because such a rule must therefore be mandatory as a matter of customary international law. Such an idea does not seem ever to have been propounded." Ibid., 33. Indeed, it was not until

after the matter had been referred to a committee of hydrographic experts, which reported in 1953, that equidistance began to take precedence over other considerations. When equidistance was propounded by these experts, it was as one of four "methods" of delimitation between adjacent states, "the other three being the continuation in the seaward direction of the land frontier between the two adjacent States concerned; the drawing of a perpendicular to the coast at the point of its intersection with this land frontier; and the drawing of a line perpendicular to the line of the 'general direction of the coast.' Furthermore, the matter was not even put to the experts directly as a question of continental shelf delimitation, but in the context of the delimitation of the lateral boundary between adjacent territorial waters, no account being taken of the possibility that the situation respecting territorial matters might be different." Ibid., 34. Moreover, the experts conceded that use of an equidistance line might not result in an equitable solution, which should then be sought through negotiation. This manner of treating the ILC proposal of equidistance was characterized by the Court as "almost impromptu, and certainly contingent." Ibid., 35.

69 The Truman Proclamation on the Continental Shelf stated that delimitation between adjacent states should be "determined by the United States and the [adjacent] State concerned in accordance with equitable principles." Cited ibid., 33.

70 Ibid., 41, 45.

71 Ibid., 53–4.

72 On the 1974–80 period of the UNCLOS III debate on delimitation, see Jagota, *Maritime Boundary*, 223–39.

73 On the "romantic" period of international legal development, see Johnston, "Political Thought in International Law," 198–200.

74 *Case concerning the Delimitation of the Continental Shelf between the United Kingdom and France*, decision of 30 June 1977, 18 *Reports of International Arbitral Awards* 1.

75 Ibid., 271.

76 Ibid., 52–3.

77 Ibid., 57.

78 Ibid., 60–1.

79 Ibid., 61.

80 "A 'simplified' median line is one in which, in order to make the line less complicated, the number of its turning points is reduced by using straight lines between the original points. When this is done, an advantage to one State in one area is usually compensated by a roughly equivalent advantage to the other State in another area." Ibid., 61, note 1.

81 Ibid., 61–2.

82 Ibid., 24–5.

83 Ibid., 75.

84 Ibid., 75–6.
85 Ibid., 78.
86 Ibid., 80.
87 Ibid., 80–1.
88 The United Kingdom invoked the particular character of the Channel Islands as not rocks or islets but populous islands of a certain political and economic importance. It emphasized the close ties between the islands and the United Kingdom and the latter's responsibility for their defence and security. These considerations were held out as sufficient to justify a judicial linkage between the shelf of the Channel Islands and that of the United Kingdom. Ibid., 93.
89 Ibid., 94.
90 Ibid., 94–5.
91 Ibid., 97.
92 Ibid., 98–110.
93 Ibid., 112–13.
94 Ibid., 113.
95 Ibid., 113–14.
96 Ibid., 116.
97 Ibid., 117. "Just as it is not the function of equity in the delimitation of the continental shelf completely to refashion geography, so it is also not the function of equity to create a situation of complete equity where nature and geography have established an inequity." Ibid., 116.
98 Although the decision was unanimous, one of the arbitrators, Professor Herbert W. Briggs, made a declaration setting out his points of difference from his colleagues in their evaluation of the French reservations to article 6 of the 1958 Convention on the Continental Shelf.
99 *Anglo-French Continental Shelf* award, decision of 14 March 1978, 18 *Reports of International Arbitrated Awards* 275.
100 Ibid., 276–7.
101 Ibid., 277–9.
102 Under article 10(1) of the arbitration agreement the two governments agreed "to accept as final and binding upon them the Decision of the Court on the question specified in Article 2," but article 10(2) provides that "either Party may, within three months of the rendering of the Decision, refer to the Court any dispute between the Parties as to the meaning and scope of the Decision." The United Kingdom argued that the rendering of the Court's decision must be deemed to have taken place on 18 July 1977, although it was dated 30 June 1977. France maintained that the application was submitted after the expiry of the three-month period and that in that period no "dispute" had arisen. Both of France's preliminary objections were rejected by the Court. Ibid., 286–9.
103 Ibid., 291–6.

104 Ibid., 297.

105 Ibid., 299–300.

106 Ibid., 300–17.

107 Ibid., 329. For commentaries on this arbitration, see McDorman, Beauchamp, and Johnston, *Maritime Boundary Delimitation*, passim. See also Jagota, *Maritime Boundary*, 140–63.

108 The "enclave" method seems to have been first used in the 1968 boundary treaty between Italy and Yugoslavia, nine years before the Anglo-French arbitration. It appeared again in the following year in the 1969 boundary treaty between Qatar and Abu Dhabi.

109 Without resorting to a great deal of geometric measurement, it is virtually impossible to identify the first use of the "partial effect" technique applied to islands in boundary delimitation negotiations. It may have originated in the Arabian-Persian Gulf, at least no later than the 1958 boundary treaty between Bahrein and Saudi Arabia.

110 "Abatement" means the reduction, or if possible the elimination, of a nuisance or defect. Accordingly, the concept of equity can be used remedially to correct a deficiency as reflected in the test of proportionality. Equity, by this approach, serves the function of final adjustment to ensure an equitable result or solution.

111 Greece and Turkey have also been in dispute over the limits of their territorial sea in the eastern Aegean, over military and civil air traffic zones in the area, over the remilitarization of various Greek islands, over the protection of ethnic minorities, and of course over Cyprus. Wilson, *Aegean Dispute*, 2, 16–21.

112 For the texts of these and subsequent *notes verbales*, see ICJ Pleadings, *Aegean Sea Continental Shelf*, 21–33.

113 Ibid., 25.

114 Ibid., 30–1.

115 Ibid., 33, 36.

116 Security Council Resolution 395, 25 August 1976, cited in *Aegean Sea Continental Shelf* judgment, ICJ Reports 1978, 10. This latter phrase was the product of a delicate diplomatic exercise in international ambiguity. From a Greek perspective, it can be interpreted as approval of the Greek government's resort to the ICJ. From a Turkish perspective, it can be interpreted as a recommendation that the parties return to the negotiating table to seek agreement on the issues to be submitted to the Court on an alternative intermediary procedure. Wilson, *Aegean Dispute*, 9. For a criticism of the Security Council's resolution, see Gross, "Dispute between Greece and Turkey," 38–9.

117 ICJ Reports 1976, 3.

118 ICJ Reports 1978, 5–6.

119 Ibid., 6.

120 Ibid., 13.

121 Ibid., 13–38.

122 Ibid., 35–6.

123 Ibid., 38–44.

124 The dissenting judges were Judge de Castro and Judge (ad hoc) Stassinopoulos.

125 ICJ Reports 1978, 12.

126 In his separate opinion, Vice-President Singh argued that there could be "no question ... of the incompatibility of negotiation with judicial settlement at any stage in the course of the dispute." Ibid., 48. See also the separate opinion of Judge Lachs, ibid., 52–3.

127 The 1982 UN Convention on the Law of the Sea provides, in article 83: "1. The delimitation of the continental shelf between States with opposite or adjacent coasts shall be effected by agreement on the basis of international law, as referred to in Article 38 of the Statute of the International Court of Justice, in order to achieve an equitable solution. 2. If no agreement can be readied within a reasonable period of time, the States concerned shall resort to the procedures provided for in Part XV."

128 The revised single negotiating text had been issued in the spring of 1976 with major revisions of the delimitation provisions. Oxman, "The 1976 New York Sessions," 267–8.

129 "For the purposes of these articles, the term 'continental shelf' is used as referring (a) to the seabed and subsoil of the submarine areas adjacent to the coast but outside the area of the territorial sea, to a depth of 200 metres or, beyond that limit, to where the depth of the superjacent waters admits of the exploitation of the natural resources of the said areas; (b) to the seabed and subsoil of similar submarine areas *adjacent to the coasts of islands* [emphasis added]." It might be argued that it remains ambiguous under the language of article 1 whether *all* insular formations are intended to generate a continental shelf. Symmons, *Maritime Zones of Islands*, 140–2. Because of the definition in article 1, Turkey has refused to sign the 1958 Convention on the Continental Shelf.

130 Symmons, *Maritime Zones of Islands*, 141–2.

131 Ibid., 143–5.

132 1982 UN Convention on the Law of the Sea, article 121: "1. An island is a naturally formed area of land surrounded by water, which is above water at high tide. 2. Except as provided for in paragraph 3, the territorial sea, the contiguous zone, the exclusive economic zone, *and the continental shelf* of an island are determined in accordance with the provisions of this Convention applicable to other land territory. 3. Rocks which cannot sustain human habitation or economic life of their own shall have no exclusive zone

or continental shelf" (emphasis added). Chiefly because of the unacceptability of this provision, Turkey voted against adoption of the 1982 Convention and since then has declined to sign it or accede to it.

133 Wilson, *Aegean Dispute*, 14.

134 On the "settlement" side of a solution, lines could be drawn in such a way as to give a continental shelf area to each that bears a mathematical relationship to the length of their respective coastlines, or "maritime façades." One suggested method of measurement would produce a ratio of approximately 2:1 in favour of Greece. Karl, "Islands and the Continental Shelf," 669–72. Such an approach would give Turkey "fingers" of jurisdiction between the Greek islands. Wilson, *Aegean Dispute*, 14, 26–7. On the "arrangement" side of a solution, some kind of joint regime might be designed with a view to facilitating joint development or management in a disputed area whose boundaries simply cannot be negotiated. Wilson, *Aegean Dispute*, 14, 26–7.

135 Articles 74 (on delimitation of the EEZ) and 83 (on delimitation of the continental shelf) are identical in language. By reference to customary international law, attempts may be made to argue that different "rules and principles" apply to these two different kinds of boundary delimitation. From a functionalist viewpoint, such efforts should be governed by consideration of the different ocean development and management purposes intended to be served under these two different regimes.

136 Evensen, "La délimitation entre la Norvège et l'Islande du plateau continental dans le secteur de Jan Mayen," 718–23.

137 "Report and Recommendations to the Governments of Iceland and Norway of the Conciliation Commission on the Continental Shelf Area between Iceland and Jan Mayen" (hereinafter "Report and Recommendations"), reproduced in 20 *International Legal Materials* 797 (1981).

138 Ibid., 799.

139 All three commissioners were prominent specialists in the law of the sea. Iceland appointed Hans G. Andersen, chairman of the Icelandic delegation to UNCLOS III. Norway appointed Jens Evensen, chairman of the Norwegian delegation to UNCLOS III. The governments agreed jointly to appoint Elliott Richardson, chairman of the U.S. delegation to UNCLOS III, chairman of the Concilation Commission. Clearly, it was intended that they should bring to the task their legal knowledge in the field as well as their diplomatic and political experience.

140 "Report and Recommendations," 803.

141 The commission was influenced by the fact that the concept of "natural prolongation" has two facets, morphological and geological. Morphologically, the northern part of Jan Mayen Ridge can be considered a southern extension of the Jan Mayen shelf, but not a northern extension of the Icelandic shelf. Geologically, Jan Mayen Ridge is a micro-continent that

predates both Iceland and Jan Mayen Island, which are composed of younger volcanic formations. Therefore, the ridge is not a natural geological prolongation of either Jan Mayen or Iceland. If the concept is used in its morphological sense, there is no scientific foundation for Iceland's claim to an continental shelf extending to the Jan Mayen Ridge.

142 The Conciliation Commission made specific references to six types of solutions: natural prolongation, proportionality ("on the basis of distance and other relevant factors"), median line, special circumstances, joint development zones, and island weightings (full effect, partial effect, trade-off, and enclave techniques).

143 *North Sea Continental Shelf* decision, ICJ Reports 1969, 51, quoted in "Report and Recommendations," 825.

144 "Report and Recommendations," 825, 827.

145 That is, concession contracts with joint venture arrangements, service contracts, production-sharing contracts, and entrepreneur contracts.

146 "Report and Recommendations," 839.

147 Churchill, "Maritime Delimitation," 23–5.

148 Ibid., 28–31.

149 Ibid., 25–6.

150 See notes 142 and 145 supra. For commentary, see Jagota, *Maritime Boundary*, 165–8.

151 Jagota, *Maritime Boundary*, 220.

152 Ibid.

153 For an account of the difficulties encountered between 1974 and 1980, see ibid., 223–39.

154 Ibid., 242–3.

155 See, for example, Oxman, "The Tenth Session (1981)," 14–15.

156 *Continental Shelf (Tunisia/Libyan Arab Jamahiriya)*, judgment, ICJ Reports 1982, 18.

157 This language is the court registry's English translation of Tunisia's French translation of the original Arabic text of the special agreement. Ibid., 21. For the English translation of article 1 supplied by Libya, see ibid., 23.

158 Ibid., 21, 22, 23.

159 The Court reached its decision by a majority of ten votes to four. Those dissenting were Judges Forster, Gros, and Oda and Judge (ad hoc) Evensen.

160 Supra note 156, 38.

161 Ibid., 38, 39–40.

162 For Tunisian references to the doctrine of natural prolongation, see ibid., 26–9; for Libyan references, see ibid., 29–32. Both parties took the view that the delimitation had to be effected "by agreement in accordance with equitable principles, and taking account of all the relevant circumstances in such a way as to leave as much as possible to each Party *all those parts of the*

continental shelf that constitute a natural prolongation of its land territory into and under the sea, without encroachment on the natural prolongation of the land territory of the other [emphasis added]." Ibid., 43.

163 Ibid., 48.

164 For the final formulation, see 1982 UN Convention on the Law of the Sea, article 76(10).

165 Supra note 156, 49.

166 Ibid.

167 Ibid., 53–4.

168 Ibid., 58.

169 Ibid., 59.

170 Ibid., 61–2.

171 ICJ Reports 1969, 54.

172 Supra note 156, 65–78.

173 Ibid., 77.

174 Ibid., 79. See also the separate opinion of Judge Jiménez de Aréchaga, ibid., 106–9, which concludes with these words: "Therefore, it is legitimate to take into consideration that the whole process of the Conference is indicative of a new accepted trend, which is to minimize and 'tone down' the role assigned to Article 6 of the 1958 Convention. These Conference texts signify that *equidistance is a method and not a principle; that it is no longer a privileged method or one having pride of place; that, like all others, it must be judged by its success in achieving an equitable solution*; and finally, that the application of equidistance and of equitable principles are not to be viewed as two distinct and successive phases, nor as requiring that equitable principles are only to be resorted to after applying equidistance, in order to connect its result. There is no such succession in time and the process must be a simultaneous one. *All the relevant circumstances are to be considered and balanced*; they are to be thrown together into the crucible *and their interaction will yield the correct equitable solution of each individual case* [emphasis added]." Ibid., 109.

175 Ibid., 82.

176 Ibid., 84.

177 Ibid., 87–8, 88–9.

178 Ibid., 92.

179 Judge Gros observed that the Court, in its majority decision, had contented itself with "some generalities on the equidistance method without giving the reasons why it has not been employed ... The reasons referred to in ... the 1969 Judgment [of the ICJ] for discarding equidistance, which 'in certain geographical conditions [could lead] unquestionably to inequity,' were based on particular geographical configurations and on their unquestionably inequitable effect, two factors that require examination. Yet in the present case nothing was done to investigate the precise effect on an equi-

distance line of the relevant geographical features in the area of the continental shelf under consideration, the 'unreasonable' ... results which the equidistance method might produce and any modifications to be therefore envisaged." Dissenting opinion of Judge Gros, ibid., 148–9.

180 The logic of the "equitable solution" approach, he suggested, required the Court to check against the facts the equitable effect of each method that might be applied. "No method should be exempt from this control, when equity is involved ... It is not enough to say that the equidistance method would not have resulted in the most equitable delimitation, when the conditions for excluding it were neither ascertained to exist nor even given proper thought, and the Court has failed to examine the extraordinary, unnatural and unreasonable results of its own manner of proceeding." Ibid., 151.

181 Ibid., 154.

182 Ibid., 156.

183 The dissenting opinion of Judge Oda (at 157–277) is exactly twice the length of the analysis presented in the majority judgment (at 34–94).

184 Ibid., 157.

185 "In point of fact, all the efforts deployed in the great workshop of UNCLOS III have been directed towards constructing an imposing edifice representing a regime of the ocean likely to be voted into existence irrespective of what it may bode for the future. Unable to cling to the aim of true world harmony, the delegates have felt compelled to content themselves with cobbling together a patchwork of ideas which are not necessarily harmonious ... Whether the result produced by this great laboratory of international law will prove to be really workable is something that will have to be judged in the future. The Court was not in a position, at least while the experiment was still going on in the laboratory, to depend on a half-finished product, and did not have to regard a simple glance at the formulated text of the draft convention as indicative of established or embryonic principles and rules of international law." Ibid., 171–2.

186 Ibid., 190.

187 Ibid., 190–7. "The ... merit of an equidistance line was not as such reported in the 1969 Judgment. However, the Court then seems to have fallen short of a proper appreciation of the equidistance method and, in particular, to have ignored the full potential of the formula contained in Article 6 of the Convention." Ibid., 197.

188 Ibid., 222–47.

189 "Although no delegate seems to be recorded as ever having challenged the concept of the exclusive economic zone or cast doubt on its 200-mile limit, the very concept and the operation of its regime are still not clear-cut, and a more scrupulous scrutiny will be required before it can be regarded as part of the established principles and rules of international law." Ibid., 249.

190 Ibid., 269.

191 Dissenting opinion of Judge Evensen, ibid., 288. "To my mind, it is somewhat doubtful that a practical method for the delimitation of the areas concerned should be based solely or mainly on continental shelf considerations."

192 Ibid., 294.

193 Ibid., 295.

194 Ibid., 296.

195 Ibid., 297.

196 Ibid., 302, 305, 309–11, 314, 319.

197 Ibid., 320–2.

198 ICJ Pleadings, *Continental Shelf (Tunisia/Libyan Arab Jamahiriya)*, vol. 3, application for permission to intervene by the Government of Malta, 258–9.

199 *Continental Shelf (Tunisia/Libyan Arab Jamahiriya)*, application to intervene, judgment, ICJ Reports 1981, 19–20.

200 Separate opinions were given by Judges Morozov, Oda, and Schwebel.

201 *Case concerning the Continental Shelf (Tunisia/Libyan Arab Jamahiriya)*, application for revision and interpretation of the judgment of 24 February 1982, paragraph 6.

202 Ibid., paragraph 7.

203 Ibid., paragraph 50.

204 Ibid., paragraphs 55, 56.

205 Application for revision and interpretation of the judgment of 24 February 1982 in *Case concerning the Continental Shelf (Tunisia/Libyan Arab Jamahiriya)*, judgment, ICJ Reports 1985, 18–19. The Court also held that the "new fact" relied upon by Tunisia to support its application for revision was not "of such a nature as to be a decisive factor" in the Court's disposition of the boundary-making issue. Ibid., 25–6.

206 Ibid., 219-20.

207 In its majority judgment the Court found it necessary to make the usual protestation that it could not decide *ex aequo et bono* unless asked to do so by the parties and to deny the discretionary or counciliatory nature of its approach. "Application of equitable principles is to be distinguished from a decision *ex aequo et bono*. The Court can take such a decision only on condition that the Parties agree (Article 38, para. 2 of the Statute) and the Court is then freed from the strict application of legal rules in order to bring about an appropriate settlement. The task of the Court in the present case is quite different: it is bound to apply equitable principles as part of international law, and to balance up the various considerations which it regards as relevant in order to produce an equitable result. While it is clear that no rigid rules exist as to the exact weight to be attached to each element in the case, this is very far from being an exercise of discretion or conciliation; nor is it an operation of distributive justice." ICJ Reports 1982, 60.

208 Perhaps the most appropriate way for the ICJ to develop the criteria of effectiveness in ocean boundary delimitation would be by spelling out the elements of the "duty to negotiate" in the specific context confronting the parties. That is, the Court could suggest types of joint development or other cross-boundary arrangements that should be negotiated as part of the process of "boundary maintenance."

209 For commentaries on this decision, see Wiktor and Foster, eds., *Marine Affairs Bibliography*, passim. See also Jagota, *Maritime Boundary*, 168–206.

210 This "declaration" was appended to the Canadian instrument of ratification deposited on 6 February 1970. Text reproduced in 716 UNTS 390 (1970).

211 For a detailed account of the fishery implications of the Gulf of Maine dispute, see VanderZwaag, *Fish Feud*.

212 Instead of submitting their dispute to the full court, litigants have the option to resort to the chamber procedure, whereby five members of the ICJ are selected by the parties to form a panel. This innovation was introduced in the 1970s in the hope of encouraging reluctant states to use the machinery of the ICJ for the peaceful settlement of their disputes. By giving the parties a degree of control over the selection of the adjudicators, the chamber procedure of the ICJ might be said to represent an intermediate mode of adjudication between full court litigation before the ICJ, which gives the parties no such control, and traditional ad hoc arbitration outside any existing framework, which permits the parties to exercise unlimited control over the choice of arbitrators and virtually all other features of the adjudicative process. For a discussion of the chamber procedure of the ICJ, see Rosenne, *Procedure in the International Court*, 38–47.

Critics of the chamber procedure have noted that resort to it might be construed, or misconstrued, as a vote of non-confidence in the Court as a whole, or in certain judges sitting on the Court, thereby lowering the morale of that body at a time when it needs to be protected and strengthened. Defenders of the chamber procedure argue that the Court suffers mostly from under-use, and that the innovation is a welcome response to the need to expand the options of potential litigant states. Canada and the United States have not made known the reasons for their resort to the chamber procedure in the *Gulf of Maine* dispute, but it might be speculated that one of the reasons is the recent tendency of the judges of the ICJ to split between western and non-western blocs – or at least to be pulled in different directions. In the context of ocean boundary-making, this split might be compared, if not identified, with the growing schism between "legal" (or "unitarian") and "equitable" (or "functionalist") approaches to boundary-making. A similar rift is apparent in the *Gulf of Maine* decision, where the dissenting opinion of Judge Gros espouses a "unitarian" approach and rejects the "equitable" approach of the majority. All five members of the chamber were western international lawyers! (See the discussion in the text below).

213 Special agreement, article 2, paragraph 1, reproduced in *Delimitation of the Maritime Boundary in the Gulf of Maine Area*, judgment, ICJ Reports 1984, 252–5.

214 Ibid., article 2, paragraphs 2 and 3. Subsequently, at the request of the parties, Commander Peter Bryan Beazley of the United Kingdom was appointed technical expert to assist the Court.

215 In article 4 of the special agreement, the following technical provisions were included: (a) All geographic co-ordinates of points referred to shall be rendered on the 1927 North American Datum. (b) All straight lines shall be geodetic lines. Curved lines, including parallels of latitude, if necessary for the judgment, shall be computed on the 1927 North American Datum. (c) Notwithstanding the fact that the Parties utilize different vertical datums in the Gulf of Maine area, the two datums shall be deemed to be common. (d) Should reference to the low water baseline of either Party be required, the most recent largest scale charts published by the Party concerned shall be utilized. (e) If a point or points on a particular chart are not on the 1927 North American Datum, the Chamber shall request the Agent of the appropriate Party to furnish the Chamber with the corrected datum points. (f) In recognition of the fact that the Parties do not utilize the same standard set of symbols on nautical charts, the Chamber or any technical expert or experts shall, if necessary, confer with the Agents and other advisers to insure proper interpretation of the symbol or feature. (g) The Chamber or any technical expert or experts is requested to consult with the Parties as may be necessary concerning any common computer programs of the Parties for technical calculations, and to utilize such programs as appropriate.

216 Special agreement, article 3.

217 Ibid., article 7.

218 ICJ Reports 1984, para. 19 (hereinafter cited by paragraph number in the text). This rather strange comment raises questions about the chamber's interpretation of the concept of functional jurisdiction in the new law of the sea.

219 "There is, for example, the criterion expressed by the classic formula that the land dominates the sea; the criterion advocating, in cases where no special circumstances require correction thereof, the equal division of the areas of overlap of the maritime and submarine zones appertaining to the respective coasts of neighbouring States; the criterion that, whenever possible, the seaward extension of a State's coast should not encroach upon areas that are too close to the coast of another State; the criterion of preventing, as far as possible, any cut-off of the seaward projection of the coast or of part of the coast of either of the States concerned; and the

criterion whereby, in certain circumstances, the appropriate consequences may be drawn from any inequalities in the extent of the coasts of two States into the same area of delimitation." Ibid., paragraph 157.

220 The U.S. presented detailed scientific evidence in support of its contention that there existed three indentifiable and distinct oceanographic and ecological "regimes" in the water of the area, each with its own type of hydrological circulation, temperature, salinity, density, vertical stratification, and tidal activity. These three "regimes" were thus divided by "natural boundaries."

221 "Undeniably," the chamber added, "a degree of simplification is an elementary requisite to the drawing of any delimitation line in such an environment" (paragraph 203).

222 On the construction of the three segments of the Chamber's line, see Cooper, "Delimitation of the Maritime Boundary."

223 The majority of the chamber calculated the ratio to be 1.38 to 1 in favour of the U.S. coast, a calculation that included most of the Canadian coastline on both sides of the Bay of Fundy.

224 For other views, see entries in Wiktor and Foster, *Marine Affairs Bibliography*, passim.

225 Text reproduced in 17 *International Legal Materials* 646 (1976).

226 Text reproduced ibid., 632–3.

227 At that time Argentina and the United Kingdom were engaged in various political difficulties, including the Falkland/Malvinas Islands dispute. On previous occasions when Argentina and Chile had resorted to arbitration under the 1902 treaty, the arbitrator had appointed an all-British tribunal of its own choice, which was instructed to report back to the British government. Chile was prepared to accept this system under the 1902 treaty, but over the years Argentina increasingly emphasized its preference for recourse to the International Court of Justice. Note, "The Beagle Channel Affair," 71 *American Journal of International Law* 733, at 734 (1977).

228 Text reproduced in 17 *International Legal Materials* 636 (1976).

229 Text reproduced in 24 *International Legal Materials* 29 (1985).

230 The judges selected were Hardy Dillard (USA), Sir Gerald Fitzmaurice (UK), André Gros (France), Charles D. Onyeama (Nigeria), and Steve Petren (Sweden). Fitzmaurice was chosen by the Court as its president, presumably as a concession to the special nature of Britain's role in the settlement process.

231 Article 1(7), supra note 228, 639.

232 Articles 9 and 14, ibid., 640.

233 Article 14, ibid., 673–4. For a summary of the arguments presented, see Note, 71 *American Journal of International Law* 733 (1977).

234 Text of Argentina's Declaration of Nullity reproduced in 24 *International Legal Materials* 738 (1985). For an evaluation of this controversial action,

see Himmelreich, "Beagle Channel Affair." The author concludes that although the Argentine Declaration of Nullity does not contain valid legal arguments for rejection, "it does indicate weaknesses in the Court's opinion that make it vulnerable to rejection for political reasons ... If the members of the International Court of Justice are to play a more important role in resolving future heated international disputes they will have to speed up the procedure of the bodies on which they serve, improve their judicial style, and pay more attention to the symbolism of international politics."

235 Text of Declaration of Puerto Montt reproduced in 24 *International Legal Materials* 3 (1985). It was agreed that in the second stage of the negotiation process the parties would examine not only the boundary question, but also (1) "the adoption of joint or separate measures for the promotion of policies of physical integration, economic complementarity and the exploitation of natural resources, including the protection of the environment"; (2) "the consideration of common interests in Antarctica, the coordination of policies for the frozen continent as well as the legal defense of the rights of both countries and studies, on the progress of bilateral agreements or joint neighborhood policies in the Antarctic"; (3) "questions that either Party may bring up concerning the Straits of Magellan, taking into consideration relevant treaties and principles of international law"; and (4) "questions relating to straight baselines." Ibid., 4.

236 Text of the Agreement of Montevideo, reproduced ibid., 5–6.

237 Text of the papal proposal, reproduced ibid., 7–10.

238 Texts of relevant documents reproduced ibid., 30–1.

239 Text of the joint declaration, reproduced ibid., 10; text of the Treaty of Peace and Friendship, reproduced ibid., 11–28.

240 Ibid., 17–23.

241 For commentaries on the Beagle Channel dispute, see entries in Wiktor and Foster, *Marine Affairs Bibliography*.

242 Guinea nominated Kéba Mbaye and Guinea-Bissau nominated Mohammed Bedjaoui; those two members chose Judge Manfred Lachs of the International Court of Justice as chairman.

243 Both Guinea and Guinea-Bissau were non-parties to the Vienna Convention on the Law of Treaties, but neither objected to the application of articles 31 and 32 of the convention to the two questions of treaty interpretation submitted to the tribunal. Article 31 prescribes the "ordinary meaning" and related criteria of treaty interpretation, and article 32 permits resort to "supplementary means of interpretation, including the preparatory work of the treaty and the circumstances of its conclusion" for certain limited purposes.

244 Arbitration Tribunal for the Delimitation of the Maritime Boundary between Guinea and Guinea-Bissau, award of 14 February 1985, text repro-

duced in 25 *International Legal Materials* 252 (1986), paragraph 84 (hereinafter cited by paragraph number in the text).

245 For a relevant regional perspective, see Underwood, "Ocean Boundaries and Resource Development."

246 *Case concerning the Continental Shelf (Libyan Arab Jamahiriya/Malta)*, Application by Italy for Permission to Intervene, judgment, ICJ Reports 1984, paragraph 15 (hereinafter cited by paragraph number in the text).

247 The "new" participants in judicial boundary making were Judges Ruda, Jennings, de Lacharrière, and Judge (ad hoc) Valticos.

248 The three dissenting judges were Mosler, Oda, and Schwebel.

249 *Continental Shelf (Libyan Arab Jamahiriya/Malta)*, judgment, ICJ Reports 1985, paragraph 18 (hereinafter cited by paragraph number in the text).

250 The following considerations were offered by the ICJ as "equitable principles": (1) the principle that there is to be no refashioning geography, or compensating for the inequalities of nature; (2) the "related principle" of non-encroachment by one party on the natural prolongation of the other ("which is no more than the negative expression of the positive rule that the coastal State enjoys sovereign rights over the continental shelf off its coasts to the full extent authorized by international law in the relevant circumstances"); (3) "the principle of respect due to all such relevant circumstances"; (4) the principle that although all States are equal before the law and are entitled to equal treatment, "equity does not necessarily imply equality," nor does it seek to make equal what nature has made unequal; and (5) "the principle that there can be no question of distributive justice." Ibid., paragraph 46.

251 ICJ Reports 1985, separate opinion of Judge Valticos, paragraphs 13, 15–27.

252 Ibid., separate opinion of Judge Sette-Camara, 60–75.

253 Ibid., separate opinion of Judges Ruda, Bedjaoui, and Jiménez de Aréchaga, 76–92.

254 Ibid., separate opinion of Judge Mbaye, 93–103.

255 Ibid., declaration of Judge El-Khani, 59.

256 "The judicial task is to make the law more determinable by objective criteria, and thus more predictable to potential parties ... It is admitted that certain subjective elements in evaluating and balancing facts and circumstances can hardly be excluded. But it is the duty of the Court, if it is not explicitly authorized by the parties to judge *ex aequo et bono*, to reduce these elements to a minimum." Ibid., dissenting opinion of Judge Mosler, 114–15.

257 "I fail to see for what reason the information given by a third State to the Court on its claims regarding maritime zones also claimed by one or both parties to a pending dispute is taken as a fact restricting the Court's juris-

diction and as a technical means to indicate the direction of the delimitation line. It does not matter whether the claim of the third State is *prima facie* not unreasonable, or that the parties did not comment on the claims. These points were not among the factual and legal questions involved in the dispute. The competence of the Court to decide on the delimitation of the area lying between the coasts of the Parties cannot depend on the pretensions of a third State brought to the Court's notice. On the contrary, the Court, in my view, has no power to take into account a line which it is not even entitled to examine. The legitimate goal of not prejudicing Italy's rights must not have the effect that not the whole of the case of the Parties is decided." Ibid., 117.

258 Ibid., dissenting opinion of Judge Schwebel, 172–87. Judge Schwebel was especially critical of the majority's apparent but unacknowledged use of the "proportionality" criterion in an opposite-state situation in a manner he found inconsistent with the chamber's treatment of the adjustment problem in the *Gulf of Maine* case.

259 Ibid., dissenting opinion of Judge Oda, 123–71.

260 Johnston and Saunders, *Ocean Boundary Making*, passim. For commentaries on this case, see entries in Wiktor and Foster, *Marine Affairs Bibliography*, passim.

261 For a recent evaluation of treaty-making from a legal perspective, see Simma, "Consent."

262 This latter agreement concerned the Dodecanese Islands. Greece seems to have accepted this treaty-based boundary when it acquired sovereignty over these islands. The treaty data analysed in this section of the monograph are derived from two listings, namely those in McDorman, Beauchamp, and Johnston, *Maritime Boundary Delimitation*, 157–95, and Jagota, *Maritime Boundary*, 331–44. However, no treaty listing is totally comprehensive. It is certain that more than two ocean boundary delimitation agreements were negotiated before the Second World War, and it is arguable that they are still in existence, though they are rarely, if ever, referred to in official records or communications. For example, on 18 January 1908 Italy and France signed a partial boundary agreement designed to delimit fishery zones between Corsica and Sardinia. Moreover, many old boundary agreements chiefly applicable to land territory also extend explicitly to territorial waters, or may be interpreted to do so. For several examples and sources, see Chircop, *Co-operative Regimes in Ocean Management*, passim.

263 For a detailed treatment of most existing agreements, see Prescott, *Maritime Political Boundaries*, passim. For a shorter account, see Jagota, *Maritime Boundary*, 69–124.

264 The exceptions are the tripartite boundary provisions adopted by Chile, Ecuador, and Peru in 1952 and 1954 (*LITS* 86 and 88), the 1971 trilateral boundary agreement concluded by Thailand, Indonesia, and Malaysia

(*LITS* 81), the 1976 trilateral agreement signed by India, Sri Lanka, and the Maldives (*New Directions VIII*, 102), and the 1978 trilateral agreement signed by India, Indonesia, and Thailand (*LITS* 93, 1981).

265 Already it is apparent that it is only a matter of time before the facts of geography accelerate the trend to plurilateral ocean boundary agreements in circumstances where three neighbouring coastal states have to negotiate the trijunction points for their offshore boundaries. This point is illustrated in various regions in Johnston and Saunders, *Ocean Boundary Making*, passim.

266 The five ocean boundary agreements with an arbitration clause are three between the Federal Republic of Germany and the Netherlands (1964), Denmark (1965), and the United Kingdom (1971), one between Japan and Korea (1974), and one between France and Spain (1979). The three providing for reference to the ICJ are two between Italy and Spain (1974) and Greece (1977), and one between Saudi Arabia and Sudan (1974). The two providing for peaceful settlement according to article 33 of the UN Charter are between Haiti and Cuba (1977) and Colombia (1978). The agreement between Colombia and the Dominican Republic (1978) calls for disputes to be settled peacefully through means recognized in international law.

267 Francalanci et al., *Atlas of Baselines*, 50, 55.

268 Ibid., 42, 34.

269 Lay et al., *New Directions*, 215.

270 See Prescott, *Maritime Political Boundaries*, 190–1; Jagota, *Maritime Boundary*, 90–2; and Prescott, *Australia's Maritime Boundaries*, 119–23. For evaluation, see Ryan and White, "Torres Strait Treaty," and Burmester, "Torres Strait Treaty."

CHAPTER TWELVE: THE THEORY

1 This is disputed by some scholars, however. See, for example, Tringham, "Territorial Demarcation."

2 For strictures on the "mystique of the frontier," see Falk, *This Endangered Planet*.

3 Gottman, ed., *Centre and Periphery*, passim.

4 See generally Clingan, ed., *Law of the Sea*.

5 See, for example, Young, *Resource Regimes*.

6 The term "co-operative ethic" encompasses the entire range of "expectations" of co-operative action generated by the UNCLOS III Convention, whether in the form of "obligations," "responsibilities," or some other type of commitment by contracting parties. For a deep analysis of the implications of the co-operative ethic in the new law of the sea, see Chircop, *Cooperative Regimes*.

7 On region-building implications, see Johnston and Saunders, "Ocean Boundary Issues." For a fully developed study of ocean development trends in the Mediterranean, see Chircop, *Cooperative Regimes*. See also Young, *Resource Management*.

8 "Boundary behaviour" can be defined as any form of official or officially sanctioned behaviour designed to affect boundary-related activities and issues.

9 For example, "functionalism" is a familiar term in sociology, where it refers to Bronislaw Malinowski's theory of social change. For an analysis, see McLeish, *Theory of Social Change*, 15–28.

10 For recent "policy science" contributions to international law, see McDougal and Reisman, *International Law in Contemporary Perspective*, and *International Law Essays*.

11 See, for example, Jenks, *The World beyond the Charter*; Friedmann, *Changing Structure of International Law*; Schachter, *Sharing the World's Resources*; and Falk, *The End of World Order*.

12 In political theory "functionalism" may be said to have evolved from, if not originated in, the writings of Henri de Saint-Simon, who envisaged as early as the 1830s the development of a system of international welfare co-operation to combat the threat to human welfare inherent in nationalism. Weiss, *International Bureaucracy*, 3–5. The concept of the League of Nations emerged from the Saint-Simonian idea of an international agency charged with welfare responsibilities, which was promoted initially by legal idealists such as James Lorimer and later by writers such as Gilbert Murray, Elihu Root, Leonard Woolf, Norman Angell, Robert Cecil, and G.D.H. Cole. The theory of functionalism in modern political theory was first advanced by David Mitrany, who argued in favour of international organization according to activity or "function" rather than according to territory (in the federalist fashion) or formula (in the tradition of legal idealism). See Mitrany, *Progress of International Government*, "Functionalist Approach to World Organization," and *Working Peace System*. See also Weiss, *International Bureaucracy*, 7–9.

13 Between the early 1960s and the early 1970s functionalism (or neo-functionalism) was taken up mostly by American political scientists interested in the emergence of organizations devoted to the purposes of regional integration. See, for example, Lindberg, *Political Dynamics*; Haas, *Beyond the Nation State*; Sewell, *Functionalism and World Politics*; Haas, "Regional Integration"; Scheingold, "Consequences of Regional Integration"; Lindberg and Scheingold, eds., *Regional Integration*; and Nye, *Peace in Parts*. On the contributions of the "neo-functionalists," see Weiss, *International Bureaucracy*, 9–17; and Deutsch, *Tides Among Nations*.

14 Young, "International Regimes"; "Regime Dynamics"; and *Resource*

Regimes. See also Krasner, ed., *International Regimes*, and Sollie et al., *Challenge of New Territories*. "At the most general level, a regime is a set of agreements among some specified group of actors spelling out: (1) a well-defined distribution of power and authority for the relevant social structure or geographical region, (2) a system of rights and liability rules for the members of the social structure, and (3) a collection of behavioral prescriptions or rules which indicate actions the members are expected to take under various circumstances. In short, a regime is a system of government, though it need not involve the existence of a written constitution or the presence of any formal institutional arrangements." Young, *Resource Management*, 44–5. Compare Haas, "On Systems and International Regimes." For a systematic application of functionalist logic to ocean regime-building, see Chircop, *Cooperative Regimes*.

15 Most functionalists would probably agree that "the nation-state, while still successfully fulfilling some functions, is thought to promote values in high politics and national prestige at the expense of public welfare; international or cross-national organisations which are created to satisfy felt needs without regard for national frontiers could produce greater welfare benefits for individuals; and their work could eventually undermine popular loyalties to the state through the creation of a working peace system and the satisfaction of felt needs on a non-national basis; the central axiom is that form should follow function." Taylor and Groom, "Functionalism and International Relations," 1. Hopes for progress along functionalist lines will, of course, often be disappointed. See, for example, Coll, "Functionalism and the Balance of Interests."

16 "Functionalism stresses the plenitude of relationships of a legitimised character between all manner of diverse actors which forms the very fabric of world society: a working peace system exists and functionalism seeks to remove impediments to its growth. The assumptions of functionalism ... are different from those of strategic studies, or crisis management, or foreign policy analysis. The billiard ball analogy of international society is rejected; greater significance is attached to the emergence of an increasing range of inter-, cross-, and trans-national systems of inter-dependence; the term 'world politics' or 'world society' is preferred to 'international politics'; the role of governments is to be progressively reduced by indirect methods, and integration is to be encouraged by a variety of functionally based, cross-national ties ..." Taylor and Groom, "Functionalism and International Relations," 2. Moreover, statist analysis, whether in the form of foreign policy analysis or otherwise, often leans too heavily on the concept of "state policy" or "national interest." "In fact, the state is not a purposive actor making rational choices about well-defined alternatives in an attempt to maximize any identifiable value. Rather, the state is an institutional arena

or framework of rights and rules within which a variety of competing actors and interests seek to hammer out social and collective decisions affecting the society at large." Young, *Resource Regimes*, 14.

17 *Los tecnicos* are those persons forming the administrative, scientific, and technical élites that operate the governmental and industrial systems on a day-to-day basis. *Los politicos* are those who dominate the senior level of management in governmental and industrial systems through the use of personality, will-power, and intelligence rather than knowledge and technical skills.

18 Young, *Resource Management*, passim. But even in the context of ocean boundary-making, few are able to share David Mitrany's utopian vision of "making frontiers meaningless through the continuous development of common activities and interests across them." Mitrany, "Working Peace System," 62.

CHAPTER THIRTEEN: THE PROCESSES

1 Jagota, *Maritime Boundary*, 219–72.

2 UN conferences such as UNCLOS III and the 1972 Conference on the Human Environment have given rise to a proliferation of research and training programs in resource and environmental management, both of a sectoral (such as fishery management) and a cross-sectoral kind (such as coastal zone management). Since the late 1970s training requirements in ocean management have received increasing attention, both inside and outside the UN system.

3 On the tensions between *los tecnicos* and *los politicos* at the national level, see Etzioni-Halevy *Political Manipulation*. For studies of similar tensions at the international level, see McLaren, *Civil Servants and Public Policy* and Jordan, *International Administration*. For important conceptual contributions to the study of bureaucratic politics, see Allison, *Essence of Decision* and Halpern, *Bureaucratic Politics and Foreign Policy*.

4 For recent listings, see McDorman, Beauchamp, and Johnston, *Maritime Boundary Delimitation*, 157–95; and Jagota, *Maritime Boundary*, 331–44.

5 See Druckman, *Human Factors in Negotiations*.

6 Raiffa, *The Art and Science of Negotiation*.

7 See Letalik, "Boundary Delimitation in the Mediterranean"; Nelson, "The Delimitation of Maritime Boundaries"; Rhee and James MacAulay, "Ocean Boundary Issues in East Asia"; and Townsend Gault, "Offshore Boundary Delimitation in the Persian-Arabian Gulf."

8 Underwood, "Ocean Boundaries and Resource Development in West Africa."

9 For a global review, see Oellers-Frahm and Wühler, *Dispute Settlement*.

10 For an evaluation of this western bias, see Johnston, "Heritage of Political Thought."
11 McWhinney, *United Nations Law Making*, 105–32.
12 On the need for de-westernizing the IJC, see Falk, *Reviving the World Court*.
13 On differing attitudes to the role of international tribunals, see Gordon, "Changing Attitudes," and McWhinney, *World Court*.
14 On the jurisprudential split in the IJC, see the section entitled "Modern Dispute Management" in chapter 11.

CHAPTER FOURTEEN: THE FACTORS

1 1982 UN Convention on the Law of the Sea, articles 3, 33, and 57.
2 Johnston, "Foundations of Justice."
3 In the fall of 1985 the Federal Republic of Germany extended the seaward limits of its territorial sea within a box-shaped area sixteen miles seaward from its baseline so as to include a deep-water anchorage which lies outside the twelve-mile limits. This unilateral extension of a territorial sea beyond the twelve-mile limits seems difficult to justify under contemporary international law, which countenances no "special case" exceptions. In functionalist theory, such a deviation from the globally approved twelve-mile limit would have to be justified by uniquely compelling considerations of port administration; otherwise, all other port states with deep-water anchorage areas might follow suit, putting the twelve-mile rule under intolerable stress.
4 It has been suggested that technical boundary experts in geography, hydrography, geodesy, and related disciplines should co-ordinate their efforts in ocean boundary studies. Alexander, "Identification of Technical Issues."
5 Outside the context of the "normal" coastline, where the low-water mark has been established for a long time in customary international law, three kinds of straight lines have been applied to "abnormal" coastal configurations: closing lines (drawn across the mouths of some rivers and bays); straight baselines (drawn along sections of complex coastlines whose features render the use of individual closing lines inappropriate); and archipelagic baselines (applicable only to states that qualify as "archipelagic"). The concepts of closing lines and straight baselines were established in customary international law long before UNCLOS III. Although the concept of archipelagic baselines is relatively new, and might be regarded as still dependent on the status of the 1982 Convention, it is difficult for non-party states to repudiate, since it is part of the UNCLOS III "package." Many jurists are prepared to argue that the UNCLOS III consensus on the package is to be interpreted as "state practice, and therefore that all parts of it, including the concept of archipelagic baselines, are in the process of

incorporation into general (customary) international law.

6 For concerns regarding the future of the freedom of navigation under the new law of the sea in the post-UNCLOS III period, see Van Dyke, *Consensus and Confrontation*, 281–311.

7 See generally Johnston, *Marine Policy*.

8 Prescott, *Delimitation of Marine Boundaries, Baselines* and Prescott, "Straight Baselines." See also *Limits in the Sea*, "Standard Guidelines."

9 In September 1985 Canada promulgated baselines around its Arctic archipelago in a manner that raised questions about their conformity with the UNCLOS III provisions on straight baselines and archipelagic baselines. The matter is unclear because of the absence in the Convention of any provisions for "coastal" archipelagoes.

10 1982 UN Convention on the Law of the Sea, articles 74 and 83.

11 The requirement for an "equitable solution" belongs to the first paragraph, which contemplates only delimitation "by agreement": that is, by negotiation, not adjudication.

12 The UNCLOS III system of dispute settlement embraces all means indicated in article 33(1) of the UN Charter and any other peaceful means that may be chosen by the parties to a dispute under the convention. 1982 UN Convention on the Law of the Sea, articles 279 and 280. For an analysis of these options, see chapter 18 infra. See also Irwin, "Settlement of Maritime Boundary Disputes."

13 Johnston, "Equity and Efficiency in Marine Law and Policy."

14 Charney, "Ocean Boundaries between Nations," at 588–9, note 40.

15 It seems unnecessary to debate whether an equity-based decision would be *contra legem* or *intra legem*, since that would involve restricting discussion of the role of equity within a "unitarian" framework of rules. Compare Rosenne, *The International Court of Justice*, at 427–8, cited in Charney, "Ocean Boundaries between Nations," at 593. It must be conceded, however, that some recent ICJ decisions, such as that in *Case concerning Military and Paramilitary Activities in and against Nicaragua* (between Nicaragua and the United States) have raised the concerns of western states regarding the tendency to *excès de pouvoir* on the part of international tribunals. See, for example, Reisman, "Has the International Court Exceeded its Jurisdiction?"

CHAPTER FIFTEEN: THE RELEVANCE OF OCEAN ZONING

1 1. In North America, for example, functionalist logic, applied to resource and environmental problems, seems conspicuous in writers as diverse as Boleslaw Boczek, Elisabeth Mann Borgese, William T. Burke, Aldo Chir-

cop, Richard A. Falk, Robert Friedheim, Myres S. McDougal, Edward Miles, John Norton Moore, Arvid Pardo, Michael Reisman, Jan Schneider, Mark J. Valencia, and Oran Young.

2 Johnston, "Heritage of Political Thought."

3 In this context it is unnecessary to take a strong position for or against the law-and-economics movement in contemporary jurisprudence. But it might be noted that the adherents of this school emphasize the value of efficiency and give it a broad meaning equivalent to maximization of net benefits. See, for example, Polinsky, *Introduction to Law and Economics*, chapter 1. Those who accept the centrality of administrative logic in ocean zoning may be tempted to apply law and economics to ocean boundary-making in general, or at least to the bureaucratic decision-making involved in the delineation of baselines and closing lines. In the case of a bureaucracy that is sensitive to coastal community values, interests, and attitudes, it is difficult to see why equity considerations would necessarily be underweighted in such an analysis.

4 It must be assumed that what is perceived to be the appropriate balance between efficiency and equity considerations will change over time as one's perception of the "situation" changes. Admittedly, a functionalist position that gives a pivotal role in ocean boundary-making to the administrative test of functionality, conceived in terms of social equity and efficiency, also assumes that the relevant sector of bureaucracy reflects the views of the appropriate sectors of science and industry and of the affected communities.

5 Criticisms of law and economics, and economics generally, often arise from the critic's conviction that the economic method of measuring all costs and benefits, in monetary terms, is insufficient.

6 Johnston and Saunders, "Ocean Boundary Issues and Developments."

CHAPTER SIXTEEN: THE RELEVANCE OF OCEAN SCIENCE AND TECHNOLOGY

1 1. On the relationship between ocean science and ocean management policy, see Ross, "Changing Ocean Policy Horizon." No one has so far developed a systematic theory of "ocean management" or worked out in detail the informational and conceptual elements of a comprehensive "managerial framework" for the making and maintenance of ocean boundary-making. For comments on the latter, see Charney, "Ocean Boundaries between Nations." For a Canadian perspective on the management responsibilities of a highly developed coastal state, see Johnston, *Canada and the Law of the Sea*, passim.

2 See various contributions in Johnston, *Environmental Law of the Sea*. On

the conjunction of science, law, and politics in marine pollution control, see M'Gonigle and Zacher, *Pollution, Politics, and International Law*. On the relationship between scientist and lawyer generally in the field of international environmental law, see Johnston, "Systemic Environmental Damage." See also Organisation for Economic Co-operation and Development, *OECD and the Environment*.

3 See the new introductory essay in Johnston, *International Law of Fisheries* (1987), pp. xxv–lxxx. For a conservationist critique of the UNCLOS III fishery provisions, see de Klemm in Johnston, *Environmental Law of the Sea*, 71–92. On the prospective use of new science and technology for the extraction of food and other benefits from the sea, see Colwell and Greer, "Biotechnology and the Sea."

4 1982 UN Convention on the Law of the Sea, articles 238–265.

5 Kindt, "Limiting Marine Research."

6 Resort to geology and geomorphology for continental shelf boundary-making was the more or less direct result of the doctrine of natural prolongation, first advanced by the ICJ in the *North Sea Continental Shelf* cases. This now-abandoned doctrine encouraged lawyers to use these sciences in the identification of deep depressions and other features of the continental margin that could be viewed as constituting a "natural" ocean boundary for settlement purposes. The same ICJ decision suggested the relevance of "unity of deposits" in the distribution of hydrocarbon reserves, which seemed to underline the importance of co-operative arrangements for management and conservation of such resources in transboundary areas of the shelf. In light of these considerations, the United States government argued by analogy that environmental factors should govern, or contribute to, the choice of a single maritime boundary in the Gulf of Maine, but this line of argument failed, despite the wealth of ecological information made available to the chamber of the court. "The Chamber decided that it had to find both a natural boundary on the continental shelf, a geological break which the United States admitted did not exist, and a natural boundary in the water column, before a natural boundary might govern the case ... Nevertheless, the Chamber went on to say that even if there had been a natural division in the seabed, the facts did not show a natural boundary in the water column ... It cast doubt on the whole notion of natural boundaries in the marine environment, stating: 'The Chamber is not however convinced of the possibility of discerning any genuine, sure and stable 'natural boundaries' in so fluctuating an environment as the waters of the ocean, their flora and fauna,' (para. 54). And *it indicated that the legal boundary need not follow a natural boundary if the location of the natural boundary is inequitable* (para. 56) [emphasis added]." Colson, "Environmental Factors." Colson suggests that the chamber declined to accept the natural boundary argument on the ground that "it did not want to open up this new area of

the law to the same type of inconclusive scientific debate that had come out of the Court's reference to natural prolongation in 1969."

7 In the *Gulf of Maine* case the United States also argued that delimitation should facilitate the management and conservation of fishery resources, and minimize the potentiality for international disputes in the Georges Bank area. Environmental facts were selected to show that the bank was an "integrated ocean ecosystem" and that the living resources in the area were "common pool resources in economic terms." But the chamber resisted this resort to functionalist logic simply by denying the existence of a rule of international law requiring that a boundary should "make it possible to ensure the optimum conservation and management of living resources and at the same time reduce the potential for international disputes." Ibid. For a cogent analysis of the relevance of socio-economic considerations in the quest for an equitable solution to an ocean boundary problem, see Sharma, "Relevance of Economic Factors."

8 In the case of the seaward limits of the shelf extending beyond two hundred miles, the scientific content of the formula provided in article 76 of the 1982 Convention ensures that the sciences of geology, geomorphology, and hydrography will play a central role in that type of ocean boundary-making. In the case of lateral boundaries, the role of science will vary with the parties to the dispute and with the vagaries of diplomacy and adjudication.

9 The rationale of the EEZ regime is not explicitly expounded in the 1982 Convention, but it seems to pivot on the recognition of the coastal state's "sovereign rights" to all ocean resources within these limits. Since the regime is essentially a response to nation-building demands from developing coastal states, it can be said to have a developmental rationale. Blatant overfishing immediately outside two-hundred-mile limits can therefore be characterized as an intolerable affront to the adjacent coastal state.

10 1982 UN Convention on the Law of the Sea, article 76.

11 See, for example, Talbott, " 'Science Court.' "

12 "The limit of territorial waters ... is not a chalk line on the surface of the sea. Its determination is a matter of difficulty even in clear weather, for legally the limit follows every promontory and indentation of the coast. The difficulty of making sure whether or not a vessel is in territorial waters at a given moment was demonstrated during the Great War. In some cases the Prize Courts deliberated for long hours, and the question resolved itself into one of a few yards." Edwards, *Grey Diplomatists*, 268. At present the attainment of precision in measurement is less difficult in distance than in depth. See chapter 9, note 108. On the prospects of sea floor measurement, see Hoskins, "Delimitation of Marine Mining Areas," 179 ff.

13 Williams, "Editorial: Marine Survey"; Cailliau, "North-South Dialogue"; Holden, "Technical Cooperation."

14 Indeed, it might be argued that "factual" disputes arising from a science-

based transboundary arrangement should be referred to a "science court." See Talbott, " 'Science Court.' "

CHAPTER SEVENTEEN: THE RANGE OF CHOICES IN DIRECT BILATERAL DIPLOMACY

1 Pruitt, *Negotiation Behavior*, 71-89.

2 Smith and Wells, *Third World Minerals Agreements*, 3.

3 Pruitt, *Negotiation Behavior*, 99-135.

4 Ibid., 16. For an early analysis of the theory of integrative bargaining, see Walton and McKenzie, *Behavioral Theory of Labor Negotiations*.

5 Johnston, "Chinese Treaty Behaviour."

6 For an earlier version of these options, see comments in Park and Park, *East Asian Perspective*, 83-8.

7 For many years the "do nothing" option has apparently been forced on coastal states in the Yellow and East China Seas, which are perceived as belonging to a region characterized by a high risk of conflict. See Rhee and MacAulay, "Ocean Boundary Issues in East Asia."

8 Joint communiqués issued after high-level talks between the governments of Greece and Turkey between 1976 and 1978 were essentially agreements to disagree on the Aegean Sea continental shelf boundary delimitation dispute. These joint communiqués were succeeded by exchanges of notes that essentially belong to the same category. For texts, see *Aegean Sea Continental Shelf Case* (Greece versus Turkey), ICJ Pleadings 1980, oral arguments, documents, 511-22.

9 Perhaps the closest to this option in practice is the designation of "neutral zones," such as those established on the shoreline and hinterland of the Dardanelles, straddling the approaches to the Sea of Marmora and the Black Sea, after the First World War. Edwards, *Grey Diplomatists*, 46, 54-66.

10 Belonging to this category is the exchange of notes between Italy and France of 20 January 1981, which created a relatively informal "mixed commission" to "contribute to the solution of frontier problems" on each side of their border (which apparently includes their undelimited ocean boundary in the Mediterranean). It is expected to meet only once a year to consider the need for recommendations to the two governments on the basis of technical reports. The text is in *Gazzetta Ufficiale della Repubblica Italiana*, no. 174, (26 June 1981), 4092.

11 Pending resolution of the *Gulf of Maine* boundary dispute, Canada and the United States, in the 1970s and early 1980s, entered into a series of provisional fishing agreements granting reciprocal rights of access to the other party's side of the disputed line. Somewhat indirectly, Italy and Malta might be said to have entered into a provisional access agreement for

exploratory purposes in the continental shelf area between Malta and Sicily by virtue of their *notes verbales* of 31 December 1965 and 29 April 1970.

12 Perhaps the closest to an actual example is the tripartite agreement of 1976 concluded by France, Italy, and Morocco for the protection of the Mediterranean coastal waters. In the ESCAP region of Asia and the Pacific, many governments have been participating in a pooling of data from joint prospecting of offshore hydrocarbon resources.

13 See, for example, the 1974 joint development agreement between Saudi Arabia and Sudan. Similar co-operation is envisaged in the joint development agreements between Japan and the Republic of Korea (1974) and between Thailand and Malaysia (1979).

14 For example, Canada and the United States have negotiated agreements on the co-ordination of Coast Guard and other government services for cleaning up after a major oil spill in boundary waters.

15 For example, some agreements of this kind are limited to "oceanographic co-operation," such as the agreement between Spain and Portugal of 27 May 1971 (UN Legislative Series, ST/LEG/SER B/16), and that between France and Spain of 11 December 1975 (UN Legislative Series, ST/LEG/SER B/19).

16 Perhaps the best-known example of such a treaty is the Boundary Waters Treaty of 1909, which established the International Joint Commission for management purposes in the Great Lakes region and other boundary waters between Canada and the United States. For an assessment of this treaty and subsequent boundary-related arrangements, see Spencer, Kirton, and Nossal, *Seventy Years On*. It should be recalled, of course, that the boundary line was also drawn.

17 The most sophisticated ocean boundary settlement/arrangement in existence is the multipurpose Torres Strait Treaty concluded between Australia and Papua New Guinea in 1979. See the section entitled "Modern Treaties and the Pattern of State Practice" in chapter 11; see also Prescott, *Australia's Maritime Boundaries* 119–23; Jagota, *Maritime Boundary*, 90–3; and Prescott, *Maritime Political Boundaries*, 190–1.

18 Johnston and Saunders, "Ocean Boundary-Making."

CHAPTER EIGHTEEN: THE RANGE OF CHOICES IN RESORT TO INTERMEDIATION

1 Statute of the International Court of Justice, article 38(1).

2 Ibid., article 38(2).

3 1982 UN Convention on the Law of the Sea, Annex VI.

4 Ibid., article 4(3).

5 Ibid., article 293(1).

6 Ibid., article 293(2).

7 Ibid., Annex VI, article 16.
8 Ibid., article 15(2).
9 Ibid., article 15(3).
10 Compare the four arbitrations of ocean boundary delimitation disputes: the *Grisbadarna* arbitration between Norway and Sweden (1909); the *Beagle Channel* arbitration between Argentina and Chile (1977); the *Channel Islands* arbitration between France and the United Kingdom (1977); and the *Gulf of Guinea* arbitration between Guinea and Guinea Bissau (1985). See the section entitled "Modern Dispute Management" in chapter 11.
11 1982 UN Convention on the Law of the Sea, article 287(1).
12 Ibid., Annex VI, article 2(1).
13 Ibid., Annex VII, article 2(1).
14 The distinction between mediation and "good offices" in so slight that it has virtually been abandoned. Cot, *International Conciliation*, 31–2.
15 1982 UN Convention on the Law of the Sea, article 284(4).
16 Ibid., article 284(1).
17 Ibid., Annex V, article 4.
18 Ibid., article 5.
19 Ibid., article 2.
20 Ibid., article 5.
21 Johnston and Saunders, "Ocean Boundary-Making."
22 On cultural patterns in the avoidance of adjudication, see Nader and Todd, *The Disputing Process*.
23 1982 UN Convention on the Law of the Sea, article 298(1)(a)(ii).

CHAPTER NINETEEN: CONSIDERATIONS IN THE TREATMENT OF OCEAN BOUNDARY PROBLEMS

1 In theory, it is possible to distinguish three basic types of *compromis*: (1) the type that assigns to the tribunal a minimal *declaratory* role, and thus reserves to the parties the maximal scope in subsequent boundary-related initiatives; (2) the type that assigns to the tribunal a *resolutive* role (such as the drawing of the line), and thus reserves to the parties a role that is chiefly related to the negotiation of subsequent boundary arrangements; and (3) the type that assigns to the tribunal a discretionary *facilitative* role, and thus reserves to the parties the role of selecting from the tribunal's observations what seems to be the most appropriate kind of linear settlement and/or institutional arrangement. A "hybrid" *compromis* is one that combines two or all three of these elements. The choosing of the type of *compromis* is part of the problem of procedural strategy facing each party to an ocean boundary dispute that cannot be settled through direct bilateral diplomacy.
2 On "lateral thinking" as an approach to problem-solving, see the writings

of Edward De Bono, such as *The Mechanism of Mind* (1969), *The Use of Lateral Thinking* (1967), and *Lateral Thinking: A Textbook of Creativity* (1970).

3 For a recent study of these special issues, see Westerman, *Juridical Bay*.

4 See Johnston and Saunders, *Ocean Boundary Making*, passim.

5 1982 UN Convention on the Law of the Sea, article 123.

6 Legal norms are clearly "extrinsic": they have to be imported into the "situation". Historical facts and "considerations" are less easy to categorize. The more distant the time, the more difficult it is to characterize the facts and considerations as inherent in the contemporary situation that must be dealt with. It is suggested, however, as a matter of common sense, that recent history as reflected in current political and economic relationships within the affected region should be treated as intrinsic, and given some weight along with other situational factors.

7 Although highly abstract and somewhat arbitrary, this Lasswellian catalogue of value categories might serve to remind an ocean boundary-maker of the human wants or needs at stake, and of the ultimate demands to be met in the treatment of the problem. Above all, it serves to remind an authoritative decision-maker of the obligation to look beyond the technical "issues" associated with the "problem."

8 This behavioural approach to an ocean boundary problem would require the boundary-maker to evaluate the "legitimacy" of the motivation that appears to influence the boundary claims of the parties to the delimitation dispute. Because of the legitimacy of national security considerations in and adjacent to the twelve-mile territorial sea, the claims to the baseline and seaward limits of such a zone might be regarded as properly motivated by the desire for autonomy. In more remote areas, on the other hand, where ocean use should be regulated in some degree under a regime of joint or regional management, boundary claims might be assessed with a view to the need for co-operation.

9 For the most recent authoritative articulation of the "basic norm" for ocean boundary delimitation, see the decision of the ICJ chamber in the *Gulf of Maine* case between Canada and the United States, as summarized in chapter 11.

10 Functionalist reasoning suggests that legal norms should be treated in one of two ways: either "promoted" as fundamental principles to the level of the "basic norm" and treated along with other (non-legal) value considerations; or "relegated" as techniques to the final, instrumental stage of problem-solving and treated as such along with criteria and methods. The so-called median line rule should be treated as a method; the so-called principle of proportionality should be treated as a criterion (or test) of equitableness; and so on. Wielding Occam's razor in this rationalist manner makes it difficult to say what is left in the category of secondary-level "principles."

11 It seems incompatible with functionalist reasoning to assign any *a priori* precedence to any of these four kinds of elements in the situation. The saliency given to these elements will, and should, depend on the way the boundary-maker chooses to characterize the situation.

12 See note 10, supra.

13 An island may be given no effect (except for an appropriate territorial sea enclave, if it satisfies the legal criteria for such treatment); partial (half) effect; or full effect.

14 The use of a zoning technique, involving the creation of a joint development, joint management, or alternative zone, places faith in some kind of co-operative arrangement instead of a linear settlement. See chapter 17. Some of these diplomatic options may, of course, be addressed by an intermediary that has been given a facilitative mandate.

Bibliography

This bibliography consists of all the sources and references included in the notes to this book. It has been expanded slightly beyond the author's research base to assist other multidisciplinary studies in the field of boundary-making in general, and ocean boundary-making in particular. A key is provided below to indicate the field or fields of interest to which each title is chiefly related.

A International law
B International politics, organization, and relations
C Physical and political geography
D Legal, diplomatic, and economic history
E Cartography
F Oceanography and mathematics
G Hydrography and geodesy
H Ocean engineering and technology
I Public administration (bureaucracy)
J Negotiation
K Adjudication (and other third-party modes of dispute settlement)
L Sociology, anthropology, psychology, and ecology
M Bibliography
N Biography

A Adami, Vittorio. *National Frontiers in Relation to International Law*. Translated by T.T. Behrens. London: Oxford University Press 1927.

D Agricola, Georgius. *De Re Metallica*. Translated by H.C. and L.H. Hoover. New York: Dover Publications 1950.

C,G Alexander, Lewis M. "The Identification of Technical Issues of Maritime Boundary Delimitation within the Law of the Sea Convention Context." In Brown and Churchill, 1988.

B Alexander, Lewis M., and Lynn Carter Hanson, eds. *Antarctic Politics and*

Marine Resources: Critical Choices for the 1980s. Kingston: University of Rhode Island Center for Ocean Management Studies 1984.

B Allison, Graham T. *Essence of Decision: Explaining the Cuban Missile Crisis*. Boston: Little, Brown 1971.

M Amato, Luciano, Tullio Scovazi, Tecia Faranda, and Tulio Treves. *La legislazione italiana sul diritto del mare/Italian Legislation on the Law of the Sea*. Milan: Giuffré 1981.

G Amin, M. "On the Conditions for Classification of Tides." 63 *International Hydrographic Review* (no.1) 161 (1986).

B Anand, Ram P. *Cultural Factors in International Relations*. New Delhi: Abhinav Publications 1981.

B Ancel, Jacques. *Géopolitique*. Paris: Delagrave 1936.

N Anderson, Bern. *Surveyor of the Sea: The Life and Voyages of Captain George Vancouver*. Seattle: University of Washington Press 1960.

F Anderson, Lee G., ed. *Economic Impacts of Extended Fisheries Jurisdiction*. Ann Arbor, Mich.: Ann Arbor Science 1977.

A Andrassy, Juray. "Les relations international de voisinage." 2 *Recueils de Cours* 77 (1951).

K "Arbitration Concerning Territorial and Maritime Jurisdiction Issues in the Beagle Channel Between Argentina and Chile, Decision of 2 May 1977." 17 *International Legal Materials* 634 (1978).

K "Arbitration Concerning the Delimitation of the Continental Shelf Between the United Kingdom of Great Britain and Northern Ireland and the French Republic, Decision of 30 June 1977." 18 *Reports of International Arbitral Awards*, reproduced in 18 *International Legal Materials* 397 (1979).

K "Arbitration Concerning the Delimitation of the Continental Shelf Between Guinea and Guinea-Bissau, Decision of 14 February 1985," 25 *International Legal Materials* 251 (1986)

L Ardrey, Robert. *The Territorial Imperative: A Personal Inquiry into the Animal Origins of Property and Nations*. London: Collins 1967.

A,K "Argentina's Declaration of Nullity." 24 *International Legal Materials* 738 (1985).

I Armstrong, John A. *The European Administrative Élite*. Princeton: Princeton University Press 1973.

A,C Aurrecoechea, I., and J.S. Pethick. "The Coastline: Its Physical and Legal Definition." 1 *International Journal of Estuarine and Coastal Law* 29 (1986).

G Babbedge, N.H. "The Oceans from Space." 41 *The Hydrographic Journal* 21 (July 1986).

J Bacharach, Samuel B., and Edward J. Lawler. *Bargaining: Power, Tactics and Outcomes*. San Francisco: Jossey-Bass 1981.

E Bagrow, Leo. *History of Cartography*. Revised by R.A. Skelton. Cambridge: Harvard University Press 1964.

F Baram, Michael S., David Rice, and William Lee. *Marine Mining of the Conti-*

nental Shelf: Legal, Technological and Environmental Considerations. Cambridge, Mass.: Ballinger 1978.

F Bardach, John E., John H. Ryther, and William O. McLarney. *Aquaculture: The Farming and Husbandry of Freshwater and Marine Organisms*. New York: Wiley-Interscience 1972.

F Barnett, T.P. "The Estimation of 'Global' Sea Level Change: A Problem of Uniqueness." 89 *Journal of Geophysical Research* 7780 (1984).

N Barrow, John, ed. *Captain Cook's Voyages of Discovery*. London: J.M. Dent; New York: E.P. Dutton 1941, 1944.

A Baxter, Richard R. *The Law of International Waterways, with Particular Regard to Interoceanic Canals*. Cambridge: Harvard University Press 1964.

K "Beagle Channel Dispute: Papal Proposals of 12 December 1980." In 24 *International Legal Materials* 7 (1985).

N Beaglehole, John C. *The Life of Captain James Cook*. London: A. and C. Black 1974.

A Beauchamp, Kenneth P. "The Management Function of Ocean Boundaries." 23 *San Diego Law Review* 611 (1986)

G Beazley, P.B. *Maritime Limits and Baselines*. 2d ed. The Hydrographic Society, August 1978.

G – "Maritime Boundaries: A Geographical and Technical Perspective." In Brown and Churchill, 1988.

B Bekiashev, Kamil A., and Vitali V. Serebriakov. *International Marine Organizations: Essays on Structure and Activities*. Translated by Vitali V. Serebriakov. The Hague: Nijhoff 1981.

B,C Bell, Frederick W. *Food from the Sea: The Economics and Politics of Ocean Fisheries*. Boulder: Westview Press 1978.

F Bell, Frederick W., and E. Ray Canterbery. *Aquaculture for the Developing Countries: A Feasibility Study*. Cambridge, Mass.: Ballinger 1976.

C Birot, Pierre. *General Physical Geography*. Translated by Margaret Ledésert. London: Harrap 1966.

H Bjono, Leif, ed. *Underwater Acoustics and Signal Processing*. Dordrecht and Boston: Reidel 1980.

C Blake, Gerald H. "Maritime Boundaries and Political Geography in the 1980s." 1 *Political Geography Quarterly* 171 (1982).

A,B,C Blake, Gerald H., ed. *Maritime Boundaries and Ocean Resources*. London and Sydney: Croom Helm 1987.

E Blakemore, M.J., and J.B. Harley. "Concepts in the History of Cartography: A Review and Perspective." Edited by Edward H. Dahl. 17 *Cartographics* (formerly *The Canadian Cartographer* and *Cartographic Monographs*) (Winter 1980).

A Blum, Yehuda Z. *Historic Titles in International Law*. The Hague: Nijhoff 1965.

A – *Secure Boundaries and Middle East Peace in the Light of International Law and Practice*. Jerusalem: Hebrew University of Jerusalem 1971.

A Blumann, Claude. "Frontières et limites." In *La frontière*, 1980.

C,G Boggs, S. Whittemore. "Delimitation of the Territorial Sea." 24 *American Journal of International Law* 541 (1930).

C,G – "Problems of Water Boundary Delimitation: Median Line and International Boundaries Through Territorial Waters." 27 *Geographical Review* 445 (1937).

C,G – *International Boundaries: A Study of Boundary Functions and Problems*. New York: Columbia University Press 1940.

N Boorstin, Daniel J. *The Discoverers: A History of Man's Search to Know His World and Himself*. New York: Random House 1983.

B Booth, Ken. "Naval Strategy and the Spread of Psycho-Legal Boundaries at Sea." 38 *International Journal* 373 (1983).

D,F Borgese, Elisabeth Mann. *Seafarm: the Story of Aquaculture*. New York: Abrams 1980.

F – *The Mines of Neptune: Minerals and Metals from the Sea*. New York: Abrams 1985.

A Bouchez, Leo J. "The Fixing of Boundaries in International Boundary Rivers." 12 *International and Comparative Law Quarterly* 789 (1963).

A – *The Regime of Bays in International Law*. Leiden: Sijthoff 1964.

J *Boundary and Constitutional Agreement for the Implementation of Division of the Northwest Territories*. Iqaluit, Nunavut: 1987.

D Braudel, Fernand. *The Mediterranean and the Mediterranean World in the Age of Philip II*. Translated by Sian Reynolds. New York: Harper and Row 1972.

A Briggs, Herbert W. *The International Law Commission*. Ithaca, NY: Cornell University Press 1965.

C Brigham, Albert P. "Principles in the Determination of Boundaries." 7 *Geographical Review* 201 (1919).

A,B Broder, Sherry, and Jon Van Dyke. "Ocean Boundaries in the South Pacific." 4 *University of Hawaii Law Review* 1 (1982).

F Brown, E. Evan. *World Fish Farming: Cultivation and Economics*. Westport, Conn.: AVI 1977.

A Brown, Edward D. *The Legal Regime of Hydrospace*. London: Stevens 1971.

A – "The Continental Shelf and the Exclusive Economic Zone: The Problem of Delimitation at UNCLOS III." 4 *Maritime Policy and Management* 377 (1976–77).

A – "Rockall and the Limits of National Jurisdiction of the UK." 2 *Marine Policy* 181 (1978).

A – "Delimitation of Offshore Areas: Hard Labour and Bitter Fruits at UNCLOS III." 5 *Marine Policy* 172 (1981).

A Brown, Edward D., and Robin Churchill, eds. *The Law of the Sea: Impact and Implementation*. Honolulu: University of Hawaii, Law of the Sea Institute 1988.

E Brown, Lloyd A. *The Story of Maps*. Boston: Little, Brown 1949.

C Brown, Peter G., and Henry Shue, eds. *Boundaries: National Autonomy and Its Limits*. Totow, NJ: Rowman and Littlefield 1981.

A,D Brownlie, Ian. *African Boundaries: A Legal and Diplomatic Encyclopedia*. London: C. Hurst; Berkeley: University of California Press 1979.

A Burmeister, Henry. "The Torres Strait Treaty: Ocean Boundary Delimitation by Agreement." 76 *American Journal of International Law* 321 (1982).

H Burns, G.E. "Offshore Platform Concepts." In *Joint Exploration and Development of Offshore Hydrocarbon Resources in Southeast Asia*, edited by Ian Townsend Gault and Susan J. Rolston. (Halifax: International Institute for Transport and Ocean Policy Studies 1988).

B Burton, John. "The Nature of Aggression as Revealed in the Atomic Age." In *The Natural History of Aggression*, edited by John D. Carthy and F.J. Ebling Jr. New York: Academic Press 1964.

B Buzan, Barry G. "Naval Power, the Law of the Sea, and the Indian Ocean as a Zone of Peace." 5 *Marine Policy* 194 (1981).

B Buzan, Barry G., and Danford W. Middlemiss. "Canadian Foreign Policy and the Exploitation of the Seabed." In *Canadian Foreign Policy and the Law of the Sea*, edited by Barbara Johnson and Mark W. Zacher. Vancouver: University of British Columbia Press 1977.

G Cailliau, E.J. "Hydrography in the North-South Dialogue." 64 *International Hydrographic Review* (no. 1) 25 (1987).

B Calvert, Peter. *Boundary Disputes in Latin America*. London: Institute for the Study of Conflict 1983.

D Campen, S.I.P. van. *The Imperator: Consequences of Frustrated Expansion*. Alphen aan den Rijn: Sijthoff and Noordhoff 1978.

G Carrera, Galo. "A Method for the Delimitation of an Equidistant Boundary Between Coastal States on the Surface of a Geodetic Ellipsoid." 64 *International Hydrographic Review* (no. 1) 147 (1987).

G Carter, James R. *Computer Mapping: Progress in the 80s*. Washington, DC: Association of American Geographers 1984.

N Cartier, Jacques. *Voyages en Nouvelle-France*. Edited by Robert Lahaise and Marie Couturier. Quebec: Hurtubise 1977.

D Cartwright, Frederick F., in collaboration with Michael D. Biddiss. *Disease and History*. New York: Crowell 1972.

A Chao, K.T. "Legal Nature of International Boundaries." 5 *Chinese Year Book of International Law and Affairs* 29 (1985).

A,K Charney, Jonathan I. "The Delimitation of Lateral Seaward Boundaries Between States in a Domestic Context." 75 *American Journal of International Law* 28 (1981).

A – "Ocean Boundaries Between Nations: a Theory for Progress." 78 *American Journal of International Law* 582 (1984).

A,K – "The Offshore Jurisdiction of the States of the United States and the Provinces of Canada: A Comparison." In Johnston and Letalik, 1984.

A – "The Delimitation of Ocean Boundaries." 18 *Ocean Development and International Law* 497 (1987).

D Chiang, Tao-Chang. "The Salt Industry of Ming China." 65 *Geographical Review* 93 (1975).

A,B Child, Jack. "Antarctica: Issues and Options." 10 *Marine Policy Reports* 1 (Sept. 1987).

A,B,C,D Chircop, Aldo. "Cooperative Regimes in Ocean Management: A Study in Mediterranean Regionalism." JSD dissertation. Dalhousie University 1988.

C Chorley, Richard J., and Barbara A. Kennedy. *Physical Geography: A Systems Approach*. London: Prentice-Hall 1971.

A,B,I Christie, Donna R. "Georges Bank: Common Ground or Continued Battleground?" 23 *San Diego Law Review* 491 (1986).

A Churchill, Robin R. "Maritime Delimitation in the Jan Mayen Area." 9 *Marine Policy* 16 (1985).

D Clark, Richard E. *Point Roberts, USA: The History of a Canadian Enclave*. Bellingham, Wash.: Textype Publishing 1980.

A Clingan, Thomas A. Jr., ed. *Law of the Sea: State Practice in Zones of Special Jurisdiction*. Honolulu: University of Hawaii, Law of the Sea Institute 1982.

A Coll, Alberto R. "Functionalism and the Balance of Interests in the Law of the Sea: Cuba's Role." 79 *American Journal of International Law* 891 (1985).

A Colombos, Constantine J. *The International Law of the Sea*. 6th rev. ed. London: Longmans 1967.

A,F Colson, David A. "Environmental Factors: Are They Relevant to Delimitation?" In Brown and Churchill, 1988.

C,F Colwell, Rita R., and Jack R. Greer. "Biotechnology and the Sea." 17 *Ocean Development and International Law* 163 (1986).

J "Convention on Fishing and Conservation of the Living Resources of the High Seas." 559 UNTS 285. In von Münch and Buske, 1985.

J "Convention on the Continental Shelf." 499 UNTS 311. In von Münch and Buske, 1985.

J "Convention on the High Seas." 450 UNTS 82. In von Münch and Buske, 1985.

J "Convention on the Territorial Sea and the Contiguous Zone." 516 UNTS 205. In von Munch and Buske, 1985.

G Cooper, John. "Delimitation of the Maritime Boundary in the Gulf of Maine Area." 16 *Ocean Development and International Law* 59 (1986).

K Cot, Jean-Pierre. *International Conciliation*. Translated by R. Myers. London: Europa 1972.

C Cotter, Charles H. *The Physical Geography of the Oceans*. London: Hollis and Carter 1965.

C Couper, Alastair D. "The Marine Boundaries of the United Kingdom and the Law of the Sea." 151 *Geographical Journal* 228 (1985).

F Couper, Alastair D., and H.D. Smith. "The North Sea: Bases for Management and Planning in a Multi-State Sea Region." In Johnston and Letalik, 1984.

H Cronan, David Spencer. *Underwater Minerals*. New York: Academic Press 1980.

C Crone, Gerald R. *Backgrounnd to Geography*. London: Museum Press 1964.

E – *Maps and their Makers: An Introduction to the History of Cartography*. 4th rev. ed. London: Hutchinson 1968.

C – *Modern Geographers: An Outline of Progress in Geography since A.D. 1800*. Rev. ed. London: Royal Geographical Society 1970.

A,G Crosby, Donald G. "Definition of the Continental Shelf: Application to the Canadian Offshore." In Johnston and Letalik, 1984.

I Crozier, Michel. *The Bureaucratic Phenomenon*. Translated by the author. Chicago: University of Chicago Press 1964.

A Csabalfi, Imre A. *The Concept of State Jurisdiction in International Space Law: A Study in the Progressive Development of Space Law in the United Nations*. The Hague: Nijhoff 1971.

A Cukwurah, A.O. *The Settlement of Boundary Disputes in International Law*. Manchester: Manchester University Press 1967.

I Curtice, John, and Michael Steed. "Turning Dreams into Reality: The Division of Constituencies between the Liberals and the Social Democrats." 36 *Parliamentary Affairs* 166 (1983).

D Curzon, George N. *Frontiers*. 1907 Romanes Lecture, 2d ed. Oxford: Clarendon Press 1908.

A D'Amato, Anthony. "Manifest Intent and the Generation by Treaty of Customary Rules of International Law." 64 *American Journal of International Law* 892 (1970).

I Dalby, Michael T., and Michael S. Wertham, eds. *Bureaucracy in Historical Perspective*. Glenview, Ill.: Scott, Foresman 1971.

L Darling, Frank Fraser. "Social Behaviour and Survival." 69 *Auk* 183 (1982).

K Dawson, James. "Ancient Charts and Modern Mariners." 4 *Marine Geodesy* 113 (1980).

B Day, Alan J., ed. *Border and Territorial Disputes*. London: Longman Group 1982.

L De Bono, Edward. *The Use of Lateral Thinking*. Harmondsworth: Penguin 1967.

L – *The Mechanism of Mind*. New York: Simon and Schuster 1969.

L – *Lateral Thinking: A Textbook of Creativity*. London: Ward Lock Educational 1970.

A,B De Martini, Raymond J. *The Right of Nations to Expand by Conquest*. Washington, DC: Catholic University of America Press 1955.

A De Visscher, Charles. *Problèmes de confins en droit international public*. Paris: A. Pedone 1969.

B,F Degenhardt, Henry W. *Maritime Affairs: A World Handbook*. Detroit: Gale Research Co.; Harlow, Essex: Longman Group 1985.

B Deutsch, Karl W. *Tides Among Nations*. New York: Free Press 1979.

B Deutsch, Morton. *The Resolution of Conflict: Constructive and Destructive Pro-*

cesses. New Haven: Yale University Press 1973.

E Dickinson, Gordon C. *Maps and Air Photographs: Images of the Earth*. 2d ed. New York: Wiley 1979.

C Dorion, Henri. *La frontière Quebec-Terreneuve: Contribution a l'étude systématique des frontières*. Quebec: Les Presses de l'Université Laval 1963.

G Douglas, G.R., and S.B. MacPhee. "Hydrography for the Year 2000." 63 *International Hydrographic Review* (no. 1) 21 (1986).

C Downing, David. *An Atlas of Territorial and Border Disputes*. London: New English Library 1980.

G Dragomir, V.C., and others. *Theory of the Earth's Shape*. Amsterdam and New York: Elsevier 1982.

J Druckman, Daniel, ed. *Negotiations: Social-Psychological Perspectives*. Beverly Hills: Sage Publications 1977.

E Drummond, Scott E. "The Nautical Chart: Friend or Foe?" 1 *Marine Geodesy* 207 (1977).

J Dunlop, John T. *Dispute Resolution: Negotiation and Consensus Building*. Dover, Mass.: Auburn House 1984.

E Dutton, Geoffrey H., and William G. Nison. " The Expanding Realm of Computer Cartography." *Datamation* (June 1978).

C East, W. Gordon. *The Geography behind History*. Rev. ed. London: Nelson 1965.

F Eckert, Ross D. *The Enclosure of Ocean Resources: Economics and the Law of the Sea*. Stanford: Hoover Institution Press 1979.

I Eckhoff, Torstein E., and Knut Dahl Jacobsen. *Rationality and Responsibility in Administrative and Judicial Decision-Making*. New York: Humanities Press 1960.

A Economides, Constantine. "The Contiguous Zone, Today and Tomorrow." In Rozakis and Stephanou, 1983.

D Edwards, Kenneth. *The Grey Diplomatists*. London: Rich and Cowan 1938.

L Eibl-Elbenfeldt, Irenaus. *The Biology of Peace and War: Men, Animals and Aggression*. Translated by Eric Mosbacher. New York: Viking Press 1979.

A Elkind, Jerome B. *Non-appearance before the International Court of Justice: Functional and Comparative Analysis*. Dordrecht: Nijhoff 1984.

G Emery, K.O. "Geological Limits of the 'Continental Shelf.'" 10 *Ocean Development and International Law* 1 (1981–2).

I Etzioni-Halevy, Eva. *Political Manipulation and Administrative Power: A Comparative Study*. London and Boston: Routledge and Kegan Paul 1979.

L Evans, Peter. *Ourselves and Other Animals*. New York: Pantheon Books 1987.

A Evensen, Jens. "Certain Legal Aspects Concerning the Delimitation of the Territorial Waters of Archipelagos." UN Preparatory Document 145, A/Conf. 13/18, 29 November 1957.

A – "La délimitation entre la Norvège et l'Islande du plateau continental dans le secteur de Jan Mayen." 27 *Annuaire Français de Droit International* 711 (1981).

A Falk, Richard A. *This Endangered Planet: Prospects and Proposals for Human Survival*. New York: Random House 1971.

A – *The End of World Order: Essays on Normative International Relations*. New York: Holmes and Meier 1983.

A – *Reviving the World Court*. Charlottesville: University Press of Virginia 1986.

C Fawcett, Charles B. *Frontiers: A Study in Political Geography*. Oxford: Clarendon Press 1918.

A,D Fenn, Percy Thomas, Jr. *The Origin of the Right of Fishery in Territorial Waters*. Cambridge: Harvard University Press 1926.

E,G Fillmore, Stanley, and W.R. Sandilands. *The Chartmakers*. Toronto: NC Press in association with the Canadian Hydrographic Service 1983.

A Finlay, Luke W. "The Outer Limits of the Continental Shelf." 64 *American Journal of International Law* 42 (1970).

G Fischer, Irene. "Marine Geodesy: A New Discipline or the Modern Realization of an Ancient Endeavour?" 1 *Marine Geodesy* 165 (1977).

G – "Mean Sea Level and the Marine Geoid: An Analysis of Concepts." 1 *Marine Geodesy* 37 (1977).

J,K Folberg, Jay, and Alison Taylor. *Mediation: A Comprehensive Guide to Resolving Conflicts without Litigation*. San Francisco: Jossey-Bass 1984.

A Francalanci, Giampiero, Daniel Romano, and Tullio Scovazzi, eds. *Atlas of the Straight Baselines*. Part 1. Milan: Giuffré 1986.

A François, Jean Pierre Adrien. *Handboek van het Volkenrecht*. Vol. 1. Zwolle: W.E.J. Tjeenk Willink 1931–3.

A Friedmann, Wolfgang G. *The Changing Structure of International Law*. New York: Columbia University Press 1964.

N Friendly, Alfred. *Beaufort of the Admiralty: The Life of Sir Francis Beaufort, 1774–1857*. New York: Random House 1977.

A,D Fulton, Thomas Wemyss. *The Sovereignty of the Sea*. Edinburgh: W. Blackwood 1911.

C Fuson, Robert H. *A Geography of Geography: Origins and Development of the Discipline*. Dubuque, Iowa: W.C. Brown 1969.

G Gardiner, Piers R.R., and K.W. Robinson. *Technology Ireland*. Dublin: Institute for Industrial Research and Standards 1977.

G Gardiner, Piers R.R. "Reasons and Methods for Fixing the Outer Limit of the Legal Continental Shelf Beyond 200 Nautical Miles." *Iranian Review of International Relations*, no. 11–12 (Spring 1978).

A Gidel, Gilbert C. *Le droit international public de la mer*. 2 vols. Chateauroux: Établissements Mellottée 1932.

L Gilligan, Carol. *In a Different Voice: Psychological Theory and Women's Development*. Cambridge: Harvard University Press 1982.

C Glantz, Michael H., ed. *Desertification: Environmental Degradation in and Around Arid Lands*. Boulder: Westview Press 1977.

C Glassner, Martin Ira, and Harm J. de Bilj. *Systematic Political Geography*. 3d ed. New York: Wiley 1980.

A,D Gold, Edgar. *Maritime Transport: The Evolution of Marine Policy and Shipping Law*. Lexington, Mass.: Lexington Books 1981.

A – "Vessel Traffic Regulation: The Interface of Maritime Safety and Operational Freedom." 14 *Journal of Maritime Law and Commerce* 1 (1983).

A Gold, Edgar, and Douglas M. Johnston. "Ship-Generated Pollution: The Creator of Regulated Navigation." In Clingan, 1982.

J,K Goldberg, Stephen B., Eric D. Green, and Frank E.A. Sander. *Dispute Resolution*. Boston and Toronto: Little, Brown 1985.

A Goldblat, Jozef. *French Nuclear Tests in the Atmosphere: The Question of Legality*. Stockholm: Stockholm International Peace Research Institute 1974.

A Goldie, L.F.E. "A Lexicographical Controversy: The Word 'Adjacency' in Article 1 of the Continental Shelf Convention." 66 *American Journal of International Law* 829 (1972).

A Gordon, Edward. "Changing Attitudes toward Courts and Their Possession of Social Decision Prerogatives." Dobbs Ferry, NY: Oceana 1976. In Gross, 1976.

C,L Gottmann, Jean. *The Significance of Territory*. Charlottesville: University Press of Virginia 1973.

C,L – ed. *Centre and Periphery: Spatial Variation in Politics*. London and Beverly Hills: Sage Publications 1980.

D Green, Lewis. *The Boundary Hunters: Surveying the 141st Meridian and the Alaskan Panhandle*. Vancouver: University of British Columbia Press 1982.

A,B Greenfield, Jeanette. *China and the Law of the Sea, Air, and Environment*. Alphen aan den Rijn: Sijthoff and Noordhoff 1979.

N Greenhalgh, Peter A.L. *Pompey: The Roman Alexander*. London: Weidenfeld and Nicolson 1980.

B Groom, A.J.R., and Paul Taylor, eds. *Functionalism: Theory and Practice in International Relations*. London: University of London Press 1975.

A,D Gross, Leo. "The Peace of Westphalia, 1648–1948." 42 *American Journal of International Law* 20 (1948).

A – ed. *The Future of the International Court of Justice*. 2 vols. Dobbs Ferry, NY: Oceana 1976.

A – "The Dispute between Greece and Turkey Concerning the Continental Shelf in the Aegean." 71 *American Journal of International Law* 31 (1977).

A,D Grotius, Hugo. *Mare Liberum* (1609, 1633).

C Guichonnet, Paul, and C. Raffestin. *La géographie des frontières*. Paris: Les Presses Universitaires de France 1974.

J Gulliver, P.H. *Disputes and Negotiations: A Cross-Cultural Perspective*. New York: Academic Press 1979.

B Haas, Ernst B. *Beyond the Nation State: Functionalism and International Organization*. Stanford: Stanford University Press 1964.

B – "The Study of Regional Integration: Reflections on the Joy and Anguish of Pretheorizing." 24 *International Organization* 607 (1970).

B – "On Systems and International Regimes." 27 *World Politics* 147 (1975).

B – "Why Collaborate? Issue-Linkage and International Regimes." 32 *World Politics* 357 (1980).

H Haines, Gregory. *Sound Underwater*. New York: Crane Russak 1974.

A Hall, H. Duncan. "The International Frontier." 42 *American Journal of International Law* 42 (1948).

H Hall, Stewart, ed. *Drilling and Producing Offshore*. Tulsa, Okla.: PennWell Books 1983.

Halperin, Morton H., with the assistance of Priscilla Clapp and Arnold Kanter. *Bureaucratic Politics and Foreign Policy*. Washington, DC: The Brookings Institution 1974.

G Hamon, B.V., and J.S. Godfrey. "Mean Sea Level and Its Interpretation." 4 *Marine Geodesy* 315 (1980).

A Hardy, Michael, Ann L. Hollick, Johan J. Holst, Douglas M. Johnston, and Shigeru Oda. *A New Regime for the Oceans*. Trilateral Commission, The Triangle Papers (No. 9) 1976.

D Harper, R.W. *The Port of London Act, 1908: With an Introduction and Notes*. London: Stevens and Sons 1910.

J,K Harrington, Christine B. *Shadow Justice: The Ideology and Institutionalization of Alternatives to Court*. Westport, Conn.: Greenwood Press 1985.

G Harris, P.A. "Towards a Total Navigation Control System." 51 *International Hydrographic Review* (no.2) 83 (1984).

C Hartshorne, Richard. "The Functional Approach in Political Geography." Reprinted in Glassner and de Bilj, 1980.

B,C – "A Survey of the Boundary Problems of Europe." In *Geographical Aspects of International Relations*, edited by Charles C. Colby. Freeport, NY: Books for Libraries Press 1938.

G Haskins, G.L. "Delimination of the Boundaries of Marine Mining Areas in International Waters." 62 *International Hydrographic Review* (no.2) 179 (1985).

C Haushofer, Karl. *Grenzen in ihrer geographischen und politischen Bedeutung*. Berlin: K. Vowinckel 1927.

G Hedberg, Hollis D. "Limits of National Jurisdiction over Natural Resources of the Ocean Bottom." In *The Law of the Sea: National Policy Recommendations*, edited by Lewis M. Alexander. Kingston: University of Rhode Island, Law of the Sea Institute 1970.

G – *National-International Jurisdictional Boundary on the Ocean Floor*. University of Rhode Island, Law of the Sea Institute 1972.

G – "Ocean Floor Boundaries: The Base-of-Slope Boundary Zone Formula Gives the Most Acceptable Jurisdictional Limit for Mineral Resources." 204 *Science* 135 (1979).

G – "A Critique of Boundary Provisions in the Law of the Sea." 12 *Ocean Development and International Law* 337 (1982–3).

A,K Herman, Lawrence L. "Proof of Offshore Territorial Claims in Canada." 7 *Dalhousie Law Journal* 3 (1982).

C Hidore, John J. *Physical Geography: Earth Systems*. Glenview, Ill.: Scott, Foresman 1974.

A Hill, Norman L. *Claims to Territory in International Law and Relations*. Westport, Conn.: Greenwood Press 1976.

A Himmelreich, David M. "The Beagle Channel Affair: A Failure in Judicial Persuasion." 12 *Vanderbilt Journal of Transnational Law* 971 (1979).

C,E Hodgson, Robert D. "Islands: Normal and Special Circumstances." In *Law of the Sea: The Emerging Regime of the Oceans*, edited by John King Gamble, Jr. and Giulio Pontecorro. Kingston: University of Rhode Island, Law of the Sea Institute 1974.

C – "Maritime Limits and Boundaries." 1 *Marine Geodesy* 155 (1977).

C,G Hodgson, Robert D., and Lewis M. Alexander. *Towards an Objective Analysis of Special Circumstances: Bays, Rivers, Coastal and Oceanic Archipelagoes and Atolls*. Kingston: University of Rhode Island, Law of the Sea Institute 1972.

C,E Hodgson, Robert D., and E. John Cooper. "The Technical Delimitation of a Modern Equidistant Boundary." 3 *Ocean Development and International Law* 362 (1976).

C Hodgson, Robert D., and Robert W. Smith. "The Informal Single Negotiating Text (Committee II): A Geographical Perspective." 3 *Ocean Development and International Law* 225 (1975).

C – "Boundary Issues Created by Extended National Marine Jurisdiction." 69 *Geographical Review* 423 (1979).

G Holden, Graham J. "Establishing a National Hydrographic Service with United Nations Technical Cooperation." 63 *International Hydrographic Review* (no. 1) 7 (1986).

C Holdich, Thomas H. "Political Boundaries." 32 *Scottish Geographical Magazine* 501 (1916).

C – *Political Frontiers and Boundary Making*. London: Macmillan 1916.

A,D Hollick, Ann L. "The Origins of 200-Mile Offshore Zones." 71 *American Journal of Interantional Law* 494 (1977).

A Hosenball, S. Neil, and Jefferson S. Holgard. "Delimitation of Air Space and Outer Space: Is a Boundary Needed Now? 57 *University of Colorado Law Review* 885 (1987).

C House, John W. *Frontier on the Rio Grande: A Political Geography of Development and Social Deprivation*. Oxford: Clarendon Press 1982.

D Hull, Felix, ed. *A Calendar of the White and Black Books of the Cinque Ports, 1432–1955*. London: HMSD 1966.

A Hurst, Cecil J.B. "Whose Is the Bed of the Sea? Sedentary Fisheries Outside the Three-Mile Limit." 4 *British Yearbook of International Law* 34 (1923–4).

A Hyde, Charles C. "Maps as Evidence in International Boundary Disputes." 27 *American Journal of International Law* 311 (1933).

G Ingram, A. *Sea Surveying*. 2 vols. New York: Wiley 1975.

K International Court of Justice. *Continental Shelf (Malta/Libyan Arab Jamahiriya)*, ICJ Reports 1985, 13.

K International Court of Justice. *Continental Shelf (Tunisia/Libyan Arab Jamahiriya)*, ICJ Reports 1982, 18.

K International Court of Justice. *Delimitation of the Maritime Boundary in the Gulf of Maine Area*, ICJ Reports 1984, 246.

K International Court of Justice. *Fisheries Jurisdiction*, ICJ Reports 1974, 3, 175.

K International Court of Justice. *North Sea Continental Shelf*, ICJ Reports 1969, 3.

B,D Ireland, Gordon. *Boundaries, Possessions and Conflicts in Central and North America and the Caribbean*. New York: Octagon Books 1971.

B,D – *Boundaries, Possessions and Conflicts in South America*. New York: Octagon Books 1971.

A Irwin, Paul C. "Settlement of Maritime Boundary Disputes: An Analysis of the Law of the Sea Negotiations." 8 *Ocean Development and International Law* 105 (1980).

F Iversen, Edwin S. *Farming the Edge of the Sea*. 2d ed. Farnham, UK: Fishing News Books 1976.

A Jagota, S.P. *Maritime Boundary*. Dordrecht and Boston: Nijhoff 1985.

K "Jan Mayen Island Dispute: Report and Recommendations of Conciliation Commission." 20 *International Legal Materials* 797 (1981).

B,D Jenks, Clarence Wilfred. *The World beyond the Charter in Historical Perspective: A Tentative Synthesis of Four Stages of World Organization*. London: Allen and Unwin 1969.

A Jennings, Robin Y. *The Acquisition of Territory in International Law*. Manchester: Manchester University Press 1963.

A,D Jessup, Philip C. *The Law of Territorial Waters and Maritime Jurisdiction*. New York: G.A. Jennings 1927.

D Jessup, Ronald F., and Frank Jessup. *The Cinque Ports* n.d., n.p. 1952.

A Jiménez de Aréchaga, Eduardo. "The Conception of Equity in Maritime Delimitation." In *International Law at the Time of Its Codification: Essays in Honour of Roberto Ago*, edited by Piero Ziccardi. Milan: Giuffré 1987.

C Johnson, D.W. "The Role of Political Boundaries." 4 *Geographical Review* 118 (1917).

A,K Johnson, David H.N. "International Arbitration Back in Favour?" 34 *Year Book of World Affairs* 305 (1980).

A,F Johnston, Douglas M. "New Uses of International Law in the North Pacific." 43

Washington Law Review 77 (1967–8).

A,B – "Chinese Treaty Behaviour: Experiments in Analysis." In *Advancing and Contending Approaches to the Study of Chinese Foreign Policy*, edited by Roger L. Dial. Halifax: Dalhousie Centre for Foreign Policy Studies 1973.

A,F – "Equity and Efficiency in Marine Law and Policy." In Johnston, *Marine Policy and the Coastal Community*, 1976.

A,F – ed. *Marine Policy and the Coastal Community: The Impact of the Law of the Sea*. London: Croom Helm 1976.

A – "The Foundations of Justice in International Law." In *The International Law and Policy of Human Welfare*, edited by Ronald St. John Macdonald, Douglas M. Johnston, and Gerald L. Morris. Alphen aan den Rijn: Sijthoff and Noordhoff 1978.

A,D – "The Scottish Tradition in International Law." 16 *Canadian Yearbook of International Law* 3 (1978).

A,D – *The Environmental Law of the Sea*. Gland, Switzerland: IUCN 1981.

A,D – "The Environmental Law of the Sea: Historical Development." In Johnston, 1981.

A,B – "The Heritage of Political Thought in International Law." In Macdonald and Johnston, 1983.

A – "Maritime Boundary Delimitation and UNCLOS III." In *International Symposium on the New Law of the Sea in Southeast Asia*, edited by Douglas M. Johnston, Edgar Gold, and Phipat Tangsubkul. Halifax: Dalhousie Ocean Studies Programme 1983.

A – *Canada and the New International Law of the Sea*. Toronto and Buffalo: University of Toronto Press 1985.

A – "Systemic Environmental Damage: The Challenge to International Law and Organization." 12 *Syracuse Journal of International Law and Commerce* 255 (1985).

A – "Comment." In *The Law of the Sea: Problems from the East Asian Perspective*, edited by Choon-Ho Park and Jae Kyu Park. Honolulu: University of Hawaii Law of the Sea Institute 1987.

A,D,F – *The International Law of Fisheries: A Framework for Policy-Oriented Inquiries*. New Haven: Yale University Press 1965. Reprinted with new introductory essay; New Haven: New Haven Press; Dordrecht: Nijhoff 1987.

A – "The International Law of Fisheries: A Post-Classical Review and Assessment." In Johnston, *The International Law of Fisheries*, 1987.

A Johnston, Douglas M., and Edgar Gold. "Extended Jurisdiction: UNCLOS III on Coastal State Practice." In Clingan, 1982.

A Johnston, Douglas M., and Norman G. Letalik, eds. *The Law of the Sea and Ocean Industry: New Opportunities and Restraints*. Honolulu: University of Hawaii, Law of the Sea Institute 1984.

A,B Johnston, Douglas M., and Phillip M. Saunders, eds. *Ocean Boundary Making: Regional Issues and Developments*. London: Croom Helm 1987.

A,B – "Ocean Boundary Issues and Developments in Regional Perspective." In Johnston and Saunders, *Ocean Boundary Making*, 1987.

G Jones, Harold E., ed. *Surveying Offshore Canada Lands for Mineral Resource Development*. 3d ed. Ottawa: Department of Energy, Mines and Resources, Surveying and Mapping Branch 1983.

C,G Jones, Stephen B. *Boundary-Making: A Handbook for Statesmen, Treaty Editors and Boundary Commissioners*. Washington, DC: Carnegie Endowment for International Peace 1945.

C – "Boundary Concepts in the Setting of Place and Time." In Glassner and de Bilj, 1980.

B,I Jordan, Robert S., ed. *International Administration: Its Evolution and Contemporary Applications*. New York: Oxford University Press 1971.

A,B Juda, Lawrence, ed. *The United Sates without the Law of the Sea Treaty: Opportunities and Costs*. Narragansett, RI: Times Press 1983.

A Kaikobad, Kaiyan Homi. "Some Observations on the Doctrine of Continuity and Finality of Boundaries." 54 *British Yearbook of International Law* 126 (1983).

G Kapoor, D.C., and Adam J. Kerr. *A Guide to Maritime Boundary Delimitation*. Toronto: Carswell 1986.

A,C Karl, Donald E. "Islands and the Delimitation of the Continental Shelf: A Framework for Analysis." 71 *American Journal of International Law* 642 (1977).

A,B,C Kent, George, and Mark J. Valencia, eds. *Marine Policy in Southeast Asia*. Berkeley: University of California Press 1985.

A,D Kent, H.S.K. "The Historical Origins of the Three-Mile Limit." 48 *American Journal of International Law* 537 (1954).

E,G Kerr, Adam J., R.M. Eaton, and N.M. Anderson. "The Electronic Chart: Present Status and Future Problems." 63 *International Hydrographic Review* (no. 2) 97 (1986).

G Kerr, Adam J., and Michael J. Keen. "Hydrographic and Geologic Concerns of Implementing Article 76." 62 *International Hydrographic Review* (no. 1) 139 (1985).

A Kindt, John Warren. "The Claim for Limiting Marine Research: Compliance with International Environmental Standards." 15 *Ocean Development and International Law* 13 (1985).

H King, Cuchlaine A.M. *Introduction to Marine Geology and Geomorphology*. New York: Russak 1975.

A Kish, John. *The Law of International Spaces*. Leiden: Sijthoff 1973.

A Kiss, Alexandre-Charles. "La frontière–Co-opération." In *La frontière*, 1980.

F,I Knecht, Robert. "Coastal Zone Management: Recent Developments in the U.S." In *The Law of the Sea: Conference Outcomes and Problems of Implementation*, edited by Edward Miles and John King Gamble Jr. Kingston: University of Rhode Island, Law of the Sea Institute 1977.

A,B Koers, Albert W. *International Regulation of Marine Fisheries: A Study of Regional Fisheries Organizations*. West Byfleet, UK: Fishing News 1973.

C Kolars, John F., and John D. Nystuen. *Physical Geography: Environment and Man*. New York: McGraw-Hill 1975.

G Kolata, Gina Barl. "Geodesy: Dealing with an Enormous Computer Task." 200 *Science* 421 (28 April 1978).

B Krasner, Stephen D. ed. *International Regimes*. Ithaca, NY: Cornell University Press 1983.

A,B Kratochwil, Friedrich, Paul Rohrlich, and Harpreet Mahajan. *Peace and Disputed Sovereignty: Reflections on Conflict over Territory*. New York: Columbia University, Institute of War and Peace Studies 1985.

A Kriangsak, Kittichaisaree. *The Law of the Sea and Maritime Boundary Delimitation, with Special Reference to South-East Asia*. Singapore and Fairlawn, NJ: Oxford University Press 1987.

B Kristof, Ladis K.D. "The Nature of Frontiers and Boundaries." 49 *Annals of the Association of American Geographers* 269 (1959).

A *La frontière*. Société française pour le droit international, colloque de Poitiers. Paris: A. Pedone 1980.

A Lagoni, Rainer. "Oil and Gas Deposits across National Frontiers." 73 *American Journal of International Law* 215 (1979).

A – "Interim Measures Pending Maritime Delimitation Agreements." 78 *American Journal of International Law* 354 (1984).

J Lall, Arthur. *Modern International Negotiation: Principles and Practice*. New York: Columbia University Press 1966.

J – *How Communist China Negotiates*. New York: Columbia University Press 1968.

D Lamb, Alastair. *The McMahon Line: A Study in the Relations between India, China, and Tibet, 1904 to 1914*. London: Routledge and Kegan Paul; Toronto: University of Toronto Press 1966.

D – *Asian Frontiers: Studies in a Continuing Problem*. New York: Praeger 1968.

A Langeraar, Wijnand. "Delimitation of Continental Shelf Areas: A New Approach." 17 *Journal of Maritime Law and Commerce* 389 (1986).

A Lapradelle, Paul Geoffre de. *La frontière: Étude de droit international*. Paris: Les Editions Internationales 1928.

A,B Larkin, Bruce D. "East Asian Ocean Security Zones." 2 *Ocean Yearbook* 282 (1980).

D Lattimore, Owen. *Inner Asian Frontiers of China*. 2d ed. Boston: Beacon Press 1962.

D – *Studies in Frontier History: Collected Papers, 1928–1958*. London and New York: Oxford University Press 1962.

A,B *Law of the Sea Bulletin*. New York: United Nations 1983–.

A Lay, S. Houston, Robin Churchill, and Myron Nordquist. *New Directions in the Law of the Sea*. 11 vols. Dobbs Ferry, NY: Oceana 1973–81.

Leanza, Umberto, ed. *The International Legal Regime of the Mediterranean Sea*. Milan: Giuffré 1987.

Lee, Yong Leng. *The Razor's Edge: Boundaries and Boundary Disputes in Southeast Asia*. Singapore: Institute of Southeast Asian Studies 1980.

Leiner, Frederick C. "Maritime Security Zones: Prohibited Yet Perpetuated." 24 *Virginia Journal of International Law* 967 (1983–4).

Leipziger, Danny M., and James L. Mudge. *Seabed Mineral Resources and the Economic Enterests of Developing Countries*. Cambridge, Mass.: Ballinger 1976.

Le Marquand, David G. *Boundary Water Relations and Great Lakes Issues*. Ottawa: Environment Canada 1985.

Letalik, Norman G. "Boundary Making in the Mediterranean." In Johnston and Saunders, *Ocean Boundary Making*, 1987.

Lim, Joo-Jock. *Territorial Power Domains, Southeast Asia, and China: The Geo-strategy of an Overarching Massif*. Singapore: Institute of Southeast Asian Studies 1984.

Lindberg, Leon N. *The Political Dynamics of European Economic Integration*. Stanford: Stanford University Press 1963.

Lister, Raymond. *Antique Maps and Their Cartographers*. Hamden, Conn.: Archon Books 1970.

Livingstone, D.N., and R.T. Harrison. "The Frontier: Metaphor, Myth and Model." 32 *The Professional Geographer* 127 (1980).

Lorenz, Konrad. *On Aggression*. Translated by M.K. Wilson. New York: Harcourt, Brace and World 1966.

Luard, Evan, ed. *The International Regulation of Frontier Disputes*. London: Thames and Hudson 1970.

Luban, David. "Bargaining and Compromise: Recent Work on Negotiation and Informal Justice." 14 *Philosophy and Public Affairs* 347 (1985).

Lyman, S.M., and M.B. Scott. "Territoriality: A Neglected Sociological Dimension." 15 *Social Problems* 236 (1967).

Lyon, Peter. "Regional Organizations and Frontier Disputes." In Luard, 1970.

Macdonald, R. St. J., and Douglas M. Johnston, eds. *The Structure and Process of International Law: Essays in Legal Philosophy, Doctrine, and Theory*. Dordrecht: Nijhoff 1983.

– "International Legal Theory: New Frontiers of the Discipline." In Macdonald and Johnston, 1983.

McDonnell, Porter W., Jr. *Introduction to Map Projections*. New York: Dekker 1979.

McDorman, Ted L. "The New Definition of 'Canada Lands' and the Determination of the Outer Limit of the Continental Shelf." 14 *Journal of Maritime Law and Commerce* 195 (1983).

McDorman, Ted L., Kenneth P. Beauchamp, and Douglas M. Johnston, comps. *Maritime Boundary Delimitation: An Annotated Bibliography*. Lexington,

Mass.: Lexington Books 1983.

A,I McDorman, Ted L., Norman G. Letalik, Hal Mills, Douglas M. Johnston and Edgar Gold. *The Marine Environment and the Caracas Convention on the Law of the Sea*. Halifax: Dalhousie Ocean Studies Programme 1981.

A McDougal, Myres S., and William T. Burke. *The Public Order of the Oceans: A Contemporary International Law of the Sea*. New Haven: Yale University Press 1962.

A McDougal, Myres S., Harold D. Lasswell, and James C. Miller. *The Interpretation of Agreements and World Public Order: Principles of Content and Procedure*. New Haven: Yale University Press 1967.

A McDougal, Myres S., Harold D. Lasswell, and Ivan A. Vlasic. *Law and Public Order in Space*. New Haven: Yale University Press 1963.

A McDougal, Myres S., and W. Michael Reisman. *International Law in Contemporary Perspective: The Public Order of the World Community*. Mineola, NY: Foundation Press 1981.

A – *International Law Essays: A Supplement to International Law in Contemporary Perspective*. Mineola, NY: Foundation Press 1981.

C McEwen, Alec C. *International Boundaries of East Africa*. Oxford: Clarendon Press 1971.

A,B M'Gonigle, R. Michael, and Mark W. Zacher. *Pollution, Politics and International Law: Tankers at Sea*. Berkeley: University of California Press 1979.

A,G McKelvey, Vincent E. "Interpretation of the UNCLOS III Definition of the Continental Shelf." In Johnston and Letalik, 1984.

B,I McLaren, Robert I. *Civil Servants and Public Policy: A Comparative Study of International Secretariats*. Waterloo, Ont.: Wilfrid Laurier University Press 1980.

L McLeish, John. *The Theory of Social Change: Four Views Considered*. London: Routledge and Kegan Paul 1969.

A,D McMahon, Matthew M. *Conquest and Modern International Law: The Legal Limitations on the Acquisition of Territory by Conquest*. Washington, DC: The Catholic University of America Press 1940.

G McMillan, Duncan J. "The Extent of the Continental Shelf: Factors Affecting the Accuracy of a Continental Margin Boundary." 9 *Marine Policy* 148 (1985).

A McNair, Arnold D. *The Law of Treaties*. Oxford: Clarendon Press 1961.

A McWhinney, Edward. *The World Court and the Contemporary International Law-Making Process*. Alphen aan den Rijn: Sijthoff and Noordhoff 1979.

A,B – *United Nations Law Making: Cultural and Ideological Relativism and International Law Making for an Era of Transition*. New York: Holmes and Meier 1984.

D Mahan, Alfred Thayer. *The Influence of Sea Power upon History, 1660-1783*. 25th ed. Boston: Little, Brown 1923.

F Mandelbrot, Benoit B. *The Fractal Geometry of Nature*. San Francisco: W.H. Freeman 1982.

Marston, Geoffrey. "Extension and Delimitation of National Sea Boundaries in the Mediterranean." In *The Mediterranean Region: Economic Interdependence and the Future of Society*, edited by Giacomo Luciani. London: Croom Helm 1984.

Marston, R.P., and P.W. Birnie. "The Falkland Islands/Islas Malvinas Conflict: A Question of Zones." 7 *Marine Policy* 14 (1983).

Martinez, Oscar J., ed. *Across Boundaries: Transborder Interaction in Comparative Perspective*. El Paso: Texas Western Press 1986.

Menon, P.K. "Settlement of International Boundary Disputes." 8 *Anglo-American Law Review* 24 (1979).

Miles, Edward. "The Dynamics of Global Ocean Politics." In Johnston, *Marine Policy and the Coastal Community*, 1976.

Minghi, Julian V. *Some Aspects of the Impact of an International Boundary on Spatial Patterns: An Analysis of the Pacific Coast Lowland Region of the Canada-United States Boundary*. Ann Arbor, Mich.: University Microfilms 1962.

– "Boundary Studies in Political Geography." 53 *Annals of the Association of American Geographers* 140 (1963).

Mitrany, David. *The Progress of International Government*. New Haven: Yale University Press 1933.

– *A Working Peace System: An Argument for the Functional Development of International Organization*. 4th ed. London: National Peace Council 1946.

– "Functionalist Approach to World Organization." 24 *International Affairs* 350 (July 1948).

– *The Functional Theory of Politics*. London: M. Robertson 1975.

Mommson, Theodore. *The History of Rome*. Translated by W.P. Dickson. Rev. ed. 5 vols.. New York: Charles Scribner's Sons 1895.

Montagu, Ashley, ed., *Man and Aggression*. 2d ed. New York: Oxford University Press 1968.

Morgan, Frederick W. *Ports and Harbours*. 2d ed. Revised by James Bird. London: Hutchinson University Library 1958.

Moritz, Helmut. *Advanced Physical Geodesy*. Karlsruhe: H. Wichman 1980.

Mouton, Martinus W. *The Continental Shelf*. The Hague: Nijhoff 1952.

Multhauf, Robert P. *Neptune's Gift: A History of Common Salt*. Baltimore: Johns Hopkins University Press 1978.

Münch, Ingo von, and Andreas Buske, eds. *International Law: The Essential Treaties and Other Relevant Documents*. Berlin and New York: De Gruyter 1985.

Munkman, A.L.W. "Adjudication and Adjustment: International Judicial Decision and the Settlement of Territorial and Boundary Disputes." 44 *British Yearbook of International Law* 1 (1972–3).

Murty, T.S. "Evidence on Traditional Boundaries and Some Problems in Its Interpretation." 8 *Indian Journal of International Law* 475 (1968).

G Myres, J.A.L. "Survey Tasks Arising from the United Nations Convention on the Law of the Sea." 63 *International Hydrographic Review* (no. 1) 65 (1986).

J,K Nader, Laura, and Harry F. Todd, eds. *The Disputing Process: Law in Ten Societies*. New York: Columbia University Press 1978.

H Nairn, Alan E.M., and Francis G. Stehli. *The Ocean Basins and Margins*. 7 vols. New York: Plenum Press 1973–85.

A,B *National and International Boundaries*. Thesaurus Acroasium of the Institute of Public International Law and International Relations of Thessaloniki, vol. 14 (1985).

H Needham, Joseph. *Science and Civilization in China*. Vol. 1. Cambridge: Cambridge University Press 1954.

A Nelson, L.D.M. "The Delimitation of Maritime Boundaries in the Caribbean." In Johnston and Saunders, *Ocean Boundary Making*, 1987.

E,G Newson, D.W. "Nautical Chart Standardization." 61 *International Hydrographic Review* (no. 2) 111 (1984).

C Nicholson, Norman L. *The Boundaries of the Canadian Confederation*. Toronto: Macmillan 1979.

A Note, "The Beagle Channel Affair." 71 *American Journal of International Law* 733 (1977).

B Nye, Joseph S., Jr. *Peace in Parts: Integration and Conflict in Regional Organization*. Boston: Little, Brown 1971.

A Obieta, Joseph A. *The International Status of the Suez Canal*. The Hague: Nijhoff 1960.

A,K O'Connell, Daniel P. *State Succession in Municipal Law and International Law*. Cambridge: Cambridge University Press 1967.

A,D – *The Influence of Law on the Sea Power*. Annapolis: Naval Institute Press 1975.

A – *The International Law of the Sea*. 2 vols. Edited by Ivan Anthony Shearer. 2 vols. Oxford: Clarendon Press 1982.

B *OECD and the Environment*. Paris: Organization for Economic Co-operation and Development 1986.

A Oellers-Frahm, Karin, and Norbert Wühler, comps. *Dispute Settlement in Public International Law: Texts and Materials*. Berlin and New York: Springer Verlag 1984.

H Oller, Cliff. *Tectonics and Landforms*. Edited by K.M. Clayton. London and New York: Longman 1980.

A Oppenheim, Lassa F.L. *International Law: A Treatise*. Edited by Hersh Lauterpacht. 8th ed. London and New York: Longmans, Green 1955.

C,I Oram, Robert B., and Christopher C.R. Baker. *The Efficient Port*. Oxford and New York: Pergamon Press 1971.

G Orlin, Hyman. "Offshore Boundaries: Engineering and Economic Aspects." 3 *Ocean Development and International Law* 87 (1975).

D Owen, Edgar Wesley. *Trek of the Oil Finders: A History of Exploration for*

Petroleum. Tulsa, Okla.: American Association of Petroleum Geologists 1975.

A Oxman, Bernard H. "The Preparation of Article 1 of the Convention on the Continental Shelf." 3 *Journal of Maritime Law and Commerce* 245, 445 (1972).

A – "The Third United Nations Conference on the Law of the Sea: The 1976 New York Sessions." 71 *American Journal of International Law* 247 (1977).

A – "The Third United Nations Conference on the Law of the Sea: The Seventh Session (1978)." 73 *American Journal of International Law* 1 (1979).

A – "The Third United Nations Conference on the Law of the Sea: The Tenth Session (1981)." 76 *American Journal of International Law* 1 (1982).

A Pardo, Arvid, and Carl Q. Christol. "The Common Interest: Tensions Between the Whole and the Parts." In Macdonald and Johnston, *Structure and Process of International Law*, 1983.

A Park, Choon-Ho. "The 50-Mile Military Boundary Zone of North Korea." 72 *American Journal of International Law* 866 (1978).

A – *East Asia and the Law of the Sea*. Seoul: Seoul National University Press 1983.

A,B Park, Choon-Ho, and Jae Kyu Park, eds. *The Law of the Sea: Problems from the East Asian Perspective*. Honolulu: University of Hawaii, Law of the Sea Institute 1987.

N Parry, John H. *The Age of Reconnaissance*. New York: New American Library 1964.

E Percotte, Roland. "A Review of Coastal Zone Mapping." In 23 *Cartographics* 3 (1986).

F Pillay, T.V.R. *Aquaculture Development: An Introductory Guide*. Rome: FAO 1977.

A,B Pinto, M.C.W. "The International Community and Antarctica." 33 *University of Miami Law Review* 475 (1978–9).

A Plender, Richard. *International Migration Law*. Leiden: Sijthoff 1972.

K Polinsky, A. Mitchell. *An Introduction to Law and Economics*. Boston: Little, Brown 1983.

L Porteous, J. Douglas. "Home: The Territorial Core." 66 *Geographical Review* (1976).

D Pounds, Norman J.G. "The Origin of the Idea of Natural Frontiers in France. 146 *Annals of the Association of American Geographers* 41 (1951).

D – "France and 'Les Limites Naturelles' from the Seventeenth to the Twentieth Centuries." 44 *Annals of the Association of American Geographers* 51 (1954).

C Prescott, J.R.V. *The Geography of Frontiers and Boundaries*. Chicago: Aldine 1965.

C,D – *The Evolution of Nigeria's International and Regional Boundaries: 1861–1971*. Vancouver: Tantalus Research 1971.

C – *Boundaries and Frontiers*. London: Croom Helm; Totowa, NJ: Rowan and Littlefield 1978.

A,B – *Australia's Maritime Boundaries*. Canberra: Australian National University, Department of International Relations 1985.

A,C – "Maritime Jurisdictional Issues." In Kent and Valencia, 1985.

A,C – *The Maritime Political Boundaries of the World*. London and New York: Methuen 1985.

A,C – "Delimitation of Marine Boundaries by Baselines." 8 *Marine Policy Reports* (January 1986).

A,C – "Maritime Boundaries and Issues in the Southwest Pacific Ocean." In Johnston and Saunders, *Ocean Boundary Making*, 1987.

A,C – "Straight Baselines: Theory and Practice." In Brown and Churchill, 1987.

I Pross, A. Paul. *Group Politics and Public Policy*. Toronto: Oxford University Press 1986.

J Pruitt, Dean G. *Negotiation Behavior*. New York: Academic Press 1981.

A Pufendorf, Samuel. *De Jure Naturae et Gentium* (1672).

E Putnam, Robert. *Early Sea Charts*. New York: Abberike Press 1983.

B Quigg, Philip W. *A Pole Apart: The Emerging Issue of Antarctica*. New York: McGraw-Hill 1983.

L Raglan, FitzRoy Somerset. *The Temple and the House*. London: Routledge and Kegan Paul 1964.

J Raiffa, Howard. *The Art and Science of Negotiation*. Cambridge, Mass.: Belknap Press of Harvard University Press 1982.

A,D Ralston, Jackson H. *International Arbitration from Athens to Locarno*. New York: Garland 1929.

A Ramakrishna, Kilaparti, Robert E. Bowen, and Jack H. Archer. "Outer Limits of the Continental Shelf: A Legal Analysis of Chilean and Ecuadorian Island Claims and U.S. Response." 11 *Marine Policy* 58 (1987).

A,B Raman, K. Venkata. *The Ways of the Peacemaker* (UNITAR 1975).

J,K – ed. *Dispute Settlement through the United Nations*. Dobbs Ferry, NY: Oceana 1977.

A Ranjeva, Raymond. "L'océan indien et le nouveau droit de la mer." 84 *Revue Générale de Droit International Public* (1980).

C,L Ratzel, Friedrich. *Politische Geographie*. Munich: R. Oldenbourg 1897.

F Reay, P.J. *Aquaculture*. London: Arnold 1979.

D Reddie, James. *Researches, Historical and Critical, in Maritime International Law*. 2 vols. Edinburgh: Clark 1844–55.

I Rehfuss, John A. *Public Administration as Political Process*. New York: Scribner 1973.

A Reisman, W. Michael. "Has the International Court Exceeded Its Jurisdiction?" 80 *American Journal of International Law* 128 (1986).

C Reitsma, Henrik-Jan A. "Boundaries as Barriers: The Predicament of Land-Locked Countries." In *Pluralism and Political Geography: People, Territory and State*, edited by Nurit Kliot and Stanley Waterman. London: Croom Helm 1983.

G *Report of the Group of Experts on Hydrographic Surveying and Nautical Charting*. UN Doc. E/CONF. 71/L1, dated 12 May 1978.

G Research in International Law. *Nationality; Responsibility of States; Territorial Waters*. Cambridge Mass.: Harvard Law School, 1929 (supplement to the 23 *American Journal of International Law*, April 1929).

A,D Rhee, Sang-Myon. "Sea Boundary Delimitation Between States Before World War II." 76 *American Journal of International Law* 555 (1982).

A – and James MacAulay. "Ocean Boundary Issues in East Asia: The Need for Practical Solutions." In Johnston and Saunders, *Ocean Boundary Making*, 1987.

D Rickard, Thomas A. *Man and Metals: A History of Mining in Relation to the Development of Civilization*. 2 vols. New York and London: McGraw-Hill 1932.

A,D Reisenfeld, Stefan A. *Protection of Coastal Fisheries under International Law*. Washington: Carnegie Endowment for International Peace 1942.

G Rinner, Karl. "Concepts and Development of Marine Geodesy." 11 *Marine Policy* 3 (1987).

E Ritchie, William. *Mapping for Field Scientists: A Problem-Solving Approach*. Newton Abbot, UK: David and Charles 1977.

E Robinson, Arthur H., and Barbara B. Petchenik. *The Nature of Maps: Essays toward Understanding Maps and Mapping*. Chicago: University of Chicago Press 1976.

A Robinson, Davis R., David A. Colson, and Bruce C. Rashkow. "Some Perspectives on Adjudicating before the World Court: The Gulf of Maine Case." 79 *American Journal of International Law* 578 (1985).

F Robinson, I.S. *Satellite Oceanography: An Introduction for Oceanographers and Remote Sensing Scientists*. Chichester, UK: Wiley 1985.

A Rogers, Ann Berkley, and Albert E. Utton. "The Ixtapa Draft Agreement Relating to the Use of Transboundary Groundwaters." 25 *Natural Resources Journal* 713 (1985).

A Rolston, Susan J., and Ted L. McDorman. "Maritime Boundary Making in the Arctic Region." In Johnston and Saunders, *Ocean Boundary Making*, 1987.

A,B Rosenne, Shabtai. *The International Court of Justice: An Essay in Political and Legal Theory*. Leiden: Sijthoff 1957.

A – *Procedure in the International Court: A Commentary on the 1978 Rules of the International Court of Justice*. The Hague: Nijhoff 1983.

F Ross, David A. "A Changing Ocean Policy Horizon for Marine Science." 15 *Ocean Development and International Law* 221 (1985).

L Ross, P.D. "Jurisdiction: An Ethological Concept" 21 *Human Relations* 75 (1968).

I Rourke, Francis E. *Bureaucracy, Politics and Public Policy*. Boston: Little, Brown 1969.

A Rozakis, Christos L., and Constantin A. Stephanou, eds. *The New Law of the*

Sea. Amsterdam: North-Holland 1983.

J,L Rubin, Jeffrey Z., and Bert R. Brown. *The Social Psychology of Bargaining and Negotiation*. New York: Academic Press 1975.

A,B Ryan, K.W. "The Torres Strait Treaty." 7 *Australian Year Book of International Law* 87 (1981).

M Sander, Frank E.A. *Mediation: A Select Annotated Bibliography*. Washington, DC: American Bar Association 1984.

H Sarton, George. *A History of Science*. 2 vols. Cambridge, Mass.: Harvard University Press 1952–9.

L Sayers, Janet. *Biological Politics: Feminist and Anti-Feminist Perspectives*. London and New York: Tavistock 1982.

A Schachter, Oscar. *Sharing the World's Resources*. New York: Columbia University Press 1977.

B Scheingold, Stuart A. "Domestic and International Consequences of Regional Integration." 24 *International Organization* 978 (1970).

B Schelling, Thomas C. *The Strategy of Conflict*. Cambridge, Mass.: Harvard University Press 1960.

H Schlee, Susan. *The Edge of an Unfamiliar World: A History of Oceanography*. New York: Dutton 1973.

B Schurmann, Herbert Franz. *Ideology and Organization in Communist China*. Berkeley: University of California Press 1966.

G "Scientific Considerations Relating to the Continental Shelf." Memorandum by the Secretariat of the United Nations Educational, Scientific and Cultural Organization. UN Doc. A/Conf. 13/2 and Add. 1, 20 September 1957, reprinted in First United Nations Conference on the Law of the Sea, *Official Records*, vol. 1.

A,K Scott, James B., ed. 1 *The Hague Court Reports* (1916).

A Scovazzi, Tullio, ed. *La linea di base del mare territoriale*. Studi e Documenti sul Diritto Internazionale del Mare no. 17. Milan: Giuffré 1986.

H Scrutton, R.A., and M. Talwani, eds. *The Ocean Floor*. Chichester and Toronto: Wiley 1982.

A,D Selden, John. *Mare Clausum* (1635).

B Sewell, James P. *Functionalism and World Politics: A Study Based on United National Programs Financing Economic Development*. Princeton: Princeton University Press 1966.

C,G Shalowitz, Aaron L. *Shore and Sea Boundaries*. 2 vols. Washington DC: U.S. Dept. of Commerce, Coast and Geodetic Survey 1962.

I Sharkansky, Ira. *The Routine of Politics*. New York: Van Nostrand-Reinhold 1970.

A Sharma, Surya P. *International Boundary Disputes and International Law: A Policy-Oriented Study*. Bombay: N.M. Tripathi 1976.

A,D – "Relevance of Economic Factors to the Law of Maritime Delimitation between Neighbouring States." In Brown and Churchill, 1988.

Siegfried, André. *Germs and Ideas: Routes of Epidemics and Ideologies*. Translated by J. Henderson and M. Clarasco. Edinburgh: Oliver and Boyd 1965.

Simma, Bruno. "Consent: Strains in the Treaty System." In Macdonald and Johnston, *Structure and Process of International Law*, 1983.

Smith, David N., and Louis T. Wells Jr. *Negotiating Third World Minerals Agreements: Promises as Prologue*. Cambridge, Mass.: Ballinger 1975.

Smith, Robert W. "A Geographical Primer to Maritime Boundary-Making." 12 *Ocean Development and International Law* 1 (1982).

Sollie, Finn, ed. *The Challenge of New Territories*. Oslo: Universitetsforlaget 1974.

Sommer, Robert. *Personal Space: The Behavioural Basis for Design*. Englewood Cliffs, NJ: Prentice-Hall 1969.

Spencer, Robert, John Kirton, and Kim Richard Nossal, eds. *The International Joint Committee Seventy Years On*. Toronto: University of Toronto Centre for International Studies 1981.

Spiess, F.N. "Acoustic Techniques for Marine Geodesy." 4 *Marine Geodesy* 13 (1980).

Spinnato, John M. "Historic and Vital Bays: An Analysis of Libya's Claim to the Gulf of Sidra." 13 *Ocean Development and International Law* 65 (1983–4).

Spooner, Brian, and H.S. Mann, eds. *Desertification and Development: Dryland Ecology in Social Perspective*. London: Academic Press 1982.

Sprout, Harold, and Margaret Sprout. *The Ecological Perspective on Human Affairs, with Special Reference to International Politics*. Princeton, NJ: Princeton University Press 1965.

– *An Ecological Paradigm for the Study of International Politics*. Princeton, NJ: Woodrow Wilson School of Public and International Affairs 1968.

Stahl, Ingolf. *Bargaining Theory*. Stockholm: EFI 1972.

Stansell, Thomas A., Jr. "The Global Positioning System." 63 *International Hydrographic Review* (no. 2) 51 (1986).

Stea, David. "Space, Territoriality and Human Movements." 15 *Landscapes* 13 (1965).

Stevenson, John R., and Bernard H. Oxman. "The Third United Nations Conference on the Law of the Sea: The 1974 Caracas Session." 69 *American Journal of International Law* 1 (1975).

– "The Third United Nations Conference on the Law of the Sea: The 1975 Geneva Session." 69 *American Journal of International Law* 263 (1975).

Storr, Anthony. *Human Aggression*. London: Penguin 1968.

Strahler, Arthur N. *Physical Geography*. 2d ed. New York: Wiley 1960.

Strange, Susan. "Cuba and After." 17 *Yearbook of World Affairs* 1 (1963).

Strassoldo, Raimondo. "The Study of Boundaries: A Systems-Oriented, Multi-Disciplinary, Bibliographical Essay." 2 *Jerusalem Journal of International Relations* 81 (1977).

– "Centre–Periphery and System–Boundary: Culturological Perspectives." In

Centre and Periphery: Spatial Variation in Politics, edited by Jean Gottman. London: Sage Publications 1980.

B Strausz-Hupe, Robert. *Geopolitics: The Struggle for Space and Power*. New York: Putnam 1942.

A Strohl, Mitchell P. *The International Law of Bays*. The Hague: Nijhoff 1963.

A,D Stuyt, Alexander M. *Survey of International Arbitrations, 1794–1970*. Leiden: A.W. Sijthoff; Dobbs Ferry NY: Oceana 1972.

A Symmons, Clive R. *The Maritime Zones of Islands in International Law*. The Hague: Nijhoff 1979.

A – "The Canadian 200-Mile Fishery Limit and the Delimitation of Maritime Zones Around St. Pierre and Miquelon." 12 *Ottawa Law Review* 145 (1980).

A – *Marine Boundary Disputes in the Irish Sea and Northeast*. 9 *Marine Policy Reports* (September 1986).

K Talbott, Richard E. " 'Science Court': A Possible Way to Obtain Scientific Certainty for Decisions Based on Scientific 'Fact'?" 8 *Environmental Law* 827 (1978).

A Tangsubkul, Phiphat. *The Southeast Asian Archipelagic States: Concept, Evolution, and Current Practice*. Honolulu: East-West Environment and Policy Institute 1984.

B,C Tanzer, Michael. *The Race for Reserves: Continuing Struggles over Minerals and Fuels*. New York: Monthly Review Press 1980.

I Taylor, Peter J., and Graham Gudgin. "A Fresh Look at the Parliamentary Boundary Commissions." 28 *Parliamentary Affairs* 405 (1975).

G Teicholz, Eric. "Processing Satellite Data." *Datamation* (June 1978).

G Thamsborg, Milan. "Geodetic Hydrography as Related to Maritime Boundary Problems." 51 *International Hydrographic Review* (no. 1) 157 (1977).

A,B Theutenberg, Bo Johnson. *The Evolution of the Law of the Sea: A Study of Resources and Strategy with Special Regard to the Polar Regions*. Dublin: Tycooly International Publishing 1984.

I Thompson, Victor A. *Bureaucracy and the Modern World*. Morristown, NJ: General Learning Press 1976.

E Thrower, Norman J.W. *Maps and Man: An Examination of Cartography in Relation to Culture and Civilization*. Englewood Cliffs, NJ: Prentice-Hall 1972.

D Tod, Marcus N. *International Arbitration amongst the Greeks*. Oxford: Clarendon Press 1913.

A Townsend Gault, Ian. "Offshore Boundary Delimitation in the Persian-Arabian Gulf." In Johnston and Saunders, *Ocean Boundary Making*, 1987.

B,D Touval, Saadia. *The Boundary Politics of Independent Africa*. Cambridge: Harvard University Press 1972.

D Trakman, Leon E. "The Evolution of the Law Merchant: Our Commercial Heritage." 12 *Journal of Maritime Law and Commerce* 1 (1981).

L Tringham, Ruth. "Territorial Demarcation of Pre-historic Settlements." In *Man, Settlements, and Urbanism*, edited by Peter J. Ucko, Ruth Tringham, and

G.W. Dimbleby. London: Duckworth 1972.

G,K Troop, P.M. "The Legal Liability of the Chartmaker." 62 *International Hydrographic Review* (no. 1) 115 (1985).

D Turner, Frederick J. *The Frontier in American History*. New York: H. Holt 1920.

A Underwood, Peter C. "Ocean Boundaries and Resource Development in West Africa." In Johnston and Saunders, *Ocean Boundary Making*, 1987.

F UNESCO. Intergovernmental Oceanographic Commission. *Ocean Observing System Development Programme*. Paris: UNESCO 1984.

F – Intergovernmental Oceanographic Commission. *Ocean Science for the Year 2000*. Paris: UNESCO 1984.

F – Intergovernmental Oceanographic Commission. *Reports of Governing and Major Subsidiary Bodies*. Thirteenth Session of the Assembly, Paris, 12–28 March 1985. Paris: UNESCO 1985.

B,I United Nations. Ocean Economics and Technology Branch. *Coastal Area Management and Development*. Oxford: Pergamon Press 1982.

J "United Nations Convention on the Law of the Sea." In *The Third United Nations Conference on the Law of the Sea: Documents*, vol. 3, compiled by Renate Platzöder. Dobbs Ferry, NY: Oceana 1982.

A,C United States. Department of State. Office of the Geographer. *Limits in the Seas*. Washington, DC: U.S. Government Publication Series, 1970– .

– *Limits in the Seas*. "Developing Standard Guidelines for Evaluating Straight Baselines." (31 August 1987).

H Urick, Robert J. *Principles of Underwater Sound*. 3d ed. New York: McGraw-Hill 1983.

B,F Valencia, Mark J., ed. *The South China Sea: Hydrocarbon Potential and Possibilities of Joint Development*. Oxford and New York: Pergamon Press 1981.

A,B – "Taming Troubled Waters: Joint Development of Oil and Mineral Resources in Overlapping Claim Areas." 23 *San Diego Law Review* 661 (1986).

A,F Valencia, Mark J. and Masahiro Miyoshi. "Southeast Asian Seas: Joint Development of Hydrocarbons in Overlapping Claim Areas?" 16 *Ocean Development and International Law* 211 (1986).

A Van Dyke, John M., ed. *Consensus and Confrontation: The United States and the Law of the Sea Convention*. Honolulu: University of Hawaii, Law of the Sea Institute 1985.

C VanZandt, Franklin K. *Boundaries of the United States and the Several States*. St. Clair Shores, Mich.: Scholarly Press 1972.

A,I VanderZwaag, David L. *The Fish Feud: The U.S. and Canadian Boundary Dispute*. Lexington, Mass: Lexington Books 1983.

A Vukas, Budislav. "The LOS Convention and Sea Boundary Delimitation." In *Essays on the New Law of the Sea*, edited by Budislav Vukas. Zagreb: Sveucilsna Naklad Liber 1985.

J,K Wall, James A., Jr., and Dale E. Rude. "Judicial Mediation: Techniques, Strategies, and Situational Effects." 4 *Journal of Social Issues* 4 (1985).

A,D Walter, Wyndham L. "Territorial Waters: The Cannon Shot Rule." 22 *British Yearbook of International Law* 210 (1945).

J Walton, Richard E., and Robert B. McKenzie. *A Behavioral Theory of Labor Negotiations: An Analysis of a Social Interaction System*. New York: McGraw-Hill 19665.

A,D Warbrick, Colin J. "The Boundary between England and Scotland in the Solway Firth." 51 *British Year Book of International Law* 163 (1980).

G Watson, W.F. "Ocean Charting." 63 *International Hydrographic Review* (no. 1) 119 (1986).

F Weeks, Wilford F., and Frank D. Carsey. "Remote Sensing of the Arctic Seas." 29 *Oceanus* 59 (1986).

C Weigert, Hans W. *Generals and Geographers: The Twilight of Geopolitics*. Freeport, NY: Books for Libraries Press 1942; reprinted 1972.

B,I Weiss, Thomas George. *International Bureaucracy: An Analysis of the Operation of Functional and Global International Secretariats*. Lexington, Mass.: Lexington Books 1975.

A,D Westerman, Gay. *The Juridical Bay*. New York: Oxford University Press; Oxford: Clarendon Press 1987.

D Wheaton, Henry. *A Digest of the Law of Maritime Captures on Prizes* (1815).

C Whittlesey, Derwent S. *The Earth and the State: A Study of Political Geography*. New York: H. Holt 1939.

M Wiktor, Christian L., and Guy Tanguay, eds. *Constitutions of Canada: Federal and Provincial*. 4 vols. Dobbs Ferry, NY: Oceana Publications 1979.

F Wildsmith, Bruce H. *Aquaculture: The Legal Framework*. Toronto: Emond-Montgomery 1982.

E Wilford, John N. *The Mapmakers*. New York: Vintage Books 1982.

G Williams, Owen W. "Editorial: Marine Survey." 6 *Marine Geodesy* 1 (1982).

N Williamson, James A. *The Cabot Voyages and Bristol Discovery Under Henry VII*. Cambridge: Cambridge University Press 1962.

A,B Wilson, Andrew. *The Aegean Dispute*. London: International Institute for Strategic Studies 1979.

G Wong, R.V.C. "Integration of Inertial and GPS-Satellite Techniques for Precise Marine Positioning." 9 *Marine Geodesy* 213 (1985).

C,D Wyman, Walker D., and Clifton B. Kroeber, eds. *Frontier in Perspective*. Madison: University of Wisconsin Press 1957.

A,B Young, Allan. "Antarctic Resource Jurisdiction and the Law of the Sea: A Question of Compromise." 11 *Brooklyn Journal of International Law* 45 (1985).

J Young, Oran R., ed., *Bargaining: Formal Theories of Negotiation*. Urbana: University of Illinois Press 1975.

B – *Resource Management at the International Level: The Case of the North Pacific*. London: F. Pinter; New York: Nichols 1977.

B – "International Regimes: Problems of Concept Formation." 32 *World Politics* 331 (1980).

B – "Regime Dynamics: The Rise and Fall of International Regimes." 36 *International Organization* 227 (1982).

B – *Resource Regimes: Natural Resources and Social Institutions*. Berkeley: University of California Press 1982.

B Zam-Azreal, Datuk. "The Malaysian Perspective." In *Antarctic Politics and Marine Resources: Critical Choices for the 1980s*, edited by Lewis M. Alexander and Lynne C. Hanson. Kingston: University of Rhode Island, Center for Ocean Management Studies 1985.

B Zoppo, Ciro E., and Charles Zorgbibe, eds. *On Geopolitics: Classical and Nuclear*. Boston: Nijhoff 1985.

Index